ENGLISH EDUCATION

1789–1902

ENGLISH EDUCATION

1789—1902

by

JOHN WILLIAM ADAMSON

*Fellow of King's College, London. Emeritus Professor
of Education, University of London*

CAMBRIDGE

AT THE UNIVERSITY PRESS

1964

CAMBRIDGE UNIVERSITY PRESS
Cambridge, New York, Melbourne, Madrid, Cape Town, Singapore, São Paulo, Delhi

Cambridge University Press
The Edinburgh Building, Cambridge CB2 8RU, UK

Published in the United States of America by Cambridge University Press, New York

www.cambridge.org
Information on this title: www.cambridge.org/9780521109420

First published 1930
Reprinted 1964
Grateful acknowledgement is made to the Library of
the University of Tasmania, which kindly made
available the copy from which this reprint is taken.
This digitally printed version 2009

A catalogue record for this publication is available from the British Library

ISBN 978-0-521-04006-8 hardback
ISBN 978-0-521-10942-0 paperback

CONTENTS

PREFACE

In 1789 it could not be said that England possessed an educational system; yet there was provision for all stages of education, from the university to the school which taught the rudiments. In the two Universities the Church was paramount and all schools of a public character were Church institutions. The uniform control involved a common aim; the great outstanding purpose to be realized was the religious purpose, to which other objects, however important, were ostensibly subordinate. The situation was not novel; ever since England had had any educational organization whatever, its direction had been the business of the Church which had framed the organization and, directly or indirectly, had brought into being its concrete instruments—colleges, schools, teachers.

In 1902 a national system had at length been organized, but direction had then passed from the Church to the State. As a consequence of political and social conditions, religion could no longer be said to·be the leading aim of English education. Indeed, it might be said that the religious purpose had virtually disappeared, while no other had definitely taken its place, except perhaps that, in the earlier days of this social revolution, the aim had been the attainment of knowledge and ever more knowledge.

The present work seeks to trace amidst conflicting opinions the slow development of this revolutionary change in the national life. The stages of that development become most evident when its progress is surveyed from the side of administration; hence the frequent reference in the following pages to legislation, and to attempts at, or preparation for, law-making—in a word, to machinery. But behind the slow building of the machine stood ideas and a creed, which owed their existence to thoughts and beliefs that had acquired momentum from the French Revolution. The study of nineteenth-century education begins in the *Émile* of Rousseau and in the *Essai d'éducation nationale* of La Chalotais, that is, in the origin of the lay school controlled by the State, the substitution of moral instruction for Christian divinity, and other changes in a curriculum which hitherto had suffered little or no change, for some three centuries at least. The seed sown by Rousseau and La Chalotais bore fruit in the formula of the French revolutionaries which, in its final form, ran, "public instruction, universal, compulsory, gratuitous, secular". With some vacillation in reference to the word "secular", the formula expresses the Radical policy which directed the development of English education during the century, until it gained an imperfect triumph in the Act of 1902, passed by a Conservative Government in the teeth of bitter Radical and Liberal opposition.

In the England of the early nineteenth century the Radical educational policy was identified with the Benthamites, the "education-mad party", and with the doctrines of utilitarianism which the party held. Schooling, it was said, should aim above everything else at imparting knowledge, "*useful* knowledge"; "Knowledge is power" was a constant theme of public speeches, leading articles, and the like. But when that policy was at length embodied in material institutions, "knowledge" had manifestly outgrown the possibility of any one's mastery; knowledge, moreover, was still in the making. Concurrently, utilitarianism had lost much of its authority as a doctrine of practice; men cherished other ends and their desires multiplied in direction. Neither religion nor utility was accepted as the dominant purpose in education. The revolution had displaced one educational end only to lose another, while putting nothing commensurable in place of either. The consequent confusion of purposes and ideals was at first masked by the belief that any kind of movement is necessarily movement forward. "Progress" was a convenient catch-word; if it could be said that education was "making progress", all was well. The enlargement of the machine and the increasing numbers subjected to it were from this point of view reassuring.

The growing interest in the study of psychology on experimental lines, and the attainment by the study of a position more independent of philosophy, took immediate effect upon educational theorizing. But the effect was necessarily upon means, not upon ends. Here again the *Émile* was potent. Rousseau saw in a child's disposition and instincts keys to a correct method of educating him, a view which assumes that the educational end is an open question. Means and ends are susceptible of being confused; and for many the satisfaction of instincts was regarded as the great thing to aim at in education. This return to the jungle is by no means absent from the educational practice of to-day.

But it is in vain to seek the educational end in the means of educating; what is wanted is an objective, not a purely subjective, standard. To demand a comprehensive standard is to ask for a statement of the *summum bonum*, and the experience of the ages teaches that agreement on that head cannot be expected. Yet a purposeless system is a contradiction in terms, and the State system, having displaced the paramount purpose of its predecessor, could only offer a number of diverse, subordinate aims such as commend themselves to the individual educator or administrator.

While the great fact of English educational history during the period is an administrative revolution, it is of course possible to view the story from other standpoints. On the political plane, it is a phase of the relations existing between the State and the citizen. How to reach a compulsory system of instruction while maintaining due respect for personal freedom, especially religious freedom, was the problem whose difficulty is reflected in the length of time which it took to attain, not a solution, but the compromises of 1870 and 1902.

Again, the immense advance in knowledge of the physical world which was made in the nineteenth century was reflected by the changes wrought in the curricula of schools of all grades. These changes are especially, but by no means exclusively, noticeable in schools above the elementary grade. The literatures of Greece and of Rome, from being an education in themselves, have become mere "subjects" in a long list of other subjects, most of which concern the human environment rather than humanity itself. Briefly, the history of the curriculum is the advance of modern, at the expense of classical, studies.

Viewed simply as the growth of an administrative scheme, the changes of a century are impressive, whether we consider the money expended, the numbers instructed, the undoubted progress in knowledge made by the population generally, the wide diffusion of culture, or the extension of discipline. But the weak spot lies in the absence of any generally recognized purpose for all this activity, beneficent as the activity was so far as it went. The consequence is that a responsibility is thrown upon the individual educator which can only be fully discharged by men and women who are not only well-informed, skilful instructors, but who are also persons who bring to their task wisdom, the habit of reflexion and an experience of life as it is outside the schoolroom.

Psychology is an indispensable foundation for a sound method of education; on the other hand, aims, purposes, ends, can only be understood in the light of philosophy illustrated by history. But the history should be that of the national education, and the philosophy ought to envisage the national conditions. The cardinal sin of schools has always been the creation of a world for themselves remote more or less from the general, and theory has often encouraged the evil. Apart from history, educational theorizing may flourish *in Platonis Republica*, but it will be of limited value in English schoolrooms. Attention lavished upon "educational reformers", without reference to the type of education they would reform, often ends in a confused eclecticism, and always in an altogether distorted picture of social history, for the student is apt to conclude that education in the past has been invariably bad. Theories of equal application to the young Japanese, the youthful American and the English boy or girl are not calculated to help any one of them very much, saving the help which is to be got from the widest generalizations. In the study of educational principles a place must therefore be found for a due consideration of the aims which have directed the national education in the past and of their relation to contemporary needs and conditions. This book is presented in the hope that it may be helpful to that end.

J. W. A.

August, 1930

INTRODUCTION

Public education spreads its roots in many different directions and draws its life from many different sources. In settled countries at least it is a growth whose beginning lies far back in the country's history. There is therefore a certain hesitation in selecting a starting-place when the comparatively recent history of education is being considered. The choice of a particular year, even of a particular century, is more or less arbitrary. The story of English education during the nineteenth century does not begin in 1801, nor is it confined to the doings of schools and universities.

Amongst the many factors which go to the making of educational practice, ideas are certainly not the least influential. It may therefore be well to begin a study of the period, 1789–1902, by a brief review of certain thoughts which were current in the preceding generation, conceptions which may be traced back to John Locke and to others of his way of thinking. In this connexion *Some Thoughts Concerning Education* (1693) naturally suggests itself, as also to a less degree does the unrevised and somewhat fragmentary *Of the Conduct of the Understanding*, which appeared in print in 1706, two years after its author's death. But neither of these equalled in effect the great truly epoch-making *Essay Concerning Human Understanding*, a seminal book in philosophy which Locke published in 1690. Its psychology in particular governed thought respecting education throughout the eighteenth century and during most of the hundred years which followed.

That psychology may be summarily expressed as the doctrine that mental development is conditioned almost entirely by the experience of the individual. The mind at birth is as a blank sheet; subsequent experience, especially the experience of which the sense organs are the channels, changes the blank into a written document, a mind more or less developed. It is in this sense that most of Locke's contemporaries and their immediate successors appear to have interpreted his teaching; the modifications tending to assign a part in development to nature as well as to nurture, which Locke introduced into his books, were commonly disregarded.

Inferences of the first importance were drawn from this doctrine of the *tabula rasa*. In the first place humanitarian feeling was fostered.

If every human being entered life unaffected by antecedent conditions, it might be hoped to ameliorate the human lot simply by improving the environment. In the eighteenth century philanthropy became almost a catch-word, and its practice influenced both private persons and statesmen. It extended to education. Pestalozzi was deeply troubled by the miserable state of the Swiss peasants of his neighbourhood long years before he sought a remedy in educating them. Joseph Lancaster was as much a philanthropist as an educator. Robert Owen's educational theory and practice grew from sympathy with his workpeople and a whole-hearted acceptance of the *tabula rasa* doctrine. This earliest of British Socialists argued that, if the particular mode of experience called education could do everything, then it was within its power to frame a new order of society. From the same premises the autocratic princes of the Continent, "the benevolent despots", as they have been termed, deduced that public education might be employed to maintain autocracy. The belief that nurture is everything led all such optimists to endorse the truth of Helvétius' emphatic assertion, "L'éducation peut tout" (*De l'esprit*, 1758).

Locke taught that experience worked in two ways to bring about the development of mind, namely, through sensation and reflection. The psychologists, English and French, who derived their inspiration from the *Essay*, tended to concentrate upon the first and to minimize or ignore the second. Thus, David Hartley (*Observations on Man*, 1749) traces all ideas to sensation, either directly, as in perception, or mediately through the force of association, as in the forming of general notions. The simpler ideas acquired through the senses are combined, compounded or otherwise reshaped in consequence of their similarity, dissimilarity or mere frequent juxtaposition. A sensationalist psychology and the doctrine of association as a sufficient explanation of intellectual and emotional life were the generally accepted foundations for the educational theorizing of the nineteenth century.

Locke's best-known educational work, *Some Thoughts Concerning Education*, assigns great importance to utility as a standard of value amongst branches of study. "Since it cannot be hoped that the pupil should have time and strength to learn all things, most pains should be taken about that which is most necessary; and that principally looked after which will be of most and frequentest use to him in the world" (Section 94). This doctrine was pushed to extreme lengths by Basedow and the "Philanthropinists" of the last decade of the eighteenth century. It dominated most of the suggestions which came from the "education-mad party" in England during the half-century which followed. The economic situation, dependent as it was upon mechanical, industrial and commercial progress, seemed more than to justify it; and, whatever its intrinsic short-comings, considerations of usefulness certainly helped to break down the monopoly held by Latin and Greek and so favoured the introduction of modern studies.

The principle of utility regarded as the criterion in morals, otherwise "the greatest happiness principle", is by some traced back to Locke as its originator. Leslie Stephen deduced it from Locke's *Two Treatises on Government*; Henry Sidgwick thought Locke's utilitarianism was "latent or unconscious". However that may be, the student of nineteenth-century affairs is constantly reminded of the vogue attained by the philosophy which saw the standard of moral value in "the greatest happiness of the greatest number". The principle is more closely associated with the names of Bentham, the two Mills and the members of the group known as the "Philosophical Radicals". In point of fact it is the teaching of their eighteenth-century predecessors. Francis Hutcheson, who died in 1747, said in his *Inquiry concerning moral good and evil*, "Moral evil or vice is as the degree of misery and number of sufferers; so that action is best which procures the greatest happiness of the greatest number". These are the words of an academic teacher; but much the same was being written by a widely read publicist, Dr John Brown, Vicar of Newcastle. In 1751 Brown published *Essays on the "Characteristics" of the Earl of Shaftesbury*, a work which reached its fifth edition in 1764. The second of the three essays ("On the motives to virtue", etc.) defines virtue ("which is no other than the conformity of our affections with the public good") as "the voluntary production of the greatest happiness", "of the greatest public happiness". *The Principles of Moral and Political Philosophy* (1785; 7th edition, 1790) by William Paley, Archdeacon of Carlisle, was a book which was very familiar to the early nineteenth-century reader. As a text-book prescribed to Cambridge undergraduates, "Paley" like "Euclid" almost ceased to be a personal name and designated a subject of examination. Paley's position in the Church and in the University gave a sort of religious sanction to the utilitarian philosophy. "So then actions are to be estimated by their tendency. Whatever is expedient is right. It is the utility of any moral rule alone which constitutes the obligation of it." When Paley speaks of "our principle that the criterion of right is utility", he is asserting Bentham's "fundamental axiom" that "the greatest happiness of the greatest number is the measure of right and wrong". In the early nineteenth century the utilitarian theory of morals and the cult of useful knowledge (in Locke's sense) were championed by the same persons.

The utilitarians argued that a man best served the common good by pursuing his own real as distinguished from his apparent good; enlightened self-interest in the individual tended to the greatest happiness of the greatest number. The theory of individualism when translated into practice underlay the many triumphs, as well as some of the failures, of the nineteenth century. It forms the woof and warp of an eighteenth-century book which still remains a leading authority in economics and politics, a book which was a veritable oracle for the majority of those who dealt in public business. *The Wealth of Nations* (1776), safely based upon a humble estimate of human nature, regarded self-interest as the mainspring of behaviour, and competition as a necessary stimulus to exertion. Its standpoint was thus strongly individualist; "natural liberty" meant freedom to exercise individual preference in most if not in all fields. Compulsion is contrary to "natural liberty". In the fifth book of the treatise Adam Smith discusses the matter of public instruction, which was at that time to be found on a comprehensive scale north of the Tweed and there only in Great Britain. Schooling should pay its own way, because endowments make for inefficiency, and dependence upon public funds renders the teachers obsequious to the public authorities who may direct in matters of which they are ignorant. "The labouring poor, that is, the great body of the people" tends to become "as stupid and ignorant as it is possible for a human creature to become...because no exertion of understanding" is needed to perform the simple, monotonous daily task.

Now a man "without the proper use of the intellectual faculties... seems to be mutilated and deformed in an essential part of the character of human nature", a momentous statement which remained little regarded by England for another century. The State derives "from the instruction of the inferior ranks of people" the advantage that, when instructed, these humble ranks are less liable "to the delusions of enthusiasm and superstition which among ignorant nations frequently occasion the most dreadful disorders. An instructed and intelligent people, besides, are always more decent and orderly than an ignorant and stupid one". The main argument then for the instruction of "the labouring poor" seems to be one of police. But a Scot could scarcely leave it at that; so Adam Smith associates himself with Comenius in asserting that instruction is a human necessity. It is but a short step to assert that it is a human right. Kant and Pestalozzi ranged themselves in this matter with the author of *The Wealth of Nations*, but English public opinion was slow to follow their example.

Smith outlines the organization of public instruction which he would approve. For "a very small expense", the community can facilitate, encourage and even compel the general mastery of the three R's. In every parish there should be a little school, whose master should be paid in part by voluntary contributions, in part by the pupil's fees, these being such as to be within the means of "a common labourer". The contribution from public funds to the upkeep of the school and the payment of the teacher must only make good any deficiency in these other sources. The school should teach the elements of geometry and mechanics as well as reading, writing and arithmetic. Small prizes for attainment should be paid for by public money; those who failed to pass an examination ought not to be permitted to practise a trade. A more difficult State examination should guard entrance to the professions.

Smith sets so high a value on utility that he finds great merit in the meagre education customarily given to girls at that time. "There are no public institutions for the education of women, and there is accordingly nothing useless, absurd or fantastical in the common course of their education. They are taught what their parents or guardians judge it necessary for them to learn and they are taught nothing else. Every part of their education tends evidently to some useful purpose; either to improve the natural attractions of their person or to form their mind to reserve, to modesty, to chastity and to economy; to render them both likely to become the mistresses of a family, and to behave properly when they have become such. In every part of her life a woman feels some conveniency or advantage from every part of her education" (Bk. V, article ij).

The eighteenth century abounded in examples of the "give and take" between this country and France which has so long marked the cultural relations of the two countries. John Locke, when made widely known to Frenchmen by Voltaire, became the leading philosophic thinker of Western Europe; and Locke's philosophy found a natural development in the deism, naturalism and political conceptions of Rousseau and of those Frenchmen whose writings did so much to precipitate and direct the French Revolution. That great unheaval in turn reacted upon English thinking; and English ideas respecting education, its purpose, character and public organization were influenced by what was happening across the Channel.

Although Rousseau has much in common with Locke, especially in psychology and educational theory, the French writer in some important respects represents a reaction from the rationalism of his English predecessor. Both are agreed as to the duty incumbent upon the educator to observe the character of mental development as exhibited in children, and to base method on such observation. Both find the root of the development in the exercise of the sense organs. Both denounce the curriculum of their time for its purely literary character and its omission of modern studies. But while Locke is all for trusting reason, Rousseau looks for enlightenment to feeling and sentiment; the preference shown by many educators to-day for the indulgence of instincts, rather than for their rational control and the discipline of reason, is a legacy from Rousseau quite foreign to Locke. In spite of the tendency of his thought, Locke was personally one whose religion rested upon the assumption of the supernatural. Rousseau's naturalism, on the other hand, is so literal that it explains, but does not excuse, the patent defect in his suggestions for moral training. The sentimentality of Rousseau had an earlier parallel in the English romantic literature represented by Richardson's novels; it is reflected in the birth, or rebirth, of German literature in the writings of Lessing, Goethe, Schiller, and in the almost contemporary movement in England.

The *Emile* of Rousseau appeared in 1762; in the following year La Chalotais published his *Essai d'Éducation nationale*. Rousseau influenced subsequent educational theory and method; La Chalotais suggested the idea of the lay, secular school and so introduced a revolutionary train of thought into educational administration. Hitherto public instruction had been considered the business, even the monopoly, of the Church; La Chalotais would transfer the monopoly to the State. The teachers were to be laymen, religious teaching was to be excluded from the schools and confined to the home and the clergy; but the schools were to give moral and civic instruction.

The politicians of the French Revolution were not very successful in establishing educational institutions, but they succeeded in framing a formula which for a hundred years after their time defined Liberal policy in the administration of public instruction. "Education, universal, compulsory, gratuitous and secular", was the statement of policy which was gradually developed through discussion under the different types of French revolutionary government. With one exception (if it be an exception) this formula describes the aim in the educational sphere which English Radicals and Liberals strove to attain throughout the nineteenth century. The exception is the principle that public education must be "secular", that is, must not include religious instruction. The English substitute ran, "education, as to religious teaching, must be undenominational, but such teaching may be omitted at the option of the child's guardian".

The compromise called undenominationalism was in effect a denial of an essential corollary of Liberal doctrine, namely, the freedom of the individual to be of what religion he pleased, or none; and the vagueness of what Joseph Lancaster called "general Christianity" proved to be as potent a solvent as secularism itself in destroying any belief in the possibility of a common end attainable by national education. The French were more logical: on Liberal principles public education must be lay, "secular"; and this has been an agreed policy in English higher education for the past fifty years.

State control of education was a principle familiar to Greek thinkers, and it had been discussed in England before La Chalotais mooted it in France. But whereas Plato and Aristotle virtually take the principle for granted, in England it met with adverse criticism. Englishmen were not blind to the fact that State-controlled instruction, not one whit less than Church-controlled instruction, involved very much more than an administrative arrangement for economizing spiritual forces and material supplies. The teaching of the *Republic* of Plato and of the *Politics* of Aristotle was not forgotten; the point at issue was the precise nature of the relation between the individual and the community.

The *locus classicus* occurs at the opening of the fifth book of the *Politics*. "That the education of the young is a matter which has a paramount claim upon the attention of the legislator will not be disputed.

The neglect of it in existing states is prejudicial to their politics. For the educational system...must always be relative to the particular polity which is its habitual preservative, as it is in fact the original cause of its creation, e.g. a democratic character of a democracy, an oligarchical of an oligarchy and so on....Again, as the end proposed to the State as a whole is one, it is clear that the education of all the citizens must be one and the same, and the superintendence of it a public affair rather than in private hands, as it now is, when each individual superintends his own children privately and with such private instruction as he thinks good....And further, it is not right to suppose that any citizen is his own master, but rather that all belong to the State; for each individual is a member of the State, and the superintendence of any part is naturally relative to that of the whole. This is one point in which the Lacedaemonians deserve praise; they devote a great deal of attention to the educational needs of their children and the attention takes the form of action on the part of the State."[1]

That is, the State, or community, once established, should remain static in character; Sparta is praised to the detriment of Athens. Education is intended to *preserve* the established order; the State undertakes it, and allows no private agency or the wishes of an individual to intervene. The doctrine that education is a political preservative is one which has been acted upon time and again, although it has not always been frankly avowed. Montesquieu held "that the laws of education should be relative to the principles of the Government". The doctrine was repeated by Thomas Sheridan (*British Education*, 1756) and by Dr John Brown (*Thoughts on Civil Liberty, Licentiousness and Faction*, 1765), both of whom asserted it emphatically. Contradiction promptly came from Joseph Priestley (*Essay on the First Principles of Government and on the Nature of Civil and Religious Liberty*, 1768), who held that an education administered on that principle would cramp the growth of a community and destroy its civil and religious freedom; the principle should be resisted in the interest alike of the individual and of the community.

The extreme length to which some of the French revolutionary leaders would take the Aristotelian principle is illustrated in the proposal of Michel le Peletier, that all children between the ages of five and eleven, if girls, or twelve, if boys, should be brought up in

[1] Welldon's translation, pp. 222–3.

common by the Republic, clothed, fed and taught on one uniform plan. The alleged ground for this proposal was that in a public institution "the entire existence of the child belongs to *us*". But there were prominent revolutionaries who saw to what end such a declaration tended. Condorcet, reporting to the National Assembly in April, 1792, said, "no public body should have authority to prevent the development of new truths, the teaching of theories contrary to its own policy or to its interests of the moment.... A power which would prohibit the teaching of an opinion contrary to that which had served as basis for established laws would directly attack the liberty of thought, would contradict the purpose of every social institution, the perfection of the laws, which is a necessary consequence of the conflict of opinion and of the march of enlightenment".[1]

In the same year Romme agreed that it is of the essence of executive power to possess very great authority, "yet it should never direct public opinion at its will, for only opinion can keep ward efficaciously over the executive". A Government possessing such unrestricted power could poison the very source of social life long before the mischief could be detected and remedied.[2]

This was a view of State-controlled education which could not fail to be appreciated in contemporary England, particularly by Nonconformists (Protestant or Catholic) who still suffered political or educational disabilities, notwithstanding the partial relief afforded by the Acts of 1778, and 1779, 1791, parliamentary measures which permitted Protestant Dissenters and Roman Catholics to teach publicly but not in the Universities and older Public Schools. They were, however, debarred from university education; Roman Catholics were in addition excluded from political office and the public services. Jews shared these disabilities to the full.

In England the Dissenter was in a minority which was made to feel its position and which might well fear that that position would become worse. The French revolutionary, if not in a numerical majority, was in possession of the executive power which he meant to use to turn the tables on the old *régime*. Add to this difference in the point of view the strong individualism of the Englishman, and we have the explana-

[1] C. Hippeau, *L'instruction publique en France pendant la Révolution: Discours et Rapports*, pp. 190 and 248.
[2] For the sequel see *Modern France*, 1922 (Arthur Tilley, ed.), pp. 376–82.

tion of the paradox, that those English Radicals who were the friends, even the enthusiastic friends, of the French Revolution were precisely the men who most strenuously opposed State-controlled education in England as being opposed to religious and political freedom.

Thomas Paine had a ready ear for the abstract principles of the Revolution, whose most redoutable propagandist in England he was generally accounted. In *The Rights of Man* (1791–2), on whose publication he found it expedient to fly to France, he affirms that "a nation under a well-regulated government should permit none to remain uninstructed". Yet he is careful to limit the State's action either to compelling parents to pay their children's school fees or to remitting taxes as a set-off to fees; in needy cases a State grant might be paid for the purpose to the individual parent. This is a roundabout way by which the State avoids responsibility for the particular kind of instruction given. In April, 1791, Joseph Priestley publicly used the phrase "the glorious revolution in France"; but he remained of the same opinion concerning State-controlled education as that which he held in 1768, when he unreservedly condemned it. The general principle advocated in William Godwin's *Enquiry concerning political justice* (1796) is an anarchistic individualism—a principle which would forbid any form of public instruction; "the project of national education ought uniformly to be discouraged on account of its obvious alliance with national government". Paine, Priestley and Godwin are all of dissenting origin and breeding.

Mary Wollstonecraft (*A Vindication of the Rights of Women*, 1792) was singular amongst English friends of the Revolution in giving whole-hearted support to national or State-directed instruction; but she was also singular amongst French admirers of that plan in her advocacy of co-education.

The fears of Priestley and his friends were justified by so uncompromising an utterance as that made by John Bowles in *A Letter addressed to Samuel Whitbread* (1807). "With regard even to the very few who feel any concern upon this subject [the religious education of their children] and who wish their children to be brought up in a particular persuasion, if they would obtain for them the advantages of charitable instruction, they cannot reasonably expect any deviation on their account from the system of religious education which is adopted in the school where that advantage is bestowed." Bowles believed that this enforced conformity would not "in the least encroach upon parental rights", and he continued, "I trust, Sir, that effectual means will now be taken to secure the full operation of the principle. . . that when education is made a national concern, youth must be brought up as members of the national church". Such a letter explains why the English State did not establish earlier than 1870 even a partial scheme of national education, why the voluntary system and the conscience clause were necessary elements in the compromise which was reached in that year after acrimonious debates of the "religious question" prolonged over two generations. It will be noticed that according to Bowles public instruction is "charitable", not a genuine public service of universal application, and that it is the function of the Church to supply it. These opinions largely affected policy and procedure in the subsequent years.

The second half of the eighteenth century witnessed an entire reorganization of English life so revolutionary that it had no equal in our previous history. Primarily industrial, this revolution was also to a high degree moral, religious, political and intellectual. The mainspring of the industrial revolution was constituted by the great advance in mechanical invention which was a marked feature of the earlier part of the third George's reign. The consequence was the supersession of handwork, of home industries, of the small master and his few journeymen by machinery, the great factory, the mill owner and his crowd of "hands". Concurrently with this change a similar revolution took place in agriculture. Scientific farming and the employment of greatly improved machinery required large enclosed farms, which displaced the open-field tillage that for centuries had been carried on by yeomen, or small farmers, and their labourers.

The new order stimulated, as nothing had done hitherto, the production of coal and iron and the increase and redistribution of population. Where coal and iron were found together, villages became great towns and new centres of population were created to which the workless were attracted. The population of England and Wales, which was estimated at six millions in 1700, was only increased by half a million fifty years later. The first census, that of 1801, showed a population of nine millions; ten years later it exceeded ten millions. Population increased beyond the subsistence limit. Whereas in the early years of George III England was still exporting corn, the conditions brought about by the industrial revolution made the country a corn importer.

In the congested manufacturing areas population outpaced the growth of suitable housing; large numbers of the people occupied insanitary dwellings whose condition was virtually unaffected by law or regulation.

An enormous improvement in transport was effected. During the second half of the eighteenth century a network of canals joined the manufacturing towns and districts. Mediaeval trackways, traversed for centuries by packhorses, became broad "metalled" roads, which bore not only heavy wagons but comparatively rapid stage coaches. The invention of the steam locomotive and the opening of the first railway (1825) may be regarded as the first step in the evolution of transport facilities which continues to-day in unabated vigour.

Great fortunes were amassed in industry and a well-to-do middle class, engaged in manufacture and in commerce, was created. The magnate of an earlier day was a landed proprietor with interests rooted in the soil; the "new men" and the "coming men" of the late eighteenth century were industrialists of the mill, the factory, and the exchange. This industrial middle class was largely Methodist in sympathy, where it did not consist of actual dissenters from the doctrine and ritual of the Church of England. Dissenters had no share in university education; many of them made no use of the grammar schools which were distinctly "Church" institutions. Politically, Dissent was against all forms of privilege, particularly such as were enjoyed by the nobility and "landed gentry". Those of them who were not sympathizers with the small but active Radical party were yet as a rule in opposition to the Government. Their growing importance in the State is exemplified by the relief legislation passed between 1778 and 1791.

The material prosperity of one section of the people was counterbalanced by an industrial population which was often overworked and not infrequently sweated. Mills and factories were usually unhealthy, and the employment of little children in such places and in mines was carried on in conditions which to-day seem incredible. Even as late as 1824 there were in mills at Macclesfield child workers under five years of age; it needed half a century's desultory agitation (1788–1840) to bring to an end the employment of the chimney-sweep's "climbing boys". Rousseau's callous abandonment of his five illegitimate children, while it is in cruel contrast with his exhortation to parents and educators to "study the child", is not unrepresentative of the attitude assumed by many towards children at that time and for many years afterwards.

PART ONE
PRE-VICTORIAN

CHAPTER I

The People and the People's Education

The close of the eighteenth century and the opening of the next was a period of war, first with the French Republic and afterwards with Napoleon, which strained the nation's resources to the utmost and left an aftermath of the kind which is only too familiar to-day. The profound social changes brought about by the industrial revolution and the disturbing consequences of the wars of 1793–1815 made the first forty or fifty years of the nineteenth century a time of stress which affected English life in all its aspects. It was during this half-century that the national system of educational administration had its beginning.

That system was very slowly constructed from below upwards; on that account it seems desirable in the first place to note the circumstances amidst which the majority of English parents and children were then living. Then, as now, a variety of causes issued in unemployment and consequent destitution. Rioting, arson, the destruction of machinery on the one side were countered by bloodshed, the suspension of the Habeas Corpus Act and rigorous prosecutions on the other. Some hoped to find a remedy in parliamentary reform, others in revolution sometimes after the French pattern. The task of government was very difficult and it was not always discharged with wisdom.

The Elizabethan Poor Law of 1601 still directed the administration of relief; but it broke down under the burden of poverty which followed the conclusion of the long struggle with France. To cope with unemployment, high prices and low wages, outdoor relief was stretched to the utmost. Wages were supplemented and doles were given from the rates on the instructions of justices and overseers; payment from the rates was made in respect of wives, of children legitimate or illegitimate. Where the wages of the family fell below the local standard, the deficit was made good from these same parish rates, a procedure which further depressed wages and corrupted employer and employed alike. The absolute pauper was often better off than the independent workman. In 1803 one person in every seven was receiving parish relief. The annual cost of relief between 1818 and 1832, when a Commission of Inquiry was appointed, varied between seven and eight millions. The Commission, which reported in 1834, discovered that whole parishes were pauperized; one parish of 139 persons included in that number 104 persons in receipt of relief.

The Poor Law Amendment Act of 1834 abolished outdoor relief, imposed a workhouse test and made over the administration to local boards of guardians and a central board of commissioners. Great distress accompanied even the gradual discontinuance of outdoor relief; yet it seemed the only way in which to break a vicious circle.

The working classes were politically impotent; at the same time large numbers of them were sufficiently instructed to understand that the cardinal doctrines of the French Revolution, the sovereignty of the people and the denial of privilege, greatly concerned themselves. Attempts at an extension or redistribution of the parliamentary franchise date from the early years of the long reign of George III. The first Reform Act (1832) was a triumph of the middle classes, not of the manual workers.

During the nineties of the eighteenth century there was much revolutionary propaganda originating at home and in France, with corresponding repressive measures by the English Government, which were directed against treason, sedition and the activities in general of the numerous revolutionary associations. This policy was continued after the Peace of 1815 in order to defeat political disaffection and industrial disorder. The Combination Act of 1800, which reaffirmed and amended a similar statute of 1799, in effect made illegal any association of the nature of a trade union. The Act was repealed in 1824, chiefly by the contriving of Francis Place and Joseph Hume, members of the small party of "philosophical Radicals", of whom more must be said hereafter. But in 1825 all combinations of that kind, save those for re-gulating wages or hours of labour, were made illegal by Act of Parliament.

The law laid a heavy hand upon offenders. In the year 1805 sixty-eight persons suffered capital punishment, of whom only ten had been convicted of murder. Amongst the offences for which the remaining fifty-eight paid the extreme penalty were burglary (15), forgery or uttering forged notes (13), horse or sheep stealing (12), larceny, wounding, arson and highway robbery. It was so late as 1832 that the death penalty was abolished in the cases of forgery, coining, sacrilege, horse or sheep stealing.

Poverty and the grievous sorrows of the English poor did not originate in the industrial revolution, although some writers of to-day seem to think so. Nor must it be assumed that there were no bright colours to relieve the gloom of the picture outlined above. The memoirs of a contemporary working man like Samuel Bamford (*Early Days* and *Passages in the Life of a Radical*) tell of a happy childhood spent in an industrial town, and they prove that the Lancashire "operative" and his wife, or sweetheart, contrived to get a good deal of jollity at least out of the greater holidays of Easter, Whitsuntide and Christmas as well as from the "Wakes" and other local feasts. Then he was as care-free and as interested in "best clothes" as are his great-grandchildren to-day. Schools were neither plentiful nor very efficient, yet the children whose schooling was meagre did not invariably grow to be "brute beasts" and nothing more. Bamford joined a "rude and simple set" of "lads from factories and dyehouses" who, about the year 1807, tramped from Manchester to South Shields in order to engage them-selves as apprentices in the coasting trade. On their arrival at York their conductor showed them over the Minster; some, of whom Bamford was one, spent their first day ashore in London visiting St Paul's, Tower Hill and the Abbey. In their attempts to better their condition working men did not lack leaders of their own class; William Cobbett, William Lovett, Francis Place, were men of outstanding ability but they were not singular in their capacity to lead. Leslie Stephen thought that in reference to the years 1760–1830 "there is probably no period in English history in which a greater number of poor men have risen to distinction", and he enumerated a list of writers, men of science and learning, social reformers, all sprung from this class of the community, the paucity and indifferent quality of their schools and the shortness of school life notwithstanding.

Neither was English society divided horizontally. Amongst the well-to-do and the wealthy, philanthropy and active benevolence were not wanting; on the contrary, these were a feature of public life through-out Western Europe in the second half of the eighteenth century. Not all mill owners were indifferent or hostile, as some were, to the material or spiritual condition of their work-people. Some provided schools and institutes for their employees and employees' children. The first Factory Act ("Peel's Act," 1802) was the joint production of two mill owners, Sir Robert Peel, the first baronet, and Robert Owen, of whose place in the history of education more remains to be said.

The title of this Act is worth noting: "An Act for the preservation of the health and morals of apprentices and others employed in cotton and other mills and cotton and other factories". Its provisions were intended to cover a wide field. All mill rooms were to be ventilated, and twice a year whitewashed. An apprentice was to receive a suit of clothes once a year; the working day was not to exceed twelve hours exclusive of meals, and no work was to be permitted between 9 p.m. and 6 a.m. Boys and girls were to sleep in separate rooms, and not more than two apprentices must occupy the same bed. The mills were to be inspected by visitors appointed by the justices, and medical attendance was to be provided in cases of infectious disease. Religious teaching was obligatory, and during the first four of the seven years' apprenticeship instruction must be given in reading, writing and arithmetic.

The Act was unpopular; manufacturers' petitions to Parliament described it as "injurious", "harsh", "oppressive", "impracticable". It was evaded by employing children who were not indentured apprentices. In truth, conditions under the factory system were radically different from those which had held under the domestic system of sixteenth-century apprenticeship. In any case these new conditions would have presented formidable obstacles to the Act's operation.

By the close of the eighteenth century Methodism had become an accepted factor of national life; its teaching permeated the new middle class and the labouring folk of the large towns and mining centres. The popular preaching of George Whitefield (1714–70), of John Newton (1724–1807), the poet Cowper's associate at Olney, of Henry Venn (1725–97), and of the numerous lesser lights who gathered about them gave birth to a very similar movement within the Church of England. Increased social importance was attached to Evangelicalism, as this movement was called, by the adhesion of Wilberforce, Granville Sharp, John Venn and others of the "Clapham Sect". This later Evangelical school, dating from about 1787, was largely a Cambridge movement, whose organizing chief was a Cambridge incumbent, Charles Simeon (1759–1836).

Evangelicalism conceived religion primarily as the intimate, personal relation between God and the individual soul, a conception which had its effect upon educational principle and practice. Narrow-minded and illiterate as were the earliest founders of the school, the Evangelicals were possessed by a philanthropy which found expression in a "burning love of souls", as they phrased it. This love of their fellow-men was manifested in missionary zeal, in a horror of the slave trade and its iniquities, in solicitude for the physical well-being of prisoners, a desire for the betterment of the poor and for the conversion of individuals. The "Clapham Sect", whose leading members were men of wealth, supported the work of Bell and Lancaster, maintained schools, savings banks and village libraries. The abolition of the slave trade in 1833 was due to the long-continued advocacy of its members. Their zeal for the spread of Christianity led to the foundation in 1797 of the Church Missionary Society, and in 1804 of the British and Foreign Bible Society. They ardently desired the establishment at Calcutta of a bishopric and "the removal of all restraints on the diffusion of Christianity within its limits".[1] Remembering the prominent place in the Clapham Sect which was taken by Zachary Macaulay, it does not seem extravagant to trace in this missionary zeal directed to India the beginning, in the mind of his son, the future Lord Macaulay, of that policy of Westernizing Indian education that has had such portentous consequences, whether for good or evil it is hard to tell. In the education of the people and in care for the prisoner and the slave the members of the Society of Friends were the associates of the Evangelicals.

The motives were various which induced private persons and privately initiated societies, at first, and, later, the Government itself, to undertake the work of educating the people on the great scale. The desire to raise the standard of the national life by removing ignorance, or by advancing morals, or by disseminating religious training, or by all of these means, was for many the impelling force. Attempts to reconcile the poor with their lot or to enable them to make the best of it, to counteract the teaching of "the democrats", as sympathizers with the French Revolution were called, were more powerful influences with others. The excesses in France, rebellion in Ireland, and mob violence at home sufficiently account for this motive of police which is evident enough in the writings and speeches of persons in authority; but it

[1] Sir J. Stephen, *Essays in Ecclesiastical Biography* (1860), p. 556.

would be unfair to human nature and untrue to the facts to regard
police measures as the chief function of popular education as understood
by all its advocates of that day.

Certainly the first movement made during the late eighteenth
century, that which established Sunday schools in all parts of the
country, was purely religious and philanthropic. The earlier charity
schools had lost the impetus with which they started, they no longer
enjoyed the popularity which had offended Bernard Mandeville, and
in some cases their endowments, like the endowments of some schools
of a higher grade, were the emoluments of teachers who had few pupils
or none. In any case their number was insufficient. But the Sunday
school movement started at Gloucester in 1780 by Stock and Raikes,
and organized chiefly by the Sunday Schools Union of 1785, spread to
all parts of the country with great rapidity. In 1784 John Wesley found
these schools everywhere in the course of his diverse perambulations;
by the close of the century timid Churchmen saw in the numerous
Sunday schools supported by Dissenters a menace to the Church. In
the "thirties" of the nineteenth century it was commonly said that one
million pupils, children and adults, attended school on Sundays; these
schools were always included in any survey of the national provision
for education. Kay-Shuttleworth, writing in 1847 under the direction
of the Committee of Council on Education, did not hesitate to declare
that the Sunday school had "laid the foundations of public education
for the poor deeply in the religious organizations of the country. The
type of this school has to a great extent predetermined the constitution
of the daily school, and provided the fabric which by a natural transition
may be employed in the establishment of an efficient system of elementary instruction tending in harmony with the Sunday schools to complete the work of Christian civilization, which has been so auspiciously
commenced".[1]

Sunday school teachers, some of whom were paid for their services,
were often persons of very humble attainments with crude ideas
respecting method; much of the religious teaching was confined to rote
learning of texts, catechisms and hymns. The teaching of reading was
carried on in all these schools, the aim being the reading of the Bible,
which was used as a child's primer and reading-book. Some schools
taught writing and a smaller number added summing; but in most of

[1] J. Kay-Shuttleworth, *Four Periods of Public Education* (1862), p. 441.

the schools these two arts were felt to be out of harmony with the day and the aims of the school. Some religious bodies forbade such teaching. A few Sunday schools in the north aroused so great an enthusiasm for elementary instruction that they opened their doors on week-day evenings also.

At a very early stage in its history the Sunday school passed beyond the limits of purely religious instruction. The school which Mrs Trimmer founded at Brentford in 1786 soon added spinning on weekdays to the usual teaching of Sunday; Mrs Trimmer's reputation as a writer of children's books and the Queen's patronage made the Brentford experiment known throughout the country. Still more influential were the labours of Hannah and Martha More in Somerset. Beginning with a Sunday school at Cheddar in 1789, these ladies, aided by philanthropists like William Wilberforce, within ten years were directing the instruction of some 3000 children, parents and aged relatives, assembled in schools scattered over twelve parishes. Knitting and spinning were added to the customary religious teaching and Bible-reading; some of the schools were open daily, some twice or thrice a week, others on Sundays only. In twenty-five years 20,000 children, mainly from the families of miners and colliers, had been taught in these Mendip schools. In connexion with this philanthropic attempt the "religious difficulty" made an early appearance (1799–1801); certain local clergy protested that the schools favoured Methodism to the prejudice of the Church.

To encourage a habit of industry and to relieve distress benevolent persons started schools whose chief aim was, in the language of the old Poor Law, "to set the poor on work" Various forms of handwork were taught, as spinning, winding, knitting, straw-plaiting, sewing, shoe-making, gardening. To some schools of this sort little ones of two, three, five years of age were admissible; seven seems to have been the upward limit for admission. Arrangements were sometimes made, as at Lewisham in 1796, to admit pauper children, and in some parishes the workhouses included schools of this kind to which only the workhouse children were admitted. The usual practice under the old Poor Law (abrogated in 1834) was to mix the children indiscriminately with the adult paupers, some of whom acted as the children's instructors; this plan almost always proved to be scandalously bad. But whether supported by private benevolence or by the Poor Law, it seems to have been the general expectation that these "schools of industry" would be maintained by the profits of the children's labour. In some cases there was a surplus after providing the children with a dinner daily, which was either returned in cash to the children who had earned it, or credited to their savings bank account. The parish rates of Birmingham were reduced by the removal of the children from the workhouse to the school of industry where their diet seems to have been more liberal than the workhouse fare.

As a rule, to which there were one or two notable exceptions, the schools of industry confined their scholastic instruction to the teaching of reading. But they were not singular in this respect; to be able to read was commonly regarded as sufficient schooling for the poor. "In all large day-schools there are many who have not acquired this art [sc. writing], and who are sent to the school solely to learn to read."[1]

During the last five or six years of the eighteenth century there was widespread interest in the schools of industry. In 1796 Pitt, then Prime Minister, proposed that there should be in every parish in England "a school or schools of industry for instructing children or poor persons to work"; but nothing of the kind was done. A return of 1802 showed that there were 188,794 children between the ages of five and fourteen receiving parish relief, of whom 20,336 were "in schools of industry and receiving education". It should be added that some mill owners provided a measure of schooling for the children in their employ, sometimes under circumstances which must have made learning a burden for pupils already tired by long hours of work. Owen's experiment at New Lanark, of which more must be said presently, was by far the most notable of these "works' schools".[2]

A more comprehensively educational aim was in the mind of William Gilpin (1724–1804), vicar of Boldre, Hants, when he founded (1791) and subsequently endowed his parochial schools for twenty boys and as many girls. Gilpin had been the proprietor of a private school at Cheam for thirty years before coming to Boldre; while the clergyman

---

[1] *Of the Education of the Poor*; a digest of the reports of the Society for bettering the condition of the Poor (1809), p. 165. The remark occurs in a report on the Borough Road School introducing Lancaster's plan (and Bell's) for teaching reading and writing in combination.

[2] See pp. 98 f. below.

gave due place to religious instruction, the retired schoolmaster felt constrained to see that the boys were taught to read, write and cipher, the girls to read, knit and sew. The discrimination between the sexes reflects the general opinion then current that for girls the barest minimum of instruction sufficed. Children were admitted to the Boldre school between the ages of seven and nine, provided they could "read tolerably a chapter in the New Testament", the master and mistress being too fully occupied to "teach first rudiments". A catechism, written by Gilpin to be learned by rote, recited the elements of religion, some points in natural history intended to illustrate "the argument from design", and an account of Jewish customs. The profits derived from the sale of the girls' work were paid over annually to the girls themselves, to each according to her earnings. The school was maintained for about forty guineas per annum, the master's salary being twenty guineas with house and garden, that of the mistress ten guineas.

The example set by Gilpin's school caused several little schools to be set up in its neighbourhood, and wide publicity was given to it throughout the country. It had many imitators in the north of Yorkshire, in Lancashire, Westmorland, and Cumberland.

The type of parish school commonly conducted by the clergy is exemplified in that of West Street, St Giles's, London, which was opened in 1802 to teach children the "three R's", in addition to that religious instruction which was traditionally since mediaeval times the principal aim of all parish schools. West Street taught 240 boys and girls, each of whom paid thirteen shillings annually; there were also 100 children in the Sunday school who of course paid no fee. The premises were overcrowded, otherwise the numbers could have been more than doubled. There were three teachers, a master and two mistresses whose salaries, with board, were £50, £32 and £30 respectively; 90 children were clothed at a charge of £90 a year. The entire cost of the establishment, clothing grant included, was between £280 and £290 per annum, a sum which was met by pupils' fees, voluntary subscriptions and "collections" at four charity sermons.[1]

In 1807 Samuel Whitbread, who then led the party which advocated popular instruction, introduced a Bill for Poor Law reform, which failed to become an Act of Parliament. Amongst many other matters

[1] *Of the Education of the Poor*, pp. 150 ff.

this Bill proposed to establish parish schools supported by a parish rate and supervised by the parish clergy.

A very similar proposal was made in 1820 by Brougham, and some progress was effected with a Bill in Parliament; but this was withdrawn in deference to the objections of the Dissenters. The Bill gave effect to what had long been both common law and canon law, namely, that education was the business of the clergy. In his introductory speech, Brougham said, "I might almost say that a parson was a clerical schoolmaster, and a schoolmaster was a lay-parson". Accordingly, parish clerks were to be encouraged to take the masterships of the parish schools which the Bill proposed to set up everywhere. This return to mediaeval practice was to be tempered by a most unmediaeval laxity of doctrine. "It was not necessary that the schoolmaster should teach any particular religion"—one of the earliest and most comprehensive assertions in this country of what was later to be known as undenominationalism.

Brief mention of Owen's works' school at New Lanark has been made above. Its one permanent contribution to English education was the introduction of the infant school, which from that time onward secured an established place in the national scheme. Owen's disagreement with his partners put an end to the New Lanark schools as Owen had conducted them; but the idea of the infant school survived under the fostering care of such men as Brougham, Wilberforce, James Mill, Zachary Macaulay and the brothers Wilson. In 1818 Brougham and others set up in Westminster an infant school, putting it in charge of James Buchanan, who had been the schoolmaster at New Lanark. Next, in 1820, Joseph Wilson opened a school in Spitalfields, the master of which was Samuel Wilderspin, who later carried on a most successful propaganda on behalf of schools of this kind, acting as agent for the London Infant School Society, founded in 1824. The first secretary of this society was the mystic, James Pierrepont Greaves (1777–1842), to whom Pestalozzi addressed the *Letters to Greaves*; Greaves had taken part (1817–18) in Pestalozzi's last educational experiment, the Poor School at Clendy, undertaken when the Yverdon Institute was coming to a disastrous end.[1] But the English infant school owed very little to the Swiss reformer, save perhaps a vague conception of the principle that the elements of instruction are language, form and number.

[1] See J. A. Green, *Pestalozzi's Educational Writings* (1912), pp. 211–66.

William Wilson (the brother of Joseph Wilson), vicar of Walthamstow, gave his parish the third infant school to be set going in England; in 1834 Lord Brougham asserted that this school was "the best to be seen anywhere". By that date, or very soon after, the London Infant School Society had ceased to exist and Wilderspin was acting on his own behalf. In 1836, when the Home and Colonial Infant School Society was instituted to train teachers, there were in England, largely in consequence of the zealous labours of Wilderspin, 150 schools of this kind.[1]

Night schools taught by independent teachers, or by teachers attached to some Sunday schools, gave instruction in reading and sometimes also in writing and summing. For the less normal there were schools for the blind and for the deaf and dumb, and reformatory schools for children in danger of becoming habitual criminals; these were maintained by philanthropic societies.

Teaching to read had not in the past been confined to the schoolroom; indeed, the old grammar schools had at one time refused to regard such teaching as part of their business. The new economic and social conditions of the late eighteenth century accentuated and extended the demand for such rudimentary instruction. Dames' schools, night schools and still humbler and less organized forms of teaching arose to meet the demand, the supply coming from independent, private teachers in return for a weekly fee of about fourpence per scholar. Mrs Trimmer asserted that in 1801 "every town and most villages" had a sufficiency of private teaching of this elementary sort and that poor parents were eager to employ it. Joseph Lancaster opened a school of this kind in the Borough Road, Southwark, in 1798, to teach 100 boys and girls, the children of mechanics, reading, writing, and summing. By the employment of pupils to "teach" their fellows, by a strictly parsimonious provision of books and the employment of a very mechanical type of instruction, he reduced the expense of his school to less than seven shillings and sixpence per annum per pupil. With the help of well-to-do sympathizers he was able to give free places and, in some cases, dinners also to necessitous children. This was in 1801; eight years later the school had 500 pupils, and arrangements were being contemplated to accommodate another 200.

[1] For the early history of English infant schools, see David Salmon and Winifred Hindshaw, *Infant Schools, Their History and Theory* (1904).

The provision of elementary instruction on the national scale was due to the great popularity of the mutual, monitorial, or Madras system —it was known by all these names. For the honour of its introduction, or invention, Andrew Bell (1753–1832), Joseph Lancaster (1778–1838) and their respective partisans carried on a bitter controversy, the two rivals in effect representing the Church and Dissent. Bell's *An Experiment in Education* (1797) recounted his use of this "system" at Madras as early as 1789; in 1800 Lancaster read this book and in 1803 organized on similar lines the school which he had opened in Southwark in 1798. In 1804 he visited Bell to whom at this time he acknowledged his indebtedness; the quarrel about priority, fomented by others, came later. But there was in reality very little to quarrel about. The employment of praepostors, prefects or monitors to assist in the discipline of a school, or even to give casual help in teaching, is an ancient device of unknown origin. The peg on which the mutual system hung was the employment of one sole master who taught monitors only, these passing on to their schoolfellows the instruction so received. Neither Bell nor Lancaster could claim patent rights in the plan. In December, 1792, F. Lanthenas had presented a report to the French National Convention on behalf of the Committee of Public Instruction. In this report the following passage occurs: "The schoolmasters as well as the schoolmistresses will make use of the help of those scholars whose intelligence has exhibited the most rapid advance. In that way they will very easily be able, at one and the same sitting, to bestow upon four classes of pupils all the care needed for their progress. At the same time the attempts of the most capable children to teach their schoolmates what they themselves know, and to inculcate it upon them, will instruct themselves much more effectively than would their master's lessons".[1]

However excusable such a procedure may seem in view of an excessive shortage of teachers, the mechanical character of the teaching implied a very obvious defect. Yet contemporaries professed to regard this as a virtue. "The grand principle of Dr Bell's system", said Sir Thomas Bernard, "is the division of labour applied to intellectual purposes.... The principle in schools *and manufactories* is the same."[2]

[1] C. Hippeau, *L'instruction publique en France pendant la Révolution: Discours et Rapports* (1881), p. 294.
[2] *Of the Education of the Poor*, pp. 35, 36.

Lancaster himself described his "invention" as "a new and *mechanical system* for the use of schools". It was claimed that the individual pupil in a mutual school received very much more attention than was possible in a comparatively large school, taught by one or two teachers only, that in a mutual school it was easier to control children, that competition was in full operation throughout the school hours, that each pupil was forced "to use and exercise his own faculties"—how, and on what were not specified. This mechanical idea of teaching led the advocates of the plan to say that it met the shortage of "intelligent and qualified schoolmasters".[1]

Its shortcomings and positive defects notwithstanding, the work of Bell and Lancaster had important consequences. It made the provision of popular instruction on a national scale feasible, it compensated to a certain degree for the absence of a body of teachers, provided a rough scheme of teachers' training and prepared the way for the pupil-teacher system. Out of the controversy between Bell and Lancaster grew the voluntary system, which was at once a makeshift solution of the "religious difficulty" and a compromise between sheer individualism and State-controlled compulsory instruction. The friends of Lancaster organized themselves in 1808 into a committee which became in 1814 "The British and Foreign School Society". The "British schools" supervised and supported by this society confined their religious instruction to Bible-reading and to what Lancaster called "general Christian principles", but which is now known as undenominationalism, the preference of Dissent and the Radical party as against the clean cut of the lay or secular school advocated by the French revolutionaries. On the other hand, the much more numerous "National schools" of "The National Society for promoting the Education of the Poor in the Principles of the Established Church throughout England and Wales" taught religion as expressed by the Catechism and the Book of Common Prayer. Many of these National schools had in their trust deeds, or in their practice, as early as 1816 a conscience clause which permitted the children of Dissenters to be withdrawn from lessons in religion. From 1839 the conscience clause became obligatory upon new trusts at least; in Prussia such a clause dated from 1803.

For a time, the mutual system had a great vogue generally and in

---

[1] As illustrating the esteem in which contemporaries held the mutual system, see Chapter IV below.

quarters where to-day we should not look for it. Jeremy Bentham was for extending it to schools of all grades; it was tried for five years (from 1813) at Charterhouse, and Pillans applied it in the High School of Edinburgh. It was introduced into private schools and was a fashionable craze in some families. It was tried but soon abandoned in Denmark, Germany, France, Spanish America and under the enlightened Père Girard in Fribourg (Switzerland).

At the beginning of the nineteenth century Prussia and other German States, France, Switzerland, Holland and Denmark all accepted the principle that the State was responsible for public primary instruction. In France State supervision, if not State control, was in operation, though its form and efficiency varied with political exigencies as the First Consul became Emperor, or Emperor was displaced by King. In German-speaking lands the "religious difficulty" was met by the provision of denominational teaching given by the clergy, or other accredited teachers, under the safeguard of a conscience clause which permitted exemption from religious instruction. Other solutions proposed were the total secularization of the curriculum and, in contradistinction to secularism, the prohibition of any form of religious teaching which it was thought could not be accepted by all bodies of Christians or, according to Basedow, by all Theists. In both these cases religious education was regarded as primarily the duty of the ministers of religion and of the home; but the more common plan on the Continent was to treat the problem on denominational lines.

In Great Britain the great majority denied that the State had a responsibility for the instruction of its individual members; if England in particular could be said to possess a national system, it was controlled either by semi-public or wholly private agencies. Ostensibly the hindrance to the erection of a real State system was the fear that it would destroy civil and religious liberty. The dust of controversy hung over the "religious difficulty" for the greater part of the century, only to be momentarily laid in 1870 and in 1902. It had no existence in the Public Schools where teaching was, or readily might be, "denominational". Away from platforms, parents, while asking for the religious instruction of their children, seemed as time went on to be careless of its form. The one thing which seemed to be clear as the result of some seventy years' acrimonious discussion of the public elementary school was that English people were averse from the purely secular solution.

The dispute raised the political issue of the Individual *v.* the State; the irreconcilables were those who regarded the individual as the political unit and those who saw that unit either in the community or, at least, in a social group. At the opening of the period individualism was the overwhelmingly predominant creed, but its dominance grew less as the years passed. By 1870 the growth of knowledge and the great cost of any adequate kind of schooling, which only the State purse could meet, compelled the adversaries to compromise.

Statistical detail respecting schools and school attendance in the thirties is far from exact, only rough approximations being available. But these come near enough to the facts to show two things; large numbers of English children were growing up without schooling, and some European countries were in advance of us educationally. A Select Committee of the House of Commons, over which Henry Brougham presided in 1816, estimated the proportion of the population attending school. Taking as a basis that one-ninth of the population falls within the school age, seven to thirteen, the school attendance in Switzerland was one-eighth of the population of the country, in Scotland and Holland one-tenth, in England one-sixteenth, in Wales one-twentieth, in France one twenty-eighth. Of 12,000 parishes in England and Wales, 3500 had no sort of school, 3000 had endowed schools of different grades, 5500 had unendowed schools.

On the other hand, where provision existed, the multiplicity of authorities sometimes caused an extravagance of administration and of overhead charges, which is illustrated by the state of things at Carlisle in the year 1834. The population of the city and suburbs was about 20,000, with a school population of 2680, a number which might have been taught in eight or nine small schools or departments. The actual number was one infant school, nine private schools "for youth of the higher classes", about forty private schools "such as dames' schools for the lower classes", one National school, one Lancasterian school, one Roman Catholic school, a school of industry and twelve Sunday schools. Some, an unknown number, of the 2680 pupils received all their instruction in Sunday schools. As the private schools numbered nearly half a hundred, some, if not most, of them must have taught very few children, and it is very improbable that they were all efficient. Carlisle at this time also had a mechanics' institute with 350 members, five libraries (a "gentleman's", law, medical and two religious) and three public newsrooms.[1] Here is no indifference to education, but wastefulness in conducting it. Bolton, with a population of nearly 42,000, had at this date about eighty day schools instructing 3828 children; yet "there must be several thousands of children without instruction", an obvious exaggeration.[2]

The Select Committee of 1816 stated that in all parts of the country, in villages as well as in the great towns, the poor were increasingly anxious to secure education for their children, and, it may be added, for themselves. Hence the popularity of Sunday schools, the numerous associations of work-people for mutual improvement, and, within the last decade of the eighteenth century, the rise of what were later called "adult schools". There is also the evidence, written in 1791, of the *Memoirs* of James Lackington, a well-known bookseller whose business was very considerable. He says that "the general desire for reading" was "prevalent amongst the inferior orders of society".[3] "According to the best estimates I have been able to make, I suppose that more than four times the number of books are sold now than were sold twenty years since. The poorer sort of farmers and even the poor country people in general, who before that period spent their winter evenings in relating stories of witches, ghosts, hobgoblins, etc., now shorten the winter nights by hearing their sons and daughters read tales, romances, etc.... In short all ranks and degrees now read. But the most rapid increase of the sale of books has been since the termination of the late war."[4] He names Sunday schools, book clubs and circulating libraries as contributors to this result. His daily business allowed him to remark "that the introducing histories, romances, stories, poems, etc., into schools had been a very great means of diffusing a general taste for reading among all ranks of people". A few years earlier the children in schools only read the Bible "and did not make so early progress in reading as they have since", when "they are pleased and entertained as well as instructed".[5]

In May, 1833, on the initiative of Lord Kerry, the House of Commons called for a return relating to schools throughout the country. The

[1] *Quarterly Journal of Education*, vol. VIII (1834), p. 189.
[2] *Ibid.* vol. IX, pp. 73–4.   [3] Jas. Lackington, *Memoirs* (1791), p. 350.
[4] *Ibid.* pp. 386 f.   [5] *Ibid.* pp. 350, 390 f.

figures compiled during the course of the inquiry proved far from trustworthy, but it seems a necessary inference from the available evidence that, at that date and for a few years later, the proportion of children of the working classes who were entirely without any sort of schooling ranged between two-fifths and one-half, that is, only three children in five, or one in two, entered a schoolroom. The proportion of girls was less than that of boys. In 1834–5 Manchester reported that "two-thirds of all the children of the lower orders who are under course of daily instruction" received it in "dame and common day schools".

The duration of school attendance was apparently from two to three years, from eight or nine years of age to eleven. In the mutual schools the course comprised reading, writing, simple arithmetic and religious teaching, denominational or otherwise. In some "British schools," geography, geometry and the elements of surveying were taught; but this was exceptional and the pupils were not from the ranks of "the labouring poor". In some "National schools" trade instruction was given, instruction which was said in 1836 to be "spreading": it included weaving, straw-plaiting, basket-making, gardening, printing, needlework and housework, the aim being primarily economic, and educational only in a minor degree. Most schools other than the mutual were content to stop at teaching children to read. The use of the Bible or New Testament as a primer for this purpose represented a traditional practice which went back to days when whole Bibles were not books which could be put into the hands of children. At a later time the Protestant view of the Bible in its relation to the individual gave it a necessary place in religious instruction, one great object of which was to enable a child to read that book as soon as possible. In the early nineteenth century more suitable primers were available, but the Bible was preferred because, owing to the activities of religious societies, Bibles were the cheapest of books.

"Speaking of the schools generally, we cannot hope that more is acquired than an imperfect power of reading (not sufficient in many cases to enable a child to read with pleasure to itself), a yet more imperfect power of writing, and an acquaintance with the first three or four rules in arithmetic."[1] The cost was estimated at about one pound *per annum* per child, the parent paying about one-third of the amount in fees.

[1] Frederic Hill, *National Education* (1836), p. 72.

There were at this time many close students of foreign education. The Manchester Statistical Society enabled F. Hill to draw the following comparison. "While in Prussia and several of the German states all children of every class between the ages of 7 and 14 are obliged by law to attend school, and it is shown by statistical returns that they actually do so; it appears by this Report that in Manchester not quite two-thirds of those between the ages of 5 and 15 receive nominal instruction. That while, in the countries above referred to, schools are carefully provided in every district and placed under the superintendence of a master who has himself been educated for the profession and has not been allowed to assume his office till found by strict examination to be qualified for the duties of it; the education of the lower classes in this country is left, with the few exceptions of public charity schools, in the hands of ignorant and uneducated men, who are often destitute of every qualification for their office, and have undertaken it only because they found this the easiest means of gaining a subsistence, and frequently in consequence of accident or bodily infirmity. That the course of instruction in the above countries is as superior as the mode of it. That every complete elementary school is there required to teach the Christian religion, the German language, the elements of geometry, the general principles of drawing, arithmetic, the elements of natural science, geography, general history (particularly the history of the country), singing, writing, gymnastic exercises and the simple kinds of manual labour. That no elementary school is considered complete which does not teach all these branches of knowledge and that a large proportion of those schools actually do so; and that no school is allowed to *exist* which does not teach in an efficient manner, religion, reading, writing and singing. That in this town, on the other hand, and generally throughout this country, the acquisition of reading, writing and arithmetic seems to be considered as constituting the finished education of the children of the lower classes of the people. That even these are often very imperfectly taught; and that the real cultivation of the mental powers, the softening of the manners, the improvement of the character, instruction on moral and religious subjects and all the more valuable *objects* of education are totally neglected and forgotten."[1] One must avoid the mistake here made of comparing the actual condition of things in one country with the official statement of what ought to be

[1] Quoted by F. Hill, *op. cit.* pp. 257 f.

done in another. But when allowance is made for the error, the difference in the aims of the two countries is extraordinary.

At the passing of the first Reform Bill (1832) England possessed some provision for all grades of education, but it could not be said that any State organization, still less any true State system, then existed. Oxford and Cambridge, the only English universities, were associated with some secondary schools, but the primary schools stood in no sort of relation with any educational institution other than the Church and the religious bodies. There were secondary schools of ancient foundation and private secondary schools recently created; but speaking generally they represented two different ideals so far as curriculum was concerned. Both types of school were insufficient in number and badly adjusted in distribution to the centres of population; they varied greatly in efficiency. No one executive authority existed which could remedy these defects, bring about co-ordination of the different grades or affect change in any one of them.

Englishmen were not agreed as to whether the State or the individual parent should be held responsible for a child's education, whether or no education should be one of the great public services, and how religious liberty could be reconciled with a State-controlled system of schools. The primary school was the centre of these controversies. The voluntary system was an attempt to close controversy by compromise. Not the State but great corporations of private citizens were to administer the primary schools, thus giving them less straitened resources and a quasi-public sanction without committing the State itself in any way. While the National Society supported denominational teaching, its rival, the British and Foreign School Society, stood for undenominational instruction, which really meant Bible-reading only, a practice that in itself seemed sufficient to a generation which held the doctrine of verbal inspiration very literally. But the conflict of opinion remained in spite of all compromise. A formidable gap in educational provision was the absence of a sufficient number of primary school teachers. The mutual system was an attempt to fill it. The first reputed virtue of that system was that it was cheap; only by second thoughts did its advocates make themselves believe that it had other and more educational recommendations.

The Reform Act of 1832 was the first of a series of measures continued in the Acts of 1867, 1884 and 1918 which by successively extending the parliamentary franchise turned England into a *de facto* democracy. The series required, if it did not imply, a parallel series whose aim should be the building up of an instructed democracy. The parallel is formed by Parliament's money grant in 1833 and by the Education Acts of 1870, 1902 and 1918. The reformed House of Commons which met in the early days of 1833 soon found itself considering educational policy. Before and after that date petitions were sent up from some of the great towns praying for the creation of a national system. On May 24th, Lord Kerry moved an address asking for a return of the number of schools and a statement of the conditions under which they were working. The return, completed in 1835, proved to be defective and incorrect, but it was an attempt to achieve an absolutely necessary preliminary to successful action. Reliable statistics were then unattainable; they were secured after 1870, when not only a central Education Department but local School Boards also existed. On June 28th, 1833, Guizot, the French Minister of Public Instruction, carried a law making it imperative upon every commune to set up a State-inspected school with provision for religious teaching in accordance with the wishes of the majority of the parents in each commune; attendance was not compulsory. On July 30th, J. A. Roebuck, the member for Bath, moved a resolution in the House of Commons which expressed the educational policy of the Benthamite or philosophic Radical party of which he was a member. Its terms were as follows: "That this House, deeply impressed with the necessity of providing for a due education of the people at large, and believing that to this end the aid and care of the State are absolutely needed, will early during the next session of Parliament proceed to devise a means for the universal and national education of the whole people".

The comprehensive scope of this resolution, the speech which commended it and the action which followed throw a bright light on the conflict of opinion, both as to ends and means, which then divided the country. The resolution fell through; its implied doctrine of compulsion went against the sense of the House, as expressed by Sir Robert Peel who, like Roebuck, was in opposition to the Government. "A compulsory system appeared to him to trench upon religious toleration, for it must almost of necessity interfere with religious opinion." Lord Althorp, Chancellor of the Exchequer, "was of opinion that they might give a father the means of educating his children, and put it in the power of a man who could not afford the expense to do so without the expense; but the actually punishing a man for not having his child properly educated would in his mind be going further than they ought".

These speakers on opposite sides of the House give the prevailing individualist view. Roebuck's lengthy speech took the State position. The provision of education he regarded as a State service, whereas primary instruction at least was commonly deemed the business of charity. In Roebuck's opinion education ought to take precedence of the Navy, the Army, the Diplomatic Service, the Home Government; "in short, I would curtail every officer in the State from the highest to the lowest rather than be parsimonious on this most important of all the services of the State". If times favoured he would set up a national system complete from the infant school to the university. He appreciated the interdependence of the various parts of such a system. "The infant school will never be properly conducted while the university is imperfect." But the times being as they were, he planned only for the poor and their teachers. This was but reasonable prudence; "the hitherto subject many are about to become paramount in the State". Yet they were ignorant and acted in flagrant disregard of political principle and economic law; they should be taught the elements of both. In strong contrast with the "three R's" of the English elementary school, Roebuck suggested a liberal course of study and of manual training, appealing to foreign practice in justification.

He would pass a law making it compulsory throughout Great Britain and Ireland that all boys and girls between the ages of six and twelve should be educated either in a State school or elsewhere. In the interests of the poor and of their educators there should be three or four types of State school—infant schools, schools of industry, "normal schools" (écoles normales, teachers' training colleges) and evening schools. A Government certificate of ability should be given to the men and women who successfully completed the "normal school" course. The country should be divided into school districts, each supervised by an elected school committee. At the head of the system should be the Minister of Public Instruction, "whatever might be his name". It should be one of the Minister's duties to arrange for the preparation of school books. This was an attempt to compensate for the shortage of teachers; it had been proposed by Pestalozzi and by

Comenius before him, and was adopted in Ireland with the consequent dissatisfaction one would expect.[1]

It was not sheer indifference which caused Roebuck's resolution to be shelved. On August 17th, 1833, Lord Althorp "procured the consent of the House of Commons to a vote of £20,000 (afterwards made annual) for the building of school-houses in England and Wales, as well as the sum of £10,000 for similar purposes in Scotland. The appropriation of these grants was confided to the Treasury, by which in England and Wales they were distributed through the National and British and Foreign School Societies",[2] £11,000 by the former, the remainder through the latter. The Treasury laid it down that the building only of schoolrooms could be aided, that preference should be given to large towns and cities where the need was most pressing; and after inquiry whether existing charitable funds would not suffice for the purpose, grants would be made on the recommendation of one or other of the two societies, provided that a given school was likely to be permanently maintained, that its private contributions would at least equal, "pound for pound", the amount of its grant, and that the school account would be audited. A similar scheme of administering an educational grant of £30,000 annually had been carried out between 1814 and 1831 in Ireland; in the latter year the Board of Commissioners of National Education in Ireland was established and the annual Parliamentary grant transferred to it.

Thus a step was taken which admitted State responsibility; yet it was a short step and taken hesitatingly. The scheme was permissive and, where a school was set up under it, no child was compelled to attend, nor was the school subject to inspection by State officials. Yet in another field the Government had no hesitation in applying inspection and compulsion. By the Factory Act of 1833 children under nine were not to be employed in mills or factories, children under thirteen might not be employed for more than eight hours daily, workers whose ages ranged from thirteen to eighteen might not be

[1] Roebuck's speech should be read; it marked out very accurately the subsequent course of opinion and practice throughout the century. The speech is in Hansard, xx, cols. 139 ff. and in De Montmorency, *State Intervention in English Education*, pp. 325 ff. Professor De Montmorency gives a full account of the important debate on Roebuck's resolution, *op. cit.* pp. 236 ff.

[2] J. Kay-Shuttleworth, *Four Periods of Public Education* (1862), p. 235.

employed more than twelve hours in a day nor more than sixty-nine in a week. The measure required the appointment of factory inspectors and the provision for factory children of two hours' schooling daily.

In May, 1835, Lord Brougham moved in the House of Lords a series of resolutions dealing with the insufficient provision of elementary instruction, as exhibited in Lord Kerry's Return of that year. In the course of his speech he deprecated the establishment of parish schools at the public expense and under public regulation, phrases which describe a general Benthamite policy, and preferred a larger method of support to the voluntary system. The country, he said, was insufficiently provided with schools, especially with infant schools, the schools were badly distributed, the number in attendance instead of being one-ninth of the population (i.e. the number of children between the ages of seven and thirteen) was only one-eleventh over the whole country. In London and in Lancashire a little more than one-fifteenth and, in more densely peopled areas, one-eighteenth or one-nineteenth was the ratio, that is, in these parts only half of the children were at school. Nevertheless he would not replace the voluntary system by a national system. The voluntary plan had justified itself by doubling the number of children at school within fourteen years.[1] All that was necessary was to supplement that plan by filling gaps and by instituting "normal schools", or "seminaries", to train teachers—the French and German terms should be noted. Any general provision by the State would extinguish all these benevolent efforts; but infant schools should be erected in large numbers —they would prevent the creation of criminals.

Great economic changes necessarily exercise a great influence upon education. It was a change of this kind which in the fourteenth and fifteenth centuries led to the creation in Western Europe of vernacular instruction and the primary school; economic prosperity was a dominant factor in the revival of classical learning in Italy. The conditions of English industrialism at the end of the eighteenth century sharpened the worker's wits and sometimes made him alive to the peril of ignorance; they also too frequently gave him a standard of living with which he could not remain content. The French Revolution continued this process of educating the majority of the nation. In spite of its excesses,

[1] By Lord Kerry's Return it appeared that for two children at school in 1820 there were three in 1830 and five in 1834. See Sadler, *Special Reports on Educational Subjects*, vol. II, p. 456.

it was impossible that the political ideas of the Revolution should not affect the thoughts of a people to whom the idea of personal freedom was more than familiar. It is therefore not surprising that, from the end of the eighteenth century, there were sporadic movements, usually beginning in the great towns, directed to the instruction of adult workers.

These were sometimes religious in motive, sometimes industrial, sometimes of a more general, educational character. The great religious revivals of the eighteenth and early nineteenth centuries stimulated a desire for instruction amongst working people. The "class-meetings" of the Wesleyans provided a model for the organization of such instruction. Night schools, adult Sunday schools, book clubs, discussion and mutual improvement societies sprang up in the great towns and industrial districts. These were sometimes conducted by men outside the ranks of the manual workers; but the majority were managed and taught by working men themselves.

"The earliest indication which has come to our knowledge of the desire of those engaged in mechanical employments to receive instruction, and the first attempts known to us to gratify this desire was at Birmingham previous to the year 1790. A society was there established called the Sunday Society. This society arose into being soon after the establishment of Sunday Schools; its object was to watch over the mental and moral improvement of youth, to give them useful instruction, to exercise their minds and feelings, and to impart consistency and permanence to their moral character. A society for mutual improvement existed some years previous to this, in which lectures were delivered by its members on several branches of natural philosophy; and many of them being actively engaged in the ingenious trades of Birmingham had constructed apparatus to illustrate the principles of mechanics, hydrostatics, pneumatics, optics, electricity and astronomy. The lectures were not always confined to themselves; they were made accessible to young persons employed in the manufactories of the town.

"Both these societies were in 1796 merged in the Brotherly Society; the operations were more satisfactorily and systematically carried on than before. Lectures were delivered at certain intervals, classes were formed for drawing, geography and for the pursuit of those scientific inquiries, in the application of which many of the members were constantly engaged.[1] In 1797 a library for the use of the working classes was established and called the Artisans' Library, by which all persons who chose to avail themselves of its advantages were supplied with useful reading at the expense of a penny a week. With very few exceptions, the individuals who took the lead in these varied plans for the amelioration of the class of mechanics were themselves employed in trades and chiefly dependent on their personal exertions for a livelihood; they had but little leisure for purposes thus beneficent in their tendency, their means were circumscribed, yet they laboured for many years and witnessed the good effect which followed their exertions."[2]

The religious motive was conspicuous in what came to be known as "adult schools", amongst the earliest of which were the classes conducted between 1790 and 1800 by Hannah and Martha More with the object of teaching Somerset miners to read the Bible. An adult school at Nottingham in 1798 taught labouring men to read the Bible, to write and to cipher. Bristol became prominent by the number of its schools of this kind, of which in 1813 it had forty-six, teaching 1297 men and women. The originator of this activity was William Smith, whose weekly wage was eighteen shillings earned as "door-keeper" of a Methodist chapel. Smith was moved to start a school by what he heard at a local meeting of the British and Foreign Bible Society (founded 1804): he quickly enlisted a number of influential supporters who in 1812 formed the "Bristol Society for instructing adult persons to read the Holy Scriptures". By 1815 there were adult schools in twenty English towns, some of which taught writing as well as reading. But the movement languished after 1818; competent teachers were lacking, some schools admitted children and this discouraged adult attendance. A prejudice grew amongst the allied religious bodies against the association of Bible-reading and the teaching of writing, which in itself was an inducement to many to attend the schools.

From 1817 to 1820 a number of London workmen maintained a society for debate and mutual instruction.[3] Although short-lived, this "Mechanical Institution" represented a type of association which was

[1] J. William Hudson (*History of Adult Education*, 1851) adds, "natural and civil history and morals".

[2] Central Society of Education, Publication, vol. I (1837), pp. 216 f.

[3] Central Society of Education, *op. cit.* pp. 216–17.

often repeated in later years, particularly by the co-operative societies and the Chartists.

The mechanics' institutes were directed to purposes which were neither religious nor political, but utilitarian and industrial. It is true that their originator, George Birkbeck, proposed to himself the purely educational aim of conveying to mechanics "a few systematic philosophical ideas" which underlay the use of tools and machinery; but the institutes did not develop quite in that direction. Birkbeck was at that time professor of natural philosophy and chemistry in the Andersonian Institution of Glasgow. Touched on one occasion by the interest and want of knowledge displayed by a group of workmen who were examining a model of the centrifugal pump, he determined, as he said, to open to them those gates of science which poverty closed against them. In spite of the objections of doubting friends, he delivered a course of lectures to mechanics which proved highly successful; and the courses were continued from 1800 to 1804, when Birkbeck removed to London. Dr Ure, his successor in Glasgow, continued these popular lectures.

In 1823 seceders from Ure's courses and other Glasgow workmen organized a "Mechanics' Institution" of which they made Birkbeck the honorary president; they had a membership of over 600, paying annual subscriptions of a guinea and half a guinea, and they paid a lecturer on mechanics and chemistry £150 per annum. The purpose of the institution was declared to be "instructing artisans in the scientific principles of arts and manufactures", "diffusing useful knowledge" (the phrase has meaning) amongst mechanics. At this time workmen's classes were also being taught in Edinburgh and at Haddington.

In the same year Thomas Hodgskin and J. C. Robertson published a weekly (later a monthly) periodical, *The Mechanics' Magazine*, to give publicity and support to working-class movements. One of its earliest suggestions was that a great centre of working-class adult education should be formed in London, where Birkbeck was now practising medicine and devoting his leisure to the activities of the group known as the "Philosophical Radicals" of whom Henry Brougham, Francis Place and the Benthamite circle were the chief members. Before the year was out, the "London Mechanics' Institution," the parent or predecessor of the present Birkbeck College, was founded on the initiative of Hodgskin and Robertson and by the efforts of Birkbeck,

Brougham and their political friends. The membership exceeded 1000, at a quarterly subscription of five shillings; the course of instruction and the material equipment were of a comparatively advanced kind. Elementary classes were formed for teaching mathematics, English, French and Latin: lectures were given on "natural philosophy" (that is, in the different branches of physics), in literature and languages. In addition to a library the institution possessed a museum, a laboratory and a workshop. At this date two-thirds of the members were weekly wage earners. London's example was speedily followed elsewhere, and mechanics' institutions, more or less resembling the London model, sprang up in all parts of the country, more especially in the industrial towns of the north. These had imitators in Ireland, France, Holland and America; within a couple of years Scotland had added six to the original Glasgow institution.

General attention was drawn to adult popular education by the appearance in 1825 of Brougham's *Practical Observations upon the Education of the People addressed to the Working Classes and their Employers*. The scheme there described had two main branches, of which the first was the establishment of institutes like those of Glasgow and London, equipped for elementary teaching in small classes, for public lectures to large audiences and for mutual instruction by means of discussions, while subsidiary to the lectures were the library and reading-room, laboratory, workshop and drawing classes. The second branch of Brougham's plan was realized in the work of the "Society for the Diffusion of Useful Knowledge" founded by him and others in 1827 as a means for giving effect to utilitarian principles. This society during the nineteen years of its existence published a number of popular works such as *The Penny Magazine*, *The Penny Cyclopaedia* (a periodical originally issued in penny numbers), *The Library of Entertaining Knowledge*, *The Library of Useful Knowledge* and the like. *The Quarterly Journal of Education* (1831–5) is a mine of information respecting the educational conditions and movements of the time throughout the civilized world.

These publications undoubtedly diffused amongst their many readers in all parts of the country knowledge of a kind not otherwise readily accessible. They also affected the ideals of national education long after the disappearance in 1846 of the society which gave them birth. The virtues of individualism, utilitarianism in concrete shapes and the advantage to an industrial community of a widely diffused knowledge of natural science were lessons deeply impressed upon the English mind; and these represented the chief aims of the "education-mad party" under Brougham's leadership.

The patronage of the London Mechanics' Institution by a royal duke (Sussex) and the predominant part played by prominent middle-class men in its management indicated that it was being modelled on other lines than those followed by the earlier working-class adult schools. Amongst the agencies of education above the elementary grade which were in existence in the early nineteenth century were the many "Literary and Philosophical Institutes", one of the earliest to be established being that which was opened at Manchester about 1780. By 1836 Hill reported that the "Lit. and Phil. Institutes" were "rapidly extending themselves" and that "few large towns" did not possess one at least. There were many in London, the greatest being the London Institution founded in 1809 for the diffusion of science, literature and the arts, Birkbeck being one of the projectors. The premises invariably included a reading-room and library; the London Institution had a museum also. Courses of lectures were delivered and classes were held in ancient and modern languages and in drawing. The usual annual subscription was two guineas and the aims, conduct and atmosphere of the institute were distinctly those of the middle classes.

Perhaps insensibly the Mechanics' Institutions tended to imitate the "Lit. and Phil. Institutes"; whether or no, within ten years from the foundation of the London Mechanics' Institution they had ceased to deserve their distinctive name. "The workshops of the London, Manchester, Newcastle Institutions had a short career; and indeed whatever industrial education has been attempted in these institutions has proved a signal failure."[1] The story is almost invariably the same; an enthusiastic beginning, a cooling as the novelty wore off, the sad discovery by many of the artisans that their rudimentary attainments were unequal to the demands of lecture and library, the entry of men and women better prepared for these and of a different social tradition, the falling away of the artisan students, some of whom set to work to form classes better adapted to their needs.

[1] J. W. Hudson, *History of Adult Education* (1851), p. 57. Hudson was secretary of the Manchester Athenaeum, a typical "Lit. and Phil. Institute" founded in 1836.

Addressing the Manchester Athenaeum in 1835 Lord Brougham lamented the abstention of the working classes and their want of appreciation of the advantages which the institution offered.[1] Yet in the same year, speaking at Liverpool, he said, "I have no hesitation in saying that of all the improvements which have been made of late years in the condition of the people of this country, the diffusion of knowledge, both in science and in the other principles of their art, amongst the *industrious portion of the middle classes, to whose use Mechanics' Institutes are more especially devoted*, stands in the first rank amongst the very foremost".[2]

The change of membership sometimes turned the so-called Mechanics' Institutions into centres of social entertainment, a purpose remote from the desires of the founders, however desirable *per se*. In 1851 Hudson described the London Mechanics' Institution as "little more than an association of shop-keepers and their apprentices, law-copyists and attorneys' clerks" for whom it provided "a more valuable and refining *amusement* than their ordinary habits and indulgences lead them to select".[3] He is enthusiastic about the Liverpool Mechanics' Institution, founded in 1825, but confesses that "the working mechanics, who generally prefer the sterner studies, have given place to others who attend the dancing and the essay and discussion classes, as more congenial to their tastes".[4] Both institutions were then in financial straits.

A general hindrance to the spread of knowledge, and one from which the poorer classes especially suffered, was the high cost of newspapers. The Government charges on these were originally imposed to fetter the expression of opinion; they were exacted long after the time when opinion was supposed to be free. Between 1819 and 1836 the stamp duty on newspapers was 4*d.* per copy; *The Times, The Globe, The Morning Chronicle*, cost 7*d.*; *The Morning Advertiser* and the *Public Ledger* 6½*d.* per copy. In 1836 the stamp duty was reduced from 4*d.* to 1*d.*; the duty was abolished in 1855. An excise charge on paper of 3*d.* per pound avoirdupois remained until 1861. Certain publications, as books published by the University Presses, Bibles and Prayer Books, were exempt from this paper duty; newspapers were not exempt.

---

[1] Hudson, *op. cit.*
[2] *Opinions of Lord Brougham…as exhibited in his speeches, etc.* (1837).
[3] Hudson, *op. cit.*   [4] *Ibid.* p. 98.

Between 1836 and 1855 no London daily paper was sold at less than 5*d*. The *First Report of the Poor Law Commissioners* (1834) contained the following: "The dearness of newspapers in this country is an insurmountable obstacle to the education of the poor. I could name twenty villages within a circuit of a few miles in which a newspaper is never seen from one year's end to the other".[1] On the other hand, there existed in the great towns "an illicit press which the law, unsupported by public opinion, is wholly unable to put down".[2]

The formation at York in September, 1831[3], of the British Association for the Advancement of Science points to the diffusion of an interest in science amongst the educated classes at this time. So distinguished a *savant* as Sir David Brewster would not have exerted himself as he did to establish the Association, if he were merely leading a forlorn hope. Hudson testifies to "a general taste for chemical science" in less educated circles as shown in the success of the laboratories of the Leeds, Bradford, Wakefield, Manchester, Westminster, York, Glasgow and Newcastle Mechanics' Institutions.

[1] F. Hill, *National Education* (1836), p. 110, quoting Appendix A of the Report.
[2] *Ibid.* p. 111.
[3] First meeting, Oxford, 1832.

CHAPTER II

Higher Education

While purely elementary instruction was left to semi-public or to wholly private agencies, higher education at this period was provided, as it had long been provided, by bodies which were formally at least public. These were the two Universities and the endowed schools, most of the latter being grammar schools, including the Public Schools' group formed by Winchester, Eton, Shrewsbury, Westminster, Rugby, Harrow, Charterhouse, St Paul's, Merchant Taylors'. Numerous private schools supplemented this provision. The higher education of girls was confined to private schools which were almost invariably boarding schools.

The grammar school by its very name announced the survival within its walls of that rhetorical instruction which was as old as the Roman Empire in its details, and in principle older still. In strict law, such a school was a foundation for teaching the "learned languages", Latin and Greek, and nothing else, although Hebrew might be added. On that ground the Lord Chancellor, Eldon, in 1805 ruled that it was incompetent to Leeds Grammar School to use its endowment, as its governing body desired, to teach arithmetic, writing and modern languages in addition to Latin and Greek. Opposed in this by the head master, the governors petitioned the Court of Chancery and the Court gave its sanction to the addition to the curriculum. On appeal, however, Eldon overruled the recommendation and rejected the governors' petition. The school had been founded in 1552 "for the free teaching of all young scholars, youths and children, who should resort to it". In Eldon's opinion a free school meant a free grammar school, and a grammar school as defined in Johnson's *Dictionary* was a school for teaching the learned languages. The governors therefore could not lawfully use the endowment for teaching anything else. This judgement, a striking instance of that power of the dead hand which at that time tended to paralyse all higher education in England, Eldon repeated in another case decided in 1826. As the Taunton Commissioners (1864–7) pointed out, the judgement permitted a master of an endowed school to refuse to teach anything other than Latin or Greek, or alternatively, to exact his own terms for instruction outside these two languages. Where there was no local demand for instruction in "the tongues" a master might in effect close the school and yet retain the statutory stipend. Instances were not wanting.

But the Lord Chancellor's judgement did not remain unchallenged, and by 1840 public opinion was sufficiently advanced to overset it. Sir Eardley Wilmot's Grammar School Act of that year gave the Courts power to regard not only the intentions of a particular school's founder, but also to consider its existing condition and circumstances and, if necessary, to introduce other branches of knowledge in addition to the ancient classics. The consequent changes in the school's statutes must be made, or at least mooted, within six months after a vacancy in the head-mastership occurred. A grammar school according to this Act was one founded, endowed or maintained to teach Latin and Greek or one of them.

In the pre-Victorian time, Eldon's decision represented tradition and usage. A grammar school taught the classics; in the school jargon of the day these were "business," "school business"; any other studies were mere "accomplishments" or the occupation of leisure hours. In order to lay a firm and durable foundation for all that was to follow, the boy of seven, or thereabouts, began by memorizing the pages of a grammar book, written in Latin, either the text of the sixteenth-century "Lily" or a later adaptation of it. As an exercise ground an easy Latin book, such as the Latin New Testament, Nepos or Phaedrus accompanied the learning of grammar. In due course Latin prose (of the Ciceronian tradition), verse-making in Latin and Greek followed; instruction in the latter language began with the use of a grammar book (in Latin) and reading in the Greek New Testament. The completeness with which this programme was carried out and the range of classical literature covered in reading of course varied from school to school. The authors with whom the grammar school boy seems to have been most familiar were Ovid, Virgil, Horace, Cicero, Homer and, in one or two orations, Demosthenes. The boy's only apparatus for the construing lesson was a plain text, or at most, a text with scanty *Latin* notes, chiefly textual; for preparation, apart from the surreptitious use of a "crib", he must depend upon grammar, dictionary and mother-wit. The French "Delphin Classics", as they gradually came into English use, tempered "by their interpretative notes" the rigour of the construe. Spoken Latin was encouraged by the use of dialogue books such as the *Colloquies* of Corderius and Erasmus. The position which Latin in particular occupied in higher education is reflected in the frequent and apposite quotations from Latin authors, poets especially, which formed a familiar oratorical device of parliamentary speeches.

Of studies outside "business", and therefore pursued only on half-holidays, arithmetic was chief; this humble position was conceded to a useful practical art, as a modern school might find time for shorthand or typewriting. Mathematics belonged to the university rather than to the school. The standard text-books were Ludlam's *Rudiments of Mathematics* (1785) and in arithmetic Walkinghame's *Tutor's Assistant*. Innumerable editions of the latter were published during the hundred years which followed the appearance of the first in 1751; its long-continued popularity and extensive circulation are demonstrated by "Alfred Crowquill's" "comic edition" of 1843. In the more successful grammar schools, which almost invariably were boarding schools, the French language and some English literature formed favourite interests more or less self-chosen, to be followed in leisure time. History, ancient and modern, was a member of the same group.

By statute, tradition and daily worship the endowed schools were closely associated with the Church of England, but the character of their religious instruction, as distinct from chapel services and the like, varied from school to school. Lyte goes so far as to say that at Eton there was "an entire absence of religious teaching" until 1829, when the foundation of the Newcastle Scholarship made it possible "to substitute a lesson in Greek Testament for the repetition of Virgil or Juvenal on Sunday mornings".[1] In 1802 William Vincent, then head master of Westminster, felt enforced to write *A Defence of Public Education addressed...to the Bishop of Meath in answer to a charge annexed to his Lordship's discourse preached at St Paul's on the anniversary meeting of the Charity children, etc.* This charge, the systematic neglect by the Public Schools of Christian instruction, had previously been made by the Master of the Temple, Dr Rennell (an Etonian and father of an Etonian).

Vincent describes the Westminster practice and adds a word or two on Winchester. In the Lower School (ages eight to twelve) the boys

---

[1] H. C. Maxwell-Lyte, *History of Eton College*, p. 398.

read the Psalter and Gospels in Latin, both presumably in the Latin version of the Prayer Book, they learned the Catechism and *A brief exposition of the church Catechism by way of question and answer*, a little duodecimo costing 6*d*., and written by Bishop John Williams of Chichester, who died in 1709. Both the Lower and the Upper School used a book compiled particularly for Westminster by Joseph Wilcocks. This was the *Sacred Exercises in Four Books*, a collection of Biblical passages illustrating the Christian virtues, with appropriate prayers. Its author says that "it is intended that it should be constantly used (not only in school for translations and other exercises but) in the several boarding houses as part of the daily prayers" The English Bible, Greek Testament and Hebrew Psalter were read in the Upper School; to these the Sixth added "a Grotius lesson on Monday explained at large". The work in question, a book on Christian evidence, is the *De veritate religionis Christianae* of 1627, but Vincent does not say whether it was read in Grotius's Latin or in the English translation by J. Clarke, of which there was a tenth edition in 1793 and a fourteenth in 1815. It took two years to complete the reading of the book.[1] The rite of confirmation was held once every two years, the preparation of candidates occupying a week. The foundationers, the King's Scholars, heard Saturday lectures by one of the prebendaries, received the Sacrament four times a year and were prepared on each occasion for its reception. It is impossible to say whether the extent of the religious instruction and training which were customary in the endowed schools approximated to the Westminster or to the Eton model. At Winchester Grotius was read and explained every Sunday evening and the "Upper Boys" received the Sacrament once a month; "catechetical lectures" were "regularly read".

So full a scheme of secular study as has been outlined above could only be attempted in the Public Schools and in the few other endowed schools which retained pupils till the age of eighteen or nineteen. The work of these schools found adverse critics who became more numerous, influential and sweeping in their complaints as the nineteenth century advanced. Schools, which still bore the name of "free grammar school", had reduced their free pupils to a small proportion of their strength by the admission of fee-paying pupils not on the foundation;

[1] Westminster examination papers of 1832 seem to show that at that date Grotius was displaced by Paley in the Upper School.

and the change usually transformed a local day school into a non-local boarding school. The schools were unsuited both in curriculum and topographical position to nineteenth-century needs; it was not possible to adapt the local distribution of these schools to the changed situation caused by the industrial revolution. Almost invariably their head masters were clergymen, even in cases where a layman was eligible for the office; the fact was one more obstacle to the use of these schools by the children of Dissenters.

These complaints were in part met by the practice of the less prosperous endowed schools. In spite of the law and tradition, of 500 grammar schools at work in 1818, 120 (whose pupils numbered some 10,000) taught "every variety of study". Fifty-six of the schools taught "English" subjects only, their pupils numbering 4000. In eighty grammar schools the parents were allowed to choose between an "English" and a classical course of studies. The authority for these statements—which there is no reason to doubt—is "A letter to Henry Brougham...on the best method of restoring decayed grammar schools" by "M.A. Queen's College, Oxford".

The disturbance of the classical monopoly of studies and an amendment of the defective distribution of schools were mainly caused by the institution of purely private schools. They were of all grades of efficiency, good and bad, and their social range was comprehensive, from the dames' schools with a fee of 4d. per week, through the country boarding schools where board and education were offered in 1798 at fourteen to fifteen guineas per annum, and so onward to small, exclusive schools whose fees only the wealthy could afford. Their number was increased by the masters of decayed endowed schools who used their office to create private boarding schools of their own. But one consequence of the existence of these privately established institutions was the foundation of a curriculum which first found a place for modern studies, and in the end made English grammar and history, elementary mathematics, geography, drawing and a branch of science (usually chemistry) the staple courses of study in schools of their type. They were not fettered by ancient statutes or traditional methods of teaching; but they were very susceptible to the opinions which ruled beyond the school walls, especially as these were held by parents. During the nineteenth century the conception of what constituted secondary instruction underwent a profound change; so far as professional theory and practice influenced the change, it was due, not to any Public School or Public School master, but to the enterprise of the private schools.

Vicesimus Knox, who had been master of Tunbridge School from 1778 to 1812, represents what may be described as the "left centre" professional opinion of his time; firmly convinced of the supreme educational value of the classics, he is not averse from modifying the curriculum by admitting other studies, provided these are not allowed to rank as "business". In 1820 he published *Remarks on the tendency of a Bill now in Parliament to degrade Grammar Schools*, a widely circulated pamphlet attacking Brougham's Bill of that year.[1] His cue here is to belittle any possible rivals of the grammar school; but his statements help the reader to understand what had called those rivals into being. He contemptuously regards the "academies" as "schools for the shop, the warehouse, the counting house and the manufactory". "However superficial the attainments in classics at the scientific, mathematical and arithmetical academies, all defects are supplied in the money-making world, by the superior excellence of dancing, French, drawing, fencing and music masters, all of them far-fetched and richly remunerated. These instructors fill the academies with pupils and the grammar schools are comparatively deserted. Though it should be remembered that in most grammar schools all such masters, and masters also in writing and ciphering, hired by the master and altogether under his control, are actually employed at this moment in the *horae subsecivae*, in the intervals of classical study"—that is, they are no part of "business". To "most grammar schools", in this passage, should be added "of the standing of Tunbridge", the statement was certainly not true of grammar schools in the mass.

"At present", says Knox, "the sciences seem to have attracted the attention of the great and fashionable, in preference to polite literature; a knowledge of chemistry seems to have become a female accomplishment; and the rising generation of studious youth devote much attention to it, as they do to geology, mineralogy and, perhaps, craniology", a cut at the popularity of Spurzheim, George Combe and their "science" of phrenology. "I urge an attention to the Belles Lettres the more earnestly, because it appears that, in imitation of the French, especially since the Revolution, the sciences which Bonaparte encouraged (chiefly

[1] P. 22, above; and p. 53 below.

for the sake of raising engineers, gunners, surgeons and all other descriptions of people who assist in sieges and the work of slaughter) are becoming in England the fashionable study to the exclusion or at least the comparative neglect of polite literature." All this means that the private schools were simply instruments for supplying the needs, real or imaginary, of the time, and that the grammar schools were either doing this unsatisfactorily or not at all.

The professional view, more generously worded, appears a few years later in a letter written by Dr Arnold in 1832. The studies of the "commercial schools" are here said to be reading, writing, arithmetic ("I believe it often happens that boys in the lowest form of a commercial school require absolutely to be taught to read"), history, geography, English grammar and composition, the rudiments of physical science "carried to a greater or less degree of advancement"; and, alternatively, land-surveying or book-keeping. Religious instruction varies with the instructor. "Sometimes the boys are required to analyse grammatically any sentence in an English book and to give the derivations of the several words in it, just as boys at classical schools are called upon to do in Greek and Latin. And doubtless there may be many commercial schools, especially in the manufacturing districts, where the course of study far surpasses what is here given, and where the instruction in scientific subjects, in chemistry and in mechanics is carried to a high degree of proficiency."[1]

English, usually as grammar and "composition", was always a prominent study in the private schools. The number and popularity of such schools may be inferred from the extraordinary circulation of their favourite text-book, Lindley Murray's *English Grammar*, of which forty-six editions were published between 1795 (the first) and 1832, not counting American editions. An abridgement, first issued in 1797, was in its fifty-fourth, or reputed fifty-fourth, edition in 1817. In short, Frederic Hill declared that in 1836 the private schools were "as is well-known, the common medium of instruction for the children of our middle classes".

Towards the close of the period now being considered, an old practice in school provision was revived, but on a larger scale than heretofore. Small groups of English parents had occasionally employed a schoolmaster to teach their children either in his own house or in

[1] Thos. Arnold, *Miscellaneous Works* (1845), pp. 230 ff.

that of one of the members of the group. "The expense...of the grammar schools and private schools in highest repute, and the indifferent character of many grammar and private schools where pupils are boarded at lower rates, combined with the opinion that few of these schools furnish all the kinds of instruction that are now requisite, have led to the foundation of various Proprietary Schools."[1] In the private school the principal was also the proprietor; in the schools here referred to he was a salaried officer employed by a committee of persons—the proprietors—who were interested in higher education. Early examples are "London University" School (the original form of University College School), 1828, King's College School, 1829, and Blackheath Proprietary School, 1830. The West Riding Proprietary School, founded at Wakefield in 1834, accommodated 100 boys taught by a head master, second master, both of these being graduates, and an assistant master, with masters for French and German. Flogging and fagging, time-honoured marks of a Public School education, were strictly forbidden at Wakefield. A suggestion for the organization of "Bristol College", another proprietary school of this date, bears clear indication of a knowledge, on the part of those who made it, of the contemporary German Gymnasium and Realschule. The school was to "divide" about the age of twelve to fourteen. Those who stood below the dividing line were to follow a common course in Latin, arithmetic, geography, French or German, or both languages. Above the line was a bifurcation. Boys intended for the Universities should study together Latin,.Greek, algebra, geometry and "mixed mathematics as studied at universities". Other boys should be grouped together for instruction; Greek should be omitted from their course, which was to include mathematics, physics or natural history, spoken and written French and German.

The outbreak of war in 1793 between England and the French Republic made it impossible for the numerous schools hitherto maintained on French soil by English Catholics to remain there. In consequence a considerable number of schools, most of which educated boys but some of which were girls' schools, returned to England from the Low Countries, where their work had begun in the sixteenth and seventeenth centuries. While on foreign soil these schools had been almost aggressively English in their adherence to the matter and mode of

[1] *The Quarterly Journal of Education*, vol. IX (1835), p. 254.

instruction followed at home; nevertheless they brought back a readier disposition than commonly actuated English schools, "Public" and endowed, to admit modern studies to the curriculum.[1] Resentment was general in this country against the manner in which all religious bodies had been treated by the French revolutionaries, and this feeling strengthened the more tolerant attitude that had previously found definition in the laws which removed the disabilities of Protestant Dissenters and Roman Catholics. Among the colleges and schools which passed (1794–5) from the Low Countries to England were Stoneyhurst, St Edmund's College, Ushaw and Oscott.

The private schools conducted by the Hill family from about 1802–3 to 1877 may be noticed at this point, not, however, as typical of that kind of school, but as illustrating the neglect into which the ideas of English educators have sometimes been allowed to fall, until they have been revived as sheer novelties under a foreign *cachet*. The system of education was established by 1817 in their first school, "Hill-top", Birmingham, which was changed for larger premises, "Hazelwood", in 1819. In 1826 the family conducted two schools, Hazelwood and Bruce Castle, Tottenham; from 1833 the latter was the Hills' only school. The education conducted in all these establishments is described in *Public Education; Plans for the government and liberal instruction of boys in large numbers, as practized at Hazelwood School*, 1822, and *Sketch of the system of education, moral and intellectual, in practice at the schools of Bruce Castle, Tottenham, and Hazelwood near Birmingham*, 1833.

The main principles of the system were that boys should be trained to educate themselves and that the discipline of the school should be administered through them. The second principle received effect in the appointment of a boys' committee, elected by the boys, with a master or two as assessors; in this committee the "laws of the school" were proposed, discussed and enacted. Infractions of these laws, if slight, were brought before a boy "magistrate", if more serious, before a judge and jury, all boys. Punishment was by fine and, "very rarely", by short imprisonment. The fines were paid in counters which represented the "marks" scored in studies and in conduct by the holder. Committees of boys directed the numerous societies and social acti-

[1] Wm. F. Hastings, *The Education of English Catholics*, 1559–1800, thesis presented to the University of London, 1923.

vities which formed a great feature of the school life; one of these was a "charitable fund", an early anticipation of the Public School Mission. The aim of the instruction was to help boys to teach themselves, and to disabuse them of the thought that learning ceased at the close of school or college life. A careful employment of the then popular mutual system was made, the boys being grouped in small classes whenever a boy became an instructor, and a master supervised his doings. But the Hills were well aware of the limitations of such a plan; the monitors merely "heard" the repetition of a lesson.

The studies, not all of which were followed by every pupil, included geography, history, English grammar, arithmetic, mensuration, algebra, geometry, trigonometry, the geometry beginning in "practical geometry", whereas "Euclid" was the text-book in the few other schools which professed the study. In languages the subjects were French, Latin and Greek; the highest class in the first was conducted in French. In most subjects weekly examinations were held; there was also a weekly staff conference where the business was more concerned with method of teaching than of government. Most schools were then conducted in one large room or in two rooms; the Hills adopted the form room plan. In addition to the principal schoolroom and a room for the little boys, who remained there for all their instruction, there were six classrooms, which permitted a separate classification of the older boys for almost all the subjects, or groups of allied subjects. Mapping and surveying were out-of-door exercises; gymnastics and swimming were taught.

The Hills understood that their business was to educate all sorts of aptitude. The "intellectual" boy could attain merit, marks and counters by the use of books. The non-bookish pupil could by undertaking "voluntary labour" secure the same tokens of ability. A long list of the forms these labours might take, at the option of the boy, includes printing (the school printed its own magazine), penmanship, drawing, etching, painting, mapping, making surveys, mathematical diagrams, reading up topics for discussion, music, modelling animals and machines, sharing in committee-work, rote-learning, reporting trials in the school court, reporting debates, composition in prose or verse "in various languages". The school periodically held exhibitions and gave dramatic performances. Nearly all the boys were members of the Church of England; but arrangements were made by which other pupils attended either a Dissenters' or a Roman Catholic chapel on Sundays. All the above-named activities were followed within the period 1817–33.

In pursuance of its anti-Tory policy, the *Edinburgh Review* over a long course of years made a series of attacks upon English education as it was practised in the endowed schools and at the two Universities; its hostility to these Church strongholds was particularly marked during the period 1807–11, when the assault was led by Henry Brougham, sometime pupil of the Edinburgh High School and graduate of Edinburgh University, and by Sydney Smith, Wykehamist and member of New College, Oxford, but then resident with a pupil in the Scottish capital. The charge levelled at the Universities was that they produced no men eminent in letters or in science, that the monopoly enjoyed, more especially at Oxford, by the two classical languages made men indifferent to useful knowledge, and that Cambridge studied mathematics by antiquated methods. The plan of teaching by college tutors, and the existence of colleges themselves as rivals to the University, were decried in favour of the non-collegiate organization of the Scotch universities and their professorial teaching, conducted in classes often unwieldy in size and encumbered by the presence of youths who still should have been at school. Brougham's abortive Bill of 1820 was an attempt to get the *Edinburgh's* ideas into English practice and to Scotify schools south of the Tweed.

Brougham was convinced that the boarding school readily lent itself to the abuse of ancient endowments by affording a satisfactory income to the endowed schoolmaster, who neglected the local poor, ignored their primary interest in the foundation and devoted himself to well-to-do "foreigners" from outside. Hence also the neglect of elementary instruction and of useful knowledge, and a deeper entrenchment of Latin and Greek. His Bill "for Improving the Administration of Endowments connected with Education and for the better fulfilling the Intentions of the Founders thereof" took as its model the Scottish parish school, a day school which ostensibly covered the whole gamut of pre-university instruction. English endowed schools were to be empowered to teach "reading, writing and accounts", as well as grammar. Brougham himself would disendow the boarding schools and with the money open a large number of schools insufficiently equipped with funds. Here are passages from the speech with which he introduced his Bill. "It was practicable upon a proper plan to educate 35,000 children in 100 schools at an expense of £2,500 a year." "There were now £4,500 a year belonging to the Tunbridge school, and a decree had been made to that effect, but £500 a year was twice as much as was wanted for that school. The remaining £4,000 would endow as many as were now in the whole of that county".[1]

The Bill assigned so dominating a position to the parochial clergy and to the parish clerks that it was withdrawn in consequence of the opposition of the Dissenters. But apart from that, Brougham's Scotch parish school would certainly have been rejected as failing to reflect English social conditions. This criticism is naïvely revealed by Knox in the pamphlet (*Remarks*, etc.) already mentioned. The union of English and Latin schools would be "degrading"; it is neither necessary "nor even desired by the common people". There is no need to interfere with the grammar schools which are so well suited to "those who can live without manual labour". Those schools are for the well-to-do and for the poor "with talents and diligence and friends to enable (them) to proceed to a great length in (their) studies". For the great majority of the poor something very like a caste system is sufficient, an opinion in which Knox was not singular amongst schoolmasters of his day; indeed, it may not unfairly be termed the general opinion amongst educated men. Knox says that the poor man "ought to be made sensible that there is an attainable good in this life superior to animal gratification; that there are pleasures more refined, exalted and durable than those of the senses, and that a life of faith and obedience affords hope of a happy immortality. Of this every poor man in the nation should be made sensible, and for this purpose the humble schools prepared for him are sufficient; for, I believe, they never neglect reading the scriptures, catechetical instruction and daily supplication". For the well-to-do and the intellectually able poor, the endowed school; for the "labouring poor", the charity school and similar humble primary schools. A century after Knox's time English public instruction is embarrassed and so rendered less effective than it might be by the failure to regard the community as a whole, irrespective of social distinctions.

In the Public Schools the eighteenth century had been a time of stagnation; the number of boys in attendance underwent startling fluctuations with a general movement towards a low level. The closing

[1] *The Pamphleteer*, vol. XVI (1820), p. 260.

years of the century and the twenty or thirty years which followed were a period of recovery. A greater stability marked the numbers on the rolls. Harrow and Rugby ceased to be merely local schools and advanced to a national standing. Shrewsbury experienced a phoenix-like revival under Butler, whose head-mastership initiated great reforms in the life and studies of this group of endowed schools, and through them on all English education above the primary grade.

The general comments made above on the studies, accomplishments and leisure-time occupations of the more successful endowed schools apply also to the Public School group. In the early part of the period we are considering, hostile critics admitted that the teaching in these latter schools succeeded in making boys expert in versifying and in writing Latin prose. But they complained that this success was gained at the expense of that vivid presentation of ancient society which was the aim of contemporary, Continental scholars. Butler of Shrewsbury and Arnold of Rugby were fully alive to the justice and value of this complaint. The most serious charge, however, which was brought against the Public Schools was not that of intellectual so much as of moral defect. The *Quarterly Journal of Education* did not hesitate to assert that "before an Eton boy is ready for the University he may have acquired at a place of education, where there is much less effective restraint than at a university, a confirmed taste for gluttony and drunkenness, an aptitude for brutal sports and a passion for female society of the most degrading kind, with as great ease as if he were an uncontrolled inhabitant of the metropolis and were responsible neither to governors, teachers, spiritual pastors and masters".[1] This is the language of an overt enemy of the English Public School; yet, however exaggerated, it reflects the opinion then held by a large number of persons who regarded the schools as communities of undisciplined young barbarians precocious in the knowledge and practice of ill-living. Reform in this field was Thomas Arnold's especial achievement.

In common with all schools at that time, the Public Schools were understaffed and in consequence were badly organized; the fact is at the root of their moral deficiencies. John Keate, head master of Eton from 1809 to 1834, who rivalled Busby as the greatest flogger in English scholastic history, had more than 100 boys in the division of the school which he took for "business". This was in 1820, after a

[1] *Op. cit.* vol. VIII, p. 286. The date is 1834.

reform of organization which had redistributed the numbers throughout the school. The Upper School at this time consisted of some 450 boys whose "business" was conducted by Keate and five assistant masters. When masters, acting as tutors, were in charge of "private business" (that is, preparation for "business" or studies outside the classical routine) their pupils numbered sixty or seventy. In 1833 the Upper School numbered 570 boys, with nine masters. To compensate for the intellectual and moral shortcomings entailed by understaffing, wealthy parents employed private tutors, unconnected with the schools, to supervise the morals and the studies of their children. Farington, writing in his *Diary* in October, 1807, refers to Lord Malpas "a boy of 15...goes to Eaton School, but there has a private Tutor and is not likely to be roughed into manhood by intercourse with other boys". Again, in October, 1811, there is a reference to the young Duke of Dorset and his private tutor at Harrow. In Keate's time thirty-two of these private tutors were employed at Eton.[1] Teachers of modern subjects like mathematics, or French, were without the necessary authority to exercise efficient control, and at Eton their work clashed with the demands of "business", owing to badly arranged time-tables.

In these large classes, "business" became little more than the repetition of lessons previously prepared, or ostensibly prepared; and the performance therein of any given boy was necessarily infrequent. The teacher's problem was two-fold. Some semblance of order and attention had to be enforced. Gladstone, a short time before his death, told how Keate used to give a Sunday morning lecture to Upper School. "During this lecture it was the custom of the bigger boys to make almost continually a kind of humming noise with the lips closed, so that the culprits could not be discovered."[2] "Songs, and even choruses, used to be sung in school, but Keate was seldom able to ascertain whence the sounds proceeded."[3] Secondly, the teacher sought a guarantee that, while only a fraction of the class could be put up either to construe or to repeat by rote, all present were duly prepared for business. Hence the readiness of resort to flogging, "impositions", and to penalties generally. The problem of good government was complicated by the considerable number of vacant hours from which

[1] See H. C. Maxwell-Lyte, *A History of Eton College* (1899), pp. 396 f.
[2] D. Hunter-Blair in *Eton College Chronicle*, October, 1921.
[3] Maxwell-Lyte, *loc. cit.*

the boys suffered. There were blanks in every day, and all red-letter days in the Church calendar were play days. No sport enjoyed the recognition which has since been extended to all games; some games, cricket and football not always excepted, were taboo. The practice of calling the roll several times during the day did not prevent boys from making their own disposal of leisure time, nor were its hours invariably devoted to "accomplishments" or other duly recognized employment of spare moments.

In these circumstances it is not wonderful that on the side of the masters there was a severity which sometimes became cruelty, and on the part of the boys a simmering insubordination which broke out into open mutiny. There were "rebellions", that is, risings *en masse* against the masters, at Eton in 1810 and 1832, at Harrow and at Winchester in 1818, at Rugby in 1822; the eighteenth century had seen even a greater number of these mutinies. They were pretty general in 1818. As always, the boys' homes had their share of responsibility for the character of the school life. In 1806 Dr Gretton, then master of a private school at Taplow, told Farington that "the bane of the Public Schools is that the parents of many of the boys fill their pockets with bank notes, and opportunity is allowed for the expenditure of it viciously".[1] Dr Keate shared this belief. He "found himself unable entirely to check the riding and tandem-driving; the frequent resistance to constituted authority at Eton, as at Winchester, Harrow and other schools, being in his opinion due to imperfect control of parents over their sons at home, and to the large allowances of money granted to mere boys".[2]

The domestic conditions under which boys on the foundation lived resembled those of the sixteenth rather than those of the nineteenth century. The dirt, discomfort, riot and rats of "Long Chamber", the lodging of the Eton "collegers" (foundationers), were notorious; wherever Eton was known, Long Chamber was a "proverb and reproach". The rough life of the school in general which was typified by this unsavoury dormitory caused a *Quarterly* Reviewer of 1834 to assert that it was "almost impossible for a lower colleger to be a gentleman". But there was another opinion, to which Farington gave expression when he said that the daily ill-disciplined intercourse "roughed boys into manhood". A juster view is that of the Etonian,

[1] *Diary*, September 26th, 1806.　　　[2] Maxwell-Lyte, *op. cit.* p. 388.

Edward Thring, who, while admitting the possible advantage of sharing in this life, called attention to the dangers which it entailed upon the average boy. "At the opposite pole to (the Ilminster private School) the old Long Chamber at Eton, now done away with for years, may be placed, with its seventy boys locked up from 8 p.m. to next morning utterly without supervision, left entirely to themselves in the great, bare, dirty room in which they were supposed to live and did sleep. Who can ever forget that knew it the wild, rough, rollicking freedom, the frolic and the fun of that land of misrule, with its strange code of traditional boy-law, which really worked rather well as long as the sixth form were well disposed or sober?... This wild college life was certainly a very different type from the sneak-as-you-please, but never-wet-your-feet existence of the private school, and it was the better of the two, for freedom is better than slavery; but alas! for the waste and ruin in the future, the wretchedness and coarseness and idleness at the time which it brought on the majority of those cast into its whirl."[1] What a boy took from his Public School greatly depended upon what he brought to it; certainly the boy who was determined to work had opportunity and sympathetic teachers at Eton. In the passage just quoted Thring also speaks of the house life of the "oppidan", the non-foundationer with no claim upon Long Chamber, as passing "on the whole in a satisfactory, humanising, effective way". The home of the oppidan was his boarding house kept by "dame" or "domine" and, from Keate's time, by an assistant master.

Some of the praise which is commonly given to Thomas Arnold as a reformer of the Public Schools rightly belongs to Samuel Butler (1774–1839) who was head master of Shrewsbury from 1798 to 1836. Butler, the greater practical schoolmaster of the two, had been in office for a generation when Arnold went to Rugby in 1828. Beginning with all the vigour of four and twenty, he went straight from Cambridge to an ancient school then at the lowest ebb of its fortunes. He not only made it in time a great and flourishing school, but his management of it became an accepted model for other Public Schools, his pupils made distinguished places for themselves at Oxford and Cambridge, and not a few of them carried his spirit and his methods into the schools of which they became head masters. He introduced into Shrewsbury a

[1] G. R. Parkin, *Edward Thring* (1900), pp. 22 f. Thring was at Eton from 1832 to 1841, being a colleger from 1835.

habit of hard work by the systematic practice of periodical examinations; the success of Shrewsbury boys in the scholarship examinations of the Universities was extraordinary—some of his contemporaries thought that these examinations bulked too largely amongst his ideals. He was a skilful and stimulating teacher, yet he was quite within the English tradition of giving a lower place to learning than to character. Writing to the father of a pupil in May, 1827, he said: "I cannot force them all to be first-rate scholars, because all have not the same capacity; but if I train them to be honourable and virtuous men, I am conferring a greater benefit upon themselves and on society than by all the learning I can give them".[1] It was this principle which caused him to throw responsibility for part of the school government upon the praepostors, and to endeavour to train initiative in all members of the school. "The leading idea which seems to have animated Dr Butler's whole plan of dealing with boys in intellectual as well as in moral matters was his desire to make them *self-reliant*. The praepostorial system, of which he was in all essential respects the originator, his persistence in urging the importance of *private work* as distinguished from work prepared for school, or done under his supervision, and the large amount of liberty which boys enjoyed out of school-hours are all illustrations of Dr Butler's anxiety to promote *self-reliance* among them."[2]

Butler was accessible to new ideas, as witness his championing of the claims of Catholic and of Protestant Dissenters to be released from political and educational disabilities. It is therefore not surprising that, while himself a good classical scholar and an unusually good teacher of the classics, he found a recognized place in the ordinary studies of Shrewsbury for mathematics, modern languages, modern history and modern geography. Yet there was a limit to his sympathies; he disapproved the principle of universal instruction, which throughout his professional career was so prominent a subject of public discussion. In a *Charge* which, as archdeacon, he delivered to the clergy in June, 1826, he said: "Now if it be true that solid and substantial learning is a plant of slow growth, even in minds that are best prepared to nourish it, I would ask to what really *useful* purpose can the *general*

---

[1] S. Butler, *Life and Letters of Samuel Butler* (1896), vol. I, p. 38.

[2] G. W. Fisher, *Annals of Shrewsbury School* (1899), p. 362. But the Merton College statutes of 1274 and those of Winchester, 1400, prove that Butler did not originate the "praepostorial system".

education of the poor, beyond the acquirements of reading, writing and plain religious instruction be applied? Nothing is so dangerous to the possessor, or so irksome and offensive to his neighbours as superficial knowledge".[1] It would be unfair to say that Butler resisted the movement for an *education* open to all. His point was that the attainment of knowledge is a very lengthy process for which the majority have not the necessary leisure. Remembering that the average school life at that time of the children who *did* attend schools for the poor was about two years, and that these children perhaps formed a minority in their social class, Butler's attitude may be understood.

But in this same *Charge* he deprecated the removal of obstacles to the pursuit of knowledge, on the ground that such hindrances stimulated and disciplined the mind. "Mighty difficulties make mighty minds; it is the struggle with obstacles apparently insurmountable that strengthens the intellect, that throws it upon its own resources—baffled, it is true, in many a conflict, but still rising with fresh vigour from every fall." Here the archdeacon of Derby would seem to have swallowed the head master of Shrewsbury, for his argument raises a dilemma. Either Shrewsbury and the University of Cambridge, indeed all schools and all universities are superfluous and mischievous institutions, or, alternatively, it is their function to hinder the attainment of knowledge. Possibly the orator, for the moment forgetting institutions, was thinking only of that essential factor in all education which is called self-education.

While this was Butler's position in reference to proposals for making elementary instruction more general in its distribution, in the matter of university studies he was a reformer. Early in January, 1822, he wrote under the pseudonym of "Eubulus" a pamphlet entitled *Thoughts on the Present System of Academic Education in the University of Cambridge*. Here he urged that the University spent too much time and labour in the study of mathematics, and that the range of classical study was too restricted. The only tripos at that time was in effect a mathematical tripos; but late in May of the same year a grace passed the Senate instituting a classical tripos, the first examination for which was held in 1824. As will be inferred from the following passage which occurs in his pamphlet, Butler favoured a tripos which would resemble

[1] Quoted by J. E. B. Mayor, *History of St John's College, Cambridge* (1869), vol. II, p. 946.

the Oxford "Greats", a school of *literae humaniores*. The quotation indicates the nature of the difference between classical study as pursued throughout the eighteenth century and as it developed in the century which followed: "I must add a few words on the classical examination. It would of course comprise not merely the construing Greek and Latin, but a variety of questions connected with the passages selected, and depending on history, antiquities, chronology, geography, metrical and philological criticism and ancient philosophy. And this leads me to a remark which will perhaps be unpalatable to some of our distinguished scholars, but which truth compels me not to omit. I mean that our range of Greek reading is at present too much confined. We labour about the dramatic writers too much to the exclusion of the rest. We weary ourselves with adjusting iambics and trochaics and anapaests, and twisting monostrophics into choruses and dochmiacs, and almost seem to neglect the sense for the sound. I do not mean to disparage these labours, which are sometimes learned and often ingenious, but I wish merely to hint that, if these things are good, there are also better things than those. We must not forsake the critics, philosophers, orators and historians of Greece for a mere branch of her poets; and I say without risk of contradiction from the most able and competent judges that Plato, Aristotle, Xenophon, Thucydides, Polybius and Demosthenes afford more improvement to the taste, more exercise for reflection, more dignity to the conceptions and enlargement to the understanding than all the Greek tragedies that were ever penned."[1] This is not said in depreciation of Greek drama—Butler had edited Aeschylus—it is the assertion that the content of literature has a higher educational value than its form. It is a protest echoed twelve years later by Adam Sedgwick, the Woodwardian Professor of Geology at Cambridge: "I think it incontestably true that for the last fifty years (with much to demand our undivided praise) we have been too critical and formal, and that we have sometimes been taught, while straining after an accuracy beyond our reach, to value the husk more than the fruit of ancient learning".[2]

"Eton and Westminster" was in the eighteenth century the accepted formula which represented the ancient Public Schools as a class; in

---

[1] S. Butler, *op. cit.* vol. I, p. 215.
[2] A. Sedgwick, *A discourse on the studies of the University of Cambridge* (1834), p. 37.

the early years of the nineteenth century the phrase was, as it still is, "Eton and Harrow". After Vincent's head-mastership (1788–1802) Westminster entered upon a period of decline; Sargeaunt marks the years 1819–46 as "the saddest in the annals of the School". There were several reasons for this, not the only one being the reign of head masters unequal to trying times. The school was restricted in its finances and within its physical boundaries; there was a proposal, frequently renewed, to remove the school to a more rural site at Putney, but it was negatived partly on grounds of sentiment, partly owing to lack of money.

The finances of Westminster School as administered by the Dean and Chapter, like the finances of many other endowed schools, were largely ruled not by current prices but by the sixteenth-century values of money, little or no account being taken of the great fall in the purchasing power of the pound which had occurred in the interval. Ten pounds, a sufficient annual stipend for a grammar school master of Henry VII's time, remained in many cases the statutory salary under George III; sporadic applications to the Court of Chancery for a readjustment were neither so many nor so successful as to alter the position of grammar school teachers in general. To secure a more equitable income, masters, where circumstances were favourable, availed themselves liberally of their statutory power to admit boarders, whose fees were not subject to statute. In course of time these "foreigners" from a distance outnumbered the foundationers, the sons of local residents, and the character of the school, and particularly its studies, tended to be governed by the requirements of the outsider rather than by local needs. Harrow is a case in point.

The transformation of this school from a local institution to a non-local one occurred during the late eighteenth century; in 1810 and again in 1833 formal protest was made on the local behalf. In the earlier year the protest took the form of an action in the Rolls Court against the governing body for failure to carry out the terms of their trust. The suit on the whole was decided in the governors' favour. It is clear from the regulations laid down by John Lyon, the founder, that his entire bequest was a charitable one in the accepted sense, and in particular that the school was primarily for Harrow children, with special solicitude for those of them who were "of the most apt and most poore sorte that be meete, the poore kinsfolk of me the said John

Lyon (if any such be) and such as are borne within the said parish of Harrow, being apt to learn, poore, and meete to go to the university to be preferred before others". But besides giving large discretionary powers to his trustees there were provisions in his own regulations whose tendency was to defeat his primary intention. First, the stipends of the master and usher were fixed at forty marks (£26. 13s. 4d.) and twenty marks respectively, with a yearly allowance of five marks in each case for wood and coals. In the second place governors and master were empowered, if not encouraged, to admit "foreigners" on payment. "And a meete and competent number of schollers, as well of poore, to be taught freely for the stipends aforesaid, as of others to be received for the further profitt and comoditie of the said schoolemaster, shall be sett downe and appointed by the discrecon of the said keepers and governors, from time to time." In the Rolls Court in 1810 the governors pleaded "that the school is a school for classical learning; that however wise the intentions of the founder might have been, the school is not now adapted generally for persons of low condition, but better suited to those of a higher class". They went on to say that "more children do not come from Harrow parish because few of the inhabitants are desirous that their children should be educated in classical learning"; they conceived that "this was intended as a school for teaching grammatically the learned languages, and not for the instruction of the children of Harrow in general learning". This last contention merely stated the law as it had been laid down some five years previously by Eldon; the endowment of a grammar school could only be drawn upon to teach grammar. In effect the Master of the Rolls repeated this judgement, with the added statement that the school clearly was not intended solely for Harrow parish; it was for the gratuitous instruction of such as chose to receive the kind of education there offered, and for other scholars not of the parish who might choose to resort there.[1]

The position was this. Lyon left property to provide what he thought the best education for Harrow parish, with special consideration for such of its poor as were competent to profit from it. In course of time that type of education proved not to be the best for the generality of Harrow; nevertheless, this type of education, ill-suited or not suited at all to Harrow parish, was being maintained for the benefit of those

---

[1] The quotations in the foregoing paragraph are from the summary of the case in the *Quarterly Journal of Education*, vol. IX (1835), pp. 80 ff.

who were neither poor nor Harrow parishioners. The governing body had adopted the principle that the school was suitable only for boys "of a higher class", a principle contrary to Lyon's intention, which required capacity not social standing in his beneficiaries. Otherwise they were acting within the limits of the discretion allowed them. But whether they desired it or not, they were powerless to change the type of education in view of Eldon's judgement of 1805. The Chancery Court might deal with the minor difficulties of individual schools; but the *impasse* in which English secondary education now found itself could only be turned by one great administrative body empowered to deal with the schools as a whole. Brougham's Select Committee of 1816 to inquire "into the education of the lower order" had its terms of reference enlarged from time to time down to 1831, so that they covered educational endowments in general; but the Universities and Public Schools were expressly exempted from its investigation. By way of protest, the Harrow Vestry in 1833 published Lyon's original orders and a statement of the local grievance.

But at that date the grievance was of long standing. At the close of the eighteenth century Harrow was second only to Eton of all the Public Schools in point of numbers. In 1831 its roll numbered 214 boys, of whom only 15 were on the foundation. The annual fee varied from 131 to 135 guineas if the boy lived in a tutor's house, from 101 to 105 guineas if in the head master's house; the payments included twenty guineas for tuition as distinct from "schooling", or business, which was charged ten guineas a year and was also included. "Masters in French, Italian, mathematics, drawing, fencing and music attend the school regularly", that is, these studies were "extras" and their teachers were paid separately by those who employed them; such teachers formed no part of the regular school staff. The 15 foundationers of 1831 were exempt from the payment of the fee for "schooling" and the annual guinea which non-foundationers paid for "school charges", possibly a survival of the payment in respect of light, firing and cleaning. The foundationers were in every respect on the same footing as other boys.[1] Clearly not much was being done to educate the poor of Harrow in Lyon's own school, albeit the governors paid an annual subscription to the National school.

Part of the complaint brought before the Master of the Rolls in 1810

[1] *Quarterly Journal of Education*, vol. III (1832).

was that the "foreigners" who were prejudicing local interests were "chiefly the sons of the nobility and gentry of the kingdom". The grievance was two-fold; a local school had become non-local and its benches were no longer occupied by boys of the lower middle class or by children from humble homes. This was a state of things not peculiar to Harrow. Whatever the reason, the Public Schools were ceasing to find pupils in these ranks and were seeking recruits only from "the nobility and gentry". The explanation no doubt takes several forms. The increased efficiency under Etonian masters of Rugby and of Harrow in the eighteenth century and the reforms later introduced into Shrewsbury under Butler, together with the improvements in the Public Schools in general, would once more bring these schools into the favour of the socially prominent and wealthy classes. On the other hand, the ever-growing gap between their curriculum and the demands of a utilitarian society tended to make them less attractive to poor and ambitious boys, who could find other and more accessible ways to a career.

Perhaps also the disappearance from these schools of boys from the humbler ranks of society is a symptom of that sharper segregation of classes which was a consequence of the social revolution then in progress. Among eighteenth-century Wykehamists were the poet William Collins, son of a local hatter, and William Whitehead, poet laureate in 1757, a Cambridge baker's son; both boys were at Winchester in 1735. William Crowe, public orator at Oxford, 1784–1829, a Winchester scholar in 1758, was a carpenter's son. William Carey, head master of Westminster, 1803–14, and educated at Westminster, was the son of a Worcester tradesman. Amongst Eton collegers were John Foster, head master, 1765–73, and his successor, Jonathan Davies, 1773–91; the former was the son of a Windsor tradesman, the latter was of humble birth, his nickname, "Barber Davies," perhaps pointing to his father's occupation. Lyte says that during Davies' head-mastership "the ranks of the Collegers were largely recruited from the sons of tradesmen in Windsor and Eton".[1] Richard Porson who entered Eton in 1774, and who was Regius Professor of Greek at Cambridge eighteen years later, was the son of a parish clerk. On the other hand, the advantages, actual and prospective, of the Eton collegers' standing induced well-to-do parents to enter their boys as oppidans at an early

[1] *Op. cit.* p. 360.

age, in the hope that at the latest possible moment, and no earlier, they would secure nomination to a place on the foundation. Edward Thring, whose father owned a considerable landed estate in Somerset, at the age of eleven entered as an oppidan in 1832, became a colleger for the remainder of his Eton career in 1835 and quitted the school for a scholarship at King's College, Cambridge, in 1841. His elder brother was an oppidan throughout his time at Eton.

Rugby's position as a great non-local school dates from the head-mastership (1778–94) of an Etonian, Thomas James, who came into office at a critical stage in the school's history. The number of pupils at that time was 52; but a large increase of income accrued by the falling-in of leases on the London estate of the trustees. A new con-stitution was given to the school in 1777 and steps were taken to increase the school staff and to enlarge the buildings. Under James's able management the numbers steadily increased; there were 245 boys in the year of his retirement. Samuel Butler, who was greatly indebted at the outset of his career at Shrewsbury to James for advice on school management, was a pupil from 1783, at the age of nine, till he went up to Cambridge in October, 1791. James was succeeded by Henry Ingles (1794–1807) and John Wooll (1807–28). During the latter's tenure Rugby reaped the fruit of reforms initiated a generation earlier; the school of 52 numbered 381 in 1818. Wooll's successor was Thomas Arnold.

Some of Arnold's younger contemporaries placed him upon a pinnacle to which few, if any, other schoolmasters could claim to have attained; Mr Lytton Strachey conveys the impression that Arnold was a prig and an ineffective prig.[1] No explanation is given of the fact that Arnold's life and character made the strongest appeal to Thomas Hughes and to others like him to whom cant and priggishness were repellent. A fair estimate of Arnold cannot be reached without taking into account, not only Rugby, but the state of the Public Schools before and after his tenure of the head-mastership (1828–42). There is no indication in *Eminent Victorians* that its author had made any serious study of English education as it was a hundred years ago. The recognized defect of the Public Schools in the reign of George III was a moral rather than an intellectual one; Arnold's intense earnestness of character and fidelity to principle became great agencies in transforming

[1] *Eminent Victorians*, 1918.

the life, not only of Rugby, but of the Public School group. The Clarendon Commission of 1861–4 noted the moral change that had passed over these schools within the preceding generation; it affected the proprietary schools which were being founded in the latter part of Arnold's life, and subsequently it passed through Rugby boys to Oxford and Cambridge and so to English education as a whole. Arnold's principles and practice became patterns for the English schoolmaster.

A study of Arnold's life from 1828 to its end in 1842 is no mere excursion into the biography of a dead-and-gone worthy. A discussion is due, if not imminent, respecting the purpose, or purposes, of English public schooling and the studies and occupations best fitted to effect that purpose, or purposes. On these subjects Arnold had steadfast convictions. For him, education was above all the religious and moral training of human nature. "Undoubtedly he is perfectly educated who is taught all the will of God concerning him, and enabled through life to execute it. And he is not well educated who does not know the will of God, or, knowing it, has received no help in his education towards being inclined and enabled to do it."[1] "Some perhaps have been puzzled...how to reconcile with a profession of religious or Christian education the devotion of so much time to studies not supposed to be religious and certainly not in themselves necessarily Christian. Now the reason is, because the words of a rule are much sooner learnt than the power of applying it universally; and that whilst the Scripture itself alone furnishes the former, the latter must be sought for in sources exceedingly various, and extracted from them by long and laborious process. Undoubtedly that is useless in education which does not enable a man to glorify God better in his way through life; but then we are called upon to glorify him in many various ways according to our several callings and circumstances; and as we are to glorify him both in our bodies and in our spirits with all our faculties, both outward and inward, I cannot consider it unworthy either to render our body strong and active, or our understanding clear, rich and versatile in its powers; I cannot reject from the range of religious education whatever ministers to the perfection of our bodies and our minds, so long as both in body and mind, in soul and spirit, we ourselves may be taught to minister to the service of God."[2]

[1] J. J. Findlay, *Arnold of Rugby* (1897), p. 132, quoting the "Sermon on Christian Education".   [2] *Ibid.* pp. 136 f.

Arnold is rightly ranked with those who, while retaining the essentials of the old classical curriculum, supplemented these by such modern studies as history, geography and spoken languages. But to stop there is to miss the point of most importance. Instruction in these things was not simply given to add to the sum of knowledge or as to ends in themselves. They were parts of a discipline which aimed at moral and religious advancement. Arnold's principle and reservations call for observance more imperative to-day than during his life-time. The demands of knowledge now distort the claims of education. We are driven to selection within its wide fields; and a successful choice can only be made in the light of a clear conception of what we expect education to accomplish in particular cases under particular conditions.

Arnold's active sympathy with modern studies did not betoken hostility to the old curriculum. On the contrary it sprang from an intense belief in the value of classical studies as instruments of education. He was deeply affected by the change in the aims of classical students which was brought about in Germany during the second half of the eighteenth century. Whereas the strength of British scholarship from Bentley to Porson had lain in verbal scholarship, in the emendation and criticism of texts and in metrical study, the new object was a fuller understanding of the ancient civilization, its history, art and institutions. Arnold was "the scholar who (in the *Quarterly Review* of 1825) introduced the first edition of Niebuhr's *History of Rome* to the English public". He maintained intercourse with German scholars from 1827 onwards and was always an admirer of German scholarship. Yet Butler had anticipated him in noting the changed direction of classical study. Arnold's generation indeed was becoming alive to the rise and growth of German literature, an awareness largely due to the efforts of Samuel Taylor Coleridge to introduce the new writers to his countrymen after his sojourn in Germany in 1798-9.

Because of his conviction that the true aim of education was religious and moral, Arnold found the chief value of a classical training in its application to the everyday affairs of English life. It is not an accident that so many of his pupils became workers for social and political reforms. Here again knowledge, learning, scholarship were instruments, not ends. Arnold's retirement from the Senate of the University of London in 1838 was caused by that body's avowal of a principle to which he was totally opposed, "namely, that education need not be connected with Christianity",[1] a contravention of "the great principle that Christianity should be the base of all public education in this country".[2] His attitude illustrates the application of his principles to the relations of Church and State at that moment; he was opposed to the removal of Jewish civic disabilities.

[1] Letter to Bishop of Norwich, February 17th, 1838, in Stanley's *Life*, p. 324.
[2] Letter to the Earl of Burlington, November 7th, 1838, *op. cit.* p. 327.

CHAPTER III

The Universities—Oxford, Cambridge, London, Durham

At the beginning of the nineteenth century England had two universities only; both were objects of attack from external educational reformers, or would-be reformers, both had yielded to the pressure for reform from within which had been a feature of their history in the preceding century. When Arnold asserted that all English public education was based upon religion, he was stating not a purely personal opinion but the general conviction of wellnigh everybody connected with the educational institutions of the country. A manifesto of certain members of the Oxford Convocation stated unreservedly in April, 1834, that "the University of Oxford had always considered religion to be the foundation of all education". A reviewer in the *Quarterly Journal of Education*, of the same date, pointed to the intimate association between the colleges and the Church, intimacies which would persist were the University no longer to require a profession of faith from its members. "There remains the chapel system which in Oxford is regarded as an essential part or instrument of college discipline; next the religious instruction which is regularly given, at least in form, and regarded as an equally essential part of the tutorial course of instruction; then there is the examination in the rudiments of religion, considered to be the most essential part of the examination for the degree of B.A.; and lastly there is a sort of general recognition of religion as the leading principle in all university institutions and forms whatsoever." These statements had a general application to Cambridge also.

The government of both Universities was in each case in the hands of a clerical oligarchy, and from the standpoint of religious belief the society of Oxford and Cambridge was exclusive. Membership of Oxford, and at Cambridge graduation with its privileges, were impossible for men who would not subscribe to the Thirty-Nine Articles of the Church of England. College emoluments were restricted by obligations to particular counties, particular schools and particular persons in the character of founder's kin. The university statutes of Cambridge were those in force in Elizabeth's time (1570), those of

Oxford went back to 1636–8, when Laud was Chancellor; some college statutes were of yet older date. Of course, some of these statutory provisions were quite unsuited to nineteenth-century conditions. There were many traps for those who desired to contravene them, since university men had taken oath to observe them and any breach exposed the culprit to a criminal charge of perjury. This legal possibility was sometimes alleged as an excuse for avoiding change; yet the governing bodies of both Universities and of their colleges did not hesitate, when it suited them, to allow some statutes to lapse and others to be disregarded.

There were special circumstances at this time to which members of universities so constituted would be disposed to attend whenever their religious exclusiveness was in question. The recent growth of Unitarianism, a growth in which Cambridge had played no small part, alarmed the friends of orthodoxy. Some Cambridge graduates, who were conspicuous by their Unitarian opinions, had at an earlier time led the agitation for the removal of religious tests in the University, and they were now active in the troubled sea of current politics. One of these, William Frend, was in 1793 "banished" (he could not be expelled) from his fellowship at Jesus College and from the University, in consequence of his pamphlet, *Peace and Union recommended*, in which he denounced the war on the French Republic, discussed parliamentary reform and spoke flippantly of Christianity. The majority found it difficult to discriminate between orthodox and heterodox Dissenters, between those whose opinions were subversive of the existing order in Church and State and those who were not actively hostile to either. Hence the language of the Oxford manifesto of 1834: "In thus stating it to be their solemn duty to provide for a Christian education, they feel that uniformity of faith upon essential points is absolutely necessary".[1] Insistence upon orthodox Church of England belief seemed the only line of safety.

This accounts for the utterances of such an extremist as William Sewell, Fellow and Tutor of Queen's College, whose *Thoughts on the admission of Dissenters to the University of Oxford*, 1834, excited attention by its vehemence and intolerance. "I deny the right of liberty

---

[1] The manifesto is given in the *Quarterly Journal of Education* (April, 1834), vol. VIII, p. 83. It was signed by about 100 persons, 900 members of Convocation concurring; 22 heads of houses signed a similar statement. *Ibid.* p. 179.

of conscience wholly and utterly. I deny the right of a child to poison itself; the right of a man to ruin himself; the right of a nation to indulge itself in any caprice or madness....I deny the right of any sect to depart one atom from the standard which I hold to be the truth of Christianity. And I deny the right of any legislative power, of any minister of God, of any individual on earth, to sanction or permit it, without using every means in my power to control and bring them back from their errors" (p. 96).

In the supposed interest of conformity daily attendance in chapel was compulsory. A complainant of 1794[1] describes the services as "slovenly", and men who were in residence about 1820 in one great college draw scandalous pictures of "the habitual desecration", in the words of one of them, "of a service which ought to be religious and is converted into a muster".[2] The disorderliness and insubordination which had marked the Public Schools in the eighteenth century were not overcome by the discipline of the Universities. "Fellow-commoners" and "gentlemen-commoners", young men of rank and fortune, formed a considerable part of the undergraduate community. Many of them were idle and dissipated, all of them were exempt from examinations and other salutary exercises which demanded at least a minimum of work. Their presence made life in College expensive; and every member of the University was perforce a member of a college. The character of the examinations at which a candidate aspired to honours was such as to require the services of a private tutor. In 1789 Vicesimus Knox wrote a letter to the Chancellor of Oxford in which he asked for the intervention of Parliament to enforce discipline and to reduce the expenses of university education.

But a university is a world and not a community moved by a single principle or devoted to one narrow ideal of life. While some men wasted their time and their fathers' money, others were differently employed. In a manuscript note written in the margin of a copy of Connop Thirlwall's *Letter to the Revd. Thos. Turton on the*

---

[1] *Strictures upon the discipline of the University of Cambridge addressed to the Senate.*
[2] "University Reform", p. 29, an article in *The British and Foreign Review* (1837), of which the author was probably the editor, J. M. Kemble. See also *Alma Mater or Seven Years at the University of Cambridge* (1827), vol. I, pp. 32 ff., of which the author was perhaps J. M. F. Wright. There may be exaggerations in these pictures, but of the slovenliness and irreverence there seems to be no doubt.

admission of Dissenters to academical degrees (1834), J. M. Kemble (?) gives the following account of an undergraduates' club, the Conversazione Society *alias* The Apostles. "No society ever existed in which more freedom of thought was found consistent with the most perfect affection between the members, or in which a more complete tolerance of the most opposite opinions prevailed. I shall say nothing of what the actual and former members of that society have done; but very few of the distinguished Cambridge men of our time have not been members of it; and it existed to remedy a fault of our education. Its business was to make men study and think on all matters except mathematics and classics professionally considered. Its metaphysical tendency has altered (first in Trinity) the system of university examination itself.... To my *education* given in that society I feel that I owe every power I possess, and the rescuing myself from a ridiculous state of prejudice and prepossessions with which I came armed to Cambridge. From 'the Apostles' I, at least, learned to think as a *free man*." This was written in 1847 when the society had existed "nearly forty years".[1] The Cambridge Union Society, which celebrated its centenary in November, 1921, had one or more ineffective and short-lived predecessors in the years immediately following Waterloo; the Oxford Union also had a predecessor, the "United Debating Society", which held its first debate in April, 1823. Both Unions had to live down a good deal of prejudice in their early years, and their infancy was a troubled one. The author of *Alma Mater*, who was at Cambridge from 1815 to 1822, asserts that through a letter to the Vice-Chancellor he, an undergraduate apparently in his fourth term, was instrumental in terminating the life of "The Union Society", a "mass of noisy ignorance". The United Debating Society at Oxford came to grief over a debate on religious disabilities.

During the first thirty or more years of the nineteenth century the Universities evolved a scheme of examination which powerfully stimulated their intellectual life, deeply affected the choice of studies and in the end established in the country at large a firm belief in the value of formal examinations as instruments of education no less than as tests of instruction. That belief exercised its full influence upon subsequent policy, administration and daily practice. The success or

[1] *D.N.B.* ascribes its foundation to F. D. Maurice and John Sterling. This would seem to refer to a revival or second foundation in the early twenties.

failure of the mediaeval student in pursuing the courses which he was required to attend was tested orally; in that way his seniors examined him in his books, and in their presence at stated periods he maintained or disputed a thesis. He "kept an Act" as respondent when he maintained a "question", or an "opponency" when he took the opposing side; both respondent and opponent used a sort of Latin as the vehicle of the dispute. As the old statutes enjoining these exercises were still in force, these "acts" and "opponencies" survived at both Universities down to the nineteenth century, by which time keeping an Act had become a formality to be complied with rather than a useful element in university education. On occasion able disputants could make the Act a display of wits which exercised the keenest intelligences; yet it was as ill adapted to the times as was the barbarous Latin (a contemporary calls it an "infamous practice") in which it was traditionally conducted. Even the habitual selection of theses from modern authors and modern studies could not confer vitality upon the ancient forms.

In his third year the Cambridge undergraduate who was reading for honours kept two Acts as respondent, maintaining three subjects of dispute on each occasion; he also made six "opponencies". The respondent called upon to keep an Act gave notice to the two moderators, who were to preside at the exercise, that the questions would be, for example:

"i.   Recte statuit Newtonus in nona sectione libri primi.

ii. Recte statuit Woodius de radicibus impossibilibus.

iii. Recte statuit Paleius de suicidiis".

The moderators would then appoint three opponents to argue respectively against the passages indicated in Newton, Wood and Paley. A fortnight's preparation was allowed during which the three opponents usually met to concert measures in common and to avoid mere repetition of arguments. The course of the debate enabled the moderators, assisted by the tutors' reports, to make a rough classification of the candidates which served as a guide in examining them for the tripos in the following year.

Formal as these exercises were, they sometimes presented a serious side even to the ablest men. Augustus De Morgan, fourth wrangler in 1827, has left the following account of the Act which he kept in the previous year. "The real disputations were very severe exercises. I was badgered for two hours with arguments given and answered in

Latin, or what we called Latin, against Newton's first section, Lagrange's derived functions and Locke on innate principles. And though I *took off* everything, and was pronounced by the moderator to have disputed *magno honore*, I never had such a strain of thought in my life. For the inferior opponents were made as sharp as their betters by their tutors, who kept lists of queer objections, drawn from all quarters. The opponents used to meet the day before to compare their arguments, that the same might not come twice over. But after I left Cambridge it became the fashion to invite the respondent to be present, who therefore learnt all that was to be brought against him. This made the whole thing a farce; and the disputations were abolished."[1]

Even the poll man did not escape the formality, although he was allowed to make it ridiculous by what was called "huddling". That ceremony was thus described in 1837—the last Cambridge Act was performed in 1839: "Thomas Styles, from the Respondent's seat, speaking in Latin: 'Newton was correct; Wood was correct; Locke was correct'. John Noakes, from the Opponent's seat, likewise speaking in Latin: 'If your disputations are false, they fall; but they are false; therefore they fall'. These words are repeated (that is, on one and the same occasion) until Thomas Styles has kept the requisite number of Acts, and John Noakes the requisite number of Opponencies. They then change places and Thomas Styles refutes John Noakes with John Noakes's own syllogism, and *Da capo ad libitum*."[2] In similar fashion the Oxford B.A. of the year 1800 proceeded to the master's degree by "doing Austins", "quodlibets", reading "sex solemnes lectiones" (vulgarly termed "wall lectures", in default of hearers), delivering two declamations and undergoing examination, a series of exercises originally intended to extend over three years, but which were "huddled" into a single occasion. On his road to the bachelor's degree the Oxonian had also kept Acts by disputing in grammar or logic, rhetoric or politics; he had had an examination which was "quite private" and he usually chose his own three examiners.

Disputation at this date was a mode of driving a coach and four through the statutes and must not be taken too seriously. It was a university, not a college, exercise; and it was the college studies,

---

[1] *A Budget of Paradoxes* (1872), p. 305.

[2] B. Dann Walsh, *A historical account of the University of Cambridge and its colleges in a letter to the Earl of Radnor*, 1837.

exercises and examinations which were the real instruments of university education. Nor were disputations the only university requirements at the opening of the nineteenth century. In the mid-eighteenth century Cambridge had instituted the Senate House examination, and from 1780 onwards that examination was the effective test of scholarship, to which Acts and Opponencies were subsidiary in fixing places in the class list. At Oxford the Public Examination Statute of 1800 was in operation by 1802; a revolution in studies and in examination followed in due course, although this statute failed to establish, as it proposed, an examination for the M.A. degree.

The Senate House examination was taken by all candidates for the B.A. degreè, whether potential honours men or not; but the preliminary sifting by college tutors and the prescribed university exercises, such as the Acts and the like, drew a clear line between those who aspired to honours and "the poll". The tests proposed to individual candidates differed accordingly. The subjects examined were mathematics (including "arithmetic, algebra, fluxions, the doctrine of infinitesimals and increments, geometry, trigonometry, optics, astronomy"; and, by the close of the period 1789–1837, mechanics and hydrostatics), natural religion, moral philosophy, "Locke". Till 1824 this was the only tripos; in spite of the presence of questions in ethics and metaphysics, it was a mathematical tripos, since mathematics outweighed everything else. Much of the examination was in the nature of a *viva voce*, questions were dictated, printed papers of questions were sparingly employed until about 1836, when the whole machinery had been recast. At this date the examination, which was conducted by printed question papers and written answers, extended over six days, and the pass men had a separate examination from the honours men. In 1822 it was decided to institute a second tripos, and two years later the first examinations for the Classical Tripos were held. This honours examination covered the whole range of the strictly "classical" authors, Greek and Latin, and included translation and *miscellanea* associated with the two literatures. But this second tripos was open only to those who had secured mathematical honours, a rule which of course must have excluded not a few men whose attainments should have entitled them to classical honours. Yet it remained in force till 1850, so hard was it to diminish the importance which Cambridge attached to mathematical study.

At Oxford the modern system of examination was introduced by the Public Examination Statute of 1800, a statute which underwent some considerable modifications in the course of the next thirty years. The examination for the B.A. degree covered a wide range within the two classical literatures; it also ostensibly included grammar, rhetoric, logic, moral philosophy and the elements of mathematics; but classics formed the essential subject, with mathematics in the second place. A proposal was made in 1833 "to render imperative some part of the elements either of geometry or of algebra, arithmetic or some branch of natural philosophy as a qualification in all candidates for the degree of B.A." This was vetoed by the Vice-Chancellor, heads of houses and the proctors, the governing body of the University, with whom it rested to bless or ban every legislative proposal submitted to Convocation. As at Cambridge, and for the same reason, all candidates for the first degree attended the same examination, because their college tutors had lectured them, or taught them together. Candidates who "gained a class", that is, passed with honour, were placed in Class I or Class II, the latter being divided between a first and second bracket. In the early days of the statute of 1800 the second bracket, virtually a third class, included the majority of the honours men. Of all the successful candidates more than one-third as a rule gained a class; the remainder simply passed. The examination was largely oral; composition, English, Latin or Greek, was of course a written exercise, as also was mathematics "if the student had advanced far in those studies",[1] that is, if he took the separate mathematical school.

Copleston protested that the *Edinburgh Review* was wholly wrong in asserting that Oxford mathematics only meant the elements of geometry; on the contrary in 1810 it comprised "plane and spherical trigonometry, conics, conchoids, cycloids, the quadratrix, spirals, fluxions, natural philosophy in all its branches, astronomy". In any case, the mathematical candidates for an Oxford degree were sufficiently numerous and the study itself of sufficient importance to cause the degree examination to be divided into two schools, *literae humaniores* and mathematics, each having its classified list of the successful. Copleston says that a "double honour" was "very frequent", a man appearing in both lists. In 1830 Oxford decided to hold separate examinations for honours and pass; effect was given to the decision in Easter Term, 1831.

[1] (E. Copleston) *A Reply to the Calumnies of the "Edinburgh Review"* (1810).

The requirements for a "pass" at the B.A. examination at the two ancient Universities show the bias of studies in their respective cases. At Cambridge in 1800 two books of Euclid, simple and quadratic equations and the early parts of Paley's *Moral Philosophy* were amply sufficient. By 1837 a more extensive range was demanded from the poll: the subjects were mathematics, pure and mixed, the Acts of the Apostles in Greek, one Greek and one Latin author, Paley's *Moral Philosophy*. At Oxford in 1834 the pass man was expected to translate from any four classical authors of his own choosing, to show a competent knowledge of the Christian religion and to be examined in logic or in the first four books of Euclid; the classics were essential and few candidates offered Euclid. At neither University was the standard for a "pass" severe.

From its foundation the members of New College, Oxford, were privileged to take degrees without supplicating the House of Congregation; the college, not the University, judged the candidate's fitness for a degree. At first, New College did not come into the scheme initiated by the Public Examination Statute of 1800, but itself examined its candidates. In spite of a high standard of examination New College, graduates suffered in repute by their anomalous position, and in November, 1834, the college relinquished its privilege. King's College, Cambridge, possessed a similar right, but was slower in abandoning it. Boys went up from Eton to King's, held scholarships and, in due course, fellowships, all by seniority;[1] they were exempt from the ordinary University tests and were given their degree on the recommendation of the college tutors. In spite of agitation within the society itself in favour of the change, this very questionable advantage was retained till 1851. Before that date Eton boys were admitted to King's College scholarships on the result of an examination and not by mere seniority.

Neither University examined men on admission; such tests as were applied were at the discretion of the particular college. But at the time now being considered both Universities examined undergraduates midway in their course. Oxford held an examination of men of not less than six and not more than nine terms' standing; in spite of its mediaeval name, Responsions, its subjects were one Greek and one

---

[1] The author of *Alma Mater* (1827) in his "advice to parents" roundly asserts "King's College is for Eton men only".

Latin author, logic or Euclid, books I, II, and III. A candidate might take both logic and Euclid; the majority took logic only. At Cambridge "an examination termed the Previous Examination was established in 1830, at which all students are required to acquit themselves in a satisfactory manner in the middle of their second year".[1] The subjects of this examination were one Greek and one Latin classic, a Gospel or the Acts of the Apostles in Greek and Paley's *Evidences of Christianity*. At an earlier date than 1830 it would seem that Trinity College examined its undergraduates on very similar lines—the larger colleges anticipated the Universities in the development of the examination system—for the author of *Alma Mater* describes a course of reading which he took up in his fifth term (1817), the topics of which closely resemble the requirements of the Previous Examination. It should be noted that the inclusion of Greek in both of these intermediate examinations made some study of that language compulsory upon all candidates for the degree of B.A.

At the close of the pre-Victorian era the examination system was fully developed at the Universities. College examinations were the general practice; at Cambridge the University examinations were conducted by means of papers of printed questions. A day's work occupied six hours divided into two equal periods.

How completely studies were being directed by examination sylla-buses may be inferred from the regulations of the University of London, whose charter (1836) empowered it "to perform the functions of the Examiners in the Senate House of Cambridge". These regu-lations provided for examinations at matriculation, and for the degrees of B.A. and M.A.; separate examinations were to be held for "pass" and "honours" at matriculation and at B.A., candidates for honours being required to succeed at the corresponding "pass" examination as a qualification for taking the more advanced test. The matriculation examination included mathematics, natural philosophy ("mixed" or "applied" mathematics and physics), chemistry, natural history, Greek, Latin, English language, outlines of history and geography. The B.A. test comprised (i) mathematics and natural philosophy; (ii) chemistry, physiology, animal and vegetable, structural botany; (iii) one Greek and one Latin author, history, Greek, Roman and English, the French or German language; (iv) logic and moral philosophy. There were

[1] W. Whewell, *On the Principles of English University Education* (1837), p. 79.

three branches of examination for the M.A. degree, a candidate being permitted to offer one or more, viz. classics, mathematics, and natural philosophy, and a third branch, whose boundaries were less well defined. For this third branch the regulations named "logic, moral philosophy, philosophy of the mind, political philosophy, political economy", their relative importance being left to the examiner to decide. The University was also prepared to grant "certificates of proficiency" in respect of "post-graduate" studies, so-called, of a more or less professional nature.

The development of the examination system had proceeded so far as to exhibit its weaknesses, and complaints were rife on that account. Some critics thought that an unhealthy rivalry was being fostered; "love of excelling, not the love of excellence is made the basis of our studies".[1] Students' intellectual interests were being narrowed and only what would "pay" in the examination secured their attention; professorial lectures which had no bearing on the "schools" or the tripos secured few hearers, or none, however intrinsically valuable the subject-matter or distinguished the professor. The services of the "coach" were necessary to ensure conspicuous success or, when the candidate was of moderate ability, even a place in the list. The fees paid to these private tutors, who held no officially recognized position in the academic economy, added to the expense of university life; and expense had been a ground of complaint in the preceding century also.

Some of the evil had already extended downwards to the schools. "The last ten years [1827–37] have sufficed to strike a fatal blow at the whole system of school education. Learning is now become the sole object and the whole generation will suffer for it; it is a concealed but not the less dangerous approach to the chrestomathic system [i.e. the utilitarianism of Bentham]. For this evil course Cambridge is deeply responsible, much more so than Oxford."[2] The schoolboy who aims at a college fellowship "is sent up to the University deep in the technical part of scholarship, well acquainted with all the *passages* likely to be set in examinations, practised in the writing of alcaics or the building up of Greek iambics, master of the letter but not imbued with the spirit of the great authors of antiquity; sacrificed to a professional or special education of the narrowest kind, stunted in mind, old before his time and without having developed those physical qualities, the complete education of which is essential to the completeness of the intellectual, without which you may be a book-worm, but never dare to become a man".[1] This was written in the days of the extraordinary successes scored in university scholarship examinations by Samuel Butler's boys from Shrewsbury.

During the early years of the nineteenth century Oxford and Cambridge were the objective of two converging lines of attack, one of which was a protest against the exclusion of Dissenters, the other, adverse criticism of university studies and the collegiate system of instruction. The *Edinburgh Review*, as part of its proposals for scotticizing English education generally, led the attack on the colleges and the studies pursued in them; the reformed Parliament concentrated the struggle to remove the academical disabilities of Nonconformists. The two lines met in Sir William Hamilton's contributions of 1831 and 1836 to the *Edinburgh Review*; they were in fact two operations of one and the same attack. "The *Edinburgh*", said its editor, Jeffrey, to Sir Walter Scott, "has but two legs to stand on. Literature is one of them, but its right leg is politics." The *Review* stood on its right leg whenever it confronted the Church of England, the Universities, the Public and Endowed Schools, all of which it regarded as parts of one objectionable political institution. These attacks failed; and those who shared in them next tried private initiative and activity, in the fashion characteristic of their day. What could not be wrung from Oxford and Cambridge they determined to create in London for themselves.

The requirements for a first degree at Oxford and at Cambridge show that at the former classical studies, at the latter mathematical, occupied a position which left little room for physical science, modern literature or modern history. This was one of the complaints of the *Edinburgh Review*. Yet modern studies were not absolutely neglected. In the late eighteenth century the Regius Professors of Modern History regularly employed teachers of modern languages, although they themselves scarcely ever lectured on history; in the early years of the nineteenth century the Oxford professor gave a course in political economy, while his confrère at Cambridge also lectured and formed a library. William Farish, Professor of Chemistry at Cambridge, lectured on the applications of science to industry, his courses being well attended,

[1] "University Reform", 1837, p. 15.

as also were those of Professor E. D. Clarke (*Stone* Clarke) on mineralogy. The last seem to have afforded rather more amusement than instruction. At this time Cambridge numbered amongst its University teachers, *Bone* Clark (anatomy) and *Tone* or *Stick* Clark (music). At Oxford, professors or lecturers taught "experimental philosophy", astronomy, chemistry, mineralogy, political economy, Anglo-Saxon, oriental studies.

There were at both Universities very able private teachers of French, Italian and Spanish, but they were wholly unconnected with the University within whose precincts they taught. The Cambridge *Calendar* for 1802 expressed the opinion that the classical authors of Greece and Rome afforded the college tutor ample opportunities "to display his taste on the best writings of antiquity and to compare them with parallel works in the modern languages".[1] A similar opportunity was given to the undergraduate by the college rule that periodically he should write essays to be read in the college chapel. Thus at Trinity College, "in the second year each man has to compose two declamations, one in Latin and the other in English, upon some historical subject generally, but occasionally in the other branches of polite literature. This he has to deliver a fortnight afterwards in the chapel, immediately after evening prayers, before the Dean, Head-lecturer and all such others as happen to be present, and against an opponent right opposite. It is usually considered a bore, this declaiming, not only to the declaimer himself but also to the numerous audience....The Reading Men are generally much annoyed at the interruption in their studies caused by these declamations, and the Non-reading Men, poor fellows! are generally so incompetent themselves to write that they buy, beg or borrow the ideas of others".[2]

The professorial lectures on miscellaneous subjects at both Universities, like the Trinity declamations, "interrupted the *studies* of the Reading Men". They formed little or no part, certainly no direct part, in the classical or mathematical routine which alone led to the B.A. degree. As a rule, therefore, they were scantily attended; about 1790 only one professor in three lectured at Oxford, at Cambridge one in two. The later development of the examination system tended to depress professorial teaching still lower and to make the college tutors

[1] C. Wordsworth, *Scholae Academicae*, p. 118.
[2] *Alma Mater*, vol. I, p. 200.

yet more responsible for the instruction of the undergraduates. This again was part of the adverse criticism levelled against Oxford and Cambridge by the *Edinburgh Review*, whose contributors, preferring the Scottish plan of professorial lectures, saw little that was good in the college system of education. That system in their opinion also explained the obstinate adherence to an outworn tradition which gave a monopoly to classical and mathematical studies and neglected that useful knowledge which the times demanded. Moreover, according to the Reviewer, Cambridge taught mathematics on obsolete methods, and Oxford confined mathematical study to the bare elements of geometry.

Edward Copleston, tutor of Oriel College and Professor of Poetry in the University, published anonymously *A Reply to the Calumnies of the "Edinburgh Review" against Oxford* (1810), following it by *A Second* (1810) and *A Third Reply* (1811). But the opponents hardly got to grips, the Reviewers directing attention to the studies of the pass man, Copleston setting out the value of the honour requirements and the opportunities for what he called "miscellaneous knowledge" which were open to all. He omitted to state how infrequently advantage was taken of those opportunities or how little they did to break the monopoly of Greek, Latin and pure mathematics. His real defence was based on the principle that the prime purpose of university education was not the accumulation of knowledge, but a mental gymnastic which would make a man the master of intellectual powers trained to their highest capacity. Such a discipline was best affected by classical or mathematical study.

The ablest replies to the strictures of the *Edinburgh* came at a later date, when that journal published (1831) an acrimonious attack on the English university system by Sir William Hamilton, metaphysician and Edinburgh professor, sometime Snell Exhibitioner of Balliol. Yet the apologists, while insisting upon the merits of English university education as then conducted, admit its serious faults. Baden Powell, Savilian Professor of Geometry at Oxford, contributed a volume (*History of Natural Philosophy*, 1831, the year in which the British Association was founded) to Lardner's "Cabinet Cyclopaedia", a series "on popular and practical sciences" for "the educated classes". In this work he says that English mathematicians have neglected analytical geometry and the differential calculus, and refused to budge beyond Newton. "It is not twenty years since we have begun to perceive that we were far behind all the rest of Europe in these (mathematical) sciences; not from want of abundance of first-rate talent, but from a misapplication of that talent to unworthy objects, or at least to such as were of a nature not calculated to lead to any great advance in the state of knowledge. Within the period named, the works and inventions of the great continental mathematicians have been introduced and studied; and it is needless to say, no sooner were they understood and appreciated than they have called forth in turn an ardent spirit at least for the cultivation of those methods, though perhaps that spirit has been shown rather in detailed improvements and amended treatises than in any extensive original researches. Yet these have not been altogether wanting; and we need not fear to plead in competition with the inventions of the Continent the analytical researches of Messrs Woodhouse, Bromhead, Ivory, Babbage and Herschel" (p. 367).

William Whewell, at that time a Tutor of Trinity College, Cambridge, published *Thoughts on the study of mathematics* (1835), in which he described the mathematical teaching of his University as defective in that it limited itself too strictly to pure mathematics. He would willingly sacrifice some of the algebra in exchange for mechanics and hydrostatics, studies which should form part of every B.A. examination. "These sciences are examples and excellent examples of that great system of knowledge which has been steadily advancing ever since the revival of learning in Europe, and with the character and nature of which no liberally educated man ought to be unacquainted." A study of modern experimental, inductive science would fittingly supplement the knowledge of ancient literature which was part of a liberal education.

Hamilton in the *Edinburgh Review* had condemned the English Universities on the grounds that they assigned a monopoly to the study of classics and mathematics, and that the plan of committing the work of instruction to college tutors resulted in defective teaching. For classics and mathematics he would substitute the study of philosophy, and in common with his fellow-Reviewers for twenty years past he would dismiss the college tutor with his small band of pupils and install the university professor and the large audiencies of the Scottish and German universities. To Hamilton's criticism Whewell addressed himself in a book published in 1837 *On the Principles of English University Education*. He distinguished two forms of teaching which he named the "practical" and the "speculative" respectively. In the former there was abundant opportunity for the activity of the pupil and for free interplay between the minds of teacher and taught; it was what the practical schoolmaster calls "teaching" as distinct from "lecturing". Such practical teaching was possible only in small classes, and mathematics, Greek and Latin were kinds of knowledge best adapted for instruction wherein the pupil always played an active part. Speculative teaching is without these advantages; it is very ill adapted to instruction in mathematics and languages, and it provokes a minimum of intellectual activity in the pupil. "In one country of Europe, the universities give up their habits of practical teaching and return to the speculative method. They make *philosophy* their main object. Their professors deliver from their chairs system after system to admiring audiences. The listener may assent or criticize; but he is not disturbed by any demands on his mind such as the teaching of mathematics gives rise to. And what is the class of men thus produced, in their bearing upon the progress of sure and indestructible knowledge? They are such men as to be utterly incapable even of comprehending and appreciating the most conspicuous examples of the advance of science. Those who are universally allowed to be the greatest philosophers of our own day in the German universities, Hegel and Schelling, cannot understand that Newton went further than Kepler had gone in physical astronomy, and despise Newton's optical doctrines in comparison with the vague Aristotelian dogmas of Goethe respecting colours" (pp. 24–5). The relatively stable position of mathematics, Latin and Greek well fitted them to be instruments of education. "In *philosophical* doctrines on the contrary a constant change is going on. The commentator supersedes the original author, or at least becomes equally important: the systematiser is preferred to him who first threw out the same thoughts in a less regular form. Or else a revolution takes place, the old system is refuted, a new one is erected to last its little hour and wait its certain doom like its predecessor. There is nothing old, nothing stable, nothing certain in this kind of study" (p. 46).

Whewell's book of 1837 marks the complete evolution of the examination system, "warts and all". He regarded examinations not merely as tests but also as means through which men were instructed;

this was a function more especially of the college examinations where the examiners were in close touch with the teachers (when they were not identical) and with the examinees. Such examinations often included subjects which, while forming part of the college tuition, had no place in university programmes. The university examinations tyrannized over the examinee's intellectual interests and encouraged a defective mode of teaching, which confined ideas to verbal definitions and fostered a premature advance to purely symbolical calculation. It was as a corrective of these defects that Whewell suggested mechanics and hydrostatics as compulsory degree subjects.

All that has since been said in condemnation of purely "external examinations", of examinations conducted by those who are entirely dissociated from the related teaching, will be found in this book of 1837. Whewell does not name the Examining Board chartered in London in 1836, but it is obviously referred to in the following passage. "The establishment of a board of examiners independent of the teachers converts the system from one of direct to one of indirect teaching; and must be avoided or modified, except we are prepared to give up direct instruction altogether. If we do this and trust entirely to the force of examinations, using only the honour and disgrace which they bring as the means of stimulating indolence and calling forth exertion, we come to an intelligible system, but one very different from any which has ever prevailed in the English universities. We need then make no demand for attendance at lectures nor even for residence. One final examination, or several examinations at certain intervals, must be all the evidence we require of the student's proficiency and of his fitness to receive the stamp of university approbation.[1] In this system all the influences of our direct college teaching...are entirely abandoned. There may be persons who would think this an advantage; who would prefer the uncollegiate system of foreign universities to ours, or who would think that we might sufficiently supply any deficiencies which may exist in them by university examinations properly devised. Such a system is quite intelligible; but it behoves us to understand what it is before we decide in its favour. It is right that we should see clearly that it never has been our system; and that when we talk of its establishment among us, we propose, not

---

[1] Whewell here anticipates exactly the practice of the University of London from 1858 to 1898.

the improvement but the destruction of our college practices, not a modification but a revolution in our English university education" (pp. 66–7).

The war on privilege, of which the Reform Act of 1832 was a token and a powerful weapon, was soon directed against the Church Establishment, of which the Universities were regarded as especially vulnerable bulwarks. Petitions were addressed to Parliament praying that the law might be so amended that Dissenters might be eligible for admission to Oxford and Cambridge; these came from places so wide apart as Norwich, Plymouth, Nottingham, Bridgwater, Nuneaton and Skipton. The last town was careful to add to the two ancient Universities the name of Durham, then scarce born; it was opened in October, 1833, with an "entry" of nineteen, and it was still without a charter. In March, 1834, a petition from Cambridge, signed by two heads of houses, nine professors, eleven tutors and forty-one other members of the Senate, was presented to the House of Lords by Earl Grey, the Prime Minister, and to the Commons by Mr Spring Rice on behalf of the Government. The petitioners, after expressing their attachment to the Church and the University and their belief that the benefits of the latter should "be communicated to all classes as widely as is compatible with the Christian principles of its foundation", went on to suggest "the expediency of abrogating by legislative enactment every religious test exacted from members of the University before they proceed to degrees, whether of bachelor, master or doctor, in arts, law and physic.[1] ...Your petitioners conscientiously believe that if the prayer of this petition be granted, the great advantages of good academic education might be extended to many excellent men who are now for conscience' sake debarred from a full participation in them, though true friends to the institutions of the country".[2]

There followed immediately from the pens of prominent Cambridge men a series of pamphlets for and against the prayer of this petition. One of the petitioners, Connop Thirlwall, Fellow and Lecturer of Trinity College, afterwards (1840–75) Bishop of St David's, in *A Letter...on the admission of Dissenters to academical degrees*, suggested that compulsory attendance in college chapels might be "omitted

---

[1] Since 1772 the test at Cambridge was a declaration by the suppliant for a degree that he was "a *bona fide* member of the Church of England as by law established".

[2] *Quarterly Journal of Education* (1834), vol. VII, p. 370.

without any material detriment to religion," and that the omission would be the only change in college organization made necessary by the admission of Dissenters. The counterstroke to the suggestion was a request from Dr Christopher Wordsworth, the Master of Trinity, that Thirlwall would resign his lectureship. Whewell in *Remarks* and *Additional Remarks* on Thirlwall's *Letter* deprecated any change in the rule of compulsory chapels as dangerous to the principle of compulsion in general and to the Established Church and compulsory Greek and Latin in particular. A similar division of opinion was manifested in Oxford. Baden Powell, the Savilian Professor, considered ("Reasons for not joining the Declaration") that the University was or ought to be a national establishment and that therefore members of all "persuasions" alike should share its advantages. On the other hand, about 100 members of the University, upwards of 900 members of Convocation afterwards concurring, made a formal declaration (April, 1834) that "the admission of persons who dissent from the Church of England would lead to the most disastrous consequences, that it would unsettle the minds of the younger members of the University, would raise up and continue a spirit of controversy, which is at present unknown, and would tend to reduce religion to an empty and unmeaning name or to supplant it by scepticism and infidelity". Certain heads of houses and others to the number of twenty-two were of opinion that if the proposed admission were made lawful, it would "violate our legal and prescriptive rights and subvert the system of religious instruction and discipline so long and so beneficially exercised by us".[1]

The explanation of this forcible language lay in the fact that a Bill was at the moment before Parliament to remove the disabilities of Dissenters in taking degrees at the Universities. It passed its third reading in the Commons by a two-thirds majority; a similar majority in the Lords threw it out (1834). The University Conservatives had scored a victory, but the struggle was not ended. In 1836 Hamilton's *Edinburgh Review* article reopened the question of the survival of colleges in the English universities and the allied question respecting the position of Dissenters in reference to Oxford and Cambridge. In the following year the attention of Parliament was again directed to that quarter. A motion to appoint a Commission of inquiry into the statutes

[1] *Quarterly Journal of Education* (April, 1834), vol. VIII, p. 179.

of the two Universities was moved by the Earl of Radnor in the House of Lords and in the Commons by Mr Pryme, member for Cambridge, formerly Professor of Political Economy. Both motions were withdrawn, on the understanding in the first case that the matter would be further considered by the Ministry, in the second case in the belief that the Universities themselves would initiate changes. There the matter rested; nothing was done either by the Ministry or by the Universities.

The exclusiveness of Oxford and Cambridge and the restriction of their main interests to Greek, Latin and mathematics were menaced, and in the end destroyed, by a combination of forces whose power became evident in the reign of George IV. A demand for higher education arose amongst social classes to whom the ancient Universities were prohibitive by reason of expense. In an age of applied science and great industrial expansion a call for the pursuit and wide dissemination of "useful" knowledge naturally made itself heard. The growing political power of the Nonconformists confronted the clerical rule of the Universities, from which they were shut out. These "causes", movements and demands took shape in the activities of Bentham, James Mill, Henry Brougham, George Birkbeck, Hume, Grote, Zachary Macaulay, Lord John Russell and other Whigs and Radicals who determined to create a university in London, on the model of the professorial non-collegial universities of Scotland and Germany. The prejudices of their own education, political feeling and the practical exigencies of their project seem to have blinded these advocates of a non-collegial university to its defects. From the standpoint of educational efficiency there could be no comparison between the college practice of individual instruction to small groups of pupils and the large classes, from which ill-prepared young boys were not absent, that attended the Scottish professors' lectures. But mass-instruction by monitors was then regarded as a great and beneficent invention for schools; and Bentham in particular thought it could be applied with success to instruction above the elementary grade. In the event, however, London's university was not non-collegial.

The idea of establishing a university in the metropolis originated with the poet, Thomas Campbell, at that time editor of a literary miscellany, *The New Monthly Magazine*. A graduate of Glasgow and an interested observer of the new universities of Berlin and Bonn,

Campbell mooted his scheme as early as 1824 and discussed it in the following January at a dinner arranged by Brougham. This was followed on February 9th by a letter to *The Times*, and later by an article in the *New Monthly*, both by Campbell. A provisional committee was formed and the Dissenting communions were invited by Brougham to a conference at which "delegates of almost all the dissenting bodies in London"[1] attended. At this conference it was proposed, contrary to the desire of the original projectors, who would omit theology from the curriculum, to set up two theological chairs, one of the Church of England, the other, Presbyterian. Campbell warmly protested that, if this were done, "the whole beautiful project was likely to be reduced to a mere Dissenters' university". Later, when the provisional committee was replaced by a council, that body while describing "religious discipline" as "the great and primary object of education" were compelled to omit it from the course of study and leave it to "the natural guardians of the pupils". By so deciding the council ceased to follow the German models; but a precedent was created that completely secularized all English institutions of higher education which were publicly established during the nineteenth century.

Some encouragement to the movement came from Lord Liverpool's Government, the Chancellor of the Exchequer going so far as to say that a charter was "by no means impossible"; in point of fact half a dozen Governments came and disappeared before the college was incorporated. A joint-stock company was formed in 1826 with a capital of £150,000 in £100 shares, and a council was created of twenty-five members, nearly all of whom were men eminent in political life (most, but not all, as "Benthamites" and "Philosophic Radicals"), in finance, in philanthropy and in letters. The Duke of Sussex, chairman of the council, laid the foundation stone of the building in Gower Street early in the following year, and in October, 1828, the "London University" received its first students; the curriculum comprised "languages, mathematics, physics, the mental and moral sciences, together with the laws of England, history and political economy, and the various branches of knowledge which are the objects of a liberal education". Upwards of 300 young men were admitted to the courses.

There were aspects, educational and political, which were certain

[1] *Life and Letters of Thomas Campbell*, 1849, vol. II, under date April 30th, 1825.

to arouse opposition to the new institution. The completely secular nature of its studies shocked those who held the principle then generally recognized, that at all stages of education religion was an essential element of its practice. The members of the council included a number of public men, amongst whom were a royal duke, several peers and wealthy persons, as well as some very active politicians; it was therefore impossible to regard this London University as a merely private body, whatever its lack of formal status. The political threat to the Church which some detected in the *personnel* of the council, and in the movement as a whole, was not an imaginary one. The point is plainly put by Mrs Grote, wife of the banker-historian; her husband was a member of the council and a prominent benefactor of the college. "The Philosophical Radicals, as the followers of Bentham were designated, naturally lent themselves to a project tending to separate education from the management of the clerical body, whilst the leaders of the Whig party gladly accepted the alliance of the Radicals and Dissenters, who, they hoped, might assist them in turn to arrive at power."[1]

In consequence, Churchmen and others who valued the religious element in public education began to take counter-measures some months before the "London University" opened its doors. In June, 1828, it was resolved at a public meeting presided over by the Duke of Wellington, then head of the Government, "that a college for general education be founded in the metropolis; in which, while the various branches of literature and science are made the subjects of instruction, it shall be an essential part of the system to imbue the minds of youth with a knowledge of the doctrine and duties of Christianity as inculcated by the United Church of England and Ireland". It was further resolved to ask the King to become the patron of such a college and to permit it to be entitled "King's College, London". A "liberal and enlarged course of education" was to be pursued, comprising "religious and moral instruction, classical learning, history, modern languages, mathematics, natural philosophy, medicine and surgery, chemistry, jurisprudence etc., [*sic*] and to be so conducted as to provide in the most effectual manner for the two great objects of education, the communication of general knowledge and specific preparation for particular professions"—with which "objects" the rival institution concurred.

[1] Harriet Grote, *The Personal Life of George Grote* (1873), p. 56.

A charter was granted in August, 1829, by which the government of the college was vested in a council made up of ex-officio governors holding high office in Church and State, life governors (eight peers, of whom the Duke of Wellington was one) and a numerous body of elected governors chosen by the proprietors. Three-fourths of the council were laymen, including distinguished members of the legal and medical professions. The college was formally opened "in a very unostentatious manner" on Saturday, October 8th, 1831. "The medical school was opened on the following Monday, and the senior department (the courses of which are assimilated to those of Oxford and Cambridge) as well as the school on the 18th of the same month." Nearly 500 students had entered either for the general course of education or for special lectures.[1] The reference to King's College School will be noted; the "London University" also had its school (now University College School) which began its sessions in 1828.

In the meantime, "London University" applied to the Crown for a charter of incorporation, but although the draft passed the Privy Seal in February, 1831, nothing further was done until March, 1835, when the charter passed the office of the Home Secretary. Both Oxford and Cambridge were amongst the bodies opposing the petition for a charter. In 1831 the Cambridge Senate prayed that "London University" be not empowered to grant degrees; in March, 1835, "in a very full [Oxford] Convocation...it was agreed, with one dissentient only, that the University seal should be affixed to a petition to his Majesty, praying that he would withhold his royal sanction from the proposed form of a charter of incorporation for a literary and scientific institution, lately established, under the title of 'The University of London'". The opposition ended in a compromise by which, while the college in Gower Street received its charter, another charter created a distinctly separate body to which alone the title, "the University of London", applied and by which alone degrees could be conferred.

On November 28th, 1836, two charters of incorporation took effect. "The London University" of 1827–36 was incorporated as "University College, London". An entirely new body, the University of London, was created to confer the degrees of A.B., A.M., B.L., D.L., B.M., D.M. The relation of University College and King's College to the University was thus defined: "Pupils from University and King's Colleges to be

[1] *Quarterly Journal of Education*, vol. III, p. 183.

admitted on certificates of having gone through a course of study at those establishments and having obtained a proficiency to pass for a degree and having conducted themselves to the satisfaction of the Governing Bodies of those Colleges to be examined and to be classed according to their relative merits". Other bodies, whether incorporated or not, might be added to the two colleges for these purposes.

The degrees in law and medicine which the new University was empowered to confer were the tokens of that professional education which was from the outset given by the two London colleges. In 1832 out of a total of 386 students in the then "London University", 226 were students of medicine; there were then 80 boys in the school.[1] A preponderance of medical students is also noted at King's College in 1834, when there were in the general department 104 men pursuing a complete course of general education and 101 taking occasional lectures, whilst the corresponding categories in the medical department numbered 66 and 175 respectively. King's College School then had 404 pupils, and seven other schools were affiliated to the college.[2] In that year University College had 104 students in arts, 18 in law, 347 in medicine; there were 284 boys in the school.[3] A proposal was made to the "proprietors" of this college in 1833 that a "Professor of Education" should be appointed to train teachers,[4] but it was not entertained; in an obscure fashion it was felt that the proposal involved the "religious difficulty", and had better be avoided. Notwithstanding its intimate connexion with the Church of England, King's College made no provision for the professional training of the clergy till 1847, when it established a theological department for that purpose. Engineering followed (1838) medicine in the development of professional education.

The Senate of the University as constituted in 1836 consisted, in the words of the charter, of "persons eminent in literature and science to act as a Board of Examiners and to perform the functions of the Examiners in the Senate House of Cambridge; this body to be termed the University of London". Arnold of Rugby was one of those who at government invitation (for the office was in all cases a Crown

---

[1] *Quarterly Journal of Education*, vol. III, p. 381.
[2] *Ibid.* vol. VIII, p. 183.   [3] *Ibid.* vol. VII, p. 371.
[4] *Ibid.* vol. VII, pp. 55 ff., reviewing an *Address to the Proprietors of the University of London* by J. M. Morgan.

appointment) accepted a fellowship involving membership of this body. The University's predecessor, the unchartered association which had now become University College, London, had shirked the problem of religious education while admitting its importance. The matter had been allowed to drop and the omission had not been resented; these were days when the political disabilities of dissentients from the Church of England were being removed. In December, 1837, the Senate passed a motion which Arnold had moved "that as a general rule the candidates for the degree of B.A. shall pass an examination either in one of the four Gospels or the Acts of the Apostles in the original Greek and also in Scripture History". Arnold's intention was to affirm the principle that as a public institution of a Christian country the University was itself Christian; its charter affirmed that it was a purpose of the University "to promote religion and morality", and Arnold held that it was the Christian religion which should be promoted. The examination therefore should be Christian while not being sectarian, open and agreeable to Christians of all denominations. But the resolution aroused much opposition and neither University nor King's College favoured it, though for different reasons. In consequence a second and more largely attended meeting in February, 1838, where Arnold was in a minority of one, passed the following resolution: "That examination in the Hebrew text of the Old Testament and in the Greek of the New Testament shall be instituted in this University; to be followed by certificates of proficiency; and that all candidates for degrees in Arts may, if they think proper, undergo such examination".[1]

Arnold, had in effect, raised *the* crucial issue of English education in the nineteenth century. He felt that a voluntary examination would not vindicate the position for which he stood, and he therefore resigned his fellowship and ceased to be connected with the University. London, as an examining body, was committed to a completely neutral position with reference to religious education. The fact became a precedent. The three Queen's Colleges of Belfast, Cork and Galway, which were founded between 1845 and 1849 and incorporated as the Queen's University in 1850, gave "an improved academical education equally to all classes of the community without religious distinction", that is, no religious teaching was included in the curriculum. When in 1879

[1] See A. P. Stanley, *Life of Arnold*, chapter VIII.

the Queen's University was abolished, the Royal University of Ireland (1880), a purely examining body, adopted the same policy of neutrality. That also was the policy of the university colleges which arose in England after 1870.

From time to time the foundation of a university in the north of England had been mooted, and in 1832 the Dean and Chapter of Durham announced their intention to devote to such a purpose a portion of the cathedral property, stated later to be of the value of £94,000, and the Bishop made donations and promised annual subscriptions for the maintenance of the projected university. In the same year an Act of Parliament authorized this diversion of ecclesiastical funds and the scheme was embodied in a prospectus. The University of Durham was to be governed by the Dean and Chapter of the Cathedral, the Bishop being Visitor. The course of study laid down included divinity and ecclesiastical history, the Greek and Latin literatures, mathematics and natural philosophy, to which studies three chairs were assigned. There were to be readers in law, medicine and history, and teachers of modern languages. Provision was also to be made for the preparation of candidates for holy orders, although these divinity students were not to be "actual members of the College". The duration of the course was to be fixed at four years; the University of London permitted graduation after two years from matriculation. The University opened on October 27th, 1833, "when", says the *Quarterly Journal of Education*, "nineteen young gentlemen were admitted on the foundation". The charter of the University of Durham was signed on June 1st, 1837, this being one of the very last official acts of William IV.

CHAPTER IV

Educational Opinion

A book which, first published in 1798, attracted sufficient notice to be re-issued as late as 1822, has fallen into unmerited oblivion, although it anticipated the principles of Froebel and tried to place the practice of education upon a scientific basis. This is the *Practical Education* of R. L. Edgeworth and his daughter, Maria Edgeworth, the popular novelist.

The Edgeworth family, of Edgeworthstown, West Meath, in effect formed a group of educators, of which the centre was Richard Lovell Edgeworth (1744–1817), though the family interest in education began with his mother, Jane Lovell, who, her son tells us, "had read everything that had been written on the subject". Edgeworth was married four times and was the father of eighteen children. His first child, born in 1764, was brought up, like Pestalozzi's only child, in accordance with the principles of *Émile* and with the same unsatisfactory result. "It was difficult to restrain him from what he wished to follow. In short he was self-willed from a spirit of independence which had been inculcated by his early education, and which he cherished the more from the inexperience of his own powers."[1] The experiment was abandoned when the pupil reached the age of eight; but its effects remained.

Edgeworth's second wife, Honoria Sneyd (married 1773, died 1780), regarded education as "an experimental science". From 1776 she began to register observations upon children, a register which Edgeworth was still keeping a quarter of a century later. This record formed the basis of *Practical Education* and it performed a similar function for *The Parent's Assistant*, a collection of stories published by Maria Edgeworth in 1796, as well as for a number of children's books, or books about children, which she wrote between that date and 1825.

As a teacher of his own children Edgeworth was "patient, candid, stimulating, sympathetic, adapting himself to individual capacity", so his daughter tells us. Like his mother he was well read in books on education; and he acquired a knowledge of educational administration,

[1] M. Edgeworth, *Memoirs* (1844), vol. 1, pp. 273 f.

nation-wide, while serving as a royal commissioner (1806–12) on Irish education. As a member of the Irish Parliament he had previously introduced a Bill upon that subject. In 1809 he suggested the formation of an association which, like Joseph Lancaster's Committee, should establish schools throughout England, but these were to be what he called "secondary schools".

The Edgeworth theory and practice are expounded in *Practical Education* and in *Professional Education* (1809); of the latter Edgeworth was sole author. The psychological groundwork is the psychology of Locke and the general attitude is that exhibited in Locke's *Some Thoughts concerning Education*. The title "*Practical*" *Education* is double-edged. In the first place, it pleads the necessity of encouraging initiative, spontaneity, activity of mind and of body rather than a purely intellectual absorption, thus anticipating the cardinal principle of Froebel. With Locke, Edgeworth insists on the educative nature of play—Froebel again—and, like Locke, gives a prominent place to utility as a standard when estimating the value of a particular study. While Edgeworth advocates the acquisition of positive knowledge, of natural phenomena particularly, and shows how such knowledge in its rudimentary form may be acquired by children, he is more concerned to train the mind to the habit of alert attention, a mental function to which he attaches the highest importance. To cultivate this habit, the pupil must be furnished with adequate motives to attend, an anticipation of the present-day stress laid upon purpose which he may have taken from Locke. As a keen advocate of an active type of learning, Edgeworth makes great use of handwork; he is also much interested in teaching children to speak as well as to write good English. As an aid to the attainment of reading he invented a phonetic scheme of notation. He was even more concerned to mould character; the cultivation of good habits and instilling moral principles are primary objects of *Practical Education*, a matter in which the book differs profoundly from *Emile*.

In the second place, the title of Edgeworth's book is an intimation of the author's belief that education as usually conducted was not practical. Still, Edgeworth was sufficiently a man of his day to hold that oratory was essential to a public man, and consequently "a knowledge and a taste for classical literature" were requisite in such a man's up-bringing. This opinion is expressed in *Professional Education*, a work which describes the preparatory stage of an education intended for the country gentleman, the statesman and the prince. In other words, the book is an addition to the long line of works on "the doctrine of courtesy" to which Elyot, Milton and Locke, amongst many others, had contributed; incidentally it furnishes an argument for vocational *education*.

It is not possible to point to any one institution which was directly influenced by the Edgeworths; but their popular writings must have affected contemporary opinion amongst educated persons, and so prepared the way for a kindly reception of similar teaching when it was propounded by foreigners such as Pestalozzi and Froebel. In one respect their influence is to be regretted: like Locke, they distrusted the creative imagination and banned all such things as fairy tales. "Why", asks Maria Edgeworth, "should the mind be filled with fantastic visions instead of useful knowledge?" But they were not singular amongst their contemporaries in this matter as Wordsworth complained; and to-day there are still literal-minded pedants to keep the Edgeworths in countenance.

Reference has already been made to the institution of the infant school by Robert Owen at New Lanark.[1] David Dale, Owen's father-in-law, who founded the cotton mills at that place in 1783, had in his employ some 400 or 500 children drawn chiefly from the workhouses of the south. For these he provided such schooling as was intended to teach all to read and the eldest to write; but as the teaching came at the end of a long day's work the result was naturally poor. In 1800 Owen took over the direction of the mills and soon turned his attention to the unsatisfactory instruction of the children; between 1809 and 1816 he was engaged in forming an elaborate educational machine whose operations would embrace not only the children of his work-people but the workers themselves. There was an infant school for children of ages three to five or six, who were educated by methods of play and the observation of familiar things, their instruction being carried on in the open air whenever possible. A school for boys and girls between the ages of six and twelve taught reading, writing and accounts, the girls also being taught sewing. The building occupied by these schools during the daytime served at night as a place of instruction and a social centre for the men and women employed in the mills. This

[1] Pp. 20 and 22, above.

organization was completed in 1816 and was in full operation for the next eight years; it attracted thousands of visitors during that period from all parts of the world, the Grand Duke Nicholas, afterwards the Russian Tsar, being one of them. But in 1824 Owen's co-directors effected an alteration, and he himself transferred his efforts for social change to a wider theatre.

Whether the pupils were children or adults, Owen insisted upon music, dancing and military discipline as essential parts of the curriculum; his fellow-directors included three Quakers, to all of whom these activities were distasteful, the first two as frivolous, the last as dangerous to peace, for Owen intended the military discipline "to assist men to bear arms in the country's defence". But this was not the most serious cause of discord amongst the directors. William Allen, a prominent member of the Society of Friends, and one of Joseph Lancaster's principal supporters, more than distrusted Owen's influence as an educator. In the course of his own development Owen had acquired the conviction that all forms of religious belief are equally mischievous and unnecessary; and in characteristic fashion took great pains to make his conviction widely known. The consequence was that the distinctive character of the New Lanark Schools was changed and they were placed under the British and Foreign School Society's patronage from 1824 onwards.

Apart from his repute as "the father of British socialism" and later as a spiritualist, Owen is chiefly remembered in educational history as the founder of the infant school, a type which has ever since formed part of English educational organization. But the infant school at New Lanark was only the base of a very ambitious "New Institution for the Formation of Character". The blank sheet represented the child's mind more completely for Owen than for Locke; character is purely the result of circumstances, it will be good or bad as these are favourable or the reverse. "The New Institution", which was planned to educate from very early infancy to the adult age, was regarded by its deviser as an experiment "to ascertain whether, by replacing evil conditions by good, man might not be relieved from evil, and transformed into an intelligent, rational and good being".[1] Like Rousseau, he replaced the old theological teaching by the dogma of original righteousness. "By my own experience and reflection I had ascertained"

[1] *The Life of Robert Owen*, by Himself, p. 60.

7-2

—the tense should be observed—"that human nature is radically good and capable of being trained, educated and placed from birth in such manner that ultimately (that is as soon as the gross errors and corruptions of the present false and wicked system are overcome and destroyed) society must become united, good, wise, wealthy and happy."[1] An opinion so simple was congenial to a mechanical age and to a man whose successes had been those of organization conducted on the established principles. The belief in machinery comes out in his account of the two chief instructors of his infant school. The master, James Buchanan, was "a poor simple-hearted weaver...who had been previously trained by his wife to perfect submission to her will and who could gain but a scanty living by his own oppressed trade of weaving common plain cotton goods by hand. But he loved children strongly by nature and his patience with them was inexhaustible....Thus the simple-minded, kind-hearted James Buchanan, who at first could scarcely read, write or spell, became the first master in a rational infant school".[2] Molly Young, aged seventeen, was the "nurse to assist the master"; "in natural powers of mind" she "had the advantage over her new companion in an office perfectly new to both".[3] Here, with the most simple means as agents, two untaught persons, not having one idea of the office in which they were placed or of the objects intended to be attained, accomplished unknown to themselves results which "surprised, astonished and confounded the most learned and wise and greatest men of their generation".[4] The easy credulity of this passage reflects, not the mid-nineteenth century when it was published, but the days when "the Mutual System" was thought to be a great discovery and when its essential weakness had not yet been detected.

Owen's autobiography appeared when he was in his eighty-sixth year (1857); he died in the following year. His memory is not always trustworthy and his optimistic temperament and abounding self-confidence are additional sources of error. That he had learned from Pestalozzi and from Oberlin is probable, although the learning may not have been direct; he does not acknowledge a debt to either. He makes a significant confusion between the Alsatian, Oberlin, an earlier inventor of infant schools, and Girard, a Swiss, who had no special association with schools of that kind. The instruction given in the

[1] *The Life of Robert Owen,* by Himself, p. 131.   [2] *Ibid.* p. 139.
[3] *Ibid.*   [4] *Ibid.* p. 141.

New Lanark infant school was based on the Pestalozzian principle of intuition; objects, pictures, models were studied rather than books, oral descriptions or narratives. It was the aim of the teaching also to make as much use of play as possible. Owen may have learned these two principles from a foreign source; but it is equally possible that they were the children of his own mother-wit or of a study of Locke.

Owen's doings and opinions attracted much attention and had their share in sustaining the interest of public men in the welfare, including the instruction, of the people at large. His *A new view of society: essays on the formation of character* (1813), was forwarded semi-officially by the Home Secretary to the English and Irish bishops and to the leading European Governments. Owen gradually moved on to larger problems of social life and in 1834 created the organized secularist movement, so adding a new "school" to those already considering public education.

Individualism, "self-help", competition were cardinal principles of English life during the major part of the nineteenth century, and naturally they played their part in public education. It is something of a paradox that these self-regarding principles were elements in a philosophy whose leading doctrine was that the moral *summum bonum* consisted in "the greatest happiness of the greatest number". This greatest good was to be attained by the pursuit of whatever could be regarded as "useful", or, as Comte would say, "positive". The emphasis laid by the utilitarian philosophy upon useful knowledge deeply influenced early nineteenth-century conceptions of curriculum; its disciples were opposed to one which was purely literary, particularly to an educational course confined to Greek and Latin. Their zeal for modern studies was apt to favour forms of these which led critics like Wordsworth and Coleridge to say that the utilitarians undervalued or even ignored the spiritual element in man, that they preferred the material good of society before all other "goods".

The account of mental process accepted by the utilitarians combined the sensationalist psychology of Locke with the associationist theory of David Hartley (*Observations on Man*) and of Thomas Reid (*The Intellectual Powers*, 1785, *The Active Powers*, 1788). These psychological theories maintained a preponderating influence in English educational theory which outlasted even the popularity of utilitarianism, with a corresponding effect upon practice and administration.

Politically the utilitarians trusted mainly to legislation to achieve their aims; laws could do well-nigh everything. Jeremy Bentham, the most distinguished member of the school, taught that all "rights" are the creation of law. Rousseau, the French Constituent Assembly of 1791, the American Declaration of 1776 had talked of "natural rights"; and some English "democrats" (a name then in ill repute) repeated the phrase which for Bentham was simple nonsense. "Natural and imprescriptible rights" he denounced as "rhetorical nonsense", "nonsense upon stilts". Some of the legislative projects advocated by the Benthamites were meant to institute universal, national instruction with an eye to enlightenment so general that all adult males could be trusted to cast a parliamentary vote by ballot intelligently.

The preacher of the utilitarian philosophy who succeeded best in impressing his contemporaries and the generation that followed was Bentham (1748–1832); one of its most effective exponents was James Mill (1773–1836). Their teaching reached the wider public through the small but very active group known as the "Philosophical Radicals", including such men as Brougham, Joseph Hume, Roebuck, Francis Place, George Grote and others, to whom their opponents gave the nickname of the "education-mad party".

Bentham and James Mill both wrote on education. The former planned in connexion with a reformed Poor Law an education for the poorer classes which comprised moral training, intellectual discipline and the learning of a trade; the institution of prison schools was one of many fruitful suggestions which were incorporated in his extensive schemes of penal reform. He would extend the parliamentary franchise to all *men* who could read and would confine it to them; it was a settled conviction of the Benthamites that the possessor of knowledge derived from books, or discussion, could be trusted to act rationally.

In 1816 Bentham published a work whose title is best quoted in full: "*Chrestomathia:* being a collection of papers explanatory of the design of an institution, proposed to be set on foot, under the name of the Chrestomathic Day School or Chrestomathic School, for the extension of the New System of Instruction to the higher branches of learning for the use of the middling and higher ranks of life". Bentham explains that "chrestomathic", meaning "conducive to useful knowledge", is a neologism of his own, but that its occurrence "in a book of the 17th century" had been noted. The "new system of instruction"

is the mutual system of Bell and Lancaster, which Bentham extra-
vagantly admired. "The matchless excellence, as well as novelty, of the
New Instruction System, is a matter too universally recognized, to need
mention in any other way than that of simple allusion. Of its applica-
bility to the higher, not to say the highest, branches of intellectual
instruction, the fullest persuasion is, over and over again, expressed in
the works of its illustrious inventor, whose anticipations have, in every
point, received such ample and undisputed confirmation from experience."[1]

Chrestomathia is not a book but, as its author says, a collection of
papers. Of these the chief are two formidable-looking tables which
set forth the marrow of the work; the rest consists of notes on, and
appendices to, the tables. The Second Table lays down the principles,
so-called, of "School Management" in accordance with which the
proposed institution is to be conducted; the other table is virtually
a chart of the intellectual world, or of so much of it as is to concern
the "Chrestomathic School".

Bentham's school management is expressly founded upon the
Elements of Tuition (1815) of Andrew Bell, and it reflects the meticulous
and misdirected care of its original. Like any other factory, the school
is to save time by mass-production and to economize money by
employing "teachers" (the monitors) whose special merits are that
they are "tractable" and "unpaid"; the nearer the level of the "teacher's"
knowledge to the pupil's, the better the teaching. Bentham had
devised a building, the Panopticon, serving equally well as school or
prison, which was so constructed that "every human object in the
whole building" was "throughout within the reach of the Head
Master's eye—or the Prison Governor's".[2] The head master was himself to be within view of the eyes of official visitors who represented
the proprietors of the school. Discipline was to be largely based upon
emulation, and place-taking with a right of appeal by any aggrieved pupil
was to be the invariable accompaniment of all class exercises ; corporal
punishment was proscribed, all forms of punishment were to be reduced
to a minimum and rewards were to be used sparingly. Schoolboy juries
were to try offenders, thus fostering a sense of responsibility in the
pupils and exonerating the master from any suspicion of "partiality or
tyranny". Careful record of progress was to be kept, a "black-book"

[1] *Chrestomathia*, Appendix 1.   [2] *Ibid.* p. 11.

was to register delinquencies; the master was to seek assistance in this part of his duties from what Bentham characteristically names "the Universal Delation principle or Non-connivance-tolerating principle", but which schoolboys more concisely call "sneaking". (Bentham entered Westminster at the age of six and went up to Oxford six years later, but he seems to have missed boyhood altogether.)

So certain, in Bentham's opinion, was the operation of the mutual system that proficiency could be guaranteed by the master and was expected in the pupil. Perfect performance was exacted in all exercises, which were to be rendered easier by graduation, sufficient repetition and short lessons. Advanced pupils were to practice note-taking; all were to mend their own quill pens and sharpen their own pencils. The schoolrooms were to be so arranged that nothing external could distract the pupil's attention; the walls were to be covered with tables, pictures, diagrams and objects to which the children might direct their eyes in the infrequent intervals which were free from prescribed tasks. Great attention was to be paid to the grouping of the children in classes. "A scholar belongs to *as many classes*, at the same *time*, as there are different *branches* in which he received instruction: *put back* in one, he may be *advanced* in another",[1] that is, pupils were to be classified afresh for each branch of study. This mode of classification was adopted in University College School, which was in some respects a partial realization of the "Chrestomathic School". In the elementary class of his proposed school Bentham insisted that care should be taken to secure distinct utterance by the children; they were to use a stick and sand-tray when learning to write, a practice which Bentham could not resist calling the "Psammographic principle".

The First Table, "shewing the several branches of intellectual instruction included in the aggregate course...and branches of instruction omitted", is in effect a map of the intellectual world or sphere of knowledge. It recalls those mediaeval encyclopaedias which contained little more than concise statements of the meaning of the terms designating branches of knowledge; indeed, Bentham says that the table "may, in some measure, serve the purpose of an *Encyclopedical sketch*". For example, one of the omitted branches is thus described. "*Balistics*. From a Greek word, which signifies to *cast*: called also the theory of *projectiles* from a Latin word of the same signification. The

[1] *Chrestomathia*, p. 21. The italics are Bentham's.

mass projected is either in a *solid* or in a liquid state: in so far as it is in a *solid* state, the art of Gunnery is included in it: an art, which, in so far as it concerns the *motion* produced, belongs, since the invention of gunpowder, to *chemistry*; and in so far as concerns giving *direction* to that motion, to *Mechanics*. In so far as the mass projected is in a *liquid* state, the art is that of making *Jets d'eau*, i.e. *playing fountains*: a branch which by its perfect innocence and comparative insignificance, forms a striking contrast with the other."[1] No room could be found for teaching dancing or music, although these were regarded by the higher classes as indispensable, and by the middling ranks as desirable if not indispensable.

The field covered by this table is so very extensive, and even the senior pupils are so very young, that any schoolmaster to whom this table was given as a guide would be sorely tempted to that very verbalism or psittacism, as Bentham might say, the substitution of words for ideas and things, with which the Benthamites, in common with most scholastic reformers of the time, were continually charging the schools.

The "Chrestomathic School" was to be the property of a joint-stock company of ten-pound shareholders, a scheme to which effect was afterwards given in the foundation of "London University", King's College, London, and the proprietary schools which were established in the early years of Victoria's reign. The buildings were to be after the fashion of the National Society's Westminster Free School, that is, there was to be one large schoolroom for 600 boys and another to accommodate 400 girls. It was thought that the rooms could be built and furnished and lodgings provided for the master and mistress at a cost of £5000. The age of pupils was to range from seven to fourteen, the fees were to be either four pounds or eight pounds (presumably *per annum*); the exact amount had not been fixed when the prospectus was issued.

It has been thought advisable to devote so much space to this abortive scheme, partly because of the eminence of its author, but chiefly as illustrating the extraordinary hold which the mutual system in its early days secured upon men of the first intellectual standing. Like much of Bentham's published work, it contained *passim* ideas which afterwards bore fruit; his recommendations respecting the care of health—"*Hygiastics* or *Hygiantics*"—are a case in point.

[1] *Ibid.* p. 35.

James Mill's chief contribution to educational opinion was the article, "Education", in the *Encyclopaedia Britannica*; its date is about 1825. According to the author of this essay, education is addressed to the mind, not to the body; its end is happiness, first, of the person being educated and, next, of others through him. The several agencies which conduct it are the family, the school and the political institutions of the society in which the individual lives; that is, education is domestic, scholastic or *technical* (the term is to be noted) and social. Political or social education is "the keystone of the arch"; it affects the other two modes. "It is education wholly which constitutes the remarkable difference between the Turk and the Englishman, and even the still more remarkable difference between the most cultivated European and the wildest savage. Whatever is made of any *class* of men, we may then be sure is possible to be made of the whole human race.[1] What a field for exertion! What a prize to be won!" This out-Lockeing of Locke is the eighteenth century over again; with Helvétius, Mill believes that *l'éducation peut tout*.

To attain happiness, there must be acquired or developed three qualities or virtues, of which the first is intelligence, that is, sagacity illuminated by knowledge. This is the special function of "technical" education; the schooling of the poor should be continued till the age of fifteen or sixteen. The remaining virtues necessary to happiness are temperance, or control of appetite, and justice and generosity, in a word, benevolence. The statement that the end of education is happiness is seriously damaged by Mill's own admission that it has not been determined wherein happiness consists. It may be added that there is a widespread belief amongst men, based on experience, that an excellent method of missing happiness is deliberately to seek it. "Ask yourself whether you are happy and you cease to be so. The only chance is to treat, not happiness, but some end external to it, as the purpose of life" (J. S. Mill, *Autobiography*, p. 82). Happiness, in short, is a by-product, not an end.

[1] His son says that "in psychology" his father's "fundamental doctrine was the formation of all human character by circumstances, through the universal Principle of Association, and the consequent unlimited possibility of improving the moral and intellectual condition of mankind by education. Of all his doctrines none was more important than this, or needs more to be insisted on; unfortunately there is none which is more contradictory to the prevailing tendencies of speculation, both in his time and since." J. S. Mill, *Autobiography* (1873), new edition, p. 61.

Mill founds his educational method upon that psychology, sensationalist and associationist, of Locke, Hume, Condillac and Hartley, which still gives tokens of survival. The educator's purpose is to ensure that certain sequences or trains of ideas shall possess the pupil rather than others. These sequences are largely conditioned by custom and by pleasure and pain; hence the great power of domestic and political (or social) education, of the human environment. The defective food and excessive labour of the majority of men are deleterious to their intelligence. Mill is thinking particularly of the "labouring poor", the class for which public, elementary instruction was thought to be especially intended. He notes the evil effect of the division of labour and the mill-horse grind imposed upon many. "The minds therefore of the great body of the people are in danger of really degenerating, while the other elements of civilization (i.e. the other social classes) are advancing, unless care is taken, by means of the other instruments of education to counteract those effects which the simplification of the manual processes has a tendency to produce."

Mill not only places the body outside the province of education; he sometimes uses language about it which would seem more natural upon the lips of a mediaeval ascetic who contemned or feared the body. Health, strength, beauty are marked down as possible dangers to their possessors. Mill asserts and calls to witness Georges Cabanis (1757–1808), the French physician and materialist, that "muscular strength is liable to operate unfavourably upon the moral as well as the intellectual trains of thought". At a later day Charles Kingsley upheld the ideal of "muscular Christianity"; Cabanis and James Mill apparently believed that there was a muscular rascality, a rascality which was a consequence of muscle.

Like Edgeworth, James Mill was the educator of his children. John Stuart Mill has given a detailed account of his father's method which will be noticed later. But it may be observed that the theoretical presentation of education which the son advanced in his *Inaugural Address* at St Andrews (1867) is in some measure that stated in the father's *Encyclopaedia* article of some forty years earlier. Alexander Bain's *Education as a Science* (1879) is not unfairly described as the work of a belated utilitarian who continues the teaching of the elder Mill.

The younger Mill has a passage in his *Autobiography* which witnesses to the popularity of Benthamism amongst young Cambridge men of the period 1820–30. "Charles Austin was but a few years older than myself and had just left the University (1824) where he had shone with great *éclat* as a man of intellect and a brilliant orator and converser. The effect he produced on his Cambridge contemporaries deserves to be accounted an historical event; for to it may be traced the tendency towards Liberalism in general, and the Benthamic and politico-economic form of it in particular, which showed itself in a portion of the more active-minded young men of the higher classes from this time to 1830" (*op. cit.* p. 44).

Of course, those who opposed Benthamism as an ethical or political philosophy would look askance at any educational scheme advanced by Benthamites. Accordingly we have writers like Wordsworth and Coleridge appearing as hostile critics of a utilitarian education; nor were they solitary voices but spoke for a minority which was never entirely silent during the nineteenth century. Wordsworth was no reactionary in reference to public education; in that matter he took the standpoint of Comenius and of Pestalozzi. Education he declares is "a sacred right", "a universal plea". He looks forward to "that glorious time" when

> ...this imperial realm,
> While she exacts allegiance, shall admit
> An obligation on her part to *teach*
> Them who are born to serve her and obey;
> Binding herself by statute to secure
> For all the children whom her soil maintains
> The rudiments of letters, and inform
> The mind with moral and religious truth
> Both understood and practised, so that none,
> However destitute, be left to droop
> By timely culture unsustained; or run
> Into a wild disorder; or be forced
> To drudge through weary life without the aid
> Of intellectual implements and tools;
> A savage horde among the civilised,
> A servile band among the lordly free! [1]

Wordsworth joined in the almost universal hope which was aroused by the introduction of the mutual system of instruction; he was an enthusiastic supporter of that system as it was propounded by Bell and maintained by the Church of England. But in 1843 he grieved "that

[1] *The Excursion*, bk. IX (1795–1814, published 1814).

so little progress (had) been made in diminishing the evils deplored or promoting the benefits of education" [anticipated]. He and his friend, Coleridge, alive to the danger of a merely material civilization, opposed the educational schemes of the Utilitarians. Wordsworth draws a picture of the model pupil as imagined by the Benthamites, "a miracle of scientific lore" but a stranger in the realm of Fancy (*Prelude*, bk. v), not an unfair summary of the educational aim as it was understood by the Edgeworths, who were as stoutly opposed to fairy tales *et hoc genus omne* as Signorina Montessori is to-day. Coleridge thus contrasts the old and the new pedagogy: "Instead of storing the memory, during the period when the memory is the predominant faculty, with facts for the after exercise of the judgement; and instead of awakening by the noblest models the fond and unmixed love and admiration, which is the natural and graceful temper of early youth; these nurslings of improved pedagogy are taught to dispute and decide; to suspect all but their own and their lecturer's wisdom; and to hold nothing sacred from their contempt but their own contemptible arrogance; boy-graduates in all the technicals, and in all the dirty passions and impudence of anonymous criticism".[1] The passage is perhaps reminiscent of the controversy with the *Edinburgh Review* and the advocates of "useful" knowledge.

Wordsworth's *Prelude*, though written between 1799 and 1805, was not published till 1850, the year of its author's death. The poet remained as hostile as ever to the utilitarian school; a passage in book v, which on internal evidence could not have been written earlier than 1826–30, reproves "these mighty workmen of our later age" who

> have the skill
> To manage books and things, and make them act
> On infant minds as surely as the sun
> Deals with a flower; the keepers of our time,
> The guides and wardens of our faculties,
> Sages who in their prescience would control
> All accidents, and to the very road
> Which they have fashioned would confine us down
> Like engines.

William Cobbett (1763–1835), whose *Political Register* (1802–35) was a trenchant instrument throughout its career in moulding opinion, influenced his contemporaries to an extent and to a degree which could

---

[1] *Biographia Literaria* (1817), bk. I, p. 6: finished at Highgate in 1815.

not be equalled by a Wordsworth or a Coleridge. A congenital Tory who devoted the second half of his life to propagating Radical principles, Cobbett in vision looked backward to a golden age of the English labourer, its date being suspiciously near to that of his own boyhood and early youth. The persistent advocate of the agricultural labourer and of the town artisan, he was the irreconcilable opponent of all schemes which involved the use of public money for the instruction of the workman's child. Such schemes were for the most part advocated by the Benthamites and by men whom Cobbett scornfully styled "Scotch Feelosofers", men whom he utterly mistrusted. To be advocated by an enemy was a sufficient reason, in Cobbett's mind, for condemnation; but there was more than that in his hostility to the "education-mad party". He denounced these schemes, partly as an expression of indignation, partly because he distrusted schools, school-masters and their doings.[1] Like Edgeworth, he was a sedulous educator of his children and in his manner of doing it a disciple of Rousseau; the *Advice to Young Men* makes clear that his pedagogical principles were opportunity, suggestion, and a strict avoidance of any compulsion. Education must be conducted in the home. Cobbett may rightly claim also to be an educator of the public who read his *Political Register* and the crowd of pamphlets and manuals, chiefly of a technical kind—for Cobbett was of his day in his enthusiasm for "useful knowledge"—which he was continually publishing. But "this education-work" of the Benthamites seemed to him no more than teaching children to read books, and of "book-learning" he had but a poor opinion. He put character and an active life before the learning taught in schools. "It is not little books that can make a people good, that can make them moral; that can restrain them from committing crimes. I believe that books of any sort never yet had that tendency" (*Rural Rides*, vol. 1,

---

[1] "If I had been brought up a milksop, with a nursemaid everlastingly at my heels, I should have been at this day as great a fool, as inefficient a mortal, as any of these frivolous idiots that are turned out from Winchester and Westminster School, or from any of those dens of dunces called Colleges and Universities" (*Rural Rides*, edn. 1885, vol. 1, p. 125). See also the frantic outburst against Oxford, *ibid.* vol. 1, p. 41. The *Rural Rides* reveals Cobbett, the master of English prose, and Cobbett, the man, egotistic in the extreme, splenetic, full of reactionary prejudices and remorselessly cruel to a defeated foe, faults which are scarcely counter-balanced by the sincerity of the burning indignation which any oppression of the poor aroused in him.

p. 130). He denied that the mere ability to read would secure those advantages, religious, moral and political, which some anticipated from them.

His indignation was aroused by the charge of ignorance which was so frequently levelled against the labouring man. The literate may yet be ignorant and the illiterate is not necessarily ignorant. Sergeant-major William Cobbett of the 54th Regiment remembered illiterate corporals, men of character, to whom the "scholars" of the regiment served as clerks. "A great deal of deception has been practised upon the working people under the pretence of giving them education, by which the parties practising it choose always to mean *learning from books*.... The truth is, this talk about education of the people is a piece of insolence arising out of the stupid pride of idlers whose knowledge consists in books, or the contents of books. Learning means knowledge; and a hedger that understands hedging perfectly is learned in his profession. The pride or vanity of literature despises all knowledge but that which belongs to itself; and you shall frequently hear a miserable fribble of a wretch, who could hardly disentangle his carcase if clasped by a couple of stout branches, and who hardly knows a rough sheep-dog from a sheep, speaking of the *'peasantry'*, as if they were creatures born without brains" (*Twopenny Trash*, April, 1831).

This was written towards the close of his life; twenty-four years earlier the following passage had appeared (September, 1807) in his *Political Register*: "A man may first become completely skilled in all the business of husbandry; he may next learn to fell and hew timber and convert the several woods of the coppices into hoops, staves and shingles; then he may take the corn into the mill and go through the several stages of making it into flour; next he may become a soldier, may learn all the laborious duties of that profession, marching, shooting, riding, sapping and mining; transferred from the army to the fleet he may learn to hand, reef and steer, to sound the sea, and to man the guns in battle; in the course of his life, he may see all the quarters and countries of the world, the manners of all the different nations, and may feel the effects of all the climates; and yet, when he comes home, with his mind necessarily stored with ideas, of which that of his neighbour must be totally destitute, he is to be called *ignorant*, in comparison with that neighbour, if he cannot read in a book, and if that neighbour can read in a book. Such a notion never surely could have entered the mind of a man, whose trade it was not to teach reading, and who did not view what he calls education through the deceitful medium of self-interest".

Cobbett knew the educative power which lies in the full exercise of a handicraft. His protest serves as a reminder that, when their education is being considered, schooling, or its absence, is not the sole difference between the skilled rural labourer and the factory "hand" of Cobbett's own time or the present-day victim of the division of labour. The craftsman of an earlier day possessed a manual versatility, a variety of interest in his work, a personal pride in doing it perfectly and a complete understanding of its place in his world, which could not fail to broaden his intelligence, maintain his self-respect and generally raise and strengthen his character, an education which came but rarely to the "hand" through his daily task in mill or factory.

Foreign theories of education and foreign plans for its public administration received considerable attention in England at this date; and interest was increased by the abnormal volume of foreign travel which followed Waterloo. The theories and practice of certain Swiss educators in particular attracted Englishmen to their study. Rousseau's *Émile* had its adverse critics here as well as its fervent admirers, and the consequent discussion was directed and intensified by familiarity with the work of Pestalozzi and of Fellenberg, work which was known throughout Europe, and beyond, before the nineteenth century was twenty years old.

John Henry Pestalozzi, who was born at Zurich in 1746 and died in the neighbouring townlet of Brugg in 1827, was before all else a philanthropist. It was philanthropy which led him in the early days of his married life on his farm of Neuhof (1774–80) to try to educate destitute children by a combination of agricultural labour with elementary schooling. "I lived", says he, "the year through surrounded by more than fifty beggar-children, shared my bread with them in poverty, and lived myself as a beggar, to teach beggars to live like men". His love of men brought him his first public charge as an educator at Stanz in 1799 and made him at the age of fifty-three a schoolmaster for the remainder of his long life. Quitting Stanz, he taught for some four years at Burgdorf, where he was visited by J. F. Herbart who in later years attained fame as a psychologist and educator. From 1805 to 1825 Pestalozzi conducted a school in the castle of Yverdon on the Lake of Neuchâtel, an establishment which attracted notice throughout Europe and North America.

Pestalozzi's early manhood coincided with the period when Rousseau's ideas were widely disseminated, and he was in the prime of life during the days of the French Revolution. Readily responsive to great ideas and willing to experiment with ideas that were novel, the principles of Rousseau and the French revolutionaries could not fail to move him. But in the course of his development he diverged widely from these teachers, from Rousseau more especially. Like Edgeworth and many others, he tried to apply the teaching of *Emile* in the upbringing of his son and was not satisfied with the result. By nature a deeply religious man, it was inevitable that he should be repelled by the naturalism of his Genevese compatriot; the greatest disagreement between them occurred in the field of moral and religious education.

It was fundamental to Rousseau's educational theory that liberty was the greatest of goods; and the liberty of the individual meant the absence of all authority save that of "necessity", the nature of things, to which every finite being must bow. Therefore the appearance of human authority over the pupil must be eliminated; the sanction of moral training is not the authority of parent or of educator, not such a discipline of praise and blame as Locke had advised, but the so-called discipline of natural consequences, *les suites naturelles*. Adherence to this doctrine raises the question whether obedience is to be required to the educator's will. For a few weeks in 1774 Pestalozzi kept a diary which noted the progress of his child's education—Jäcobli was then four years old. The closing pages discuss this question of obedience and decide against Rousseau. "Freedom is good, but so is obedience also. We must bring together what Rousseau has separated. Convinced that the wretchedness of man came from restrictions to his liberty, he assigned no limits to freedom. Let us make use of what is wise in his principles. Let the teacher recognize that freedom is good; let him not try to force on his young charges just to gratify his own vanity....But when it is necessary to teach him to obey, then let his freedom itself prove the need. Remember that all restraint is a sign of mistrust....He should have confidence in you....The child has much necessary and seemingly meaningless labour in preparing for the duties, conventions and accomplishments of social life. I cannot

A E	8

make a citizen of him without, for example, setting him early to work, and there is much that he cannot yet quite understand and which is contrary to his principle of doing nothing which he does not himself see to be necessary. What is to be done in such cases?...The more you strive to reduce both work and discipline to a minimum, the more imperative it is that your commands when given should be obeyed. Duty and obedience should be indissoluble bonds and should lead to pleasure. But blind obedience is necessary in some cases."[1]

In later years Pestalozzi described *Émile* as "the impracticable dream-book of education"; but in matters of method and of intellectual training generally he remained its debtor. He heartily endorsed its condemnation of contemporary modes of instruction as a mania for books and a persistent disregard of the realities of which, so he thought, words were but the ill-defined shadows. His cardinal principle he shared with Comenius, Kant, Adam Smith and comparatively few men of his own day: education was neither a luxury for the few nor a charity to be bestowed upon the many, but a necessary process without which the human animal cannot attain to the stature of manhood. "We have spelling schools, writing schools, catechism schools; what we lack is *men* schools."

The ideas and practices which ruled at Yverdon attracted so much attention from educators in general, including Englishmen who were planning schemes of elementary education, that some statement of the Pestalozzian theory is necessary. Education so understood is the process of assisting the development of intellect, emotion and will; and development follows use, exercise. "It is life that educates", the educator simply playing the part of "benevolent superintendent" or of a gardener who fosters, or who may obstruct, the growth of the plant, but cannot create it. The first principle of method follows; instruction concerning things must be given directly by the things themselves or through suitable substitutes which appeal to one or more of the senses. This is the distinctively Pestalozzian principle of intuition, *Anschauung*, "the absolute foundation of all knowledge", a principle which, in its direct claim upon the active participation of the pupil and in its demand for the exercise of first-hand observation on his part, was applied by Pestalozzi to the spheres of sentiment and behaviour as well as to that of the intelligence. All this involves what

[1] J. A. Green, *Life and Work of Pestalozzi*, pp. 39–44.

Froebel afterwards called self-activity, that is, self-initiated activity in the pupil. The Prussian Minister, Stein, in a memorandum of 1810 spoke of "the Pestalozzian method which elevates the self-activity of the mind, stimulates the religious sense and all noble human feelings, promotes life in the idea and diminishes the inclination to life in enjoyment".[1]

Self-activity involves an association between school and life. Of his work with the orphan children at Stanz, his first essay in school-mastering, Pestalozzi says that he tried to secure his object "simply by the influence exercised on the children by nature and by the activity to which they were aroused by the needs of their daily life".[2] "I still made use of the impressions and experiences of their daily life to give my children a true and exact idea of right and duty."[3] "I tried to connect study with manual labour, the school with the workshop, and make one thing of them."[4] Hence the beggar children on his farm school, Neuhof, learned fieldwork and spinning; at Yverdon the well-to-do pupils were taught bookbinding, cardboard work and gardening. Self-activity and the principle of intuition require the use of the heuristic method, the pupil learns by discovery, he analyses and "finds out" for himself. A strict embargo is laid upon rote-learning.

Because the success of education is greatly dependent upon sympathy and insight in the educator, the home is the best school. "The basis of education is love." Emile in spite of his tutor was shut out from the home. The physical life of an organism man shares with the other animals and with the plants; unlike plant or animal, man is a moral being, and to that fact education must be primarily addressed. But while the process is definitely social, the individuality of the pupil must not be engulfed in it; the development of personality is one of Pestalozzi's primary objects. Such an education is a universal need, since only through it can the moral, which Pestalozzi sometimes also calls the divine, be fostered and developed. This view of the matter was shared by very few at that time, although philosophers like Adam Smith and Kant had enunciated it. Indeed, Pestalozzi was before his

---

[1] F. Paulsen, *Geschichte des gelehrten Unterrichts*, vol. II, p. 279.

[2] De Guimps, *Life of Pestalozzi*, John Russell's translation, p. 152. This and the following two quotations are from Pestalozzi's chief educational work, *Wie Gertrud ihre Kinder lehrt* (1801).

[3] *Ibid.* p. 162.　　　　　　　　　[4] *Ibid.* p. 167.

time not only in his conception of education as a whole but also in his belief that the instruction of the people at large could and should be liberalized.

The smashing blows which Napoleon gave to Prussia at Jena and Auerstädt (1806) and the subsequent occupation of Berlin by the French troops drove her statesmen to the task of national reconstruction, and popular education was at once regarded as an essential instrument of their policy; the army was another. The enthusiasm with which the renovation was carried on found no place for the question of the individual *versus* the State. Although in earlier years Humboldt had vigorously asserted the right of the individual to be free from State interference in so intimate and spiritual a thing as his own education, events made him the administrative chief of a system which, before all others, was State-maintained and State-directed.

These were the early years of Pestalozzi's work at Yverdon (1805 and onwards) when his name was familiar in Western Europe. The Prussian Government sent student-teachers to Yverdon to learn Pestalozzi's principles and to acquire something of the spirit in which he applied them. Herbart received his first official recognition, the chair of philosophy at Königsberg (1809), on the express ground that in the opinion of the Prussian Ministry of Instruction he would "be useful in the reform of education after the principles of Pestalozzi". The Prussian was not the only Government which showed a lively interest in the work of the Swiss educator; Austria, Holland, Russia also sent students to learn from him at Yverdon.

Other visitors came on their own initiative. Froebel was such a visitor; in 1805 he spent a fortnight in the Institute and he returned in 1808 bringing with him three private pupils of his own. This time he remained for two years discharging a two-fold duty as teacher and as pupil. Andrew Bell of the mutual system spent some days with Pestalozzi in the summer of 1816. He had but a poor opinion of Pestalozzian method but a very high one of Pestalozzi. Bell was characteristically impressed by the discouragement of emulation in the Institute. He also bore witness to the widespread popularity of the school whose pupils were drawn not only from Switzerland but also from Germany, France, England, Spain, Portugal, Italy and elsewhere. In 1819 the English pupils were so numerous as to make it expedient to provide them with a chaplain. This was Dr Charles Mayo (1793–1846) who in

1822 set up a Pestalozzian school under that name at Epsom and removed it four years later to Cheam. Mayo was the moving spirit in establishing (1836) the Home and Colonial School Society and its training college for schoolmistresses. His sister, Elizabeth Mayo, by her text-books made English teachers familiar with the Pestalozzian "object lesson" and its underlying principle of intuition, the pupil's personal observation. Chiefly through the activities of the Mayos and their adherents, English infant schools adopted the Pestalozzian triad, "Number, Form and Language", as the elements of instruction.

During the first half of the nineteenth century Switzerland was a land of pilgrimage for students of education. Robert Owen, Henry Brougham and, at a later date (1839), Kay-Shuttleworth were amongst the English pilgrims. Pestalozzi was not the only magnet; those who shared the opinions of Owen and Brougham found a more congenial mentor in Philipp Emanuel von Fellenberg (1771–1844), the founder of the Hofwyl Institute, a great educational colony in Canton Berne, which embraced all grades of schooling and all social classes. Owen's two sons were educated at Hofwyl.

Fellenberg, a member of a Bernese patrician family, like Pestalozzi began his educational labours by a purely charitable effort to ameliorate the condition of the poor. In 1799 he opened at Hofwyl a free "Poor School" which in character but not in history resembled Pestalozzi's experiment at Neuhof. Andrew Bell, who visited Hofwyl in the summer of 1816, speaks thus of the Poor School: "His school for the poor consists of 32 boys who work about ten hours a day and study two. They are chiefly employed in agricultural labour, sometimes in mechanical work. They learn to read, write, cipher, draw, music and the elements of geometry". Some seventeen years later the pupils numbered 100 boys and 100 girls who were virtually indentured labourers engaged in cultivating 250 acres of arable land. Apparently the time given to schooling was then less than two hours each day, but the number of studies had increased. The children made a close study of the neighbourhood of the school ("Heimatkunde") including flora and fauna, specimens of which were deposited in the school museum. They also studied "some of the most useful of chemical phenomena", they were trained to observe and the attempt was made to quicken moral and religious sentiment. Carpentry and blacksmith's work supplemented field labour. Religious instruction was given in accordance with the denominational adherence of the parents.[1]

The economic and what without offence may be termed the police motives were seldom absent from the thought of educational reformers who at that time concerned themselves with popular instruction. However much Fellenberg was originally moved by pure philanthropy (he began with a single pupil), as his Poor School developed the instruction aimed at so enlightening its pupils that they were less likely to trust demagogues, while it did not induce in them "imaginary wants" which would make them discontented with the labourer's lot. M. Pictet, a contemporary observer, says that Fellenberg's purpose was to make his pupils happy in themselves and useful to society. "The poor should acquire in the course of their education an assured means of livelihood and their instruction should be confined to what is in accord with that necessity of their position".

At the date of Bell's visit Hofwyl included also an "Agricultural Institute", started in 1807, for the instruction of young men in the theory and practice of agriculture, and, dating from 1808, a "Scientific Educational Institution for the Higher Social Classes". This latter had at times as many as 100 pupils from all the countries of Europe and from America; Robert Owen's two sons were educated in this institution. The subjects taught included all that was then usually taught in German secondary schools other than classical, and the first importance was attached to moral and physical training. In 1828 Fellenberg added to his establishments a "Realschule" for the middle class, most of the pupils being Swiss. He continued to plan schools and institutes to the end; but the Bernese Government were always strongly opposed to his schemes and Hofwyl rapidly declined after his death in 1841, the last of his institutes coming to an end by the closing of the "Scientific Educational Institution" in 1848.

To return to Bell's account of Hofwyl as he found it in 1816. "Music and drawing (designing) are in great request in their schools and also geometry. The new[2] school has but one master, Verhli [Wehrli], of distinguished merit. The excellency of both institutions [i.e. Yverdon

---

[1] An account of Hofwyl c. 1833 will be found in the *Quarterly Journal of Education*, vol. VI, pp. 336 ff. and 351.

[2] This seems to refer to a new organization of the "Poor School" by Wehrli who, taking it over in 1810, first made it successful.

and Hofwyl] and their superiority about which, Fellenberg's particularly, an immensity of pamphlets and philosophical disquisitions have been published, consists in both of a single point, which is not much noticed. Every class and every scholar has his master always at his side, whether at study, work or play. I had almost forgotten the gymnastics which constitute a principal part of the instruction at both these schools and which deserve imitation to a certain degree."[1]

Bell's reference to the schoolmaster of "distinguished merit" is to be noted. Johann Jakob Wehrli came to the Poor School in 1810 at the age of twenty and laboured there with the greatest success for twenty-three years, when he returned to his native canton to become the head of the cantonal training college at Kreuzlingen where he laboured for twenty more years. Training teachers to labour in schools for the poor had been familiar to him at Hofwyl, the Poor School under his direction being recognized by other Swiss cantons as an efficient training ground for such teachers. When Kay-Shuttleworth visited Wehrli in 1839 the latter had had a long and successful career in training teachers on Pestalozzian lines. His experience and his personal distinction greatly impressed his visitor; Wehrli and Kreuzlingen did much to shape the first ideals and early practice of the "Training School at Battersea" which Kay-Shuttleworth and his friend Carleton Tufnell founded in 1840.

In the account which Kay-Shuttleworth has given of his Swiss tour, so important in its consequences for English popular education, he says: "At Fribourg we spent some time in the Convent of the Capuchin friars, where we found the venerable Père Girard officiating at a religious festival.... The Père Girard has a European reputation among those who have laboured to raise the elementary instruction of the poorer classes, consequent on his pious labours among the poor of Fribourg."[2] Andrew Bell had also sought the acquaintance of this Franciscan friar; and it would seem that Robert Owen had met him, if the confused account given by Owen in his old age can be trusted.

[1] Southey, *Andrew Bell*, vol. III, pp. 89 ff. Imitation by England was slow in coming. "It is strange in the light of present practice to find that the gymnasium opened (by Thring at Uppingham) in 1859 and the gymnastic master put in charge was the first possessed by any public school in England" (G. Parkin, *Edward Thring*, p. 76). Gymnastics was taught in University College School in 1840 under a gymnastic master. See F. W. Felkin, *From Gower St. to Frognal* (1909), p. 12.

[2] J. Kay-Shuttleworth, *Four Periods of Public Education*, p. 301. "First Report on...the Training College at Battersea (1841)."

Jean-Baptiste Girard (b. 1765), known as le Père Girard and Père Grégoire, was "préfet des écoles", or director of the primary schools of Fribourg from 1804 to 1823. He so improved these schools that, as Kay-Shuttleworth said, his fame was European. France, Italy and Germany joined Fribourg and Switzerland in erecting a monument to this "benefactor of the people and of suffering humanity", after his death in 1850. He is remembered for his advocacy of the mother tongue as a potent educational instrument and for his attempt to acclimatize the mutual system of Bell in an unfavourable atmosphere. His book on the former subject, *De l'enseignement régulier de la langue maternelle dans les écoles et les familles* (1844), was "crowned" by the French Academy and awarded a special prize of 6000 francs. He was also the author of half a dozen volumes, *Cours éducatif de la langue maternelle*, which appeared within the period 1840–8. But his earlier and greater reputation rested upon his direction of the schools of his native town. He achieved this success and was regarded in Switzerland as an authority on primary education years before it occurred to him to experiment with the mutual system. He told Bell that he first heard of that system and of the work of the National Society in 1815; the system was in operation in Fribourg in June of the next year. Nine months later Girard was writing to his English visitor. "My school, sir, glories in being a Madras school. The system has been introduced into the schools of the canton and teachers from Berne and Neuchâtel have come to Fribourg to learn about it."[1]

Bell was enthusiastic over his disciple. "From Yverdon I was invited to Fribourg in Switzerland, the capital of the Roman Catholic canton of that name. There I found the new schools in a most flourishing state; the scholars multipliéd, as is the case in the ratio of its improvements. Père Girard, a priest who deserves to be recorded in history as an amiable, benevolent and indefatigable friend of humanity and of youth, has the superintendence of these schools....This liberal father felt the true spirit of the Madras system and had introduced none of the fooleries, absurdities, noise and nonsense which are found in other schools or in the models from which they are chiefly taken. [An obvious hit at Lancaster.] In none of them were the arrangements [wanting] requisite to give due scope to the principles of imitation and emulation, which promise to render his school equal to the best in

[1] Southey, *Andrew Bell*, vol. III, pp. 110 ff.

England. He imbibed with eagerness the instructions which I gave and pledged himself to follow them."[1]

In addition to its inherent defects the mutual system had certain associations which were likely to arouse opposition where the first and highest place in education was assigned to a strictly denominational form of religious instruction and training. The Jesuits in Fribourg and the bishop of the diocese set on foot an inquiry, the outcome of which was a declaration that the mutual system was "immoral and irreligious". Girard was relieved of his office as director of schools and sent to Lucerne to teach philosophy. This was in 1823; he returned to Fribourg in 1834 and lived there till his death.

English interest in foreign education was by no means restricted to those who could make personal observation abroad. The Society for the Diffusion of Useful Knowledge published a *Quarterly Journal of Education* from 1831 to 1835 in whose pages not only were established systems described but periodical reports kept readers informed of what was being done in education throughout the civilized world. The Central Society of Education, an association which had many public men of diverse opinions in its membership, proposed to inquire "what is and what ought to be the education of both sexes of all classes",[2] and with this inquiry in view its publications (of which there were two volumes, 1837–8) gave information respecting foreign as well as British education. Fellenberg was an honorary member and wrote an explanatory memorandum which was printed in the volume for 1838. There was in fact a great deal of knowledge concerning foreign educational theory and practice available for English public men when the first Reform Bill became an Act.

[1] *Op. cit.* vol. III, pp. 89 ff.
[2] The Society's publication (1837), vol. I, p. 3.

PART TWO
EARLIER VICTORIAN (1839–1867)

CHAPTER V

The Committee of Council and the Voluntary System

A little more than two years after Lord Brougham delivered his speech in the House of Lords deprecating interference with the voluntary system,[1] a Select Committee of the House of Commons was appointed (November 30th, 1837) "to consider the best means of providing useful education for the children of the poorer classes throughout England and Wales". This Committee reported in the following July that "in the Metropolis and in the great towns of England and Wales there exists a great want of education among the children of the working classes"; and that it was "desirable" that schooling should be accessible to not less than one-eighth of the entire population.[2] The Committee were not prepared, "under existing circumstances and under the difficulties which have beset the question", to go further than recommending an extension of the Treasury grants which reached the schools through the National Society and the British and Foreign School Society.

The satisfaction felt by Brougham in the voluntary system and the tolerance extended to it by the Select Committee were not shared by the Government. The grounds of dissatisfaction were stated by the Home Secretary, Lord John Russell, in a letter to the President of the Council (Lord Lansdowne) which was laid upon the table of the Commons on February 12th, 1839. "Much remains to be done," said Lord John, "and amongst the chief defects yet subsisting may be reckoned the insufficient number of qualified schoolmasters, the imperfect method of teaching which prevails in, perhaps, the greatest number of the schools; the absence of any sufficient inspection of the schools and examination of the nature of the instruction given; the want of a model school...and finally the neglect of this great subject among the enactments of our voluminous legislation."[3]

[1] See Chapter i above, p. 35.

[2] In 1831 the census return was 13,896,797, increased by more than two millions in 1841.   [3] Kay-Shuttleworth, *Four Periods*, pp. 445–6.

The first step in the forward policy thus foreshadowed was taken on April 10th, 1839, when it was "ordered by Her Majesty in Council that the Most Hon. Henry, Marquis of Lansdowne, Lord-President of the Council, the Rt. Hon. John William, Viscount Duncannon, Lord Privy Seal, the Rt. Hon. Lord John Russell, one of Her Majesty's Principal Secretaries of State, and the Rt. Hon. Thomas Spring Rice, Chancellor of H.M.'s Exchequer, be and are hereby appointed a Committee to superintend the Application of any sums voted by Parliament for the purpose of promoting public education".

This "Committee of the Privy Council on Education", usually known as "the Committee of Council", consisted of four Ministers of the Crown, the Lord-President naturally being its chairman. Its ostensible function was purely financial but the course of events made it something like, although incompletely like, a Ministry of Public Instruction. For sixty years until superseded by the Board of Education Act, 1899, it was the only semblance of such a Ministry that the country possessed. Its first secretary was Dr James Phillips Kay (1804–77), later and better known as Sir James Kay-Shuttleworth (from February, 1842), who had previously served as secretary to the Manchester Board of Health and as Assistant Poor Law Commissioner. He was a close student of the poor in several European countries, paying particular attention to the conditions of their health and education. His tenure at the "Committee of Council" extended from 1839 to 1849 during which period he was its moving spirit. He has been called "the founder of English popular education".[1]

In the opinion of the Government, the lack of qualified teachers and the absence of any official inspection of the schools which were aided by the Parliamentary grant were the most urgent administrative problems, and to these the newly created Committee at once addressed itself. Within three or four days of its institution the Committee formulated a scheme for a "normal school", "a school in which candidates for the office of teacher in schools for the poorer classes may acquire the knowledge necessary to the exercise of their future profession and may be practised in the most approved methods of religious and moral training and instruction". The "candidate teachers" were to be resident in the institution, where they were to receive

[1] For Kay-Shuttleworth see Dr Frank Smith's *The Life and Works of Sir James Kay-Shuttleworth* (1923).

instruction in "the theory of their art" and in "whatever knowledge is necessary for success in it". Two schools for children were to be associated with the normal school. A day school of 150–200 children of both sexes and of all ages was to serve as a practising school "in which the candidate teachers may realise the application of the best methods of instruction, under the limitations and obstructions which must arise in a small village or town day school". To serve as a pattern for general imitation a model school of "120 infants, 200 boys and girls receiving ordinary instruction" was to form an integral part of the establishment. All these children were to be resident and their ages were to range from three to fourteen.

At this stage the Committee had not thought out a complete curriculum either for the candidate teachers or for the children of the two schools. References to "simultaneous method classes", "simultaneous instruction" and the employment of a gallery suggest that the Committee favoured the principles and practice of David Stow's "training system."[1] But the economic factor was kept in mind, since it was decided "to give such a character to the matter of instruction in the school as to keep it in close relation with the condition of workmen and servants", "to include instruction in industry as a special department of the moral training of the children."[2]

But the great aim of the whole establishment was clearly conceived as the furtherance of religious and moral training and instruction; and it was this aspect of the scheme which ensured its destruction. In the model school, religion was to be "combined with the whole matter of instruction and to regulate the entire system of discipline". Times were to be set apart for "such peculiar doctrinal instruction as may be required for the religious training of the children". At these times a chaplain was to teach children whose parents or guardians belonged to the Church of England; a licensed minister, or ministers, might be appointed to teach others on the request of the dissenting parents, provided that the number of such children was "such as appear to this Committee to require such special provision".[2]

The Committee foresaw opposition to their plan but failed to gauge

[1] See pp. 135 ff., below.
[2] The minute describing the proposed "National Normal School" is printed in full in Sir J. Kay-Shuttleworth's *Four Periods of Public Education* (1862), pp. 179–81.

its intensity; it believed that the differences between Churchmen and Dissenters were not so deep as they seemed and it underestimated the objection to State-controlled education. Popular instruction was regarded by the Government as an urgent need which the voluntary system could not satisfy; support or at least assistance from the public funds was as essential in England as it had proved to be in Germany and in France. Enlightenment soon came. The scheme of religious instruction proposed for the model school appeared to Churchmen as an infringement of the Church's legal right to superintend national education, while to the Dissenters it was contrary to religious liberty. An opposition, which Kay-Shuttleworth called "unqualified and persevering",[1] was offered by the Church of England, the Kirk of Scotland, the Wesleyan Conference and by Wesleyan congregations. The very existence of the new Committee of Council was endangered and with it what little had been achieved in the way of State control. In debates on the subject in the House of Commons in June, 1839, the Government majority sank to five, and the renewal and increase to £30,000 of the annual grant of 1833 was carried by a majority of two only.

On June 3rd, the Committee formally abandoned the plan for a national normal school "until greater concurrence of opinion is found to prevail", and its secretary was instructed to draw up and publish "an explanation of the intentions of H.M. Government" in putting forward the measures of 1839.[2] Nor did controversy end with the Committee's surrender. The opponents of State education were alarmed by the Government's attempt to evade Parliament and to attain their end by an Order in Council. During this same month of June in the House of Lords the Archbishop of Canterbury (Howley) moved an address to the Crown, which was carried by 229 to 118, pleading that no plan for the general education of the people should be set up which had not been fully considered by the House.

The attempt to provide a supply of qualified teachers through a purely national channel was utterly defeated; but the Committee of Council carried the second object of its policy after some opposition. Between 1833 and 1839 the National Society and the British and

---

[1] *Op. cit.* p. 502.

[2] "The Explanation of the Measures of 1839" is printed in Kay-Shuttleworth *op. cit.* pp. 185–286. So lengthy a document shows that the Government was very much on its defence. See pp. 131 f. below.

Foreign School Society had been the distributors to the schools of the annual Parliamentary grant. This duty now devolved upon the Committee and, to ensure that the schools complied with the conditions, it proposed to appoint inspectors. "The Committee recommend that no further grant be made, now or hereafter, for the establishment or support of normal schools or any other schools, unless the right of inspection be retained in order to secure a conformity to the regulations and discipline established in the several schools, with such improvements as may from time to time be suggested by the Committee."[1]

Religious instruction was an integral part of the curriculum of every grant-aided school; the fact would bring these State inspectors of schools into some sort of relation with that instruction and the relation might infringe the principle of freedom from State interference in this particular. In 1840 the National Society was placated by an agreement that the Archbishops should have a veto upon the appointment of inspectors of Church schools; but it was not till 1843 that the British and Foreign School Society reluctantly accepted the power of vetoing the visit of any particular inspector to a British school. In the end it became the practice to appoint clergymen as inspectors of Church schools and laymen as inspectors of non-Church schools; the lay inspectors did not examine the religious instruction given in Dissenting schools.

The State had now fairly committed itself to the partial support. and, in a measure, to the supervision of popular education; but the conduct of individual schools remained with the voluntary subscribers who at this time supplied about two-thirds of the money for their upkeep. To the two original societies which represented these subscribers there were added in course of time the Home and Colonial School Society (1836), the Wesleyan Education Committee (1840), the London Ragged School Union (1844), the Catholic Poor School Committee (1847), the Church Education Society (1853), the London Committee of British Jews and various diocesan boards of the Church. The schools of these bodies and their administration constituted the "voluntary system". The Congregational Board of Education (1843) and the Voluntary School Association, being opposed to State interference, stood outside that system.

[1] Kay-Shuttleworth, *op. cit.* p. 183. The minute is of the same date as that which abandoned the Normal School scheme.

Nineteenth-century England was deeply interested in theological and ecclesiastical controversy, a feature of the national life very noticeable from 1833 onwards for some fifty years. The Evangelical movement of an earlier time was succeeded by Tractarianism (1833–45), the revival of High Church doctrine and practice, its prominent figures being John Keble, John Henry Newman and Edward Bouverie Pusey. In a general sense, as fostering religion and directing its practice, this movement continued the educative influence exercised by Methodism and Evangelicalism. But whereas these laid emphasis on the individual aspect of religion, the relation of each to God, the newer teaching recalled the older conception of man's relation to God through a social organization, the Church and its offices. The tendency of Tractarianism therefore was to accentuate the claim of the Church of England to be the national educator, to support the opponents of the State-controlled school and to strengthen the position of the voluntary system.

On the other hand, the great advance in the physical sciences had changed the conception of the universe and of their own relation to it in the minds of the educated. The material and social conditions of the time conspired with this new order of thought to convince many that between science and religion there was irreconcilable conflict and that in the struggle religion had been worsted. Such an opinion was evident amongst the working people of the industrial centres, where it was known as secularism.

The revival of religious feeling and the growth of secularism necessarily prolonged the struggle over the religious problem in administering the schools. From 1833 onwards there were acrimonious debates and prosecutions of clergymen on charges of theological or ritual irregularity. The very year (1843) in which Newman quitted the Church of England saw the disruption of the Church of Scotland on a question of Church government. In England widespread interest and support were given to ecclesiastical controversy by the formation of societies with large memberships. Such bodies as the Liberation Society (1844), the National Secular Society (1846), the Church Association (1865), lent point and edge to the weapons of those who shared in the bitter fighting over religious instruction in schools. While religious disabilities, especially as these affected Jews, were being removed, some with an educational consequence remained; there were still religious tests at Oxford, Cambridge and Durham.

The stages of the struggle are illustrated by the story of the "conscience clause", the proviso in trust deeds that schools should exempt from religious instruction those who desired exemption, without prejudice to their membership of the school. Incidentally, the earliest pronouncement on this head enumerates the subjects which were regarded as forming the curriculum of studies to be followed in grant-aided schools. In December, 1839, the Committee of Council decided that a school which, not being in connexion either with the National Society or with the British and Foreign School Society, desired to share in the annual grant from the Treasury must insert in its trust deeds a clause to the following effect: "And it is hereby declared that the instruction at the said school shall comprise at least the following branches of school learning, namely reading, writing, arithmetic, geography, Scripture history and (in the case of girls) needlework: and it is hereby further declared that it shall be a fundamental regulation and practice of the said school that the Bible be daily read therein and that no child shall be required to learn any catechism or other religious formulary or to attend any Sunday School or place of worship to which respectively his or her parent or other person having the custody of such child shall on religious grounds object, but the selection of such Sunday School and place of worship shall in all cases be left to the free choice of such parent or person, without the child's thereby incurring any loss of the benefits and privileges of the school the trusts whereof are hereby declared".[1]

The Committee was content at first to suggest the insertion of such a clause in all trust deeds of schools in receipt of grant. But in 1847 it took power to require the inclusion of this or a similar clause in such deeds; yet it appears that the insertion was not pressed till about the year 1853. The problem which the conscience clause was intended to solve was of course most acute in what, during later controversies, were known as "single-school areas", districts, that is, which possessed but one school for the community as a whole. In nearly all cases this school was a Church school. In 1847 the Committee of Council would venture no farther than to make an indefinite and discreetly veiled threat against school authorities in a single-school area who maintained an intolerant attitude. "If it should be found that in any parish a Church of England school alone exists, that this school is aided by

[1] A. Garfit, *The Conscience Clause* (1868), p. 4.

Government, and that there are communicants of dissenting congregations too poor to provide for the education of their children, and who cannot conscientiously permit them to attend a school in which instruction in the Catechism and Liturgy is required from (*sic*) all the scholars; it would become their Lordships to inquire whether the managers of the school feel themselves under the obligation of duty to enforce this condition. Such a result would be to be regretted and it is believed would be rare; but if it existed, it would become the Government to deliberate in what way education could be provided for the children of religious parents who conscientiously objected to permit their children to be taught the Catechism and Liturgy of the Church".[1]

Most of the clergy were willing to act on the principles of a conscience clause; some had done so in their parish schools in the preceding century. But the terms of the clause as recommended in 1839 suggested that some were not ready to adopt the principle; and of these the firebrands roused the National Society to protest against a conscience clause as derogatory to the Church's office of national educator. The controversy was brought to a head by the inclusion of a clause (art. 22 b) in the Committee of Council's Revised Code of 1862 which required the observance of the principle in the management of all grant-aided schools. The Newcastle Commission of 1859–61 had had evidence of the Dissenter's grievance in single-school areas and the Committee was forced to find a remedy. But article 22 b led to a rupture between the Committee and the National Society; the controversy rose and fell between 1862 and 1870, when the principle became statute law by the Elementary Education Act of that year.

"The labouring poor" in whose behalf so much educational activity was being displayed were in sad case during the early years of the period now being considered. The beneficial effects upon industry, commerce and employment which were to follow the introduction of railways (1825), the invention of the electric telegraph (1837) and of the penny post (1840), were not immediately felt. The earliest effect of the use of labour-saving machinery was to increase the amount of unemployment. The new Poor Law of 1834 withdrew the old form of outdoor relief without allowing for the inevitable economic disturbance which followed, and the wretchedness which the disturbance entailed.

[1] Kay-Shuttleworth, *Four Periods*, pp. 513–14.

Taxes were heavy, unemployment was rife, wages were low, prices, until the abolition of the Corn Laws and the introduction of Free Trade in 1846, were high; conditions of labour in mines and factories and in the homes of workers in the industrial centres were, in the absence of sanitary laws or regulations of a kind which to-day would be called inhuman.

Political power was conferred by the Reform Act of 1832 upon those who were being enriched by the cheapness of labour; the Act left the manual workers as politically impotent as before. Hence their demand for that more drastic series of Parliamentary reforms which were summarized by the People's Charter of 1838 and supported by the abortive Chartism of the next ten years. Yet Parliament itself refused to consider petitions in favour of the Charter.

The wretchedness of the poor found expression in strikes and in rioting; a riot at Newport under John Frost in November, 1839, led to considerable loss of life and the transportation of the leaders on their conviction of high treason. Violence, or the apprehension of violence, was met on the Government side by repressive measures which badly strained the conception of individual liberty. In 1843 the Home Secretary, Sir James Graham, spoke of "a social insurrection of a very formidable character".

A semi-official publication, whose author was Kay-Shuttleworth, appeared in 1839 as "an explanation of the intentions of H.M. Government".[1] By way of exhibiting the backwardness of this country, the book described the primary systems in vogue upon the Continent, emphasizing their State character and the fact that religion formed an integral part of their instruction, while State inspection was found to be compatible with religious freedom, features which the Committee of Council earnestly desired to incorporate in English practice. One motive, probably a very strong one, which caused the Government to embark upon an educational policy was the fear of Chartism and the discontent of which it was a symbol. "We are far from being alarmists," says the author, "we write neither under the influence of undue fear nor with a wish to inspire undue fear into others. The opinions which we have expressed are founded on a careful observation of the proceedings and speeches of the Chartists and of their predecessors in

[1] "Recent Measures for the Promotion of Education in England" in *Four Periods*, pp. 185 ff.

agitation in the manufacturing districts for many years as reported in their newspapers; and have been as deliberately formed as they are deliberately expressed. We confess that we cannot contemplate with unconcern the vast physical force which is now moved by men so ignorant and so unprincipled as the Chartist leaders; and without expecting such internal convulsions as may deserve the name of *civil war*, we think it highly probable that persons and property will, in certain parts of the country, be so exposed to violence as materially to affect the prosperity of our manufactures and commerce, to shake the mutual confidence of mercantile men and to diminish the stability of our political and social institutions....It is astonishing to us that the party calling themselves Conservative should not lead the van in promoting the diffusion of that knowledge among the working classes which tends beyond anything else to promote the security of property and the maintenance of public order. To restore the working classes to their former state of incurious and contented apathy is impossible if it were desirable. If they are to have knowledge, surely it is the part of a wise and virtuous Government to do all in its power to secure to them useful knowledge and to guard them against pernicious opinions. We have already said that all instruction should be hallowed by the influence of religion; but we hold it equally absurd and short-sighted to withhold secular instruction on the ground that religion alone is sufficient".[1]

These aims of 1839 are different from those which actuated the founders of the voluntary system; and the attitude of "a wise and virtuous Government" towards "pernicious opinions" goes part of the way at least in justifying the contention of the individualists in education from Priestley's day onwards.

There were attempts, some successful, to ameliorate the conditions of labour. Between 1840 and 1847 Lord Ashley (afterwards better known as the Earl of Shaftesbury) forced inquiry and legislation respecting those conditions in mines, factories and on the land, particularly as these concerned women and children. In 1840–2 little children spent twelve or thirteen hours daily in the dark, opening and shutting doors in the mines; boys and girls on hands and knees dragged trolleys of coal along the ways, children of six and seven carried coal in sacks. In many trades children were apprenticed at the ages of

[1] *Four Periods*, pp. 231–2.

seven, six, five and even four; they received food and clothing but no wages.

Sir James Graham's Bill of 1843 (its author was then Home Secretary in Peel's second ministry) was designed to regulate the employment of children in factories and to ensure for them a measure of instruction; religious instruction was to be that of the Church with a conscience clause as safeguard. The British and Foreign School Society, the Sunday School Union and the Congregationalists united with the Wesleyan Conference and its congregations in so vigorous a protest and resistance that the Bill was withdrawn. During its discussion Roebuck moved "that in no plan of education maintained and enforced by the State should any attempt be made to inculcate peculiar religious opinions" since the contrary course would render "the cordial co-operation of all sects and denominations...impossible".[1] The motion was defeated.

The "voluntaryists" did more than protest; they did their best to furnish an alternative to Graham's Bill by enlarging the scope of their labours. An opponent of voluntaryism says: "The greatest voluntary efforts ever made were those which took place after the rejection of Sir James Graham's Educational Bill, when nearly a quarter of a million was raised by the joint efforts of Churchmen and Dissenters" (*National Education* (1847), p. 26, by Rev. John Dufton).

The principle of State-controlled education, and particularly of State education based upon religion, was confronted by such active and determined opposition that the question suggests itself: Why was the policy initiated in 1839 resolutely upheld by three successive ministries, two Whig and one Conservative? The Committee of Council persisted in strengthening its hold upon the schools, and in attempting a reconciliation of Churchmen and Dissenters rather than cut the knot by making the schools purely secular. The answer to the question seems to be that, in the opinion of responsible statesmen, popular ignorance and irreligion were amongst the gravest features in what was known as "the condition of England" problem. Kay-Shuttleworth allows us to see what was in the mind of the Council. "The state of the manufacturing poor is that which awakens the greatest apprehension. The labour which they undergo is excessive and they sacrifice their wives and infants to the claims of their poverty and to the demands of the

[1] *Four Periods*, p. 504.

intense competition of trade. Almost everything around them tends to materialise and enflame them. They are assembled in masses, they are exposed to the physical evils arising from the neglect of sanitary precautions and to the moral contamination of towns, they are accustomed to combine in trades unions and political associations, they are more accessible by agitators and more readily excited by them.... The time for inquiry into their condition is past, the period for a sagacious national forethought is at hand. We (i.e. Shuttleworth and E. C. Tufnell) therefore felt that the imminent risks attending this condition of the manufacturing poor established the largest claim on our institution (the Training School at Battersea) founded to educate Christian teachers for the people".[1]

The Utilitarians, notwithstanding the central principle of their philosophy, deprecated interference with contract and the operation of economic law; they were therefore opposed to much of the labour legislation and to the proposals of its advocates. After a good deal of resistance from those who trusted to pure individualism and *laisser-faire* (amongst whom were Roebuck, Cobden, John Bright, and other champions of Free Trade), the employment of children under eight and of night work by boys and girls under thirteen was prohibited by law. This was in 1845; two years later a ten hours' day was made the maximum for women and young persons.

The reference above to the Training School at Battersea makes it necessary to hark back to earlier years. When the Committee of Council was instituted, the elementary schools of the country were still being conducted for the most part on the "mutual system", and the defects of that system had by that time become patent. Bad as the system was, it was often made worse by the unqualified masters and mistresses who directed the doings of the monitors. As a rule these adult practitioners were persons of scanty knowledge and no great force of character. As Kay-Shuttleworth pointed out, nothing but a sense of religious vocation could ensure the presence of suitable men and women in the schools. There were no material attractions. The schoolmaster had no social standing, his income was scanty and precarious, dependent upon fluctuating fees and a contingent share in voluntary subscriptions. Even though he sought and found other

---

[1] "Second Report on the Schools for the training of parochial schoolmasters at Battersea, December, 1843" in *Four Periods*, p. 428.

posts and occasional jobs to supplement his income from the school, he could only look forward to "hopeless indigence" (Shuttleworth's phrase) in old age. "To entrust the education of the labouring classes of this country to men involved in such straits is to condemn the poor to ignorance and its fatal train of evils. To build spacious and well-ventilated schools, without attempting to provide a position of honour and emolument for the masters is to cheat the poor with a cruel illusion."[1]

To make a beginning in reforming this state of things, the Committee of Council brought forward its scheme for a national normal school, and the language in which that scheme was propounded indicates that the Committee had been made acquainted with the work of the Glasgow philanthropist and educator, David Stow (1793–1864), one of the most influential men in British elementary education, notwithstanding the oblivion into which his name has now fallen. A practical educator whose interest in popular education originated in his philanthropic labours for the poor, he was no mere empiric; unlike Bell and Lancaster he had a formulated theory upon which his practice was based. A well-to-do Glasgow merchant, his first efforts to help the poor were centred in the Sunday schools of the city; and it was from his experience with the poor children in those schools that his theory developed.

Stow's sphere was throughout confined to elementary education and the training of teachers to serve in elementary schools. His theory was embodied in the "training system", a term which describes one of Stow's principles; the phrase has nothing to do with the expressions, "the training of teachers", "training college" and the like. The training system trained the pupil, whose teachers Stow preferred to call "trainers". The early, preparatory stage of Stow's labours occupied the years 1807–27; he aimed at forming habits and found that one day a week in the Sunday school was insufficient for such a purpose. He therefore opened evening schools for his ragamuffins and through them tried to influence their parents. He was very prompt in noting the relation of the newly introduced infant school to the principles which had been forming in his mind, and about 1826–8[2] he formed the Glasgow Infant School Society.

---

[1] *Four Periods*, pp. 473–5.
[2] There is some doubt as to the exact date. See R. R. Rusk, *The Training of Teachers in Scotland: An Historical Review* (1928). Dr Rusk has established the date of the opening of the Drygate Infant School as April 23rd, 1828.

But too much was expected from infant schools in the early days of their history and the consequence was that the little ones were over-burdened with schooling or, as the enthusiasts regarded the matter, with "studies". In April, 1828, Stow opened an infant school in which also he trained a few teachers, men and women. From this small beginning was evolved the Glasgow Normal Seminary, opened in 1836, the first of its kind in Great Britain. From the outset the seminary trained but did not educate teachers; its founder protested against the English training colleges because of their mixing general education with technical instruction, maintaining that these were distinct things and should be kept distinct. It took England nearly a century before its Board of Education adopted that view and put it into practice. Stow was equally opposed to the monitorial system, to the employment of pupil teachers and to the English Revised Code of 1862. History has justified him on all these counts. In 1840, when Kay-Shuttleworth and Tufnell were planning the first English training school, they visited the Glasgow Normal Seminary, and from it they took the first tutors for their normal school at Battersea. At a little later time, students were sent from England to be trained under Stow; the Wesleyan body before it acquired its own training institutions regularly sent its intending teachers to the Glasgow seminary. In the second half of the nineteenth century the works of John Gill (1818–1910), a sometime Glasgow student, were the standard manuals of method and of educational ideas which formed the professional reading of elementary school teachers not only in Great Britain but in the Colonies. In ways such as these David Stow exercised an incalculable influence upon the conduct of English elementary schools long after his death.

It is therefore expedient to say something of the "training system". In 1831 a small tract, *Physical and Moral Training*, set out Stow's ideas as they then were. This became a larger work, *The Training System in the Glasgow Normal Seminary* (new edn. 1840), which in its turn was transformed into *The Training System of Education*, of which an eleventh edition appeared in 1859. The aim óf religious and moral education as here described is the formation of character; its most powerful agency is the good family, since in the family sympathy and real life are necessarily to be found. A catch-phrase of the training system was "the sympathy of numbers", a phrase which sometimes misled Stow and his followers. Stow had noted that public opinion amongst the very poor in large industrial centres sometimes made for evil; he desired to create a better opinion and to support it by the sympathy of numbers. What the modern psychologist calls by the derogatory name, "the herd instinct", Stow tried to apply to the simultaneous acquisition of knowledge by large numbers of children seated together on galleries, an essential structure of schools conducted under his system. The teacher of a class, numbering it might be 200 children, addressed to them an ellipsis, and then awaited the "missing word" which completed the imperfect sentence, and so answered his pretended question. Stow relied upon the sympathy of numbers to ensure that all the 200 would simultaneously reply with the right word or words. He does not seem to have realized that the educational value of the response was in inverse proportion to the unanimity: only the very obvious could be expected. In brief, the question was not worth putting except as an occasional "shake-up" to a lethargic class. Yet Stow knew the danger of a merely verbal knowledge. Learning, he insisted, is not cramming but doing. "What we mean by training is causing children *to do*, whether doing be an exercise of the head, the heart or the hand." To secure understanding and not mere memorizing, Stow's trainers became uncannily expert in what they called "picturing out", that is, drawing pictures in words, a device which they did not confine to plain narrative, but used also to explain texts of Scripture, sometimes of an abstruse nature. Abstract ideas were always so explained. A fault of the system was the excessive use of oral teaching, a fault neither peculiar to the system nor extinct at the present day. Stow was of the opinion that "the Master is the best book".

The playground with its garden borders for work, its "circular swing" or giant stride, and open space for play was indispensable to the training system. This was the field of moral training; the master noted the characteristic behaviour of the several children and traits of good or bad conduct were made the test for a lesson given to all on their return to the schoolroom. Here in what Stow called "the uncovered school" habits and principles of conduct could be formed and developed in a way and to an extent not feasible in the less unrestrained intercourse of the schoolroom. Stow was as much alive to the necessity of controlling the habits of the young as were Aristotle or John Locke.

"It is imagined by some that infants can learn nothing. Certainly they cannot learn Greek, but they can learn evil." In spite of what may be called the mass methods of his system, Stow was not forgetful of the claims of individuality and to those claims his "trainers" were taught to attend in the duties of the uncovered school. Stow notes how early the germs of character appear. Great numbers of wooden "bricks" lay in the playground for use by the children in "building" as part of their spontaneous play. He observed that some children were satisfied to be barrow-men day after day, serving others who must be builders or nothing, whilst yet others played the architect. Stow's use of these bricks is a point to remember; a contemporary print of an early English infant school shows a playground with children building with wooden blocks.[1] At this date Froebel was unknown in this country; his "gifts" and "occupations", if then invented, were not part of the English or Scotch teachers' apparatus or art.

So convinced was Dr Kay[2] of the necessity to create a corps of qualified trained teachers that he refused to be rebuffed by the failure of the Committee of Council to institute its national normal school in 1839. What he could not achieve as secretary of the Committee he determined to attempt as a private person. When assistant Poor Law commissioner (1835–9) he had had to face the problem of the education of pauper children; as the result of that experience he initiated a plan of apprenticing promising boys to the workhouse schoolmasters, the plan from which the pupil-teacher system of 1846 was evolved. In January, 1840, he and his friend, Carleton Tufnell, took a number of boys from the Poor Law school at Norwood to be trained as teachers in an old manor house by the Thames at Battersea; to these boys were added a few young men sent by private patrons. This was the first English training school or training college, as the term afterwards ran; Dr Kay, its first principal, had studied the plans for educating poor children and for the professional preparation of their teachers as practised in Holland, Prussia, Saxony, France and Switzerland. The "Training School at Battersea" was modelled upon the normal schools of the last, more especially perhaps upon that of Kreuzlingen on the Lake of Constance, of which Wehrli was rector, a very frugally

---

[1] Reproduced in C. Birchenough's *History of Elementary Education in England and Wales* (1914), p. 238.
[2] By royal licence of February 24th, 1842, he took the name of Shuttleworth.

conducted establishment in which the rule of life was hard work and hard living. Twenty years later Herbert Spencer condemned on personal observation a similar regimen which was then being followed by an unnamed English training college.[1]

The Battersea course was planned to run through three years, including general education and technical instruction and training, the necessary practice being afforded in the "village school"; education and training went on concurrently. Kay and Tufnell were assisted by a few private persons in meeting the cost and maintenance of the institution; but in November, 1842, the Committee of Council included in its Parliamentary estimate a vote of £1000 and in 1843 one of £2200 towards the expenses of establishing and enlarging "the schools for the training of parochial schoolmasters at Battersea". Within some three years the purpose of training Poor Law teachers had given place to the more general one of preparing for their office the teachers in elementary schools.

The upkeep of the training school proved too onerous for Kay and his supporters, and at the close of 1843 its management was transferred, with the concurrence of the Committee of Council, to the National Society. At that date it was not the only such institution, the number of training colleges being considerably increased after 1843 and the failure of Sir James Graham's Bill in that year. The course of training varied in length at different colleges between eighteen months and three or even four years.

The Committee of Council took another short step in the direction from which it had been diverted in 1839. A "school of method", at first held in Exeter Hall, London, and later in St Martin's Lane, gave lectures on teaching to teachers and to others interested in music and drawing. These courses were apparently maintained by the fees of the pupils and the more or less gratuitous services of the lecturers; but the history of this school of method is obscure. Most of the particulars furnished by Kay-Shuttleworth relate to Hullah's singing classes only;[2] we are not informed as to where the teachers who attended came from, but there was a close association between the school and Battersea, of which Kay remained principal till the close of 1843,[3]

[1] H. Spencer, *Education*, chp. iv.
[2] Kay-Shuttleworth, *Four Periods*, pp. 414, 417.
[3] Frank Smith, *Life and Work of Sir James Kay-Shuttleworth*, p. 121.

while he also held the post of secretary to the Committee of Council. An amusing illustration of a national foible is seen in the choice of the model methods proposed to teachers by the Exeter Hall lecturers. Hand-writing was to be taught on the method of Mulhäuser of Geneva, music on that of Wilhem of Paris, model-drawing on that of Dupuis, another Parisian; arithmetic followed the method of Pestalozzi. Of course all these exotics are now antiquarian curiosities only.

The reports made to the Committee of Council by its newly-appointed inspectors, although not wanting in terms of encouragement, yet revealed defective premises, deficiency of apparatus, and teachers, rarely competent, assisted by what Kay-Shuttleworth in private corre-spondence called "the monitorial humbug". The voluntary system was financially at least unable to cope with the requirements of popular education on a truly national scale; and from its earliest days it had been the policy, though not the avowed policy, of the Committee of Council to supersede the voluntary system. "I understood your lordship's Government to determine in 1839", Kay-Shuttleworth wrote to Lord John Russell on April 30th, 1843, "to assert the claims of the civil power to control the education of the country".[1] Not-withstanding the rebuffs which the Committee experienced in its early days, the Committee's secretary did not cease to meditate measures by which effect might be given to its policy as against the voluntary system. In 1843 he was contemplating the institution of apprenticeship to the business of school-teaching; in the next year he was privately urging that an Address to the Queen be moved in the House of Com-mons, lamenting the lack of "proper schoolmasters" and of "means to render the profession honourable".[2] From the sequence of events it would appear that in the spring of 1846, when the Conservative Government was making very heavy weather and an early accession of the Whigs to office seemed probable, Kay-Shuttleworth and Dr W. F. Hook, then Vicar of Leeds, were acting in concert with the two-fold object of replacing the voluntary system by a State system of secular instruction and of building up a corps of State teachers.[3]

The result was that on June 1st, 1846, Dr Hook published a pamphlet which was evidently intended to test public feeling; it took the form

---

[1] Frank Smith, *op. cit.* p. 148.
[2] F. Smith, *op. cit.* pp. 163 f, 170 f.
[3] Compare F. Smith, *op. cit.* pp. 174–9

of a letter to Connop Thirlwall,[1] Bishop of St David's, entitled *On the means of rendering more efficient the education of the people*. The pamphlet aroused many opponents and supporters; within a very short time it reached the fourth edition. Its main themes were first, a proposal to make the popular schools wholly secular in so far as they were Government-aided, with arrangements for separate denominational religious instruction by special teachers, clerical or lay; and, second, the creation of a body of teachers who should virtually be civil servants of the Crown. This teaching corps was to be developed through a five years' apprenticeship, the novices being called "pupil teachers"; masters and mistresses were to receive payment direct from Government in respect of the instruction of such apprentices as were individually indentured to them, the stipends of the apprentices also being drawn from the same Government central fund. The money necessary for the maintenance of the schools was to come from Government grants and from county rates, each county having its board of management to administer the schools within its area. The school books would be selected or prepared under the direction of the Committee of Council.

Hook drew a depressing picture of schools and schoolmasters as they then were, and he denied the spiritual value of most of the religious instruction then being given. He suggested that Government "should establish a board of examiners without a diploma from whom no master should ever be appointed to a Government school"; admission to the examination was to be conditional upon attendance at a normal school for at least two years. Let the Churches, he said, continue to make themselves responsible for maintaining teachers' training colleges, and for the religious education of the children; but literary and scientific education, otherwise "secular" education, should be solely under the direction of the State. To have proposed that the various religious bodies should be invited to continue to train teachers, who would pass from denominational colleges direct to a purely secular State-maintained service, is less a token of Hook's impracticability than a sign of the haste and the animus with which his letter was written. Indeed, he naïvely reveals what was in his mind. "If it be objected that neither Churchmen nor Dissenters would be inclined to maintain their normal schools under such an arrangement, I can only say, let the experiment be first made, and, if it fail, then the Government might undertake

[1] See Chapter III above.

the support of normal as well as primary schools" (p. 65). This was, in truth, "to assert the claims of the civil power to control the education of the country".

The significance of Hook's *Letter* was appreciated at once by the "voluntaryists". The secretary of the London Diocesan Board of Education (Richard Burgess), in *A Letter to the Revd. W. F. Hook, Vicar of Leeds* (July 18th, 1846), denied the validity of Hook's figures and the conclusions which he based upon them; under the voluntary principle the shortage of schools was not so serious as Hook inferred from erroneous statistics, and the existing schools were improving in character. Incidentally, Burgess puts the average length of school life in the elementary schools throughout the country at eighteen months, and at an even shorter period in the large towns and the manufacturing districts; "the average cost of each scholar all over England is eleven shillings and twopence *per annum*", two-fifths being paid by the children's pence. "A sum not falling short of £250,000 is at this time annually supplied by the members of the Church."

But the most forcible protest against Dr Hook's scheme came from the Dissenting side. In a series of twelve "Letters to the Right Hon. Lord John Russell, First Lord of the Treasury, on State Education", which ranged in date from July 24th to October 16th, 1846, Edward Baines, proprietor of the *Leeds Mercury*, and at one time M.P. for Leeds, made a vigorous defence of the voluntary system. He neither addressed the Vicar of Leeds, nor his old friend and fellow-Nonconformist, Kay-Shuttleworth, but directed his criticisms to Lord John Russell, who had become Prime Minister since Hook's pamphlet had appeared. The foundation principle of these "Letters" is that it is no function of a Government to educate the people. Baines denies, too, that there was any need for the State's intervention in any form, the denial extending to the annual Parliamentary grants of 1833 and onwards. He calls detailed attention to the achievements of voluntaryism in the many educational institutions of all grades with which the characteristic self-help of the English people had covered, and continued to cover, the country. There was reason to believe that education would not be more efficient under Government direction. "The tendency of all things committed to Government is to become stagnant, frozen, bound in chains which it requires a Hercules to break. Is not this the very genius of Downing Street, and Somerset House?...At first, infinite diligence, excellent arrangements and the most charming annual reports. By and by, stiffness, formality and indifference. Ere long a positive hostility to all reform, complaint or disturbance." What reception would the Government office accord to a Lancaster, a Pestalozzi, a Fellenberg, a Robert Raikes, a Wilderspin, or a David Stow? "All experience is belied if they would not be discountenanced" (pp. 59–61). Religious and secular education ought not to be divorced, because religion is not a "subject" but "an all-pervading principle" which cannot be shut out from secular instruction. The popular schools are not "for the teaching of mathematics, chemistry or other abstract study, but mainly for the rearing of thought and moulding of character."

The Continental systems are not old enough to allow us to profit from their example, neither are they so successful as their English admirers report. They are compulsory, are administered in the interest of the Governments and in consequence are hostile to freedom. All this is particularly true of Prussia, the *Kulturstaat* and exemplar in educational administration. Lord John is reminded that by an "invariable law", when the public purse is open, the private purse shuts; State education is destructive of voluntary education. Moreover, should the State supersede the voluntaryists, "Englishmen would then find that they had been seduced into a surrender of the first prerogative of freemen and had committed the training and keeping of their souls to a set of official Mandarins" who "would issue Chinese edicts from Downing Street" (p. 119). A broad hint is administered to the Prime Minister that he will lose old and tried political friends if this policy is adopted.

But when these words were penned the first public step towards that policy had been taken. The Committee of Council by Minute of August 25th, 1846, resolved to appoint three additional inspectors of schools, to institute a scheme of apprenticeship for teachers together with regulations for the instruction and examination of the apprentices and the payment of annual grants to the masters who instructed them. It was also resolved that small gratuities be annually distributed to schoolmasters distinguished by zeal and success. It was also deemed "expedient to make provision in certain cases by a retiring pension for schoolmasters and schoolmistresses who, after a certain length of service, may appear entitled to such provision". These resolutions were elaborated into a matured scheme in Minutes of December 21st,

1846, which did not displace the voluntaryists—Kay-Shuttleworth unkindly quoted "political circles" as describing Hook's scheme as "impracticable"[1]—but began in a very practical way to create a professional body of teachers. Boys and girls of at least thirteen years of age and of good moral character were to be indentured for five years as apprentices to head teachers, provided that these boys and girls showed capacity to teach and passed a very elementary examination. A schedule of studies and of annual examinations set forth the following: arithmetic, English grammar, composition and history, geography, Scripture and religious knowledge, vocal music, teaching, school method and organization. To these were added, in the case of boys, algebra, mensuration, surveying and levelling, the elements of mechanics. Grants would be made from Government direct to the instructors of these "pupil teachers"; the rate of pay would be increased in cases where the masters had taught their apprentices gardening or a mechanical art, and where the mistresses similarly gave instruction in sewing and in cutting-out, in knitting, cooking or in laundry work. These December Minutes of 1846 offered to assist school managers who were prepared to add to their premises, "field-gardens, workshops for trades, school-kitchens and wash-houses"; the manual instruction which might be given to the pupil teachers was proposed with an eye to staffing the "schools of industry" thus constituted.

On completion of the apprenticeship, pupil teachers were to be admissible to a competitive examination, the successful candidates, or "Queen's Scholars", being awarded exhibitions of £20–30, to be held for three years or less at a normal school. Certificates were to be awarded on examination at the end of one, two or three years' training, the successful Queen's Scholars becoming certified teachers. Untrained teachers were to be admissible to the Acting Teachers' Certificate Examination, success in which conferred the same standing. The first Certificate Examination of the Committee of Council was held in December, 1847. A further step in the institution of a teaching corps under the control and, in a measure, in the employ of the Council was taken by the decision to pay direct to the masters an augmentation of salary varying from £15 to £30 per annum, according to the duration (one, two or three years) of the master's training. The payment was to depend on the school managers providing a house rent free and paying

[1] *Four Periods*, p. 506.

a salary of at least twice as much as the augmentation payment from the Council. Mistresses were to receive two-thirds of these emoluments. In cases of disablement by age or infirmity after fifteen years' service a teacher might be awarded by the Committee of Council a pension, not exceeding two-thirds of the pensioner's average salary and emoluments.

At the date of these Minutes, Holland had long possessed in its primary schools a body of trained teachers, masters, assistant masters and apprentices; the last continued their education under their several masters and learned their art through its daily practice in school. By a law passed in 1806 the Dutch Government established an examination for intending teachers and an inspectorate for schools which became a most important instrument in developing a national system.[1] This Dutch scheme was familiar to Kay-Shuttleworth who has written more than one brief account of it in his *Four Periods of Public Education*, and it is clear that he bore it in mind when meditating the policy which found expression in the Minutes of 1846. By direction of the Committee of Council he wrote "an explanation" of those Minutes under the title *The School in its Relations to the State, the Church and the Congregation* (1847). In this anonymous work he expressed the belief that "combined education", the plan by which the State supervised secular instruction only, leaving religious instruction to the religious bodies, a plan carried out in the Dutch schools since 1806, was one of the causes which brought about the revolution of 1830 and the separation into the two distinct kingdoms of Holland and Belgium.[2] He attributed a share in that upheaval to the hostility of the Belgian clergy to "combined education"; yet it was that form of State action which he and Lord John Russell desired to introduce into Great Britain and which Hook's pamphlet was intended to facilitate. The opposition of Church and Dissent made the plan impossible in the English elementary school; but partial effect was given to it in the secular and undenominational Queen's Colleges of Belfast, Cork and Galway founded by Peel's Government in 1845 and opened during Russell's Administration in 1849. These Colleges, neither separately nor combined in the Queen's University of 1850, really solved their special problem, the religious difficulty.

[1] *Special Reports on Educational Subjects* (1902), vol. VIII, p. 313.
[2] *Four Periods*, pp. 450 f; *Special Reports*, vol. VIII, p. 317.

In spite of opposition the Committee of Council adhered to its belief that "voluntary efforts for the education of the people" were of necessity inadequate, and that the business was "too vast or too complicated or too important to be entrusted to voluntary associations" —opinions which the secretary inserted in the *apologia* of 1847, *The School*, etc. The Committee was engaged during 1846–7 in framing trust deeds adaptable to the various conditions of "National", "British", Wesleyan and Roman Catholic schools. Every school receiving Government aid must be governed by an instrument of this kind which in all cases required a considerable lay element in the managing committees; provision must be made for religious instruction and the schools must accept Government inspection. These "management clauses" were deemed objectionable by the National Society, at whose annual meetings for several years they were subjects of discussion. Suspicion was perhaps not unnatural in Churchmen when it was remembered that the very energetic secretary of the Committee of Council was a Nonconformist and that the then Prime Minister, Lord John Russell, had been and remained as long as he lived an active supporter of the British and Foreign School Society. The steadily growing participation of the State in public education is reflected by the rise in the annual Parliamentary grant to elementary schools during the period under consideration. In 1839 this stood at £30,000; in 1842 it was increased by £10,000, which was also the sum voted in 1844, while in the intervening year it reached £50,000. In 1845 the amount was £75,000, which was raised to £100,000 in 1846, 1847; from 1848 to 1850 the yearly vote was £125,000.[1] Sir James Kay-Shuttleworth ceased to be the secretary of the Committee of Council in 1849.

Thomas Carlyle (1795–1881) was an implacable enemy of the prevalent utilitarianism, whose ideal he satirized as being the maximum quantity of "hog's wash"; he was for ever insisting that there were "eternal verities" which no measures of expediency and no regard for popular clamour or material advantage could set aside. He voiced the opposition to most of the political, economic and social cure-alls of his time, and he had in his character of "the sage of Chelsea" a great following down to the day of his death. Although on quitting the university he had begun life as a schoolmaster, he expressed no opinions at any great length upon education; yet the subject was implicit in

[1] *Special Reports on Educational Subjects* (1898), vol. II, p. 524.

almost everything that he wrote. The key to his conception of national education lies in such a phrase as this from *Sartor Resartus* (1833): "All prosperity begins in obedience; obedience is an universal duty and destiny; wherein whoso will not bend must break". In the *Inaugural Address* which in 1866 he delivered as Lord Rector of the University of Edinburgh, he committed himself to the untruth that "the true university of our days is a collection of books". He had made *Sartor* more wisely declare that mind grows "like a spirit by mysterious contact of spirit". "My teachers", says Teufelsdröckh, "were hide-bound pedants, without knowledge of man's nature, or of boys'; or of aught save their lexicons and quarterly account-books. Innumerable dead Vocables (no dead Language, for they themselves knew no Language) they crammed into us, and called it fostering the growth of mind. How can an inanimate mechanical Gerund-grinder, the like of whom will, in a subsequent century, be manufactured at Nürnberg out of wood and leather, foster the growth of anything, much more of Mind, which grows, not like a vegetable (by having its roots littered with etymological compost) but like a spirit, by mysterious contact of spirit, Thought kindling itself at the fire of living Thought? How shall *he* give kindling in whose inward man there is no live coal, but all is burnt-out to a dead grammatical cinder? The Hinterschlag Professors knew syntax enough; and of the human soul thus much: that it had a faculty called Memory, and could be acted-on through the muscular integument by appliance of birch-rods. Alas! so is it everywhere, so will it ever be; till the Hodman is discharged or reduced to hod-bearing; and an Architect is hired, and on all hands fitly encouraged; till communities and individuals discover, not without surprise, that fashioning the souls of a generation by Knowledge can rank on a level with blowing their bodies to pieces by Gunpowder; that with Generals and Field Marshals for killing, there should be world-honoured Dignitaries and, were it possible, true God-ordained priests for teaching."

From generalities such as these the events of the late 'thirties' and early 'forties' brought Carlyle to the utterance of more explicit, concrete opinions. In *Chartism* (1839) two "great things" are said to be in "all thinking heads in England...Universal Education is the first great thing we mean; general Emigration is the second". As to education, its purpose is to humanize; a man uneducated is a man mutilated—language which recalls Adam Smith. "Who would suppose that Education were a thing which had to be advocated on the ground of local expediency, or indeed on any ground? As if it stood not on the basis of everlasting duty, as a prime necessity of man. It is a thing that should need no advocating; much as it does actually need. To impart the gift of thinking to those who cannot think, and yet who could in that case think: this, one would imagine, was the first function a government had to set about discharging. Were it not a cruel thing to see, in any province of an empire, the inhabitants living all mutilated in their limbs, each strong man with his right hand lamed? How much crueller to find the strong soul, with its eyes still sealed, its eyes extinct so that it sees not! Sight has come into the world, but to this poor peasant it has come in vain."

Education, then, should be a national service directed by Government; and it should include religion. "For in very truth how can Religion be divorced from Education? An irreverent knowledge is no knowledge; may be a development of the logical or other handicraft faculty inward or outward; but is no culture of the soul of man." It cannot be "taught" by institutions or by their apparatus of formularies. "To 'teach' religion, the first thing needful, and also the last and the only thing, is finding of a man who *has* religion. All else follows from this." It is an infection, an inspiration, not the absorption of propositions. But Government or its official representatives are not capable of this; such teaching must be left alone by the State which must confine itself to the "Alphabetic Letters", teaching all its members to read and write, a task not to be obstructed by "Churchism" or "Dissenterism". It is not at all clear whether these 'isms have any part to play in the national system as Carlyle envisages it, except a negative one. "Reconcile yourselves to the Alphabet or depart elsewhither!" Presumably the religious bodies are to be entrusted with the care of "that last priceless element by which education becomes perfect"; but Carlyle is evidently doubtful about their success. His emphatic assertion of the premier place of religion in education notwithstanding, he gives no support whatever to the "voluntaryists"; Lord John Russell, Kay-Shuttleworth and the Committee of Council generally must have seen in him an ally.

Carlyle deprecates the advocacy of public education on the ground of local expediency. But that reason for action was not absent from his mind. "These Twenty-four million labouring men, if their affairs remain unregulated, chaotic, will burn ricks and mills; reduce us, themselves and the world into ashes and ruin. Simply their affairs cannot remain unregulated, chaotic; but must be regulated, brought into some kind of order." This police-motive reappeared in *Past and Present* while Sir James Graham's Factory Bill of 1843 was as yet not rejected by the Noncomformist interest. "This one Bill, which lies yet unenacted, a right Education Bill, is not this of itself the sure parent of innumerable wise Bills—wise regulations, practical methods and proposals, generally ripening towards the state of Bills? To irradiate with intelligence, that is to say, with order, arrangement and all blessedness the Chaotic Unintelligent: how, except by educating, *can* you accomplish this? That thought, reflection, articulate utterance and understanding be awakened in these individual million heads which are the atoms of your Chaos; there is no other way of illuminating any Chaos. The sum-total of intelligence that is formed in it determines the extent of order that is possible for your Chaos—the feasibility and rationality of what your Chaos will dimly demand from you, and will gladly obey when proposed by you. It is an exact equation; the one accurately measures the other. If the whole English people, during these 'twenty years of respite' be not educated with at least schoolmaster's educating, a tremendous responsibility before God and men will rest somewhere! How dare any man, especially a man calling himself minister of God, stand up in any Parliament or place, under any pretext or delusion, and for a day or an hour forbid God's light to come into the world, and bid the Devil's Darkness continue in it one hour more! For all light and science, under all shapes, in all degrees of perfection, is of God; all darkness, nescience, is of the Enemy of God. 'The schoolmaster's creed is somewhat awry?' Yes, I have found few creeds entirely correct; few light-beams shining white, pure of admixture; but of all creeds and religions now or ever before known, was not that of thoughtless, thriftless Animalism, of Distilled Gin, and Stupor and Despair unspeakably the least orthodox? We will exchange *it* even with Paganism, with Fetishism; and, on the whole, must exchange it with something. An effective Teaching Service I do consider there must be; some Education Secretary, Captain-General of Teachers who will actually contrive to get us *taught*."

The novels of Disraeli (*Sybil, or the Two Nations*, 1845) and the *Mary*

Barton (1848) of Mrs Gaskell must be reckoned amongst the forces which, in the decade 1840–50, made for amendment in the circumstances of the working classes. In a very real sense such books educated the English people since they touched the public conscience. They put *laisser faire* on trial and questioned the worth of utilitarianism as it had been taught by Bentham and James Mill.

But the fiscal revolution of 1846, the abolition of the Corn Law and the introduction of Free Trade, was a logical consequence of the individualism of the utilitarian philosophy; and coincidentally with this change an era of commercial and industrial expansion began. The earlier improvements in transport were now followed by their natural effects. With more regular employment and an increased purchasing power of wages the conditions of working-class life changed for the better; the co-operative movement expanded and trade unionism developed the "friendly society" side of its operations. The first and terribly needed Public Health Act was passed in 1848 largely owing to the untiring advocacy of Edwin Chadwick. The years between 1850 and 1870 were a time of general prosperity in England, during which public interest in education was displayed on a scale hitherto unprecedented.

After 1846 the principle that the State should supervise public education and aid it by money grants met with ever-increasing agreement; but it was commonly denied that public instruction ought to rank as a public service from which all might directly benefit. The old belief persisted that such instruction was merely a charitable relief to "the labouring poor", as the phrase ran. The practical questions now requiring solution were, how and to what extent public supervision should be exercised. These questions formed the educational politics of 1850–70. Hitherto the popular schools had been supported by voluntary subscriptions and by grants from the taxes. During these twenty years the much-disputed question was whether resort should be made to a third source, the local rates. Rate aid of course implied a responsibility in the local communities for the local schools; and many of these local populations were without any but the vaguest forms of local government. The Municipal Corporations Act of 1835 had conferred the municipal franchise on ratepayers and had made great reforms possible in the administration of towns; but there seems to have been a fairly general agreement that town councils were too "political", that is, partisan, to be entrusted with the oversight of education. The counties, that is, the rural areas, were governed by magistrates acting in quarter sessions, petty sessions or individually; democratic feeling was sufficiently strong to forbid the notion that education should be administered from the magistrates' bench. It was not until an Act of 1888, taking effect in the following year, created County and County Borough Councils, that local government, urban and rural, was based upon a more democratic franchise.

Opinion was gravely divided during 1850–70 as to whether local educational responsibility should be discharged through denominational schools in which a conscience clause was enforced, or in free, secular schools supported by the rates. The latter, in so far as it meant secular education, was the opinion of the minority. The objection to the denominational solution was that members of the community who would be called upon to pay the rate were deeply divided in matters of religious belief. Consequently A would be paying for the teaching of B's children doctrines which A himself disapproved; B, C, and the rest of the denominational alphabet would be in like case. This was the standing grievance, in another form, of the church rate which was paid by all ratepayers until its abolition in 1868. The odium attached to that impost was of course attached to a proposal to give rates to denominational schools. That is to say, the question of rate aid was the religious question; and a conscience clause did nothing to solve it.

The conflicting opinions were championed by societies like the London Committee of Friends of Voluntary Schools, the Manchester and Salford School Committee, and, opposing these in the interest of secular instruction only, the National Public Schools Association and the Lancashire Public Schools Association. Their principles were embodied in Bills and rejected by the House of Commons between 1851 and 1854; from 1853 to 1868 a series of Bills, some being Government measures, some only formally private, occupied the attention of Parliament. While none of them became law, most of them contributed to the ideas upon which the Act of 1870 was constructed. It will be sufficient to indicate the principles and projects which these apparently abortive measures introduced to the consideration of the country, but which eventually found their way into legislation. It being assumed that the schools should be under the control of local committees, it was debated whether the members of these committees should be elected or nominated; further, whether the rates should be allocated to schools under denominational control, the system of "rate aid", or whether they should be restricted to providing schools. The conscience clause and the limits to its advantageous use also were much discussed.

Rate aid raised the very contentious question, What part, if any, should the rating authority take in managing the denominational school? In the debate on Sir John Pakington's Education (No. 2) Bill of March, 1855, it was said by one member that rate-supported and voluntary schools cannot co-exist and that rate aid would lead inevitably to the destruction of the schools of the religious communions—a dictum largely borne out by twentieth-century experience of the working of the 1902 Act. But the supporters of the voluntary principle were forced to recognize that the financial demands of public instruction could not be satisfied by free-will offerings. When introducing his Bill, Pakington asserted that "by the voluntary principle alone we cannot educate the people of this country as they ought to be educated; you can no more do it than you can carry on a great war[1] or defray all the annual expenses of Government by a voluntary contribution instead of taxation. We cannot go on as we are. The voluntary system has broken down. It is harassing and vexatious, and the only legitimate mode in which you can provide education for the people is by calling on the people to contribute a rate for it". The comparison of the requirements of national instruction with those of the Armed Forces and the Civil Service is significant. However unmixed the intention to legislate only for "the labouring poor", the logical issue of a measure so introduced was the institution of an educational service whose operations would not be confined to any one section of the community. In other words, the Bill admitted a national responsibility in that respect; yet Pakington's Bill was permissive only, its adoption depending upon the will of the particular borough council or Poor Law union. The Free School Bill, introduced a fortnight later than "No. 2", implied the responsibility of all localities for secular instruction only. It also proposed a Board of Public Instruction for England and Wales (anticipating the Board of Education Act of 1899), one of whose duties should be a periodical review of popular instruction as it existed

---

[1] The Crimean War lasted from March, 1854, to March, 1856; the twelve months' siege of Sebastopol was in progress while Pakington was speaking.

at home and abroad, a scheme which was realized in 1896 by the formation of the Office of Special Inquiries and Reports, under the Education Department.

Early in April, 1853, an important change was introduced into the mode of allocating the Government subvention. The Capitation Minute offered a grant varying from three to six shillings per head on condition that the income from other sources amounted to twelve (in girls' schools) or fourteen shillings (in boys' schools), that attendance reached 192 days a year per scholar, that a Certificated Teacher was employed and that three-fourths of the scholars passed an examination graded apparently according to three age groups, 7–9, 9–11, 11–13. Premises and apparatus might also come under review. The benefit of this Minute was at first confined to "agricultural districts and incorporated towns not containing more than 5,000 inhabitants"; but in January, 1856, it was extended to all parts of England and Wales, urban as well as rural. The conditions laid down were of course regarded as at least practicable; they imply a great advance since 1833 in the length of school life, the standard of attainment and the material circumstances of the school building.

Less than a week after the passage of this Minute Lord John Russell, then a member of Aberdeen's Coalition Ministry of Whigs and Peelites, became sponsor of an Education Bill, one of three rejected in 1853, which amongst other things proposed the establishment of school committees by borough councils. The Bill was part of a big scheme which involved a review of all charitable trusts for the benefit of education, the enlargement of the School of Design, which had been created as part of the Board of Trade in 1836, its transfer as a Science and Art Department to the Committee of Council, and the reform of Oxford and Cambridge in the light of the inquiries then being conducted by the respective Royal Commissions. Of these projected changes only the setting up of the Science and Art Department was immediately (1853) effected; the offspring of the Great Exhibition of 1851, it was appropriately housed in South Kensington.

In the course of the debate on Russell's Bill some remarks were made incidentally by W. Johnson Fox which bore bitter fruit nine years later. An advocate of compulsory, secular education, the member for Oldham expressed the opinion that "to make the application of national grants most conducive to the improvement of education, remuneration should be given, not in reference to the number of children or the mere amount of attendance [an allusion to the Capitation Minute], but in reference to the attainment; that it should be the result of something like an inquiry by the inspectors into what was actually taught. Let all the schools retain their present denominational character if they would, but if they were always rewarded in this way, if the amount were proportioned to the amount of education realised in the school, that would be a stimulus which would operate very strongly indeed towards raising the character of education". The stimulus was applied in 1862, but the result was not the expected one.

Palmerston's Ministry (which succeeded the Coalition of 1852–5) by an Order in Council, February 25th, 1856, established the Education Department to include the education establishment of the Privy Council Office and the Science and Art Department. This new Department thenceforth, till its absorption into the Board of Education at the very end of the century, controlled the fortunes of the public elementary schools. The Lord President of the Council was to be chairman both of this Department and of the Science and Art Department; but as the President was always a peer, the office of Vice-President of the Council was instituted so that the new body should have a responsible representative in the House of Commons, the Vice-President always being a member of the Government at the moment in power. It will be observed that the Education Department was not a Ministry of Education in the Continental sense nor was the Vice-President a Minister of Public Instruction. These foreign terms have never been adopted by England although our newspapers habitually make use of them.

CHAPTER VI

The Workman's Self-Education

The great and fatal defect of the Mechanics' Institutes as places of education for working people lay in the fact that the men and women for whose benefit they were established were too often destitute of a general elementary education. Lectures on scientific topics demanded a background of culture and knowledge which were lacking. All, or nearly all, of the Institutes possessed libraries, some also had tutorial classes; but these agencies could not correct the deficiency. The Institute at Hastings reported that it was "difficult to obtain members from the lowest class of operatives". Lewes found that *elementary* knowledge was "much needed amongst its members". In 1835 at Manchester, out of a membership exceeding 1500 less than 400 were handworkers. At Sheffield, in the following year, of a membership counting 305, the handworkers numbered 250; a year later while the total membership had increased to 527 the number of manual workers had only increased by 7, that is to say that more than half of the members were not mechanics. Everywhere there was a falling off in the attendance at continuous classes as distinct from occasional courses. The number of Mechanics' Institutes in Great Britain in 1850 was 610 with a membership of about 600,000. In that year the Ewart Act made possible the institution of free libraries and local museums maintained by the rates.

The adult education movement throughout the nineteenth century was due to private initiative at a time when the State either accepted only a limited liability for public instruction or else denied that responsibility entirely. Indeed, at the origin of the movement the State, by its treatment of the newspaper press, deliberately hindered such instruction. The Mechanics' Institutes by their individual origin and utilitarian aims were distinctly of their day. Their chief, although not their sole, aim was to make their members more efficient industrially; they aimed at "useful knowledge" in full sympathy with the prevailing philosophy of which their middle-class promoters were the leading exponents.

Beginning in the first quarter of the nineteenth century a different type of adult education appeared, of which the chief supporters were the working men themselves, whether they acted as Chartists, as co-operators or as trade unionists. Following the teaching of Robert Owen, these working-class organizations endeavoured to teach children as well as adults, and much of their teaching was necessarily very elementary. Yet, as their ultimate object was not industrial efficiency but the rights and duties of citizenship, they favoured social and political studies; and these cannot be pursued successfully without reference to the whole range of humanist culture. It is not meant that vital contact was attained in many cases, but that such was the tendency; and in consequence there were notable achievements by men of exceptional character and of ability above the average.

Probably no more striking instances of such outstanding merit are discoverable than those of William Lovett (1800–77), the founder of Chartism, and Thomas Cooper (1805–92), an early, enthusiastic and leading Chartist. Both wrote autobiographies[1] which tell a tale of manful yet pathetic struggles for self-culture in circumstances which might well daunt the bravest and strongest; incidentally these books reveal a desire amongst working men for a type of education of which, in its range, only the minority of men had a vision. Societies of English working men whose purpose was culture were indeed not an entire novelty in the nineteenth century, although there was then a greater stimulus to their formation and increased opportunity for attaining their object. In 1845 the Astronomical Society became the residuary legatee of a "Mathematical Society" which had been founded in Spitalfields in 1717 by artisans and maintained chiefly by them for the greater part of its existence, although at the later date "the artisan element had been extinct for many years".[2] Lovett says that before the year 1826 he had been a member of several "mutual improvement societies", the members of which devoted their funds to the upkeep of collections of books; always an incorrigible talker he had also belonged to more than one debating society. One such, known as "the Liberals", met in Soho twice a week to discuss "literary, political and metaphysical subjects". In the years 1820–4 Cooper joined a draper's assistant named Winks, an unnamed grocer's assistant and one other in conducting at Gainsborough an "Adult school on Sundays for

---

[1] *The life and struggles of William Lovett in pursuit of bread, knowledge and freedom* (1876); *The life of Thomas Cooper written by himself* (1872).

[2] A. de Morgan, *A Budget of Paradoxes*, p. 232.

teaching the poor and utterly uneducated to read". Twenty years later, when Cooper was at the head of the Leicester Chartists, he held an adult Sunday school which was crowded, morning and afternoon, to hear him lecture on English literature, geology, phrenology and teetotalism.

In their young days both men pursued very strenuous courses of study at the cost of great personal sacrifice. Lovett was amongst the first members of the London Mechanics' Institute and attended lectures very regularly. As a schoolmaster in his later years he taught anatomy and physiology, and wrote school books on astronomy, geology and natural history. Whilst a working shoemaker, "never earning more than ten shillings a week", Cooper carried out a comprehensive course of study which included ancient and modern languages and literature, as well as mathematics. Before beginning his shoemaking at 7 a.m. it was his daily practice to study for three or four hours, winter and summer; he read at his frugal breakfast and dinner, and from 8 p.m. was engaged in rote-learning till sheer exhaustion sent him to bed. Luckily he loved trees, flowers, birds, "and above all the silver windings of the Trent", and these were the surroundings of his studies in favourable weather. Yet he often swooned at the end of the day's labours, and broke down seriously before he was three and twenty. In the course of his long life Cooper's studies included Greek, Latin, French, German and Italian; music was his delight. Before he became a journalist (and a Chartist in consequence) he spent nine successful years in Gainsborough and Leicester as the proprietor and principal of private schools.

The teaching and the personality of Robert Owen were very influential amongst working men during the early decades of the nineteenth century, and from New Lanark days some provision for instruction had formed part of his schemes for improving the circumstances of labour. Reading, writing and dancing formed the evening occupations of his mill hands after the day's work was done; the last was regarded as something more than recreation or amusement. "Dancing, music and the military discipline will always be prominent surroundings in a rational system for forming characters", says Owen (*Life*, p. 142). The co-operative societies, most of which were established to give effect to Owen's socialism, included amongst their objects the education of their members and members' children. Lovett asserts that in the first thirty years of the century there were from 400 to 500 of these societies, most of them being short lived. The Birmingham Co-operative Society (established in 1828) maintained a library and a debating club and proposed to arrange concerts and lectures for the members. The Rochdale Society, founded in 1844 and usually regarded, as indeed its full title claimed, to be a pioneer amongst modern co-operative societies, instituted an "Educational Department" which it supported by regular quarterly grants; in 1852 it proposed to give ten per cent. of its profits to the work of this department, but reduced the percentage to two and a half in reluctant obedience to the Government Registrar, who thought the high rate excessive.[1] Some trade unions also supported this policy of education by establishing libraries and mutual improvement societies. The solicitude of the early co-operators for education, particularly for the education of children, is easily understood when it is borne in mind that they were, first and foremost, the champions of the new social and industrial order taught by Owen, wherein a brotherly co-operation was to replace the competition of individualism.

Although public instruction was not one of the "six points" of the Charter of May, 1838, universal education was necessary to the Charter's complete success as understood at least by the "Moral Force Chartists". Manhood suffrage was the root idea of Chartism; moral and social reformation and, more especially, amendment of the manual worker's lot could only come through a political reformation, which would make the Parliamentary franchise universal in respect of men. And, in Lovett's words, "those who possess the power to elect must have knowledge, judgement and moral principle to direct them, before anything worthy of the name of just government or true liberty can be established". The formulation of educational policy was the work of Lovett; it appears in an *Address on Education by the Working Men's Association* (1837), is elaborated in *Chartism*,[2] written during Lovett's

[1] *Final Report, Adult Education Committee* (1919), p. 21, quoting Webb, *Industrial Co-operation*, p. 69. The editor is Miss Catherine Webb.

[2] "*Chartism*; a new organization of the people, embracing a plan for the education and improvement of the people, politically and socially; addressed to the working classes of the United Kingdom, and more especially to the advocates of the rights and liberties of the whole people as set forth in the People's Charter. Written in Warwick Gaol by William Lovett, Cabinet-maker and John Collins, Tool-maker" (2nd edn, 1841).

imprisonment (1839–40) and repeated (1840) in a prospectus of the "National Union of the United Kingdom for the Promoting the Political and Social Improvement of the People".

"Public education ought to be a *right*, a right derivable from society itself, as society implies a union for mutual benefit, and consequently to provide publicly for the security and proper training of all its members." But the function of society's executive should be very strictly limited. "While we are anxious to see a *general* system of education adopted, we have no doubt of the impropriety of yielding such an important duty as the education of our children to any government, and the strongest abhorrence of giving any such power to an irresponsible one", that is, to one not placed in power by universal suffrage. Continental systems, that of Prussia in particular, are "centralizing, State-moulding, knowledge-forcing schemes". Government should build schools; but the provision of teachers, the making of school books, the prescription of methods and of rules of management should be entrusted to local school committees elected by universal suffrage and empowered to strike a rate. There was a difference in the earlier and later statements of policy with reference to the central authority. At first it was suggested that Parliament (itself elected annually) should every three years appoint twelve persons to be a Committee of Public Instruction. The later proposal was the appointment of a "Central Board of Instructors" popularly chosen who should excogitate a scheme of education; when completed the scheme was to be considered by a representative body, each county electing by universal suffrage two of its members. When this second body had passed the scheme, it was to be sent down to the local school committees who might or might not adopt it.

It was further proposed to establish throughout the kingdom "Public Halls or Schools for the People" for the physical, mental, moral and political instruction of children and adults. During the day-time these Public Halls were to be schoolrooms; in the evening they were to be reserved for public lectures on physical, moral and political science, for readings, discussions, musical entertainments and dancing. Two playgrounds were to be attached to each Hall, as well as a pleasure garden, where this addition was practicable. There were to be apartments for teachers, hot and cold baths, a small museum, a laboratory and general workshop "for experiments in science and first principles of the most useful trades". As early as 1837 Lovett and his friends were proposing the erection of "normal or teachers' schools" in different districts; the instruction was to be gratuitous and certificates of having been educated and trained in a normal school were to be required from candidates for appointment as teachers. They regarded the "art of simplifying knowledge" as an essential part of the teacher's training.

The object of the school should be the harmonious development of the physical, moral and intellectual powers of each child, "so as to enable him to enjoy his own existence and to render the greatest amount of benefit to others". A school was to be divided into three sections, one for infants from the age of three to that of six; between six and nine they were to be pupils in the "preparatory school" from which they were to pass to the "high school", remaining there for three years. For pupils above twelve years of age "finishing schools or colleges" were suggested, but these had no place in the scheme of public halls; instruction here also was to be gratuitous. All sincere revolutionaries are optimists and the Chartists were no exception to the rule. It was hoped to enlighten infants as to the why and wherefore of the moral training which they received, to teach the preparatory children moral laws, social and political relations, and to give the boys and girls of the high school, whose ages ranged from nine to twelve, a general knowledge of geology, mineralogy and the most useful applications of social science, physiology, the laws of health and "the outlines of such other sciences as may be useful". Topography, the pursuits and resources of the country, physical and natural phenomena, chemistry and its application in arts and trades also figured in the high school programme. The scheme is as doctrinaire as any sketched by the seventeenth-century methodizers, like whom Lovett was filled with praiseworthy intentions and blind to the evils of smattering. But extravagance was by no means the only feature of Lovett's plan, and extravagance was itself to be checked by the saving clause that the curriculum was to include "every other science" provided it "is suited to the capacity of the scholars". Much of the time of the infants was to be spent in the open air, the children in the sections above the infants were to learn "to express themselves in writing"; all the schools were to be provided with tools and workshops, in suitable circumstances gardening and agriculture were to be learned. The mark of Pestalozzi is visible in the inclusion of "the use and properties of common things" in the preparatory school studies. As to more advanced instruction "the acquisition of living languages should also be preferred to the dead; we do not want to neglect the latter, but to break down the national barriers which tyrants use to foment the evils of wars"—a singularly modern touch, this last! The *Address* of 1837 says that "no particular forms of religion should be taught in the schools". The preference seems to be for purely moral instruction, but the point is not clear; perhaps the vagueness was intentional. Schools were to be both cheap and efficient, the teachers were to be trained for their profession and provided with "a handsome and comfortable subsistence". All this was to be contrived on an income derived from school fees, public money being spent upon buildings alone. Naturally, the proposals of men destitute of administrative experience were vague, doctrinaire and largely impracticable; nevertheless, the Chartists in their educational creed, as in the political "six points" of their Charter, anticipated in a remarkable manner the subsequent course of history.

But to what extent was that educational creed translated immediately into actual fact? In July, 1842, what had been Gate Street Chapel, Holborn, was adapted to the purposes of a "National Hall", that is, for public meetings, concerts, lectures and "classes of different kinds", Lovett, Cooper and W. J. Fox being amongst the lecturers. In the following year a Sunday school was held in the Hall, and for four years Lovett and others instructed children on Sundays in the "three R's", grammar, geography, and "such other kinds of information as it was in the power [of these teachers] to bestow". In 1846 an anonymous donor offered funds for starting a day school; this was established late in 1848, Lovett being its superintendent. The aims of this day school were said to be "to provide for the children of the middle and working classes a sound, secular, useful and moral education" which would prepare them for the business of life and enable them to understand and perform their duties as members of society, "to enable them to diffuse the greatest amount of happiness among their fellow-men". In 1850 the philanthropic William Ellis undertook to introduce into the day school "social science, the science of human well-being". Lovett attached great value to the teaching of anatomy and physiology. How he attained the requisite knowledge apart from reading, he does not say;

but he taught these sciences to teachers and children in the National Hall and, after its collapse, in other schools in which he found employment. Anatomy and physiology were introduced, Lovett thinks in consequence of his example, into the Birkbeck Schools of William Ellis, into University College School, London, and into the School of Design, an off-shoot of the Board of Trade, and the germ of the Science and Art Department. A set of anatomical drawings, Marshall's diagrams, were prepared for the School of Design and long remained standard. In 1851 Lovett's second schoolmaster resigned and Lovett notes that it was difficult to secure for a secular school the services of a *trained* teacher, that is an alumnus of one of the then fairly numerous training colleges; he therefore added the duties of second master to his own.

The National Hall from the beginning was always in financial straits. In 1857 its site was coveted, its would-be rival dispossessed it, its belongings were sold and the society dissolved. Lovett protests with indignation: "Thus after labouring for about fifteen years to establish and uphold this place, did it pass out of our hands to be converted into a gin palace". A school of about 300 children and an institution for "the instruction and improvement of great numbers" of adults gave way to one "for corrupting the rising generation".

A passing reference must be made to the utilitarian philosopher, William Ellis (1800–81)[1], who was associated with Lovett and the National Hall. Ellis regarded careful moral training and instruction in social well-being as the most beneficent tasks open to popular education; attention to health and careful economy in money and material resources were in his view the measures best calculated to improve the labouring man's condition. In support of these opinions he lectured, wrote, opened schools, instructed their teachers and lavished his fortune. After the beginning made in the National Hall, he established his first school on the premises of the London Mechanics' Institution, calling it in honour of the Institution's president the Birkbeck School, a name which was also applied to the other six schools which Ellis maintained in London between 1848 and 1862. His work and his ideas attracted general attention; they so far interested the Prince Consort that Ellis was called upon to give instruction to the children of the Royal Family.

Characteristic of the newer ideal of adult education which was arising at this time was the People's College at Sheffield, initiated by

[1] See E. K. Blyth, *Life of William Ellis* (1889).

the Rev. R. S. Bayley, an Independent minister, who proposed for "youth of the middle and working classes" an education aiming at culture through language and literature, ancient and modern, mathematics, logic, elocution and drawing. From 1842 to 1848, evening classes, taught mainly by Bayley himself, were conducted on these lines, during the first year in a "ghastly, whitewashed, unplastered garret", destitute of conveniences for study. The weekly class fee was ninepence and the pupils included women. Bayley's removal to London threatened to bring his college to an end; but, whatever degree of success or failure had attended his intellectual instruction, he had implanted in his pupils the desire to pursue knowledge independently of himself or any other teacher, and had taught them something of the power of a corporate spirit. Sixteen of these lads and young men determined in the middle of October, 1848, to give the People's College a fresh start; before the end of the month there were nearly 200 students, and at the close of the first year's work 426 men and 104 women had been enrolled. The institution was self-supporting and self-governing, the teaching, under a monitorial system, was largely, if not entirely, in the hands of the members themselves. Occasional public lectures were given by outsiders, but they were not suffered to interrupt the routine of the class-work which was carried on from 6.30 to 7.30 on three mornings a week and every evening between 7 and 9.30. In the second year day classes were opened for boys.

Beyond a few necessary books of reference there was no library; available funds were spent upon a collection of scientific instruments. Bayley's curriculum had been in the main humanist; but under the new direction something like a reversion to the ideal of the early Mechanics' Institutions took place. "There was something more required for the artisans of Sheffield than purely mental discipline, however excellent in itself that might be, and that to be really a college for the people, it must include in its classes studies that would have a direct bearing upon the industrial pursuits that distinguish the town." Haywood, an eminent local chemist, gave a course of lectures with these pursuits in view; but the project of an industrial department of the college fell through after his death by accident. In order to secure a standard of attainment and to give a systematic character to the courses, the students were encouraged to become candidates at the examinations of the Society of Arts; in 1856 there was one such candidate, in 1858 of fourteen candidates, twelve took certificates, three in the first class, two of these gaining prizes of £5 in Latin and Roman history and English literature. In 1859, the candidates numbered twenty-three.

During the first ten years of its second establishment the People's College expended £4000, the money of the students themselves, for they stood absolutely by their principle of self-support and self-government. Yet when the sixteen young men began their adventure in 1848 they did not possess a single book nor one farthing with which to buy furniture; "at the first meeting of the Committee the room was illuminated by a halfpenny candle inserted in an earthenware inkstand". The uphill struggle waged by these enthusiasts is reflected in the complaint that "ignorance, deep and general prevailed" and "a pervading apathy on the subject of education seemed to possess the multitude". Even the 530 students of the year 1848–9 maintained an average attendance at the classes of only 135, a little above 25 per cent. As in all similar institutions, the rolls were inflated at the outset by the idle curiosity or want of staying power or of true intellectual interest characteristic of many who soon fell away. When Maurice and his fellow Christian Socialists were planning the Working Men's College, they applied to the People's College of Sheffield for information and advice.[1]

Nottingham also had its People's College, founded in 1846 by George Gill and others with the purpose of ensuring "the mental and moral improvement of the labouring population, clerks, warehousemen and others receiving wages or salaries for their services". Elementary instruction of a general character was given in evening classes and a day school for boys and girls later became a part of the institution.[2]

Chartism came to an abrupt end upon Kennington Common on April 10th, 1848; the fact only stimulated some of the working-man's friends to try other ways than the political of bettering his condition. A small knot of professional men, of whom Frederick Denison Maurice, Charles Kingsley, J. M. Ludlow, Edward Vansittart Neale and Thomas Hughes were prominent, associated themselves under the name of Christian Socialists, choosing the name in order to make clear,

[1] See "An account of the origin and progress of the People's College at Sheffield", by Thomas Rowbotham (one of its leading members) in *The Working Men's College Magazine*, vol. 1, April, May, 1859.

[2] Edith M. Becket, *The History of University College, Nottingham* (1928), p. 13.

as Maurice said, their readiness to combat "the unsocial Christians and the unchristian socialists", their object being "the practical application of Christianity to the purposes of trade and industry". As they saw the matter, the road to amendment lay through a changed economic order and a liberal education for the workman. They were all enthusiastic co-operators of the school which would replace the employer and his wage earners by an association of operative producers combining in their own persons the several positions of manager, foreman, manual worker and profit taker. Following the model of the *associations ouvrières* which in 1849 Ludlow introduced from Paris, the Christian Socialists started some twelve associations of this type, each confined to a single industry and operating in a "self-governing workshop". Lack of discipline and of business experience, or aptitude, together with a lively appreciation of individual profit, soon closed these shops and disbanded the associations. A series of tracts and periodicals, of which *The Christian Socialist* (1850–1) was the chief, was equally short lived. Kingsley's tract denouncing "sweating" (*Cheap Clothes and Nasty*) and his novels *Yeast* (1848) and *Alton Locke* (1850) had the success which may be measured by controversy and bitter opposition.

But while the attempt at economic change failed, the educational policy proved successful and secured permanent results. In the year of the Kennington fiasco the Christian Socialists engaged a mistress to teach infants in rooms in Little Ormond Yard and themselves taught men and boys in these rooms in the evenings. Maurice at this time was Professor of English Literature and Modern History in King's College, London, and he enlisted some of his colleagues as well as young graduates from Oxford and Cambridge in this teaching. A library and reading-room were added in 1851, but the attraction of the scheme proved too great for its accommodation and a "Hall of Association" was built and enlarged premises secured in Castle Street East. Here classes were held in grammar, French, English history, drawing, singing, book-keeping, and lectures were delivered on Shakespeare, Burns, photography, architecture, astronomy, entomology and other subjects suitable for popular discourses.

Yet neither the elementary tutorial classes nor the lectures satisfied the ideal which was shaping itself in Maurice's mind. The titles of the People's *Colleges* of Sheffield and Nottingham struck his imagination. At a meeting held in January, 1854, "a conversation took place concerning the establishment of a People's College in London in connection with the Associations and Mr Vansittart Neale read a letter received from Mr Wilson, secretary of the People's College, Sheffield, as to its origin and history and also the five annual reports of that institution". The following resolution was carried. "That it be referred to the Committee of Teaching and Publication to frame, and so far as they think fit, to carry out a plan for the establishment of a People's College in connection with the Metropolitan Associations."[1] The result of the deliberations of this Committee was the issue in February, 1854, of a twelve-page statement which clearly differentiates the (London) Working Men's College from the working-class organizations which had preceded it.

"Education", the pamphlet declared, "should be regular and organic"; it is not effected by "miscellaneous lectures or even by classes not related to each other". The teachers, and by degrees the pupils, should form "an organic body", self-governed and self-supported, to which the name, college, should as rightly apply as to University College or King's College. Since the fundamental principle of Christian Socialism was that the operations of trade and industry lie under the moral law, the college is obliged "to regard social, political, or to use a more general phrase, *human* studies as the primary part of our education". Membership of the college was open to the working classes generally, it being a condition of admission that a man could read, write and manipulate the first four rules of arithmetic. An entrance fee of half a crown was to be paid and the fees for courses of instruction varied between that amount and five shillings, the Sunday Bible lessons being free. The first students were limited to males above sixteen years of age, but it was "very desirable that provision should in due time be made for the teaching of boys and females". The teachers were to give their services gratuitously, all tuition fees going to the common fund of the college, for whose reception

[1] See F. J. Furnivall, *Early history of Working Men's College*, 1891, a fifteen-page reprint from *The Working Men's College Magazine*, vol. I, 1859. The committee included several noteworthy men, amongst them Maurice himself, Viscount Goderich, M.P. (afterwards Earl de Grey and Ripon), William Johnson (the Eton master, William Cory, author of *Ionica*), Charles Kingsley, A. Macmillan (the publisher), C. Kegan Paul (then curate of Banbury, afterwards the well-known publisher), John Westlake (then a law-student, afterwards Q.C., and Professor of International Law at Cambridge).

a house had been rented in Red Lion Square. Every great town should have such a college, London required half a dozen at least; the college which it was proposed to institute was meant to serve North London in particular.

Friction had existed for some time between the Principal (Dr Jelf) of King's College and Maurice, who had become Professor of Divinity in 1846; disagreement at length reached the breaking-point and the opinions expressed by Maurice in a volume, *Theological Essays*, which appeared in 1853, led to a charge of heterodoxy and a request for his resignation. He was dismissed from his chair in October of that year. Twelve months later saw him as Principal of the Working Men's College presiding at a public meeting held to inaugurate the institution. On the following evening (that is on October 31st, 1854) the college began its work, not, as had been anticipated, with thirty pupils but with four times that number.

A time-table of lectures was arranged for every evening of the week, including Sunday, when the Principal lectured on St John's Gospel; on Wednesday evenings his subject was "Political terms illustrated by English literature", and on Fridays Shakespeare's *King John* in illustration of English history. Other teachers dealt with arithmetic, algebra, geometry, natural philosophy, astronomy, geography as related to English history (J. S. Brewer), the law of partnership, public health (Walsh and T. Hughes), machines, drawing—the last by John Ruskin, an offer to teach being his response to an invitation to subscribe to the college funds. It had been proposed to hold a singing class on Saturday evenings, but possibly on account of the small number of candidates this class was not held at first. Applicants were referred to "Mr Hullah", then Professor of Music at King's College; in view of what had befallen Maurice in 1853, there is significance in the prominence of King's College professors and lecturers amongst the teachers of the Working Men's College in its early days. A similar rally by his colleagues around Maurice had been equally noticeable a few years earlier in connexion with the establishment of Queen's College.[1]

Early in 1855 an adult school was opened at the Hall of Association under a paid teacher who taught the elementary subjects necessary for admission to the college. In 1856 women's classes were started at the college, but they were "not numerously attended"; the teachers

[1] See Chapter XII below.

were women friends of Maurice and other members of the college council. A girl's school was begun early in 1858. From the beginning it was hoped to effect some kind of association with the universities; in December, 1856, affiliation to the London University opened the university examinations to suitable candidates. In the following year the college moved into the premises in Great Ormond Street which housed it until it removed in 1904 to its present site in Camden Town.

Working Men's Colleges more or less on the London model were set up between 1855 and 1862 in Manchester, Salford, Ancoats, Leicester, Halifax, Liverpool, Wolverhampton, Oxford and Cambridge. As in the case of the Mechanics' Institutes, the insufficiency and ineffectiveness of the primary instruction generally available are reflected in the fact that the manual workers ("the working man" as the phrase is usually understood) did not form the majority of the students of these Working Men's Colleges. Furnivall gives the following table for the London College.

	1854	1855	1856	1857	1858	1859	1860
Operatives	72	101	103	119	109	121	150
Clerks, etc.	73	132	113	151	133	181	246

At Salford in 1858 warehousemen and clerks numbered 79 in a total of 170, while "packers, mill-hands and labourers" were but 14, all told, the rest being made up of small numbers in a variety of trades and 28 described as "miscellaneous". At Manchester in the same year the numbers for the three terms were:

Clerks, book-keepers, warehousemen, shop-keepers, shop-assistants, and teachers		149	135	109
Miscellaneous		24	3	0
Operatives		70	57	54

Furnivall says that when the London College was in process of formation the trade societies committees, that is, the trade union executives, were canvassed for pupils, "but without much success, I fear".

Nevertheless, there existed amongst adults a widespread desire for the schooling which may be obtained from books. In 1850 John Cassell, a self-taught lecturer on teetotalism, began publishing popular works of instruction in London, his *Popular Educator*, the most notable of these, continuing in successive editions to appear in penny weekly numbers for many years after his death in 1865. Edward Baines giving evidence before a Parliamentary committee in 1852 thus testified to

Cassell's early success and the desire amongst working men for education of an advanced kind. "I consider", said Baines, "that Mr John Cassell is doing more at the present time than any other individual to supply the increasing demand of the operative classes for useful knowledge, and in supplying works peculiarly adapted to their circumstances and condition. His popular mode of education is receiving an extended and an extraordinary circulation and is highly estimated by a large number of the operative classes. For a penny per week the working-man is supplied with lessons in grammar, arithmetic, mathematics; in Latin, French and German; and he has had enquiries for lessons in Hebrew and Greek, that the working-man may endeavour to read the Scriptures in the original text. In these penny numbers are also furnished lessons in ancient history, natural history, geology and physiology; and such lessons and such subjects are being entered into by many with great avidity. Mr Cassell has published two volumes of literature by working-men. This work contains essays upon various subjects, such as 'The education of the working classes' by a gardener, 'On the education of taste among the working classes' by a chainmaker, 'The educational apparatus' by a cutter, 'On biography' by a wool-carder, 'The peasant's home' by a labourer, 'Botany' by a working-man's son under fifteen years of age, 'Temperance and intemperance' by a labourer, 'The rise and fall of the Roman Empire' by a workman at a colliery, 'The working women of Britain' by a shoemaker's wife, 'On Geology and atheism' by a dyer, 'On reasoning and logic' by a labourer; and various other subjects, to show that there are those among the operative classes that can both think and write."[1]

In 1855 King's College, London, instituted an Evening Class Department, under that name, to provide systematic or, as Maurice would say, "organic" courses of higher instruction; standards of achievement were laid down and to those men who satisfied the tests the diploma of Associate of the college was awarded.[2] This was at a time when the connexion between the college and the University

---

[1] *Report of Select Committee on the education bills of the Manchester and Salford and National Public Schools Associations* (1852), Q. 2261.

[2] The College held evening classes during the year 1848–9, but they were not continued. See F. J. C. Hearnshaw, *The Centenary History of King's College, London* (1929), p. 195.

of London had become very weak. John Henry Newman, as President of the then newly instituted Catholic University in Dublin, had in the previous year anticipated this step. One of his first official acts was to institute a system of evening lectures, which were soon after suspended; but in, or about 1856, he induced the Academical Senate to make these evening classes statutory and their members eligible for degrees on passing the necessary examinations.[1] In 1854 also the Birmingham and Midland Institute was founded and maintained by subscriptions. Its evening classes attracted students in large numbers and the development of the curriculum, literary and scientific, in response to their demands transformed the Institute in the course of a generation into a people's university.

[1] See "Discipline of the Mind, an Address to the Evening classes, 1858" in *The Idea of a University* (1912 ed.), pp. 480 ff.

CHAPTER VII

The Universities in the Mid-Century

The turn of the economic tide came in 1850, the year which marked the beginning of a long period of commercial and industrial prosperity; the great place occupied by public education in the minds of responsible persons during the years from 1850 to 1870 appears in a series of Royal Commissions and the consequent legislation, or regulation, arising out of them. Oxford and Cambridge were the earliest objects of inquiry; Acts of Parliament followed within the years 1854–6. In 1858, after many failures to legislate on behalf of elementary education, the Newcastle Commission was appointed to consider the subject. It reported in 1861, the year in which the Public Schools, or Clarendon, Commission began an inquiry into the state of the nine Public Schools. This Commission reported in 1864, and in the same year The Schools Inquiry, or Taunton, Commission began its labours on behalf of secondary schools. The Taunton Commission reported in 1867; the Public Schools Act, 1868, and the Endowed Schools Act, 1869, followed. The careful inquiries which these Commissions caused to be made on the Continent and in the United States are evidence of the earnestness and thoroughness with which their task was performed. Both political parties, Liberal and Conservative, were responsible for initiating these measures, but great interest in public education was by no means restricted to Governments; on the contrary, Parliamentary action was stimulated and supported by a volume of public opinion expressed through the discussions and controversies of many influential associations of private citizens. Of course, Parliament possessed the power to affect public education in any or all of its grades; the Royal Commissions of the 'sixties' were signs that it meant to exercise the power. The establishment of a national system appeared to be imminent; yet its consummation was still nearly half a century distant.

The most general conclusion to be drawn from the inquiries of the Commissions is that no grade of instruction, elementary, secondary or university, reached all the persons who stood in need of it. In particular, the majority of the children attending elementary schools ceased attending at, or before, the age of eleven, and the instruction which they received was pronounced to be "too ambitious and superficial"; on the other hand, the defect of secondary school and university teaching lay in narrowness of range.

Nevertheless there was no falling off in the demand for higher education; the causes which had contributed to the establishment of the Universities of London and Durham still operated and with even greater effect, and the demand could not be satisfied by those two institutions. Men were beginning to ask what were Oxford and Cambridge doing for a class, possibly a large class, to whom education in an expensive collegiate life was prohibitive. That the expense of education so conducted debarred men from university education was illustrated in the case of Durham, which in its early years consisted of a single college conducted on the Oxford model. In 1846 Bishop Hatfield's Hall was founded with the object of rendering life in a college much less expensive and its discipline more strict. In four years this hall increased its numbers from nineteen to between fifty and sixty; a year later it had to refuse twenty applicants on the ground that it had no room for them. A second hall, established in 1851, filled all its rooms at once and on its enlargement in the following year its admissions were doubled. This growing demand was not a purely local one; candidates came from other parts of England and from beyond the four seas.[1]

Expense, however, was not the only bar; the mode of government, the distribution of emoluments, the studies and the principles in accordance with which those studies were pursued, all hindered the access to the two ancient Universities of "a class, probably a large class" as the Oxford tutors admitted, "for whose education there was a general demand". A Cambridge degree with its academic privileges, and the entire Oxford career, were reserved for those who could profess membership of the Church of England. It was exceptional for college scholarships and fellowships to be open without restriction to those who could win them by intellectual merit alone. In most cases they were reserved by statute for men who came from particular localities, from particular schools or even from particular families; "founder's kin" was a common title to college emoluments. For centuries, Queen's College, Oxford, took its fellows from Cumberland and Westmorland only. At Pembroke College, in the same University, fellowships of the

[1] *Papers published by the Oxford Tutors' Association* (Oxford, 1853, 1854), Report No. 1, p. 14.

old foundation were mostly open only to members of particular families or, failing them, to former pupils of Abingdon Grammar School. As late as 1850 a would-be benefactor of Magdalen College, Oxford, left £20,000 to found fellowships which were to be reserved for founder's kin, or failing kin, to those bearing the founder's name or to residents in the county of Hereford.[1] The Winchester, Westminster or Eton schoolboys gained their scholarships at school, were transferred to New College and Christ Church, Oxford, or to King's College, Cambridge, respectively, and except through misconduct were sure to succeed to fellowships in due course. The New College and King's College scholars also attained their degrees by the same simple efflux of time.

From the fellows thus chosen in accordance with greatly varying standards were selected, by the heads of their respective societies, the college tutors, those members of the teaching body whose influence upon university education was greatest. Their academic antecedents made it inevitable that the tutors were in a measure specialists in classics and mathematics, as the one or the other had been learned at school and during undergraduate years: there was not sufficient inducement, other than the hope of a college living falling vacant, to retain the fellows in residence long enough to make the work of tutor a profession and a life occupation. Tutors, therefore, were rarely specialists in any strict sense; they not only controlled the teaching but also the examinations which depended upon the teaching. It was to little purpose that the University instituted new professorships or added new optional studies to the ancient. The specialist teaching of the professors, who had been appointed to instruct all members of the University, did not attract the undergraduate desirous of doing well in "Greats" or in the tripos, preparation for which was provided by his non-specialist college tutor, or more frequently by an expensive private "coach". The professors of newly introduced studies had few or no pupils; of the thirty-two Oxford professorships the greater number were very badly paid sinecures. On the other hand, adverse critics asserted that the college tutors were incompetent to teach outside the classical or mathematical routine. Research and learning were at a discount.

[1] *Letter to…Lord John Russell…on the constitutional defects of the University and Colleges of Oxford with Suggestions for a Royal Commission of Inquiry into the Universities by a Member of the Oxford Convocation* [C. A. Row] (London, 1850), p. 35 n.

The same narrowness which made entrance to the University, its studies, degrees and emoluments matters of privilege turned its government into an oligarchy. The Oxford Hebdomadal Board and the Cambridge Caput, both constituted mainly by *ex officio* members, were clerical bodies, pure and simple; a contemporary critic described the Hebdomadal Board as "an organized torpor", and Board and Caput alone had the power of initiating university legislation.

Yet measures of reform were being advocated or actually carried to completion by resident members of both Universities. As early as 1839, A. C. Tait (Archbishop of Canterbury, 1869–82), a tutor of Balliol, and A. P. Stanley (Dean of Westminster, 1864–81), of the same college and Fellow of University, were associated in a project by which the degree examination might be taken at the end of the second year, the third year being spent by the student in specializing and, for that purpose, attending professorial lectures. Tait, it should be remembered, was a Glasgow student before he went up to Oxford and was therefore familiar with the practice of a professorial university, he was also a very influential college tutor. Convocation, the assembly of Oxford graduates non-resident as well as resident, rejected this scheme; but the proposal was again made in 1848 in a pamphlet published by Stanley and Benjamin Jowett, at that time a very energetic tutor of Balliol. The last named in the same year endeavoured to pave the way for a great advance in professorial teaching by planning, with Stanley and others, courses of lectures on early Greek history and philosophy, on Livy, on "scholarship" and on Latin and Greek literature. One of the men invited to contribute lectures was R. R. W. Lingen, a Balliol man then in the service of the Education Office of the Privy Council and Kay-Shuttleworth's successor when the latter resigned the secretaryship in 1849.

Two Cambridge colleges, Trinity in 1844 and St John's in 1849, succeeded in obtaining new statutes. In 1848 a syndicate was appointed to consider the introduction of studies other than mathematical or classical; as a consequence two new triposes, or honours schools, were instituted in the same year, the first examinations being fixed for 1851. The Moral Sciences Tripos included moral philosophy, political economy, modern history, jurisprudence, the laws of England; the Natural Sciences Tripos was similarly comprehensive, anatomy, comparative anatomy, physiology, chemistry, botany, mineralogy and geology all falling within its confines. The agglomeration of "subjects" reflects the undeveloped condition of these studies regarded as instruments of education. A memorial, signed by the greater number of the Oxford tutors, was presented in 1848 to the Hebdomadal Board asking for a revision of the University's examination regulations. The result was the Examination Statute of 1850 which amongst other things set up an "intermediate" examination, the First Public Examination before Moderators ("Mods."), Oxford thus following the pattern of the Cambridge "Previous".[1] "Mods." came between Responsions and the final Second Public Examination *in Literis Humanioribus*. It was an examination, pass or honours, in the two classical languages, together with elementary logic or mathematics. Ancient history, philology and more advanced logic were postponed till the final examination. Two new "schools", or honours courses, were instituted, one in law and modern history, the other in natural science. The first examinations were to be held in 1852, but the statute was not in full operation until the following year. However, it was one thing to make examination programmes, and quite another to secure effective teaching. In March, 1850, Cambridge appointed a syndicate to revise the University statutes.

These internal movements in favour of reform had their parallels outside the Universities, which, however, were not in all cases spontaneous. In 1835 the Duke of Wellington, the Oxford Chancellor, assured the House of Lords that the Universities were reforming themselves. Six years later W. D. Christie moved in the House of Commons that the Crown issue a Commission of Inquiry; in February, 1846, Stanley was coaching him as to the questions which should be asked of the Universities. In the following July there was a change of Government and Lord John Russell became Prime Minister. His very active sympathy with educational liberalism was well known and he had already performed considerable services to its cause. The Minutes of the Committee of Council of 1846 had founded a profession of teachers in elementary schools, made these teachers *quasi* civil servants and consequently had gone some distance in making elementary education an affair of the State. Those who feared that there was a deliberate purpose to bring all English education from top to bottom under the

---

[1] The London Intermediate Examinations date from 1859 (Arts) and 1861 (Science).

control of a Government department would not have been reassured had they been permitted to look behind the scenes. Jowett wrote from Balliol on an unspecified Sunday in 1847 to Lingen: "Your master 'master Doctor Caius' [Kay-Shuttleworth, Lingen's chief], not the French Doctor, paid a visit of inspection to our Normal School [i.e. Balliol College] yesterday. You can guess his object". Jowett goes on to say that he and Stanley are willing to be guided by Lingen's judgement. "Shuttleworth's name is, I think, an omen of success in the scheme; at the same time he is as unfit as the two barbarians, Hengist and Horsa,[1] to reform the University, and the prospect of good is really how far he will be advised by others. We think that if we and others undertake the somewhat invidious part he assigns to us, we ought to have some understanding with the Ministry that they are to support us, time and opportunity favouring, with a friendly measure of reform; in other words that we are not simply made a cat's paw of by Kay-Shuttleworth in a private speculation of his own."[2] Clearly Lord John and his henchman had their own ideas as to the reform of Oxford and Cambridge. In an earlier letter to Lingen, Jowett had said that he thought the Universities seemed "a more promising nucleus for reform, if we could but educate them first, than Dr Kay-Shuttleworth and Privy Council schemes".[3]

In 1849 a memorial signed by members of both Universities and by Fellows of the Royal Society was addressed to the Prime Minister in which it was complained that "the system of the ancient English universities had not advanced and was not calculated to advance the interests of religious and useful learning to an extent commensurable with the great resources and high position of those bodies". The memorialists therefore urged that a Royal Commission should be issued to inquire into the condition of the two Universities. In April, 1850, Mr Heywood, Radical M.P. for North Lancashire, moved in the House for a similar inquiry, which was opposed by the two University burgesses, W. E. Gladstone and Sir R. Inglis. Lord John Russell promised that a Commission should issue.

[1] Messrs Christie and Horsman, Members of Parliament, who were interesting themselves in university reform.
[2] E. Abbott and L. Campbell, *Life and Letters of Benjamin Jowett, M.A., Master of Balliol College, Oxford* (1897), vol. I, p. 188.
[3] *Ibid.* p. 187.

"A Member of the Oxford Convocation" [the Rev. C. A. Row, Head Master of Mansfield Grammar School] came opportunely to the Prime Minister's support by publishing *A Letter on the constitutional defects of the University of Oxford with suggestions for a Royal Commission of Inquiry into the Universities* (1850) addressed to Lord John. The *Letter* set out in detail the defects and abuses of University administration, warmly advocated professorial teaching as against the existing practice of instruction by college tutors, claimed for Parliament the undoubted right to interfere in the affairs of the University and of its several colleges, and maintained that only through Parliamentary action could reforms be really effected. To these ends he urged the issue of a Royal Commission of Inquiry. Sir Robert Inglis, M.P. for Oxford University, had spoken against Heywood's motion made in the House of Commons requesting the appointment of such a Commission; Row again came forward and repeated the arguments of his earlier letter in *A letter to Sir Robert H. Inglis...in reply to his speech on University Reform, April 23rd*, 1850. One suspects, as in the case of Dr Hook and Kay-Shuttleworth, collusion between the Government and the author of these two elaborate *Letters*. However that may be, Row had a personal grievance to whet his zeal for reform. On the occasion of a fellowship election at Exeter College, the College "after advertising for candidates and testimonials as usual, elected to a Cornish fellowship a gentleman who produced no testimonials, who did not even offer himself as a candidate, was not examined, and was not even present in the University at that time; whilst the candidates who were there submitted to an examination of four days' continuance, and performed all other prerequisites. One of them had previously taken a second class degree, and the elected party had only been in the third class".[1] The rejected second-class man was Row himself, as W. D. Christie stated in the House of Commons.[2] The legality of this election was questioned and an appeal addressed to the College Visitor, the Bishop of Exeter; but the Bishop dismissed the appeal on the ground that "the election fulfilled all the conditions imposed by the statutes of the College". Nevertheless, in a private, informal letter he strongly condemned the proceedings.

[1] *A Letter to...Lord John Russell...by a Member of the Oxford Convocation* (1850), pp. 40 ff.

[2] W. D. Christie, *Two Speeches in the House of Commons* [1843, 1845] *on the Universities of Oxford and Cambridge* (1850).

On the last day of August, 1850, the Royal Commission was issued for inquiry "into the state, discipline and revenues" of the two Universities and their colleges; both Commissions reported in 1852, that for Oxford in April, the other in August. The Oxford Commissioners met with a great deal of hostility in the prosecution of their inquiry, the University authorities disputing the legality of the Commission. "The Governing Body has withheld from us the information which we sought from the University through the Vice-Chancellor as its chief resident officer; and, as has since been intimated to us, with the purpose of disputing the legality of Your Majesty's Commission....From the majority of Colleges, as societies, we have received no assistance" (*Report*, p. 1). All the Oxford Commissioners, of whom A. C. Tait was one, were Oxford men who held, or had held, official positions in the University, were well acquainted with its conditions and were desirous of securing fundamental alterations. Jowett, Stanley, Goldwin Smith and W. C. Lake (Dean of Durham, 1869–94) had previously sent a private communication to Lord John thanking him for the intention of advising the issue of the Queen's Commission and expressing their readiness to give every information in their power.[1] Stanley was made secretary to the Commission and Goldwin Smith occupied the same office to the Executive Commissioners who were subsequently appointed by Parliament to give effect to the recommendations of the Royal Commission.

It was Cambridge's good fortune to have as its Chancellor[2] Prince Albert, who was popularly thought of as "the great patron of all arts and sciences". Every public office to which the Prince was called he took very seriously and in the case of the University the fact made him a keen, well-informed critic of its studies. Without ostentation he initiated or took part in changes which required every candidate for a degree to make the acquaintance of one in a long list of special subjects outside the beaten track of mathematics and classics. The Moral Sciences and Natural Sciences Triposes date from his Chancellorship.

The relations between Commissioners and University authorities at Cambridge were markedly cordial and the recommendations of the former were much less drastic than those of the Oxford Commission. The *Report* was careful to note any measures of reform which had been spontaneously carried out or mooted; the appointment of the syndicate

[1] *Report*, vol. I, p. 178.   [2] Installed March 1847.

of March, 1850, to initiate new University statutes under Crown sanction, the readiness of the Colleges to seek modifications of their statutes and to surrender valueless or injurious privileges, such as that exercised by King's College to secure the first arts degree for its members without examination, a privilege spontaneously abandoned in 1851—all these are duly chronicled. In reference to one burning question the Cambridge *Report* asserts that "a great majority of the College fellowships have long been open to free competition".

The number of Cambridge residents in November, 1851, was returned as 1923 of whom 1187 were lodged in colleges, the remainder in private lodgings. Owing to lack of information the Oxford Commission could only estimate the number of residents at the older University; they are put down as 1300. Contrary to the strong recommendation of the Oxford *Report*, the Cambridge Commissioners deprecated the revival of the non-collegiate, or unattached student, as "not expedient". Men in that position would be cut off from the mixed society of a college, an important element in education. The syndicate for the revision of the statutes had proposed a "relaxation" of the requirement that all candidates for degrees and fellowships must subscribe a declaration of membership of the Church of England. The Commissioners agreed with the recommendation, but did not go further than the expression of a hope that the difficulties in the way of admitting Dissenters to full University standing might be overcome. The chief difficulty was seen in the belief that the domestic discipline of the Colleges would be embarrassed by the formal, constitutional admission of men who were not members of the Church.

Cambridge studies as regulated by the courses leading to the B.A. degree are described in detail. The course for the Previous Examination comprised a Greek Gospel, Paley's *Evidences*, Old Testament history, a portion of the works of one Greek and one Latin classic, Euclid, bks. I and II, arithmetic. For the poll degree the requirements were a portion of the Acts of the Apostles in the original, a Greek Epistle or Epistles, classical authors as in the "Previous", three of the six books of Paley's *Moral Philosophy*, Church history to the Council of Nicaea (A.D. 325), the history of the English Reformation, arithmetic, the rudiments of algebra, Euclid, bk. III and part of bk. VI, the elementary principles of mechanics and hydrostatics. To be admissible to the examination for the ordinary degree, candidates had to produce certificates of at least one term's attendance at the lectures of one of the following professors and of having passed an examination therein, viz. law, physic, moral philosophy, chemistry, anatomy, modern history, botany, geology, natural and experimental philosophy, the laws of England, medicine, mineralogy, political economy.

The examination for the Mathematical Tripos, still "*the* tripos", was divided into two stages, the first lasting for three days, the second coming eight days later and lasting five days. Candidates also attended the general examination in Paley's *Moral Philosophy*, the New Testament and ecclesiastical history. "Disputations, being no longer usefully applicable to the present improved and extended course of study, have been reduced to a mere nominal form, sufficient to carry with it an appearance of conformity to the Statutes. The duties of the Moderators are now confined to the Public Examinations according to the existing regulations of the University" (*Report*, p. 22). The aspirant for honours, whether in the Classical Tripos or in those only just instituted, Moral Philosophy and Natural Sciences, must first pass in the Mathematical Tripos or, if he failed to gain mathematical honours, in the ordinary "poll" degree. Graduates might also offer themselves for a theological examination which included the Greek New Testament, Church history, the Thirty-Nine Articles and Liturgy of the Church of England and assigned portions of the patristic writings. There was a further examination in Hebrew.

The Commissioners reported that "a very general feeling of dissatisfaction" prevailed in reference to the system of tuition. The scanty emoluments and brevity of tenure of fellowships were great obstacles to the retention of good men as college tutors, and the improvements in the examinations and courses of study intensified the defects of tutors who were not good. The competition for honours and prizes had led to the growth of private tuition, which caused "serious interference with other forms of instruction", at the cost of from forty to sixty guineas per annum to the student who resorted to it. Indeed, the evidence goes to show that the private "coaches" and not the lectures of college tutors were the effective instruments in preparing men for their examinations. It is significant that since 1838, when a new programme for the poll had been promulgated, the number of private tutors preparing men for the ordinary degree had "unhappily become more numerous" (*Report*, p. 78). However, a grace to abolish private tuition was not likely to pass in the Senate, a great number of whose members were interested in the system either as private tutors or as examiners. Whewell, then Master of Trinity, evidently regarded the private tutor as a mere crammer, who not only caused his pupils considerable expense but also produced "enervating effects" upon their minds—the kind of partial truth perhaps to be expected from one in Whewell's position when commenting upon the doings of irregular practitioners. Philpott, the Master of St Catharine's, was a more helpful critic when he suggested a system of inter-collegiate lectures, a classification of attendants at college lectures instead of massing together for instruction all men of the same "year", honours and pass-men indiscriminately, and lastly the institution of more triposes. The last suggestion was in effect intended to enlarge Cambridge teaching so that it would serve other forms of mentality and interest than the mathematical, classical or theological.

To the long list of professorial chairs, largely instituted in the eighteenth century, the nineteenth century had added professorships of the laws of England and of medicine (at Downing, 1800), of mineralogy (1818), political economy[1] (1828) and archaeology (1851). In reference to the professorships generally, the Commissioners stated that the detailed regulations imposed by the founders of chairs had frequently made the duties impracticable or very inconvenient. "If the professors are to continue to form useful and essential members of the University, their duties must be completely assimilated with its system and be modified therefore from time to time to suit the changes which it undergoes" (*Report*, p. 70). As we shall see, the Oxford Commissioners held much stronger opinions on the relation of the professors to the University. Apart from the duly equipped and very efficient astronomical observatory, apparatus and laboratories were deficient or lacking. "In strong and unfavourable contrast with such a statement stands the provision made for the manipulative instruction of students in King's College, London, where there is also a museum of philosophical instruments, and in the Birkbeck laboratory of University College in that metropolis" (*Report*, p. 117).

In the Commissioners' opinion, the blame for the expensive character of college life lay upon parents and guardians and upon early habits formed at home, a repetition of the charge levelled against the family

[1] The existing chair dates from 1863.

by Public School head masters earlier in the century. As Whewell said, "If boys cost £200 or £300 a year at Eton or Harrow, they are not likely to cost less at Cambridge". At Trinity College a tutor estimated the annual expenditure of an undergraduate at £150 to £250. £61. 2s. 10d. is a low estimate of yearly expense; at Trinity Hall it was £68, at Christ's £80. 3s. 9d., at Trinity £73. 18s. 4d.—these are estimates of minimum expenses. At Emmanuel it varied from £65 to £90; the actual expenditure at Pembroke of a pensioner (a member of the College not on the foundation) from his admission to the taking of the B.A. degree was £305, exclusive of the cost of private tuition. Of 104 pensioners residing at Christ's for eleven terms, say three and a half years, the sums actually paid through the tutors ranged from £155. 11s. 6d. to £1015. 12s. 6d. It is added in the *Report* that of these 104 men the first perhaps himself paid for many things while the last paid through his tutor.

The opening of all scholarships and fellowships to free competition, the enlargement of the professoriate and the addition of more triposes and branches of study to the curriculum were the chief recommendations of the Cambridge Commission. The suggested new chairs were two in theology and one each in jurisprudence, laws of nations and diplomacy, Latin, anatomy, chemistry, zoology, engineering and descriptive geometry. For the upkeep of these ten chairs, with stipends varying from £400 to £800 per annum, contributions were to be levied upon the income of non-resident fellows who were absent from Cambridge in order to travel or to prepare for the legal or medical professions, for which purpose the University did not furnish adequate provision. It was recommended that law should be separated from the Moral Sciences Tripos and be made a separate tripos, and that the University should encourage the teaching of German, French and Italian.

The Cambridge Commissioners' *Report* as a whole was complaisant, even indulgent; that of Oxford was characterized by severe condemnation and the recommendation of drastic change. The pages of the latter reflect the persistent war upon English higher education which, from the early days of the *Edinburgh Review* to the date of the inquiry and beyond, was waged by the friends of educational liberalism and utilitarianism and by the Radical party in general. The Oxford *Report* is not always innocent of the charge of partisanship. The opposed ideals differed greatly, not only in respect of modes of university administration and methods of teaching, but even more in reference to the vital matter, the very purposes of education and the consequent character of the studies which are its most effective instruments. In particular, the Radical principle involved great additions to the studies pursued at school and university and a great increase in the number of students, together with the liberation of education from clerical control even at the cost of excising theology and religion altogether from public instruction. The point in dispute was, virtually, should public education be controlled, as hitherto it had been controlled, by the Church or by the State, to which all forms of religious belief were alike indifferent. The increasing power of control which the State had assumed in elementary education since 1833 had undermined but had not destroyed the Church's position. The dispute continued down to 1870, when Radicalism gained what proved to be but a temporary triumph; the twentieth century is still faced by the problem, although in an altered form.

Superficially the struggle now presented itself as one between the English collegiate system conducted by college tutors, and the professorial system which was destitute of colleges, the type which its opponents regarded as distinctly German or Prussian, and therefore bureaucratic, although in fact it was the system adopted in Scotland and almost universally on the Continent. The college tutor gave catechetical teaching as well as instruction by lecture, or monologue, to a comparatively small group of pupils; his practice was in essentials the mediaeval one of expounding a book, or author, Aristotle or Thucydides. The opposite, "un-English" system consisted in lectures to large numbers of students delivered by specialists who did not expound authors but taught "subjects" and made no use of catechetical forms. This difference in method followed a difference in aim. The purpose of the professor with his large audience was to communicate knowledge, more particularly a knowledge of modern science and learning, "useful knowledge" as many advocates of the system regarded it. The primary aim of the tutor was mental discipline, the communication of knowledge being subordinated to this main object; hence the small classes, whose members might conveniently be questioned and individual minds tested, exercised and fortified, for which purposes the Greek and Latin classical authors and mathematics were thought to be unrivalled instruments.

Again, while the one party was content to educate an intellectual *élite*, the other desired a wide diffusion of knowledge. It was not enough that the University should educate the future clergyman and, in much smaller numbers, the lawyer and the physician; provision should be made for the future banker, merchant, solicitor, surgeon, and for the members of those scientific occupations, indispensable in modern life, which were claiming to rank with the learned professions. It was thought that this extension of university education could not be effected so long as Universities were under clerical control. Here a general political principle, the denial of privilege, intervened to suggest that freedom from control could only be attained by separating education, regarded as the process of acquiring knowledge, from all ecclesiastical ties or indeed from religion itself.

This attempt to analyse the dispute, of which the Universities' Commissions of 1850–2 are a particular illustration, must not be taken to imply that the opponents were ranged, man for man, in two clearly distinguished camps; there were individual thinkers who advocated from conviction some of the measures supported by those to whom on the whole they were opposed.

Grave dissatisfaction with the constitution and procedure of the Hebdomadal Board was felt alike by the Commissioners and by resident members of the University, who for twenty years past had in vain attempted to introduce reforms into this supreme governing body of the University, with whom alone lay the initiation of its legislation. The heads of houses, who formed the great majority of the Board, stood socially apart from the other members of their respective societies, they took no share in tuition beyond appointing the tutors, yet, notwithstanding the leisure which they enjoyed, as a body they were not eminent in learning or in science. Commissioners and residents agreed that the Board ought to consist of members chosen from a wider field and elected periodically. But the Commissioners differed from the tutors in their desire to give a preponderant place on the Board to the professors, a proposal which they advanced as part of their plan to depress the collegiate system and, so far as might be in the circumstances of Oxford, replace it by a professorial system of the foreign type. The professors as such had no part in academic business; the Commissioners recommended that a standing delegacy of professors (Crown nominees in the Commissioners' scheme) should supervise studies, examinations, libraries, thus subordinating the tutorial to the professorial body. "A better arrangement of study under a well-organised professoriate will remedy many evils." Very naturally the tutors objected that "the independence and equal co-operation of the tutorial body is the only available mode of preventing the evils of an unrestricted professorial system".[1] "To make professorial instruction the main education of the University, to substitute general lectures on subjects for special study of books, would be to deteriorate the mental discipline of education and to subvert all the present energies and old associations of Oxford for a very doubtful benefit."[2] Professors examining their own pupils would be in the position stigmatized at a later date in another University as "branding their own herrings", and the tutors call to witness the Commission of Visitation of the Scottish Universities (1826, 1830), on the effect of such a procedure upon the value of the degree. "The utter contempt in which the degree of M.A. is held in Scotland and the notorious inefficiency of the examinations under the existing system have appeared to us [the Scottish Visitation Commissioners] to require that the examination of candidates shall be conducted on a different footing."[3] E. A. Freeman, destined in later years to become a most distinguished member of the professorial body, took the middle way in the controversy, tutors *v.* professors. "The professors ought to be, though only one class amongst several, a highly honourable and influential class in the University and, as such, are entitled to a distinct representation [on the Hebdomadal Board]. And a feeling which, I think, does exist, an abstract dislike to professors, appears to me just as childish and unreasonable as the abstract love of them which possesses the Commissioners and their followers."[4]

One difference of opinion between the Commissioners and the tutors reveals in the latter a limitation of view with respect to the function of a university in the nineteenth century. For the tutors, Oxford was, above and beyond all, a place of education; the Commissioners would assign to it a second duty, that of advancing knowledge. While the endowment of its chairs was not sufficient "to command the services

---

[1] *Papers published by the Oxford Tutors' Association* (1853), Report No. III, p. 67.
[2] *Ibid.* pp. 76 f.   [3] *Ibid.* p. 72.
[4] F. H. Dickinson and E. A. Freeman, *Suggestions with regard to certain proposed alterations in the University and Colleges of Oxford* (Oxford, 1854), p. 133. This pamphlet was published as part of the Tutors' *Papers* already quoted.

of the ablest men", the University needed a professoriate with leisure and opportunity to cultivate learning as well as teaching; professors should be freed from more elementary teaching by the appointment of assistant professors and they should look to academical not ecclesiastical preferment as their fitting reward. The tutors chose to regard these recommendations of the Commissioners' *Report* as meant to be a refusal to bind professors "to make the University the field, or lecturing the method of their instruction", and to leave them "at liberty to work or not as they please, receiving at the same time a large stipend and having the right to direct and control the whole course of academic study".[1] Yet in the pamphlet which contains this animadversion, the tutors confess that the members of their body are neither encouraged to exert themselves while in office "nor enabled to hold it for a sufficient time to acquire real eminence as a scholar". They continue: "It is on this point that the English Universities contrast most unfavourably with those of Germany.... The German teacher is a scholar or a philosopher by profession, instead of being compelled, as is too often the case in Oxford, to take up scholarship or philosophy as a mere temporary occupation" (p. 63). Mark Pattison and Thomas Huxley said the same thing a quarter of a century later.

The studies of the University as set forth in the programmes of examination under the statute of 1850 may be summarily stated. At Responsions, an examination held between the third and seventh terms of the undergraduate's residence, candidates offered a Greek and a Latin author, each represented by two or three "books", not "works", Euclid, books I and II, or algebra to simple equations, translation from English to Latin. At Moderations a Greek Gospel was added to these requirements, and logic was alternative to three books of Euclid and "the first part" of algebra. These were "pass subjects"; candidates for classical honours offered four Greek and four Latin authors, with logic, while "pure mathematics" was exacted from those who read for mathematical honours. Translation into Greek and Latin was an obligatory part of the examination and verse-making, Latin and Greek, was encouraged. For the ordinary, or pass, degree the examination comprised four plays of Euripides, four or five books of Herodotus, six books of Livy, "half of Horace", four books of Euclid, Aldrich's *Artis Logicae Compendium* "to the end of Reduction of Syllogisms".

[1] *Papers published by the Oxford Tutors' Association*, Report No. III, p. 78.

Candidates were also expected to translate from English into Latin, to construe any passage from the Greek Gospels, to repeat and illustrate from Scripture any of the Thirty-Nine Articles and to answer questions on Old Testament and New Testament history. This imposing programme sinks to modest dimensions when the comments of examiners are added. The Commissioners learned, what most of them knew well enough already, that the examiners were "satisfied with a very slight exhibition of knowledge as regards many of these subjects". The classical authors were commonly "got up" from cribs, candidates displaying a very meagre acquaintance with logic and, in the opinion of one examiner, "if decent Latin writing should be insisted on, the number of failures would be more than quadrupled". There were four honours schools: *Litt. Hum.*, mathematics and physics treated mathematically, natural science, law and modern history from A.D. 1 to 1789. To attain honours a candidate must pass in *Literae Humaniores* and in one other school.

The Commissioners were of opinion that *Litt. Hum.* should not be compulsory; for the majority of young men the exaction of classics made the University "a mere grammar school from first to last". Compulsory Latin and Greek should end at "Mods."; thereafter the student should, if he so desired, begin the preparation for his future profession. With that object in view a professorial university would need more honours schools. The four schools recommended were: theology; mental philosophy and philology; jurisprudence, history and political economy; mathematics and physical science. Philology should not be restricted to Greek and Latin; Sanskrit and modern languages should have a place. The requirements in the mathematical school, which included mixed as well as pure mathematics, were considered too wide, and a reduction of reading in mixed mathematics was suggested. The Commissioners regretted the absence of a common matriculation examination for all entrants into the University; "the best Colleges have one".

To the complaint that Oxford assigned undue importance to the two classical languages and literatures, whilst modern knowledge was either ignored or not sufficiently pursued, Oxford opinion, as voiced by its associated tutors, made it clear that there was a fundamental difference on first principles. The tutors considered it "wise and salutary" to make *Literae Humaniores* compulsory while allowing an option of some one of the other schools; the Commissioners' proposal to make all the final schools equally optional involved "an injudicious sacrifice of the principal end of University education, as a discipline of the mind, in favour of its subordinate end as a training school for particular professions".[1] Freeman expressed this opinion very emphatically: "I am sure nothing is better for the mind than our comprehensive course of the ancient languages and the masterpieces of philosophy and history which they contain....These studies tend to produce a certain combination of power and clearness in reasoning, a breadth of view, and especially a power of sifting analogies and differences, which does not seem to be the result of any other process". He contrasts to its disadvantage "the bauble of taking up all history before the year 1789" (a "bauble" constructed by the examination statute of 1850) with "a solid course of Herodotus and Thucydides".[2] For Freeman, historical study and Aristotle's *Ethics* were humane letters *par excellence*.

The assertion that mental gymnastic is the purpose of university study, old as Plato as it is, is one of those historically *ex post facto* challenges of which educational theorizing is full. That, however, does not necessarily impugn its truth; those who maintained it might rightly claim that academic education in the course of its natural development had reached that stage and condition. Yet those who thought so were uneasy under the charge of neglecting useful knowledge, while they were too ready to doubt the possibility of any disciplinary value in studies outside Latin and Greek. Both sides perhaps forgot that much of the educational value of the two ancient languages lay in the method, perfected through an age-long routine of trial and error, of employing them in schools and universities; contrariwise, modern studies had no such tradition.

One consequence of the disregard of modern knowledge is touched upon by Freeman, when he comes to discuss the pass man. Humane letters, especially as the term was understood before 1850, are excellent for the honours man; but the pass man needs another sort of culture, as also do members of "that most important class with which at present it [the University] has no connexion...the great middle class of England". At present undergraduates belong to one or other of three classes: prospective parsons, prospective lawyers, or young men

---

[1] *Reports of the Oxford Tutors' Association*, No. III, p. 89.
[2] Dickinson and Freeman, *Suggestions, ut supra*, pp. 133 ff.

of rank and fortune. "A lay member of the University not coming under one of these two heads is something quite exceptional." Yet "the intellect of England" is not confined to "the territorial aristocracy, the clergy and the bar"; but Oxford studies do not attract those who are looking forward to one of the many professions bred by modern civilization. That Freeman classed the members of "the great middle class" with the Oxford pass men was not meant as a reflexion on their intellectual capacity; no doubt he had in mind the type of school in which so many boys received the kind of instruction which made Matthew Arnold a few years later declare that the English middle classes were nearly the worst educated in the world. The University, as Freeman saw it, included a vast proportion of men disqualified "by nature or by habit" from pursuing a course in honours. For these, the pass men and the men of the neglected middle class, he made two not very well-defined proposals. First, a matriculation examination should bar the way to the quite incompetent on account of ignorance: he hoped that the existence of this obstacle would force the schools into more effective teaching and into the adoption of a discipline which would inculcate industry. The University course should be shortened, but it should enforce two years of "solid *work*" on studies different from the classical, but not specified, except for a passing reference to the use of English translations of Greek history and ethics.[1]

The Oxford Commissioners saw little but defect in the practice of confiding all, or nearly all, the recognized teaching to college tutors. It was objected that the choice of suitable teachers was limited, that those chosen were not specialists and that even good teachers were hampered by the absence of a satisfactory classification of their pupils; all these causes of inefficiency made the expensive private tutor necessary. The Commissioners were in favour of "measures calculated greatly to raise the importance of the professorial body so that we may hope to see its ranks filled with able and active men in all departments" (*Report*, p. 16). The tutors saw in this proposal a deadly blow to the cherished belief that education was especially the province of the clergy. Many of the professors, perhaps a majority, would be laymen. "The effect and indeed the avowed object of this recommendation is largely to remove education from the hands of the clergy", and they added that they could sanction no proposal having that effect. Freeman's

[1] *Suggestions, ut supra*, pp. 136 ff.

objection to a professorial university was not of this kind, but one which voiced the misgivings of many Englishmen who took note of the activities of the Committee of Council and what seemed likely to happen with Lord John Russell as Prime Minister. Freeman was for giving a distinct and honourable place to the professors in University administration; but, said he, "we do not want *an irresponsible board of oligarchs under that name, sent down by the minister or prince of the day to carry out whatever additional Germanisms may be most acceptable to a bureau of public instruction*".[1] The italics are not Freeman's, but his words are of the first importance, since they embody a then widely shared distrust of State schemes of public education. All teachers, whether university professors or teachers in infant schools, were to be Government nominees armed with full powers to indoctrinate their pupils with principles favoured by those in authority. Such a system could not fail to be bureaucratic; and bureaucracy was hateful to the Victorian Englishman, who regarded it as un-English, German, Prussian. It may be noted that England has never possessed a Ministry of Public Instruction nor a Minister of Education under those names. Freeman here in effect tells us why. His allusion to "the prince of the day" with his "Germanisms" is, of course, a very thinly veiled reference to the Prince Consort, whose attempts to improve English culture were not always appreciated as they deserved.

Accepting neither mental discipline nor disinterested culture as the full and sufficient purpose of a university education, the Commissioners declared that Oxford prepared her *alumni* for the ministry of the Church of England but otherwise did not contribute to their advancement in life. That Oxford education was unnecessarily expensive was in their opinion due to the college system. Life in a college encouraged idleness and extravagance, especially in gambling, in furniture, tobacco, driving, riding and hunting, hobbies or amusements indicating the presence of young men of wealth. The University's recognition of distinctions of rank had had a bad effect; but the *Report* itself shows that the day of the gentleman-commoner (too often a licensed loafer) was almost over. "Young men of the best families and of great wealth or expectations are frequently entered as commoners." The expense of college life was one explanation of the number of the vacant rooms in the colleges, which, it was said, reached 60 or 70 in

[1] *Op. cit.* p. 159.

1846, and the Commissioners believed that the number was now greater. Owing to the attitude adopted by the authorities, it was not possible to cite exact figures; but it appeared that Oxford, with more colleges and more money than Cambridge, yet had fewer students.

The Oxford Commission experienced great difficulty in getting even partial accounts of finance. "It is however certain that the whole expenses of prudent and well-conducted students greatly exceed £300" for all charges, the cost of books excepted. £370 seems to be an average sum which does not include caution-money, travelling, clothes, wines or amusements. Fees to private tutors are not counted in the foregoing estimates; these were usually £30 per year for three hours' tuition every week and £50 for six hours weekly. "On the whole, we believe that a parent who, after supplying his son with clothes and supporting him at home during the vacations, has paid for him during his university course not more than £600 and is not called on to discharge debts at its close, has reason to congratulate himself" (*Report*, p. 33).

The Commissioners had been instructed not to entertain the question of the admission of Dissenters. "Several members of the University have recorded in their evidence a strong opinion that the present policy in this matter should be abandoned" (*ibid*. p. 54). The Commissioners believed that subscription as then practised habituated the mind to a careless assent to truth; it did not exclude some who were not Churchmen and did exclude those Churchmen who scrupled to give assent to the Thirty-Nine Articles of Religion.

It was generally agreed that as matter of public policy the Universities should be accessible to greater numbers and that the cost of a university education could, and should, be reduced considerably. To this end several suggestions were offered. The Commissioners recommended the opening of "halls", that is, students' hostels presided over by a master of arts whose property the hall would be—a return to an early and much-used mediaeval form; alternatively to the self-contained hall, the Commissioners also proposed the opening of halls by individual colleges, the chapel, dining-hall and tuition of the college being accessible to residents in the associated hall. The Oxford Commission, contrary to the judgement of the Cambridge Commissioners, strongly favoured a return to the practice of recognizing unattached, i.e. non-collegiate, membership of the University; such students would in no way be connected with a college, but would receive the necessary instruction from the lectures of the university teachers, the professors. This recognition would, it was said, tend to re-instate the University, which had "been absorbed in the Colleges". It is significant of the improved standing of the master in the elementary school, which followed the Minutes of 1846, that the Oxford *Report* hazarded the guess that "the training institutions for masters for schools for the poor are likely to produce pupils of great powers, who would probably desire a university education, if they considered it within their reach, and [that they] would submit to great privations in order to obtain it" (p. 49). Outside the Commission the suggestion was made that an "External" scheme for granting degrees should be set up. The institution of theological colleges, virtually another mediaeval revival, was favoured by many at this time; it was proposed that attendance at these colleges, or at the similar institutions connected with the cathedrals, should qualify for an Oxford degree. William Sewell, a senior tutor, would establish professorships at Birmingham and Manchester for the purpose of preparing men to take the degree. But the Commissioners were alive to the evil example then being set by London. Their reply to Sewell and the advocates of the "External" scheme was, "the examination and the degree...do not form a part of the education itself". An Oxford degree is a certificate that its possessor "has undergone the training which cannot be secured without residence" (*Report*, p. 54)—a concession to the doctrine of formal training which the Commissioners did not often make.

To Freeman's thinking "the great question of all" was that of University Extension. "Shall the University endeavour to influence the great middle class of England?" "Surely the University hardly fulfills its mission as a great national institution, a corporation charged with the guidance and nurture of the national intellect, unless it at least attempts to extend its benefits to these most important classes. Surely it is hardly true to itself if it does not endeavour to gain by all honourable means the vast accession of strength which would be conveyed by the adhesion of those orders of men who now possess the primary political influence in the country." To this consideration, "poor scholars, poor clergy, poor colleges" (i.e. colleges for poor students) are entirely subsidiary; poverty and good moral conduct alone are not sufficient evidence that a man would profit from education at a university. Freeman was altogether opposed to the revival (after more than four centuries) of the "unattached students," the "nomads" who are to be sacrificed as a sort of καθάρματα (offscourings, scape-goats) for the good example of undergraduates in general. But to connect the professional classes with the University by almost any means is "the University Extension which we really need". He proposed a shortened course to last two years, at the entrance of which it would be necessary to pass a matriculation examination held by the University, a following of London's example which he rightly saw would raise *school* education to a higher level of efficiency. After passing an examination analogous to Responsions or Moderations, these students would devote the remainder of their residence to preparation for their professions, in so far as Oxford was able to prepare them.[1]

Such a document as a Royal Commission Report is by its nature restricted to broad and fairly general assertions of fact and of principle with little or no dwelling upon the exceptional behaviour of individuals, even when that behaviour "proves" the general statements by contradicting them. The result is that the reader is disposed to assume that there are in truth no redeeming features in a picture which only reflects failure or worse. That the adverse statements, repeated so often in the foregoing pages, do not tell the full story of contemporary Oxford life, becomes clear when we scan the memoirs and correspondence of the time. For example, Benjamin Jowett, a Balliol tutor from 1842 to 1870, is a contradiction of the belief that all college tutors then lived only for examinations and class lists. Jowett's course on the history of philosophy "became from year to year more comprehensive. It had no immediate relation to the examination system as then [1846–50] constituted, but helped to quicken men's intellects and gave them larger views about the books they were reading.... Hitherto in Greek philosophy at Oxford the *Ethics* and the *Rhetoric* of Aristotle had been all in all. By lecturing on Plato, Jowett infused new life into the study of Greek and of philosophy. He had been doing so at least as early as the Lent Term of 1847, although the practice of 'professing' the *Republic* became general only with the inauguration of the new system in 1853",[2] that is, the system established by the examination statute of 1850. "In those days the University was not so much in the grasp of its

---

[1] Dickinson and Freeman, *Suggestions, ut supra*, pp. 145–9.

[2] E. Abbott and L. Campbell, *Life and Letters of Benjamin Jowett*, 2 vols. (1897), vol. I, pp. 131 f.

examination system as it has since come to be; we kept the Schools but they were not the Alpha and Omega of our reading as undergraduates." The speaker is W. L. Newman, a one-time pupil of Jowett's. G. C. Brodrick, afterwards Warden of Merton, thus testified to the character of Jowett's tuition; the date is 1850–4, when Brodrick was a Balliol undergraduate: "No other tutor in my experience has ever approached him in the depth and extent of his pastoral supervision, if I may so call it, of young thinkers; and it may be truly said that in his pupil room, thirty, forty or fifty years ago, were disciplined many of the minds which are now exercising a wide influence over the nation".[1]

The strong affirmations for, and against, the reliance upon college tuition or professorial lecturing, obscure the possibility of a middle course. Yet "Jowett never admitted the broad distinction that is sometimes drawn between professorial and tutorial teaching. All teaching that is worthy of the name appeared to him to involve close dealing with individual minds. He regretted the decay of catechetical instruction in the University and the substitution of lectures to large classes for the college lectures of old times; though this perhaps was an inevitable result of the inter-collegiate system which he approved"[2]— a system which followed the legislation of 1854. Not all tutors were inefficient nor were all undergraduates idle, dissipated or extravagant; they could even spare thought for, and interest in, the life of the time outside the confines of Oxford. Thus Canon North Pinder says of the Oxford of 1848, "Christian Socialism was taken up ardently by the few, who for a testimony were content to wear strange-patterned and ill-fitting trousers made in the workshops of the Christian Socialist tailor. Foremost among these was John Conington, then Fellow of University and afterwards Professor of Latin in Oxford".[3]

Effect was given to the work of the two Commissions by the Oxford University Act of 1854 and the corresponding Act for the sister University passed in 1856, and by the labours, continued until 1858, of the Statutory Commissioners created by those Acts. The two governing bodies, the Hebdomadal Council at Oxford and the Council of the Senate at Cambridge with whom lay the initiative in legislation, virtually became elected bodies, the number of *ex officio* members being greatly reduced. The two legislative bodies with whom it rested to accept or

[1] E. Abbott and L. Campbell, *op. cit.*, p. 202.
[2] *Ibid.* p. 243 n.   [3] *Ibid.* p. 135.

reject proposals initiated by the Councils, became real deliberative assemblies in virtue of the right to discuss measures in English; hitherto the use of Latin was compulsory in the Congregation and Senate. The two Acts made all obstructive oaths illegal and permitted the Universities and the several colleges to amend their statutes; failing such amendment, the Statutory Commissioners were authorized to make the necessary changes. The Universities might alter the terms of any trust older than fifty years; or the Statutory Commissioners were empowered to do this, if the University took no action. The Acts sanctioned the institution of private halls and no oath or declaration might be exacted either at matriculation or graduation; the Nonconformist was thus able to become a member of a college and to take the degree of B.A., but he could not obtain a fellowship or a degree qualifying for office in the Church of England. The vested interests of particular schools might be respected, if the school governors or the Charity Commission (created by the Charitable Trusts Act of 1853) so desired; in case of dispute, Parliament was to be the arbitrator. Winchester and Eton were for the purposes of the two Acts to be regarded as colleges of Oxford and Cambridge respectively. The ordinances of the two Statutory Commissions and the changes in their statutes effected by the Universities and colleges themselves brought it about that the great majority of fellowships and scholarships were thrown open to free competition, the professoriate was enlarged, endowed from college funds, and generally given a much greater importance in administration and in teaching. The office of college tutor opened out a career to which a man might devote himself as to a profession. In brief, these great changes gave a new atmosphere to the life of Oxford and Cambridge and enlarged their membership, making it more representative of the country as a whole. A newer curriculum afforded opportunity for a better appreciation of modern studies and for their advancement at the hands of an increased number of resident scholars and *savants*, the professors and college tutors.

As was said in an earlier chapter, the University of London began in 1836 as an examining board which conferred degrees on the students of the two London colleges, University and King's. By a supplemental charter of 1850 the University was empowered to affiliate other institutions both within and without the London area. Under these powers colleges of different degrees of merit, from the Working Men's

College to Owens College, Manchester, were from time to time so affiliated. But the system broke down and in 1858 the examinations of the University were thrown open without reserve to all comers of the masculine sex. The teaching at the two London colleges got out of touch with the University examinations, and these in turn were somewhat "in the air", partly owing to this dissociation and partly because the syllabuses became antiquated. The higher education of London suffered extremely from this state of things. It was part of the general chaos which existed in English educational affairs during the closing years of the nineteenth century. Some admirers of a purely external examination system were wont to speak of the University as "Imperial", because it examined candidates in places so far away as Ceylon. But after all it was the University of *London* and it was not discharging its most obvious duty. Unfortunately it formed the pattern on which the Indian universities were modelled; it is only within recent years that teaching and examining have become closely united in them.

In 1852 when the controversies aroused by the appointment of the Universities' Commissions were still warm and their *Reports* had not yet appeared, a course of lectures was being delivered in Dublin by an Oxford man which were not only "topical" in the truest sense but, in virtue of at least two of the subjects discussed, retained, and still retain, a more permanent interest. The lecturer was John Henry Newman (1801–90) and the lectures were subsequently published under the title, *On the Scope and Nature of University Education* (London, 1859). This was described as the second edition. Originally the lectures were printed as they were delivered week by week, and on the completion of the course they were published as *Discourses on University Education addressed to the Catholics of Dublin* (Dublin, 1852). These ten discourses, with omissions, rearrangement and verbal changes, formed the eight chapters which constituted the second edition of 1859. In the interval Newman had published *The Office and Work of Universities* (1856) and *Lectures and Essays on University Subjects* (1859). The *Discourses* and the *Lectures* next appeared as one book, published in 1873, under the title *The Idea of a University defined and illustrated, I: in nine discourses addressed to the Catholics of Dublin, II: in occasional lectures and essays addressed to the members of the Catholic University*. This was described as the third edition. Six other editions were issued before 1890, the year of Newman's death.

The work, in all its different forms, traverses the principles of that educational Radicalism which was in 1852 moving steadily to its partial victory and, in the course of the argument, considers the questions, Is a university primarily concerned with mental discipline or with the inculcation of useful knowledge? and What place does religion necessarily occupy in a satisfactory scheme of education? These questions, the second more especially, are scarcely less insistent to-day than they were when Newman discoursed in Dublin.

Somewhat half-heartedly the Irish Catholic hierarchy had proposed in 1850 to set up in that city a Catholic university, of which Newman was invited to be President, and in that capacity he delivered these lectures. At that time the "religious difficulty" was even more acute in Ireland than in England. Two schemes, one dealing with elementary, the other with higher education, had met with only a qualified success. The scheme of 1831 was planned to give literary and moral teaching to Protestants and Catholics in common, whilst religious instruction was to be given separately to the members of different communions, a conscience clause forming part of the scheme. This "mixed" or "combined elementary education" was not universally acceptable. At the three Queen's Colleges, which were federated as the Queen's University in this same year, 1850, the London precedent of 1828 was followed and the instruction was wholly secular. Only a small number of Catholics resorted to these colleges, and it was decided by the hierarchy to establish a private university independent of Government assistance.

The question which most seriously divided Irish opinion was the place and function of religion in a scheme of education. The Government or official view was that of educational Radicalism; it was exemplified in the Irish national schools. This view might also be termed the Protestant view, although some of the most cultivated Irish Catholic clergy in a measure shared it as it was applied in the Queen's Colleges. According to this opinion religion was merely one "subject", howbeit a peculiarly important one, amongst many others which formed the curriculum, and the influence of religion upon those other studies, and their influence upon religion, were immaterial. On these principles a conscience clause, or the right of exemption from religious teaching, made a common public education possible for all varieties of religious conviction.

Newman expounded the Catholic opinion which was based upon the philosophical principle that a curriculum deserving the name is not a fortuitous group of "subjects", but an organized unity whose parts mutually affect each other for a common purpose. The teaching of religion, on this view, will influence the teaching, for example, of history or of science, and these in turn will influence the teaching of religion. That being assumed, a conscience clause is obviously ineffective to ensure the religious liberty of a pupil; and exemption from religious instruction makes a breach in the unity of the curriculum. The College at Maynooth, founded in 1795 and assisted by annual grants from public funds, embodied the Catholic principle; but Maynooth had been almost throughout its history a purely clerical seminary and, therefore, was not suitable for transformation into a university, had its transformation been desired. "Mixed education" seemed to the Protestant both desirable and feasible; to the Catholic it was neither.

To this burning question Newman devoted the first four of his discourses. His treatment of it is academic not controversial; not the religious instruction of the schoolroom but the teaching of theology in the university is his theme. As Newman sees it, faith is a matter of reason, not of sentiment, and theology is part of the sphere of knowledge. That being so, a university must teach theology or fail to fulfil its proper function, which is to teach "universal knowledge"—an attempt to carry the point by a mistaken etymology. But in any case a university teaches more than one branch of knowledge; and Newman goes on to show how theology bears on other knowledge and how other knowledge bears upon theology. "Summing up what I have said, I lay it down that all knowledge forms one whole, because its subject matter is one; for the universe in its length and breadth is so intimately knit together, that we cannot separate off portion from portion, and operation from operation, except by a mental abstraction."[1]

The leading topic of the last five discourses is the nature of knowledge, and in particular the differences between liberal and useful knowledge, between a "liberal education" and a "useful education". Here again is a topical, controversial subject treated academically.

[1] For convenience of reference the citations in the text are from *The Idea of a University defined and illustrated* (1912); but, with the one exception mentioned below, they are all in the edition of 1852. The above passage occurs on p. 50.

True to his Oxford traditions, Newman follows Aristotle in drawing the distinction, quoting the *Rhetoric* to this effect: "Of possessions, those rather are useful which bear fruit, those liberal which tend to enjoyment. By fruitful I mean which yield revenue; by enjoyable, where nothing accrues of consequence beyond the using".[1] Liberal knowledge, which Newman holds to be the knowledge with which a university concerns itself, is an end in itself. "That alone is liberal knowledge which stands on its own pretensions, which is independent of sequel, expects no complement, refuses to be *informed* (as it is called) by any end, or absorbed into any art, in order duly to present itself to our contemplation".[2] The purpose of liberal knowledge is neither morals nor religion but an intellectual excellence which gives "illumination" and "enlargement" of view, not learning or "mere knowledge" nor "mechanical production". Its attainment forms neither the Christian nor the Catholic but the "gentleman", described as a person of "cultivated intellect, a delicate taste, a candid, equitable, dispassionate mind, a noble and courteous bearing in the conduct of life". It is disconcerting to learn that the "gentleman", so understood, may nevertheless be a profligate and heartless man of the world.[3]

The aim of university teaching then is to educate "the intellect to reason well in all matters, to reach out towards truth and grasp it".[4] "It is, I believe," says Newman, "as a matter of history, the business of a university to make this intellectual culture its direct scope or to employ itself in the education of the intellect."[1] Since he appeals to history it is relevant to remember that the earliest universities were established to teach what, according to Aristotle and to Newman, is "useful" rather than liberal; their Faculties of Arts were occupied with studies, however liberally followed, which found their fruit, complement or sequel in the professions of divinity, law and medicine. Perhaps unconsciously Newman testifies that the separation of liberal and useful may be undesirable, when he contrasts the seminary with the university, a contrast deliberately presented to his hearers who were more familiar with the narrower institution. "This I conceive to be the advantage of a seat of universal learning considered as a place of education. An assemblage of learned men, zealous for their own sciences and rivals of each other, are brought by familiar intercourse

[1] Newman, *The Idea of a University defined and illustrated* (1912), p. 109.
[2] *Ibid.* p. 108.   [3] *Ibid.* pp. 120 f., 198.   [4] *Ibid.* p. 125.

and for the sake of intellectual peace to adjust together the claims and relations of their respective subjects of investigation. They learn to respect, to consult, to aid each other. Thus is created a pure and clear atmosphere of thought, which the student also breathes, though in his own case he only pursues a few sciences out of a multitude. He profits by an intellectual tradition which is independent of particular teachers, which guides him in his choice of subjects and duly interprets for him those which he chooses. He apprehends the great outlines of knowledge, the principles on which it rests, the scale of its parts, its light and its shades, its great points and its little, as he otherwise cannot apprehend them. Hence it is that his education is called 'liberal'....A habit of mind is formed which lasts through life, of which the attributes are freedom, equitableness, calmness, moderation and wisdom; or what in a former discourse I have ventured to call a philosophical habit. This then I would assign as the special fruit of the education furnished at a university, as contrasted with other places of teaching or modes of teaching. This is the main purpose of a university in its treatment of its students."[1]

Such language was scarcely congenial to an age whose outstanding experience was an extraordinary advance in material prosperity and in the application of mechanism to the intercourse and comfort of men. The railway, the electric telegraph, the submarine cable and photography were all inventions of the time of Newman's own middle life. The Atlantic had been crossed under steam, great advances had been made in the study of heat, light and chemistry. Murchison and Sedgwick, Faraday and Hooker were familiar names, speaking of progress in men's knowledge of the natural world. All these things had been reflected in educational projects, and there was a disposition to think that mechanical invention and civilization were co-terminous if not identical.

It is therefore easy to see why Newman paid such close attention to useful knowledge in the course of his argument and why he identified it with the study of science, the practice of the inductive method and the philosophy of Francis Bacon.[2] He was alive to the danger which

[1] Newman, op. cit. pp. 101 f. This passage was not in the original edition of 1852; it occurs in Discourse IV of the edition of 1859.

[2] But as knowledge, and particularly scientific knowledge, developed, it became increasingly difficult to disentangle the "liberal" from the "useful". Newman himself admits that the two may overlap.

this sudden outburst of material prosperity might throw in the way of sound mental cultivation at its more advanced stages. There is a passage (pp. 142 f.), much too long for quotation in which he describes what he terms "the practical error of the last twenty years", namely, sciolism, smattering.

Newman regarded the university as an institution for the free communication of all kinds of knowledge which can be deemed liberal; but it had no concern with morals.[1] A university therefore did not educate, except perhaps indirectly. Neither did it attempt to advance knowledge; research is the business of institutions specially founded for that purpose. Contrariwise, the English notion of a university was, and is, that it is before all else a place of education; while the German conception is that universities are places of learning maintained to advance knowledge but not for providing education, which is the proper business of schools. Newman differs from both ideas.

Having decided that a university ought to teach theology, Newman goes on to ask what is the Church's office in this connexion. He replies that the Church must act as a steadying force while the intellect is being freely exercised and knowledge attained. He anticipates a time, which he compares with the thirteenth century, in which much questioning on the gravest concerns of humanity will arise; the publication (1859) of Darwin's *Origin of Species* was still in the future. The progress of science and the materialist ideals then prevalent made such questioning unavoidable. The competent place for its discussion is not the platform or the popular press, but the university where at least there is some guarantee of knowledge, method and free inquiry. But Radicalism, the Queen's Colleges and those who shared their notion of theology made free inquiry impossible by their exclusion of what man has learned about the nature of God. The schoolmen, aided by the Church, reconciled such learning with the teaching of Aristotle; a similar reconciliation of science and theology, or rather of knowledge of the congruent seen and unseen worlds, would be attained in a university which gave its rightful place to theology and was fortified by the Church.

[1] Enough has been said in this chapter to indicate the presence in university life of elements which depressed the moral level. See Walter Besant, *Autobiography* (1902).

CHAPTER VIII

"Sound and Cheap Elementary Instruction"

During the 'fifties' of last century the Parliamentary advocates of a national scheme of popular education were divided into the opposing camps of those who pressed for denominational schools rate-aided as well as tax-aided, and those who were for schools, undenominational or wholly secular, supported entirely by public funds. To these dissentients were added the many, 'in Parliament and without, who in other respects were dissatisfied with the scheme of the Committee of Council as it was then being administered. In the first place there was the steady and considerable increase in the demands which that scheme made upon the public purse at a time when the Crimean War had cost the country nearly £78,000,000 in three years. The annual Parliamentary grant for public education, which in 1851 stood at £150,000, was £541,233 in 1857 and £663,435 in the following year.[1] In 1851 £15,474 had been spent in augmenting the salaries of certificated teachers, pupil teachers had cost £78,000 and the administrative expenses of the Committee of Council itself had been £22,117. Six years later these respective sums stood at £64,491, £192,248 and £53,814.[2]

Some demanded a halt if not a reduction in this expenditure; others thought that it secured an insufficient return in superficial instruction given by teachers whose education and training were ill-suited to their task. Again it was feared that these teachers and still more their recruits, the pupil teachers, were potentially so many agents of a bureaucratic executive whose aim it was to drill Englishmen, as the German people were being drilled, into dependence on the Government. Such a fear was not allayed by the threat of compulsory universal instruction under the control of the Committee of Council, a body which no less than its office, the Education Department, had been constituted, not by Act or Resolution of Parliament, but by an Order in Council, an origin which to some appeared ominous. In short, the Committee of Council was on its trial.

[1] *Special Reports on Educational Subjects*, vol. II (1898), p. 524.
[2] *Ibid.* p. 527.

In the last days of Palmerston's administration, February, 1858, Sir John Pakington moved a resolution in the House of Commons asking for the appointment of a Commission of inquiry, and in the following June under a new Ministry the Commission was issued, its terms of reference being "to inquire into the present State of Popular Education in England, and to consider and report what Measures, if any, are required for the Extension of sound and cheap elementary instruction to all classes of the People". The chairman was Henry Pelham, fifth duke of Newcastle, from whose title the Commission gets its name; the keynotes of the inquiry were the two words, "sound", "cheap". The Commissioners began by studying the reports of the inspectors of schools from 1839 onwards, in the meantime appointing ten assistant commissioners each to "examine minutely" the educational condition of a "specimen district", agricultural, manufacturing, mining, maritime and metropolitan, two of each. James Fraser, tutor of Oriel and afterwards Bishop of Manchester, was sent to report on German primary education, and to Matthew Arnold, an inspector of schools of seven years' standing, was committed a like duty in France. The Commissioners also received information from Upper Canada (Ontario) and from the United States of America. Mr P. Cumin made inquiry respecting English charities which were applied or applicable to education. The major part of the Commission's *Report* dealt with "the education of the independent poor", the main subject of its inquiry; but the education of pauper, vagrant and criminal children also received attention, as also did the elementary schools under the Admiralty and the War Office, charity schools and the lesser endowed schools.

The *Report* of the Newcastle Commission, which was signed on March 18th, 1861, contains a great array of statistics; in addition to the figures which occur in the body of the *Report* there is a section extending to 127 pages wholly devoted to the statistical aspects of English education at that time. But the circumstances under which these were compiled did not permit the Commission to present a precise educational census of schools or of pupils. In many cases statements are frankly described as "estimated", and some of these are estimates whose basis consists in turn of other estimates. Distinguishing schools as "public", that is, directed by religious societies and other bodies of persons but not conducted for profit, and "private", that is, the property of their principals who conducted the schools for profit, the Commissioners give the prominence of heavy type to the following enumeration.[1] Of public schools there were 24,563 instructing 1,675,158 children; in spite of their designation more than two-thirds of these schools received no money from public funds, owing to poverty, scanty population or apathy. Of the private schools (which were "of all degrees of merit", but "it is to be feared that the bad schools are the most numerous") there were 34,412 with 860,304 pupils. The Commissioners stated that 573,536 private school pupils were being taught in places "for the most part inferior as schools for the poor, and ill-calculated to give to the children an education serviceable to them in after life". Of the 7646 public schools inspected by the officers of the Education Department, 75·4 per cent. were ranked in one or other of the categories, excellent, good, fair.[2]

Public and private schools together numbered 58,975 with 2,535,462 pupils; to these must be added 2036 evening schools (a number "altogether inadequate to the wants of the population") instructing 80,966 pupils, two-thirds of whom were men and boys. As in the earlier returns of the century, Sunday Schools are included as part of the national provision; 33,872 of these taught 2,411,554 pupils. The clauses of the Factory Act of 1833 which had set up the half-time system, the children's work alternating with schooling, were said by the Commissioners to be eminently successful where good schools were employed, but there was no guarantee or compulsion which made it certain that a school for "half-timers" was not very bad. Any room might be called a school, any person a schoolmaster empowered to certify school attendance, and the law was satisfied.[3]

In public week-day schools, 82 to 91 per cent. of which were controlled by the Church of England, the daily average attendance throughout the year of 220 days was 76·1 per cent. of the number on the school rolls. The large majority of the pupils left school before attaining the age of eleven; "attendance diminishes rapidly after 11, and ceases almost entirely at 13, only 5·4 per cent. of the children

[1] See *Report of the Commissioners appointed to inquire into the State of Popular Education in England*, 6 vols. (1861), vol. I, p. 591.

[2] *Ibid.* pp. 91, 210, 279, 294.

[3] *Ibid.* pp. 204 ff.

remaining after that age".[1] The Commissioners believed that the school life of these children was "about four years" and that the average, reckoning all grades of schools, did not exceed six years. At the date of the *Report* the Government had expended on national education in round numbers £4,400,000; voluntary subscriptions for the same purpose had reached double that sum.[2]

Of a population estimated for 1858 by the Registrar-General as 19,523,103, the number of children of school age and attending school should have been 2,655,767; it was estimated as actually 2,535,462, a discrepancy of 120,305 or 4·5 per cent. only. Contrast with other countries appeared to be even more reassuring. In Prussia, where elementary schooling was compulsory, one pupil in every 6·27 persons was attending school, one in 7·7 in England and Wales, one in 8·11 in Holland, one in 9 in France. In the opinion of the Commission, "the means of obtaining education are diffused pretty generally and pretty equally over the whole face of the country (i.e. England and Wales) and the great mass of the population recognizes its importance sufficiently to take advantage to some extent of the opportunities thus afforded to their children".[3] These insufficiently informed opinions were of the unduly optimistic kind which in 1870 led Forster to assert that a threepenny rate would meet the local charges which the Elementary Education Act of that year made necessary.

Yet the Newcastle Commissioners did not draw too much comfort from their opinions. "The presence of this proportion of the population in school implies...that almost everyone receives some amount of school education at some period or other, but it also implies that the average attendance is far shorter than it ought to be; and it is perfectly consistent with the incompetency of a large proportion of the schools in the country to give really useful instruction, or to have considerable influence in forming the character of those who attend them."[4]

The annual cost of educating a child in an elementary, inspected school varied from twenty-eight to thirty shillings, of which thirteen shillings and sixpence was derived from the Government grant. The entire charge per child to the public, including the cost of training

---

[1] *Report*, vol. I, pp. 68, 172. "They obtain situations very generally between 11 and 12. I have ascertained that at that age steady and intelligent lads gain from 3/- to 7/- weekly in London" (p. 187).
[2] *Ibid.* p. 309.   [3] *Ibid.* pp. 84, 86, 293.   [4] *Ibid.* p. 88.

teachers, inspecting schools and administering the Education Department of the Privy Council, was eighteen shillings. School pence contributed between one-fourth and three-fifths of the cost, subscriptions and endowments, one-third to one-fourth. In "British" schools the fees were higher and subscriptions, etc., lower than in "National" schools. For a year of forty-four weeks the weekly cost was eightpence per child; in the majority of schools the fee was less than threepence. The Commissioners' comment shows how far they were from regarding elementary instruction as a national, public service. "The difference between what he actually pays and eightpence a week is in the nature of a charitable donation."[1] "If the fees are too high [the Commissioners were inclined to raise them] the poor will be driven from the school, and it will be frequented by children of a higher class, for whom the Government grant is not intended." Some schools graduated their fees in accordance with the social position of the parents, farmers and shopkeepers paying more than mechanics and labourers. Managers in general were not unwilling to make special terms to meet exceptional cases.[1]

In order to give an idea of what was being taught in English elementary schools generally, the *Report* sets out the branches of instruction followed in 1824 public schools situated within the ten specimen districts with the percentage of pupils studying each branch. From these returns it appears that in some of the schools the curriculum was confined to religious instruction and reading; that less than four-fifths of the children were taught to write and to sum and, in the case of girls, to ply the needle; that less than two-fifths learned geography, grammar and history; that the number studying drawing, music from notes, and the elements of physical science, was inconsiderable; and that an insignificant number of boys carried mathematics beyond arithmetic. In this connexion, the definition of "public" schools must be borne in mind; the details are not confined to inspected schools in receipt of grant, but include schools of all grades of efficiency which made a return as to their numbers and studies.[2] A similar return,

[1] *Report*, vol. I, pp. 71–5.
[2] The details are as follows (the figures are percentages of pupils following the study): religious instruction 93·3; reading 95·1; writing 78·1; arithmetic 69·3; needlework 75·8; other industrial work 3·8. Geography 39·4; English grammar 28; English history 19·5. Elements of physical science 3·1; music from notes 8·6; drawing 10·8. Mathematics (boys only), mechanics 1·1, algebra 1·5, Euclid 1·4. See *Report*, vol. I, pp. 662 ff.

similarly varied with reference to efficiency, was made from 3495 "private" schools; here the percentages were lower, sometimes markedly lower, than in the "public" schools. Clearly, the efficient private schools were swamped in a welter of dames' schools and of even less useful pretences at instruction. The real significance of these figures, "public" and "private", lies in the indication of the great number of so-called schools which had no valid right to the name.

On the other hand there were inspected schools which surpassed general expectation. Mr Cook reported that "the principles of political economy with especial reference to questions which touch on the employment and remuneration of labour, principles of taxation, uses of capital, etc., effects of strikes on wages, etc., are taught with great clearness and admirable adaptation to the wants and capacities of the children of artisans, in the reading books generally used in the metropolitan schools".[1] In rural schools at this time there was a noticeable development in the teaching of gardening and of household management, while in the better schools land-surveying was not an uncommon branch of instruction.[2]

Although the school was in no sense typical, reference may here be made to the village school of King's Somborne which was conducted by the vicar, Richard Dawes (1793–1867), afterwards Dean of Hereford. Dawes was one of those English educators who, being in advance of their own time, have been forgotten by later generations. Under his direction and instruction, the children of this Hampshire village were trained to observe and reflect upon the common experiences and surroundings of their everyday life; they wrote "compositions" on familiar topics, learned English grammar inductively and not by mere rule, studied geography, geology and astronomy in the field and from the heavens, while natural history and the elements of geometry were learned in the same direct, intuitive way. Dawes has left an account of his labours in *An improved and self-paying system of national education suggested from the working of a village school in Hampshire* and *Suggestive hints towards improved secular instruction making it bear on practical life* (1847). In his "General Report" to the Education Department for the year 1853 Matthew Arnold called attention to the exceptional character of this school and of its organiser and inspirer.

[1] *Report*, vol. I, p. 237.
[2] *Report of the Board of Education* (1910–11), p. 4.

It was a condition of the payment of the capitation grant[1] to a school that three-fourths of its pupils should pass an examination. The inspectors were kept fully employed in the schools and there was insufficient time to do more than test whole classes rather than individuals, a procedure which the Commissioners considered a "defect"; yet even these class examinations were thought by teachers to prejudice the instruction in the direction of cram. The reports which were made of these periodical tests furnished the material out of which a case was constructed unfavourable to the scheme of elementary instruction as it was being conducted. In good schools what was professedly taught was really learned; the Commissioners themselves affirmed that, in four-fifths of the inspected schools, children who remained at school till eleven or twelve, and reached the first class, received "a sound and useful education".[2] But the majority left school at eleven, or earlier, and did not reach the first class, and it was upon these children that the Newcastle *Report* was centred. Here the elementary knowledge was defective, reading being especially unsatisfactory; the teachers were not incompetent in any way, but in the Commissioners' judgement they shirked the necessary drudgery. The teachers themselves claimed to be judged by the performance of their first classes, which contained the pupils whose school lives were longest, and some inspectors supported that claim, although the Commissioners scouted it. Yet given the irregular attendance of the children, their short school life, the defective organization of most schools under one certificated teacher and a number of apprentices, the teachers' claim was not unreasonable. What was achieved in the first class was bringing order out of chaos, a business which cannot be hurried; and 80 per cent. of these classes gave evidence of having received sound, useful education at the early age of twelve.

The causes of such inefficiency as existed were obvious and their proper remedies were equally patent. "Mass production" and factory methods generally are not educative, or even efficient as so much instruction; the certificated teacher assisted only by pupil teachers was scarcely free to employ a more individual method. Yet as the trained, certificated teachers increased in number this defect was being gradually remedied; the system was not twelve years old when the Newcastle Commission began, its inquiry. Voluntary school attendance ter-

---

[1] See p. 153, above.   [2] *Report*, vol. i, p. 238.

minating before eleven years of age must, if public instruction were to be generally diffused, give way to universal compulsion and a school life prolonged to an age much beyond eleven. But on no account would the Commission recommend compulsory school attendance, to which they raised objections, some of which were social, some political, others merely fanciful—and all, it may be added, in the event mistaken. The Commissioners were not disturbed by the thought that children of ten and eleven were no longer schoolchildren but wage-earners whose formal education had ceased. On the contrary they proposed measures which rendered such a brief school life possible, covering this betrayal of principle by a delusive scheme of evening schools, in which such tired children as cared to resort to them after the day's work might receive the instruction which the day schools had not succeeded in giving them, but which even the Commissioners considered was either necessary or desirable. Some of the inspectors wished to make the English elementary school as efficient and as educative as the Prussian primary schools were generally believed to be. The Newcastle Commissioners preferred the ideal of Mr Fraser, the future bishop of Manchester. "We must make up our minds to see the last of him, as far as the day school is concerned, at 10 or 11. We must frame our system of education upon this hypothesis; and I venture to maintain that it is quite possible to teach a child soundly and thoroughly, in a way that he shall not forget it, all that is necessary for him to possess in the shape of intellectual attainment, by the time that he is ten years old." He goes on to specify these intellectual possessions: to spell the words the boy will have to use, read a common narrative or newspaper paragraph, write a legible and intelligible letter, make out or test a shop bill, have "some notion" where foreign countries lie on the habitable globe, be sufficiently acquainted with the Bible to follow "a plain Saxon sermon", remember enough of the Catechism to know his duty to God and man. "I have no brighter view of the future or the possibilities of an English elementary education floating before my eyes than this."[1] This is either clap-trap, or, at best, a house of cards, since, while "we" see the last of the boy in school at 10 or 11, it is not said when we see him there first, nor is there any guarantee that we shall see him there at all.

The Commissioners in making their final recommendations seem

[1] *Report*, vol. I, p. 243.

to have felt that they had not done full justice to the schools or to the teachers in animadverting upon their intellectual shortcomings, for they say "the religious and moral influence of the public schools appears to be very great, to be greater than even their intellectual influence. A set of good schools civilizes a whole neighbourhood. The' most important function of the schools is that which they best perform".[1] If that were so, there was not much that was seriously wrong with the elementary schools under inspection. But the explanation of these conflicting pronouncements lies in the fact that the Newcastle *Report* is the result of a compromise between a majority who accepted the principle of State-aided education and a minority who would give State aid only in very exceptional circumstances such as did not exist in England at that time. Moreover, majority and minority combined only numbered seven persons.

The *Report* makes no secret of the situation. The question of State grants in favour of public instruction and, more especially, the manner in which such grants were being administered by the Committee of Council were arraigned at the bar of public opinion; the Commissioners came to their inquiry not as judges with open minds but as adherents to one, or other, of two opposed sets of principles. "The greater portion of the members of the Commission are of opinion that the course pursued by the Government in 1839, in recommending a grant of public money for the assistance of education, was wise; that the methods adopted to carry out that object have proved successful" and, although considerable changes in the manner of giving aid are expedient, the amount of money grant for this purpose should neither be withdrawn nor largely diminished. The minority "hold that in a country situated politically and socially as England is, Government has ordinarily speaking no educational duties, except towards those whom destitution, vagrancy or crime casts upon its hands". "It must not be inferred that this is the only matter on which we differ...universal concurrence was not to be expected and has not in fact been obtained." In short, "there exists among the members of the Commission as among the nation at large deeply seated differences of opinion with regard to the duty of Government in this country towards education".[2]

As the inquiry proceeded it became clear that the powers of the Committee of Council on Education could not be curtailed, but should

---

[1] *Report*, vol. I, p. 273.   [2] See the *Report*, vol. I, pp. 297–299.

perhaps be enlarged; in this the minority acquiesced on the understanding that the Committee's expenditure should be reduced and its help extended to the barest rudiments only of instruction. So great a change in policy called for explanation and this was found in the relation of the teachers to their junior pupils. Careful instructions were given to the inspectors on this head. "Being instructed", says Mr Hare, "to ascertain whether trained teachers are disinclined to bestow proper attention upon reading, writing and arithmetic, particularly reading,. I have made this a subject of special inquiry and close examination." It is both curious and enlightening in this connexion to note that one inspector was astonished at his own discovery that "the language of books is an unknown tongue to the children of the illiterate".[1]

The operation of the Minute of 1846 which created the staff of certificated teachers was closely studied. The apprentices, those pupil teachers who, so Matthew Arnold said, were "the sinews of English primary instruction", were accounted by the Commission as "undoubtedly the most successful feature of the system" and presumably well worth the fifteen pounds which each annually cost the State.[2] The studies pursued in the training college were regarded in some quarters as being of a kind which was too advanced for persons who were to teach in elementary schools; and, further, it was believed that the large number of subjects which demanded attention within the compass of two or three years led to superficiality and conceit. In addition to instruction and practice in the art of teaching, religious knowledge, geography and history formed part of the student's education; to these, men students added science, mathematics, Latin, while the women took domestic economy and sewing. Drawing was an optional subject. Moseley and Temple (Archbishop of Canterbury, 1896–1902) were the authors of this curriculum; the former defended its breadth because its aim was "enlarging, strengthening and storing their minds, so as to enable them to teach with intelligence, force, readiness of application and fulness of illustration". The *Report* admits that there was ground for the complaint that too many subjects were taken up in the time available, yet regret is expressed that political economy and physiology were not included, studies which might be admitted even at the expense of the elementary subjects. The two voices of the Com-

---

[1] See the *Report*, vol. I, pp. 253, 255. [2] *Report*, vol. I, pp. 107, 346.

mission are here doubtless finding utterance. The general conclusion reached as to the training college curriculum was that it gave training which on the whole was sound, though there were several drawbacks to its value. The *Report* prints a salutary warning which is just as pertinent to the present day as it was to 1861. "It is also a common mistake to forget that the students on leaving the training college are only beginning their profession, and that thorough skill can only be obtained by practice. A training college can be expected to give its pupils only the power of learning their business. It cannot give actual proficiency in it."[1]

From apprentices and students in training the *Report* turned to the certificated teachers who, having passed the Certificate Examination of the Committee of Council, were actually conducting schools under inspection. In the schools of the displaced mutual system the best teachers (that is, the men and women in charge, not the monitors) were ignorant and unskilful, although often well-meaning and serious-minded, while "the inferior and more numerous class of teachers were unfit for their position and unqualified to discharge any useful function in education".[2] While so sweeping a condemnation could not be passed upon the teachers of inspected schools, there was a marked difference in the efficiency of the trained, certificated teacher and his confrère, whether certificated or merely registered, who had not been trained. And the trained teacher embodied the policy of the Committee of Council. Of 686 inspected schools 470 were conducted by trained teachers, the remainder by teachers untrained. Of the 470, 24 per cent. were marked good, 49 per cent. fair, 27 per cent. inferior, whereas 58 per cent. of the schools conducted by untrained teachers were inferior, 39 per cent. fair and only 3 per cent. good. Of trained teachers in general the Commissioners say: "Intellectually and morally they are far superior to untrained teachers, and there can be no doubt of their competence to teach elementary subjects thoroughly well to young children, or to see they are so taught by pupil teachers, if they had an adequate motive for doing so". Nevertheless, "they fail to a considerable extent in some of the most important duties of elementary teachers, and a large proportion of the children are not satisfactorily taught that which they come to school to learn".[3]

[1] *Report*, vol. I, pp. 116, 138.   [2] *Ibid.* p. 99.
[3] *Ibid.* pp. 155, 154.

The Commissioners were convinced that teachers avoided the drudgery involved in the instruction of the younger or less able children, and that this evasion of duty was the real and effective cause of the unsatisfactory state of children who left school at the age of ten or eleven. To drive the point home they made a quite illusory comparison between the results of teaching children in an educated home and in the elementary school, as though there were any real parallel between the two cases; the only difference of moment which they would admit is that the educated parent recognizes the absolute necessity of his child attaining the power to read. "It is natural to suppose that the same results [the conditions being quite different!] could be produced in elementary schools, if the teachers were thoroughly determined to produce them." Then follows a very inept reference to Eton, Harrow, Rugby and the many boys who leave those schools "unable to read an easy Latin book with satisfaction a year after they have left", a reference which scarcely proves their point, even if (as they put it) "to know Latin well is not absolutely essential, but to be able to read and write is so". The Public School master and the certificated teacher must suffer the same condemnation or be excused on similar grounds; or did the former regard Latin as unimportant, or teaching it as drudgery? A failure which condemned the elementary school, its teachers and the Committee of Council scheme as administered was condoned by the Commissioners when it occurred in the schools of another order. They were ready with a remedy. "There is only one way of securing this result (the successful teaching of the elementary subjects to the children under eleven) which is to institute a searching examination by competent authority of every child in every school to which grants are to be paid, with the view of ascertaining whether these indispensable elements of knowledge are thoroughly acquired, and to make the prospects and position of the teacher dependent to a considerable extent on the results of this examination.... The object is to find some constant and stringent motive to induce them to do that part of their duty which is at once most unpleasant and most important."[1]

The *Report* indeed spoke with two clearly distinguishable voices when referring to the certificated teachers. One voice said that they were skilful and competent, the other that they were neglectful of duty.

[1] *Report*, vol. I, pp. 156–7.

One denied that they were conceited in consequence of their education
or that they were lacking in good manners, a charge which the *Report*
brought against some school managers; this voice also denied that
teachers were dissatisfied with their position. The other voice com-
mented on two grievances entertained by teachers and declared both
to be ill-founded. The Minute of December, 1846, had vaguely promised
("may be granted" is the phrase) pensions to "*any* schoolmaster or
schoolmistress" rendered incapable of service by age or infirmity;
a Minute of August 6th, 1853, had limited the number of persons to
be pensioned to 270, amongst whom £6100 was to be divided annually,
with a further £400 to be distributed in special gratuities to an unspecified number of recipients. This later Minute the teachers considered
a breach of faith. Their dissatisfaction was not allayed by a circular
letter from the Committee of Council which reminded them that they
were not appointed or dismissed by Government, and informed them
that it was inexpedient to set up a compulsory superannuation fund,
but in the meantime teachers would be well advised to purchase
deferred annuities through the Post Office Savings Bank. The Newcastle
Commissioners with one of their voices declared that the action of the
Committee of Council in this matter was "satisfactory" and they urged
managers to impress upon teachers the importance of providing for
old age or disablement by saving a provision out of their "large
salaries". These were officially stated to be, in addition to a house, on
the average about £90 for men and £60 for women. The second
grievance was that the inspectorate was closed to teachers, not on the
score of inability but for social reasons. The *Report* views the exclusion
with complacency and does not scruple to quote an inspector who
said that teachers "in some cases are too apt to forget that they owe the
culture they have to the public provision made for them".[1] The statement did not come gracefully from men whose own education in
school and university had been obtained below cost price but without
any corresponding obligation of service. There was public discontent
with the policy of the Committee of Council and the chief agent of
that policy, the certificated teacher, was made the whipping-boy for
the offence: to effect his castigation the Commission recommended
a measure which gravely hindered elementary education for a
generation.

[1] *Report*, vol. i, pp. 157–164.

Since 1846 the Committee of Council had encouraged manual and industrial instruction in the elementary schools by offering contributions to the cost of field-gardens, workshops, wash-houses and kitchens; in the following year it established a scheme to assist such schools in purchasing class-books, maps and diagrams. The Committee issued a list compiled from publishers' catalogues and offered to pay one-third of the cost to schools making purchases from this list. In 1854 the average yearly number of sets of books and apparatus so purchased was said to be between 800 and 900; the grant amounted in 1860 to £5683. In addition £1000 was paid to an agency for collecting, packing and transmitting, and the Committee maintained a separate office and staff to administer the scheme.

The Committee expressly repudiated the assumption of censorship when it issued the list; there was no compulsion to purchase from it, no recommendation of the books or apparatus named in it. Yet it was difficult for the Committee to evade responsibility in the circumstances, and the Newcastle Commission reported that the books on the list, the reading-books in particular, "left much to be desired". The scheme was a modification of one introduced in 1833 by the Irish Board of National Education; but this body prepared and published a series of "readers", maps and text-books which became popular in this country on account of their cheapness and completeness. They were in fact the most popular school books used in England and they "left much to be desired". Schoolmasters complained of the difficulty of their diction, the inferiority of their poetry, dry outlines of grammar and geography, and of history in epitome "destitute of picturesqueness", "incapable of striking the imagination and awakening the sentiments of a child". "The fifth book is greatly taken up with science in a form too technical for the purpose. If science is to be taught by means of reading-books, care must be taken to translate it into familiar language, and to enlist the child's curiosity by illustrations drawn from daily life."[1]

The Commissioners unsparingly condemned the teaching of reading in classes below the first, and "reading" in school parlance means the fine art of reading aloud; yet it does not seem to have occurred to them that part of the explanation of the bad reading was to be found in their

[1] *Report*, vol. I, p. 351. On this book-distribution scheme see pp. 327 and 348 ff. of the *Report*.

own criticism of the reading-books. Matthew Arnold, in his "General Report for the year 1860", summed up the outstanding defect of these manuals as presenting "a literature such as that of the few attractive pieces in our current reading-books, a literature over which no cultivated person would dream of wasting his time".

The attention of the Commission and the major part of its *Report* were given up to the concerns of the "children of the independent poor"; but their commission bade them consider "all classes of the people" and they were not unmindful of the charge. They extended their inquiry to pauper children, to criminals and vagrants and to what they called the "State Schools", that is, the schools for the children of the fighting Services. They found that of the 44,608 pauper children under instruction, more than 84 per cent. were still being taught in workhouses, although by teachers who were not pauper inmates. It was difficult to enlist good teachers for the ill-paid, irksome duty, and the instruction given in workhouses was inefficient, while the moral defects of schools carried on in those institutions, which had been noted at an earlier day, were still apparent. On the other hand, "the success" of the district schools, founded by an Act of 1845, "was striking"; but these schools taught only 6 per cent. of the children, who were drawn from the neighbouring parishes which formed their district. The remaining 9 per cent. were in nineteen "separate schools", buildings which were often distant from the workhouse; these were "as. well managed and as successful as the district schools". There was no difficulty in procuring proper teachers for district or for separate schools. An Act of 1855 permitted Boards of Guardians, if they would, to pay for the instruction of the children of persons in receipt of outdoor relief. Comparatively few Boards exercised the right and the Commission recommended that the "may" of the Act should be converted into "must". On the other hand, they objected to the payment of school fees by Guardians on behalf of children whose parents were not receiving relief; such payments were a reversion to the conditions prevailing before 1834 and an obliteration of the distinction between the pauper and the independent labourer.

Private or semi-public benevolence long preceded State aid in furnishing the means of educating children who had been charged with crime, or whose circumstances gave reason to fear that they would become criminal. The Newcastle *Report* points to the activities of the

Philanthropic Society (founded 1788, incorporated by Act of Parliament, 1806) as including the earliest attempts to make special provision for such children; beside these there were reformatories, "homes", refuge and "ragged schools" under independent management serving the same purpose. The London Ragged School Union was formed in 1844 to safeguard the position of its individual schools; but, owing to the absence of trade instruction in 189 out of 192, their total number, ragged schools, like Sunday schools, were not thought by the Commissioners to be qualified to receive Government grants. An Act of Parliament of the last-named year extended State aid to the reformatory schools which educated children who had been convicted of criminal offences; three years later another Act gave similar help to industrial schools for children who were regarded as potential criminals. All these schools, except the ragged schools mentioned above, gave some form of industrial training.

Basing their opinion on official reports, the Commissioners believed that the garrison and regimental schools and the Arsenal school for apprentices at Woolwich were efficient. The regimental libraries and the popular and scientific lectures were well attended by the troops who shared "the wish for education now so prevalent among all classes". For the improvement of 39 per cent. of the rank and file "primary adult schools" were "indispensable"; the Army schools taught soldiers as well as the children borne on the regimental strengths. On discharge 32 per cent. were unable to sign their names. An examination of 10,000 British troops in 1856 showed that 27 per cent. were unable to write and 21 per cent. could neither read nor write. Of the German recruits in the British Foreign Legion of 1855 only 3 per cent. were unable to write, of the Italian recruits, 20 per cent. The Newcastle Commissioners at the expense of a good many platitudes express approval of the Army educational system as modified in 1846, when a normal school for training Army schoolmasters was established at the Royal Military Asylum, Chelsea, known also as the Duke of York's school, which became a "model school" for the Service.

Schooling in the Navy was another story in which the reforms of 1846 had no place. The Commission got its information through one of their number who "examined personally and by letter naval officers of distinction to whom he was commended by the Admiralty". Apparently he was not warmly welcomed. "The officers are not alive to its importance"; the Admiralty turned a deaf ear to requests for competent teachers. The "Seamen's Schoolmasters" were as a class not qualified for teaching and, unlike the Army schoolmasters, they could not look to promotion to warrant rank. The Army system was partially adopted by the Royal Marine schools at Woolwich, Portsmouth, Chatham and Plymouth; but the pay and rank of the teachers were below the Army level. The Commissioners reported that these schools did not appear to be efficient.

To advance the education of the apprentices schools had been established at Deptford, Woolwich, Chatham, Sheerness, Portsmouth, Devonport and Pembroke Dockyards, entrance to which was through an examination conducted by the Civil Service Commissioners. Their leading studies were mathematics and physical science and the Commission, while referring to them as "valuable institutions", thought they were not as efficient as they might be, owing to the teachers' shortcomings. On that ground the panacea of the Newcastle Commission was suggested. "We recommend that, if possible, the masters have more direct interest in the school and that the increase of their pay depend upon the report of the inspector"—that is, "payment by results". In connexion with these dockyard schools mention is made of an early use of the intelligence test, as applied by Mr Patrick Cumin of the Education Department. "In order to test the intelligence of the lads [Devonport Dockyard apprentices] I asked them to define an 'endowed school'".[1] Beyond furnishing a rough test of Mr Cumin's own intelligence, there is no record of the result. In the Upper School at Greenwich Hospital it was reported by an examining committee in 1859 that general education was sacrificed to mathematics and navigation. The Newcastle Commission recommended that a model school should be instituted at Greenwich like that at Chelsea and that a body of Royal Naval schoolmasters should replace the Seamen's Schoolmasters.

The *Report* states that in 1858 there were in England and Wales 22,740 public elementary week-day schools whose income, exclusive of Government grants, was £1,121,981. Of these schools 9378 were inspected by the Committee of Council's Education Department, and of this smaller number 6897 received Government grants. There were 1,101,545 pupils in the inspected schools, the Government grants being paid in respect of 917,255 children. By "school" the *Report*

[1] *Report*, vol. i, p. 438.

meant a separate school department under a separate principal teacher; thus, a school consisting of separate departments for boys, girls and infants respectively, each under its own principal, counted as three schools. The total Parliamentary grant for schools paid between 1839 and 1860 was about £5,400,000.[1]

The Commission estimated that the aggregate annual revenue of charities devoted to education was about £375,000. These were distributed for the most part according to the incidence of the population in the sixteenth and seventeenth centuries, an incidence very unlike that of the nineteenth. It was difficult to disentangle from the whole that which properly belonged to elementary education, owing to the changes in the character of individual schools in the course of time. There were, however, endowed schools which, for various reasons, were giving primary instruction only; and such rudimentary teaching formed the curriculum of endowed charity schools and such parish schools as were maintained out of the proceeds of parish property. In Wales "Madam Bevan's Charity", which had been in operation since 1809, supported thirty or forty "circulating schools", paying the masters (who went from parish to parish, remaining in each six months, two years, three years) £25 to £35 per annum. This was one of the richest charities in Wales, if not the richest; but the general opinion was that it was "in every way ineffective in the promotion of education".[2]

As a whole the endowed elementary schools were inefficient; the Bishop of Carlisle described those he knew best as "the curse of his diocese". The Commission recommended that the masters of such schools should qualify for their posts by becoming certificated teachers and that the schools should be open to H.M. inspectors. This modest recommendation seems to have suggested to its authors another, much more comprehensive and open to question. It was that the Committee of Council should supersede the Charity Commission in respect of educational trusts, and thus become the central authority for public education.[3] It was becoming recognized that the country stood very badly in want of such an authority. But the Commission's proposal

---

[1] *Report*, vol. 1, p. 574.
[2] *Ibid.* p. 466. Bevan's Charity continued the work of the "circulating schools" established in 1730 by Griffith Jones; it was sadly hindered by litigation. See J. E. G. de Montmorency, *State Intervention in English Education* (1902), pp. 203 ff.
[3] *Ibid.* pp. 481 ff.

was that the Privy Council should act through the newly instituted Education Department; and the history of that body during the generation which followed the Newcastle Commission was not such as to inspire confidence in it as administrator of English education in all its grades. A Board of Education working in conjunction with duly constituted local authorities is one thing; an Education Department playing "instans tyrannus" with a multitude of independent schools was quite another. The need of a central administrative body must be admitted; but the political conditions in 1861 were not congenial to its successful establishment. However, if the Committee of Council system was on its trial, the Newcastle Commission certainly found a verdict in its favour. The immediate purpose of the Commission's proposals, beyond the efficiency of the endowed schools, seems to have been the reduction of the Government grants that were being paid to elementary schools situated in towns which possessed school endowments. The justification for the transfer was found in the fact that "grammar learning" was not greatly in demand and in consequence these endowments were being wasted on a few pupils.

The Commissioners were of opinion that "the existing plan", that is, the voluntary system as administered by the Education Department of the Committee of Council, "was the only one by which it would be possible to secure the religious character of popular education". The feeling in the country was against secular education; indeed a clear cut between religious and secular instruction is impracticable so far as humane studies are concerned. The facts were against undenominational religious teaching; of the pupils in "public" schools, 85·6 per cent. were being taught in denominational schools attached mostly but not exclusively to the Church of England. The faults of the system were financial and administrative and the teaching of the elementary subjects was defective.[1] It cost too much and the procedure by which the Government dealt directly and individually with certificated teachers and pupil teachers in respect of their emoluments was costly, cumbrous and wasteful. This last criticism originated with R. R. W. Lingen, Kay-Shuttleworth's successor in the office of secretary to the Committee of Council; the first secretary's plan in this particular threatened to break down under its own weight. The difficulty in which the officials found themselves was made the occasion, or the

[1] *Report*, vol. I, pp. 310–13.

excuse, for abolishing a procedure which gave colour to the belief that teachers were servants of the State, and not of particular bodies of school managers.

Lingen estimated the entire expense of the *public* aid to education at eighteen shillings per child, the estimate including the cost of teachers' training, school inspection and administrative charges borne by the Education Department. The original stipulation that public grants should be met by private subventions of at least equal amount was infringed by the capitation grant of 1853 and its amount was very rapidly increasing in response to appeals. In 1854 this particular grant stood at £5957; in five years' time it had become £61,183 and the Commissioners foresaw a time when it would be £300,000 per annum.[1]

Compulsory schooling "would entail so much difficulty and danger, and give so great a shock to our educational and social system" that the Commissioners could not recommend compulsion, but would rather trust to the persuasion which might be exercised by "active and right-minded employers, land-owners, clergymen and other persons of local influence". The Commission accepted the fact that the majority of children ceased to attend school and "went to work" at ten or eleven. They not only palliated but encouraged this brief schooling by proposing that working children of eleven should attend evening schools. "If the education of the country were in a good state, they [evening schools] would be nearly universal and would serve to compensate the scantiness of the instruction given in day schools by giving more advanced instruction to an older class of scholars."[2]

But the outstanding recommendation of the Newcastle Commission is summarized in a sentence which occurs on p. 96 of the *Report*. "We think that the assistance given by the State to education should assume the form of a bounty rate paid upon the production of certain results by any person." That is "payments" should be by "results", a catch-word which commended itself to a commercial and strongly individualist community not likely to ask whether the "results" were worth paying for and, if so, whether it was possible to measure them. "There is only one way of securing this result, which is to institute a searching examination by competent authority of every child in every school to which grants are to be paid, with the view of ascertaining whether these indispensable elements of knowledge (reading, writing,

[1] *Report*, vol. I, p. 316.　　　　　　　[2] *Ibid.* pp. 201 and 86.

ciphering) are thoroughly acquired, and to make the prospects and position of the teacher dependent, to a considerable extent, on the results of this examination."[1]

The inspectors' reports, as distinct from those of the assistant commissioners, do not warrant this sweeping condemnation of the rudimentary teaching, yet the system of "payment by results" was at once made an essential part of educational administration. The *Report* itself said, "education to be good must always be expensive", that parents and "religious and charitable persons interested in the condition of the poor" could not by themselves meet this expense (p. 297) although "good elementary education cannot be obtained without considerable expense" (p. 303). Yet mindful of their commission to seek an elementary education which was to be cheap, they proposed a measure which must inevitably seriously check, if not diminish, State expenditure on popular education, while the instruction itself was to be reduced to the barest elements, since managers and teachers must in self-defence concentrate their efforts upon the "3 R's". Adverse critics of the *Report* pointed out that a lowering of the *status* and stipends of certificated teachers would end in a lowering of the teaching, since the better qualified by character and ability would cease to recruit the teachers' ranks.

The Commission desired to attain three principal objects, a diminution of the State grant, more effective teaching of the three elementary subjects in the junior classes and the stimulation of a much greater local interest in local schools. It proposed to achieve all three by making the publicly contributed funds of a particular school depend upon the individual examination of the children attending it. In every county or county division having a separate rate, and in every corporate town with a population exceeding 40,000 inhabitants, a Board of Education was to be set up. These Boards were to appoint and pay examiners, certificated schoolmasters of at least seven years' standing, by whom, and not by H.M. inspectors, the children were to be examined. The county or borough was to pay grants to its schools in proportion to their several successes in these examinations. To be eligible for a share of these county or borough rates and of the State grant, schools must be registered with the Education Department on the report of H.M. inspector of schools as "elementary schools for the education of the

[1] *Report*, vol. I, p. 157.

poor", the premises must be properly drained and ventilated and the principal room must afford at least eight square feet of floor space per pupil in average attendance. The county or borough examiners were to examine in reading, writing and arithmetic; in respect of each child who passed the examination a sum varying from 22s. 6d. to 21s. was to be paid to the school out of the local rate.[1] The total cost per child was at that time reckoned at thirty shillings per annum.[2]

Under the terms proposed a private school, equally with one conducted by a religious body or other semi-public association, could share in the State grant to schools and presumably in the local rate also. "We think that the assistance given by the State to education should assume the form of a bounty upon the production of certain results by any person whatever. We consider it unfair to exclude the teachers of private schools from a share in this bounty, if they can prove that they have produced the result".[3] The examination for certificates under the Education Department should be thrown open to teachers in private schools which satisfied the requirements for registration. State grants should be payable only to schools which were directed by a certificated teacher. The State and the local subventions must not exceed the sum of the children's school pence together with the patrons' subscriptions, or 15s. per child in attendance, whichever was the less. The Commission estimated that the annual charge on the State would be £630,000, on local rates £428,000; it was supposed that a five-farthing rate would discharge local obligations under this head.[4] This was the financial stroke which the Newcastle Commission was expected to make; an increase of £500,000 in the cost of public education was to be contemplated, but it was to come from local taxation, the charge on the Exchequer remaining as before.

The other Royal Commissions on education of this period were followed by Acts of Parliament, but the Newcastle Commission had no such sequel. The Commission's one recommendation which appealed to the Government was that known as "payment by results" and effect was given to this by the administrative action of the Education Department with the sanction of the House of Commons. Since 1839 the

---

[1] *Report*, vol. 1, pp. 328 ff. [2] *Ibid.* p. 345.
[3] *Ibid.* p. 96. The word "bounty" here surely should be "cash on delivery"; "free trade", "protection", "bounty", were popular catch-words which tended to becloud thought. [4] *Ibid.* pp. 345 f.

Committee of Council had regulated its relations to the schools by the issue from time to time of "Minutes" which were consolidated in 1858 and published as a Parliamentary paper. In June of the following year there was a change of Government, Palmerston succeeding Derby; in the new administration Robert Lowe (1811–92) was Vice-President of the Council, that is, head of the Education Department. One of the earliest pieces of work carried out during his tenure of this office was the digestion of the Minutes into the form of a code of regulations; and in April, 1860, the House of Commons directed that this document, which was subsequently named the "Old" or "Original Code", should be printed and published. Henceforward, the Vice-President annually laid the "Code" upon the table of the House, where, subject to amendment, it remained for a month; at the expiration of this time it had the force of statute law in the form it had assumed at the close of the month's probation. As a rule, Parliament accepted the Code without criticism; indeed it was often presented "in dummy". But the Old Code did not enjoy so uneventful a history.

The Newcastle *Report* appeared in March, 1861, and opposition was at once aroused. Believing that he was assisting the Committee of Council to dispose of impracticable advice, Kay-Shuttleworth addressed a letter on April 24th to Earl Granville, President of the Council, in which he defended the system of 1846 and its administration in Whitehall, and condemned the proposal to transfer two-fifths of the cost of education from the taxes to the rates. He took the ground that the transfer could only mean local control of the schools by authorities who were hostile to the denominational system which was overcoming the religious difficulty. "Payment by results" would, he maintained, limit instruction to the "3 R's" to the neglect of more liberal influences and of moral training, and that the so-called "free-trade" in instruction would displace pupil teachers and certificated teachers in favour of poorly qualified or quite unqualified persons who would be attracted by the offer of grants.

On the other hand, the *Edinburgh Review* (July, 1861), which professed agreement with the minority of the Commissioners, vigorously attacked the system of 1846; its administration by the Education Department was described as "the most entirely *bureaucratic* of all the offices now existing in this country, and we mean by that term an office in which the subordinate members of the Department do in reality exercise an almost absolute authority under the 'clarum et venerabile nomen' of the Privy Council of England". These officials dispensed "large sums of public money on principles determined by themselves"; the business employed fourteen senior officers, fifty clerks, sixty inspectors, a staff exceeding in number the whole strength of the Home Department; yet it was insufficient for its work. The certificated teachers, 25,000 in number, formed a body of extremely well-educated well-behaved and valuable members of society for many purposes; "but are they *primary* teachers?" They were not the sort of people to teach rudiments; less highly trained teachers and less artificial methods would be more to the purpose. The whole system of popular instruction was "pitched too high". Still the *Review* admitted that "it is certain that a much better education can now be obtained in a National school for twopence a week than in a middle school for one or two shillings a week".

A leading motive of Palmerston's Ministry, as voiced by Gladstone, its Chancellor of the Exchequer, was an early and drastic reduction of taxation; if an argument for economy were needed, the ominous clouds which hung about England's foreign relations in the early 'sixties' supplied it. Of a national income standing at £70,000,000, £24,000,000 being spent on the Navy and Army, the sum of £724,403 was devoted to education, more than half of it going to teachers and training colleges. The Vice-President had decided to reduce expenditure in his Department by adopting the Commission's recommendation to pay grants to schools in proportion to the attendance of individual pupils and the success of those pupils in an examination restricted to reading, writing and summing. In a speech on the estimates (July 11th, 1861) Lowe declared that it was not intended to change the voluntary or denominational system, nor to adopt the recommendation to relieve taxation by drawing heavily on the local rates, nor to abrogate the rule which made the employment of a certificated teacher obligatory upon every aided school. But some vital changes in the system of 1846 were intended. It was to be made clear to certificated teachers, to their apprentices and to lecturers in training colleges that they were not, as many deemed themselves, civil servants; they would no longer receive pay or augmentation of pay direct and individually from the Education Department but from their several managing committees with whom all future arrangements respecting stipends must be made. From this speech it appeared that in effect, if not in intention, the number of years to be spent in training for the work of teaching would be reduced from two, or three, to one. But the most drastic change foreshadowed was that summarized in the phrase "payment by results". Schools were not to be aided in proportion to their needs and their own provision for meeting those needs, but in accordance with their attainments as evidenced by the attendance of their scholars and the success of their scholars individually in examination in the three primary studies. "Hitherto", said Lowe, "we have been living under a system of bounties and protection; now we prefer to have a little free trade." These alterations were embodied in a Minute constituting a revision of the Old Code of the previous year, and the document, the Revised Code, was published on July 29th, 1861, at the close of the Parliamentary session.

For the next six months there followed a storm of protest carried on in the Press, and by much pamphleteering, by memorials, deputations and public meetings. The various societies which represented the voluntary system, in spite of their differences of religious opinion and practice, made common cause against the Revised Code; resolutions condemning it were passed by county associations of schoolmasters. F. J. A. Hort, then a Hertfordshire vicar, described it as "a reckless pursuit of cheapness", "an unobtrusive alliance with the numerous persons who hate and fear the education of the lower classes, but dare not confess their feelings".[1] The language of economics was "in the air" at this time; "supply and demand" and similar formulas were freely bandied about by the Code's supporters, who did not see that they were irrelevant. Education is not trade. Hort appropriately answered them by saying that if the poor were content to accept the "3 R's" as "education" it was all the more incumbent upon their richer fellows to correct so narrow a conception, for the poor have the greatest need of a "liberal education", not a feeble or mutilated copy of what passes under that name, but one capable of producing corresponding effects by different means. It was not the State's part to withhold supply until a demand was formulated or otherwise obvious, but to create the demand. *The Times* was one of the few newspapers which approved the Code; but in this connexion that journal meant

[1] *Thoughts on the Revised Code of Education, its purposes and probable effects,* 38 pp. (1861).

Robert Lowe himself, then one of its leader-writers. On September 26th, *The Times* announced that the Revised Code would be suspended until after March 31st, 1862.

Still the protests continued. The *Edinburgh Review* of October, 1861, reported that the "outcry" was "already vehement", that the Vice-President had substituted an entirely new system for that of 1846 and it approved payment by results as "a sound principle", "a great improvement". One pamphleteer[1] agreed that the principle was "fair and sound", but only if the right sort of results was obtained and if they were capable of being estimated. He charged the Newcastle Commission with misinterpreting the evidence and the assistant commissioners with incompetence. Professor John Grote[2] declared that the Code, if adopted in its entirety, would be injurious to education and unfairly hard upon managers and teachers; "success in teaching is a function of the recipient as well as of the communicator, a good deal of failure of it there must always, and in every system of education, necessarily be". Stupidity, idleness, irregular attendance and sickness cannot but affect the results of instruction. In the altered relation of teachers to the Education Department Grote saw a breach of faith.

In November Kay-Shuttleworth again addressed a letter to Earl Granville in which he denied the truth of the Commissioners' criticism but somewhat weakened his case by an over-statement of the illiteracy and barbarity prevailing amongst the poor in 1839, and by the admission that schools could not reach the standard of attainment needed to secure a grant. He was convinced that the Revised Code would check the recruiting of teachers, lower the standard of instruction and of the training of teachers, give money where it was less needed and withhold it from needy schools.[3] He foresaw that the more prosperous schools would be "farmed" to the teachers to make what they could out of them. Subsequent history bore out these gloomy anticipations. In short, the system of 1846 assumed that the State was responsible for public education, whereas the State's duty as envisaged in the Revised

[1] Omega, *Why is a new Code wanted?* 32 pp. (1861).

[2] *A few words on the new educational Code*, 48 pp. (1862).

[3] Another letter-writer to Granville (T. R. Birks, *The Revised Code*, 44 pp. (1862)) pointed out that under this Code schools would incur all their expenses before the payment was even measured.

Code was limited to *aiding* rudimentary instruction when and where "the poor asked for it". The State had created and supported the very system which its Code would weaken or destroy.[1] Vindication of the Code was attempted by Dr C. J. Vaughan, head master of Harrow (1844–59) and afterwards Dean of Llandaff, and by James Fraser, one of the assistant commissioners; but the attempts were refuted by John Menet of the Hockerill Training College.[2] As a practical schoolmaster, Vaughan could not approve the grouping of children for examination solely on the ground of age; he naturally suggested that examination should be based upon attainment or alleged attainment. Even Fraser saw an objection to making payments to schools depend upon the individual examination of babies of three and four. Yet Mr Lowe's Code directed the examination of school children arranged in four groups according to age, 3–7, 7–9, 9–11 and 11 onwards.

On February 13th, 1862, the Vice-President introduced the Revised Code in the House of Commons in a long speech of defence and justification. The system introduced by the Committee of Council was admittedly only experimental and in the event its administration had become "circumlocution and red tape" which must be replaced by greater simplicity. During the past year the Education Department had had 38,331 separate correspondents, the great majority of whom were unpractised in official business. The system was wasteful, money sometimes going to schools which could afford to pass it on to the children who had earned it by their attendance; at the same time only a minority of schools received Government aid. An extension of such aid was necessary and, to make extension possible, "a lower kind of teacher must be employed", security being taken that his humbler task was duly performed. Inspection of schools was not sufficient; and the examinations required by the Capitation grant of 1853 had not really been carried out. Children must be examined in the rudiments individually but infants under six would not be examined; in their case the grant would be calculated upon attendance, but both attendance

---

[1] Kay-Shuttleworth's two letters to Earl Granville are published in his *Four Periods of Public Education*, pp. 555 ff.

[2] Respectively, *The Revised Code...dispassionately considered*, 46 pp., *The Revised Code...principles, tendencies, and details*, 37 pp., both of November, 1861, and *The Revised Code*, 80 pp., January, 1862.

and success in examination would be taken into account in respect of children above that age. Compulsion to attend school was out of the question; the children's earnings forbade it.[1] The fact must be faced that most children left school at or before the age of eleven; therefore the day schools must do their best for children below that age. Evening schools could make good the deficiency by teaching children after working hours; grants would be paid to these schools in respect of the attendance and attainments (as proved by individual examination) of the pupils above twelve, not thirteen years of age as originally proposed. The general principle governing the payment of grants to schools would be a capitation grant upon attendance subject to deductions for defects of instruction or accommodation; of these deductions the most considerable would be those made for failures in examination. "We are not willing to extend grants to day schools beyond one payment to a child over eleven, because children who remain there after twelve years of age are mostly children for whom the schools were not intended. Every parent who sends a child to school is a recipient (annually) of twenty-three shillings made up of *private charity and public relief*"— the italics are not Lowe's. And this from a Liberal Minister of the Crown!

The Vice-President justified the reduction of aid to training colleges; they were started as voluntarily supported institutions whereas now Government paid 90 per cent., in one case 99 per cent., of their expenses. The payment of £100 a year to specialist lecturers encouraged the study of "subjects remote from the necessary business of the school". The augmentation of teachers' salaries, graded according to the class of their certificates, induced students unnecessarily to prolong their residence beyond one year. However, the Government would not persist in requiring a diminution in the number of Queen's Scholars and of training college lecturers.

The stormy reception accorded to the Code and the "vehement" criticism to which it had been subjected for months before this speech was delivered did not cause the Government to budge from its position. There were modifications but they were of relatively small importance. The most determined opponents, next to the teachers, were the country clergy upon whom the upkeep of the schools laid a heavy burden. By

[1] Fraser, *The Revised Code, ut supra*, called it "the peremptory demands of the labour market".

way of placating them, Lowe had said at the outset of his speech that they were mistaken in thinking that any change was intended in the position assigned to religion in aided schools; it still underlay "the whole system of Privy Council education". In view of Lowe's well-known opinion on this matter, the assurance was opportune. He announced that the Code would come into operation after March 31st, 1863, thus making a second postponement. "I cannot promise the House that this system will be an economical one, and I cannot promise that it will be an efficient one, but I can promise that it shall be one or the other. If it is not cheap, it shall be efficient; if it is not efficient it shall be cheap. The present is neither one nor the other....In this way we make a double use of our money...it is a spur to improvement, it is not a mere subsidy, but a motive of action, and I have the greatest hopes of the improved prospects of education, if this principle is sanctioned."[1]

The Code was debated during March, 1862, in both Houses of Parliament, and in the following month the controversy was closed by the Government's announcement of the only modifications which it could accept. These dealt with the way in which the payment by results was to be determined and paid, leaving the principles and main lines of the Revised Code unchanged. The *New Code* fixed the full capitation grant at 12s., 4s. in respect of a minimum of 200 attendances in the year, and 2s. 8d. on successful examination in reading, with the like payment in respect of the other two primary subjects. Children below six years of age were not to be examined and for them the grant of 6s. 6d. was to be payable on attendance. A similar scheme with lower grants applied to evening schools. The distribution of the pupils for examination into four groups according to age was superseded in the New Code by their division amongst six standards corresponding to as many years of school life, terminating at the age of twelve.

The requirements for Standard I, age 6–7, were those set in the Revised Code for Group I, 3–7; and those for Standard VI, age 11–12, repeated the original requirements for Group IV, except that simple proportion was omitted. In Standard I children were required to read narrative in monosyllables (a requirement which proved that the

---

[1] *Speech of the Right Hon. Robert Lowe, M.P., on the Revised Code...in the House of Commons, February 13th,* 1862, 91 pp., p. 65.

syllabus-maker had not grasped the difficulty of teaching children to read in English, at least), to form on blackboard or slate from dictation, letters, capital and small manuscript, to form similarly from dictation figures up to 20, to name at sight figures up to 20, to add and substract figures up to 10 orally from examples on the blackboard. At the other end of the scale Standard VI was expected to read a short ordinary paragraph in a newspaper or other modern narrative, to write similar matter from dictation and to work a sum in practice or bills of parcels. These "subjects" with plain needlework for girls were the compulsory studies, on which alone grants were payable; they virtually formed, with religious instruction, the curriculum of the public elementary school.[1]

An unsuccessful attempt, more than once repeated, was made by John Walter, M.P. for Nottingham and chief proprietor of *The Times*, to obtain the abrogation of the rule which made it compulsory for a grant-aided school to employ a certificated teacher; "free trade" notwithstanding, the attempt was obstinately, if illogically, defeated by Lowe and his successor in the Vice-Presidency. Walter's purpose, of course, was to secure Government aid for the small rural schools[2] whose managers were unable to pay the salary of a fully qualified teacher. That being the case, it was perhaps to be expected that he and his numerous supporters would insinuate that the uncertificated man was the better schoolmaster.

Payment by results began by acting as a brake upon public expenditure; the grant which stood in 1861 at £813,441 had fallen by more than £76,000 in 1865. But although it might be argued that the device secured cheapness, its outstanding defect was that it discouraged soundness. Its limited application impoverished the curriculum; and, since the teacher's reputation and very livelihood became dependent upon a high percentage of "passes" in the three rudimentary studies, cram and an even cruel concentration upon work done by the dullards, with a corresponding neglect of the more capable children, were

---

[1] The standards of examination underwent revision (and were at each revision increased in bulk and difficulty) in 1871, 1875, 1882, 1895. A Seventh Standard was added in 1882.

[2] In 1863 the unassisted schools numbered some 15,000, the assisted 8000. See John Walter, M.P., "*Education*. Correspondence relative to the Resolutions to be moved on the subject of the Education Grant on Tuesday, May 5th" (1863).

commonly noted in schools under the New Code of 1862. The adverse critics of that Code were vindicated by the fact that, for nearly thirty years thereafter, the English public elementary school was engaged in breaking the fetters or in mitigating the evils inherent in Lowe's work, until in 1890 payment by results was abandoned as an administrative principle in a sphere to which it was inapplicable.[1]

Kay-Shuttleworth's condemnation, made in 1868, although somewhat rhetorical in its phrasing, is in the main just. "The Revised Code has constructed nothing; it has only pulled down. It has not simplified the administration. It did not pretend to accelerate the rate of building schools or to improve their structure. It has not promoted the more rapid diffusion of annual grants and inspection to the apathetic parts of cities, or the founding of schools in small parishes and for the sparse population of rural districts. It has generally discouraged all instruction above the elements and failed in teaching them. It has disorganized the whole system of training teachers and providing an efficient machinery of instruction for schools. These ruins are its only monuments. It has not succeeded in being efficient; for it wastes the public money without producing the results which were declared to be its main object."[2]

The New Code's sins against sound education are obvious enough. Yet a Cabinet which included Earl Russell, a life-long supporter of the British and Foreign School Society, was ultimately responsible for it, while its author was a Vice-President who was ignorant neither of the nature of education nor of its public administration. For seven years Robert Lowe had been a very successful, hard-working Oxford "coach", alive to the difference between knowledge and smattering and fully conscious of the use which could be made of cram and of the small worth of its results. During his subsequent career in Australia he had been an opponent of compulsory gratuitous instruction and a defeated champion of unsectarian education. He had great faith in the value of examinations; as joint secretary of the Board of Control for India in the Aberdeen Ministry he had been instrumental in sub-

[1] Payment based on the individual examination of every pupil in the "three R's" ceased in 1890; an examination of selected pupils in "specific subjects" in 1897.

[2] *Memorandum on the Present State of the Question of Popular Education,* p. 30.

stituting examination for nomination in appointments to the Indian Civil Service (1853). He held that examinations for degrees at Oxford and Cambridge should be conducted by the Civil Service Commissioners who were appointed to examine, in and after 1855, candidates for certain of the public services. His life in Sydney had not impressed him favourably with democracy and he knew that only a very limited achievement could be attained by children who came from homes chiefly illiterate and who abandoned school about the age of eleven. A man of Lowe's intelligence and record could not miss the real solution of the educational problem as it then presented itself, namely, compulsory attendance at school beyond that age. But Lowe would not budge from his individualist, free trade standing ground, and compulsion was contrary to individualism and free trade. He could not apply the remedy nor frustrate "the demands of labour", otherwise the call of capital for cheap labour.

Twenty years afterwards in writing to Lingen, his second in command in 1862, Lowe described his Code and the rule of payment by results as "more a financial than a literary preference". However irrelevant the remark may be to the most serious criticism of the New Code, it recalls a fundamental factor of the political situation of the early 'sixties'. Gladstone, the Chancellor of the Exchequer, was intent upon a drastic reduction in the public expenditure, a policy warmly supported by Russell. Had Lowe so desired, a subordinate member of the Government could not oppose; the Code was intended to restrict if not to reduce (as it did reduce) the demands of elementary education upon the Consolidated Fund. Earl Russell as Foreign Secretary was scarcely able to note closely so purely domestic a business as education, in view of the condition of affairs in both hemispheres at this period, a condition which gave rise to the gravest anxiety. Moreover, the Cabinet was not so united a body as to permit any of its member to risk public disagreement with his colleagues.

But neither finance nor an unstable Ministry affords all the explanation possible of the abandonment of the policy laid down in 1846. Kay-Shuttleworth had devised an office procedure which his successor regarded as cumbrous to the extent of being unworkable; and Lingen had seized the opportunity afforded by the Newcastle Commission for effecting a radical change. Hence the new rules which cut off the teachers from any direct association with the Education Department, so destroying their standing of *quasi* civil servants. Lingen, like Lowe and Russell, was an advocate of unsectarian education; and a serious blow to the denominational schools would not have greatly distressed any of them. Lingen indeed was suspected by some opponents of the Revised Code of being the real "villain of the piece".

It was not a happy family over which Lingen presided at the Education Department. Not only were he and his staff overworked, but there was friction between the indoor and outdoor officers, disagreement as to policy between Lingen and some of the school inspectors, and disputes between the Department and the managers of schools. Neither Lowe nor Lingen thought it needful to soften the asperity or qualify the assertiveness, characteristics of both men, with which decisions were sometimes communicated. Naturally this behaviour bred enemies. In April, 1864, Lord Robert Cecil (afterwards Marquess of Salisbury), seconded by John Walter of *The Times* and supported by W. E. Forster, moved in the House of Commons "that in the opinion of this House the mutilation of the reports of Her Majesty's Inspectors of Schools and the exclusion from them of statements and opinions adverse to the educational views entertained by the Committee of Council, while matter favourable to them is admitted, are variations of the understanding under which the appointment of the Inspectors was originally sanctioned by Parliament and tend entirely to destroy the value of their reports". The motion was carried by a small majority. It has been supposed that Lingen, not Lowe, was aimed at in this resolution. The *Saturday Review*, in its issue four days after the condemnation had been passed, speaking of the two men said: "If rumour does not belie him, Mr Lingen is quite as powerful and a good deal more offensive. It is from Mr Lingen that all the sharp, snubbing replies proceed, which have imprinted upon half the rural parishes in the country a deep conviction that the Education Department is their natural enemy, whom it is their first duty to elude, baffle and disprove to the utmost of their power."[1]

Whether the culprit was the permanent civil servant or his temporary titular chief, the Vice-President of the Council, Lowe of course accepted full responsibility, resigned his office and asked that a Select Committee be appointed to inquire into the charge. This Committee

[1] A. Patchett Martin, *Life and Letters...of Viscount Sherbrooke*, 2 vols. (1893), pp. 221 ff.

exonerated Lowe and the Education Department, and on July 26th, 1864, the House rescinded its resolution of April 12th. The explanation offered in *The Times* was to the effect that what had been termed "mutilation" was only the removal of irrelevant passages and of mischievous partisan expressions of opinion.

CHAPTER IX

The Ancient Public Schools

The University Commissions incidentally exhibited the close relationship existing between the two Universities and the ancient Public Schools, a relationship so close that changes at Oxford and Cambridge in not a few cases called for corresponding changes in the schools. The association brought to a point that public interest in education which was a feature of English life at the time. The Universities and the elementary schools had had their turn and in the early 'sixties' adverse criticism of the Public Schools appeared in the Press. Amongst the most pointed was a series of three *Letters* addressed to the *Cornhill Magazine*[1] by "Paterfamilias", who based his observations upon Eton as typical of the older Public Schools in general.

The chief contentions of these *Letters* were that the school was grossly understaffed, its teachers overpaid and overworked, and that mathematics, modern languages, modern history and modern geography were of trifling importance compared with Greek and Latin, while these two languages were nevertheless inefficiently taught. The boys contracted luxurious and self-indulgent habits at this "the most expensive school in England"; the cost of their education was excessive, yet such of them as desired to enter the Army or the Civil Service found it necessary to seek the help of the crammer in order to pass the qualifying examinations. Still the school was very popular amongst the landed and propertied class.

In his first *Letter* "Paterfamilias" had thinly disguised under the name, Harchester, the school which he knew best; but after the delivery at Tiverton in October, 1860, of a lecture by a still older Etonian, Sir John Taylor Coleridge, the disguise was dropped. Coleridge agreed with "Paterfamilias" in condemning the vicious circle in which the Eton boy passed as a scholar to the other foundation of Henry VI, King's College, Cambridge, there automatically attained his fellowship and his degree and in due course by seniority returned to Eton as a master. "Paterfamilias" was too well-informed and cogent a critic

---

[1] May and December 1860 and March 1861. The writer, an old Etonian of Keate's time (1809–34), was said to be Matthew James Higgins ("Jacob Omnium").

to be ignored; replies were made on behalf of the Public Schools in the *Quarterly Review* of October, 1860, and on behalf of Eton by one of its masters, William Johnson (Wm. Cory) in a pamphlet, *Eton Reform*, which was not fortunate in its support of a weak case. Newspapers and magazines took up the dispute, mostly siding with the writer of the three *Letters*. The *Edinburgh Review* (April, 1861) declared that the only adequate remedy for the state of things existing in the schools was the appointment of a Royal Commission with full powers to visit not Eton alone, but Winchester, Westminster, Harrow and Rugby also; and it welcomed the prospect of such an inquisition.

The animadversions upon Eton were but particular illustrations of a general dissatisfaction with English higher education, more especially as it was given in the ancient schools. On July 18th, 1861, by letters patent a Royal Commission was appointed to inquire into the administration, finances, studies, methods, subjects and extent of instruction of Eton, Winchester, Westminster, Charterhouse, St Paul's, Merchant Taylors', Harrow, Rugby and Shrewsbury. The inquiries of this Commission, of which the Earl of Clarendon was chairman, extended over nearly three years during which the Commissioners held 127 meetings, examined 130 witnesses, and between May 11th and July 3rd, 1862, visited all nine schools.

At the date of the visits to the schools the total number of pupils was 2815, of whom 1815 were at one or other of the three schools, Eton (840), Rugby (500) or Harrow (475). The remaining six were small schools, only Merchant Taylors' having so many as 260 in attendance. In the year which ended at the summer holidays of 1862, 467 boys left these schools, of whom 140 went to Oxford or to Cambridge, that is roughly three in every ten. The Clarendon Commission, therefore, was directly concerned with a very small fraction of the potential school population of England and Wales. Yet the inquiry was of the first importance, partly because of the prominent positions in public life which were subsequently occupied by boys educated at the Public Schools—"the schools of the governing classes" as the phrase went, but chiefly because these schools exercised an influence hard to measure upon all other endowed grammar schools, proprietary schools and "colleges", and upon the Englishmen's thoughts as to what constituted liberal education and the mode of conducting it.

In the course of his evidence Dr Moberly, head master of Winchester, made a remark which summed up to a nicety the existing position of the Public Schools and the conditions which had made the Commission necessary. "You see", he said, "we are dealing here with a traditional system; it has grown up with circumstances." The statement found illustration in the constitution of the governing bodies and their relation to the head masters, in the number, standing and remuneration of the assistant masters, and above all in the greater or less repute of some branches of knowledge and in the omission of others from the school courses. The statutes, which in the last resort ruled these and all other conditions of school life, were three, four, even five centuries old, mitigated by occasional attempts of the Law Courts to bring their prescriptions and proscriptions into line with contemporary needs and preferences.

The only teachers recognized in most of the statutes were the head master and his second in command, the usher; their position in reference to the school's governing body naturally varied in different schools. In some the relation was helpful, in others the master was fettered in matters which to-day would be considered strictly within his own province; there were cases where it was alleged that the school and the schoolmaster were subordinated to the interests, even the personal advantage, of the governors.

The religious instruction was the least controversial of the topics brought before the Commission; the schools were generally accepted as Church institutions, the senior members of the staff at least were clergymen of the Church of England and outsiders showed no disposition to interfere with their discretion.

Divinity was an integral part of the curriculum in all the schools, the study of Scripture history and of the Greek New Testament being common to all. Merchant Taylors' was peculiar in the retention of Hebrew as a regular part of the senior boys' business; the scheme of instruction there was unusually extensive, the top form writing essays and biographies connected with Scriptural subjects and, as a preparation for the university, they committed the Thirty-Nine Articles to memory, a superfluity of naughtiness not to be expected from "the best school in London". Westminster had replaced Paley by Butler's *Analogy*; Shrewsbury studied the history of the Reformation. Colet's statutes for St Paul's created a high master, a sur-master and a chaplain; the names persisted, but the "chaplain", or third master, had no special charge of religious teaching. When giving this information Dr Kynaston, the high master, oddly added, "the School is wholly Protestant". At all the schools attendance at chapel, daily or weekly, was the rule, boys were duly prepared for confirmation, and the periodical reception of Holy Communion was the practice of the great majority of boys who had been confirmed. Communion was voluntary except at Westminster, where reception by the Queen's Scholars (foundationers) was compulsory each quarter. Scott, the head master, thought that if it were optional none would attend; but he seems to have been a somewhat disgruntled person, with no high opinion of his boys, who was carrying out a traditional system (he himself was an Etonian) or compulsorily deferring to Dean and Chapter. Dr Moberly's description of the typical Wykehamist is probably a just summary of Public School boy religion at that time: "a strong religious feeling of a very moderate, sober and traditional kind".

In all the nine schools the first, and by far the first, matter of instruction consisted in the two classical languages; grammar, composition, verse-making, translation, the study of the two literatures and the committing to memory of many masterpieces filled so many hours of preparation and of school that the excuse, "no time", was commonly alleged in explanation of many omissions from the curriculum. The same reason was put forward to account for the comparatively unimportant place occupied by mathematics and "modern languages" (a term which usually meant French only). These studies were sometimes grudgingly admitted to the standing of "business" in consequence of the pressure exerted by the examinations of the Civil Service Commission and of the Board of Military Education, supported in respect of mathematics by the recent demands of Cambridge and of Oxford. Eton in particular pleaded that no time could be spared from that devoted to classical study. In examining Edward Balston (head master, 1862–8), Lord Clarendon said, "We find modern languages, geography, history, chronology and everything else which a well-educated English gentleman ought to know given up in order that the full time should be devoted to the classics, and at the same time we are told that the boys go up to Oxford not only not proficient, but in a lamentable state of deficiency with respect to the classics". The judgement was that of the head of one of the first colleges in Oxford, and this authority thought that Eton stood prominently forward among the defaulters.

Balston could only admit the fact; "I am sorry for it". A question previously addressed to him ran, "Do you think that the boys who generally stay at Eton four or five years leave it with anything like a fair proficiency in the classics to which all their time is devoted?" His answer was, "No, not at present".[1] "I am afraid that there is really but a small literary interest among the boys", was the comment upon the neglect of the Harrow school library made by the head master, H. M. Butler.[2] No Harrovian below the age of fifteen was exempt from verse-making.

Individual proficiency is not a compensation for an inefficiency which on the evidence of these head masters was so common. Still it would be unfair to pass by the testimony given to the Commission by a Rugbeian of 1854–60, then at St John's College, Cambridge. H. Lee Warner thought that the head boys at Rugby read "more than the head boys of Eton and Harrow but not more than the head boys of Shrewsbury". Recalling his own time in the upper forms, he thus outlined the reading of the head boys of his time at school. In Greek this comprised about four plays of Aristophanes and about ten other plays, not more than two books of Thucydides, extracts from Herodotus, an oration of Demosthenes and the orators, perhaps Aeschines, a "tolerable amount" of Plato, three or four dialogues. He did not think any Aristotle was read—a fact which would have grieved Arnold. In Latin the reading covered about three books of Livy, the *Agricola* and *Germania* of Tacitus, an oration of Cicero, always some of the Tusculans and the *De natura deorum*, all Horace, but not all Virgil; he thought he "did some of the *Aeneid*" at school. Of Lucretius three books were read, and of Plautus three plays; although Juvenal was not taboo, he had not been read within Warner's experience. The authors named were all read "in school"; so much time was required for the writing of original Latin prose that little remained for private reading in Latin and Greek literature.

In English Warner's private reading included a good deal of poetry, Carlyle, Shakespeare, novels, Tennyson, not much Wordsworth, but

---

[1] *Report of Her Majesty's Commissioners appointed to inquire into the revenues and management of certain colleges and schools and the studies pursued and instruction given therein.* 4 vols. (1864). See the Eton Evidence (vol. III), QQ. 3554, 3550.

[2] *Ibid.* vol. IV, Harrow Evidence, Q. 604.

Macaulay, Scott, Kingsley, "Dickens of course", "Thackeray was not a favourite so much".[1]

All the schools taught mathematics, but the standard varied from school to school; French also was taught in all the schools, although at Eton and at Harrow it was not part of "business", that is, the general compulsory course. Rugby taught both French and German as an optional alternative to experimental science. In most of the schools, Rugby excepted, the masters who taught mathematics and modern languages, not holding offices which were named in the statutes, were regarded as mere instructors in their subjects and not as educators, a status reserved for the classical masters who had a statutory position or one which could be represented as such. The assumed inferiority of the more modern studies was emphasized at Harrow in the marks allotted for form work and examinations; classical marks were to mathematical as four to one, the ratio in the case of modern languages being nine to one. At St Paul's classical marks were three times as valuable as mathematical; the teacher of mathematics would have been satisfied with a ratio of two to one. "An inferior classical boy may... gain an exhibition over a very superior mathematical boy."[2] All this of course had its effect upon the boys' attitude towards the different studies and, it must be added, to the several teachers; exhibitions and scholarships were almost confined to the classical subjects, a fact which emphasized the inferior position of all other branches of knowledge.

Charterhouse, like Rugby, taught German as well as French; less than 10 per cent. of the Etonians included French in their school studies, while at Westminster the head master, C. B. Scott, admitted that the teaching of French was a failure. It must not be forgotten that the schools had no traditional method of teaching a modern language and that the teachers not unnaturally followed in the main the procedure employed in teaching Latin and Greek. The general scheme included grammar (which meant much learning by heart), translation and the reading of French classical authors of the seventeenth century; and two hours a week sufficed for these things. Conversation in the foreign tongue was only exceptionally employed in special classes for the purpose; the aim was not speech or writing but ability to read. Bentley, who taught French at Shrewsbury, believed that attempts

[1] *Report*, vol. IV, Rugby Evidence, QQ. 1756 ff., 1914 ff.
[2] *Ibid.* vol. IV, St Paul's Evidence, QQ. 239, 285.

at conversation had been abandoned at the schools which he knew, because the boys insisted upon all talking together and because they imitated one author's mistakes. The bear garden revealed in this opinion seems to have been familiar in a good many schools, whether "Public" or not, when French was being taught.

Rugby alone made serious and successful attempts to teach experimental science. The study formed a recognized part of the general curriculum, oddly alternating with French and German. The school had set up, a few months before the Commissioners' visit, a natural science laboratory which was presided over by "J. M. Wilson, Esq."— "clarum et venerabile nomen!"—who expected his pupils on leaving to be well up in the chemistry of the non-metallic elements, to be perfect in common qualitative inorganic analysis and "to have a fair notion of the other subjects, geology, physical geography and perhaps electricity and so on".[1] Wilson's colleague, R. B. Mayor, gave a course comprising the elements of mathematics, hydrostatics and popular astronomy. Wilson thought that if a "modern school" or "modern side" were instituted, half the school would resort to it, so great was the pressure from the Army examinations' requirements. The alternative between modern languages and science was ridiculous, since boys who desired a modern education wished to study both alternatives. In point of fact four boys were doing so. Asked whether any Rugbeians were studying in the Oxford laboratory, he said there were certainly two, perhaps more; as to Cambridge (Wilson was Senior Wrangler in 1859) his reply was, "I have not heard of any, I do not know where they could study it".[2]

In the attention given to natural science Rugby was markedly exceptional. The usual plan, where the subject secured any notice whatever, was to offer occasional lectures by distinguished scientific men invited down from London for the purpose. At Eton there was a charge of two shillings per head per lecture, and the lectures were well attended. Questions and discussion followed each, after the plan adopted by Faraday and others when lecturing to children at the Royal Institution. The hearers were of all ages; it is not surprising that only about 5 per cent. of them took part in the subsequent writing of answers to questions. A course was closed by an examination. Ten or twelve such lectures were delivered annually at Winchester on successive

[1] *Report*, vol. IV, Rugby Evidence, Q. 1412.   [2] *Ibid.* QQ. 1397–8.

Saturdays after Easter, to pupils of all ages; the head master, for whom science meant an accumulation of "scientific facts", allowed himself to believe that at the conclusion of the course a boy would be able to appreciate "the last discoveries and the present state of the sciences", much as the ultra-"scientific" man supposed that Greek and Latin were superfluous when English translations were accessible. Yet of the "scientific facts" with which his boys were thus made acquainted, Dr Moberly anticipated that the remembrance would resemble "the sort of recollection that ladies are apt to have of something they learned at school, they know there is a good deal to be said about it, but they forget what it is".[1]

At Charterhouse the lectures were given in playtime and attendance was voluntary. Harrow made no attempt to teach science; text-books were indicated in botany, geology, chemistry and electricity at the end of a school quarter and certain pages in these were to be got up for an examination in the next quarter. The number of examinees had fallen from ninety to twenty or less. The character and value of this text-book "science" may be inferred from the evidence of M. W. Ridley, who had been head of the school but was now at Balliol. "I have known some boys get firsts in an examination after a couple of night's hard reading....In a general way about three or four weeks would be devoted to it at about an hour or an hour and a half a day".[2] There was plenty of time to study these subjects without interfering with the classical studies.

Merchant Taylors' was exceptional amongst the nine schools in the time given to mathematics and in the advanced character of its mathematical reading; it did not teach or encourage natural science. Westminster, St Paul's and Shrewsbury made no pretence of teaching science. Dr Kennedy, the Shrewsbury head master, gave his reasons for the omission. The natural sciences, he said, "would not furnish a basis for education at all; I should consider them as an assemblage of facts not as supplying principles". The natural laws of science relate to the senses and not to an abstract mental discipline. They afford no basis for education, to which they are only "adjuncts".[3] It was in vain that the Earl of Devon, a Commissioner and an old Westminster, put it to Moberly that the explanation of natural phenomena involves "very elaborate processes of reasoning and memory".

[1] *Report*, vol. III, Winchester Evidence, Q. 503.   [2] Q. 1822.
[3] *Ibid.* vol. IV, Shrewsbury Evidence, QQ. 694–700.

The general assumption was that practice in translation into English was sufficient exercise in the use of the mother tongue; but English essays were written at Rugby and Harrow, and, occasionally, at Shrewsbury. Rugby boys learned a good deal of English by heart, and at Winchester there were recitations from Shakespeare and Milton before the whole school on six successive Saturdays in Easter time. The difficulty which the schools experienced respecting English literature and the way in which they hoped that its omission might be compensated were expressed by Dr Kennedy. He was asked, "Are you satisfied with the knowledge possessed by the boys of the best English literature?" to which he replied, "I am sorry to say I have not time to test this much. If I were to make it prominent I am afraid we should fritter away our power. That is my feeling. I have never seen my way. But I know perfectly well there always have been, and I trust still are, boys who are availing themselves of the opportunities they have for private reading".[1]

English history and geography presented a problem in method which some of the schools either ignored by omitting these subjects altogether, or evaded by setting them as holiday tasks; an old Harrovian who gave evidence described the geography learned under these conditions as "rather a farce". In the middle school and the two "Fifths" at Rugby, boys passed through a three years' cycle in which they studied history—Hebrew, Greek, Roman, and English.

The Clarendon Commissioners, supported by a large body of public opinion, thought that the well-nigh exclusive attention which the Public Schools paid to the languages and literature of Rome and Greece, and the consequent neglect of studies demanded by life in the nineteenth century, needed justifying. The fact that large numbers of boys failed to learn these languages effectively, and that boys whose talents lay in other directions than the literary found in the curriculum little or no encouragement, made public opinion still more impatient. The explanation, if not the excuse, rested partly upon history and tradition, partly upon a theory of education, and partly upon very practical considerations. Throughout their history the schools had been fettered by their statutes, documents which implied that the education which began in the grammar school was only completed in the university, and that the business of the grammar school, by virtue of its very

---

[1] *Report*, vol. IV, Shrewsbury Evidence, Q. 470.

name, was to teach "the learned tongues", upon which as a foundation the university course could be erected. Yet only a minority of boys ever had completed this extensive course and in the nineteenth century the minority was a small one, in whose interest the great majority were dismissed with what, *ex hvpothesi*, was an incomplete education, and one whose appeal was not universal. At Harrow the young and inexperienced head master was surprised when the Commissioners pointed out that a large number of Harrow boys left school between the ages of sixteen and eighteen, a leakage of which he was unaware. But Kynaston, after twenty-four years' service as high master of St Paul's, could talk like this: "I have no objection whatever to any boy coming to the school if there is a reasonable chance of his going to the university; but I should not like a boy to come here who is not supposed to be training for the university." Lord Devon then put two very pertinent questions: "Must it be said on the admission of a boy that he is to be trained for the university?" and "Practically speaking what proportion of the boys do go to the university?" To the first the answer was "No"; to the second, "Every year about 25 leave the school, but of these I should say not more than six go to the university. The rest go into the Army or Navy or various lines of business".[1] Even if to the six be added those who were helped by the school course in various examinations, the disproportion between intention and fulfilment is striking.

To the many critics who objected to the classical course that it found no place for useful studies, while Latin and Greek possessed no utilitarian worth, the reply was that the Public Schools existed to give a liberal, not a professional or purely useful education. They did not desire to teach the arts and forms of knowledge which Aristotle had stigmatized as "banausic", fit only for vulgar mechanics and craftsmen. The apologists for the established order abandoned the great claims of Greek and Latin to which the *humanitas* of their literatures entitles them, and instead proferred the plea that the two languages afforded a discipline of the mind incomparably superior to any which could be derived from other studies. This taking refuge in a haven of theory and of doubtful psychology was no new thing in the history of education. Practices which have begun under the stress of sheer necessity, or of convenience, survive until their usefulness has diminished or

---

[1] *Report*, vol. IV, St Paul's Evidence, QQ. 454 f.

disappeared; in due course a doctrine is propounded which asserts the intrinsic excellence of these practices and the expediency of retaining them. Throughout the inquiry there was repeated reference to "forming the mind", "mental discipline" and the like, to the exclusion of the intrinsic advantages which a study might possess other than as a gymnastic. Lord Clarendon raised the question again and again in reference to all sorts of studies. With Plato the apologists agreed that an important aim of a liberal education was the disciplining of the intellect; but their Platonism was incomplete, since the philosopher did not hold that the study of literature was all-sufficient for that purpose. In the small importance which most of the head masters attached to mathematics as discipline they were directly contradicting the thinker from whom "the doctrine of formal training" is derived.

It was assumed by men trained under the classical tradition that modern studies failed "to strengthen the mind" or did not do so comprehensively; they must therefore occupy less of school time, be taught by less completely educated teachers and, in short, take an inferior place in the school's life. And there were the statutes to support this condition of things. Rugby did not take this view of modern studies, and Rugby came out best after the ordeal of the Commission. The invitation to give evidence, which was extended to a number of distinguished men, including Faraday, Owen, Lyell and Airy, would appear to have been given in order to elicit their view as to the purely gymnastic value of modern studies, of natural science in particular. Faraday wanted to know the meaning of the phrase "the training of the mind" and denied that a literary education had a monopoly of it; he pointed out the error which conceived science as an accumulation of facts and bluntly told the Commission, "You want men who can teach [science] and that class has to be created".[1]

This was really the core of the trouble. Kennedy held that the natural laws of chemistry, heat, electricity, etc., "*are not synthetical enough for elementary instruction*, do not furnish a basis for education".[2] Dr Moberly had really raised the same objection. The sciences were, in effect, new ("not above 70 years old"). "If a man is pursuing a science practically and experimentally, so as to be making discoveries

[1] *Report*, vol. IV, pp. 377–8, QQ. 27–39.
[2] *Ibid.* vol. IV, Shrewsbury Evidence, QQ. 699–700. Kennedy put the classical and the mathematical studies on an equal footing.

and carrying it forward to greater heights of perfection, then he is indeed exercising the highest faculties a man can have." But boys in school cannot do this; they "can only be taught what other people have done, they will only get such knowledge second-hand".[1] The contrast in the mind of these head masters was probably this. Classical instruction was organized, its aims and method were perfectly familiar, it had attained its present position after the experiments of centuries; its content was practically fixed. No one of these propositions could be asserted of the modern studies, mathematics excepted; new studies still fluid as to content were not the best available instruments for the instruction of boys. Organization, clear aim and method depended upon competent teachers; and as Faraday said they had to be created. In the meantime, the universities were not doing very much to create them; and the teachers of the new subjects looked to their classical colleagues for guidance in method. The difficulty was a very real one, of much more practical importance than any question-begging theory. The schools were enclosed within a vicious circle which must be broken if the modern studies were to get their due; it could be broken by the abrogation of the old statutes and the formation of new under newly constituted governing bodies. This was in effect the remedy applied by the Public Schools Act of 1868 which gave effect to the recommendations of the Commission.

In the earlier years of the century, as already said[2], the non-local character which Harrow had assumed had been unsuccessfully challenged by the local people. The type of schooling did not satisfy them and they had no desire to send their boys to a place of education which regarded the university as its goal; nevertheless they felt that genuine Harrow residents were being unfairly deprived of the benefit of John Lyon's foundation. Butler told the Commission that the position in life of the foundationers varied extremely; "in many instances foundationers are the sons of widow ladies who come to reside in Harrow, who having previous to their husband's death been moving in affluence are now in comparatively reduced circumstances.... There is no condition as to length of residence".[3] "I believe in no instance is any son of a Harrow tradesman now a member of the great school.... It is

[1] *Report*, vol. III, Winchester Evidence, QQ. 510–12.
[2] See pp. 62 ff. above.
[3] *Report*, vol. IV, Harrow Evidence, Q. 148.

found that the English Form is accepted by them as more satisfactorily answering what they consider to be the needs of their children." In reply to the suggestion that the number of boys in the English Form—twenty-two—was small, Butler said, "The class of tradesmen and farmers in and about Harrow is small".[1] Yet some of their number preferred London schools for their sons rather than the somewhat makeshift arrangement with which the Harrow governors and head master were trying to satisfy them.

The "English Form" which had been devised by Butler's predecessor, C. J. Vaughan (head master, 1844–59), was a school dissociated from the "great school" in every respect, except that the head master, the senior mathematical master and the modern language masters periodically examined the boys, one of the classical masters assisted with the Scriptural instruction on Sunday mornings and the head master received a weekly report on each boy's progress. The schoolroom "is known as the public-room in Harrow....It is a humble room... that was used for a long time before we got our new schools as one of our school-rooms....It is a very common room. I do not know how to describe it more accurately". The master of the "English Form" was a certificated teacher trained at St Mark's Training College, Chelsea; the boys paid an inclusive annual fee of £5 and purchased "the few books" which they use.

There was a similar concession to local feeling at Shrewsbury where the "Non-collegiate Class" had been instituted by Kennedy about four or five years before the Commissioners' visit. He himself described it as "an attempt I have made of late years to satisfy that sort of call which exists, and not unnaturally exists, among the community, for an education which shall meet the wants of those classes who do not intend to send their sons to the universities. I call it a 'non-collegiate' class, because I have never allowed the word 'commercial' to enter in among us". The class numbered about a score of boys (the "strength" of Shrewsbury in 1861 was 141); their studies comprised Latin, French, English composition, modern history and extra mathematics, these modern subjects replacing Greek and verse-making in the ordinary "business" of the school proper. They had a special director who also acted as tutor to all boys below the sixth. This director thought that

[1] *Report*, vol. IV, Harrow Evidence, QQ. 177–8.
[2] *Ibid*, vol. IV, Harrow Evidence, QQ. 210 f.

the class, which had been formed to meet a pressing demand for "a more commercial style of education", "encouraged indolence to a certain extent". Kennedy testified that some of the boys were remarkably intelligent while others were "the idle boys of the school" who joined the class to escape classics, an opinion shared by the French master. One of the trustees had conscientious scruples as to the existence of such a class; it tended to turn a place of liberal education into a commercial school.[1]

Incidentally, Kennedy had a good word to say for the scholastically idle boys, "the active boys with whom play is the great end and object, but who...do not wish to fly in the face of the master and therefore wish to give him general satisfaction. They are a very valuable class of boys when their principles are good, that is, if they have a good moral character and are respectful to their masters and wish to set an example to the other boys. They are a very peculiar and a very good element in a public school".[2]

One of the witnesses, a town councillor, remembered when the school numbered 400 boys; other witnesses attributed the serious drop in the number attending to the defective school buildings. Kennedy thought that it was due to the competition of the new proprietary colleges like Marlborough, Rossall and Cheltenham.[3] He did not add that at these schools modern studies did not occupy the position assigned to them by most of their ancient rivals.

At Rugby it had been Dr Arnold's practice to hold periodical meetings of the masters at intervals of three or four weeks; occasionally the meeting took the form of a dinner. Arnold's successors, Tait (1842–9), Goulburn (1849–57) and Temple (1857–69), continued the custom, which seems to have arrested the attention of the Commissioners, who were curious to discover whether it was followed elsewhere. There were such periodical staff meetings at Harrow and at Shrewsbury, but Westminster and Charterhouse held them only when the head masters judged them to be needed. Winchester, St Paul's and Merchant Taylors' had no such practice; Eton, as usual, "had no time" for this and other novelties in Public School administration.

The importance attached to particular studies by the several schools is reflected in the standing of the masters who conducted them. The

[1] *Report*, vol. IV, Shrewsbury Evidence, QQ. 213–225, 231, 848, 862 f., 951.
[2] *Ibid*. Q. 236.   [3] *Ibid*. QQ. 377 f., 338.

two oldest schools, Winchester and Eton, adhering closely to their statutes, considered all masters, other than those who taught classics, as merely auxiliary to the work of education, whose real agents were the head master and the statutory "ushers", who like him taught Latin and Greek. In most of the schools mathematics had by this time vindicated a claim to be on an educational equality with the ancient languages; but that equality was not accorded to the modern tongues. Rugby and Shrewsbury were alone in regarding all members of the school staff, irrespective of "subject", as professionally and *socially* equal.

It was inevitable that, when masters were regarded as occupying an inferior station in the school hierarchy, the studies which they professed should be lightly esteemed by the boys; yet some head masters failed to appreciate this, and attributed to the intrinsic inferiority of the studies the comparative neglect with which the boys often treated them. As to consultation with the members of his staff, Dr Hessey of Merchant Taylors' told the Commission that he would not "for any purpose" call together the writing master, the French master or the drawing master. He also addressed the Commission as follows. "Of course you are aware that the great difficulty is to make boys respect masters who are not university men. Practically, masters who are foreigners and who are not thoroughly acquainted with the English language, and likely by occasional mistakes to excite the risibility of the boys, are the masters whom they most fail to respect. It is also very difficult indeed to make boys respect writing masters and, of course, I am applied to occasionally to enforce discipline."[1] Neither Hessey nor the Commissioners seem to have noted cause and effect here; but the facts indicate the small value attached to modern studies.

The schools were undoubtedly understaffed for what they proposed to accomplish. In most cases the number of pupils in a form exceeded thirty; Eton and Merchant Taylors' thought forty satisfactory. At Winchester Dr Moberly, following what he called "one of our old time-honoured practices", united for a construing lesson the two Sixths and the Upper Fifth, some eighty boys in all, but he later informed the Commission that this practice had "in great measure" been done away with.[2] Understaffing, entailing an excessive number of pupils in a given "form", was an ancient defect in grammar schools,

[1] *Report*, vol. IV, Merchant Taylors' Evidence, QQ. 447, 345.
[2] *Ibid.* vol. III, p. 348.

whether "Public Schools" or schools of humbler standing. At Winchester an attempt to correct it had been made by constituting every prefect a "tutor" to some half dozen junior boys, for which he was paid by the parents a fee of one guinea per half-year. It was the duty of the tutor to help his pupils in the preparation of lessons, thus presumably saving time and labour when these exercises had to be said or shown up in class later on. Charles Wordsworth, second master (1835–46), who had been educated at Harrow, protested to the warden that such tutoring was not boys' work and the practice was changed. At the time of the Commission there were three tutors in the school, one for collegers, two for commoners and the services of three others might be privately engaged; all six were assistant masters of the school. Boy tutors had charge of the little boys and the oversight of a small part of the composition exercises was still in their hands; but their chief office was to be responsible in a measure for the care of their small clients, in return for which they received the customary half-yearly guinea.[1]

By "the double system" at Eton, construes, verses and prose compositions were prepared and corrected under one master, acting as tutor, and shown up or said to another, the form master Balston, the head master, whose cue was that Eton needed no reforming, would not admit that the duplication wasted time or that the practice caused the boy to rely too much on the tutor, that it was in short a sort of intellectual coddling which tended to destroy initiative. Sir H. Maxwell-Lyte drily remarks that "this system incidentally gave every Master frequent opportunities of gauging the scholarship of his colleagues".[2] Butler of Harrow was alive to the dangers of the Eton double system, which his school partially employed, but trusted to the discretion of the tutors to avoid them; the evidence of M. White Ridley, a recent head of the school, justified that trust.[3] At Rugby a classical private tutor was necessary; parents paid a special fee of ten guineas for his services or, where there was inability to pay, the fee in respect of a foundationer came out of a reserve fund or from a small tax levied on all the classical tutors.[4] Private tutors were supplied on request at

[1] *Report*, vol. III, Winchester Evidence, QQ. 382–92, 636–7.
[2] *History of Eton College*, p. 395.
[3] *Report*, vol. IV, Harrow Evidence, QQ. 1784 ff.
[4] *Ibid.* vol. IV, Rugby Evidence, QQ. 269, 280.

Charterhouse, Shrewsbury and Merchant Taylors'; in the last case they were boy tutors as at Winchester. The Eton system was peculiar to itself.

Outside opinion either distrusted or flatly condemned as abuses three long-established Public School practices, namely, the prefect system, corporal punishment and fagging. But public opinion concerning the schoolroom is apt to be a generation at least behind the facts. It was so in 1860; and in deference to it the Commissioners made a point of seeking evidence from boys then at school or who had but recently left school for the university. The prefect, praepostor or monitorial system, through which much of the discipline of the school is administered, has long been accounted one of the most educative methods employed by the Public School; but its original purpose was undoubtedly to compensate for a staff which was under-manned. Yet a practice invented for one purpose sometimes achieves another and a greater one; the boy witnesses before the Commission invariably approved, as beneficial to school life and helpful to the younger boys, a system which invested their seniors with so much authority. The Commission as *advocatus diaboli* professed to fear that the prefect might become arbitary and domineering. Where, as at Harrow, seniority made the prefect, there seemed a possibility of such behaviour. Robert Lang, who had been six years in the school before going to Cambridge, reassured them in words which represented the Public School boy in general on the subject. "I almost doubt that, because they would be kept in check a great deal by the others." Appeal always lay from a monitor to the monitors as a body and beyond them to the head master. The prefects were regarded by the masters as "the keystone of the Harrow system". "Certainly it is quite recognized by the school and I think quite approved of, generally, as far as I can see."[1] Two masters who knew Rugby before Arnold's time and whose evidence was supported by a Commissioner, H. H. Vaughan, a Rugbeian, testified that great importance was attached to the authority of the Sixth Form when Dr Wooll was head master (1807–28) and that the exercise of that authority was a great advantage to the school.[2] Arnold legalized the administration of punishment by the Sixth, but it existed under his predecessor who, like himself, was a Wykehamist. H. Lee

[1] *Report*, vol. IV, Harrow Evidence, QQ. 1877 ff.
[2] *Ibid.* vol. IV, Rugby Evidence, QQ. 1130 ff.

Warner, an old Rugbeian, like most, if not all, of the pupil witnesses insisted on the value of the prefect system both for the school and for the prefects. Public opinion, that is, the boys' opinion, was so much in its favour that abuse of power by a monitor was virtually impossible or at most an exceedingly rare occurrence. He could not recall an instance of such abuse.

It was sometimes said that punishments in the schools were brutal and degrading; the evidence goes to show that corporal punishment was exceptional everywhere and that the prefects had a limited power of punishing, the employment of a cane not excepted. The most common form of penalty was the writing of lines, and to this the Chairman was continually raising the very cogent objection that it spoiled the culprit's handwriting.

Fagging, like the prefect system, originated in the shortage of labour. It did not exist at St Paul's or at Merchant Taylors', day schools with no need for a staff of domestic servants; conversely, it flourished at all the boarding schools, though its incidence and the duties which it involved were different in different schools. The privilege of employing the services of juniors of a defined standing belonged to the Sixth, and thus formed part of the authority ascribed by tradition to the young men who constituted that form. Those services were most required at breakfast and tea-time or about the fireplaces in winter, and they were required at those times because the school did not employ a sufficient number of domestic servants. It was only in the course of time that all sorts of moral and other educational advantages were ascribed to fagging, so true is it that practice always precedes theory. The boy witnesses—some of them actually fags when they appeared before the Commission—approved of the system, the chief complaint (never loudly made) being that the studies of the fags were greatly interrupted by frequent but irregular calls for such small offices as fetching books or carrying messages. Another source of complaint was compulsory presence at games, not as players, but as casual helpers of the players. Rumour said that at Charterhouse the fagging was "incessant in school, out of school, from morning to night". Robert Brodie, then in his third year at Oxford, who had been ten years at Charterhouse and a fag for half that time, denied the truth of this rumour or its implication. "No; I do not think we used to think it hard when we were fags; I never did."

Questions on the domestic life of the boarding schools addressed to former pupils elicited the opinion that immorality ("drink" and gambling were especially named) was confined to "a few", "a set", and that its prevalence varied at different times in the same school, but that it never stamped its character on a school as a whole. The Harrow witness agreed that in his time the tone was "honourable and gentlemanlike"; and Dr Temple was very emphatic in asserting that Rugby was sound with reference to respect for truth and condemnation of bullying. The governing bodies of the day schools accepted no responsibility for the boys' behaviour beyond the school walls. At St Paul's they made no sufficient arrangements for feeding boys at midday, leaving them to "feed where they can, some to dining rooms, some to one place, some to another".[1] The Merchant Taylors' governors did not "recognize" such boarding houses as lodged some of the pupils.[2] Both schools were then situated in the heart of London amidst a large and strenuous population of business men.

On the whole the Commission seems to have been very well satisfied with the moral condition of the schools. "The great schools...may certainly claim...a large share of the credit due for the improved moral tone of the Universities, as to which we have strong concurrent testimony."[3]

Sport was not so highly organized at the schools as it subsequently became, but its importance for health, amusement and character-building was fully recognized; indeed the Commissioners feared that some schools rated it too high. Cricket was the leading game; at Harrow, one of the sporting schools, those boys played cricket whose names were put on the list by the heads of games; football was compulsory there and Shrewsbury boys had established the rule that "all should attend at football", a rule marking the somewhat primitive development of the game at that date. Boys were not allowed in the boats at Eton, Westminster or Shrewsbury before they could swim. The Volunteer Movement of 1859 had called into existence at nearly all the boarding schools rifle corps, so called; but they were not taken seriously, their management and discipline being left almost entirely to the boys themselves; they were really rifle clubs whose members underwent a little squad drill and wore uniform.

Inclusive fees were not the rule, charges were added, or exemption from them granted and emoluments paid to masters and pupils as

[1] *Report*, vol. iv, St Paul's Evidence, QQ. 186 ff.
[2] *Ibid.* vol. iv, Merchant Taylors' Evidence, QQ. 406–8.   [3] *Ibid.* vol. i, p. 44.

circumstances and the history of the particular school seemed to demand. It is therefore not easy to discover how much parents paid at this time for their sons' education at a Public School. At Harrow the cost "to the great majority" was said to be under £150 a year, though as much as £210 was paid for boys boarding in the small houses. At Rugby the average yearly cost was placed at £130. At Charterhouse, then situated in the City of London, the total annual cost ranged from £90 to £110 for a boarder; the day boy's tuition fee was £18. 10s. The corresponding fee at Merchant Taylors' was ten guineas. It must be remembered that all the schools numbered a proportion, sometimes a very high proportion, of foundationers ("college boys", "collegers", "gown boys") who were exempt from payment.

Between these foundationers and the "commoners" or "oppidans" there was a certain antagonism confined to the younger boys but which ceased as boys reached the Middle School; it was perhaps a remnant of the feeling which possibly existed in early days when boys not on the foundation were regarded as interlopers, "foreigners" who irregularly profited from the founder's bounty. The collegers were holders of scholarships, tokens of a measure of intellectual distinction not possessed by the others. This point was put by a young Wykehamist boy witness who, when asked "Why should a college boy look down on a commoner?" replied, "Because we think we are a cleverer set". He had to admit that at games "they generally beat us". Where there were day boys, as at Charterhouse, Rugby and Shrewsbury, the cleavage was between the boarders and the day boys, who were mostly the sons of local tradesmen; in such cases the distinction was a social one.

Harrow and Rugby excepted, the governing bodies were not entirely independent bodies concerned wholly and solely with the affairs of the schools, but corporations, or closely identified with corporations, which had other interests, sometimes very personal interests, to consider. On occasion the schools were sacrificed, there was usually an absence of enterprise in meeting altered circumstances and at times a disposition in a provost or a dean to interfere with the purely scholastic functions and discretion of the head master. In the very forefront of their recommendations the Clarendon Commission placed the reformation of the governing bodies "in order to render them thoroughly suitable and efficient for the purpose and duties they are designed to fulfil".[1]

---

[1] *Report*, vol. I, p. 52.

The publication of the Commission's *Report* was followed by the passage of the Public Schools Act of 1868 which appointed a Statutory Commission of six members to carry out this recommendation. Within a given interval each of the seven boarding schools was required to submit to this Commission a new constitution for its governing body, with corresponding statutes and rules to give them effect; on approval by the Commission such schemes were to receive their final shape from the Queen in Council. Should any one of the old governing bodies fail to reform itself in this manner, the Statutory Commission was empowered to make a scheme. St Paul's School (which had no connexion with the cathedral) and Merchant Taylors' School, governed respectively by the Mercers' Company and the Merchant Taylors Company, were not included in the Act.

Desirous of knowing what the more recently established schools were doing, the Clarendon Commission had requested information from three proprietary colleges and from one large London day school, all four of which were displaying an active interest in modern studies, an interest stimulated, if not created, by the requirements of the Army and Civil Service examinations. Cheltenham, Marlborough and Wellington Colleges so chose and distributed their studies that, while the classical course remained for those (they formed the majority) who desired it, there was full opportunity for boys whose interests and capacities better fitted them to undertake a less exclusively literary course. But for all, whether on the classical or the modern side, the ideals of outlook and discipline were those of the Public School, Rugby being the pattern. These schools frankly regarded themselves as educational experiments; and in the earlier stages the results were not encouraging.[1]

Cheltenham College (founded 1841) had two distinct departments, the Classical and the Modern (otherwise the Military and Civil). While Francis Close was rector (1826–56), the town of Cheltenham was a great centre of Evangelicalism and the college was directly under the influence of that party in the Church. The principal and the assistant masters stood in no relation to the religious instruction and discipline of the pupils who, for these purposes, were under the direction of two specially employed theological tutors. At Marlborough (founded

[1] See R. L. Archer, *Secondary Education in the Nineteenth Century*, ch. III, "The Revival in the Public Schools".

1842) and at Wellington (founded 1859) all boys in the lowest forms pursued the same course; bifurcation followed. The Boys of the modern side at Wellington studied mathematics in "sets", not in forms, for ten hours a week, four hours being the minimum for the "classical" boys. French, German, and chemistry were also included in the modern course; the last-named subject was also open to "volunteers" from the classical side. The hindrances to a full and satisfactory development of the modern side at Wellington were said to be the absence of text-books and of the encouragement afforded by university examinations, and the difficulty of finding masters competent to teach up to a standard comparable with that aimed at on the classical side. At Marlborough English literature, experimental science and geometrical drawing were included in the modern courses, and Hindustani was an alternative to German; Sanscrit was an optional study on the classical side. There were special Army classes which prepared for Sandhurst and for the direct taking of a commission; of course, military sketching, surveying and fortification were taught to these pupils. The "Civil Class" learned arithmetic, history, geography, Latin, modern languages, English composition and the writing of abstracts and précis.

These proprietary colleges were less expensive than the older Public Schools. At Marlborough the annual charge was £72 or, for the sons of clergymen, £54. 10s. At Wellington it was £110 or, for Officers' sons, £80; there were foundationers who paid from £10 to £20 a year. Cheltenham charged £71 in the higher and £67 in the lower forms; at private boarding houses the cost ranged between £80 and £120.

The City of London School, which had been evolved by an Act of Parliament of 1834 from a small fifteenth-century endowment, charged an annual fee of £9. While not expressly organized, as were the three boarding schools, for modern studies, the whole school was divided into four sections for instruction in chemistry by lecture and experiment. Geometrical drawing and choral singing were optional subjects taken outside school hours. The year 1861 had witnessed a triumph for the school which Dr Mortimer, the then head master, thus chronicled: "The case of W. S. Aldis, Senior Wrangler and First Smith's Prizeman, and Edwin Abbott Abbott, Senior Classic and First Chancellor's Medallist, 1861, is singular [unique]. The four highest honours of the University of Cambridge were never before gained in the same year by men from the same school". Abbott succeeded Mortimer in 1865.

CHAPTER X

Secondary Education and its Reform

The Clarendon Commission's *Report* was signed on February 16th, 1864. On December 28th in the same year letters patent were issued for a Commission "to inquire into the education given in schools not comprised within Her Majesty's two former commissions"—the Newcastle and Clarendon Commissions. The Commissioners were "to consider and report what measures (if any) are required for the improvement of such education, having especial regard to all endowments applicable or which can rightly be made applicable thereto". All schools between the public elementary and the nine Public Schools ostensibly fell within the survey; hence the official designation, "The Schools Inquiry Commission", 1864–7. But, as the Commissioners were requested to attend in particular to the scholastic endowments to be found within this broad field, and as endowed schools were more easily identifiable than the other institutions covered by the Commission, it was more popularly referred to as "The Endowed Schools Commission" or, from its chairman, "The Taunton Commission". Amongst Lord Taunton's colleagues were Dean Hook, Frederick Temple, head master of Rugby, Edward Baines and William Edward Forster, whose name was later to be inseparably associated with public elementary education. Assistant commissioners were appointed to prosecute inquiries in England and Wales, and there were subsidiary missions to France, Germany, Switzerland, Italy, Canada and the United States of America, the last two countries being visited by James Fraser, the others by Matthew Arnold. Information was also obtained from Scotland and from Holland, from the three Universities and from their colleges.

In signing their report on December 2nd, 1867, the Taunton Commissioners thus summarized their labours. "We have investigated thoroughly the condition of nearly 800 endowed schools; we have examined 147 witnesses; we have inquired, partly by written circulars, partly by the direct inspection of our Assistant Commissioners, into the state of as many private and proprietary schools as were willing to give us information, and we have investigated the important though hitherto much neglected subject of female education."[1]

The reservation here made, in reference to schools whose proprietors were either their principals or whose principals were the servants of a private proprietary body, explains the fact that the inquiry was in the main directed to schools maintained wholly or partially by charitable endowments. According to the *Digest* of educational reports presented to Parliament in 1842 there were 705 grammar schools and nearly 2200 "non-classical" schools which belonged to the endowed category, the large majority of the second group being devoted by foundation and by actual use to an instruction purely rudimentary. The Commissioners regarded as within their special province the grammar schools and such of the non-classical schools as were giving, or professed to give, an education of a higher standard than that arrived at by the grant-aided, elementary school.

For their own guidance in considering particular schools, the Commissioners adopted a division of three grades which, while expressed in terms of length of school life, was based upon the presumed future occupations of the pupils. It was thus in effect grounded in social distinctions and incidentally reflected the general contemporary opinion as to the type of schooling which was thought fitting for particular occupations and well-marked social ranks. But in the view of the Commission exhibitions ought to be provided out of existing endowments to make possible the promotion of more able pupils from a lower to a higher grade, thus giving effect to the principle of the career open to talent, irrespective of social class. Schools of the first grade were those which retained their pupils to the age of 18–19; their principal aim was a liberal education which required a university course for its satisfactory completion. Such an education was not so frequently to be had in the grammar schools as formerly, but must be sought in the Public Schools or in boarding schools of a very expensive kind; it was predominantly classical, embracing both Greek and Latin. The schools of the second grade were those whose pupils completed the course at, or about, sixteen; they were regarded as giving the necessary preliminary education for the Army, for all but the highest branches of the legal and medical professions, civil engineering, many departments of the Civil Service "and probably for all but the wealthier gentry".

[1] *Schools Inquiry Commission Report*, 23 vols. vol. I, p. 661.

In other words, a comparatively short school life without the sequel of a university course was thought sufficient for this large and important part of the middle class. Boys in third grade schools ceased to attend after the age of fourteen, yet they were regarded as having received a secondary education in such schools, fitting them for the careers of "small tenant farmers, small tradesmen and superior artisans". The clergy, that is, the clergy of the Church of England, do not appear in the Commission's enumeration of professions; it was assumed that a first-grade school and university education prepared the clerk in holy orders for his life's work.

It is unnecessary to rehearse the strictures and recommendations in reference to the curriculum which had been made by the Clarendon Commission and which the Taunton Commission repeated. Equally with the earlier body, the Taunton Commission was prone to value a branch of knowledge from the standpoint of its real or supposed power to "train the mind" rather than by the positive worth of its content. In their view the great merit of natural science is that it is "an important agent in mental discipline", the value of geometry lies in its "exercise of severe reasoning"; drawing "strengthens habits of accurate observation"; Italian (for which there is "no effective demand") cultivates taste and an appreciation of beauty of thought and expression. William Ellis was earnestly advocating the introduction of political economy into all school courses, and amongst reasons for the adoption of the study the Commission's Report alleges that "it supplies excellent examples of reasoning". Latin was to be retained "partly because all teachers agree in praising its excellence as a mental discipline"; for that reason the schoolmistresses who gave evidence argued that a modicum of Latin or German grammar was desirable even though girls made no more extended study of the languages. When middle class parents declined to be moved by these abstract values in studies which they thought were better omitted from school courses, the Commission retaliated by remarking that "of the best means of training the mind and strengthening the faculties, they (the parents) are no judges at all".[1] A meticulous emphasis upon mental discipline, when wedded to a psychology of more or less independent "faculties", reasoning, memory, observation and the rest, was not calculated to assist the discussion of educational values; and it was just this psycho-

[1] *Report*, vol. i, p. 308.

logy with precisely that emphasis which was in fashion in the 'sixties' and for a generation later amongst those who theorized about the curriculum.

Endowed schools, like the nine which monopolized the term "Public", were too much governed by the notion that they were only preparatory schools for the university, and must therefore make one or both of the classical languages their chief, if not their sole, occupation. It was the Commission's opinion that "with some slight modification of the existing arrangements in classical schools", classics, mathematics, modern languages and natural science could all be taught, different schools making one or other of them their leading subject. Greek should be limited to first grade schools and not all of them should teach it; some might substitute a wider or deeper study of modern languages, science or mathematics. The demands of the professions or of public examinations made Latin necessary in second grade schools; and it might be made alternative with French or German in those of the third grade. Where science was taught in the endowed schools it was often taught by imperfectly equipped teachers, without suitable books or suitable apparatus, and in unsuitable rooms.[1]

On the burning question of religious instruction the *Report* makes a general statement which seems to have been true at the time and for many years thereafter. Parents, it is said, desired religious teaching for their children, but "those who are solicitous about religious teaching are not equally solicitous about the form in which it may be given". Nearly all grammar schools were Church of England institutions. In the highest schools the Greek Testament, "evidences" and Church history were usually part of the instruction; in the lower classes and in the great majority of endowed schools Bible history was studied and the Church Catechism learned by heart. From very few schools were children excluded whose parents dissented from the Church of England, nor was there any marked indisposition of these parents to use Church of England schools. But the *Report* admits that a power to withdraw from this particular teaching was desired; while schools must be denominational in respect of their religious teaching, "it would be thought unjust that institutions claiming to be national should be administered in the interest of a single section of the nation". In any case there were serious objections to a purely secular education.

[1] *Report*, vol. I, p. 34.

Parents did not want it, it would alienate sympathy and increase controversy, it would hamper or exclude able men from the profession of teaching and would prevent schoolmasters from speaking freely on the highest moral questions. The solution which commended itself seemed to be denominational teaching coupled with the right of withdrawal. The teacher should "be free and unfettered in his teaching"— presumably within denominational limits. Of the importance of religious instruction the *Report* thus testifies; it "gives a higher tone and character to the whole of school life and presents education both to parents and to boys in its only true light".[1]

The problem to which the Taunton Commission chiefly addressed itself was the general diffusion of "higher" education throughout the country in the absence of any controlling, co-ordinating power, central or, save in the narrowest sense, local. Its members were less interested in the details of curriculum except in so far as they affected this diffusion. The assistant commissioners reported that the condition of the endowed schools was on the whole unsatisfactory and the comment of the *Report* thus accounts for the fact: "Untrained teachers and bad methods of teaching, uninspected work by workmen without adequate motive, unrevised or ill-revised statutes and the complete absence of all organization of schools in relation to one another could hardly lead to any other result".[2] Contemporaries must have regarded the Commission's description of many school buildings and their appurtenances as drawing a depressing picture, one which to-day is scarcely credible. Although there were exceptions, Oxford and Cambridge colleges which had responsibilities in respect of schools were not as a whole good trustees;[3] the cathedral schools were said to be "well-taught, though the standard of instruction and the number of scholars are in some cases not so high as might be expected".[4] The Cathedral Commissioners, reporting in 1855, had said that these schools were "not in a flourishing state", accounting for this by the fact that the incomes of the schools had been fixed by statutes, or had been commuted at an early date. While in the course of time the value of the whole estate, of which the school fund was a part, had greatly advanced, the value of money had depreciated. The consequence was that the school automatically lost its equitable share of the estate and

[1] *Report*, vol. I, pp. 38–43.   [2] *Ibid.* p. 139.
[3] *Ibid.* pp. 260 ff.   [4] *Ibid.* p. 272.

its income had very considerably shrunk.[1] This was an evil by no means confined to cathedral schools or to the sharp practice of earlier generations. Dr Mortimer, the late head master of the City of London School, told the Taunton Commission that the Act of Parliament which constituted the school had directed the Corporation to pay £900 yearly to its account, that being the value of the land forming the school's estate; but while that value had appreciated in thirty years to more than £3000 per annum, "the payment to educational purposes had not increased".[2]

Apart from finance, curriculum or the distribution of the schools with reference to the existing population, there were other serious hindrances to the usefulness of not a few endowments. One of these was the indiscriminate admission of boys to the gratuitous enjoyment of a foundation's benefits; the choice of pupils by nomination was the rule, by competition the exception. Endowments were never really sufficient to educate all the pupils of a school, save on one of two alternative conditions; either the instruction must be reduced to the rudiments and the teachers be such as were incompetent to give more advanced instruction, or the teaching must be of a character that the demand for it would be very small and consequently the pupils would be few. "The only schools giving a really high education gratuitously to a large number of scholars are Birmingham, Bedford and Manchester. Manchester has £2500 a year and the whole educational system is starved by the 250 free boys who are of a class abundantly able to pay fees."[3] Birmingham spent over £9000 a year on the upper schools and even that amount was insufficient for the purpose. Bedford expended £3000 on the grammar school, with results not so good as the City of London School secured from an endowment of £900 and the pupils' fees. Generally, to be successful a school must have a very competent master and it must be large in numbers; a school which exacts no fees but depends upon its endowment can afford neither, endowments not being adequate to modern needs. Where a school has but a few free pupils amongst a majority paying fees, the few should be chosen by

---

[1] *Report*, vol. 1, p. 269.   [2] *Ibid.* p. 272.

[3] *Ibid.* p. 148. Manchester, under an able head master, was however classed by the Commission amongst the successful endowed schools. The point here is that, under different terms of admission, more than 250 boys might enjoy the good education which was being given.

competition and not admitted really or ostensibly on the ground of poverty; otherwise there is the danger of class distinction being introduced. Boys admitted on the ground of more than average ability are not likely to be the victims of this bias.

The Charity Commissioners had frequently failed to carry out schemes of reform in educational trusts in the face of strong local opposition, the motive for which may be inferred from facts alleged. In some cases the very wealth of an endowment made the trust, as interpreted and administered, an instrument of public mischief. Thus the Harpur's Charity "colours and determines the whole life of many in Bedford. It bribes the father to marry for the sake of his wife's small portion; it takes the child from infancy and educates him in a set form, settles the course of his life by an apprenticeship fee, pauperises him by doles and takes away a chief object of industry by the prospect of an almshouse".[1] The apprenticeship fees payable annually from English charitable endowments were estimated as £50,000, while the apprenticeship system was virtually extinct. Mr Fearon, an assistant commissioner, reported that one parish possessed endowed charities in the hands of the vestry worth at least £500 a year. This was some-times distributed in money, sometimes in kind. "The vestry at its meeting appoints distributors for the several districts who are generally tradesmen. Thus at one time the distributor is a baker and then the dole is the bread dole. At another time he is a coal factor and then it is a coal dole. The working of the whole system is rotten to the core."[2] A charitable loan fund in Westminster consisted of upwards of £30,000 "with very little purpose to which it could be applied". Sometimes "persons have borrowed £200 or £300 from such charities at one or two per cent., and placed it in one of the joint stock banks at five or six per cent."[3]

Beneficiaries under statutes were sometimes endowed with a freehold which brought about results clean contrary to the founder's intention. The master of the Whitgift Hospital, Croydon, who died in 1866, found no pupils when he was appointed and had none during the thirty odd years of his mastership;[4] nor was his case singular. The school at Thame with an annual income of £300 and a good house was described in the *Report* as "one of the greatest scandals in the country.

[1] *Report*, vol. I, p. 531.
[3] *Ibid.* p. 219.
[2] *Ibid.* p. 217.
[4] *Ibid.* p. 226.

There were two masters and one boy when our Assistant Commissioner visited it".[1] The school at Normanton, with a yearly income of £10, had at least twenty *ex officio* governors and eleven pupils; when visited, the master was leisurely reading *Bell's Life in London* (a well-known sporting periodical), the eleven meanwhile following their own devices.[2]

These cases of neglect and corruption do not of course tell anything like the full story of English endowed schools at this time. But they were sufficiently frequent to cause the Taunton *Report* to assert that "the fore-going review seems to show clearly that the government of schools requires to be thoroughly reconsidered and considerable alterations introduced". The appointment of special bodies of trustees for individual schools would remove many causes of mischief; but the Commission believed that more was wanted and the "more" hinted at (p. 276) was an official inspection by an inspector in touch with a number of schools, the plan in fact then being administered by the Education Department in the elementary school field. *Laisser-faire* and unrestrained individualism were found wanting.

The Commission conceived that London and the great towns needed large day schools of the first grade, some of which should resemble the Realgymnasien which Prussia had established so recently as 1859. These would not teach Greek and, while retaining Latin, would provide advanced courses in modern languages, mathematics and science. Schools somewhat similar already existed but they were mostly boarding schools under private or proprietary control. The Military and Civil Department of Cheltenham College was the most prominent example. Marlborough, Wellington, Clifton, Rossall "and some others" approached the desired type, though none of them could fairly be called "semi-classical", since they taught both Greek and Latin while affording opportunities to pursue modern studies. But the modern departments of these schools were usually small and did not receive the main stress of attention. Oxford and Cambridge were responsible for the paramount position of Greek and Latin; the introduction of other studies was "due mainly to the examination for admission to Woolwich".[3]

For boys whose schooling ceased at sixteen, fairly suitable courses had been arranged in some recently reorganized second grade boarding schools and in the recently founded proprietary County Schools,

[1] *Report*, vol. I, p. 262.   [2] *Ibid.* p. 252.   [3] *Ibid.* p. 103.

so-called. "But of the day schools it may be said that, with few exceptions, they become semi-classical [i.e. teach Latin but not Greek] by force of circumstances, not by choice...they do not teach mathematics vigorously, they teach little or no natural science and French is weighted with an extra payment or taught in a way to give little real mental training. These subjects do not get their full share of the teaching and organization of the school."[1]

But it is in reference to the type of school which the Commission termed "third grade" that the *Report* animadverts upon one of the greatest weaknesses of the existing system, a weakness which affected the vast majority of boys and girls of the critical age, 12–14. "For boys who are intended to finish their education at 14 there is very little public education excepting in the upper class of a National or British school or in an endowed school of the same general standard, but frequently of inferior quality; so that as the middle division of the boys within the scope of this Commission have to take a fragment of a classical education, the lower division has either to take a still more imperfect fragment, or to accept a distinctly lower curriculum than they might otherwise have found to their profit."[2] For children of this group "there is little good education till we come to the schools under Government inspection".[3]

The population of England and Wales in 1864 as estimated was nearly 21,000,000. So far as it was possible to gauge the numbers, the Commission put it that secondary education ought to be provided at the rate of 10 per 1000 of the population and, of the 10, 8 should be educated in third grade schools. Due provision for such schools was the country's most urgent educational need; the instruction which they were designed to give was the "indispensable preliminary to technical instruction", another urgent matter of the moment on which the Commission had already made an interim report. According to an assistant commissioner, parents expected for boys who left school at fourteen "very good reading, very good writing, very good arithmetic"; or, as another phrased it, "a clerk's education". The Commission's view was less circumscribed. For pupils of six to twelve years of age third grade schools should be elementary in character; in their upper divisions (twelve onwards) instruction ought to include such subjects as the elements of Latin or of a modern language, algebra, practical

[1] *Report*, vol. I, p. 103.   [2] *Ibid.* p. 103.   [3] *Ibid.* p. 104.

geometry, botany or experimental physics or the rudiments of inorganic chemistry, the precise subjects being at the discretion of a school's governing body. The avowed models were the Swiss Sekundarschulen and the Prussian Bürgerschulen which, like the French higher primary schools, had long been necessary parts of the educational system in their respective countries. The Commission's suggestions were in effect a complete anticipation of the "Central School" plan of the twentieth century. "It might often be desirable to attach the schools of the third grade to the present elementary schools which are subject to the inspection of the Committee of Council....It would therefore be possible to treat the present elementary schools as the lower division of schools of the third grade...to admit to the upper division without increase of fee children of labourers who could pass the prescribed examination and who seemed to deserve a longer and better education. ...And sometimes a third grade school might in this way be fed by several elementary schools. Both kinds of school would gain by this. The prospect of such a promotion would stimulate the boys in the lower school. And the third grade school would be perpetually supplied with picked scholars." Similarly the *élite* of the third grade pupils could be transferred to the grade above; it was part of the Commission's scheme that pupils should pass by a qualifying or competitive examination, as the case required, from the lower to the higher division of a grade, or from grade to grade.[1]

But such proposals demanded a centrally directed power of co-ordination which did not exist; its absence constituted the vital problem of the endowed schools. Endowments had been scattered over England and no provision for meeting changes rendered necessary by the efflux of time had been devised beyond the tinkering with individual trusts by application to Chancery or Charity Commission or to Parliament itself for a special Act. There were innumerable bodies of trustees continued in perpetuity, whose schools were submitted to no public test of an official kind, whose actions were virtually uncontrolled save by the terms of statutes which were frequently impracticable and sometimes undesirable; there was no authoritative body able and likely to detect and prevent waste, or in a position of experience to advise governing bodies in doubt as to the discharge of their trust. "Large endowments were attached to places where there are few to benefit

[1] *Report*, vol. I, pp. 82–4.

by them; and pittances only are found where the need is great. In numbers of districts schools stand near to each other doing the same work and doing it more wastefully than one school only would do it; and in the same districts, or even at the same places, there is other work to be done equally important and perfectly feasible, which meanwhile is neglected. Viewed as a whole, the conditions of school education above the primary has been called a chaos, and the condition of endowed schools is certainly not the least chaotic portion."[1] What is wanted is "good local organization guided by the supervision of a higher authority"[2]—in other words, the creation for secondary education of those central and local education authorities which were created for national education as a whole by the legislation of 1899 and 1902.

The administrative scheme of the Taunton Commission illustrates the trend of opinion and its hesitation in the face of controversy; it has historical interest only. The scheme proposed to secure a central authority for secondary education by enlarging the powers of the Charity Commission in respect of schools and by adding to it an educational committee of persons conversant with education. Subordinate to this body there should be "provincial authorities", each of which would be responsible for the schemes of instruction and of management, as well as inspection, of the secondary schools of its "province", the provinces being the several "districts" of the Registrar-General. These provincial authorities were to consist of six or eight Crown nominees, unpaid, and an "official district commissioner", a civil servant appointed by the Central Authority; his duties would include the inspection of the schools and membership, *ex officio*, of all governing bodies of secondary schools within the area of the province. The governing bodies themselves should be new modelled, the representatives of the older order being reduced to a minority. If the provincial *personnel* should seem too bureaucratic, two alternative constitutions were outlined in the *Report*. The provincial authority might take the form of a county authority, in which case it might consist of the chairman of the boards of guardians within the county with half as many members nominated by the Crown. Or, again, the greater number of the members of the provincial body might be elected directly by the ratepayers; for the Commission ventured to believe that in some places rate aid might be extended to secondary

[1] *Report*, vol. I, p. 112.   [2] *Ibid.* p. 434.

schools, the prolonged controversy about it in the elementary school field notwithstanding.[1]

As to finance the *Report* is sketchy. Buildings could be erected, maintained and furnished from existing endowments, if these were pooled in a common fund, and supplemented from "some public sources". Grants from the Consolidated Fund are not mentioned, but "we believe that recourse must be had to rates, if this object is to be effectually attained. We are not, indeed, prepared to recommend that rates for secondary education should be made compulsory; but we are of opinion that, if any town or parish should desire to rate itself for the establishment of a school or schools above the elementary, it should be allowed to do so".[2] The cost of teaching should be covered by the pupils' fees. In third grade schools £4 a year would be a sufficient fee. "This we have reason to believe the parents would not be unwilling to give, at any rate in many parts of England, if they were thoroughly satisfied with what they got in return. In some cases a judicious use of endowments or other funds under public control might relieve some of the parents of a part of this burden. To relieve them of it altogether would, according to almost unanimous testimony, be unwise."[3] But provision should be made for assisting boys who would profit from a more advanced education, but whose parents were too poor to pay the full fee. It will not be forgotten that, previous to 1891, fees were the rule in public elementary schools.

The recommendation that there might be a close and profitable association between certain third grade and certain elementary schools suggests a comment on social conditions to the writer of the *Report*. "Much of our evidence tends to show that social distinctions in education cannot at present be altogether ignored. The education of the gentry has gradually separated itself from that of the class next below them, and it is but natural that this class in their turn should be unwilling to be confounded with the labourers whom they employ. It would be better that such distinctions, as far as education is concerned, at any rate in day schools, should disappear; but an attempt to obliterate them by superior authority might both do mischief and fail of its object."[4]

The principles of State supervision and of partial maintenance out

[1] *Report*, vol. I, pp. 633 ff.   [2] *Ibid.* p. 656.
[3] *Ibid.* p. 83.   [4] *Ibid.* p. 82.

of public money, the principles which directed the system of the Committee of Council, were accepted by the Taunton Commission as applicable also to secondary education, an important advance toward the erection of a national organization of schools. It is noteworthy, too, that, some six years after the issue of the adverse Newcastle *Report*, another Royal Commission took occasion to contrast very favourably the work done in the public elementary schools with that of endowed schools whose instruction had become elementary in character.

If individualism and *laisser-faire* had failed, it was not for want of trying; but the magnitude of the task exceeded the power of private resources to achieve it. Proprietary and private schools were numerous, yet the number was insufficient and there was of course no organization of the schools as a whole beyond the rough grouping ensured by demand and supply. Of the large number of private schools[1] the efficiency varied "from good to exceedingly bad". The root difficulty was money. The expensive schools reached a good standard in buildings and in teaching staff, the best were certainly equal to the best grammar schools. "The account given of the worst of the endowed schools must be repeated in even more emphatic language to describe the worst of the private schools."[2] But the position of the poorer schools was precarious and consequently the principals hesitated to invest capital (where they had it to invest) in buildings or apparatus; fees were low and teachers were engaged at "pitiful salaries". The teaching staff was the weak spot in the private schools; the *Report* states that the assistant teachers were rarely good. Many head masters were very able men, but there were many pretenders among them and their exclusion was difficult. The Commissioners should have added that for twenty years past the College of Preceptors had been endeavouring to effect the exclusion, but public support had been wanting.

The humbler schools aimed chiefly at teaching commercial arithmetic and penmanship; those immediately above them added English and some French. These two groups made up the majority of private schools. They gave the instruction which was regarded as the necessary preparation for "business", the motive which centuries before had first called elementary schools into existence in Western Europe. The schools with greater pretensions also taught Latin or science or both. But the *Report* adds the damaging statement, "their preference for

[1] *Report*, vol. I, pp. 283–309.   [2] *Ibid.* p. 285.

what are called modern subjects is often accompanied with a substitution of superficial for sound instruction".

For a variety of reasons the Commission felt tnat private schools, however good, could not make up the existing deficiency in the supply of secondary education. Yet these and the analogous proprietary schools possessed an elasticity which made it expedient to include them in any national scheme. Mr Fitch, the assistant commissioner in the northern counties, reported that "almost all the educational enterprise of the last few years has originated with private teachers"; and the Commissioners add "and this is likely to be often the case".[1] Enterprise is a great virtue when the aim is to adapt schools to the requirements of their time, since educational processes must necessarily change as the national life changes in its more considerable manifestations; but enterprise is least to be expected from a well-established official organization. The Taunton Commission was therefore wise in recommending that private and proprietary schools, subject to two conditions, should be registered and enjoy the privileges of public recognition. The conditions were that the fees charged should not be so high as to put the schools beyond the reach of the class for which secondary education was needed, and that the schools should submit to the same inspection and examination as the Commission would impose upon public, that is, endowed schools.

The Commissioners regarded the proprietary plan[2] as the most promising method of making national provision for secondary education; but the class distinctions of the proprietary schools stood in the way of their recognition as public agents. Since schools whose pupils completed the course at the early age of fourteen were included amongst those giving secondary instruction, the objection was a serious one; that the *Report* alludes to it is an indication that social boundaries in the 'sixties' were shifting, at least, if they were not being obliterated. Though there was at this time considerable activity in opening proprietary schools, the movement was not new. The earliest group was pre-Victorian, and Cheltenham, Marlborough and Rossall (founded 1844) had more than a score of years' life behind them in the days of the Clarendon and Taunton Commissions. Their significance has already been noted.[3] Wellington (1859), Clifton (1860), Malvern

---

[1] *Report*, vol. I, p. 299. [2] *Ibid.* pp. 310–22.
[3] See Chapter II, and pp. 50 f. above.

(1862), Radley (1863) and Haileybury (1864) were contemporary with the Commissions. All these together with Brighton, Bath, Liverpool (College and Institution) and several others were first grade schools giving classical instruction and greater facilities for modern studies than were usual in endowed schools; most of them were boarding schools. From the early 'fifties' the West of England had been active in establishing for the sons of farmers and others resident in rural areas what were called "County Schools", a name which implied no connexion with Quarter Sessions or any official mode of county administration. The schools were the property of bodies of private persons interested as parents or otherwise in local secondary education. The Taunton Commission noted such schools at West Buckland (the Devon County School), Sampford Peverell, Dorchester, Hereford, Wells and Saham Toney; Trent College and Bedford County School were in the initial stage. North Tawton, Framlingham and Cranley (the Surrey County School) had permanently dedicated their buildings to education and were on that account classed amongst the endowed schools by the Commission. The school established at Wakefield in 1834 was now absorbed in the local grammar school trust.

No Greek was taught in these "county schools" nor did all teach Latin; their studies were predominantly modern. Boys were lodged and boarded in hostels, a plan initiated by Marlborough as less costly than the "house" system of the ancient Public Schools.

Proprietary schools were to be found in all three grades, from Clifton College to day schools (though these were few) like the Central School, Finsbury, which had just been started by the Middle Schools Corporation under "the active and well-directed exertions of Mr Rogers".[1] The third grade schools amongst them varied in standard from a stage just above the primary to that of the lower schools of the Liverpool Institute and the Birkbeck Schools which William Ellis established in different parts of London between 1848 and 1862. Ellis was a great advocate of the teaching of political economy to the people at large; physical training, the laws of health and "the science of human well-being" (or the practical application of economics to the daily life of the individual) were specialities of his schools.

---

[1] *Report*, vol. I, p. 185. The reference is to William Rogers ("Hang theology Rogers") then rector of St Botolph's, Bishopsgate; the corporation was a proprietary body which favoured secular education.

The *Report* of the Taunton Commission pointed out that the fortunes of the proprietary schools had varied during the thirty or forty years of their history. Depending largely upon the support of individuals for their capital outlay and charging fees which left little margin over current expenditure, it was only to be expected that some would be short-lived. Several in London and eleven outside the metropolis had either ceased entirely or had become private schools, whose principals were also their proprietors. Yet "the history of these schools is in a great degree the history of recent struggles for the improvement of secondary schools".[1] Commercially they were not successful. In the majority of cases dividends were neither paid nor expected; where they were looked for, the percentage was limited by by-law or by custom. Capital and dividends, where they were earned, were surrendered for the good of the cause. Yet "the educational character of proprietary schools stands very high....The County schools, proprietary as well as endowed, gain and deserve the favour of the public almost as rapidly as they are formed, and the schools established for the third grade of scholars are certainly no less useful, perhaps more useful, than any others of the same kind in the Country".[2]

A school opened in 1847 at New Shoreham, Sussex, by Nathaniel Woodard[3] (1811–91), curate-in-charge of that place, was the germ of a great scheme for the recovery by the Church of its position as the educator of the nation. Woodard's experience as a parish clergyman in Bethnal Green and Shoreham had convinced him that the middle classes were estranged from the Church, and that schools for the labouring poor would never be completely successful so long as the employers remained ill-educated and opposed to the Church. Although his own operations did not extend to the elementary school, Woodard grasped the conception of a *national* education. Provision existed for the advanced schooling enjoyed by a small minority and for the rudimentary instruction of the great majority; but the middle classes, politically powerful and increasing in wealth, were neglected. "Middle schools" were therefore a crying need. The good, typically English education was that given in the Public Schools, that is, in boarding schools; the day school was not intensive enough to educate. (Woodard

---

[1] *Report*, vol. I, p. 314. [2] *Ibid.* p. 318.
[3] Sir John Otter, *Nathaniel Woodard, a memoir of his life* (1925), to which the author is here greatly indebted.

himself had been educated at home and by a private tutor before he went up to Oxford at the age of twenty-three.) What was necessary therefore was the institution of a "system of boarding schools for the sons of persons of moderate or less than moderate means" and an organization of persons, independent of the State but intimately associated with the Church, to direct and govern the system.

These principles were not reached in a moment but were developed rapidly after the success of Woodard's earliest school, which was held at first in the dining-room of his vicarage. This was a day school framed particularly to meet local conditions; navigation and French, subjects of special concern to the skippers resident about Shoreham Harbour, were prominent studies of the boys. These and the other "secular" studies were conducted by an Oxford graduate; Woodard reserved to himself the religious instruction, the aim of which was "to unite them [the pupils] to the true faith of the Church". For the upkeep of the school donations were solicited and obtained; Woodard was always fortunate in securing the wholehearted support of a few wealthy men. Two features in the management of this school remained constant factors in the history of the Woodard schools; the fees exacted from parents and the stipends paid to teachers were extremely moderate. Twenty years later the Taunton Commissioners said of the three boarding schools then existing that the masters gave their services "at a very low rate" and that the success of the schools "must in some degree be ascribed to religious zeal".[1] This was at once the strength and the weakness of Woodard's scheme for education on a national scale. It secured in two or three schools the self-sacrificing devotion of a chosen few; it would fail to attract the many whose services would be necessary when the scheme became as wide as the nation itself. Woodard in effect called for the well-nigh gratuitous labour of a religious order, whereas the conditions of the time demanded the services of a profession.

The first venture proved very successful and under the stress of the political and social disturbance, which marked the year 1848, Woodard and his supporters were soon enlarging their plans from a local to a national scope. Although he studiously avoided any active participation in "politics"—his personal opinions were distinctly Tory—Woodard's relations with individual Chartists in his Bethnal Green parish gave him

[1] *Report*, vol. 1, p. 49.

an understanding of their point of view, and bred in him the desire to help them in the way he considered best. In that troublous year, so he told an audience in 1881, a party of six used to meet in a little room in Shoreham to frame schemes of amelioration. They decided that societies ought to be formed to employ university graduates to give a good, sound, Church of England education to the neglected children of the nation, a conclusion made public in Woodard's pamphlet, *A Plea for the Middle Classes* (1848). The *Plea* met with a very favourable response and in August of the same year the day school was given up, to be replaced by a boarding school lodged in a number of private houses and charging an inclusive fee varying from £30 to £40 a year. Then with characteristic energy this was followed, still in 1848, by the establishment of a society to give effect to the much greater scheme which Woodard and his friends contemplated. Taking its name from the dedication of the parish church, the society was called the Society of St Nicolas College, and the school, St Nicolas Grammar School. (The rapidity with which matters were moving may be inferred from the fact that the title first given to it was "Shoreham Grammar School", a name with far less implication.) The constitution of the "College" was intended as a model to be followed by future societies of the kind. At its head was the provost, in this instance Woodard himself, and associated with him were to be a number of fellows whose office was tenable for eight years; the first four years being probationary. On the satisfactory completion of probation, fellows were to serve in any of the society's schools to which they might be sent. The local diocesan was to act as visitor. The college proposed to undertake "the education of the sons of the middle classes at such terms as will make education available for most of them".[1]

A second boarding school was opened in the following year at Shoreham, the fee being about half that which was charged at the grammar school of the society. In 1850, in which year Woodard gave up his parochial charge in order to devote himself entirely to his scheme of national education, this second school was removed to temporary quarters at Hurstpierpoint; three years later it moved into its permanent quarters there. This school included a section in which senior pupils were trained to serve as "commercial schoolmasters", presumably professional schoolmasters not in holy orders: Woodard may have

[1] Otter, *op. cit.* p. 49.

had in mind the growing profession of elementary school teachers created by the Minutes of 1846. Property and funds were accumulating and Woodard's doings interested both clergy and laymen all over the country; it became necessary to ensure permanence by means of a deed of trust. Five men of weight were appointed trustees and the deed was duly enrolled in the Court of Chancery in 1855.

Originally the purpose was limited to founding schools of two grades only; but in 1851 Woodard addressed a letter to the clergy of the diocese of Chichester in which he propounded a scheme for schools of three grades, very much on the lines afterwards adopted by the Taunton Commission. Steps were taken to give effect to this scheme, and in 1857 St Nicolas Grammar School was removed from Shoreham to Lancing, which thenceforth became the headquarters of "The Society of SS. Mary and Nicolas, Lancing". The society's third school was at once opened in temporary premises in Shoreham and within a year it had two hundred pupils at a yearly charge per boy of thirteen guineas for board, lodging and tuition; it was known as St Saviour's, Shoreham. The three Sussex schools were thus of three grades. Lancing itself was taught and administered on the assumption that a fair proportion of its sons would pass on to Oxford or Cambridge. Hurst was a second grade school, and St Saviour's as a school of the third grade was planned with special thought for the poorer members of the middle classes whom the society desired more particularly to benefit. Long and careful preparation was made for its accommodation in suitable buildings and it was not till 1870 that the school was housed in its permanent home at Ardingly. Its teaching staff then consisted of five graduates and a number of "associates of St Nicolas College" who had qualified to teach by their course of training at Hurst. The inclusive fee was fifteen guineas. That Hurst gave Ardingly some of its teachers, and that the passage of pupils was made possible from a school of the lower grade to one of the higher, or from Lancing to the university, are facts significant of Woodard's ideal of uniting all members of the three schools in one fellowship. The great chapel at Lancing was designed to be the symbol of that unity and the centre of its corporate life.

While the Taunton Commission was bringing its labours to a close, Woodard was further enlarging the sphere of his society's influence. Hitherto tangible results had been confined to a county which could not be termed urban; and the middle classes whom he desired to reach were chiefly resident in great towns. He got into touch with men in the Midlands who were desirous of setting up in their own neighbourhoods schools like his own. In 1867 negotiations were opened to institute a Society of SS. Mary and John of Lichfield, which was to be federated, not amalgamated, with Lancing; it was to be a centre for the Midlands as the earlier society was for the South of England. Denstone, the fourth Woodard school, grew out of these negotiations.

Woodard was not greatly interested in those reforms of curriculum which at this time made the staple of educational discussion. The second head master of the Shoreham Grammar School (1849–51), C. E. Moberly, was attracted by the school's possibilities as an experiment and, before his appointment, had suggested that a more modern character than was usual might be given to the course of study. To the suggestion Woodard replied, "My view is not to introduce new elements either into our religious or educational departments, but rather to try our strength on the present system which has stood the test of many generations.... My real object, of course, is to win the people over, or back to, the Faith of the Church, and the means proposed to be employed are an education of such a sort, and communicated in such a way, as may fall in with popular prejudices".[1] Moberly's predecessor had retained office for one term only; he had resigned in consequence of what he took to be the undue prominence of the school chaplain in the moral and religious training of the boys. Like the Evangelical leader, Close, at Cheltenham, Woodard had thought it necessary to separate the moral and intellectual disciplines, entrusting their direction to different persons. Lancing at a later date lost the services of an efficient head master in consequence of a similar conception of the head master's sphere.[2] Woodard refused to make the education of girls a part of his scheme, although circumstances forced upon him a kind of morganatic alliance with a number of new girls' schools, to which he lent a somewhat tepid support. In 1880 he wrote, "Public Schools for girls are of very doubtful merit. Religious homes or convents are more in harmony with my ideas. The High School system, and knowledge without the female grace of gentleness and devotion, is another cloud in the gathering storm which is awaiting society".[3]

[1] Otter, *op. cit.* pp. 54 f.   [2] *Ibid.* pp. 51 and 329.   [3] *Ibid.* p. 274.

Not innovation but a return to an older conception of public education was what he had at heart; education must have a religious foundation and that could be secured by making Church and nation co-terminous, with the Church restored to its ancient office of national educator. A public "Letter to the Marquis of Salisbury", one of the Lancing Society's trustees, sets forth the full Woodard scheme as it was in 1869. The country was to be arranged in five divisions—north, south, east, west and midland. Each division should maintain boarding schools for three grades, respectively for the rich, for persons of good incomes, and for small tradesmen, farmers, artisans and persons who were likely to become employers. The schools of a division should be directed by a body such as the Lancing Society, each having its provost and twenty-four fellows, half of them resident clerics, half non-resident laymen. Professional schoolmasters would be trained in schools of the second grade. The five provosts and the one hundred and twenty fellows would be empowered to make by-laws for all the schools. Each bishop would be the official visitor of the schools within his diocese; and from him an appeal was to lie to the Upper House of Convocation, that is, to the whole body of bishops of a province, whether of Canterbury or York. In secondary education there would be no intervention by the State; State activity had gone far enough within the limits of elementary education. About a quarter of a million had been expended upon the Woodard schools within twenty years; Woodard believed that two and a half millions of money would be required for the scheme propounded in the "Letter" to Lord Salisbury.[1]

The Lancing Society received the support, in many cases the enthusiastic support, of a large number of men distinguished in public and in academic life. But those were times of fierce ecclesiastical wrangling, and prejudice was easily awakened at the least suspicion of anything which could be stigmatized as "Popery". Woodard's opinions and procedure aroused bitter enmity in quarters not entirely without power to obstruct, and he sometimes met indifference where he might have expected support. The scheme of 1869 was not only in opposition to the work then being undertaken by the Endowed Schools' Commissioners appointed by an Act of Parliament of that year; its principles were in flat contradiction to the trend of that Radicalism in public education which was becoming more and more dominant as the

[1] Otter, *op. cit.* pp. 208 ff.

nineteenth century advanced. The issue was the century-old one of the Church *v.* the State, and all which the controversy implied in the upbringing of the nation's youth.

However, the scheme achieved only a very partial realization. At Woodard's death the number of schools erected was seven and two were added before the year 1900; of the five projected divisions, three only, the Southern, Midland and Western, found realization in these nine schools, one school alone representing the division of the West. As Matthew Arnold had pointed out in the very friendly criticism, which appeared in his *A French Eton* (1864), private enterprise could not command resources which were adequate to the urgent needs of English secondary education.

Of the less obtrusive educational developments of the nineteenth century one of the most influential was that of the examination system. Beginning with the century at the Universities and applied at the mid-century to candidates for service under the Crown, it had come to be accepted generally as an educational institution which ensured the efficiency of teaching and of learning, and fairness in the treatment of individual candidates. So exaggerated was the public trust in examinations that from 1858 the University of London subordinated everything else to them, and after 1862, the Education Department, that is, the Government, made examinations the measure of the financial support which it extended to individual public elementary schools. Inevitably, therefore, the Taunton Commission discussed in its *Report*[1] the value, kind and functions of examinations.

The *Report* points out that a great deal of the work done in school cannot be tested by examination, and that, to be really valuable, there should be an intimate connexion between the examination and the work done in the particular school which is being examined. The examiners should be, so to say, *ad hoc* in order to avoid the vice of a purely external and general examination, which is, that the test and the matter tested, the examiner and the teacher, are liable to move on different planes. Where the efficiency of teaching, or of learning, is gauged solely by success in an examination which is destitute of such a connexion, there is a strong temptation to sacrifice real study to the tricks of the crammer and the sham of the smatterer. "The examination of a school by its own masters is in one sense the best of all", since the

[1] Vol. I, pp. 322–36.

desired intimacy is fully attained by making examiner and instructor one person. But to guide the teacher and to enable him to judge of the success of his own work is but one function of an examination. Another is to enable public authorities or the public at large to judge whether a given school, teacher or pupil is working at the level of a standard applicable to all schools and pupils of the same grade. For this purpose an outside, independent examiner must at least share in the testing.

The *Report* passes in review the different public examinations to which secondary schools were in one form or another submitting and, from the national point of view, finds them all more or less unsatisfactory. "A considerable number of private and proprietary schools" have adopted the matriculation examination of London University as their goal, with the gratifying consequence that their curriculum has comprised classics, a modern foreign language, English, Euclid, algebra and the elements of natural science. But the examination is one of persons, not schools; few schools send candidates and, of those that do so, the proportion of their pupils examined is small. The examinations of the College of Preceptors, established in 1853, "are well planned, comparatively inexpensive and have attained a fair success"; but as yet public confidence has not been completely secured. The examinations are individual; but it is becoming the practice of some masters to send up whole classes. The Local Examinations of Oxford and Cambridge, started in 1858, "seem to have done all that could be done by a purely voluntary agency to supply the schools with a fair test of the efficiency of their teaching"; but the examinations are too expensive, too difficult and too individual.

What the country needed was a general system under the direction of an entirely independent "Council of Examinations"; the *Report* proposed the appointment of such a body, consisting of twelve members, unpaid, six being nominated by the Crown, and two each by Oxford, Cambridge and London. This Council should frame rules of examination and appoint examiners of schools, the rules being such as to leave the schools as far as possible perfect independence in their work and to limit the examiners to the work professed by the school authorities.[1]

Nothing is more illustrative of the estimation in which examinations were held at this time than the second important function which the Commission would assign to this Council. The creation of new schools

[1] Vol. i, pp. 649 ff.

in large numbers and the reorganization of existing schools contemplated by the Commission called for an increased number of competent teachers. Competence is only partially testified by a university degree. "A man who is profoundly versed in science might happen to be very ill-fitted to teach." "A university degree may imply a very sufficient amount of knowledge in the subjects in which the graduate was examined. But on the other hand a university degree by no means of necessity implies that the graduate is able to teach what he knows, or that his knowledge is cast in the best form for that purpose."[1] These are the reasons which make necessary the training of the schoolmaster, irrespective of the grade of school in which he is to work. The *Report* asserted "It is to the training schools that the great improvement in elementary teachers is really due".[2]

John Stuart Mill and others of their witnesses were in favour of establishing training schools for secondary teachers; but the majority opposed the recommendation. The great objection to the establishment of secondary training colleges was that it would give the Government undue control of higher education; or so it was thought. Further, the only "training of teachers" known in England was the training mingled with a general education which made the system of the training colleges for elementary schoolmasters and schoolmistresses. The origin of those training colleges, the imperfect education of their students and the mechanical nature of much of the technical instruction were working in men's minds to the prejudice of training in the strict sense, the necessity for which the *Report* recognized. A casual sentence exhibits the Commission hovering on the brink of a solution: "it is complained that the trained masters in this country often show that they would have been the better had they been educated in company with those who were preparing for other employments."[3] It took the lapse of more than twenty years and yet another Royal Commission to drive that home.

There were, then, to be no secondary training colleges. The Taunton Commission recommended that the proposed Council of Examinations should institute a certificate of competence to teach, granted on passing an appropriate examination, the mode of preparing for which was left to the candidate himself. No head-mastership should be open to men not in possession of this certificate. Further, since the Com-

---

[1] *Report*, vol. I, p. 651.   [2] *Ibid.* p. 612.   [3] *Ibid.* p. 613.

mission evidently realized the importance of encouraging the growth of a profession of schoolmasters,[1] it was recommended that a list be kept of all successful candidates at the certificate examinations, such list becoming automatically that "Register of Teachers" for which many schoolmasters had long been asking. When secondary school-masters were thus enrolled in a profession it would become necessary not only to obtain qualified members, but also, as the *Report* bluntly puts it, "to remove those whom age disqualifies". The disqualifying age should be sixty or sixty-five; if the endowment of the particular school would bear it (the Commission seems to have regarded "endowments" as especially elastic) a pension might be paid to a retiring master. If not (and this was the more probable event) the Commissioners cheerfully bade the schoolmaster "make the necessary provision for himself".

"The general deficiency in girls' education is stated with the utmost confidence and with entire agreement, with whatever difference of words, by many witnesses of authority. Want of thoroughness and foundation, want of system; slovenliness and showy superficiality; inattention to rudiments, undue time given to accomplishments and those not taught intelligently or in any systematic manner; want of organisation—these may sufficiently indicate the character of the complaints we have received in their most general aspect. It is needless to observe that the same complaints apply to a great extent to boys' education. But on the whole the evidence is clear that, not as they might be but as they are, the girls' schools are inferior in this view to the boys' schools."[2] This was the considered opinion of the Schools Inquiry Commissioners with reference to the schooling of girls other than those who were taught in the public elementary schools. While "mental discipline" was the ostensible aim of the most expensive form of boys' education, a merely superficial attainment of so-called accomplishments (as music, dancing, deportment, fluent speech in one or more foreign tongues) was thought sufficient for their sisters. What was admittedly a fault in the instruction of boys, as for example an excessive appeal to rote while understanding was neglected, was a legitimate practice in a girls' school. That this difference between the sexes was deliberately adopted or at least consciously tolerated is a reasonable inference from the routine of some of the most expensive boarding schools for girls.

[1] Cp. *Report*, vol. I, pp. 615 ff.   [2] *Ibid.* p. 548.

Yet, when the Taunton Commissioners reported in 1867, educational reformers, revolutionaries rather, had been at work upon this matter for more than twenty years. Frances Mary Buss, Dorothea Beale and Emily Davies were unquestionably actuated by the purely educational motive; but at bottom it was the economic position of women which gave cogency to their attempts to revolutionize the then accepted ideal of girls' education. Success came to them in due course in the years following 1870.

Some time before 1843 the Governesses Benevolent Institution had been started to relieve the distress from which private governesses so frequently suffered; all governesses not employed in public elementary schools were at that time "private". In the year named the Institution was not flourishing and David Laing, a philanthropic parish clergyman of North London, accepted the office of honorary secretary. He and his friends on its council proceeded to enlarge the scope of the society by adding an employment agency, or teachers' registry, the operations of which soon revealed that many candidates were ignorant and otherwise incompetent. A proposal followed to issue a diploma to those who passed an examination, a proposal involving some scheme of preparation to undergo the test. In 1847 the teaching, examination and diploma were projects only. But in that year Frederick Denison Maurice, Professor of Divinity in King's College, London, and most of his brother-professors associated themselves in a Committee of Education in order to carry out the scheme of the Governesses Benevolent Institution. Unpaid they both taught and examined women who desired to become governesses.

Quite independently of this scheme, Miss A. M. Murray, one of the Queen's maids-of-honour, was collecting funds for a College for Women which she had planned. In 1848 the two schemes were amalgamated and Queen's College, London, was the result, the name marking Queen Victoria's express approval. Maurice was its first principal, Miss Buss and Miss Beale were amongst its first students. In 1853 the College was incorporated by charter and empowered to grant certificates of qualification "to governesses" and "to open classes in all branches of female education".

In 1847 also Mrs Reid started classes for girls in her own house; from 1849 to 1860 the classes were known as Bedford Square College, in the latter year as Bedford College for Women. The informal association between Queen's College and the staff of King's College was paralleled by a similar connexion between Bedford College and the staffs of University and King's Colleges, London. Bedford College received its charter in 1869.

The two women who from the 'fifties' of last century led the reform in girls' education were Frances M. Buss and Dorothea Beale, to whom a little later must be added Emily Davies. Miss Buss, whilst a pupil at Queen's College, taught in her own private school in Camden Street, to which in 1850 she gave a *quasi*-public standing by associating in its supervision the beneficed clergy of St Pancras; it was then known as the North London Collegiate School for Ladies. The last word was changed to "Girls" in 1871, when Miss Buss transferred her property to a body of trustees and the school became "Public" in more than one sense. The North London Collegiate School for Girls, for most of its pupils a day school, became the model of the High Schools of the Girls' Public Day Schools Company, in other words the pattern after which the reformed education of girls was shaped. Miss Beale became principal in 1858 of the Ladies' College, Cheltenham, a school which had been granted a charter some five years earlier.

It is impossible to gauge justly the influence upon feminine education exerted by those two former students of Queen's College; and that college had come into being for the sake of the better education of governesses, an economic motive in fact. When the Taunton Commission desired information on the state of girls' education above the elementary grade and advice on the measures advisable for its improvement, they summoned these two ladies and Miss Emily Davies. The last named, one of the original supporters of Bedford College, had been since 1862 secretary of a ladies' committee whose policy it was to obtain the admission of women to university examinations. In consequence of the activity of this committee girls were admitted, at first tentatively (1865) and afterwards on equal terms, with boys to the recently instituted (1858) Cambridge Local Examination. The next step was to induce the Taunton Commission to include girls' schools and girls' education within their survey. Hence the appearance of the three ladies before the Commission in 1865.

The number of endowments for secondary education appropriated to girls was less than 2 per cent. of the whole number of such endowments. The Commission made a list of fourteen schools in all, two of them in fact being for elementary instruction only; not one of them was of outstanding merit and each of the twelve secondary girls' schools had only a handful of pupils, the numbers ranging from ninety-one down to twelve, the average being fifty-two. This state of things was a reflection of public opinion; girls suffered from a widely held belief that they were less intellectually capable than boys and that in any case their instruction was economically less important.

"We cannot doubt that at present as a class the female teachers in girls' schools must be pronounced not fully equal to their tasks", [1] which is not surprising, when the circumstances of their own schooling are remembered. The following report by Mr Fearon, an assistant commissioner, is said to be concise and accurate. "We find as a rule a very small amount of professional skill, an inferior set of school-books, a vast deal of dry, uninteresting task-work, rules put into the memory with no explanation of their principles, no system of examination worthy of the name, a very false estimate of the relative value of the several kinds of acquirement, a reference to effect rather than to solid worth, a tendency to fill and adorn rather than to strengthen the mind."[2] The wealthiest class did not as a rule send their daughters to schools, but educated them at home in accordance with a tradition many centuries old.

The *Report* makes a point of describing these defects as "the less favourable side" of girls' education; over against it are the statements that there is much good in the girls' schools, that much improvement is going on in them, that still more may be looked for, admissions which the Commissioners cordially make. The work of the pioneers during the preceding twenty years was bearing fruit.

The Commission's general recommendations respecting boys' secondary schools were repeated in reference to those existing, or contemplated, for girls. In particular, a very much more equitable share of the endowments ought to be assigned to the latter, and whenever the reform of an educational endowment was undertaken, the claims of girls should always be considered in conjunction with those of the other sex. The option of examination and inspection might be offered to private girls' schools; apart from the advantages accruing to the girls, a system of inspection would tend to mitigate the professional isolation of the mistresses.

[1] *Report*, vol. i, p. 561.   [2] *Ibid.* p. 552.

The organization and curriculum of the North London Collegiate School for Ladies, of Queen's College and of Bedford Square College, as these were described to the Taunton Commission,[1] illustrate the attempts to reform feminine education. The first, then under the principalship of Miss Buss, daughter of its founder and proprietor, was established to give a good secular education on a religious basis at a moderate cost to girls of the middle class. The pupils, whose ages ranged from six to eighteen, numbered 190 "day" girls paying fees of from nine to twelve guineas, and sixteen boarders living in two houses at fees of sixty and forty-two guineas per annum. The staff of men and women teachers was a large one, "visiting teachers" predominating. The general course of studies included English, French, the elements of Latin and German, drawing, class-singing, geometry, plain needlework and callisthenics; there were opportunities also for learning arithmetic, geography and harmony. About fifty girls were studying Latin, Cornelius Nepos being their highest attainment in the language; the chief value of elementary Latin and German was thought to lie in the "mental discipline" to be extracted from their grammars. Two clergymen representing the St Pancras clergy visited the school every week; the daily prayers were those of the Church of England, Roman Catholics and Jews not being obliged to attend. From the return of parents' occupations it would seem that the daughters of trades-people were only received if their fathers did not reside on their business premises. Amongst the entries are "Fish salesman (dead)", "Zinc worker (private house) dead"; so neither the zinc nor the fish came between the wind and the school's respectability.

An account[2] of the school building as it was in 1872 very well illustrates the primitive form of school planning in vogue at an earlier time; for under the School Boards of 1870 the division of a school into separate classrooms was the type which was replacing the great schoolroom here described. "The North London Collegiate School in Camden Road occupies an unpretending building which at first sight appears only a private house, but will reward an inspection. The Secretary's entrance-room contains several boards on which are

[1] *Report*, vol. x.
[2] Mary Gurney, *Are we to have education for middle-class girls? or the history of Camden Collegiate Schools*. Published under the sanction of the National Union for improving the Education of Women of all Classes, 2nd ed. (1872).

inscribed the already numerous names of successful competitors in various public examinations....From this room a long and winding passage leads to a most attractive school-room capable of holding 120 girls. The aspect of this room is remarkably pleasant, the bright young girls are arranged at long reversible desks, and separate classes are divided by curtains on the plan of elementary schools. A dark staining of wood on walls, floors and desks below the large windows, which open on sky and foliage, gives an air of brightness and refinement to the whole room. The children can here write undisturbed by one another or may be collected for a general lesson, while the long passages give them a convenient space for the musical gymnastics which form a part of every day's work. Upstairs the house is equally well arranged, one long room stretching from end to end, while two smaller class-rooms on each floor are prepared for separate classes....There are more than 200 girls in attendance."

A liberal education for boys was understood to require attendance at a university up to the age of twenty-two or twenty-three. While this was not immediately practicable for girls, it was obvious that something different from the regimen of a school was needed where the pupils were young women in the late 'teens or early twenties. Tennyson's *Princess* (1847) never materialised in a women's university, but the combination of "school" and "college" in Bedford Square and in Harley Street made possible a more advanced instruction than could then be given in the schoolroom. There floated before the minds of the Commissioners the project of a Women's College and they considered Queen's and Bedford from that point of view. The former, "an admirable institution", was more a school than a college; its rival was careful to mark the distinction between its junior and senior sections and seemed to be "nearer the mark".

Bedford Square College, which occupied two houses in the Square, aimed at providing "a sound, liberal, unsectarian education for girls without any restriction". No religious instruction was offered; an unsectarian Biblical literature class had been tried but failed to get support. The students numbered seventy-eight, of whom thirty-two were "regular students" pursuing a four-year course; they paid an annual fee of twenty-one guineas; "occasional students", who took classes in particular subjects, paid two guineas per term per class. The studies included Latin, pure and applied mathematics, natural science, modern languages. There were seventeen professors and assistants and a body of "lady visitors", members of the governing body, who were responsible for discipline. In English studies, the pupils in the lowest class, whose average age was ten years, took Ince's *Outlines of English History*, Cornwell's *Geography*, *The Fourth Irish Reading Book*, Constable's *Third Reading Book*, Mavor's *Spelling Book*, Joseph Payne's *Selections of Poetry*, Hullah's *Manual of Singing*, a series of text-books familiar in the elementary schools.

Queen's College, which was accommodated in two houses in Harley Street, was a Church of England institution; but exemption from divinity teaching was granted on request. The full course of four years included divinity, moral philosophy, history, geography, mathematics, natural philosophy, languages ancient and modern, music and drawing. Gymnastics and callisthenics were also taught. There were 124 regular and 59 occasional students, most of whom entered at fourteen or fifteen years of age, the majority remaining for three years. In the junior division children of five were admissible.

The questions which the Commissioners addressed to these schools indicate the rising interest in school hygiene, the subject to which serious attention had been drawn by Herbert Spencer. Neither Harley Street nor Bedford Square possessed its own playground, but there were gardens attached to the two houses in Camden Street in which Miss Buss's school was lodged. But as to furniture all three schools could assure the Commission that "the seats had backs". In the two colleges the great majority of the teachers were men, and in obedience to current notions of propriety it was thought necessary that the students should be attended by a chaperone.

In both there was a body of "lady visitors" who were present in rotation at the professors' lectures; these ladies were responsible for college discipline. The implication here (as in the employment of the chaplains, to the exclusion of the head master, at Cheltenham College in its early years and in the Woodard schools), that, in education, instruction and religious or moral training can and should be separated, was one of the most mischievous ideas with which continental liberalism infected the nineteenth century. Education even more certainly than the French Republic is "one and indivisible".

These pioneer institutions assisted in forming a more intelligent public interest in feminine education and made feasible a considerable step in advance beyond the instruction given by the ordinary school for girls. Experiment and suggestion followed which, when they had borne fruit, wrought changes in the social and economic life of women that even yet have not attained their full effects. Mark Pattison, Rector of Lincoln College, Oxford, told the Taunton Commission[1] of classes begun in the university town at Christmas, 1865, by half a dozen persons, of whom he was one, for the education of girls of seventeen and upwards who had left school and were preparing to settle in life. Oxford mothers complained that there was neither a university nor suitable instruction for their daughters; whereupon Pattison and his friends, some of them women, started these classes in French, German (this was Pattison's class), history and Latin. In May, 1866, a class in mental philosophy was added. The total number of pupils was thirty-nine, of whom a score belonged to "University families". The classes were self-supporting on an annual fee of four and a half guineas per subject per pupil. In the course of his evidence Pattison referred to a similar and earlier experiment at the Midland Institute, Birmingham.

It was found that the number of pupils needed to secure the requisite support in fees could only be counted upon so long as the instruction was in "accomplishments" or was of the "useful" kind. The desire to give the girls the culture and mental discipline of a university, a desire not satisfied by the work of these classes, led Pattison to conceive a more ambitious plan which might be followed in every large town in the country. As he sketched this to the Commission, "classes" or "a college" would be set up at moderate fees under local management, ladies being in the majority on the governing body, and a grant in aid paid from the Treasury. The success of the Government Schools of Art (the Oxford classes had been started as such a "school") controlled from South Kensington suggested that there should be in London a central board to supervise these proposed classes, or colleges, for girls, to inspect their teaching and to establish a model school in which to train their teachers.

About the same time the Commission received a letter on the education of girls[2] from Miss A. J. Clough (1820–92), who stated by way of credentials that she had managed a school for the upper classes

[1] *Report*, vol. v, Part ii, Minutes of Evidence, pp. 945 ff.
[2] *Report*, vol. ii, pp. 84–7. B. A. Clough, *A Memoir of Anne Jemima Clough* (1897).

at Liverpool (1844–52), and at Ambleside (1852–62) one for the children of trades-people and farmers, and that she had known something of middle class private schools in Liverpool and elsewhere. She complained, as Woodard had done, that while public provision existed for the education of both the upper and the humbler classes, the middle classes were flagrantly neglected in that respect. She herself had started a school for middle class girls; but her experience taught her that the task of maintaining one was beyond the means of an individual, and that a local proprietary body would find it difficult, unless supported by Government help and organization, "on sufficiently liberal principles to insure the attendance of all denominations of Christians".

A permanent central board to supervise female education being postulated, and middle class girls' schools, private and proprietary, being assumed to exist, Miss Clough's letter went on to propose the erection in large towns of central schools (to be called "Victoria Schools" in order to avoid an invidious "class" reference) with lecture halls, playgrounds and libraries for teachers and pupils. In these schools girls from neighbouring schools should be assembled periodically to receive collective instruction from specially-appointed highly competent teachers. Miss Clough's letter went on to suggest the appointment by Government of university men to professorships in English language and literature, in English and general history, in scientific subjects and in art, and that these professors should periodically give courses at the central schools to elder school girls and their teachers. The latter suggestion, which was intended to give "those of riper years" an opportunity to continue their studies, was one of the seeds of the later University Extension movement.

In the meantime the advocates of an improved education for women had found a new objective. Miss Elizabeth Garrett applied in 1862 for admission to the matriculation examination of London University, but the Senate informed her that their charter did not permit them to comply with her request and they refused to seek fresh powers. The ripost was the formation of Emily Davies' "Committee for obtaining the admission of Women to University Examinations", whose first success was the participation of girls in the Cambridge Local Examination, as has already been said. A memorial[1] signed by some seven hundred persons, the majority of whom were schoolmistresses, was

[1] Printed in full in *Report*, vol. II, pp. 194 f.

sent to the Taunton Commission by the indefatigable Miss Davies, in which it was pointed out that "there are in England no public institutions for women analogous to the universities for men in which a complete education is given, and at the same time duly certified by an external body of recognised authority". The memorialists asserted that they had "reason to believe that opportunities of undergoing a course of instruction and discipline adapted to advanced students, combined with examinations testing and attesting the quality of the education received, would not only be eagerly welcomed by the higher class of teachers, but would also be made use of by many young women having no definite object in view other than that of self-improvement". They went on "to ask that in any recommendations which the Commission may see fit to make respecting the application of school endowments or other charities, special regard may be paid to the need for such an institution, and to other measures providing for the higher education of women". These and the like schemes for the better education of girls and of women received the Commission's "cordial approval". That they were conscious of the economic motive which inspired the agitation is made evident in the *Report's* comment on the memorialists' proposal: "it is connected with the subject, so much discussed of late, of new openings in branches of employment not hitherto pursued" by women.[1]

The conception of "the Universal Industrial Exhibition" held in London in 1851, and usually called "the Great Exhibition", and the earliest steps taken to give it effect were due to the Society of Arts,[2] whose President, Prince Albert, played a very conspicuous part in establishing the Exhibition. The completion of the arrangements for holding it was committed to a Royal Commission especially chartered for that purpose in August, 1850, and subsequently made a permanent body with power to administer the surplus profit of £186,000. The Commission purchased land in South Kensington with the intention of erecting there a central institution "for the dissemination of a knowledge of science and art among all classes". The Prince's scheme for

[1] Vol. I, p. 570.
[2] The formal style of the Society was, from its foundation in 1754, "The Society for the encouragement of Arts, Manufactures and Commerce in Great Britain"; in 1908 it prefixed the word "Royal" to its title by permission of the Patron, King Edward VII. See Sir H. T. Wood's *History of the Royal Society of Arts*.

realizing this project met with a great deal of opposition and in the end the Commission's estate was made the site of the South Kensington Museum and the headquarters of the Science and Art Department. The success of 1851 was not repeated by the second London Exhibition held in 1862; the Prince Consort had died in the preceding December.

The Prince and others had hoped that international Exhibitions would promote international goodwill; he probably foresaw another consequence of these lavish displays of the art and industries of Europe. Professor Lyon Playfair (1818–98), the distinguished chemist who assisted in organizing the two London Exhibitions and had served as a juror for that of Paris in 1867, was convinced that England had not made the industrial progress between the first and last of these dates that he noted in the case of some Continental countries. He saw the explanation in the fact that France, Prussia, Austria, Belgium and Switzerland possessed good systems of industrial education for employers and their managers, while England had none. As early as 1853 in a pamphlet, *Industrial education on the Continent*, he had suggested an official inquiry into the state of technical instruction abroad. He now brought the subject before the Taunton Commissioners, who discovered that there was a general assent to his view. The Commissioners thought that, since instruction in physical science was involved, the matter was partly within the purview of their own inquiry, but that it was too grave and too vast in scope to be seriously considered by themselves. To mark their sense of its importance, they issued a very brief and formal *Report relative to Technical Education* which was presented to Parliament in July, 1867. In this document they printed letters from Playfair and from a number of jurors and exhibitors at Paris, and themselves recommended the Government to consider whether an inquiry of the kind desired should not be instituted. Some of the letter-writers doubted whether the Paris exhibits afforded sufficient evidence for the conclusions reached, others saw the remedy, not in technical teaching, but in a thorough education of a more general type; yet all agreed that English industrial progress was not satisfactory and that an inquiry should be held.

The Taunton Commission was followed by the Endowed Schools Act of 1869, a measure which sadly mishandled the recommendations of the *Report*, substituting a makeshift expedient for a comprehensive scheme of reform. The *Report* envisaged English secondary education as a whole, whether endowed or unendowed, public or private, and it proposed to place that whole under a central, constitutional body presided over by a minister of the Crown. Subordinate to this central body, there should be local authorities, some of whose members might be elected by the ratepayers; and there was a further recommendation, to which great importance was attached, that a Council of Examinations be appointed to inspect schools and examine and thus register teachers. The Act ignored all the minor proposals and, instead of creating a permanent, central authority, appointed for a limited term of office three Commissioners to deal with endowed schools only. The "religious difficulty" of the elementary school had hitherto seldom been a problem for schools of another grade. But, taking note of public opinion, the Act allowed a parent, whose child was attending an endowed school, to claim for the child exemption from any lesson, or series of lessons, on a religious subject; and the teacher was forbidden, "in the course of other lessons", to teach systematically and persistently any particular religious doctrine from the teaching of which exemption had been claimed. The State was preparing to throw religion overboard.

The Commissioners were empowered to make new organizations for particular schools, including the constitution of their governing bodies, and to divert to educational uses trust funds whose original purpose had become impracticable or undesirable. An appeal from interested bodies or persons lay to the Judicial Committee of the Privy Council or to either House of Parliament.

The three Endowed Schools Commissioners, the chief of whom was Lord Lyttelton, a prominent member of the Taunton Commission, lost no time in exercising their powers; they did this with such effect that before the close of 1869 they had aroused a good deal of opposition. Their policy was to ensure a more equitable division of educational endowments between boys and girls, to introduce modern studies and to grant exemption from religious instruction to particular children on the request of parents or guardians. During their tenure of office 235 school schemes were made obligatory; the value of their work may be estimated by comparing almost any endowed school as it was about 1850 with its educational standing, buildings, staff, studies and number of pupils about 1880–90. It would be invidious to select a particular school for this purpose; but some schools which stand high to-day were doing very humble work indeed, or were paying a master's stipend and doing nothing else, before the Endowed Schools Commissioners initiated vital changes in their organization. A substantial increase was effected in the number of endowed schools for girls, but it was still quite inadequate to the country's need. However, the Commissioners offended a good many interests and the Government thought it advisable to bring their labours to an end; this was effected by an amending Endowed Schools Act of 1873, which transferred their powers to the Charity Commissioners who exercised them from 1874 to 1900.

CHAPTER XI

The Conflict of Studies

The three Royal Commissions concerned with higher education had given particular attention to the curriculum and especially to the insignificant position accorded to science, spoken languages and to modern studies in general. The Newcastle Commission had made recommendations which led to the issue of the Revised Code, a document which in effect, if not in intention, had reduced the elementary school course to reading, writing and summing, with the addition of needlework in girls' schools. The Annual Report of the Committee of Council for 1865 admits that their Code "tended *at least temporarily* to discourage attention to the higher branches of elementary instruction, geography, grammar and history". In spite of this official optimism, it became necessary in 1867 to offer an increased grant to schools which taught one or two of these studies; and "object lessons" were added to them a little later.

The last-named subject of instruction was introduced to ensure that children should grow familiar with their surroundings, but also, and chiefly, "to train Observation". One great barrier, which prevented the penetration of the school course by modern studies, was the obsession which the principle of mental gymnastic had established in the minds of the authorities, an obsession which led them to undervalue the attainment of knowledge as a substantive possession. The barrier was strengthened by the belief that a clean cut could be made between "liberal" and "useful" studies. Yet the life of the time was exhibiting some significant features which had a bearing upon the activities and inactivities of the schools. The *Origin of Species* had been published in 1859, Lister introduced antiseptic surgery in 1865, the Atlantic cable was laid in 1866, to be followed within the next twelve years by the invention of the typewriter, the telephone and the electric light. In these circumstances it did not seem reasonable either that the schools and the educational system generally should show but a tepid concern in the progress of knowledge, or to believe that mental discipline could alone be derived from the contemplation of an earlier civilization.

During the 'sixties' the discrepancy was exposed by men who commanded a hearing.

Herbert Spencer (1820–1903) had written between 1854 and 1859 a series of four magazine articles which were re-issued as a book in 1861 under the title, *Education, Intellectual, Moral and Physical*, thus completing a chain which had united French and English theorizers during three centuries. Montaigne's essays had informed and inspired Locke's convictions respecting the upbringing of youth; the Englishman in turn built a foundation upon which Rousseau constructed his conception of educational method and Spencer gave *Émile* an English, nineteenth-century setting. *Education* secured an immediate success and within less than twenty years it was translated into thirteen languages, Japanese and Chinese included.

The earliest written of the four essays comprising the book, that on "Intellectual Education", initiated a more systematic, if not scientific, study of education by teachers. It is a concise and still valuable treatise upon educational method which, it insists, must be rooted in psychology, more especially in a study of the observed mental development of children. "The education of the child must accord both in mode and arrangement with the education of mankind considered historically. In other words the genesis of knowledge in the individual must follow the same course as the genesis of knowledge in the race." This assertion, since known as the Recapitulatory Theory, has now become a commonplace of the text-books and the justification of some applications to practice for which Spencer can hardly be held responsible. He himself was content to use it as giving a broad, general guidance in the due sequence of studies; the empirical should precede the rational, self-development should be encouraged, instruction ought to arouse "pleasurable excitement". Spencer attributed the enunciation of the theory of recapitulation to Auguste Comte; but it is to be found in the writings of Pestalozzi, for whom no doubt it was an inference from the studies in embryology made by the eighteenth-century biologists. It was not unknown to Herbart and Froebel.

The essay on "Moral Education" is mainly occupied by that discipline, so-called, by means of natural consequences which was Rousseau's perversion of Locke's discipline by moral consequences. Spencer credited children with an acuter mode of reasoning than can be expected from them and his lack of experience made him insensible to the very strict limits within which natural consequences can be safely relied upon to yield discipline. Indeed some of his illustrations are cases of moral discipline and therefore do not illustrate his thesis at all.

The first chapter in the book and the last to be written—"What knowledge is most worth?"—is sheer special pleading for the teaching of science, a term very ambiguously used by the author; in fact the chapter itself is a veritable Tom Tiddler's ground for the logician looking for instances of fallacy. In it occurs the notable *ignoratio elenchi*, "When a mother is mourning over a first-born sunk under the sequelae of scarlet fever, when perhaps a candid medical man has confirmed her suspicion that her child would have recovered had not its system been enfeebled by over-study, when she is prostrate under the pangs of combined grief and remorse; it is but small consolation that she can read Dante in the original". Yet nothing less than an exaggerated championship seemed likely at that date to secure the attention of those who were responsible for the continued omission of science from the educational curriculum. Disregard of logic may therefore be excused. Not so Spencer's pontifical attitude towards humane letters which he would relegate to the leisure moments of the pupil, as though the study of mankind were merely a pastime. The explanation is furnished in Spencer's own *Autobiography* which shows him constitutionally insensible to art, and at the same time allows the reader to gauge his competence as a critic of a classical education. These are Spencer's scholastic attainments at the age of sixteen when his schooling ceased; there is no further record of any linguistic study: "In the acquisition of languages but trifling success has been achieved; in French nothing beyond the early part of the grammar and a few pages of a phrase book, in Greek a little grammar, I suppose, and such knowledge as resulted from rendering into English a few chapters of the New Testament;[1] and in Latin some small ability to translate the easy books given to beginners—always however with more or less blundering".

The chapter on "Physical Education" deals wisely with such topics as food, clothing, play, sleep and the unhealthy restriction placed upon growing girls in these matters. Spencer's counsels were much needed

[1] "My friend, Mr Herbert Spencer,...does *not* know the letters of the Greek alphabet, and as far as I can judge, manages to get on very well without them" (Grant Allen, *The European Tour*, 1899).

and they strengthened the growing desire for a more sedulous care for hygiene, personal as well as public. This essay, originally written for the *Quarterly Review* but not accepted by the editor, was published in April, 1859, in the *British Quarterly Review*. Its author says of it, "Though it makes no reference to the doctrine of evolution, its ideas are congruous with the doctrine in so far that the method of nature is emphasized as that which should be kept in view when deciding on methods of physical training—so that though this essay was not conspicuously evolutionary in its doctrines, yet its doctrines were evolutionary in their unavowed origin".[1]

Another set of four essays which appeared during the autumn of 1860 in the *Cornhill Magazine* had met with a very different reception from that accorded to Spencer's venture. Thackeray, then editor of the *Cornhill*, felt compelled to refuse any more of these assertions of "the first principles of political economy" on the ground that they were opposed to the economic orthodoxy of "Malthus, *The Times* and the city of Manchester", while the publisher of the magazine thought they were "too deeply tainted with socialistic heresy". They certainly provoked much opposition and some bitterly expressed criticism; when the essays were equipped with a preface and published (1862) under the title, *Unto this Last*, the book sold very slowly. Yet its author, John Ruskin (1819–1900), regarding the principles therein propounded as "the central work" of his life, had applied a scrupulous pruning and revising before his carefully written essays first saw the light. Twenty years later, owing to a widespread interest in socialistic teaching, *Unto this Last* attained a great circulation and was translated into French, German and Italian; selections from it were made by Thomas Barclay and published (1889) at one penny with the title, "The Rights of Labour according to John Ruskin".

Education had long been one of Ruskin's subjects of meditation. In appendices to *Modern Painters* and *The Stones of Venice* (1853)[2] he had protested that the lack of clear thinking which he believed to be common amongst Englishmen was due to the exclusively literary and rhetorical character of their upbringing. He denied that the ordinary classical course of teaching was either the only or the best instrument of mental

[1] H. Spencer, *Autobiography* (1904), p. 21.
[2] See the "Library Edition" (E. T. Cook and A. Wedderburn, editors) of Ruskin's *Works* (1904), vol. IV, pp. 482 ff. and vol. XI, pp. 258 ff.

discipline—"the science which it is the highest power to possess, it is also the best exercise to acquire". A man should learn three things: where he is, where he is going, what he had best do under those circumstances. "The present European system" ignored or despised all three; that is to say, it did not teach the physical sciences, religion or politics, "the science of the relations of men to each other". "The great leading error of modern times is the mistaking of erudition for education."[1] To his thoughts on this subject Ruskin had added practical experience in teaching. He was one of the first to volunteer his services on the unpaid staff of the Working Men's College; from its beginning in 1854 to 1858 he taught drawing there in collaboration with Lowes Dickinson, D. G. Rossetti, Ebenezer Cooke and others, and for years afterwards he gave occasional lectures and addresses to the College. When in 1858 Oxford started its "Middle Class Examinations" (the "Local Examinations" of later days) he acted as examiner in drawing; while holding that office he wrote a letter to Frederick Temple (then Inspector of Training Colleges) urging the University not to be satisfied with examining the schoolboy in drawing but to add teaching in art to the course of the undergraduate. With this purpose in view he suggested the establishment of a School of Arts to include in its purview "painting, sculpture, architecture, agriculture, war, music, bodily exercises (navigation in seaport schools), including laws of health".[2]

When the *Cornhill* essays appeared Ruskin was a recognized teacher and critic of art, but the public was not prepared to regard him as a political teacher or social prophet. To poke fun at Mill, Ricardo and the political economists generally was unpardonable at that time; a further offence, a statement of what he described as "the worst of the political creed" he was inculcating, found no place in the *Magazine*, but formed the conclusion of his preface to *Unto this Last*. Here blandly ignoring its revolutionary character he briefly outlined the new society of which he dreamed. Schools and factories should be established under State control. "First there should be training schools for youth established at Government cost and under Government discipline over the whole country; that every child born in the country should at the parent's wish be permitted (and, in certain cases, be under penalty required) to

[1] *The Stones of Venice*, vol. III, appendix 7 ("Library Edition", vol. XI, *ut supra*).
[2] T. D. Acland, *Some Account of the origin and objects of the new Oxford examinations for the title of Associate in Arts*, etc. (1858), p. 59.

pass through them; and that in these schools the child should with other minor pieces of knowledge (hereafter to be considered) imperatively be taught, with the best skill of teaching that the country could produce, the following three things: (*a*) the laws of health and the exercises enjoined by them; (*b*) habits of gentleness and justice; and (*c*) the calling by which he is to live." The manufactories and shops, "entirely under Government regulation", were to be set up "for the production and sale of every necessary of life and for the exercise of every useful art," "so that a man could be sure, if he chose to pay the Government price, that he got for his money bread that was bread, ale that was ale[1] and work that was work." Provision was to be made for dealing with the work-shy and the malingerer and for pensioning the old and destitute.

This view of the function of the State, so subversive of the individualism which then ruled English public life, was not a new element in Ruskin's teaching. In the appendix to *The Stones of Venice*, quoted above, the following occurs: "Finally, I hold it for indisputable that the first duty of a State is to see that every child born therein shall be well housed, clothed, fed and educated till it attain years of discretion. But in order to the effecting this, the Government must have an authority over the people of which we now do not so much as dream". This passage, the wellspring of those measures which have transferred so much of parental responsibility to the community as a whole, Ruskin repeated with a solemn endorsement in *Time and Tide by Weare and Tyne* (1867).

Time and Tide and *The Crown of Wild Olive* (1866–9) continued the theme. Schools should be built in the open country, where "riding, running, all the honest personal exercises of offence and defence and music should be the primal heads of this bodily education". Reverence must be inculcated through the example of the masters and the study of literature. Compassion (collateral in esteem with courage) should find ample practice; "every possible opportunity be taken to exercise the youths in offices of some practical help"—the thought which gave birth to the many Public Schools' "missions", beginning with that of Uppingham in 1870. History, natural science, mathematics will tend to cultivate an understanding and sentiment for truth. City children

---

[1] Ruskin did not live to undergo the chastening experience of "war bread" and "Government beer".

should study especially mathematics and the arts, country children architecture "practically" and the natural history of birds, insects, and plants; children whose calling will be on the sea should learn physical geography, astronomy and the natural history of sea fish and sea birds.[1]

Education must not be of the intellect alone, "which is on some men wasted and for others mischievous, but education of the heart which is alike good and necessary for all".[2] "The first condition under which it [education] can be given usefully is, that it should be clearly understood to be no means of getting on in the world, but a means of staying pleasantly in your place there. And the first element of State education should be calculated equally for the advantage of every order of person composing the State. From the lowest to the highest class, every child born in this island should be required by law to receive these general elements of human discipline"[3]—a plain statement which the writer proceeds to becloud in meaningless rhetoric and something worse.

Technical instruction, handicraft and art education were becoming pressing questions in 1867 and Ruskin, "a man of his hands", had long had his opinions on these subjects. "Every youth in the State—from the King's son downwards—should learn to do something finely and thoroughly with his hand, so as to let him know what *touch* meant; and what stout craftsmanship meant; and to inform him of many things besides, which no man can learn but by some severely accurate discipline in doing. Let him once learn to take a straight shaving off a plank, or draw a fine curve without faltering, or lay a brick level in its mortar; and he has learned a multitude of other matters which no lips of man could ever teach him."[4]

Like his great friend, Carlyle, Ruskin was the persistent adversary of commercialism and industrialism; the primary aim of any national scheme of education, as they conceived it, was the rearing of a disciplined people, a result demanded by the times, under penalty of chaos in the event of failure. Current controversy mingles with that autocratic principle in the following passage from *The Crown of Wild Olive*, (1869): "Educate, or govern, they are one and the same word. Education does not mean teaching people to know what they do not know. It

---

[1] *Time and Tide*, pp. 97 ff.   [2] *Ibid.* p. 92.
[3] *Ibid.* pp. 96–7.   [4] *Ibid.* p. 134.

means teaching them to behave as they do not behave. And the true 'compulsory education' which the people now ask of you is not catechism, but drill. It is not teaching the youth of England the shapes of letters and the tricks of numbers; and then leaving them to turn their arithmetic to roguery, and their literature to lust. It is, on the contrary, training them into the perfect exercise and kingly continence of their bodies and souls. It is a painful, continual and difficult work; to be done by kindness, by watching, by warning, by precept, and by praise—but above all—by example. Compulsory! Yes by all means! 'Go ye out into the highways and hedges, and *compel* them to come in!' Compulsory! Yes, and gratis also. *Dei Gratia*, they must be taught, as *Dei Gratia*, you are set to teach them" (Sections 144–5).

Ruskin's ideal polity was a socialist state, not a democratic, but a feudal or patriarchal organization. It was based on the belief that the Great Man (or, as Carlyle called him, the Hero) would either be disclosed by events or discovered by an enlightened people. When he appeared, he must be obeyed. Ruskin's teaching did not greatly influence the educational practice of his day, but the later effect on English politics is beyond question. The shrewdness, the self-confidence, the sentimentality, the self-contradiction and want of common fairness of that teaching, as well as its nobler elements and its fine medium of expression, make Ruskin in no small measure responsible for those class antagonisms which are only too familiar to the England of the twentieth century.

The year 1867, made remarkable in English political history by the extension of the Parliamentary franchise which the Second Reform Act of that year effected, is also notable for other outstanding pronouncements on education than the *Report* of the Taunton Commission and the lectures and articles of John Ruskin. John Stuart Mill (1806–1873), who had been elected Lord Rector of St Andrews University in November, 1865, delivered his *Inaugural Address* on February 1st, 1867. Mill's opinions on the subject are largely peculiar to himself or to himself and his father, James Mill. But father and son exercised great influence in education as well as in politics and economics; and the younger man has left a very complete account of the manner in which he was educated by his father. It therefore seems expedient to review part of J. S. Mill's *Autobiography* (1873) before passing to his rectorial address.

Described briefly, Mill's education comprised the ordinary full university course crowded into the first fourteen years of life; that is, Greek, Latin, mathematics and logic made up the formal part of this domestic schooling. Mill could not recall when he began his first foreign language, Greek; he had been told that it was at the age of three. When at the age of eight he began Latin, he had read all Herodotus, Xenophon's *Anabasis* and *Memorabilia*, parts of Diogenes Laertius, Lucian, Isocrates and Plato. He had learned arithmetic, read history, biography and travels and some "books of amusement" which he had borrowed. His father made it a practice to discuss the boy's reading during their daily walks. "My father's health required considerable and constant exercise, and he walked habitually before breakfast, generally in the green lanes towards Hornsey [1810–13]. In these walks I always accompanied him, and with my earliest recollections of green fields and wild flowers is mingled that of the account I gave him daily of what I had read the day before. To the best of my remembrance this was a voluntary rather than a prescribed exercise."

As soon as he began Latin he concurrently taught the language to a younger sister; other sisters and brothers were successively added as pupils. In 1814 the "mutual system" was in full operation, and of course attracted the admiration and allegiance of a doctrinaire like James Mill, whose master, Bentham, held it in great esteem. J. S. Mill, in mature life, thought unfavourably of "the teaching of children by means of one another. The teaching I am sure", he said, "is very inefficient as teaching, and I well know that the relation between teacher and taught is not a good moral discipline to either".

At this time he began to read his first Greek poetry, the *Iliad*, and his first English verse, Pope's translation of Homer. By the age of twelve he had read extensively in the Greek and Latin classics, had made a peculiarly careful study of Aristotle's *Rhetoric*, and in mathematics had studied geometry, algebra and the differential calculus. His private reading was chiefly in ancient history, and between the ages of eleven and twelve he compiled, on his own volition and without showing his work to anyone, a history of the struggle between the Roman plebeians and patricians. He wrote no Greek composition and only a little Latin prose; but he composed English verse, a practice encouraged by his father because "some things could be expressed better and more forcibly in verse than in prose" and, further, since "people in general attached more value to verse than it deserved, the power of writing it was worth acquiring on that account". Mill read scientific works for amusement (a reflection of the then current belief respecting science held in the Public Schools) but he made no experimental studies. At twelve he began logic in the *Organon* of Aristotle and the *Computatio* of Hobbes; political economy was taken up in the following year, reading in the classics being continued. His father wisely practised him in the art of reading aloud; but characteristically made the performance "a most painful task" both for himself and the boy. Mill was "brought up from the first without any religious belief in the ordinary acceptation of the term". Yet his father made him "at an early age a reader of ecclesiastical history", teaching him "to take the strongest interest in the Reformation, as the great and decisive contest against priestly tyranny for liberty of thought". At the age of fourteen the boy went to reside in France as the guest of Jeremy Bentham's brother, a retired General. The visit lasted for more than a year; and thereafter Mill was his own teacher.[1]

It will be seen that Mill's upbringing was wholly bookish and for the most part followed traditional lines; he was doing at home what other boys were trying to do at school and university, but he was doing it more rapidly, more extensively and more thoroughly. Like most of them he learned no modern language, no experimental science. Unlike them he was ignorant of all forms of sport; the boyish impulse to do and to make was starved to inanition. "I remained long", he says, "and in a less degree have always remained inexpert in anything requiring manual dexterity; my mind, as well as my hands, did its work very lamely when...applied...to the practical details...of daily life."

His father's aim was "the highest order of intellectual education"; Mill himself thought the course pursued was "unusual, remarkable", yet such as any ordinary healthy boy could take successfully. That the ordinary boy did not achieve as much was owing to the inefficiency of schools and schoolmasters. But what help did this severely intellectual discipline give towards realizing the utilitarian ideal of the greatest happiness of the greatest number? What was its social value? "I was not at all aware that my attainments were anything unusual at my age. ...I neither estimated myself highly or lowly; I did not estimate

[1] See Graham Wallas's *Francis Place* for Place's (and James Mill's) account of the appalling method of instructing his children which the elder Mill practised.

myself at all. If I thought anything about myself it was that I was rather backward in my studies, since I always found myself so in comparison with what my father expected from me. I assert this with confidence, though it was not the impression of various persons who saw me in my childhood. They, as I have since found, thought me greatly and disagreeably self-conceited; probably because I was disputatious and did not scruple to give direct contradictions to things which I heard said. I suppose I acquired this bad habit from having been encouraged in an unusual degree to talk on matters beyond my age and with grown persons, while I never had inculcated on me the usual respect for them. My father did not correct this ill-breeding and impertinence, probably from not being aware of it, for I was always too much in awe of him to be otherwise than extremely subdued and quiet in his presence." Is there not reason in the judgement of a French critic who describes the education of John Stuart Mill as "le chef-d'œuvre et la condamnation de l'intellectualisme exclusif"?[1]

The presiding genius of this education was a bureaucrat and pedant, who bred his son to be a bureaucrat and doctrinaire. That James Mill was virtually ignorant of men and life is seen in the picture of the Benthamites which his son draws in the *Autobiography*: "In politics, an almost unbounded confidence in the efficacy of two things, representative government and complete freedom of discussion. So complete was my father's reliance on the influence of reason over the minds of mankind, whenever it is allowed to reach them, that he felt as if all would be gained if the whole population were taught to read, if all sorts of opinions were allowed to be addressed to them by word and in writing, and if by means of the suffrage they could nominate a legislature to give effect to the opinions they adopted."

Yet his son did not resent the rigour of his upbringing. He thought that the element of compulsion, even of fear, could not safely be eliminated. He rejoiced in the change which had come over the spirit of education during his lifetime and the exchange of a "brutal and tyrannical system of teaching" for one which made learning "easy and interesting". "But when this principle is pushed to the length of not requiring them to learn anything but what has been made easy and interesting, one of the chief objects of education is sacrificed."

The profound effect which was produced upon the mind of John

[1] Louis Cazamian, *Le roman social en Angleterre* (1904), p. 57.

Stuart Mill by the education of his childhood and early boyhood is manifest in the St Andrews *Inaugural Address*.[1] When Mill published his *System of Logic* (1843) he looked forward with hope and some confidence to the possibility of elaborating a "science of the formation of character", a science to which he proposed to give the name, "ethology". This science, if it were ever instituted, would afford a firm theoretical basis, so Mill thought, to the art of education. But there is no trace of this science, or of the principles presumably allied to it, in the *Address*, which is dominated by his father's intellectualism. He lays down a course of studies, tacitly assuming that education is a process given up almost but not quite entirely to the attainment of various branches of knowledge. The general character of this extended course of studies may be inferred from the following passage in the *Autobiography*. "In this discourse I gave expression to many thoughts and opinions which had been accumulating in me through life respecting the various studies which belong to a liberal education, their uses and influences, and the mode in which they should be pursued to render their influences most beneficial. The position taken up, vindicating the high educational value alike of the old classic and the new scientific studies, on even stronger grounds than are urged by most of their advocates, and insisting that it is only the stupid inefficiency of the usual teaching which makes those studies be regarded as competitors instead of allies, was, I think, calculated not only to aid and stimulate the improvement which has happily commenced in the national institutions for higher education, but to diffuse juster ideas than we often find, even in highly educated men, on the conditions of the highest mental cultivation."

The St Andrews curriculum is put forward as the result of reflection; but, save in one important respect (its very real concern for aesthetic cultivation), it does not differ greatly from the intellectual discipline which his father had made him pursue in boyhood. Sharing the prevalent obsession of the time, Mill commends studies less for their intrinsic worth than for their capacity to serve as "sharpeners of the intellectual faculties". Greek and Latin classical authors (but no compulsory verse-making), mathematics and science are prescribed chiefly for that reason; on like grounds, no reading, it is said, is more

[1] See Wm. Knight (ed.), *Rectorial Addresses delivered at the University of St Andrews*, 1863–1893 (1894), pp. 17–78.

profitable than the works of "Hobbes and Locke, Reid and Stewart, Hume, Hartley and Brown" and this "notwithstanding that so many of their speculations are already obsolete". In connexion with Mill's dogmatism concerning mental discipline it is not irrelevant to cite from this *Address* the dictum that psychology, so far as it consists of such "laws" as those of association and certain observed laws based upon experimental evidence, "is as positive and certain a science as chemistry and fit to be taught as such".

The *Address* opens with the statement that universities are not professional or technical schools, although it is well that such schools as those of law, medicine, engineering and the industrial arts should be in the neighbourhood and under the general supervision of universities, the business of the last being "general" and liberal education. "The old English universities in the present generation are doing better work than they have done within human memory in teaching the ordinary studies of their curriculum; and one of the consequences has been, that whereas they formerly seemed to exist mainly for the repression of independent thought and the chaining up of the individual intellect and conscience they are now the great foci of free and manly enquiry to the higher and professional classes south of the Tweed." The trouble was not with them, but with the schools, on whose general inefficiency Mill does not cease to insist. The imparting of knowledge is the schools' function; the philosophy of knowledge belongs to the universities. The schools, however, fail in their office and, in consequence, the universities become schools.

Passing to the more advanced studies of the university and beyond to the sphere of self-culture, Mill recommends the pursuit of logic, physiology, psychology, ethics, politics, political economy, jurisprudence and international law. He makes short work of one stock controversy, that of literature *v.* science. Why, he asks, should a tailor be reduced to the alternative of making coats or trousers? Why not both? That such an alternative as literature or science should be proposed is evidence of the "shameful inefficiency" of schoolmasters. The Clarendon Commission asserted that classical teaching in the Public Schools was "unsatisfactory", showing "great want of grounding", "too indulgent to idleness". Mill dismisses the schools as "shams".

The *Address* lays it down that schools and universities cannot educate either morally or religiously, thus agreeing with Newman.

The latter, who knew and loved his own University of Oxford, had a thesis to uphold, the principle that all universities should teach theology; perhaps too he was influenced by the sharp line of distinction which he drew between the Catholic and the "gentleman". Mill had no experience of schools or of universities and therefore failed to understand that they are societies; they are for him, first and foremost, knowledge mongers. Here Newman lends him countenance. Religion being the most controversial of subjects, universities, as Mill thinks in opposition to Newman, should only teach ecclesiastical history. But this is only repeating his father's prescription, though no doubt without its malice.

It is not surprising that Mill betrays ignorance of the average boy living under the conditions of school life. Signs are not wanting in the *Autobiography* that his father took pains to suppress the natural boy in him. When his son confessed to an interest in the military side of history, James Mill carefully pointed out the error of such an interest; contrariwise ecclesiastical history was to be studied almost solely because it exhibited men engaged in intellectual conflict. It is characteristic of the doctrinaire in J. S. Mill that he shows neither knowledge nor sympathy with the reforms of Arnold, of Thring or of the private and proprietary schools. His partial commendation of modern methods of instruction cited above might very well have come from the equally impersonal pages' of Herbert Spencer's book. The schools which followed the lead of the *Inaugural Address* would teach no modern language, no history, no geography; in Mill's opinion it would be "absurd" for them to teach the last, because it only appeals to "memory" —one more disregard of intrinsic value when confronted by formal discipline. Private reading and a sojourn abroad to acquire French sufficed in Mill's own case; they are methods sufficient for the generality. So far as studies are concerned there was for Mill no history of education between 1806 and 1867.

There is one important exception to the predominantly literary type of education sketched in the *Address*; it owed nothing to the elder Mill. The St Andrews audience was told that "all the arts of expression tend to keep alive and in activity the feelings they express". Poetry, music, painting, architecture therefore all have high educational value. "Who does not feel a better man after a course of Dante, or of Wordsworth, or, I will add, of Lucretius or the *Georgics*, or after brooding over

Gray's *Elegy* or Shelley's *Hymn to Intellectual Beauty?*" Here at least the Benthamite spell of "useful knowledge" is broken and Herbert Spencer is answered.

In the St Andrews *Address* Mill was dealing with higher education in relation to adolescents and adults whose studies were purely voluntary. In the fifth chapter of his essay, *On Liberty* (1859), the public education of children is considered. The doctrine there expounded is that it is the father's duty to see that his child is fittingly prepared to play his part in the world, while the State should compel the education up to a certain standard of every human being who is born its citizen. The State should compel, but itself not educate; "a general State education is a mere contrivance for moulding people to be exactly like one another", a result which Mill deprecates in express, flat contradiction to the Aristotelian teaching. The State may go so far as to pay the school fees of the poorer children and defray the entire cost of educating destitute orphans; but this is not State control of the actual process. All this is Thomas Paine and *The Rights of Man* over again. If public education is established and controlled by the State, room should be left for other bodies and individuals to experiment and compete with the State system. Then, taking his cue from Bentham, Robert Lowe's *New Code* and the prevailing trust of the mid-century in examinations, Mill went on to suggest that children should be examined annually from an early age till they had attained a stated minimum of knowledge; thereafter submission to these tests should be voluntary, the examinations being confined to "facts and positive science exclusively". The enforcement of universal education in the mode described would in Mill's opinion end the disputes which made the subject "a battlefield for sects and parties".

One week after the delivery of Mill's discourse at St Andrews, F. W. Farrar (afterwards Dean of Canterbury), a Harrow master with thirteen years' experience in the work of Public Schools, was lecturing before the Royal Institution on some defects in Public School education. His chief complaint was that the monopoly accorded to Greek and Latin rendered modern studies impossible, and that the neglect of science was scandalous. He promised his audience a further elaboration of the theme, a promise which was fulfilled later in the same year, 1867, by the publication of *Essays on a Liberal Education*, of which Farrar was editor.

These *Essays* agreed in principle with Mill that educational instruments must be fashioned both from literature and from natural science; but, for the essayists, literature included modern as well as ancient classics. The book is in fact one of the earliest works to assert the possibility of a modern humanism, the possibility of extracting from modern studies, and especially from modern literature, much which was commonly thought to be derivable from a study of Greek and Latin alone.

Of the nine essayists all but one were Cambridge men, every one of whom attained high distinction in education or in public life. The only Oxford essay, "On the history of classical education", based in part on German sources, is one of the earliest attempts in English, if not the earliest, to write a history of education. Two of the essays stand out from the rest. That on the theory of classical education is by Henry Sidgwick, the Senior Classic of 1859, then assistant tutor at Trinity College; that on teaching natural science is by James Maurice Wilson, the Senior Wrangler of 1859, then a master at Rugby[1] with eight years' experience of teaching mathematics and natural science.

Sidgwick criticizes severely the exaggerated claims of the advocates of a purely classical curriculum; he dismisses many of their stock contentions as sophistical and regards as a "most singular assumption" the belief "that it is an essential part of the study of Greek and Latin to cultivate the faculty of writing what ought to be poetry in these tongues". He deals faithfully with "the enthusiast" Edward Thring (master of Uppingham, 1853–87). "How can it be said, for instance, that there is no 'false ornament' in Aeschylus, no 'tinsel' in Ovid, no 'ungracefulness' in Thucydides, no 'unshapely work' in Lucretius? In what sense can we speak of finding 'perfect form' and 'perfect standards of criticism' in such inartificial writers as Herodotus (charming as he is) and Xenophon?[2] There is perhaps no modern thinker with equal sensitiveness to beauty of expression, who (in those works of his which have been preserved to us) has so neglected and despised form as Aristotle. Any artist in words may learn much from Cicero and much from Tacitus; but the profuse verbosity of the one, and the perpetual mannerism of the other, have left the marks of their mis-

---

[1] Head master of Clifton, 1879–90; now, September, 1929, in his ninety-fourth year.

[2] For the allusions, see Thring, *Education and School* (1864), p. 71.

direction on English literature." Sidgwick urges the plea that the ancient classics are fine educational instruments just because they are *literature*, and on this ground it is reasonable to employ for a like purpose the literature of modern tongues. He is in favour of reforming the method of teaching Latin and Greek; in particular he would remove "verses" from the compulsory studies.

To keep "formal training", "mental discipline", and special exercises to secure general results, out of such a book as the *Essays* was, in 1867, impossible. Sidgwick believed that the ancient classics afforded even more of this discipline than its champions usually asserted. On the other hand, some of those who took the side of science lauded the usefulness of scientific knowledge, a quality which their opponents were prone to consider its one merit. Reaction from the narrow cult of the merely useful and a disposition to oppose the cult at all costs drove the classicists to maintain that a study acquired additional value when it was useless. Sidgwick takes this point in a distinction which he draws between what he calls a natural and an artificial education. He does not elaborate the point, but his very brief treatment of it in effect raises the question of formal training as it has been discussed in recent years. "By a 'natural education' is meant that which teaches a boy things in which for any reason whatever he will be likely to take an interest in after life." Such an education may be professional or, if its component parts are presented in the proper order, liberal. A liberal education leads "to the most full, vigorous and harmonious exercise, according to the best ideal attainable, of the active, cognitive and aesthetic faculties". "An artificial education is one which, in order that man may ultimately know one thing, teaches him another, which gives the rudiments of some learning or accomplishment, that the man in the maturity of his culture will be content to forget. This is the extreme case, but in proportion as a system of education approximates to this, in proportion as the subjects in which the boy is instructed occupy a small share of the thoughts of the cultivated man; so far the system may be called artificial rather than natural. Now I think it must be allowed that, however much historically and actually the *onus probandi* may rest on those who oppose an artificial system of education, and wish to substitute a more natural one, yet logically the position of the combatants is reversed, and the *onus probandi* rests on those who maintain the artificial system. If a boy is to be taught things which it is distinctly understood are to be forgotten, the good that they do him during the time that they remain in his mind ought to be very clearly demonstrated. In order to escape the severity of this demonstration the advocates of classical education are sometimes inclined to make an obviously unfair assumption. They assume that 'training the mind' is a process essentially incompatible with 'imparting useful knowledge'. And no doubt the attack on classical education has frequently been of so vulgar and ignorant a character that this assumption might be, if not fairly, at least safely made. The clamour has been 'useful knowledge at any rate and let the training of the mind take care of itself'. Against assailants of this sort the defence of the classics was and deserved to be victorious. But the question is now posed in a suitable form. It is now urged that the process of teaching useful knowledge affords as valuable a training in method as any other kind of teaching. However difficult it may be to appraise exactly two different kinds of training, this task distinctly devolves on those who would teach knowledge that they admit to be useless."

Three years before the appearance of *Essays on a Liberal Education*, the editor, speaking before the British Association upon the subject of classical teaching, had denounced the practice of verse composition as "a huge gilt wooden idol" meet to be cast down. Compulsory verse-making was given up at Harrow, and Farrar devotes his essay, in the general interest, to a few more hammer blows upon the image. "Elegiacs" worry the small boy in his preparatory school, "verses" confront him at the entrance to his Public School and there consume a great part of his time to small purpose in the great majority of cases. The time wasted on the practice Farrar would give to modern studies, to science more especially.

E. E. Bowen, also a Harrow master, in his essay condemns the premature introduction of the formal grammar book with its formidable rules and exasperating "exceptions" expressed in an unfamiliar and highly technical language. He would give the boy the very minimum of grammar at the outset and then "plunge him straightway into the delectus" and the actual language, Latin or Greek. Bowen's protest and proposal were not new, however necessary. John Colet had pertinently said, "In the beginning men spoke not Latin because such rules were made, but contrariwise because men spoke such Latin upon that followed the rules." But there was a timely reason for an essay on grammar teaching. The Clarendon Commission had favoured the employment by the nine Public Schools of one and the same grammar book, and the head masters decided to adopt as the basis of such a book the *Elementary Latin Grammar* of B. H. Kennedy of Shrewsbury. From this text-book and the deliberation upon it came the *Public School Latin Primer* of 1866, which Bowen regarded as "irrevocably accepted" in the nine schools, and which "the general opinion of persons interested in education" had "already condemned". Yet it remained the boy's *primer*, not a compendium for reference or use at a somewhat later stage.

J. M. Wilson's essay is a temperately expressed and weighty plea on behalf of instruction in science, the more convincing because he gives sufficient illustration and detail to show that boys can undertake serious work in the study, although they spend only two hours a week upon it.

"All that may be said on the worthlessness of science as a means of education in schools is before the world in the evidence given by Dr Moberly of Winchester." Wilson has a retort for the head master. "Sooner or later, the classicist argues thus in fact: 'Whatever the faults of an exclusively classical system may be, it turned me out as one of its results. Whatever the value of science, it is not indispensable, for I am wholly ignorant of it'. 'My dear sir,' one longs to say, 'you are the very man in whose interests I am arguing. It is you who would be so much wiser, so very much less conceited, so much more conscious of the limitations of your knowledge, if you had been scientifically educated. You are far from stupid and not uncultivated; but you lack what I consider of great value. When I speak of philology as a *science* and of comparative philology as a *science*, you imperfectly understand me; and your depreciation of those studies (the whole nation depreciates them) results from your want of proper education. You would have more power in your own subjects, and an infinitely wider range of ideas and interests, if your classical education had been less unmitigated than it seems to have been.' It is not enough therefore only to provide at school means of learning something of science, as one might demand for the flute; but it must be made one of the compulsory subjects."

The essayist is as ready as any "classicist" with arguments involving "faculties" and their "training". "The mental training to be got from the study of science is the main reason for its introduction into schools.

...In all cases the training consists in *doing*; in educating others you must make them *do* whatever you intend them to learn to do, and select subjects and circumstances in which *doing* is facilitated....Intellectual education ultimately divides itself into the training of the artistic and logical faculties....Probably no study will cultivate one of these faculties and wholly neglect the others, but all studies aim principally at one or other of these." He goes on to say that there is ground common to the methods of studying literature and science; it is in virtue of the method of the study that the possibility is asserted of "formal training", that is, the capacity to do one thing which results from learning to do another. "The methods of these studies [language and literature, science] are in many respects precisely the same. Models and exercises are given by the one, models and exercises by the other. Thucydides must be read and Latin prose must be written by the student of form and style; and the man who would cultivate his powers of thought must read his Newton and study experimental physics. And as the student of Thucydides and Plato is likely to gain in clearness and brilliance of expression, and an insight into history and humanity, in intelligent and ready apprehension of the thoughts of others, in versatility and in polish; so the student of natural science is likely to bring with him to the study of philosophy or politics, or business, or his profession, whatever it may be, a more active and original mind, a sounder judgment and a clearer head in consequence of his study."

At Rugby, Wilson asked for two hours a week for natural science with the hope that the time would be extended to three or four hours. He would have a preparatory stage formed mainly by physical geography, including the elementary principles of geology and astronomy. The course proper consisted of botany and experimental physics, "the standard subjects for the scientific teaching at schools". Chemistry, geology and physiology are not good school subjects, but belong to a later stage, albeit the first two are "frightfully crammable". The method is to be one of observation not of authority; still, Wilson believed that "laboratory work" was not likely to form an integral part of school education. Schools should possess laboratories "into which boys of some talent may be drafted".

A footnote to this essay is significant of a coming change in the study of geometry. "The extreme repulsiveness of Euclid to almost every boy is a complete proof, if indeed other proofs were wanting, that the ordinary methods of studying geometry in use at preparatory and Public Schools are wholly erroneous....It is much to be hoped that before long the teaching of practical geometry will precede the teaching of the science of geometry." This is, of course, to repeat Rousseau's *Emile*. Within the intervening century Euclid, retained alone in English schools, had disappeared from the schools of the Continent. In 1871 Canon Wilson took a leading part in founding the Association for the Improvement of Geometrical Teaching (now the Mathematical Association), an influential body which succeeded in effecting the reform that Wilson, in common with other mathematicians, had long desired.

From time to time the British Association had shown interest in schools in their general social relation or as material for statistics. From 1861 onwards this interest was focused upon the teaching of science. At the meeting of that year and again in 1862 and 1864, James Heywood called the Association's attention to the disproportionate time spent by the schools and by Oxford and Cambridge upon Greek and Latin to the detriment of the study of science. Farrar at Nottingham in 1866 presented a paper "On the teaching of science at Public Schools" in which he claimed that science exercised a different order of faculties than those which were developed by classical study, and that the teaching of science would do something in preparation for their future professions in the case of those boys, a great majority in fact, who were "naturally unsuited" for classical training and did not intend to pass to a university. He believed that most Public School masters were sympathetic but that there were practical difficulties which hindered the introduction of natural science into those schools. To remove these he suggested a joint committee of scientific men and of masters accustomed to Public School methods.

At this same meeting the Committee of Recommendations made representations to the Council of the Association which resulted in the appointment of a Special Committee to inquire and report, its membership including amongst others Professors Huxley and Tyndall, Farrar, J. M. Wilson of Rugby and Joseph Payne, a private schoolmaster, who some five years later was appointed Professor of Education by the College of Preceptors. This Committee, in the report which it presented at the Dundee meeting of 1867, stated that the study of science was encouraged by the universities, English, Scottish and Irish, that science was an optional examination subject in the tests of the College of

Preceptors and in the Local Examinations of Oxford and Cambridge, and that it had "even been partially introduced into several Public Schools". Yet the means adopted in these institutions were "capable of great improvement". The Committee believed that science should play a two-fold part in the curriculum with appropriate procedure for each. As scientific information, conveyed by lectures and by books, the course should comprise general knowledge concerning natural phenomena, particularly of astronomy, geology, physical geography and physiology. As mental training involving experiment or observation, school science should include experimental physics, elementary chemistry and botany. It was suggested that natural science should be taught in every Public School, that the hours weekly allotted to the study should be three, not two as recommended by the Clarendon Commission. Each school should employ at least one natural science master and the subject should be upon an equal footing with mathematics and modern languages. At entrance to a Public School boys should be examined in arithmetic, and an examination in natural science should be held by Oxford and Cambridge either at matriculation or at an early period in the university career.

The Committee reported that at Oxford, where the Natural Science School had been established by the Examination Statute of 1850, there were ample opportunities for the study of physics, chemistry, physiology and other branches and that a very complete chemical laboratory had lately been opened by Christ Church. The Natural Science Tripos at Cambridge covered the whole range of the natural sciences and for the ordinary, or "pass", B.A. degree the "special" optional subjects included chemistry, geology, botany and zoology. "At present public opinion in the University does not reckon scientific distinction as on a par with mathematical or classical." In the University of London "the claims of science to form a part of every liberal education have long been recognised"; there were two specially scientific degrees, those of bachelor and of doctor. Rugby and Harrow were signalized in the report by descriptions of their methods of advancing the study of science.

Thomas Henry Huxley (1825–95), at that date professor at the Royal Institution, who added to his qualities of eminent savant and great teacher of science a prominent place in public life, made vigorous attacks upon the curriculum then established in schools and univer-

sities. One such occasion was afforded by the delivery of an address
to the South London Working Men's College in 1868. "A Liberal
Education and where to find it"[1] is remarkable by reason of its professions of faith, not the least of these being an eloquent statement of
the speaker's conception of what constitutes an education deserving
to be called liberal. Amidst the many reasons then being daily advanced
for the widest extension of popular education he asserted the simplest
and most comprehensive. Politicians would educate their masters,
manufacturers wanted more efficient "hands", the clergy desired to
stem the drift towards infidelity. Huxley takes his stand with Comenius,
Adam Smith, Kant, Pestalozzi. "A few voices are lifted up in favour
of the doctrine that the masses should be educated because they are
men and women with unlimited capacities of being, doing and suffering,
and that it is as true as ever it was that the people perish for lack of
knowledge."

Huxley denounced the general attitude of educational authorities in
reference to science, denied the claim of classics to be the sole instrument
of mental discipline, and derided the aim and method of the instruction
commonly given in the schools. "I could get up an osteological primer
so arid, so pedantic in its terminology, so altogether distasteful to the
youthful mind, as to beat the recent production of the head-masters[2] out
of the field in all these excellences. Next I could exercise my boys upon
easy fossils, and bring out all their powers of memory and all their
ingenuity in the application of my osteo-grammatical rules to the interpretation, or construing of those fragments. To those who had reached
the higher classes, I might supply odd bones to be built up into animals,
giving great honour and reward to him who succeeded in fabricating
monsters most entirely in accordance with the rules. That would answer
to verse-making and essay-writing in the dead languages."

But Huxley did not desire to replace the classical by a scientific
monopoly. He told the Liverpool Philomathic Society, "there are
other forms of culture beside physical science; and I should be profoundly sorry to see the fact forgotten, or even to observe a tendency
to starve or cripple literary or aesthetic culture for the sake of science.
Such a narrow view of the nature of education has nothing to do with

[1] Thomas H. Huxley, *Science and Education: Essays* (1905). See pp. 76–110,
esp. p. 86.
[2] *The Public School Latin Primer.*

my firm conviction that a complete and thorough scientific culture ought
to be introduced into all schools. By this however I do not mean that
every schoolboy should be taught everything in science. That would
be a very absurd thing to conceive and a very mischievous thing to
attempt".[1] He then went on to outline a school course resembling
that advised by the British Association's Special Committee of 1867;
he believed that four hours a week in each class of an ordinary school
would suffice for the study recommended.

The preoccupation of the schools with courses of study almost
entirely literary and with mental training as a primary aim drew
criticism from another quarter. As noted in the previous chapter, the
great international Exhibitions of 1851, 1862 and 1867 had caused
heart-burning when the progress revealed by some of the foreign
exhibits was matched with our own. The Commissioners of the Great
Exhibition of 1851 attributed the difference to the general deficiency
of English industrialists and workmen in the more scientific and
aesthetic elements of their work. Since 1837 the Board of Trade had had
control over a number of "Schools of Design"; on the recommendation
of the Commissioners the administration of these was remodelled in
1852 as a Department of Practical Art, to which was added in 1853 a
second department, the amalgamation receiving the name, the Department of Science and Art. The Order in Council of 1856 which created
the Education Department also transferred the Department of Science
and Art to the control of the Committee of Council on Education.
After ten years' experience of its working the new Science and Art
Department with its headquarters at South Kensington met with
general approval; some took exception to the principle of "payment
by results" on which, in common with the sister department of Whitehall, its grants were made, but the chief complaint then made against
South Kensington was that its operations were not extensive enough.
By this time the progress of our trade rivals had advanced so far as
to diminish the volume of our exports. Once more the explanation
was sought in the Continental systems of public instruction and
"technical education" was the subject of daily discussion.

The Taunton Commission asked for further information and in
pursuance of this request, Lord Stanley, the Foreign Secretary, addressed a detailed questionnaire to H.M. Ministers in France, Austria,

[1] *Science and Education*, p. 122. The date is 1869.

Prussia and the other German States, Switzerland, Holland, Belgium, Sweden and Norway. Their replies formed a large octavo volume of some 500 pages which was issued to Parliament as a Command Paper in 1868. In the meantime Mr Bernard Samuelson, M.P., had made an extensive tour in search of similar information and reported to Lord Montagu, the Vice-President of the Council (that is, the titular head of the Education Department), in November, 1867. Samuelson paid special attention to the systems of primary instruction, since upon these he believed that the success of secondary or technical education must depend. The instruction was "evanescent" which children received under our Factory Acts of 1844, 1864 and 1867. He recommended that the limitation of Science and Art capitation grants to working-class pupils be removed, that larger grants should be paid for the more difficult subjects and that physiology and inorganic chemistry should be less frequently taught. The great hindrance to technical instruction was the lack of competent teachers of science and the Government should train men to make good this want.

The Vice-President circulated amongst the Chambers of Commerce of the country the following questions. What trades are now being injured by the want of a technical education? How and in what particulars are they injured? How do other countries from their greater attention to technical instruction absorb our trade? (Give instances and, if possible, statistics). What plan of technical education would remedy the evil? Lord Montagu met a deputation from the Chambers in November, 1867, and in the same month the Chambers appointed a Special Committee to deal with his four questions. The replies together with certain letters to the Vice-President were ordered by the House of Commons to be printed, March 25th, 1868.[1]

There were naturally differences of opinion and the Chambers as a whole were not well-informed respecting Continental education; statements and opinions wear an *a priori* appearance in many replies. Some Chambers desire the institution of technical schools in their towns, others take the longer view that technical instruction can only be profitably considered in its relation to national education at large, primary as well as secondary. The country was waiting for the report

[1] *Copies of Answers from Chambers of Commerce to Queries of the Vice-President of the Council as to Technical Education: and of a Letter from Mr Jacob Behrens to the Vice-President on the same subject.*

of the Taunton Commission when these replies were being considered. Kendal and Nottingham were exceptional in presenting constructive proposals; the report of the latter town, signed by A. J. Mundella (one day to be a Vice-President of the Council), is particularly to the point. Nottingham is thankful for the existence of its School of Art but regrets that the cost of attending it is beyond the poorer classes. For their local industries knowledge of art, of mechanics and of chemistry is requisite. Chemnitz in Saxony is Nottingham's rival in hosiery. In Chemnitz "a technical education of the highest class is accessible"; Nottingham has nothing to compare with it. Technical schools in no wise inferior to the Continental and as cheap and accessible should be established "immediately".

Mr James Hole put the case of Leeds in a striking fashion. "Here is a town now containing about 250,000 inhabitants, most of whom are dependent upon industries that demand for their successful prosecution an acquaintance with the principles of science. Large portions of the population are dependent for subsistence upon dyeing, bleaching, tanning, iron-founding, tool and machine-making, flax-spinning, cloth-making, coal-mining, pot-tube making and a host of smaller trades; but the whole of the scientific instruction provided is one chemistry class of about thirty pupils taught by a very good teacher, who drew from the Department last year the magnificent sum of eleven pounds, besides which he received the fees of the pupils less 10 per cent. deducted by the local committee for management. No charge has been made for the rent of the dark dingy cellar in which the class has been housed for the last twenty-five years."

Mr Behrens, whose letter is dated January 24th, 1868, after addressing his reply to the questions of the Vice-President, writes that in his town they are anxiously awaiting the report of the Taunton Commission and the replies to the Foreign Secretary's circular to Ministers abroad. "But I believe, whatever may be the tenor of these reports, the people of Bradford will be confirmed in their opinion, that technical instruction not based upon a system of sound elementary and secondary education, would not meet the wants of the country, and that Government action in this matter ought to embrace the whole system of education, and not a part only. In no other country has practical technical education been more perfect than in England, and the great number of most valuable inventions and improvements which have been made by uneducated workmen prove that this practical education has had excellent results.... I am convinced that no school can ever give the same practical education as that which is given in the real workshop; but it is evident that in places like Bradford, where this branch of education is so thoroughly satisfactory, teaching of a more scientific character would be doubly beneficial."

PART THREE

LATER VICTORIAN (1867–1902)

CHAPTER XII

Women and other Working Folk

A movement favouring an extension of the Parliamentary franchise, which arose soon after Palmerston's death in 1865, rapidly became a fever of agitation, in which the exciting microbe was Robert Lowe, the *enfant terrible* of his party. The project of reform wrecked Lord John Russell's Government and almost wrecked the Conservative Cabinet which succeeded it. The Second Reform Bill became law in July, 1867, the measure which by "the lodger vote" enfranchised the town workmen in great numbers though it left the agricultural craftsmen in most cases voteless; so considerable was the change in the social character of the electorate that Derby, the Prime Minister, described the Act of 1867 as "a leap in the dark", and Lowe from the side of the Opposition declared that "we must educate our future masters".

As in 1832 so it was in 1867; the years immediately preceding and succeeding the passing of the Second Reform Bill were a time of unusually animated and widely distributed public concern in educational policy. The demand for a great advance in the education of women, which was so marked in the 'seventies' and early 'eighties', was a phase of the question then known as "Woman's Rights". This feminist movement began in the United States of America and spread to this country about 1840, but it made little progress here until the extension of the Parliamentary franchise was mooted. In origin the English movement was economic. The disparity in the numbers of the two sexes and the instability of fortune experienced by many families during the first half of the century caused an increase in the number of women who were in whole or in part self-supporting. This state of things was in contradiction of middle class tradition and sentiment; but economic facts could not be gainsaid. Out of a total population of eighteen millions in 1851 three and a half millions of women were working for a subsistence, of whom five-sevenths were unmarried. Within the next ten years the number of self-supporting women exceeded 20 per cent. of the total population, which numbered twenty millions. The middle-class prejudice against the paid employment of women, their inferior education and the disabilities under which they suffered before the law, all tended to lower the rate of remuneration for women's work. In the language of a contemporary pamphlet, women had "the hardest drudgery and scanty pay". The remedy proposed was better education, the vote and equality before the law.

One of the foremost advocates of woman suffrage was John Stuart Mill, who in the course of the debates upon the Bill of 1867 moved an amendment with that object in view. Its rejection was followed by an increase in the number and a strengthening of the organization of societies formed to secure the Parliamentary vote for women. Mill's speeches in the House and at public meetings emphasized the inter-dependence of the economic, political and educational elements in the problem of the betterment of women. As an illustration of the prevailing indifference, he asked where are the universities, high schools or schools of any advanced kind for their advantage. "Hardly any decent educated occupation, save one, is open to them. They are either governesses or nothing."[1] Again, women teachers will be wanted if education becomes national. But, if so, they themselves must be educated, and being educated they will claim political status. "The higher education of women and their political emancipation are sure to go forward together."[2]

Charles Kingsley in the course of a magazine article written in 1869 put the case thus, "A demand for employment has led naturally to a demand for improved education fitting women for employment, and that again has led naturally also to a demand on the part of many thoughtful women for a share in making those laws and those social regulations which have, while made exclusively by men, resulted in leaving women at a disadvantage at every turn".[3] These three claims were interdependent, and at that time were generally put forward in the order of urgency, employment, education, the vote. The Act of

[1] Speech in the House of Commons, May 20th, 1867.
[2] *Report of the London National Society for Woman Suffrage* (1869), p. 12.
[3] C. Kingsley, *Women and Politics*, reprinted 1869, from *Macmillan's Magazine*, by the London National Society for Woman Suffrage.

1867 which conferred the vote upon a large number of men, "most of them altogether uneducated", was an argument the more in favour of woman suffrage.

Kingsley's plea was no novelty. A remarkable brochure first published in 1855 by Mrs Henry Davis Pochin had asserted that the exclusion of her sex from employment superinduced a defective education. Women will not want this or need to study that. "We are carefully and protectively guarded from the contamination of art, science and philosophy, and then told that woman has not yet contributed any new form to art, any discovery in science, any deep searching inquiry in philosophy".[1] "All national schemes of education, however good in themselves, will be neutralised to a great extent, if the better and more enlightened education of women be not made of paramount importance. The educational reform must begin here at the root of the matter, if it would be thoroughly efficient."[2] A lecture on the *Electoral Disabilities of Women*, delivered in 1872, by Rhoda Garrett, complained that women's education did not fit them to enter the Civil Service or a profession, more especially that of medicine. If women had the Parliamentary vote a more equitable division between the sexes of schools, scholarships and educational endowments would be made, and the defective education of the middle-class women improved.

It was reserved to the twentieth century to see the realization of Parliamentary votes for women; but in 1869 women became eligible for the vote in municipal elections, and the Elementary Education Act of 1870 gave women the same status as men in respect both of the School Board vote and (by implication) of membership of School Boards. Indeed, some women recorded a Parliamentary vote after the passing of the Second Reform Bill; but in 1868 the Court of Common Pleas ruled that a woman's vote for a Parliamentary candidate could not be accepted. The Ballot Act of 1872 removed one of the objections alleged to the participation of women in a contested election. The Married Women's Property Act of 1882 made a great advance in the standing of women, legal, social and economic, while the later invention of the safety bicycle initiated changes in their lives which fully deserve the description, revolutionary.

In the light of the foregoing, the comparative stagnation of women's

[1] H. D. Pochin, *The Right of Women to exercise the Franchise* (1855). Reprint of 1873, p. 13.   [2] *Ibid.* p. 17.

education during the twenty years preceding 1865 and the rapid movement between that year and 1876 can be understood. Speaking generally, the women who worked for a more liberal education at this time and who were sympathetic towards the feminist cause, did not prominently identify themselves with its political activity. In all probability their time and energy were fully occupied by their special interest; it is possible that they regarded the action of some advocates of Woman's Rights as not likely to commend the cause even to the friendly. However that may be, the names which stand out as champions of an improved education for women also appear amongst the supporters of the woman's Parliamentary vote. Madame Bodichon (Barbara Leigh Smith), who played a leading part in the founding and endowment of Girton, was an active writer and speaker on the political side. Amongst the *Opinions of Women on Women Suffrage*, a pamphlet of 1879, statements favourable to the exercise of the vote by women were included from Miss Emily Davies, Mrs Maria Grey, Miss Buss, Miss Emily Pfeifer, Mrs Bryant, Mrs Woodhouse, everyone of whom holds a place of honour in the history of English education. The annual report (1886) of the Central Committee of the National Society for Woman Suffrage contains the names of Miss Davies and Miss Buss amongst its subscribers and donors, but they do not appear on the Executive or General Committees.

As early as 1860 Emily Davies (whose father was Rector of Gateshead) was urging upon the North of England public two pressing claims: that more occupations should be opened to women and that the education of women should be improved. She was in her appropriate place as honorary secretary of the "Committee for obtaining the admission of Women to University Examinations" which was set up in 1862, and of that Committee, as of the similar body instituted five years later, she was the indomitable leader. She had a kindred spirit in Miss Clough, with whom she was corresponding in 1864; together they took the next forward step by starting in 1866 local societies of schoolmistresses. The first of these was formed in London on Miss Davies' suggestion, the second under an impulse from Miss Clough at Liverpool; others followed at Manchester, Newcastle and elsewhere.

Miss Clough now tried to realize in Liverpool the schemes of local lectures by university teachers which she had propounded to the Taunton Commission; but, failing to secure the assistance of Oxford or of Cambridge, she left Liverpool in discouragement. Yet early in 1867 she was addressing the schoolmistresses of London and of Manchester on the same subject. The Schoolmistresses' Associations in the northern towns adopted her plan and invited James Stuart, a junior Fellow of Trinity College, Cambridge, to give a course of lectures on "the theory and methods of teaching". He thought it advisable to take a somewhat less abstract topic and proposed a course on the history of astronomy by which he could treat "some specific thing in the way and by the methods which might be usefully adopted in other instances". The lectures were confined to elucidating the discovery and meaning of the law of gravitation.[1] The course was delivered weekly during October and November, 1867, in Liverpool, Manchester, Sheffield and Leeds, the four audiences together numbering 550, mainly schoolmistresses and their elder girl pupils. Stuart had thus in effect inaugurated what was later known as "University Extension".

Largely in consequence of Miss Clough's advocacy, a federated body came into existence in November, 1867, calling itself the North of England Council for promoting the Higher Education of Women, Miss Clough being its first honorary secretary. Its object was "to deliberate on questions affecting the improvement and extension of the education of women of the upper and middle classes, and to recommend to the several associations and societies therein represented plans for the promotion of these objects". At one time or another during the seven years of its history twelve towns were represented on this Council, James Bryce (afterwards Viscount Bryce), T. Markby, secretary of the Cambridge Local Examinations Syndicate, and others being either co-opted or representative members, and its lecturers included Stuart, J. W. Hales, Seeley, Roscoe, F. W. H. Myers, and Charles Pearson.

While they remained in cordial agreement as to the main objective, Miss Davies and Miss Clough differed as to the mode of approach. Miss Clough was keen to establish a scheme of lectures by teachers from Oxford and Cambridge addressed to women only and intended to advance feminine culture generally, but more particularly to aid schoolmistresses and women who proposed to make teaching their profession. The immediate goal of these lectures was a recognised university examination. Miss Davies deprecated plans which were limited to

[1] James Stuart, *Reminiscences* (1912), p. 49.

women. She desired to secure for them a higher education which, *mutatis mutandis*, should be in character and conditions the same as that provided for men. Special lectures or examinations for women would most certainly be of a lower standard than those demanded by men, whereas a common standard was what was necessary. "We do not want certificates of proficiency given to half-educated women. There are examinations which will do this already within reach."[1] For her the status of women was not a "Woman's Question" at all, but one which deeply affected both sexes; how could men become capable of their best so long as they were associated with women who were mistakenly kept at a lower level? As events proved, no contradiction of this opinion was involved in her acceptance of the honorary secretaryship of the Committee for establishing a New College for Women; the Committee was formed in December, 1867, but the project itself had already been brought to the notice of the Taunton Commissioners, who heard of it with approval.

There were warm friends of the movement for women's education amongst the graduates of London and of Cambridge. When it became clear that nothing less than a supplemental charter could open London examinations to women, steps were taken in Convocation to secure the necessary powers. This supplemental charter from the Crown was obtained in 1868 and under its provisions there was instituted a General Examination for women, the requirements for which were almost identical with those for matriculation. The first examination was held in May, 1869; in the following year University College, London, opened its classes to women. In 1877 the Council of King's College, London, established classes in Kensington with the purpose of giving to women instruction of a university type and of such a standard as was required by the examinations then open to women.

The admission of girls to the Cambridge Local Examinations and the success attained by the lectures which the North of England Council had arranged encouraged that society to petition the University of Cambridge for an examination which would test and attest the higher education of women. The memorialists pointed out that the absence of such a test heavily handicapped schoolmistresses and governesses. The petition was granted and the Women's Examination was instituted and

---

[1] Emily Davies, *Thoughts on some questions relating to women*, 1860–1908, with Prefatory Note by E. E. Constance Jones (1910), p. 125.

held for the first time in 1869. Although intended primarily for teachers, the examination was open generally to women over eighteen; a few years later its title was changed to the Higher Local Examination, when it was made open to both sexes. In 1880, candidates had a choice of subjects comprising English language, literature and history, mathematics, some branches of natural science, languages ancient and modern, logic, political economy, harmony and drawing.

Emily Davies and her friends declined to take part in the petition for a women's examination, but at once put into operation the scheme for a women's college. Taking a small house at Hitchin in October, 1869, they admitted six students to read the courses set for the Previous Examination and for the ordinary degree of Cambridge; the object, as avowed by the Council, was to "use such efforts as from time to time they may think most expedient and effectual to obtain for the students of the College admission to the examinations for degrees of the University of Cambridge and generally to place the College in connection with the University".[1] In December, 1870, the University was asked to permit five of the students to take the Previous Examination, which in that year included a Gospel in Greek, Paley's *Evidences*, Latin and Greek accidence, a Greek play, one book of a Latin author, Euclid, bks. I, II, III and IV, 1–6, and arithmetic, with additional papers in algebra, trigonometry and mechanics for candidates seeking honours. The University would not formally admit these women to the examination, but it raised no objection to individual examiners at their own discretion allowing them to take their papers. On these terms four of the women passed in the first class, one in the second; that is to say, they attained those standards but their names did not appear in the class list. Under this informal arrangement in 1872 one student passed the examination for the Mathematical Tripos and two that for the Classical Tripos; in subsequent years the arrangement was continued in respect of various triposes and the ordinary, or pass, degree. The college was incorporated as Girton College in 1872 with Emily Davies as its first "mistress"; in the next year it removed from Hitchin to Girton, on the outskirts of Cambridge. In 1874 a Girton woman was examined for the Natural Science Tripos.

In the meantime, largely owing to Henry Sidgwick and Mrs Millicent

---

[1] Alice Zimmern, *The Renaissance of Girls' Education* (1898), p. 106, quoting the Council's prospectus.

Garrett Fawcett, the wife of Professor Henry Fawcett, lectures had been started in Cambridge itself to prepare students for the Women's Examination. A number of distinguished university men co-operated, either as lecturers or as members of the committee of management, or as both; Professor F. D. Maurice lectured on English history, Cayley on algebra and arithmetic, J. E. B. Mayor on Latin, Alfred Marshall on political economy. James Stuart lectured to this Cambridge group of women as well as to those at Hitchin; in his *Reminiscences* he says, "the Cambridge pupils attended my class just as men would have done, but at Hitchin Miss Davies sat in the room and knitted all the time". During the first term, October—December, 1870, between seventy and eighty women attended the Cambridge lectures. Contrary to the Girton ideal and practice, these students of the "Lectures Association" did not attempt the regulation courses but prepared for the Women's Examination or its later form, the Higher Local Examination, thus avoiding the compulsory Greek and Latin of the "Previous" and giving a longer time for the initial stage preparatory to entering upon the degree course proper. Moreover, Sidgwick, at least, amongst the members of the Lectures Association, did not think that the compulsory study of Greek and Latin on the method used in schools was expedient for either sex. In far too many cases these methods failed to give a literary education, whereas if literature were really taught, the choice of the particular language to be learned would be only "a subordinate question". "We must allow all weight to the advantages which a dead and difficult language has, as an instrument of training, over a modern and easy one. But we must remember that it is a point of capital importance that instruction in any language should be carried to the point at which it really throws open a literature; while it is not a point of capital importance that any particular literature should be so thrown open."[1]

In another important respect the policy of the Lectures Association differed from that of Miss Davies and of Girton. While the latter looked to the degree courses and to the closest assimilation to the studies of the men as their aim, the Association was ready to advance women's education by means that were not strictly academic. It conducted "correspondence classes" for women unable to come up

[1] *Essays on a Liberal Education* (1867), p. 130, "The theory of Classical Education."

to Cambridge, it permitted attendance at the lectures for such short periods as one or two terms, and it kept steadily before itself the importance, to women's education generally, of the higher education of schoolmistresses. Again, while Girton was associated with the Church of England, the other group was, and remains, undenominational or neutral in reference to religious education. In 1871 a hall of residence, with Miss A. J. Clough as "Principal," was opened in Cambridge, the students numbering five; after three migrations to different houses in the town, it settled finally at Newnham Hall where students were first received in October, 1876. The Newnham Hall Company was formed to undertake the maintenance of the institution. In the meantime the Lectures Association had become the "Association for promoting the Higher Education of Women in Cambridge".

In an appeal for assistance made by Miss Clough it was said to be an essential part of the plan "to offer academic education on the lowest possible terms to those preparing to be teachers". Whereas the charge per term, exclusive of tuition fees, was £20, intending teachers were charged £15; "even this payment is somewhat heavy for the scanty resources of this class of students and we are anxious to reduce it still further".[1] Tuition fees were arranged on the scale of one guinea per term for two weekly lectures in a subject, the setting of papers and their revision by the lecturer; teacher students paid half-fees. From the first the Lectures Association and its successors received very considerable help and encouragement from resident members of the University. Not only did scholars such as Seeley, Cayley, Jebb, Sidgwick and J. S. Reid undertake tuition, but the students were admitted to most of the professorial lectures, a concession which was followed by their admission to college lectures, Christ's being the first to grant the privilege; St John's College opened its laboratory to them. "Indeed the helpfulness of men on whom the students had no claim is one of the brightest features even of the bright days of Newnham's beginnings"; the acknowledgement comes from a tutor of the college, Miss Alice Gardner.

In 1874 the Association presented two students, under the informal conditions already described, for the Moral Sciences Tripos; one was assigned by two examiners a first class, by their two colleagues a second. The other student passed in the second class. From that time

[1] B. A. Clough, *A Memoir of Anne Jemima Clough*, p. 159.

onwards Newnham students were similarly examined for different Triposes. In 1880 the Association and the Hall Company were amalgamated as the "Newnham College Association for the advancement of education and learning of Women in Cambridge" and the College was duly incorporated. This year was made further memorable by the success of Miss C. A. Scott, of Girton College, in the Mathematical Tripos, where she stood "equal in proficiency to the eighth wrangler".

This achievement fired the friends of women's higher education to petition the Cambridge Senate for the formal admission of women to the degree examinations and the granting of degrees to successful candidates. The first petition, which bore a large number of signatures, originated outside the University;[1] it was followed by petitions from within requesting that the informal examination and classifying of women should be regularized. Girton and Newnham seem to have been embarrassed by these activities for which they denied responsibility; they took the opportunity to state their case. In December a syndicate was appointed to consider the matter and on its Report the Senate by a ten to one majority passed in February, 1881, a series of graces which recognized the two women's colleges and threw open the Previous and Tripos Examinations to their students who had kept the requisite number of terms and attained the qualifying status. Success in languages or in mathematics at the Higher Local Examination was for these students made an alternative to passing the "Previous". The names of successful examinees were to be published in a separate women's list with indications of the relative positions occupied by men and women. These concessions stopped short of making women members of the University; consequently they could not receive the degree, the place of which was to be taken by a certificate setting forth the candidate's examination successes. The graces came into force in June, 1881.

Women's education at Oxford followed much the same lines as at Cambridge. Pattison's classes, to which the attention of the Taunton Commission had been invited, have already been described.[2] When these were no longer in being, their place was taken in 1873 by classes which were organized under a Ladies' Committee, a body which five years later became the "Association for the Education of Women",

---

[1] The prime movers were W. Steadman Aldis, Senior Wrangler 1861, and his wife, of Newcastle-on-Tyne, who obtained over 8500 signatures.

[2] Chapter X, p. 289.

"to establish and maintain a system of instruction having general reference to the Oxford examinations".[1] As at Cambridge, it was found necessary to establish halls of residence, and Somerville and Lady Margaret Halls were opened in 1879. The former, "Somerville College" from 1894, was "undenominational"; the sister hall, like Girton, was associated with the Church of England. The Association, unlike its Cambridge counterpart, maintained its separate existence distinct from the halls which housed its students; it made a link between the halls and the University, maintained a staff of lecturers and tutors, and formed a Board of Studies for the women students. The Local Examinations Delegacy arranged the examinations of the women, who took the undergraduates' question papers. The University had opened its Local Examinations to girls in 1870, and in 1875 it established for women the Higher Local Examinations, the first examination being held two years later. The "Higher Local" of Oxford remained till 1901 a test for women only.

The University of London obtained power in 1878 to admit women to all its examinations and to confer degrees upon them. At the first matriculation examination held (January, 1879) under this supplemental charter, the first place in the honours division was occupied by Sophie Bryant, a mistress in the North London Collegiate School for Girls. Graduates of London became eligible for membership of Convocation three years after obtaining the bachelor's degree. The new charter expressly excepted women graduates from this provision unless and until Convocation itself assented to their admission. The assent was given in 1882 and thenceforward men and women were academically equal in the University. The Reform Act of 1867 conferred on the members of Convocation the duty of electing a Member of Parliament; but women graduates had to wait until the twentieth century was well advanced before they could share in the voting.

It remains to add that the Newcastle College of Science, founded in 1871, admitted both sexes to its scientific and medical classes, that the Victoria University, founded in 1880, made no sex discrimination in reference to its degrees and other distinctions,[2] and that University College, Liverpool, incorporated in 1881, admitted women to its classes.

---

[1] The Association's prospectus quoted by A. Zimmern, *The Renaissance of Girls' Education* (1898), p. 117.

[2] A similar rule had been followed in Owens College, Manchester, since 1869.

All this activity in colleges and universities had its inevitable reaction in schools for girls, a reaction which gained strength from the provision of elementary instruction which was made by the Act of 1870. If, at the rudimentary stage, boys and girls could be educated by the same studies and the same methods, why should they not receive a similar instruction at the stage above the elementary? This was an echo from the Taunton *Report*; and the Endowed Schools Commissioners appointed by Parliament to give effect to the *Report* were busy in devising new schemes and adapting old endowments in order to increase the number of secondary schools for girls and so adjust the balance between the sexes. Moreover, much that had been attempted in the education of women had been done with an eye to the education of girls.

The years immediately following 1870 therefore constitute an epoch in the history of English girls' schools and, as in the earlier time, women played the leading part in that history. In May, 1871, Mrs William Grey (*née* Maria G. Shirreff) propounded before the Society of Arts a scheme intended to secure an "educational charter of women" which would recognize their right equally with men to an education which was "the best for human beings" irrespective of sex, which would give girls an equal share with boys in educational endowments, ancient and future, and which, by the registration of teachers, would make the schoolmistress's profession as honourable and as honoured as the schoolmaster's. To attain these objects a strong backing of public opinion was felt to be necessary and, to create this support, Maria Grey proposed with the aid of the Society to set up a central committee in London having local committees in all towns whose populations were large enough to need the establishment of girls' secondary schools. With these aims before them, Mrs Grey, her sister, Emily Shirreff, Mary Gurney, Lady Stanley of Alderley and others formed a "National Union for promoting the Education of Women", the policy of which took material shape in the Girls' Public Day School Company of 1872. The purpose of this proprietary body was stated to be "to supply for girls the best possible education corresponding with the education given to boys in the great public schools of the country". The veteran Kay-Shuttleworth was a member of the Company's Council and took an active interest in the establishment of its first "High Schools" in Chelsea (1873), Notting Hill and Croydon (1874).

The next ten years witnessed the coming of important girls' schools established by the Company, or by other proprietary associations or by private benefactors. The first-founded (1853) proprietary school for girls, the Ladies' College, Cheltenham, under Miss Beale's rule at this time, was again amongst the pioneers; its department for training schoolmistresses was opened in 1879. The Church Schools Company was started in 1883 to secure for girls' secondary schools the definite denominational education which it was not a purpose of the Girls' Public Day School Company to afford. Further reference to this Company will be found in Chapter XVI below.

The studies in which the High Schools of the Girls' Public Day School Company were prepared to give teaching comprised religious instruction, the "three R's"—pupils were admissible at the age of seven —book-keeping, mathematics, English (grammar, composition, literature), history, geography, French, Latin (or, alternatively, German), the elements of physical science, drawing, singing, needlework, gymnastics. In some schools, political economy was a "subject"; and elementary Greek was requisite for those girls who were intending to enter Cambridge or Oxford. Full opportunity was afforded to learn to play piano or violin, to paint, to take drawing beyond the early stage. Of course, it was not proposed that every, or indeed any, girl should take up all these studies or that every High School should include them all in its course. The question of curriculum as matter of detail was a question for the individual school and its head mistress. But at that date, when the High Schools began their career, belief in the paramount value of examinations was very general; and examinations had played a prominent part in the development of feminine education. It followed that the examination requirements of London, Cambridge and Oxford had a great share in deciding which studies should, indeed *must*, form the curriculum of a particular school, or even of a given pupil. Oxford and Cambridge co-operated in 1873 in framing a Joint Board whose examination might be at once a school-leaving examination and a test of fitness for admission to either University; to this examination girls were admissible from 1876 onwards and it was largely adopted by the High Schools as a guide to the studies of their senior pupils. The subjects of examination fell into four groups, languages (ancient and modern), mathematics, science and a group comprised of English, history and Scripture. From these four groups a candidate must offer at least four subjects taken from three of them, thus preventing a specialization, literary, mathematical or scientific.

The projectors of the Girls' Public Day School Company in announcing the intention to give girls an education correspondent to that given by the "great public schools" had impaled themselves on a dilemma. If they made the course identical with that followed in those schools, they must necessarily sacrifice accomplishments which were usually regarded as distinctively feminine; not only must they surrender that tyrant of girlhood, the piano, but also drawing and modern languages, studies in which schoolgirls had attained a certain standing. To retain these feminine achievements meant less time and attention to the traditional studies of the Public Schools; it was this alternative horn of the dilemma which the girls' schools chose to occupy, hoping to mitigate its pains by devoting a long morning session to the more solid studies and reserving the afternoons for art and other manual occupations.

Notwithstanding the influence of tradition and the weight of authority expressed in examinations, those who started the womens' colleges and the girls' high schools were well aware of the contemporary demand for a reform of curriculum, especially in that of the ancient grammar schools. As the schoolmistresses became experienced in their especial task, they grew less inclined to follow traditional lines, and the economic impulse, which had effected so much in beginning the women's movement, supported the disinclination. Teaching and, at a long distance from it, medicine were the only professions open to women; and for these special courses of study must be followed. Experience in the schools emphasized the truth that not all girls, any more than all boys, are fitted for these professions or likely to benefit greatly from the university education which prepares for them. The early tendency had been to think almost exclusively of the needs and capacities of "Mary"; "Martha" now secured consideration. Needlework was supplemented by "domestic subjects" and the non-academically minded girl found her opportunity.

The High Schools and the schools which followed their pattern were day schools; a much closer approximation to the Public School was effected by the proprietary and private boarding schools that were organized and conducted on the model of St Leonard's School, which a private company had established at St Andrews in 1877. An English school of this type was Roedean which the Misses Lawrence started in Brighton in 1885 as Wimbledon House School. The success of St Leonard's under its first head mistresses, Miss Lumsden and Miss Dove, both Girtonians of the Hitchin period, led to the formation of an English company which in 1896 set up Wycombe Abbey School with Miss Dove as its head mistress. In all three schools the aims were physique, character and learning—in that order, an order significant of a further advance in thought about education. With the many distracting claims made upon them in their early years, the day schools had not found it possible to do much to encourage games; these boarding schools assigned great educational value to them. The year, 1885, which saw the opening of Wimbledon House School also saw the opening at Dartford of the first Physical Training College for Women. The subsequent development of games in girls' schools, boarding and day, fostered by schoolmistresses educated at the women's colleges, was greatly advanced by the games mistresses trained at Dartford and at similar institutions. Tennis, hockey, lacrosse, cricket and gymnastics killed the dolorous "crocodile".

Quite apart from the reform which the new girls' day schools wrought in their own particular field, their organization initiated on the large scale a change for the better in the schooling of very young children. The essays of the Edgeworths and of Robert Owen in this direction have been described already. The Edgeworths are now almost forgotten, and the infant schools which were the outcome of Owen's philanthropy did not long continue to apply his principles, but were content to become mere stepping-stones to the schools for older children. The names now most firmly associated with the education of children under seven are Friedrich W. A. Froebel (1782–1852) and his Kindergarten.

Froebel's reputation as an educator is English and American rather than German, and in England and America that reputation is based upon the Kindergarten. His chief literary work, *Die Menschenerziehung*[1] (1826), is not especially related to infant education; and it is a fragment only. In this work he repeats Pestalozzi's teaching that education is development, and in the course of his exposition Froebel casually

[1] See Fletcher and Welton, *Froebel's Chief Writings on Education rendered into English* (1912).

touches upon the recapitulatory theory of which Herbert Spencer made so much. But education as practised hindered development, because educators persistently regarded the child not as a child, but as an immature little man. On that ground they tried to abridge childhood and used it as a storing time for what would be useful when the child became a man. This was to obscure the fact that the child is an organism in course of development, "the strong and perfect development of each successive stage is grounded in the vigour and completeness of all the preceding stages. Parents are too apt to overlook this".[1] The development is that of an individual; it is brought about by activity which must be spontaneous, self-initiated, "self-activity". "God created man in his own image;...therefore man should work and produce, as God does."[2] That is the pupil's part. On the educator's part, education must be "passive, following (only guarding and protecting) not prescriptive, categorical, interfering",[3] the teaching in fact of Montaigne and Locke.

Hence self-expression, "making the inner outer", should be encouraged. "We shall see that many forms of the boy's activity are as yet directed towards no definite end; his painting, for example, is not designed to make an artist nor his singing to train a musician. The purpose of all such activities is simply the complete unfolding of the boy's nature. They give that spiritual food and air without which his soul would be weakened, dwarfed and cramped....To repress any one of these capacities is to do violence to the nature of the boy. Still worse is it to try to graft another activity into the place of the one we have cut off in the belief that this will be better for his future life....But God neither excises nor grafts. He develops."[4] Once more Froebel re-echoes Montaigne: "Play is the highest expression of human development in childhood, for it alone is the free expression of what is in the child's soul....Childhood's play is not mere sport; it is full of meaning and serious import....For to one who has insight into human nature, the trend of the whole future life of the child is revealed in his freely chosen play".[5]

All this is to be found in *Die Menschenerziehung* of 1826; Froebel's distinctive work for very young children dates from 1837 to 1840, a quarter of a century after the Edgeworths and Owen, seventy years

---

[1] Fletcher and Welton, *op. cit.* p. 41.   [2] *Ibid.* p. 42.
[3] *Ibid.* p. 32.   [4] *Ibid.* pp. 167 f.   [5] *Ibid.* pp. 50 f.

after the Alsatian pastor, Oberlin. Froebel hesitated long over the name which he would give to his system of infant education, but in a moment of inspiration he used the term "Kindergarten", the garden whose plants are children, and that name it retains. To him, as to Pestalozzi, the plant, the garden and the gardener were most apt figures of the child, the educator and the special relation between them. In this system he attached an inordinate importance to certain pieces of apparatus—ball, cube, cylinder—which, he protested, were "not introduced arbitrarily"; with these and with tablets of wood, sticks, peas mounted on wire, the folding and cutting of paper, drawing, gardening and games he proposed to conduct the child through the progressive stages of development—physical, intellectual and spiritual.

Froebel died in 1852, frowned upon by the Prussian Government as the abettor of atheism and revolution; however comic this behaviour of theirs may seem, it is testimony to the German belief in the power of ideas. Two years after the master's death, the Baroness Marenholtz von Bülow and other German ladies started propaganda in England in favour of Froebel's system, and an exhibition of the Kindergarten apparatus and material with samples of little children's handiwork was opened in London. The first English Kindergarten was set up at Hampstead in the same year, 1854. Charles Dickens, always warmly interested in children and their upbringing, wrote an article, "Infant Gardens", in his periodical, *Household Words*, July, 1855, in which he described Froebel's career and recommended with enthusiasm the "gifts", or apparatus, occupations and nursery songs.

All this produced small immediate effect. Froebel's thought and practice were not congenial to a materialist, utilitarian age; and the connexion between English industrial magnates and English politicians was close. As for the majority of the people, the popular attitude towards Germany and Germans was one of hostility or of contempt. In the 'fifties' and early 'sixties' neither the people nor their Parliamentary representatives or their industrial chiefs would feel inclined to countenance a German system of education, even though it had failed to secure more than a footing in its native land. The earliest English supporters of the Kindergarten belonged to the more cultivated portion of the community, amongst whom an almost mythical conception of Germans and Germany had developed, encouraged by the prejudiced but influential writing of Thomas Carlyle, and the sympathies of

Queen Victoria, the wife of a cultivated and public-spirited German prince. It was not until 1874 that any considerable movement in favour of Froebel's teaching was made in this country. But in that year the Froebel Society was founded, largely owing to the advocacy of Emily Shirreff and her sister, Maria Grey, to make the principles of the Kindergarten better known and to train and certify teachers in its practice. In the same year a Kindergarten department was attached, under Madame Michaelis, to the Croydon High School, the third of the schools to be founded by the Girls' Public Day School Company. From that time onwards the education of very young children became, and has remained, an integral part of the business of the Company's High Schools.

At this time the School Boards created by the Elementary Education Act of 1870 were still in the experimental stage of their organization and the appreciation of their functions. The London School Board appointed Miss Bishop in 1874 to lecture on the Kindergarten to the infant-school mistresses in its employ, and, still in 1874, the British and Foreign School Society founded Stockwell Training College for the training of infant-school teachers in Froebel's principles. But throughout the nineteenth century Froebelianism remained a misunderstood exotic in the "Infant Departments" of our elementary schools. Whereas its author designed it as a systematic education of young children, those schools persisted in regarding the "Kindergarten" as one "subject" amongst others; they saw no absurdity in time-tables which confined it to two specific school times in each week. Senior inspectors of schools like Mr Joshua Fitch preferred to represent it as an amusing game which softened the rigours of the "three R's", these being the real business of children under seven.[1] A better understanding of Froebel was not attained or applied in these schools before the twentieth century, when a few unofficial enthusiasts opened "Free Kindergartens" in Scotland and in this country.

In his *Reminiscences* Professor James Stuart recalls that shortly after

---

[1] "The methods of Froebel...will have value up to the age of seven if judiciously incorporated with other forms of early instruction" (Fitch, *Lectures on Teaching*, 1880). A similar misconception, or compromise, underlay Mundella's Elementary School "Code" (1882), which ruled that infants' schools must provide "appropriate and varied occupations" for their pupils.

taking his degree (1866) he was entertaining two projects which were suggested to his mind by a comparison between English university organization and that of Scotland. The first was a scheme of inter-collegiate lectures, the second the idea of a sort of peripatetic university of professors circulating in the big towns. The latter was precisely the scheme which Miss A. J. Clough had submitted to the Taunton Commission.[1] Then came a request that he would lecture to the Schoolmistresses' Associations in Liverpool, Manchester, Sheffield and Leeds, a request which brought him into touch with the North of England Council for promoting the Higher Education of Women and with its honorary secretary, Miss Clough. A similar invitation came to him from the Mechanics' Institute at Crewe,[2] where he lectured on meteors to an audience of 1500 on the night following the great meteoric shower of November, 1867. He was so pleased with his hearers that he offered to lecture again at Crewe in the following year. The Equitable Pioneers Co-operative Society of Rochdale, desiring to expend $2\frac{1}{2}$ per cent. of their profits to the best advantage educationally, were recommended to apply to Stuart, who, in response, repeated in Rochdale the lectures which he had given to ladies in the four towns.

Stuart's experience in conducting this novel form of public teaching led to the formulation of a method which subsequently became common form amongst University Extension lecturers. On coming to a lecture, or course of lectures, each student was provided with a synopsis. Stuart would have preferred to develop his theme by questions, based upon the synopsis and put directly to his audience, rather than by way of the lecturer's customary monologue. But it was explained to him that it would be "improper" to address questions publicly to women or for them to answer questions thus addressed. So he printed his questions and offered to read written answers, and thus originated the periodical essay of the University Extension class. Another characteristic practice started almost by accident. At Rochdale after a lecture he left his astronomical drawings hanging in the room, where, in the interval before the next week's lecture, they were examined and discussed by his pupils, some score or more of whom plied him with questions at his next visit. The consequent discussion and active participation of his hearers seemed so valuable that it was made permanent in the form

[1] Schools Inquiry Commission, *Report*, vol. II, pp. 82–5.
[2] Founded by the London and North Western Railway Company.

of the class discussion, lasting an hour, which follows an "Extension" lecture.

Stuart's next step was to suggest to the different bodies for whom he lectured that they should send memorials to Cambridge requesting that a scheme of external lectures should be recognized by the University and made a part of its policy and administration. In the autumn of 1871 memorials to that effect were sent to the Vice-Chancellor and Council of the Senate from the Women's North of England Council, Crewe Mechanics' Institute, the Rochdale Co-operative Society, from the Mayor and others of Leeds, of Birmingham and of other towns. Stuart backed all this up in letters to resident members of the Senate in which he described his experiences as lecturer. His principal help in bringing the subject successfully before the University came from the town of Nottingham where a committee was formed in connexion with the Mechanics' Institute, the chief moving spirits being Mr Richard Enfield, Dr J. B. Paton and Canon Morse. Nottingham secured the co-operation of Derby and Leicester.

The result of this activity on the part of women, artisans and municipal bodies was the formation by Cambridge of a Syndicate, the approval of the scheme of lectures and examinations, the appointment of three lecturers and of James Stuart as the Syndicate's secretary. The first course of University Extension lectures under this *régime* was delivered in October–November, 1873, at Nottingham; courses were also given during this autumn at Derby, Leicester, Leeds, Bradford, Halifax and Keighley. Thus began the system of extra-mural teaching which in time was taken up by all the British universities and by some of the universities overseas.

The memorials addressed to Cambridge had asked for continuous courses under specially competent lecturers who would, in effect, as far as possible bring the University to the locality. The memorials had in view three classes of students; ladies and persons of leisure who could pay an adequate fee and attend in the day-time; young men of the middle class engaged in business; and artisans to be admitted at reduced fees to lectures delivered in the evening. In practice it did not prove possible to maintain these divisions, and the second class, young men between eighteen and twenty-five, did not attend in considerable numbers. In some towns teachers in elementary schools and pupil teachers formed a noticeable proportion of the students.

There were difficulties in the way of artisans beyond the initial difficulty (as it was in the early 'seventies') of an imperfect literary grounding, the difficulty which had daunted the Mechanics' Institutes of an earlier generation. A day of hard manual labour is not the best preparation for an evening's severe intellectual work, and intellectual distraction was not the scheme's primary object. Leisure in the case of the artisan, in times before an eight hours' day, usually meant unemployment and lack of wages and, as one of their number rightly said, "bread comes before education". But the Extension courses wisely appealed to a variety of interests, and working men in considerable numbers persevered in attending in spite of obstacles. The colliers of Northumberland distinguished themselves in this respect. It became evident to those who conducted the lectures and discussion classes that brains and character are qualities which know not social distinctions and that what was wanting in some social classes was opportunity.

At a public meeting held at the Mansion House in June, 1875, the following resolution was carried: "That the principle of the Cambridge University Extension Scheme be applied to London and that the various Educational Institutions of the Metropolis be requested to co-operate in an endeavour so to apply it".[1] It was part of the position which was occupied by the University of London at that time that it could not initiate a movement of a university character within its own borders but was constrained to leave it to a private society. Effect was given in 1876 to the Mansion House resolution by the establishment of the London Society for the Extension of University Teaching. A joint board of the Society representing the Universities of Oxford, Cambridge and London was formed to supervise the Society's teaching, and University College and King's College were represented on the Council. With the revival of teaching in London University which followed the Act of 1898, the Society's functions were transferred to that University and from 1902 were discharged by a specially appointed Board.

Oxford took up the work in 1878; but its arrangements were reorganized in 1885, when the office of secretary was occupied by Mr M. E. Sadler; the success which followed made it expedient to appoint in 1892 a special delegacy to take charge. The Universities of Durham and Victoria followed the example set by their elder sisters, and so important a place did the Extension movement take in the life of some

[1] R. D. Roberts, *Eighteen Years of University Extension* (1891), p. 77.

towns that these established colleges for its accommodation. Yorkshire College, Leeds, established in 1874 as a Scientific and Technical College, enlarged its scope so as to include the humane studies to which "Extension" was usually more addicted. Firth College, Sheffield (1879) and University College, Nottingham (1881) were largely concerned with Extension and its students. The University Extension College, Reading, was founded in 1892, the Technical and University Extension College, Exeter, in the next year; a similar college was started at Colchester in 1896. These colleges, following a customary line of development in the history of educational institutions, in a few short years outgrew their initial purposes and in the twentieth century added a new chapter to the history of English universities.

The weak spot in brief, self-contained lecture courses, whose delivery was exhausted in three or four months, was of course well understood; they might be mere channels of "interesting" information without causing any permanent effect upon the knowledge or culture of the hearers. To secure more or less unity of subject and continuous application to a study, Cambridge in 1886, and Oxford a little later, instituted "affiliated centres" in which the students were eligible for certificates of successful study which had extended over three or four years. In some cases similar certificates admitted the holders to the B.A. degree after two years' study at Oxford or Cambridge. In 1902, London, whose office of teaching had at that date been resumed, conferred a Vice-Chancellor's certificate on the completion of five years' successful "Extension" study and later instituted a diploma in humane letters studied under "Extension" conditions.

In the winter of 1883, a time of economic distress, the country was shocked and its social conscience was stirred by "The Bitter Cry of Outcast London" which appeared in the *Pall Mall Gazette*. Disraeli's "Two Nations" once more stood revealed, and official bodies as well as private citizens were anxious to bridge the chasm which separated the well-to-do from those who stood upon, or below, the poverty line. But long before "slumming"[1] became a West End fashion and an East End embarrassment, an Oxford undergraduate, Arnold Toynbee (1852–83) had begun on his own initiative to investigate the situation for himself. In the Long Vacation of 1875 he occupied rooms in

[1] The *N.E.D.* gives May 1884 as the earliest use of the word in this sense.

Commercial Road, East, got into touch with the Vicar of St Jude's, Whitechapel, the Rev. S. A. Barnett, with the teachers and school children, worked with the Charity Organization Society, joined the Tower Hamlets Radical Club and spoke at its meetings. For the remainder of his short life his chief preoccupation was the life of the poor and measures for its amelioration. In due course made bursar of his college (Balliol) and tutor of its candidates for the Indian Civil Service, he yet found time and energy for membership of the Oxford Board of Guardians. He frequently lectured on economics and politics to popular audiences in the great industrial towns. Not only an enthusiast but a singularly lovable man, he attracted many friends in the University and amongst artisans and labouring men; and his academic friends, or some of them, were in effect his disciples. "He always believed in the possibility of a democratic society whose members should be intellectual, refined, nay spiritual."[1] Never a physically strong man, Toynbee wore himself out and died in his thirty-first year.

"At the suggestion of the Revd. S. A. Barnett...who had many friends amongst us, a little university colony had already been formed in Whitechapel to *do* something for the poor, and when we came to discuss the nature of our memorial to Arnold Toynbee it was natural with many of us to urge that a University Settlement in East London would be the most fitting monument to his memory."[2] Effect was given to the proposal in 1884 by the establishment of the Universities Settlements Association and the erection of Toynbee Hall adjacent to St Jude's Church, Mr Barnett being the first Warden of the Hall. The word "Settlement" is significant; the university men who participated either gave their whole time to the work or, being professionally engaged in London, devoted their leisure hours to it. But in either case, they made their home in Toynbee Hall. They had two objects: first, the education, recreation and enjoyment of their poorer neighbours; second, an inquiry into the conditions of those neighbours' lives with

[1] F. C. Montague, *Arnold Toynbee* (Johns Hopkins University Studies, Baltimore, 1889). The foregoing details are drawn from Professor Montague's monograph.

[2] P. L. Gell in an "Appendix" to Professor Montague's monograph. Messrs Gell and Montague were Balliol contemporaries of Toynbee; the former was chairman of the Toynbee Hall Council.

the view of ultimately bettering them. They taught, conducted clubs and societies, held themselves ready to advise when their advice was sought. Oxford House, Bethnal Green, was opened in 1884 also, with similar objects but placing religious work in the forefront. Toynbee Hall set itself particularly to foster culture. Remembering the obstacles in the way of the labouring man, it is not strange that "Toynbee" in its early days exercised a greater influence outside than within its immediate neighbourhood; it was especially influential amongst the teachers of London elementary schools through whom its residents reached, although indirectly, a greater number of the comparatively poor than inhabited Whitechapel. The idea of "settlement" once realized, other embodiments of it followed; Canning Town Women's Settlement (1892), Browning Settlement (1895), Mansfield House, Passmore Edwards Settlement and others, although not "university" settlements, conducted forms of adult education as part of their work for their neighbours.

Earlier than the settlements is the London College for Working Women, Fitzroy Street, W., which was founded in 1874 to offer an education of a higher standard than that of the elementary school; its classes were held in the evening at low fees. The social relations of the students and their mostly unpaid teachers, and other features of their organization are reminiscent of the Working Men's College. It was at this time (1871–84) that Ruskin continued and elaborated the social and economic teaching of *Time and Tide* in the series of "letters to working men" to which he gave the title *Fors Clavigera*. Ruskin College, Oxford, established in 1896, marks a return to an earlier stage in the history of adult education in that it was conducted not only for "Labour", but by "Labour"; the college was a novelty in being residential and frankly propagandist. But the great days of adult education belong to the twentieth century.

CHAPTER XIII

The Compromise of 1870 and the Cross Commission

The Reform Act of 1867 added a million voters to the Parliamentary Register, thus doubling the total; and, in anticipation of the assumption of full citizenship by an unknown number of illiterates, the provision of schooling became a matter of urgency. As Robert Lowe had said, "we must educate our masters". Few understood the magnitude of that undertaking when regarded as an adequate supply of schools; accurate statistics which might make it evident were wanting. Speaking in the House of Commons in July, 1867, in support of an Education of the Poor Bill, H. A. Bruce, a former Vice-President of the Council, put the number of children who were not attending school at 1,050,000. In the autumn of 1869 the number, as estimated by partisan speakers, varied between "nearly two millions" and 333,033; one well-informed friend of denominational schools put it at a quarter of a million.[1] The truth was that nobody knew. All agreed that there was a shortage of school places and that the shortage was not trifling; subsequent inquiry by the School Boards proved that it was considerable.

Yet it would be unfair to our people to suppose that at this time they were indifferent to the things of the mind or depended in that respect upon the lead of politicians. Publishers found that the removal of "the taxes upon knowledge" (the stamp and paper duties) opened to themselves a lucrative market. A paper read at the Cambridge meeting of the British Association (1862) declared that Mr John Cassell issued between 25,000,000 and 30,000,000 copies of penny publications annually; perhaps the most noteworthy of these was the *Popular Educator*, a weekly illustrated manual of instruction which for many years was the text-book for myriads of "self-taught" students in every branch of knowledge. Edward Baines, addressing the National Education Union at Leeds in December, 1869, reminded his hearers that in 1864 he told the House of Commons that the circulation of newspapers in the United Kingdom had advanced from 38,648,314 sheets per annum in 1831 to 546,059,400 thirty years later. Within the

[1] The Census of 1871 gave the total population of England and Wales as 22,712,266.

same period the number of periodicals (literary, scientific, and religious) published weekly and monthly had increased from 400,000 to 6,004,950. Within the generation lying between the two dates the population of the United Kingdom had only increased by 20 per cent.

The first general Parliamentary election under the new Act took place in November, 1868, and the Liberals were returned with a majority of 112. Disraeli resigned office early in December and before the end of the year was succeeded by Gladstone, who then became Prime Minister for the first time. Ireland and the Irish Church formed the immediate concern of the new Government; but certain Radicals, few in number yet very resolute in pursuing their object, recognised the possibility, afforded by a Liberal majority, of displacing the "Voluntary System" by their own scheme of national education. Yet there were doubts as to the feasibility of this substitution at the moment. The Conservative Government had appointed in 1868 a Royal Commission on Irish primary education which had not yet reported; but it was believed that the majority of its members would recommend the continuance of the denominational system of schools. It was common knowledge that Gladstone's Government intended to introduce an Education Bill at an early date; and it was thought that some members of the Cabinet were not unfriendly to denominational schools and the voluntary system of maintaining them. Moreover, in January, 1868, Sir James Kay-Shuttleworth had published a *Memorandum on Popular Education* in which he proposed the maintenance and extension, by means of payment from local rates, of the denominational schools; and this suggestion for the firm establishment of the voluntary system had evoked approval from members of both Parliamentary parties. On the Liberal side these had included Gladstone and William Edward Forster; Gladstone was now Prime Minister, and Forster was Vice-President of the Council whose business it would be to introduce and take charge of a Government Education Bill.

The Radicals determined to force the hand of the Government by arousing popular enthusiasm in favour of their own programme. So closely was the group connected with one particular town that it may be designated the Birmingham group. Its most active member was George Dixon, M.P. for the borough; others taking a prominent part were John Sandford, Archdeacon of Coventry, George Dawson, who characterized himself as "a Latitudinarian avowedly", Joseph Chamberlain, eminent in Birmingham's public life, and Robert William Dale, a Congregationalist minister distinguished as a theologian. When the movement began to get active, it received the powerful support of Henry Fawcett, Liberal M.P. for Brighton.

So early as February, 1869, the group had formed a provisional committee and drafted the plan of a National Education League; by the following September it was strong enough to summon a general meeting of members to be held in Birmingham on the 12th and 13th of October. Before this meeting took place nearly 2500 "influential persons" had become members of the League, including forty members of Parliament and between 300 and 400 ministers of religion. There were branches in London and seventeen other towns, not counting the Birmingham headquarters. Twenty members, chiefly Birmingham men, had between them promised donations amounting to £14,410. Evidently a formidable engine of propaganda had been created at short notice.

The object of the League was, in the words of its own circular, "the establishment of a system which shall secure the education of every child in England and Wales". Whatever the differences of opinion which existed amongst its members, and the differences were very important, all were unanimous in their desire to set every child to school; and they were equally agreed in the conviction that such a system could not be reached through a voluntary scheme. To achieve this object local authorities must be "compelled" to ensure sufficient school accommodation within their areas; the schools thus rendered necessary must be founded and maintained by local rates and by Government grants, managed by the local authorities (that is, town councils or boards of guardians), and inspected by government officers. The instruction must be "unsectarian, free", compulsory and, of course, universal—in short, the Radical programme inherited from the France of the Revolution. The policy of the League was declared to be "to collect and disseminate information and prepare the way for such legislation as will carry out the objects of the League".

The great two-days' meeting arranged for October was duly held. Apart from general discussion of the League's aims, the chief business was the debating of the motion, "That a Bill embodying the principles of the League be prepared for introduction into Parliament early next session". This was proposed by Professor Fawcett, seconded by Professor Thorold Rogers and carried. But the speeches of these two supporters brought out the fact that the word "unsectarian" meant different things to different speakers and there was a suspicion that the leading spirits were either unaware of its ambiguity or were not quite candid in expounding its meaning. Archdeacon Sandford did not like the word, but preferred to say "undenominational". Professor Fawcett explained that unsectarian did not mean secular; that it left managers free to follow the British and Foreign School Society's plan of Bible-reading without note or comment. The less politic George Dawson bluntly declared that they meant instruction to be "purely secular. Disguise it as you may, to that complexion you must come at last". A. J. Mundella, M.P. for Sheffield and a future Vice-President of the Committee of Council, contributed the following novelty to this discussion: "The word 'secular' is scandalously abused. All truth is holy. The order, system and cleanliness of a school are the most religious influences, I think, that can be brought to bear." Professor Rogers would be satisfied by describing the teaching as "secular, unsectarian, undenominational", as though these words had one and the same meaning. Jesse Collings, the honorary secretary of the League, held that that association had "nothing to say about the Bible", while another member, the Rev. C. Clarke, thought "it would be improper and unbecoming for us of the League to say that the Bible should not be used". Finally, George Dixon, the chairman, ruled that "unsectarian" meant the exclusion of "all dogmatic, theological teaching, creeds and catechisms" but that the exclusion of Bible-reading "without note or comment" was "not necessarily" intended. At the second session Dixon read a paper, "On a system of national schools based on local rates and Government grants", which marks him as the real originator of the Elementary Education Act of 1870; here he not only outlined the Bill but sketched almost uncannily the early history of the school boards after the Bill became an Act.

The League's conference closed with a public meeting held in the evening at the Birmingham Town Hall, the Mayor presiding and the floor and great gallery being occupied chiefly by working men. The purpose of the League to make the Government "go faster" was frankly stated to this audience. Referring to the Vice-President, Dixon said: "What we are going to do is this: by means of this League and its branches, we are going to rouse the people—in whom now, happily, is placed political power—in order that we may say to Mr Forster, 'Be our leader and give us what we want; we'll support you'. But if Mr Forster should hestitate, if he will not transfer the education of this country from the voluntary and denominational basis, upon which it now rests, to the basis of the taxation and self-governing energy of this country, then, much as we respect Mr Forster, much as we esteem his strength of character, his excellent will and his great skill, it will be our duty to say, even to Mr Forster, our hitherto leader, that we can follow him no longer. We shall say, 'We have taken upon ourselves the performance of a duty than which none can be higher—the duty of seeing to the education of every child in this country; and that duty we shall perform—with you as our leader, if you will, but if not, in spite of you". Fawcett followed this intimation to the Member for Bradford by a hint to his chief, the Prime Minister. "It is our privilege at the present time to be governed by a Prime Minister who is ever ready to be instructed by the intelligently expressed public opinion of this country, and if Mr Gladstone has not made up his mind on the educational question yet, nothing is so likely to give clearness and distinctiveness of view and firmness of resolution, as the expression of opinion of such an audience as this, in favour of unsectarian, compulsory national education."

These were the aims of the Birmingham group; its fears were voiced by Mr W. R. Cremer who claimed to represent "the working class". "I fear Mr Forster is likely to bring in next session a Bill based upon the denominational system. I hope therefore that the Executive Committee will as speedily as possible frame a Bill embodying the principles of the League, and get some staunch friend of education, such as Professor Fawcett, Mr Mundella or Mr Dixon, to introduce it into the House of Commons; because its being in their hands will be the best guarantee that there will be no unholy compromise upon this question."

The League professed the modest desire to supplement the existing denominational voluntary system, which it was generally agreed had not provided a sufficiency of schools nor an efficient instruction. But the speeches at the Birmingham meeting clearly foreshadowed much more than supplementing what already existed, and the friends of denominational education were quickly on the defensive. After consultation a number of these determined to form a National Education Union and on October 1st, 1869, their secretary issued an invitation to a congress to be held at the beginning of November in the Manchester

Town Hall. The invitation met with a very favourable response and the congress was presided over by the Earl of Harrowby. The Union secured a large number of adherents including two former Vice-Presidents of the Council, and a number of peers, bishops, members of Parliament and clergy and laity of all denominations. The object of this National Education Union was announced to be the securing of "the primary education of every child by judiciously supplementing the present denominational system of national education". But when the measures proposed to attain that end are scrutinized the "supplementing" is seen to be confined to two forms of compulsion; how more schools were to be instituted does not appear. The religious instruction was to remain denominational, safeguarded by a conscience clause; but at the congress itself the Rev. G. W. Olver, of the Wesleyan Training College, Westminster, made a vigorous protest against "numbers of clergy in the Established Church, who, notwithstanding the withdrawal of that condition of membership in the National Society, do most intolerantly persist in compelling attendance at the Sabbath-school as a condition of instruction in the week-day school". School fees were to be paid by the parents as heretofore; the only charge on the local rates for such fees was to be in respect of pauper and vagrant children, charges which, by the Industrial Schools Act (1866) and Denison's Act of 1862, would be incurred by localities electing to compel such children to attend school. The Union would make these two permissive Acts compulsory upon all localities; further it would require a certificate of school attendance from all children under thirteen who were seeking paid employment. To that extent the Union was for compulsion. Partly on educational grounds, but mainly to meet the demands of parents for children's wages and of employers for child labour, the Union supported the half-time system by which half the time of the child was spent in school, half in paid employment. Under the Factory Acts the system was familiar in the industrial areas; the Union proposed an equivalent system for the agricultural districts.

A conference between the Union and the League was held in Newcastle at the end of November, but it only served to make evident the distinct cleavage in the public mind on the fundamental question. In animadverting on the League's proposals, members of the Union more than once expressed distrust of town councils and boards of guardians as education authorities; they would be too ready "to keep down the rates" at the expense of their schools. Edward Baines, of Leeds, the chairman of a Union meeting held at Leeds on December 8th, announced that the Government was pledged to introduce a measure for the good education of the whole people during the next session and the following resolution was passed: "That legislative measures ought forthwith to be taken for the comprehensive extension of the present system with such additions as may be needed to complete the education of the poorer classes".

Like their rivals of the League, the Union pursued an active propaganda by public meetings and leaflets. One of the latter thus set forth what had been accomplished by the denominational system aided by government grant but without calling upon local rates. In Great Britain it possessed nearly 15,000 inspected schools, employing 13,697 certificated teachers, 1241 assistant teachers and 13,668 pupil teachers. In 1868, 1,423,759 children had been examined in day schools, 61,292 scholars in evening schools. The annual cost of the schools was £1,552,542, undertaken by the Government to the extent of £484,000, voluntary subscribers contributing £443,000 and the parents in school fees £508,772; endowments and other sources yielded £110,000. (No doubt the government grants and subscriptions as well as the last item are given in round numbers.) But the noticeable thing is that school fees are the largest item of the total expenditure, a fact which the Union was not slow to use as an argument against free schools maintained by the rates.

The promised Government Bill was introduced in the Commons on February 17th, 1870, by the Vice-President of the Council. Mr Forster explained that the Bill sought to ensure that efficient schools should exist everywhere throughout England and Wales, and that the local authorities in charge of education should have power to compel the attendance of children when compulsion seemed to them to be necessary. These local authorities, the "school boards", would be elected in boroughs by the town councils and outside the boroughs by the vestries. The Government deemed it obligatory upon them to maintain the voluntary system of denominational schools, since public funds were not equal to the strain involved in providing all the school accommodation required; moreover it would be inexpedient to lodge in the central Government the enormous power which would reside in a State system of schools. But steps would be taken to secure the efficiency of the secular instruction, inspection would be undenominational and religious liberty would be secured by a conscience clause.

The fears of the extremists in the National Education League were thus justified, and George Dixon, their leader, challenged the Government Bill by moving at the outset of the second reading debate an amendment which, if it gained the assent of the House, would mean the rejection of the measure. The Radicals opposed the policy of a Liberal Cabinet and of a Radical Vice-President. "The effect of clause 7", said Dixon, "would be materially to strengthen denominationalism, and he thought that the object ought rather to have been to check its growth and weaken its influence so that it might ultimately vanish from the land." The existing conscience clause was ineffective for its purpose; parents were afraid to claim its protection. The only practicable form was a time-table conscience clause.[1] The amendment was warmly debated for three nights in March, but in the end it was withdrawn on the assurance of the Prime Minister that a time-table conscience clause would be favourably considered. It was during this debate that Forster committed himself to the statement that the charge thrown by the Bill upon the rates would "very rarely" exceed three-pence in the pound. This honest but entirely erroneous belief is an excellent illustration of the ignorance of the conditions of the problem then prevalent.

From this point the direction of the Birmingham League's policy passed to the small but resolute group of which Dixon and Fawcett were the protagonists. Their principle was compulsory attendance at State schools wherein instruction should be either purely secular or, if religious teaching were included, that teaching must be eviscerated of every trace of institutional religion. Their opponents of the Manchester Union declared that the real motive of the League was the elimination of religious education from the schools, and no doubt that was the solution of the "religious difficulty" which the League's moving spirits preferred. The interval between the second reading in mid-March and the Committee stage of June–July was filled by the

---

[1] That is, a clause fixing the time of religious instruction so that it immediately precedes, or succeeds, the secular instruction at a given session of the school. Such an arrangement had since 1866 been the rule in the Irish elementary schools under the Commissioners of National Education. By adhering to it, withdrawals on conscientious grounds would not disorganize the secular teaching.

propaganda of League and Union, so that it was said that the country was stirred to "its very depths", and the issue was always the same, whether raised in the Press, in pamphlets or in the great and excited public meetings held throughout the country. Should the schools be secular or, if not, should religious teaching be denominational or the reverse? The League held an especially strong meeting in St James's Hall, London, and the Union replied by holding soon after in the same building a meeting presided over by the philanthropic Earl of Shaftesbury and attended by "a vast assemblage of all ranks of society", of "different creeds and denominations" but united as one man to resist the attack upon denominational teaching and the voluntary system which supported it.

A number of Liberal members of Parliament called a conference of London schoolmasters, "Church", "British" and Wesleyan, in order to learn their opinions on the burning question. The masters agreed unanimously that the existing plan of Bible-teaching did not prevent parents sending their children to school. They were almost unanimous in repudiating the adoption of a time-table conscience clause; they were entirely unanimous in the conviction that a conscience clause was workable. It is instructive to note that these men, looking at the matter as it affected the organization of their daily work, cheered the statement that the religious difficulty was a "platform difficulty"; and Mr T. E. Heller, of the Lambeth Boys' School, gave some figures which illustrate parental opinion and practice. Mr Heller's school educated 700 boys; of these 34 per cent. belonged to no religious communion or were in bodies outside the Church of England, 25 per cent. were Wesleyans, 6 per cent. were Roman Catholics. The adherents of the Church of England amounted only to 35 per cent., and this in a Church of England school under the shadow of Lambeth Palace.[1] At an earlier meeting of "teachers of all denominations" it was agreed that while denominational teaching should be continued in the existing voluntary schools, in all schools supported by local rates catechisms or formularies should not be used.

The agitation started by the League and chiefly maintained by that body had its desired effect upon the Government. In introducing the

[1] *Report of a large conference of schoolmasters on the Education Bill* (pp. 78–9), published by the National Education Union with the Report of the meeting at St James's Hall, April 9th, 1870.

Committee stage (June 16th) Gladstone asserted that "every day which has passed has multiplied the expression of the opinion and the feeling of the country" while in Parliament the notice paper was loaded with amendments, numbering between two and three hundred, all directed to the questions of religious teaching in the schools. He announced that the Cabinet had agreed upon certain changes in the Bill. The school boards would be elected by ballot of the ratepayers, "the representatives of the parents of the children who were to receive instruction at their hands", and not by town councils or vestries. The time-table conscience clause would be adopted, and the amendment suggested by Mr Cowper-Temple, that "no catechism or religious formulary which is distinctive of any particular denomination shall be taught", would stand part of the Bill. Disraeli, leading the Opposition, declared that these alterations virtually constituted a new Bill. Yet the Radical dissentients were not satisfied, since the Cabinet persisted in its support of the denominational schools. While these were to receive no share of the rates which were to finance the board schools, they were to be qualified to receive an augmented government grant exceeding the existing subsidy by 50 per cent. as a maximum.

The Committee stage lasted from June 16th to July 21st and the Bill was read a third time in the Commons on July 22nd. The proceedings in the Lords were completed between July 22nd and August 2nd; another week was spent in discussing amendments and finally the royal assent to "33 & 34 Victoria, c. 75" was given on August 9th. On that same day Great Britain joined France and Germany (at war with each other since the middle of the preceding month) in assuring the neutrality of Belgium and of Luxembourg by a treaty which held till 1914; the Elementary Education Act of 1870 had a shorter life.

By that Act the Radical formula, "education, universal, gratuitous, compulsory", was only partially realized. It made schooling universal only in the sense that it was designed to provide sufficient schools everywhere within reach of all children between the ages of five and thirteen. If the Education Department was satisfied that a shortage of schools existed in a given locality, it was empowered to cause a school board to be elected there, whose function it would be to supplement the existing supply and, if necessary, erect new schools. The Act contemplated the possibility of new schools being started which would be outside the local school board's control; in other words the leading principle of the Birmingham League was repudiated and the voluntary system was maintained. On the other hand, no rate aid was to be extended to the denominational schools, notwithstanding the policy advocated by the Manchester Union. The education given in the schools was gratuitous only for the children of necessitous parents; all other children were to be charged a fee payable weekly. Instruction in public elementary schools, both "board" and "voluntary", was made universally gratuitous by an Act of 1891.

Again, schooling was to be compulsory only in places whose school boards ruled by their by-laws that it should be so. The boards had power to compel attendance by children of the statutory school-age; but they were not bound to use the power. A child might be excused attendance if it was "under efficient instruction in some other manner", the efficiency or otherwise being judged by the particular magistrates, or magistrate, before whom an alleged defaulter was charged. Where there was no school board there could be no compulsion by the Act of 1870; compulsion on the great scale was enacted by two measures dated 1876 and 1880. By the first of these (Sandon's Act) parents were compelled to cause their children to receive efficient instruction; penalties were imposed upon the parents of children under ten who worked for wages and upon the parents whose children, of ten to thirteen, did not hold a certificate of proficiency in the "three R's" or a certificate of due attendance at a certified efficient school. Where there was no school board, a School Attendance Committee was to be appointed to carry out the provisions of this Act. Mundella's Act (1880) made compulsory attendance universal.

The disappointment with the Government policy which was felt by their Radical supporters was expressed by Professor Fawcett while the Bill was in Committee. On July 11th he proposed that "school attendance" should mean attendance for at least 300, not 200, times in each year, to which Forster objected that that was a matter for the school board's by-laws. Whereupon Fawcett said he should say nothing further on the subject "as it appeared that there was to be permissive compulsion, permissive school aid and permissive time". He did not speak again upon the Bill.

The Act of 1870 did not create a system of national education, since it was confined to the elementary instruction of children below thirteen years of age. But it defined in loose terms the public elementary school as one in which "the *principal* part" of its teaching is elementary and whose "*ordinary*" fee does not exceed ninepence per week; there were possibilities implied in this language of which the great school boards took advantage. A dual system of administration was created, that of the school boards elected by the ratepayers, and the "voluntary system" partially maintained by private subscription. Board schools and voluntary schools both participated in government grants, both charged school fees; but only the board schools could draw upon the rates, and were therefore potentially the richer. Ostensibly the school boards were created to supplement the provision made, or yet to be made, by the voluntary system, and it was supposed that a comparatively small sum would suffice for the purpose. "Practically the Bill provides for a rate not exceeding threepence in the pound in order to the carrying out of the requirements of the Act" said Forster on the second reading. "That amount of rate would very rarely be exceeded; indeed in my opinion a smaller levy would be quite sufficient to work the Act". Threepence in the pound on the rateable value of England and Wales at that date was estimated to yield £1,250,000 and the critics of the Bill declared that the sum was insufficient. They were right; yet neither they nor Forster, still less, could foresee the action of wealthy school boards confronted by a shortage not only of elementary but of higher schools also. The rate could not be put at Forster's level; most boroughs and parishes greatly exceeded it. In West Ham at one time it stood at thirty pence.

The question which so gravely divided opinion was parried by a compromise; while recognizing the very general desire for an education which could be described as religious, Parliament carefully dissociated itself from the forms of religious instruction which might be given in the schools. By Section 7 (3) the Education Department was no longer to inspect such instruction; in the light of the Department's previous history the abrogation of this duty was a revolutionary step. From being tolerant in matters religious, the State had become neutral. But with one exception. Referring in Committee to the Cowper-Temple clause[1] Disraeli declared: "You will not intrust the priest or the presbyter with the privilege of expounding the Holy Scriptures to the

---

[1] Section 14 (2). "No religious catechism or religious formulary which is distinctive of any particular denomination shall be taught in the School", that is, the board school, the rate-supported school, to which the clause alone had reference.

scholars; but for that purpose you are inventing and establishing a new sacerdotal class. The schoolmaster who will exercise these functions and who will occupy this position will be a member of a class which will in the future exercise an extraordinary influence upon the history of England and upon the conduct of Englishmen". He might have added that the clause fathered by the member for South Hants established and endowed, if it did not create, a religious sect whose standard was the English Authorized Version and whose principle of interpretation must in practice be that any explanation was valid so long as it was not contained in a creed, catechism or other institutional formulary.

Yet Section 7 of the Act made it imperative upon all schools, "board" or "voluntary", in receipt of public funds to adopt "the time-table conscience clause" device. The inevitable consequence was that religious instruction which had at one time constituted the pivot of the teaching, became a mere adjunct thereto, which might be taken or left. The idea of a curriculum which should form an organic whole was thus destroyed, and education in the popular schools became destitute of a master purpose. It was a triumph of the Radicalism of 1793, although the victors did not appreciate the victory.

Compromise though it was, the Act placed elementary instruction amongst the public services from which all classes benefit, and removed it from the category of charities whose recipients were limited to "the labouring poor". Hitherto popular education had suffered by being framed by one social class for the service of another. The representative system in local school boards greatly altered this by making all rate-payers, who were the electors, equal. Women equally with men had the school board vote and were eligible for membership of the boards. Triennial elections and the controversies which they periodically aroused kept education before the country, though not always in the best of ways. The school boards made it possible to gauge educational shortage and the gauging induced some to supply deficiencies in secondary education. An important but less immediately obvious consequence of the institution of school boards was a salutary revolution as to what was desirable in the planning and building of schools. Inheriting a tradition centuries old, schools hitherto were simply big rooms usually ill adapted to their special purpose and not seldom very defective in point of ventilation, lighting and warming. In the vast majority of cases board schools were entirely new buildings erected under rules formed by the Education Department which were particularly directed to securing the health and convenience of children and of teachers. Thus a standard was created and lodged in the public mind.

School boards and voluntary school managers, locally, and the Education Department, centrally, between them made a rough approximation to a State system of elementary education. The Act came into force at once; the election of the first school board for London was held on November 29th, 1870.

It is worth noting that by Section 16 of the Act a school board in default is to be declared so by the Education Department; and "if any dispute arises as to whether the school board have done or permitted any act in contravention of or have failed to comply with the said regulations, the matter shall be referred to the Education Department, whose decision thereon shall be final". The identification of prosecutor and judge lodged in a government office and the consequent repudiation of the judiciary and the common law is an instance of that imposition of *droit administratif* (there is no English for it!) which a zealous Civil Service has been industriously engaged in framing during the past half century. Its practice is a reversion to seventeenth-century methods —inimical to the liberty of the subject but condoned by a heedless or indifferent House of Commons. Yet it is in complete harmony with the bureaucratic tradition that has marked the history of the State's intervention in English education from the beginning in 1839.

The two-fold administration authorized by the Act represented two conflicting ideals whose respective exponents remained as irreconcilable as before. On the one hand were those who regarded religion as a vital element in all education, on the other were the Radicals who, distinguishing between public and individual education, held that religion was more or less a matter of indifference in the former, however important it might be for the latter. From the beginning the two parties took different views of their respective functions. The voluntaryists appealed to the intentions of those who framed the Act, that it was to supplement not to suppress the existing school provision and, more particularly, to reach "that large class of outcast children whom the voluntary schools had not reached". The great school boards held themselves bound by the language of the Act. Section 18 said that, "The School Board shall maintain and keep efficient every school provided by such Board, and shall from time to time provide such additional school accommodation as is in their opinion necessary in order to supply a sufficient amount of public school accommodation for their district". The boards interpreted this to mean that the obligation of providing schools in sufficient numbers rested primarily with themselves and that they could not delegate that responsibility to others. This was the interpretation laid down by the law officers of the Crown and acted upon by the Education Department. The other side urged that this meant the subversion and absorption of the voluntary system as evidenced by the erection of schools which, while not needed to make supply good, were competing against established voluntary schools. In one notorious case the Swansea school board was permitted by the Education Department to veto the admission to the annual grant list of a newly erected Roman Catholic school at Dan-y-Craig. The Catholic clergy built the school in order to provide an education for Catholic children on denominational lines such as the schools of the neighbourhood did not offer. When application was made that it should be put on the roll of schools eligible to receive grants, the Education Department referred the application to the school board, who vetoed it, on the ground that the schools already on the roll provided the number of school seats required within the district and that the new school was therefore unnecessary.

The Birmingham "League", more than ever actuated by the Radical principle, and the Manchester "Union", the champion of the voluntary system and denominational schools, kept the country in a ferment by their meetings and the circulation of letters and leaflets in large numbers. Both encouraged the presentation of petitions to Parliament. Within two years of the passing of the Act the League had sent up 625 such petitions containing 74,199 signatures, and the Union had forwarded 1969 petitions from 215,571 petitioners.

A conference held at Manchester in January, 1872, and attended by 1865 delegates representing Nonconformist churches and institutions, condemned the "settlement" of 1870. A committee appointed by the Wesleyan Conference asked for universal school boards and an undenominational school accessible to every family. In March of the same year George Dixon, though defeated in a Liberal House of Commons by 355 votes to 94, moved a resolution to the effect that the Act of 1870 was unsatisfactory and its working defective and in consequence "provoked religious discord throughout the country" and violated the rights of conscience. The specific grounds of complaint were that the election of school boards, attendance at school and uniformity, or remission, of school fees were not universally obligatory; and school boards were allowed to pay the fees of children taught in denominational schools. Mr Dixon's opponents outside the House retorted that some school boards discarded every vestige of religious instruction, whilst others reduced it to a perfunctory minimum. Messrs Dixon and Dale having stated publicly that the elementary school teachers were opposed to religious instruction in their schools, the conference of the National Union of Elementary Teachers, held at Manchester in December, 1872, repudiated those gentlemen as having no authority to make such statements. In its report for the same year, the National Education Union complained of the injurious competition between board and voluntary schools, the erection of unnecessary board schools, the great cost of board schools and the financial strain thrown upon the rival institutions. Of course, League and Union were making *ex parte* declarations and both were careful not to expose both sides of the shield. The former body dissolved in 1876 and was succeeded by the National Education Association, whose policy was frankly secular.

Notwithstanding the expenditure of great sums voluntarily subscribed for the erection of new schools and the maintenance and improvement of old schools, it became manifest that, under the conditions then operating, the virtual extinction of denominational instruction, if not of religious education itself, in public elementary schools was only a question of time. The contest was too unequal.

The Liberal Government came to an end in February, 1874, Gladstone being succeeded by Disraeli, who made a place in the Cabinet for the Vice-President of the Council, Lord Sandon. Allusion has already been made to the Act called by his name.[1] The Vice-President was a known sympathizer with the voluntary system and in its interest the Act of 1876 abandoned the pound-for-a-pound principle which hitherto had ruled the amount of the annual grant payable to a given school. While the limit of 15s. was increased by half-a-crown, the Act decided that within the limit of 17s. 6d. the grant must not be so reduced as to

---

[1] See p. 357, above. This Act also created day industrial schools to provide industrial training, elementary instruction and one or more meals daily for the children committed to such schools by the magistrates.

equal the income per head derived from other sources, e.g. fees, subscriptions, endowment or, in the case of board schools, rates. This met the case of the voluntary school with an income apart from grants of less than 17s. 6d. per head. But the Act forged a two-edged blade. If the grant per head "earned" under the Code by examination, etc., by a given school exceeded 17s. 6d., while income otherwise derived did not exceed 17s. 6d., such excess of earned grant was not payable; if income could be shown equal to the sum earned above 17s. 6d., then the excess would be paid. Obviously the provision told in favour of the richer school. The *Annual Report* of the National Society for 1875 complained of "pressure on voluntary schools", of competition forced upon them by school boards, of falling subscriptions and rising cost of maintenance. Thereafter these complaints were repeated, in terms more or less anxious, in each succeeding *Report*, notwithstanding measures of relief introduced by friendly Governments.

Government grants were first paid to board schools in 1872, when the cost of maintenance per pupil in those schools averaged 28s. 4¼d. per annum and of that sum 7s. 5½d. was covered by the child's fee; the corresponding sums in the voluntary schools were 27s. 5d. and 8s. 9¼d. In 1885 these amounts had become 45s. 4d. and 9s. 4d., 35s. 9½d. and 11s. 2¾d.[1] respectively. In the latter year board schools received a government grant of 17s. 7d. per head, the voluntary schools' grant being 16s. 8¼d. (see below). It will be observed that the voluntary schools found it necessary to charge a fee which exceeded that of the board schools by nearly 15 per cent. Mr Patrick Cumin, Secretary of the Education Department, thus described the position in 1885 to the Cross Commission. "Although voluntary subscriptions have decreased in Church of England schools, the pence [i.e. school fees] and endowments have increased and the grant also has increased. In Wesleyan and British schools there is an increase in the fees and a diminution in subscriptions. In Roman Catholic schools both fees and subscriptions have increased. The school pence in Wesleyan schools are much higher than the average for the whole of the United Kingdom and they are largely self-supporting schools."[2]

What was happening may be inferred from the following details. The returns of the Education Department first classified the voluntary

[1] *Special Reports on Educational Subjects*, 1896–7, pp. 28, 49.
[2] Cross Commission, *Digest of Evidence*, p. 8.

schools according to their religious denomination in 1878; in that year and in 1885 these schools were distributed as follows:[1]

	Church of England	Roman Catholic	Wesleyan	British
1878	10,910	693	572	1436
1885	11,794	850	554	1387

In the seven intervening years Church schools had increased by 9 per cent., Roman Catholic schools by 22·6 per cent., but the others had decreased, the Wesleyans by 3 per cent. and the "British" group (including other undenominational bodies not specified) by 3·4 per cent. Either the Protestant Nonconformist schools were unable to withstand the competition of the board school, or their authorities were satisfied with the form of religious instruction which those schools provided. But the schools which owed allegiance to the historic creeds and formularies were not so satisfied and struggled to maintain their position.

The Cross Commission drew the following contrast between the rivals as it existed in 1885. "The percentage of [board and voluntary school] scholars presented in higher standards was almost identical, but the advantage was on the side of Board schools in the percentage of passes, Board schools having 87·07 per cent. as against 84·14 per cent. in Voluntary schools. Board schools also were receiving a larger average grant per head, earning 17s. 7d. as against 16s. 8¼d. in Voluntary schools. On each child's schooling Board schools spent 9s. 6½d. in excess of the sum paid by Voluntary ones; the amounts being 45s. 4d. and 35s. 9½d. respectively. Finally each separate institution inspected had on an average 195 scholars on the register in Voluntary schools as against 362 in Board schools."[2] The voluntary schools were evidently fighting a losing battle and something must be done if the dual administration of the Act of 1870 was to endure.

One of the last acts of the very short-lived Salisbury Government of 1885–6 was to appoint the *personnel* of a Royal Commission "to inquire into the working of the Elementary Education Acts, England and Wales" of which the chairman was Sir Richard Assheton Cross, Home Secretary and, in the next Conservative Cabinet (August, 1886, to August, 1892), Viscount Cross, Secretary of State for India. All shades of opinion upon the vexed questions involved found repre-

[1] *Special Reports, ut supra*, p. 22.
[2] *Final Report* of the Cross Commission (1888), p. 49.

sentation in the twenty-three members of Parliament, ecclesiastics and ex-officials over whom Lord Cross presided. Two former Vice-Presidents of the Council, the Earl of Harrowby (formerly Viscount Sandon) and Sir F. R. Sandford, were included and a practising school-master, Mr T. E. Heller, Secretary of the National Union of Elementary Teachers, was an active member of the body. The Commission, appointed on January 15th, 1886, reported on June 27th, 1888, and to the end continued to reflect the divided opinion of the public at large. There were two reports, that of the minority carrying eight signatures, and both reports were followed by reservations on the part of some of the signatories.

The circumstances of their appointment being what they were, the Commissioners naturally directed their inquiries to the religious teaching given in the schools. Of such teaching in the voluntary schools they reported that "the general inference we draw from the various sources open to us is that in the class of schools in which religious instruction is obligatory under their trust deeds the religious instruction is quite as good now as it was before the passing of the Education Act of 1870, if not a good deal better; and that it is effective, intelligent and practical".[1] The passage comes from the majority report; their colleagues of the minority were in substantial if not sympathetic agreement. In the board schools the Commissioners found that, where organization and sufficient time were devoted to religious teaching, it was "of a nature to affect the conscience and influence the conduct of the children of whose daily training it forms a part".[2] In many board schools the teachers accompanied systematic Bible-reading with appropriate comments and explanations. The school boards for London, Liverpool, Leeds, Bristol and Sheffield had syllabuses of religious knowledge in which they held annual examinations, the attendance at which was purely voluntary. Of the 2225 school boards, seven in England and fifty in Wales prohibited the teaching of religion in their schools, the opinion of the Welsh boards being that the Sunday schools gave what was required. In "not a few" board schools the religious training was limited to reading the Bible for a few minutes daily or to a very meagre provision for worship.

Some teachers interpreted the Cowper-Temple clause as prohibiting all reference to religion outside the times assigned by the school time-

---

[1] *Final Report*, p. 115.   [2] *Op. cit.* p. 118.

table to religious instruction. One witness held that he was debarred, during the course of "secular" teaching, from any appeal to Christian sanctions, however appropriate at the moment such an appeal might be. Another regarded as illegal the use of the name of God during the "secular" hours, while the belief was abroad that the clause forbade the singing of the National Anthem at those times. Cowper-Temple, who was a subscriber to the funds of the Manchester "Union", could not have anticipated this reading of his intentions. But this instance of its operation in practice must have revealed the danger to religious education which was latent in the clause of his inventing. The majority of the Commission thought that the teachers simply misunderstood;[1] but the misconception persisted long after the school boards had disappeared.

The minority, true to the principles of La Chalotais and to Radical politics, while regarding school-taught religion with coldness, warmly insisted upon the necessity of moral instruction being given in schools, a matter upon which both parties in the Commission agreed. The Code of the Education Department in 1876 laid upon the inspectors the duty of ascertaining "that reasonable care is taken by managers and teachers to bring up the children in habits of punctuality, of good manners and language, of cleanliness and neatness, and also to impress upon the children the importance of cheerful obedience to duty, of consideration and respect for others, of honour and truthfulness in word and act". The injunction was withdrawn in 1882 but was again in the current Code while the Commission was sitting. The minority report shows that the evidence satisfied them that on the whole the moral results of the educational system were satisfactory. The majority held that moral instruction and training formed "an essential condition of the efficiency of public elementary schools"; and recommended "that increased support should be given by the State to the moral element of training in our schools" (p. 214).

The minority noted that nearly five and a quarter million names were said to be on the Sunday school rolls with an average attendance between 66 and 70 per cent. They seemed disposed to regard the fact as a

---

[1] The fourteenth section of the Act "does not exclude from public elementary schools instruction in the religion of nature, that is the existence of God, and of natural morality which, apart from belief in the existence of God, cannot be intelligibly taught". *Final Report*, p. 119.

solution of the religious difficulty; but they record the failure of the Religious Education Society in Birmingham to teach religion in the day schools after school hours through the agency of volunteer teachers as distinct from the professional staff. Yet this of course is precisely the question at issue. School education is one, not two; and its unity is best preserved where the whole process is directed by the same educators. The majority report is clear as to this fundamental rule. "We are also of opinion that it is of the highest importance that the teachers who are charged with the moral training of the scholars should continue to take part in the religious instruction. We should regard any separation of the teacher from the religious teaching of the school as injurious to the morals and secular training of the scholars" (p. 127).

The voluntary schools in the great majority of instances stood for denominational religious teaching and of these schools the majority report noted since 1870 "a vast increase", "maintained at great pecuniary sacrifice", "held in much favour by large masses of the population" (p. 113). The minority report puts the vast increase in figures, the number of school places, or seats, being 1,878,000 in 1870 and 3,438,000 in 1886. Nevertheless the financial straits of these schools had made it expedient to appoint the Commission. Like their rivals, these schools were attempting to attain a standard of efficiency which, under the demands of the Education Department and stimulated by the achievements of the school boards, was continually rising. The attempt required money amongst other things, and its insufficient amount constituted the schools' handicap. The limitation of the government grant to 17s. 6d. per head meant that in a small but efficient school "the results are produced but the payment is not forthcoming" (p. 187). Twelve per cent. of the schools sustained deductions of this kind amounting to 5 per cent. of their grants. And the small voluntary schools were numerous. The Code of 1875 assigned an annual grant of £10 where the population did not exceed 300, of £15 where it did not exceed 200, provided the school was the only local school. There were 6398 parishes in England and Wales with populations not exceeding 300. In 1885 there were 5180 aided schools with an average daily attendance below 60; and of these less than 10 per cent. were board schools (p. 159). The lack of any reserve fund hindered, when it did not prevent, voluntary schools from that enlargement of buildings and increase in staff and apparatus which the times demanded; inability to establish cookery classes is especially instanced.

The majority believed that the voluntary system ought to be maintained and that could only be done by increasing the resources of the denominational schools. Their report recommended in the first place that grants from Government should be not less than 20*s.* per head, of which 10*s.* should be a fixed sum, the remainder a variable sum, not less than 10*s.*, dependent upon "the good character of the school as a whole and on the quality of the acquirements of the great majority of the scholars rather than on the exact number of children who attain the minimum standard of required knowledge" (p. 189)— an implicit condemnation of payment by results as practised under Lowe's Code.

But the majority of the Commission was ready to go much further, to the extent of giving voluntary schools a share of the local rates and, in view of the passage of the Local Government Bill then (March–August, 1888) before Parliament, it approved the absorption of the school boards by the county councils to be. "The time indeed seems to have come for a new departure. The country is now provided with a national system.... The supply of schools is complete; a full staff of teachers has been provided and four and a half millions of children are on the registers of inspected schools. The great majority of these schools, containing sixty-four per cent. of the scholars on the rolls, have been erected and are supported by voluntary effort; the promoters of which are nevertheless rated for the maintenance of the school board system in school board districts....It does not seem either just or expedient to allow the voluntary system to be destroyed by the competition of board schools possessing unlimited resources at their command. We therefore recommend that the local educational authority [the term was at this period indeterminate] be empowered to supplement from local rates the voluntary subscriptions given to the support of every public State-aided elementary school in their district, to an amount equal to these subscriptions, provided it does not exceed the amount of ten shillings for each child in average attendance....The school boards might in time, if not at once, be merged in the local authorities charged with the general civil administration" (p. 195).

The minority of the Commissioners denied the existence of "the intolerable strain" on the voluntary schools and repudiated the remedy proposed by the majority. "So far from the strain on the resources of voluntary subscribers having been increased, the table of subscriptions, fees and grants which we have given for Church Schools shows that the income from voluntary subscriptions is 2*s*. 3*d*. a head, or nearly 25 per cent. less than it was in 1876, when Lord Sandon's Act materially increased the grant and relieved the managers from the obligation in all cases of finding half the income of the school. In the case of other voluntary schools the voluntary subscriptions are lower than in the case of Church of England schools" (p. 368). They objected to any payment of rates to these schools as "unsound in principle, destructive of the settlement of 1870, and certain, if it became law, to embitter educational politics and intensify sectarian rivalries" (p. 246). The plea that voluntary subscribers were also compulsory ratepayers was brushed aside as irrelevant; still, during the discussion of the Act of 1870 the suggestion had been made that ratepayers should have the option of paying their educational rate to the funds of a voluntary school.

Although the Act of 1870 was expressly entitled one for elementary education, it did not define the meaning or scope of the term; and the Commissioners were now in a position to note the consequences of this want of logic. They complained that neither Parliament nor the Courts had given any authoritative explanation of the word "elementary"; its limits in terms of studies were interpreted by the annual Code of the Education Department, and those limits had been extending since 1870, until Latin, modern languages and "advanced science" had become possible studies of the elementary school.

While the Commissioners appreciated and approved the principle that schemes of study might be varied to suit local needs, they regarded certain studies as essential. The "three R's", singing, linear drawing for boys and needlework for girls, were matters of course. English should be so taught as to give an adequate knowledge of the mother tongue; English history should be studied in reading-books and the geography of the British Empire learned in a similar fashion. In the lower "standards" children should have lessons on common objects which would lead to a knowledge of elementary science in the upper standards. This self-contained course may be compared with the more elastic conception stated by the Education Department in its *Instructions* of 1886–7 to the inspectors. "The course suited to an elementary school is practically determined by the limit of 14 years of age; and may properly include whatever subjects can be effectively taught within that limit. It may be hoped that year by year a larger proportion of the children will remain in the elementary schools until the age of 14; and a scholar who has attended regularly and possesses fair ability may reasonably be expected to acquire in that time, not only a good know-ledge of reading, writing and arithmetic, of English and of geography, but also of the rudiments of two higher subjects to furnish a stable foundation for further improvement either by his own exertion, or in a secondary school." Against this vague provision for higher education the Commission recommended the erection of more secondary schools and the establishment of scholarships to them for children from public elementary schools to take effect at the age of eleven.[1] Fourteen was obviously too advanced an age for the transition to be successful in most cases.

The lack of precision in the word "elementary", the great differences between school and school, pupil and pupil in the same school, under a compulsory system had by this time forced upon administrators a lively realization of the fact that English education did not possess a true organization on a national scale. They were trying various experiments in "grading" schools, which, while ignoring the country's secondary schools, that is the endowed grammar schools, were attempts at once to define "elementary" and, under an elementary school Code, to give secondary instruction. The higher elementary school was doing, and not under the most favourable circumstances, the work of the secondary school with a modern course of studies. Incidentally it was underselling the secondary schools, whose fees had been fixed by their schemes under the Endowed Schools Commissioners or the Charity Commission. On the other hand, great school boards such as those of Manchester, Leeds, Bradford and Birmingham were linking elementary and secondary schools by the foundation of scholarships in the local grammar schools.

The "higher elementary" or "higher grade" schools possessed laboratories, apparatus, special provision for drawing; they charged very low fees. The Science and Art Department made these schools financially possible; and directed their studies into one channel. It was estimated at Manchester that a pupil who had passed Standard VII could earn for his school by examination under the Science and Art Department 74s. per annum; from the examinations of the Education

[1] *Final Report*, pp. 170 f.

Department a pupil still in Standard VII could similarly earn 22s. 6d. Most of these schools belonged to one or other of the great school boards; but some were under voluntary management, as had been the case before 1870.

These administrative attempts to improve an imperfect system of public instruction were not approved by the majority of the Commission who had not yet freed themselves from the conception of the elementary school as a more or less charitable benefit favouring "the labouring poor". The extension of studies in these schools brought into them the children of persons "in comfortable circumstances" who were thus relieved of their parental responsibility at the cost of those who paid rates and taxes. The contention of Mr Cumin and his Department that the public elementary school was open to all did not win the assent of these Commissioners nor did they agree that it was the business of the school boards to make good the acknowledged and great insufficiency of secondary schools. With Matthew Arnold, they saw that the type of institution which these higher grade schools were creating was wanting in breadth and was likely to confuse still further the public mind as to what constitutes a liberal education, and so delay a truly national provision of secondary schools.

The passing of the Act of 1870 naturally caused changes to be made in the Education Department's annual "Code", the administrative instrument which gave the measure practical effect. Such changes occurred at once, and soon initiated the policy of enlarging the public school elementary curriculum which gave misgivings to most of the Cross Commissioners. The Code of 1871 laid down a course in the three primary studies which was divided into six stages called "standards", each defining the work of one year's study between the ages of seven and thirteen.[1] To pass the examination in the sixth or highest standard, the pupil was required "to read with fluency and expression, to write a short theme, or letter, or easy paraphrase and to work sums in proportion and vulgar or decimal fractions". Several more advanced studies were enumerated, any two of which might be offered for the individual examination of pupils in the three highest standards. The same Code introduced military drill (squad and company drill) into the schools. The Commission reported in 1888 that the Birmingham school board conducted a system of physical training in its schools and

[1] Compare p. 230 above.

that the London school board had adopted the Swedish system for girls under the supervision of Mme Bergmann Osterberg. Singing became a grant-earning subject in 1872.

A more systematically ordered course appeared with the Code of 1875. In addition to the "three R's", in which all pupils qualified by attendance were examined individually, there were "class subjects" and "specific subjects". The former (grammar, geography, history and, for girls, needlework) were so called because the examination in them was by classes and not by individuals, grants being assessed upon the performance of the group as a whole. Where school authorities put forward a study which could reasonably be regarded as elementary and could be taught through reading-books, the Code of 1880 permitted such a study to rank as a "class subject".[1] The policy of expansion was expressed in the "specific subjects" open to pupils in Standards IV to VI, in which the examination was individual but was not necessarily taken by all the children of a standard; as in other studies, money grants to the school depended upon the "passes". The specific subjects were algebra, Euclid, mensuration, Latin, French, German, mechanics, animal physiology, physical geography, botany, domestic economy. To them were added in next year's Code (1876) "English literature", a title which dignified the memorizing of "lines" with a knowledge of their "allusions". The 1875 Code denounced as educationally worthless merely verbal description in branches of science, in which experiment and illustration were essential.

Further organization of the curriculum marked the Code of 1882. Since children were now remaining longer at school, to the original six standards was added a seventh and the studies were divided into three groups—"obligatory" (or elementary) in which needlework was included with the three primaries, "class subjects" and "specific subjects". To pass Standard VII in obligatory subjects the pupil must "read a passage from Shakespeare or Milton or some other standard author, or from a History of England; write a theme or letter, composition, spelling and handwriting to be considered". Arithmetic included "sums in averages, percentages, discounts and stocks".

---

[1] The time-honoured jibe respecting the Minister of Public Instruction, his watch and the geography lesson going on simultaneously throughout the land, never applied to the Education Department, still less to its successor, the Board of Education.

English and elementary science were made class subjects. If any class subject was studied in a school and submitted for examination, English was compulsory, a fact which the Commission deprecated as there was "a very general objection" amongst their witnesses to technical grammar. By the Code the course in elementary science was to consist of simple lessons "designed to cultivate habits of exact observation, statement and reasoning". Agriculture and two branches of physics were added to the specific subjects, examination in which was now open only to pupils in Standard V and upwards. The Commission reported that geography was being taught with increased skill and by methods which interest as well as inform, but that history had disappeared from all but a few schools.

The friends of the nationalist movement in Wales, which was at this time very active and successful, brought before the Cross Commission a complaint that children whose vernacular was Welsh were taught and examined in English, thus being at a disadvantage compared with children who, for these purposes, used their mother tongue. It was suggested that in Welsh schools the reading-books should be bilingual, that a specially devised English course should be a class subject in those schools, and that Welsh should be placed amongst the specific subjects and with Latin, French and German in the languages which might be taken by candidates for admission into teachers' training colleges. The advocates of these proposals stated somewhat inconsistently that the English learned at school by Welsh children was in a great measure lost soon after leaving school, but that "a considerable proportion of the adults speak English with ease" (*Final Report*, p. 144). As similar "concessions" had been made in the Scotch Code in favour of Gaelic-speaking children, the Commission recommended the adoption of these proposals and they were incorporated in later Codes.

The Cross Commission advised the retention of the seven standards, but, in order to deprive them of a rigid and somewhat cramping influence, it was recommended that teachers should classify the children according to ability and attainment, and not by age nor by compelling a passage through the standards without skipping, as the practice had been hitherto. Drawing should be made compulsory for boys in view of its great value as a technical acquirement, useful in the workshop. But the sister art, music, was valued for its own sake. On the testimony of the inspectors, Drs Hullah and Stainer, it was stated that "very substantial progress" had been made by the schools since 1870. "The development and extension of the tonic sol-fa system of teaching singing formed a distinguishing mark of the same period (1874–82), and the encouragement given to this system by many of the larger school boards formed no inconsiderable factor in the improvement which then took place" (*Final Report*, p. 143).

Both the minority and the majority reports condemned the system of "payment by results" which had been in force since 1862. The minority condemned it unreservedly, their colleagues with some hesitation. "After weighing carefully all the evidence laid before us tending to show the evils which arise from the present method of payment by results, we are convinced that the distribution of the Parliamentary grant cannot be wholly freed from its present dependence on the results of examination without the risk of incurring graver evils than those which it is sought to cure. Nor can we believe that Parliament will long continue to make so large an annual grant[1] as that which now appears in the Education Estimates, without in some way satisfying itself that the quality of the education given justifies the expenditure. Nevertheless, we are unanimously of opinion that the present system of 'payment by results' is carried too far and is too rigidly applied, and that it ought to be modified and relaxed in the interests equally of the scholars, of the teachers and of education itself" (*Final Report*, p. 183).

The modification desired was effected, with other changes advised by the Commission, in the Code of 1890. The capitation grant was made a fixed one, determined by the average number of children in attendance. Examination in the obligatory subjects was confined to sample groups numbering not less than one-third of the school; in 1895 this plan was abandoned and examination was replaced by inspection. Two years later payment for individual passes in specific subjects ceased. The last vestige of the principle of payment by results disappeared in 1900, when the block grant of 22s. or 21s. was substituted for special grants for particular studies; but payments of that kind remained in respect of cookery, laundry, gardening, dairy-work and manual instruction.

These more or less technical arts had been introduced, together with shorthand, navigation and hygiene, into the Codes issued between

[1] £3,474,072 was paid in grants to schools in 1887.

1890 and 1894. Their presence in the elementary school was partly due to the claims of technical instruction which were being urged as a crying need by a numerous section of the public, partly as a counterpoise to an instruction which was thought to bias children in favour of the black-coated occupations. The Education Department endeavoured to keep to the front the disciplinary function of these arts; the inspectors were reminded[1] that manual arts were in the schools, not to prepare children for specific trades, but to train hand and eye and to furnish a skill and a knowledge which could be employed later in a great variety of ways. There was a wider recognition of the wonderful adaptability of the human hand and of the part it had played in the advancement of mankind, and a more general appreciation of the connexion between an alert brain and a skilled hand. In 1893 the Department issued a circular on infant school instruction in which the educational value of clay-modelling, plaiting and other "varied occupations" of a like kind was emphasized. Two years later the Code, alive to the gap of three years in manual instruction existing between the infant school and the use of tools in the school above it, made object lessons and "one suitable (manual) occupation" compulsory in Standards I, II and III. Drawing had been made compulsory for boys in 1890, when the Code also added to the course manual instruction and "suitable physical exercises" (in lieu of military drill).

The classification of subjects as "obligatory", "class" and "specific" gave way in 1900 to a two-fold division, subjects to be taken "as a rule" in all schools, though not necessarily by every child, and subjects one or more of which might be taken if the inspector deemed it desirable. "In 1902 there were 23,295 departments for older children [of seven and upwards]. In practically all of these the following subjects were taught [in addition to arithmetic and writing]: English (including grammar and composition as well as reading), geography, history, 'common things', physical exercises, singing. Drawing was taught in 20,040 departments, algebra in 1355, domestic economy in 1027, French in 719, science in 574, shorthand in 537, mensuration in 395, animal physiology in 320, mechanics in 299. No other 'specific' subject was taught in more than 200 departments; several departments taught more than one subject. Of the subjects earning special grants, cookery was taught in 3776 schools ('departments') and grant earned

[1] See *Revised Instructions to H.M. Inspectors of Schools*, 1897.

in 3693 by 202,534 girls; laundry was taught in 671 departments and grant earned by 28,413 girls; grant for dairy work was earned by 9 girls in one department, gardening grant was earned by 4359 children in 289 schools, manual instruction grant by 100,932 boys in 1749 schools, and household management grant by 14,158 girls in 153 schools.... Within reasonable limits managers and teachers were now free to choose what they should teach and how they should teach it, without regard to the probable effect of their choice upon examination results and the financial stability of the schools."[1]

But to return to the Cross Commission. Technical instruction being a question of the moment, the Commissioners were careful to take evidence on the subject so far as the elementary schools were concerned. Reference to this part of the *Final Report* will be found in Chapter XIV below. Some witnesses thought that the curriculum of these schools was too literary, that the study of science was discouraged and that boys were trained to become clerks, not artisans. The Commission thought it possible to teach elementary school children something of the principles, scientific or artistic, which underlie handwork, and that, by way of object lessons and drawing, they might also learn to apply those principles. But while children under seven received instruction on natural phenomena and on common objects, no science was taught to their elders in the first four standards, and in the standards above these English was a compulsory class subject, geography usually being selected as the second study. The Commission reported on the quasi-technical instruction which some of the school boards were giving. "The curriculum in the ordinary elementary school might well include not only instruction in the elementary principles of science, but also elementary manual instruction in the use of tools; and in higher schools and in evening schools this work might be carried still further" (*Final Report*, p. 142).

The cleavage between majority and minority was marked in their references to the plan by which teachers were brought into their profession. The majority, while aware of the serious faults of the pupil teacher system, recommended that it should be upheld, since there was no "equally trustworthy source" of the supply of teachers; the minority dissented from this judgement and reported that the system was "the weakest part of our educational machinery" (p. 242). But

[1] *Report of the Board of Education for the Year* 1910–11, p. 20.

both sides of the Commission welcomed a fundamental change which had come about in some towns in the relation between the apprentices and the teachers and schools to which they were attached. Under the earlier conditions the apprentice had been, and in many cases still was, too much a teacher and a pupil under difficulties. His (and her) instruction was often insufficient and unsatisfactory in character, and the preparation for the annual examination a mere cram.

The earliest attempt to change this state of things was made somewhat earlier than 1873 by the Convent of Notre-Dame, Mount Pleasant, Liverpool, an establishment which included a women's training college. To this the nuns added a department for boarding girl pupil teachers and gave them their instruction collectively. It was noted that girls so educated took higher places in the Queen's Scholarship examination (the entrance examination to Government-aided training colleges) than did the pupil teachers engaged under the local school board who were instructed by the head teachers (whose apprentices they virtually were) at the schools in which they were serving. Accordingly the Liverpool school board adopted this collective or "centre" organization in 1876. As evidence of the superiority of "centre" teaching over the old individual plan, it was reported to the Commission that during the period 1884–7 the percentage of all candidates from England and Wales who were placed in the first class on the Queen's Scholarship list was 25 (boys) and 28 (girls), while the corresponding figures for Liverpool school board candidates was 58 and 73. By that time the collective or "centre" system had also been adopted by the school boards for London, Birmingham and Bradford as well as by some voluntary organizations connected with the Church of England. The London school board's experiments of a similar kind in 1874–5 had been stopped by the Education Department on the ground that the terms of the then current Code and of the apprentice's indenture required individual tuition from the pupil teacher's head master or mistress.[1]

The intended sequel to apprenticeship was a course of education and professional preparation, lasting two years, in a residential training college where fees were low, the cost being very largely met by government grants (the so-called Queen's Scholarships) and to a very small and diminishing extent by the subscriptions of the colleges' supporters. Yet of the 42,212 certificated teachers (16,805 men, 25,407

[1] See *Final Report*, pp. 87 ff. and 268 ff.

women) then employed, nearly half of the number were untrained, that is, had not followed the training college course, but had become certificated by examination. Thirty-five per cent. of the entire certificated body consisted of similarly untrained women.[1] "In the 43 colleges there were only 96 vacant places altogether, so nearly was their whole capacity utilized; but had all candidates who passed the entrance examination obtained admission, the colleges would have been filled twice over.... For the 1682 vacancies there were in July, 1886, 5111 candidates, of whom 3379 passed high enough to be eligible for admission. Of these many did not desire to enter college, but we have no means of ascertaining the exact number" (p. 93). There were more reasons than one explaining this absence of professional preparation in the case of so large a proportion of teachers who nevertheless held the professional certificate. But certainly one reason was the existence of the voluntary system, under which all the training colleges were managed and administered. As the figures just quoted show, the accommodation which they supplied fell far short of the demand; but the discrepancy was increased by the number of those who, though formally qualified, were debarred from entry by conscientious scruples.

The remedy therefore was not to be found in opening more denominational training institutions; and at this point some undenominational colleges were indicating what might be done. The Yorkshire College, Leeds, was giving academical teaching in evening and Saturday morning classes to acting teachers and ex-pupil-teachers, so preparing them in part for the Certificate Examination of the Education Department. The college thought it would be easy to teach purely professional subjects and to arrange for practice under "a master of method" in adjacent schools. The denominational difficulty was acute in Wales, and the Welsh university colleges urged that Queen's Scholarships should be held within their walls; Cardiff offered to provide the necessary technical instruction, and the school board was ready to afford practice in its schools. The Education Department was of course aware of this attitude on the part of the colleges, and its secretary, Mr Patrick Cumin, put before the Commission a scheme whereby holders of Queen's Scholarships might elect to attend non-residential "existing educational institutions", with which schools for practice would be associated, the Queen's Scholar receiving an annual subsidy

[1] See *Final Report*, p. 81.

of £25 and the "institution" (by which Mr Cumin certainly meant the university colleges) one of £10 in respect of him. In this way the Department hoped to add to training college accommodation at a less proportionate cost to the State,[1] while the denominational bar would be removed.

Majority and minority desired to improve the general education of the teacher and to that end they would extend the course to a third year in the case of picked students. The minority appreciated the opportunity which universities and university colleges might offer, not only to add to the number of students in training but to improve the teacher's education and to give it apart from denominational ties. The majority saw things differently. "While unanimously recommending that the experiment of a system of day training for teachers, and of day training colleges, should be tried on a limited scale, we would strongly express our opinion that the existing system of residential training colleges is the best; and this recommendation is made chiefly with the view of meeting the cases of those teachers for whom for various reasons a residence at a training college cannot at present be provided" (p. 211). They would limit the number of students admitted to such day training colleges and would not allow any of the cost to fall upon local rates. Security must be taken for the moral and religious instruction of those who were trained to be teachers.

The minority considered that the scheme deserved much heartier support than it received at their colleagues' hands, and themselves adumbrated something bigger than the stop-gap contemplated in the majority report; neither could they agree to withhold rate aid. "We are of opinion that it is desirable to give expansion to our present system of training by permitting students to lodge at home or in lodging-houses of approved character and respectability, to utilise the colleges and other places of higher instruction which are willing to aid in the training of teachers, and to encourage the formation of educational faculties in such colleges either in conjunction with or apart from the local school board" (p. 290). "Educational *faculties*" in universities and university colleges implied a study of educational principles and practice such as had not yet been attempted in this country.

Effect was given to the Commission's recommendation by the Code

[1] See *Final Report*, pp. 98 ff.

of 1890 which announced the Government's readiness to recognize and subsidize training departments at universities and university colleges, styling them, not happily, "day training colleges". Their true *differentia* was not that they were non-residential but that they were integral members of a university or university college. They were not all non-residential and none of them was a "college" in the customary sense of the word. The first of these departments, which opened in the early autumn of 1890, were attached for men, to King's College, London, and Owens College, Manchester; for women, to Mason College, Birmingham; for both sexes, to the university colleges of Newcastle, Nottingham and Cardiff. The movement extended to Cambridge in the following year and to Oxford in 1892, by which year the original six had become fourteen and the new method of training teachers for elementary schools had ceased to be experimental. In 1902 nineteen "day training colleges" were educating some 2000 students.

The Cross Commission found that considerable improvement in school attendance had taken place since 1870. In that year there were on the rolls of public elementary schools 1,693,059 children, being 7·66 per cent. of the population; in 1886 these numbers were 4,465,000, or 16·24 per cent. of the population. The average attendance of those on the roll, which in 1870 had been 68·09 per cent., was in the later year 76·27. But the large-scale activities of the school boards had necessitated the practice of grouping children under one teacher in classes inordinately large. "As a matter of fact classes are formed to contain as many as 60 or 80 children, and an assistant, we are told, has been endeavouring single-handed to teach a class of 100" (p. 86). The case was by no means singular. There was too often warrant for Sir F. Sandford's description of schools as "the huge educational factories of modern days". The half-time system, half-school, half-labour, had in the interval proved a failure; most managers and teachers were opposed to it, some thought it unfair that half-timers should be expected to satisfy the same standard of examination as those who spent the whole day in schools. Yet the thesis of its advocates of an earlier time had been that industrial work sharpened the wits and that half-timers would learn more quickly and as much as the full-timers. As an indication that denominational religious teaching might be dispensed with in the schools, the minority called attention to the statement that the Sunday schools of England and Wales had enrolled

5,200,000 pupils, 66 to 70 per cent. of whom attended every Sunday.

There was a movement afoot, almost exclusively political, for the abolition of school fees. According to the report of the Education Department for 1886–7 these amounted in the course of the year to £1,812,916, of which 97·3 per cent. came from the pockets of the parents, the remaining 2·7 per cent. being paid by Boards of Guardians in respect of parents too poor to pay. The Commission was of opinion "that the balance of advantage is greatly in favour of maintaining the present system established by the Act of 1870, whereby the parents who can afford it contribute a substantial proportion of the cost of the education of their children in the form of school fees" (p. 200). The evidence was against the belief that there was any popular demand for abolition; on the other hand the opinions of one witness were instructive, and no doubt brought conviction to some Commissioners. This was Dr Crosskey of the Birmingham school board, an honorary secretary of the Central Nonconformist Committee and an advocate of "universal board schools". His theme was that "no public aid should be given to any school where fees continue to be charged". This of course was a short and certain way to the extinction of the voluntary school; equally of course Dr Crosskey did not point that out. School fees were abolished by Act of Parliament in 1891.

The Commission found that the evening schools were not in a satisfactory condition owing to lack of funds and more especially because their curriculum was unsuited to the times. These schools first came upon the grant list in 1855, and, just as in that year the Committee of Council required them to teach reading, writing and summing, so a generation later in spite of altered circumstances it continued to examine evening school pupils in those three subjects, and to pay grants on their successes. The Newcastle Commission had regarded these schools as furnishing compensation for a too brief schooling which ended at the age of eleven; the Cross Commission, while admitting that this compensating function was still required, looked to its early disappearance, when evening schools would all be, what some were then, continuation schools, preliminary to "institute classes, science and art classes or university extension lectures". They saw another use for them which would never have occurred to the Commissioners of 1858–61. "We attach the highest importance to the development and training of the physical powers of the youth of both sexes and we therefore think that in the re-organization of evening and continuation schools moral and physical training should have as prominent a place as ordinary instruction and intellectual training" (p. 163). One of the witnesses, Dr J. B. Paton of Nottingham, who represented the "Recreative Evening Schools Association", declared that the schools could be made "a most important social civilising influence", and the Commissioners fully agreed as to the wisdom of continuing the wholesome influences of the day school after the pupil had quitted it for good, so keeping him "from the contamination of the streets". The problem of the adolescent, of which the twentieth century has heard so much, was once again emerging; in the eighteenth century it had created the Sunday school, it was now about to establish an entirely new conception of the evening school, as the name of Dr Paton's Association reminds one. It was to be "recreative", "social" and "civilising".

One obstacle seemed to hinder. Should girls attend evening schools or classes? The answer must depend upon local conditions and conventions. "This must however be a question of locality, for there are many places in which respectable girls habitually frequent the streets in the evening for the purposes of exercise and pleasure or for going on errands" (p. 163). Evidently the idea of the "social" evening school as conceived by the Commission was only in the germ.

Yet long before 1888 and the Cross Report and outside the circle of Government and officialdom the education of the adolescent had engaged attention, active sympathy and assistance of a kind which had done much to solve some at least of its difficulties. In London in particular Quintin Hogg (1845–1903)[1] had devoted his life and fortune to the cause. As a young man of nineteen not long down from Eton he had started and supported a ragged school, and in 1871 turned his attention to lads whose circumstances placed them above the social level of the ragged school. He gathered about him a number of such boys in the Youths' Christian Institute near Long Acre; in effect this was a club with educational facilities for working lads between sixteen and twenty-one. Classes giving instruction in trades were opened in the face of a good deal of opposition. Employers were indifferent or sceptical as to the trade value of the classes; the Trade Unions were

[1] Ethel M. Hogg, *Quintin Hogg, a Biography* (1904).

actively hostile. The only subject of the kind eligible to receive Science and Art grants was building construction. Nevertheless, the Institute continued to teach trades. Its success at all points was great and it rapidly outgrew the premises in Endell Street.

In 1881 the Polytechnic, Regent Street, came into the market. Established in 1838 for the advancement of "practical science", it had for nearly half a century been the recognized home of instruction tempered by amusement; then it exhausted its interest, or fashion changed, and it ceased to pay its proprietors. Hogg acquired the building and adapted it to the educational and social purposes of his Institute. It was planned to accommodate 2000 persons; between the opening day in September, 1882, and the close of the winter session in 1883, applicants for membership numbered 6800. The fee for membership was three shillings a quarter or half-a-guinea for the year, and the class fees were equally modest. The member's privileges included the use of the gymnasium, reading rooms, refreshment room, billiard room, library, admission to concerts and other entertainments, reduced class fees and ultimately free legal advice from an experienced lawyer. Members could choose their studies from a lengthy list of subjects, and there was considerable variety in the social and athletic activities open to them; in the last "the Poly" soon made a great reputation for itself. A scheme of technical education classes was drawn up by Mr Robert Mitchell, which was gradually adapted to the requirements of the boys and young men who resorted to them. Indeed, the co-operation of the members in the management and discipline generally of the institution was a part of its educational aim. Women were admissible to the classes, but they also had their own Institute (opened in 1885), in the immediate neighbourhood, presided over by Mrs Hogg. Day schools for boys and girls were opened in 1886; here the pupils received manual instruction in workshop or kitchen, and the teaching included commercial instruction.

For years the founder of the Polytechnic had to meet out of his own pocket annual deficits of £7000 or £8000; and this in spite of grants in respect of examination successes from the Science and Art Department and from the City and Guilds of London Institute "in subjects ranging from the domestic arts to carriage-building, photography and goldsmith's work".[1] Aid was also received from the Commissioners of the

[1] E. M. Hogg, *op. cit.* p. 203.

City Parochial charities and, in the early 'nineties' from the Technical Education Board of the London County Council. In the latter case the help involved some reorganization and changes in the governing body. Quintin Hogg's institution was the accepted model of the Polytechnics which, under the County Council, were distributed over London; there were twelve of these before Hogg's death.

Although the "Regent Street Polytechnic" did not carry over the title which described its predecessor, or parent, in Long Acre, it was nevertheless under the dominating personality of the founder a Christian institute for young men and women. When it came under a more public management the suggestion was made that its Bible classes and religious work in general should cease. But Hogg declared that he would rather forgo the advantage of receiving public money than abandon what had been the mainspring of his devoted life. The religious ἦθος of the place must be maintained and its religious worship and instruction remain accessible to all who desired them; but no public money would be used to maintain them. The virility which marked all Hogg's relations with his "boys", which were unaffectedly intimate, was proof against the mere cant of religion. But it was made plain to all that "the Poly" was based upon religious conviction, while no attempt was made to proselytize. All were welcome; but each was made to realize that when he acquired membership he was entering a Christian society. Amongst the men and women to whom England is in debt for the expression of its educational ideals Quintin Hogg holds a very honoured place.

While Hogg was busy with the Youths' Christian Institute and the embryo "Poly", Walter Besant was "walking about the mean monotony of the East End". The consequence of that dolorous pilgrimage was the writing of *All Sorts and Conditions of Men* and its publication in 1882. The suggestion in that work of a people's house of drama and of music, wherein entertainers and entertained should alike be of "the People", attracted Sir Edmund Hay Currie, a prominent East End public man; he "used the book as a text book" in trying to turn Besant's fantasy into concrete fact. Funds were raised and trustees were appointed, their chairman being Sir Edmund; in 1887 the People's Palace[1] was opened in the Mile End Road. But Besant was not pleased with this

[1] Now the East London College, a school of the University of London.

consequence of his dreaming. "Unfortunately a polytechnic was tacked on to it; the original idea of a place of recreation was mixed up with a place of education." This was at a time when technical education was much discussed and Currie was a keen advocate for technical schools. The customary difficulties in establishing a novel institution were experienced by the trustees, the financial difficulty not being absent. The City Companies were then taking action energetically to initiate and maintain schemes of technical instruction, and the Drapers' Company undertook to support the People's Palace. Besant's regretful comment runs: "They have turned the place into a polytechnic, and nothing else...except for one or two things which they cannot prevent".[1] It was then one of the twelve London polytechnics referred to above.

In 1844 twelve young men, of whom all but one were assistants in the same City business house, formed the Young Men's Christian Association, with the object of promoting "the spiritual welfare of young men engaged in the drapery and other trades by the introduction of religious services among them". They were keenly alive to the danger of isolation in London amidst the hardships and temptations to adopting a low standard, moral and social, which beset most young men engaged as they were. Their first aim was mutual protection of those who could show "decided evidence of conversion"; the second, the increase of the number of "the converted". The leading spirit amongst them was George Williams (1821–1905), through whose apostolic fervour and winning personality the plan took effect in other City houses and thence spread to other parts of the country. The Great Exhibition of 1851 afforded an opportunity of propaganda which was used to the full, with the consequence that similar associations were founded in America and on the Continent. These constituted a world-wide federation which sent great numbers of delegates from a variety of nations and languages to London in celebration of the Association's jubilee in 1894.

The services of "Y.M.C.A." in the field to troops engaged in the South African war (1899–1902) disclosed other channels of usefulness than the purely religious one, and from that time onward the Association employed that wider educational programme which marks its operations to-day and which proved its value in the splendid work of the Association upon all fronts during the Great War. But in the nineteenth century the Association was above all a religious society. By a curious

[1] See Walter Besant, *An Autobiography* (1902), pp. 246 f.

coincidence the original twelve members were equally divided between the Church of England, the Congregationalist, Baptist and Methodist communions. Their worship and Bible study had perforce to be "undenominational", the outward symbol and bond of their union being the reading and study of the Bible. The Earl of Shaftesbury, President of the Association, expressed this at the annual meeting of 1872 when he asserted "the great principle of holding the Word of God to be indispensable as the basis, the middle and the end of all our education". The words were spoken in the early days of the school boards; it is not fanciful to suppose that undenominationalism was the more firmly seated in the board schools and in the public mind through the widespread influence of the Young Men's Christian Association.[1]

Comment has been made *passim* on the fundamental differences in the opinions and advice of the two parties in the Cross Commission. The minority saw possibilities in the school boards which the policy of the majority would hamper or extinguish. No rate aid should be extended to the denominational schools. Parliament had placed upon the school boards alone the responsibility of making good the provision of public instruction. Those bodies were therefore merely doing their duty in establishing higher grade schools, whose business it would be to prepare for advanced and commercial instruction. The technical schools for which there was a demand ought to be controlled by the school boards since these schools were "the crown and development of elementary education" (p. 245). That is, the boards had a function beyond elementary teaching. Board schools were for all, not for a class or for the adherents of any religious creed. It was incorrect to say that the provisions of the Act of 1870 were meant to secure harmony amongst various Christian bodies; others than Christians had the right of access to board schools and their scruples in religion must be respected.[2] The minority in short stood for the Radical policy as it had been expounded by the National Education League; the uncompromising logic and the stark assertions of their report betray the pen of the man whose name comes first in the list of signatories, the Hon. E. Lyulph Stanley.

[1] See J. E. Hodder Williams, *The Father of the Red Triangle, The Life of Sir George Williams, Founder of the Y.M.C.A.* (1918).

[2] The Minority report occupies pp. 237–393 of the *Final Report*; the main conclusions are given in the first twelve of these pages.

CHAPTER XIV

Disseminating a knowledge of Science

The phrase "the industrial revolution" and the specific year, 1760, have tended to obscure the truth that English industrial history goes back to years long precedent to the accession of George III. Moreover, the interest of a small but educated lay public in the improvement of industry was never absolutely absent since Francis Bacon urged that "the relief of man's estate" was one of the two great objects of research. The spirit animating Bacon's phrase was one of several causes which led in due course to the foundation (1662) of the Royal Society. In 1754 a number of private persons formed the Society of Arts "for the encouragement of arts, manufactures and commerce in Great Britain", a purpose which they endeavoured to fulfil by offering medals and money prizes for useful inventions of all kinds. From 1829 onwards the Society undertook the periodical delivery of lectures and subsequently added the reading of "papers" and discussion thereon. Within a few months of his marriage (February, 1840) Prince Albert was elected a member of the Society and in 1843 he succeeded the Queen's uncle, the Duke of Sussex, as its President. His tenure of the office (1843–61), following "a condition of torpor and ineptitude",[1] was characterized by great advance in the usefulness of the Society, which received a charter of incorporation in 1847. In particular the Society initiated a series of industrial and fine art exhibitions whose success prompted the holding of the great international exhibitions, the first of which were held in London in 1851 and 1862; the part played by the Society in these has already been mentioned.[2]

The Society held an inquiry and issued a report upon industrial instruction in 1853 and in the same year it invited to a conference the authorities of Mechanics' Institutes and of bodies with similar aims. (It will be recalled that at that date these institutions had for the most part passed from the working men with whom they had originated.) From this conference sprang the Society's system of examinations. The meetings were repeated annually down to 1875; that in the following

[1] H. T. Wood, *History of the Royal Society of Arts*, p. 353.
[2] See p. 291 above.

year discussed adult education. During the course of the meeting of 1853 an educational exhibition was held which proved so successful that Prince Albert urged its repetition next year on a larger scale. On that occasion eleven foreign countries took part in exhibiting school books and apparatus, furniture and building-plans, thus affording an experience hitherto unknown in England but familiar to-day in all Swiss towns which are cantonal centres. The collection afterwards formed the nucleus of the educational exhibition of the Victoria and Albert Museum at South Kensington.[1]

The examinations were first held in 1854 with a too-ambitious schedule of subjects, which in 1856 was remodelled so as to include mathematics, book-keeping, branches of science, history, literature, modern languages and freehand drawing: the list is interesting as showing what at that time might, in the Society's opinion, be learned in schools or in evening classes. Drawing had always been an object of the Society's care. At the first meeting in 1754 it was resolved that prizes should be given to boys and girls under fourteen and to those between fourteen and seventeen for success in drawing, "it being the opinion of all present that the Art of Drawing is absolutely necessary in many employments, trades and manufactures",[2] all present thus anticipating the opinion of the Cross Commissioners and of those who, in 1880–90, wished to advance technical teaching. In 1857 the Society's examinations were extended to provincial centres, in that way creating *nuclei* up and down the country which greatly facilitated, if indeed they did not originate the Science and Art Department's examinations, the first of which were held in 1859. Overlapping unavoidably arose between the two schemes and it became necessary for the Society to give way. Freehand drawing disappeared from its examinations in 1860 and a recasting of its schedules was made in 1870, when seventeen out of thirty-six subjects were removed from the list of examinations. The Society thenceforward limited itself to examining in commercial subjects, interpreting the phrase liberally.[3] The Society of Arts received no monetary assistance from the State, but depended upon the subscriptions and benefactions of its supporters; yet its activities attracted public men, particularly those of scientific proclivities, and distinguished men of science served it as lecturers and examiners.

---

[1] Wood, *op. cit.* p. 371.   [2] *Ibid.* p. 15.   [3] *Ibid.* p. 430.

After nearly half a century of life the Society of Arts was confronted by what was in effect a rival body, the Royal Institution. Circumstances proved that at the opening of the nineteenth century London was unable or unwilling to support both and in the end the two societies reached success by somewhat differentiating their functions. The later body to be formed was the creation (1799) of Count Rumford (born Benjamin Thompson of Woburn, Mass.), a man of very versatile genius with a good appreciation of his own worth. Rumford, a typical eighteenth-century philanthropist, had devoted much thought to ameliorating the conditions under which the poor lived in this country and upon the Continent; many of his scientific improvements and inventions had that for their aim. At the outset the Institution's expressed purposes differed very little from those of the Society of Arts; both were the children of an industrial, utilitarian age. If there were a substantial difference it lay in the intention of the Royal Institution to improve the material conditions of the poor and in particular to increase the technical knowledge of the manual workers. This was in accord with Rumford's previous history and with the activities of Thomas Bernard and other members of the "Society for Bettering the Condition and Increasing the Comfort of the Poor"[1] from which members of the Institution's provisional committee were drawn. Rumford was careful to obtain government support for his project which was embodied in a royal charter of the year 1800 as "the Royal Institution of Great Britain". It was incorporated "for diffusing the knowledge and facilitating the general introduction of useful mechanical inventions and improvements; and for teaching by courses of philosophical lectures and experiments the application of science to the common purposes of life". In its earliest years the Royal Institution possessed an industrial school for mechanics where they might study the principles underlying their respective crafts; bricklayers, joiners, tinmen and ironplate workers were specially in the projectors' minds. The house in Albemarle Street had a large room which was the "Repository" for a collection of models intended to illustrate or exemplify inventions, especially of such as improved ventilation, heating and cooking.

From the first much was made of popular lectures in science. Writing

[1] Founded 1796. Bernard, like Rumford an American, William Wilberforce and Shute Barrington (Bishop of Durham) were amongst the first members.

to his daughter in March, 1801, Rumford said that these lectures were "frequented by crowds of the first people....In short the Royal Institution is the rage". Happily however the managers in the following June engaged as assistant lecturer "a nice able man for the place",[1] Humphry Davy (1778–1829). In the next year Rumford's connexion with the Institution ceased and he went abroad to serve his master, the Elector Palatine of Bavaria, and to marry Lavoisier's widow. The managers' policy at once underwent a change. They proceeded to develop the popular science side; while the school for mechanics and their workshop, the Repository and its models, "all the culinary and other contrivances" of Rumford were allowed to fall into disuse, it was resolved "to continue the existing scientific establishment alone". The laboratory and a large reference library became the first care. But expenditure increased as subscriptions decreased; although the fashionable audiences improved the financial position for a time, they could not be considered a permanent source of income. But the true fountain of prosperity was elsewhere. Appointed Professor of Chemistry in 1805, Davy in the two years which followed began the series of discoveries which made him and the laboratory in which he worked famous throughout Europe. It was the turning-point in the history of the Royal Institution, which henceforward engaged in the researches of pure science no less than in the diffusion of scientific knowledge. Not that the utilitarian element was forgotten. Davy's laboratory gave, in his own words, "aid upon several occasions to the useful arts" and had "afforded assistance to various great public bodies".

It was decided to change the semi-private standing of the Institution to one of a public body, with which end in view an Act of Parliament was obtained in 1810 that confirmed and enlarged its powers. Its aims are therein described as "the promotion of chemical science by experiments and lectures, improving arts and manufactures, discovering the uses of the mineral and natural productions of this country, and the diffusion and extension of useful knowledge in general".

Sir Humphry Davy—he was knighted in 1812—gave his last lecture at the Institution in April of that year and almost at once started on a prolonged scientific tour upon the Continent, accompanied by his amanuensis, Michael Faraday (1791–1867), the recently appointed

---

[1] H. Bence Jones, *The Royal Institution, its Founder and its first Professors* (1871), pp. 70 f.

laboratory assistant of the Institution. On their return in 1815 Faraday resumed his office in Albemarle Street, receiving thirty shillings a week and occupying two attic rooms in the building. The fortunes of the Royal Institution revived from the year 1824, when Faraday lectured there, and in 1831 became world famous by reason of his researches in electricity. Two years later "Michael Faraday, Esquire, Doctor in Civil Law, now the Director of the Laboratory in the Royal Institution of Great Britain" was made its first Fullerian Professor of Chemistry by the express desire of the man who endowed the chair—John Fuller. Thenceforward the history of Faraday and that of the Institution itself were one history; the honour of Founder belongs to Count Rumford, but the continued existence of the Institution and its later successful career were chiefly due to the researches and discoveries made in its laboratory by Davy and Faraday.

The protest against the neglect of science in education which was made by Spencer, Mill and Farrar's team of essayists in 1867 was not a purely personal protest; they were voicing the general discontent entertained by men of science, who regarded that neglect not only as a flagrant failure to employ a great educational instrument, but also as a positive obstacle to the country's industrial progress. Collectively and individually they had done their best to compensate for the omissions of schools and universities and to arouse the country to the serious consequences of neglect. The modification of the curriculum which was finally secured was due to many causes; but amongst them the tireless activity of individual scientific men should not be forgotten. Of these, none was more persistent and influential than Professor Huxley[1] and the small group of savants who were his fellow-advocates in the matter.

Appointed at the age of twenty-nine (1854) Professor of Natural History in the Government School of Mines, Jermyn Street, Huxley at once became a public man as well as a distinguished student and teacher of science. When the Society of Arts arranged its second educational exhibition Huxley was chosen to lecture in association with Whewell, De Morgan, W. B. Carpenter, Cardinal Wiseman, Trench and Hullah, all in the front rank of their several studies. From 1855 onwards Huxley's ordinary routine included lectures to working men, "people's lectures", as he pointedly called them, not *popular* lectures.

[1] See Leonard Huxley, *Life and Letters of Thomas Henry Huxley*, 2 vols. (1900).

Six years later when his subject in these discourses was the relation of Man to the rest of the animal kingdom, he could say, "My working men stick by me wonderfully, the house being fuller than ever last night".

Lectures, started for recreative purposes by H. E. Roscoe at Manchester during the cotton famine of 1862, became in 1866 "Penny Science Lectures", to form in succession "Science Lectures for the People" and the foundation of the Working Men's College at Manchester, an organization subsequently absorbed in the evening classes of Owens College. Roscoe and his colleagues on the staff of the college were assisted in the People's Science Lectures by Huxley, Tyndall, W. B. Carpenter, Huggins, Lubbock (Lord Avebury), Stanley Jevons, Edward Thorpe and William Spottiswoode, all of whom either were at that time, or subsequently became, Fellows of the Royal Society.

Roscoe was in full sympathy with attempts to introduce science and scientific ideas into the general consciousness. At the Bath meeting (1864) of the British Association he initiated the series of public lectures[1] which afterwards became a "fixture" of these annual gatherings. Roscoe was followed by Huxley (1866) and Tyndall (1867) in these addresses to the laity.

In 1858 Huxley, Tyndall and J. D. Hooker collaborating, attempted the publication of a periodical review of science progress for the information of the lay public; but they had to rest content with a fortnightly article in the *Saturday Review*. Then in 1859 came Darwin's *Origin of Species* with whose main teaching Huxley and his group at once identified themselves. Darwin's book aroused an interest whose equal had not been experienced in Europe since Rousseau's *Emile* sent French men and women in crowds to the booksellers and to the libraries. The attention of the readers was by no means confined to the natural history aspect of the doctrine of evolution. The book brought to a crisis the opposition between theology and scientific thought, as these terms were then understood, and the breach grew wider as the century advanced. One consequence was an aggravation of the "religious difficulty" in the schools.

The Science and Art Department had by this time begun its operations, and the aid granted by the State towards the instruction of the industrial classes comprised grants for examination successes in

[1] H. E. Roscoe, *The Life and Experiences of Sir Henry E. Roscoe* (1906), p. 133.

geometry, mechanical and machine drawing and building construction, naval architecture, physics, chemistry, geology, mineralogy, animal physiology, zoology, economic and systematic botany; there were also grants to the teachers who gave the instruction. Certificates, prizes, medals and scholarships were awarded in connexion with the scheme of public examinations.[1]

Huxley's appointment in Jermyn Street was supplemented by other engagements, one of which was to lecture for the Science and Art Department at Marlborough House; the connexion thus begun was maintained throughout his active career. He was at a very early date an examiner for the Department and was always a firm believer in the worth of the Department's examinations; he valued them as "the most important engine for forcing science into ordinary education". But his solicitude for "ordinary education" extended beyond the scientific branch of the curriculum, as he proved by joining in 1865 the recently formed International Education Society of which Richard Cobden was president. The Society, one of whose objects was to help the cause of European peace, set up at Isleworth the International College to give a liberal education in preparation for commerce and the professions. The main studies were modern languages and the elements of physical and social science. The Society had schools in France and Germany, the scheme arranging that the boys should spend part of their time at Isleworth, part in these schools, thus ensuring a mingling of boys of different nationalities who learned their English, French or German in the countries where those languages are severally spoken. There was not time for the schools on the Continent to be in effective operation when the Franco-German War of 1870 put an end to their part in the scheme.

Huxley's connexion with the British Association went back to the meeting of 1846 and he had made it historical by his crushing retort to Bishop Wilberforce's rudeness at the Oxford meeting of 1860. At Nottingham in 1866 as president of Section D he complained of the neglect of science by the schools, attributing it to the unsatisfactory position which was occupied by its study at Oxford and Cambridge. He was followed by F. W. Farrar, who read a paper on the teaching of science at Public Schools, of which a summary has been given in a

[1] Captain Donelly, Inspector for Science, reporting to the British Association meeting at Manchester, 1861.

previous chapter.[1] The special committee suggested by Farrar was appointed and its subsequent labours gave great satisfaction to the Association. At the next meeting (Dundee, 1867) it was decided to make this committee permanent with a watching brief in the interest of science teaching. A copy of its first report was sent to the President of the Privy Council as head of the Education Department, and the Association's officers were authorized to give the document general publicity.

During the discussion of Farrar's paper at Nottingham, Joseph Payne had pointed out that the greatest obstacle to the general introduction of science teaching into the Public Schools was the dearth of qualified teachers; let men of science "condescend to teach in schools" and a beginning would be made. Huxley accepted the challenge. He and Tyndall drew up a four-year scheme of instruction in science for the International College of which they both were governors. Then, in 1869, at the invitation of William Rogers, Rector of St Botolph's, Bishopsgate, who did great things in founding and reforming schools, Huxley gave a set of lessons ("not talkee-talkee lectures") to children at the London Institution. These lessons were subsequently repeated to women at South Kensington.[2]

The next step was to plan a series of shilling science primers for schools, Huxley being the general editor and contributing the introductory volume; Roscoe and other distinguished men of science took part in the series, of which experiment *by the pupil* was a characteristic. It was about this time (1869) that Huxley described a scheme of instruction which should be the basis of all science teaching. Physiography, as he called it, was not only physical geography but also included some elementary conceptions of astronomy, geology, physics and chemistry.

From the pupils Huxley passed to the teachers. In the summer of 1871 he gave lectures daily for six weeks at South Kensington to schoolmasters "with a view of converting them into scientific missionaries to convert the Christian Heathen of these islands to the true faith". More than 100 teachers took this physiology course, which proved so successful that in and after 1872 it was arranged to hold it annually; in the following year a similar arrangement was made for botany, and thereafter teachers of other sciences and of art were afforded the same

---

[1] See p. 315 above.   [2] Leonard Huxley, *op. cit.* vol. I, p. 309.

facilities. Vacation courses for selected teachers, who paid no tuition fees and received railway fares and a bonus, thus became part of the Science and Art Department's ordinary routine. At this time the Jermyn Street School of Mines (now become the Royal School of Mines) had outgrown its accommodation, laboratory space in particular being too straitened. In 1872 its biological section (Huxley's department) was transferred to South Kensington where a newly built laboratory had been prepared for it. Here it was possible to teach zoology not by lecture and illustration only but with the addition of practical laboratory work by the individual student. Huxley had long felt that this was "the only true method. It involved the verification of every fact by each student, and was a training in scientific method even more than in scientific fact".[1]

In the meantime Huxley had been elected (November, 1870) a member of the first London school board. Reasons of health and overwork caused him to resign in 1872, but he was a very active member during the brief term of office. He served prominently on the curriculum sub-committee and was instrumental in securing a place for elementary science in the board school course of instruction. He surprised his secularist colleagues on the board and the public generally by supporting the proposal (which was adopted) to make the reading of the Bible a part of every day's study in the schools. But Huxley was himself a Bible reader; his letters and his less formal writings and speeches repeatedly employ Bible phrases, always very appositely. A self-described "agnostic", he yet thought that the old theological dogmas concerning human nature "were nearer the truth" (his own phrase) than the vague and shallow optimism of popular theology. "I do not say that even the highest biblical ideal is exclusive of others or needs no supplement. But I do believe that the human race is not yet, possibly may never be, in a position to dispense with it".[2]

But this did not mean for Huxley a theology, still less denominationalism. He seems to have valued Bible-reading primarily for the moral teaching in the Bible and, next to that, for the literary merit of the Authorized Version. He looked to lay teachers to make this ethical and aesthetic use of the book. But his secularist colleagues were more logical. Bible-reading without some instruction would not, except

[1] L. Huxley, *op. cit.* vol. I, p. 378.
[2] "Science and Christian Tradition" in *Collected Essays*, vol. v.

partially, attain the ends which he had in view. And instruction involves interpretation; instead of the authoritative interpretation of a Church or of a Communion, the school board's regulations (which were those of the Cowper-Temple clause of the Act) perforce substituted the individual interpretation of the individual teacher, which might be anything from undenominationalism to unbelief. So acute a thinker as Huxley must have appreciated the point; but he probably misjudged the lay, or anti-clerical, trend of opinion in the 'seventies'.

By this time the action taken by the British Association at Dundee had begun to bear fruit. The special committee's report had been duly put before the Education Department, whence it had passed to the House of Commons and the House in its turn in March, 1868, ordered it to be printed. Public interest and Parliamentary approval made it incumbent upon Gladstone's Government to take the matter up. In May, 1870, a Royal Commission was appointed "to make enquiry with regard to scientific instruction and the advancement of science and to enquire what aid thereto is derived from grants voted by Parliament or from endowments belonging to the several Universities in Great Britain and Ireland and the colleges thereof and whether such aid could be rendered in a manner more effectual for the purpose". The Chairman was the Duke of Devonshire (William Cavendish, seventh duke, Chancellor of Cambridge University), the Royal Society was strongly represented by Huxley and other Fellows, Bernhard Samuelson stood for industry and technical instruction, Kay-Shuttleworth for education in general.

The Devonshire Commission got to work at once and between 1870 and 1875 issued a number of reports which fully covered the ground proposed to it. These are a mine of information respecting the working of particular institutions. They review the condition of the bodies which gave scientific instruction directly under government control, considered training colleges, elementary schools, science classes in connexion with the Science and Art Department, the universities and colleges of university standing,[1] museums, and similar national collections.

The government schools of pure and applied science did not work in concert and they were inconveniently and improperly housed for their special tasks. The Commission recommended that the Royal

[1] See Chapter xv below.

School of Mines and the Royal College of Chemistry[1] should be united as a School of Science and that, instead of being one in Jermyn Street, the other in Oxford Street, a house should be provided for the school in the buildings which were then being erected at South Kensington for a projected School of Naval Architecture and Science. The school proposed by the Commission should undertake the instruction of teachers of science.

Huxley was not only a member of the Commission but he was also a witness before it; in both capacities he was very influential. He was examined at great length on the operation, consequences and value of the Science and Art examinations, and in the course of his replies to Commissioners' questions broached the subject of teachers' training. "If I were to propose an ideal system—I should like to have all these teachers passed through a normal school in London, through a proper training school for teachers.—You will never get thorough scientific training in the country till that is the case." He distinguished "training to teach" from imparting knowledge of subject-matter,[2] and was apprehensive lest the former should be lost in the latter, a fear that was subsequently justified. The training which he desired should be open to teachers whether their work would lie in secondary or elementary schools. They should be instructed in pure science and there should be no pretence of giving them purely technical instruction, on the ground that arts and crafts are best learned in the workshop; lecture rooms and laboratories help to the mastery of principles but not of arts.

The evidence of Henry Cole, secretary of the Science and Art Department, revealed that most science teaching in connexion with that Department was given by certificated teachers employed during the day in elementary schools, that the teachers were in consequence overworked, but that they were underpaid in their schools and eked out an income by teaching science in evening classes. Huxley regarded

---

[1] The Royal College of Chemistry was founded in 1845 by a number of noblemen and gentlemen to encourage the study of chemistry with a view to its application to arts and manufactures. Queen Victoria permitted it to add the title "Royal" to its original name. Its managers transferred it to the Government in July 1853, when it was amalgamated with the Royal School of Mines. See *Report of the Royal Commission on Scientific Instruction and the Advancement of Science* (i.e. the Devonshire Commission), Minutes of Evidence, QQ. 5667, 5672, 5676.

[2] *Report*, Minutes of Evidence, QQ. 289, 292.

this state of things as an illustration of "the nocturnal and somewhat surreptitious position which science occupies at present".[1]

It appeared to the Commission that the Code of 1862 had had an adverse effect upon elementary schools, and upon their associates, the training colleges and the Science and Art classes. It was recommended that certificated teachers be encouraged to qualify as teachers of science, and that inspectors of schools should include in their number some men who had been scientifically instructed. The treasures in the national collections, museums and the like, should be explained in public lectures; in particular the educational collection at South Kensington ought to be employed to teach the general principles of elementary science, and to instruct working-class audiences in the application of science to arts and industries.

Occasional references were made in the preceding chapter to manual instruction, to the teaching of trades, and to technical education. The early schemes of the Society of Arts and of the Royal Institution were directed to the hand workers, with the object of improving their dexterity and giving them a knowledge of those scientific principles which underlay their several crafts. When Quintin Hogg started his trade classes in Endell Street, his chief motive was to afford congenial occupation to adolescents which would enable them to take up remunerative work. The relation of these things to education in general was scarcely considered. Masters and men were alike sceptical as to the practical worth of teaching and training carried out apart from the workshop and the inflexible conditions which ruled there. The instructor's experiences and the criticism of the experts led to a modification in the belief as to what was feasible. Playfair in a lecture at Edinburgh in 1870 said bluntly "Instruction in manipulative skill is not education at all; and, such as it is, belongs to the workshop, not to the school". This view of the limitation to the school's usefulness was shared generally by the public men and men of science who were interested in the subject. While schools might enable the boy to learn to use his hands, the only place in which a particular trade could be learned was the workshop. This was said again and again in speeches and pamphlets until it became a fixed principle with the advocates of technical instruction.

But their doctrine was grounded in a condition of things that was

[1] *Report*, Minutes of Evidence, Q. 314.

obsolescent if not quite obsolete. In the trades in which apprenticeship survived and the apprentice went through all the processes of his craft, the workshop was undoubtedly a school; with capable and conscientious masters or foremen it was the best school for the purpose. But apprenticeship was becoming exceptional, and the factory or big shop with its many machines and minute sub-division of labour was a school with very limited opportunities for instruction.

Yet even under the conditions of factory life a developed intelligence had its value for the work to be done, no less than for the man as an individual; and intelligence could be developed by the study of principles. It was agreed that principles might be learned in schools. In this connexion the principles were those of science. Most workmen had not had sufficient elementary grounding to be able to follow intelligently instruction of this sort; and the education accessible to employers and their managers and superintendents in most cases had not been of the kind which readily leads to scientific study. These were considerations of education in general; and attention was once more called to the neglect of science in most educational establishments. Technical education so understood could not be separated from the more comprehensive process; and some teaching in science was required by all ranks engaged in industry. A conference of employers, managers of works and heads of offices, arranged in January 1868 by the Society of Arts came to this conclusion.

In 1872 the Society produced a scheme of technological teaching confined to those who were actually engaged in factories and workshops; it was subsidized liberally by the Clothworkers' Company of the City of London. In the following year, on the suggestion of Captain Donelly of the Science and Art Department, the Society instituted technological examinations for artisans in the subject-matter of their industries. Candidates were required to produce certificates of practical skill from their employers and to have passed previously certain elementary examinations of the Science and Art Department. In 1878 when the Society ceased to hold these examinations the subjects included manufacture in cotton, paper, silk, steel, carriage-building, calico-bleaching, dyeing and printing, alkali manufacture and blow-pipe analysis.

The Clothworkers were distinguished by their liberality in advancing technical teaching, but they were not singular amongst the City Livery

Companies in the lively interest which they took in that aspect of public education. Dr Playfair, Sir John Lubbock and other members of Parliament tried year after year to induce Government to secure a more effective employment of science in public education, only to be met, as Huxley said, "with warm admiration for science in general and reasons at large for doing nothing in particular".[1]

But what Parliament could not be moved to do was successfully attempted by the Livery Companies of the City. In 1869 the Lord Mayor (J. C. Lawrence) summoned an informal conference of representatives of the Companies to consider the propriety of giving assistance to technical education; it was there agreed that the Companies might and should grant sums of money for the purpose. From that time technical instruction was aided by grants made year by year by the wealthier Companies.

In 1873 Sir Sydney Waterlow of the Clothmakers' Company was discussing with the secretary of the Science and Art Department the ways in which technical education might be assisted. Somewhat later the Company sent two commissioners to the Continent to make inquiry into technical instruction in textile manufactures and generally; their report was printed and circulated. By 1877 plans had taken definite shape; Waterlow, Owen Roberts and others of the Clothworkers were seeking Donelly's advice in reference to a "City Guilds Industrial University". Some of the chief Companies had formed a committee, established a large fund and sought counsel of such men as Huxley, Donelly, Sir William Armstrong and the secretary of the Society of Arts. The first executive act of this body was to take over in 1879 the system of technological examinations from the Society of Arts, to add considerably to the number of subjects for teaching which grants were made, and to establish communication with local committees throughout the kingdom, so initiating a general type and standard of instruction and examination in technical studies and making capitation grants for the purpose. In 1880 it was incorporated as the City and Guilds of London Institute for the Advancement of Technical Education.[2]

But long before this date the Livery Companies, the use which they made of their property and the matter of technical education, had

[1] Huxley, "Science and Education", in *Collected Essays*, p. 418.

[2] *Journal of the Society of Arts*, vols. XXV, XXVI. *Royal Commission on Technical Instruction*, Second Report, vol. I, Waterlow's evidence.

become a "political question", the occasion for a contest between the Radicals and their opponents. So early as 1872 a dissatisfied member of one of the minor companies made known his grievance in a pamphlet which bore on its title-page such ominous phrases as "Behold the Spoiler Cometh!" "Reform your City Guilds". Mr John Bennet, one of the sheriffs for the City, had said in a public speech that a number of the guilds had been founded to advance technical instruction (a very disputable assertion), that they had neglected their duty, were very wealthy and only needed "a little gentle persuasion" to make them devote to the purpose some of their "loads of money".

A party in the House of Commons proceeded to act on such statements as these. In 1876 William James, M.P. for Gateshead, moved that an inquiry be addressed to the Companies but was outvoted. He and his friends regarded the property of the Companies as a part of the public estate as to whose use Parliament could claim to be informed. The answer was that the Companies were societies of private persons, some of whose wealth was held in trust, the trust of course being open to the scrutiny of the Charity Commissioners; the remaining property was the private possession of the members for the time being. If there was malversation, the Courts were open and the intervention of Parliament was not necessary. James was acting on the recognized Radical principle that there was no place in a free State for privileged persons or corporations, and, as he saw them, the Livery Companies were of the privileged order. But another type of attack began to threaten. There was great dissatisfaction amongst London ratepayers respecting school board expenditure; in order to ease the burden by finding a fresh source of income, a committee of the board had been making such inquiry as they could into the property and obligations of the Companies. The third London school board was to be elected in November, 1876, and many of the candidates assured the electors that they would do what they could to secure some of this wealth for the school board fund.

In the meantime it had been made clear that such property belonging to the Companies as was free from trusts was private property with which Parliament was powerless to interfere; and it was agreed that trusts had been, and were being, more than fulfilled. The next step was the formation of a City Guilds Reform Association and William James, seconded by Arthur Pease, member for South Durham, became its

A E

spokesman in the House. In April, 1877, these two moved that it was the Government's duty to introduce "some legislative measure empowering the Crown to make full investigation into the present condition and revenues of the eighty-nine Companies". In other words, as there is no law which compels these bodies to disclose their affairs, let a law be made; the intention being to "convey" the Companies' moneys to such uses as Parliament should deem fit. But the appeal was to Disraeli's Government and the motion was negatived by a majority of 5 to 3.[1]

At the time when James was moving the first of these two unsuccessful motions the Clothworkers were being congratulated on their liberality in providing the Yorkshire College, Leeds, with a considerable sum to provide technical instruction in the textile industries. The City and Guilds Institute in 1881 opened its Technical College in Finsbury to give evening instruction to artisans and to train boys for the positions of foremen and other non-commissioned officers of industry, a function of the *école primaire supérieure* and of similar German and Swiss schools.

In 1882–4 the Central Institute at South Kensington was completed, its purpose being to train young men professionally for different forms of engineering and of manufacture and to educate and train technical teachers, the presence of this last probably being due to Huxley, who was an active member of the Institute's Council. A school of decorative art in Kennington was added later to the Institute's local establishments; its national work in testing and otherwise aiding technology was continued. The movement in support of this kind of instruction was taken up by Birmingham, Manchester, Bradford and other cities in the industrial areas. The Central Institute received its charter in the year 1900.

Concern respecting the commercial and industrial instruction of the community now extended to the general public. The Paris Exhibition of 1878, token of France's wonderful recovery after the catastrophes of 1870 and 1871, revived the misgivings which had been aroused by the previous gatherings of this kind and a time of waning industrial prosperity coincided with the decade that followed. In August, 1881, a Royal Commission was appointed "to enquire into the instruction of the industrial classes of certain foreign countries in technical and

[1] J. R. Taylor, *Reform your City Guilds* (1872), and *House of Commons, 10th April*, 1877, *Mr W. James' Motion on City Companies*.

other subjects for comparison with that of the corresponding classes in this country" and the influence of such instruction on manufacturing and other industries at home and abroad. The Chairman of this "Royal Commission on Technical Instruction" (1881–4) was Bernhard Samuelson, an ironmaster who had long been prominent in the country and in Parliament as an authority and as an earnest advocate of technical education. The Commissioners included representatives of the cotton, woollen and pottery industries, Professor Roscoe represented science, and the City and Guilds of London Institute sent its director and secretary, Philip Magnus. The Commissioners visited Germany, Belgium, Switzerland, Holland and France and inquired into all forms of technical education abroad and in this country. "Each Commissioner", so Roscoe says, "had to pay his own expenses, the Government being responsible only for the secretarial expenditure and cost of printing". The Government was a Liberal Government.

The Commission reported in 1882 and finally in 1884;[1] these reports attracted considerable attention and they were favoured by having "a good Press". Their survey was not confined to schools and colleges but also took in visits to great Continental factories and other industrial establishments. As a result of comparing the foreign institutions with our own, the general conclusion was that we neglected or used insufficiently the means afforded by our schools and colleges, but that nevertheless in invention we were still ahead of the industrial world. Amongst instances of this primacy the Commissioners unfortunately included Perkin's discovery of aniline colours, the subsequent commercial history of which affords a good argument in favour of a better technical training or a wider diffusion of scientific knowledge than were then common in England. But the Commissioners maintained that as a school of practice the English workshop had no rival.

The Commissioners were impressed by the value of drawing as a necessary part of technical instruction. They found that in English elementary schools it was taught, and taught badly, to some pupils only in about one fourth of the schools. In Manchester and elsewhere boys were taught the use of tools and one London board school had experimented in woodwork; in the latter case the official auditor had

[1] *Report of the Royal Commission on Technical Instruction*, First Report (France) (1882), Second Report, vol. I, Foreign countries and United Kingdom, Minutes of Evidence; vol. II, The Continent and America (1884); vols. IV and V (1884).

surcharged the responsible school board members for the cost of the timber. The Commissioners advised that teaching of this nature and of drawing should, in the case of elementary schools, be transferred from the supervision of the Science and Art Department to that of the Education Department, and that drawing should be made a "class subject" taught throughout the "standards" (or classes) in boys' schools. Work with tools in wood and iron should rank amongst the "specific subjects" of the Code. The rudiments of science were taught in these schools to some degree, but the hindrances to the success of the teaching were expense, insufficient allocation of hours and a lack of teachers. It was recommended that the training colleges should each year send apt students to take the courses at the Normal School of Science, South Kensington. Further, the great school boards should be empowered to set up training colleges for day students, and they should also maintain classes for young persons and adult artisans in connexion with the Science and Art Department. The second of these two recommendations was an encouragement to the school boards to act illegally, as the event proved a few years later. Private firms at Newcastle, Crewe, Manchester and Oldham had technical schools for their juvenile employees; the Commissioners regretted that there were not more of these and they noted the formation of a uniform standard in technical teaching which had followed the activities of the City and Guilds Institute.

Technical instruction above the elementary stage must wait for the appearance of improved secondary schools; the complaints of the Taunton Commission are repeated in the present *Report*. There were too many private secondary schools which were "hopelessly bad". Secondary education, in the Commissioners' opinion, ought to be in the hands of public bodies having power to draw upon rates and taxes. For his part, the chairman would authorize local authorities (that is in effect the school boards) to apply ancient endowments to the support of secondary schools which taught modern subjects, as science, mathematics, modern languages. Such bodies should establish schools of high standing to give instruction purely technical, like that given in Firth College, Sheffield and at University College, Nottingham.

The model which the Commission proposed for the most advanced teaching was the Federal Polytechnikum at Zurich, the scope of whose studies and wealth of apparatus and other auxiliaries of study constituted it a veritable technical university. "The great Colleges of the Capital, of Manchester and Liverpool have departments of applied science which, if the necessary funds were forthcoming, might be expanded into Polytechnic Schools. The Central Institute [of the City and London Guilds] might become a true Polytechnic. In short we have the nuclei of as many technical high schools [*Hochschulen*, universities] as we require."

The most general conclusions of the Commission were as follows. Technical education is a branch of national education as a whole and is dependent upon it. The first necessary step is therefore the perfection of elementary and intermediate (i.e. secondary) education. The aim is not culture but ability; the technical schools and their teaching must be carefully suited to the needs and, it might be added, the prejudices of the particular trades resorting to them. A good technical school cannot be made to "pay". It is too costly for the fees to maintain it, still less to yield a profit. Establishment charges and upkeep must be met in the main by rates and taxes. The different grades of technical schools must be co-ordinated with each other and with schools in general. To attain this there should be one central authority for technical education. It did not fall within the Commissioners' reference to assert the conclusion that the country needed one central authority for all grades of public instruction; but that conclusion was obviously implied.

Between the publication of this Commission's *Reports* in 1884 and the appointment of the Cross Commission two years later there had been a change of Government and a second change was imminent; but within the interval neither Government had introduced Parliamentary legislation respecting technical education. It fell to the Cross Commission to consider what the elementary schools were doing, or might do for this type of instruction. The Commissioners noted that a suggestion, made by the earlier Commission, that the wealthier school boards should co-operate with the Science and Art Department was being adopted. At Sheffield the Higher Central School (admission to which was by competition amongst the boys who had passed Standard V, whether in a board or voluntary school) organized classes under the Education Department's *Code* for Standards VI and VII. The pupils senior to these standards were taught under the regulations of the Science and Art Department, their curriculum embracing drawing, machine drawing and construction, chemistry, mechanics, electricity, light and heat; the course for a given boy was chosen from this list of studies, drawing being compulsory for all. The Seventh Standard School at Birmingham was "to a certain extent a technical school". The course was for three years, one year in the seventh standard, two under the Science and Art Department of South Kensington, the studies open to the choice of the pupils being mathematics, plane geometry and projection, machine construction and drawing, magnetism and electricity, chemistry, freehand drawing and woodwork. Other schools of this type, to which the Commission assigned the generic name "higher elementary school", were the Deansgate Central School, Manchester, and the large London voluntary school of St Thomas's, Charterhouse.

To cope with the problem created by the shortage of competent teachers of science, Donelly had suggested, so early as 1876 to the Liverpool school board, the employment of a few competent men who should pass from school to school giving a course of lessons in science illustrated by experiment. The suggestion was adopted and the board sought the advice of its originator and of Huxley in planning the details. Classes of boys were taught physics, girls were taught domestic economy; between the delivery in a given school of one lecture and the next the subject-matter was recapitulated by the class teachers of the school, of course in co-operation with the peripatetic teacher but without the use of his apparatus, which travelled with him. In 1880 Birmingham took up the plan; here the instruction was given to all boys and girls above Standard IV, the subject-matter in the girls' case being domestic economy and physiology. Two and a half hours were given up fortnightly to the teaching, the lecture lasting forty-five minutes, and the remaining time being spent in recapitulation. In 1885 the London school board was employing in this way four peripatetic demonstrators who were instructing 2000 children. In the London school these lectures were associated with the central classes which were formed for manual instruction; the boys made in the workshop pieces of apparatus which were used in the peripatetic lecturer's demonstrations.

But these were only local attempts to deal with a need which was national. The minority of the Cross Commission reported that "in spite of these scattered efforts, on the whole it appeared that hardly anything was done in this country in the way of workshop instruction for boys, and little in linear drawing, still less in that scientific education which is the foundation of such technical instruction as can be given in the school". Sir Philip Magnus told the Commission that the Science and Art Department and the City and Guilds of London Technical Institute were unable to get from the elementary schools sufficient recruits for "the excellent science, art and technical classes which are now organised in different parts of the country".

Attention was drawn in the *Report* to the advance in manual training which was being made in the Swedish elementary schools; the Swedish Government was sending teachers to a special college under private management there to learn an educative scheme of woodwork known as Slöjd.[1] The Commission recommended that boys should attend for one or two afternoons each week at workshops centrally situated with reference to neighbouring elementary schools.

The general control of technical instruction should, in the opinion of the majority of the Commission, be lodged with the municipal authorities, that is the rating authorities, and with the Education Department; it was not the business of the school boards or of the Department at South Kensington. The minority report advised that technical instruction should be commercial and agricultural and not purely industrial, the locality settling for itself the branches, or branch, which it would teach. Such instruction should form the staple of the curriculum in "higher elementary schools" whose pupils might, if necessary, hold scholarships from the elementary schools which they would leave at the age of eleven or twelve. "The higher elementary (or central) school would satisfy the wants of an entirely different class from those who desire really secondary education." For these, schooling is continued till sixteen or eighteen, and may be followed by the university; the pupils of the higher elementary schools begin to learn a trade or to earn a living at fourteen or fifteen. Commercial instruction in these latter schools should comprise book-keeping, shorthand, French, German, business letter-writing, précis, commercial geography and "a literary knowledge of the English Language" Nothing was said as to the compatibility of the last with "business letter-writing" or as to which of the two was the antidote to the other.[2]

---

[1] Subsequently anglicized to "Sloyd" (sleight, skill).

[2] The observations of the Cross Commission on technical instruction will be found in the *Final Report*, pp. 146 ff. and 311 ff.

The years 1884–6 were years of great political excitement and of events, at home and abroad, which were critical in the country's history. Between July, 1885, and August, 1886, three successive Governments were formed and for both Prime Ministers, Gladstone and Salisbury, there were more serious matters to consider than forms of public education. Interest in the topic fell off and nothing was done to give effect to the recommendations of the Technical Instruction Commission. But there were members of Parliament and others who were determined to press the subject upon Parliament and the country, Sir Henry Roscoe and Mr A. D. Acland being foremost amongst them in promoting bills in the Commons and stirring the public at large. In July, 1887, Lord Salisbury's Government introduced a measure intended to empower school boards and other local bodies to provide or support technical schools, but within a month it was withdrawn.

Lord Rosebery and Professor Huxley now actively co-operated with Roscoe and Acland in re-awakening general attention to the subject; public meetings were held and a fruitful agitation arose in the great industrial and commercial centres. The movement was concentrated by the formation of a National Association for the Promotion of Technical Education whose aims were to stimulate public interest, to advise local bodies and to take Parliamentary action. Writing to his friend, Hooker, at the close of the year, Huxley could say, "Manchester, Liverpool and Newcastle have now gone in for technical education on the grand scale and the work is practically done. *Nunc dimittis!*"[1]

Not many days before this letter was penned Huxley had addressed, on behalf of the National Association, a gathering of business men representing all branches of industry and commerce in Manchester. His appeal was cogent and direct—"bare and almost cynical" is his own description of it—with reference to his immediate topic. But Huxley never took a narrow view of educational aims, and he did not forget the broader aspect on this occasion. In his peroration he made his audience see the narrower issue in its true perspective. While putting the case of industrial education plainly and forcibly, he bade his hearers, the employers of Manchester, "have a care, at the same time, that the conditions of industrial life remain those in which the physical energies of the population may be maintained at a proper level; in which their moral state may be cared for; in which there may be some

[1] L. Huxley, *Life and Letters of T. H. Huxley*, vol. II, p. 181.

rays of hope and pleasure in their lives; and in which the sole prospect of a life of labour may not be an old age of penury".[1]

Technical Instruction Bills were fathered by Roscoe in February, 1888, and in 1889, these being followed by a third, the work of Acland in March, 1889; they had varying fortunes in the House but none became an Act. Finally, Sir William Hart Dyke, then Vice-President of the Council, brought in a government measure which in three weeks (August, 1889) became the Technical Instruction Act.

The Act permitted the levy of a penny rate by the newly created county councils and by urban sanitary authorities in support of technical teaching, the curriculum to be supervised by the Science and Art Department. Aid of this kind was not to be extended to public elementary schools, and the county council or other body granting aid was to be represented on the governing body of the institution so assisted, whether school, college, institute or polytechnic. This was the first blow struck at the school boards, to which no part was assigned by the Act. Technical instruction was defined as the teaching of the scientific and artistic principles that are applicable to industry and special trades, but not the practice of these industries or trades. By manual instruction was meant exercise in the use of tools. In the following year Roscoe attempted by a Bill in Parliament to remove the disqualification of elementary schools to receive aid in respect of the technical teaching authorized by the Act; but he was unsuccessful.

The National Association had by this time added "secondary education" to its purview and in 1889 held a conference at Manchester with delegates from the county councils, a meeting which subsequently had an important bearing on ways and means. The Local Taxation (Customs and Excise) Act of 1890 allotted to local bodies certain surpluses with which it was at first intended to compensate publicans whose licences had not been renewed; the name "whisky money" was popularly applied to these sums. Acland proposed as an amendment that the money should be ear-marked for technical education; the amendment was negatived, but three weeks later the Chancellor of the Exchequer (Goschen) moved that the "whisky money" should be assigned to the county councils, or equivalent local bodies, to be expended on technical education or in relief of the rates, at their option.

[1] "Science and Education", in *Collected Essays*, p. 449.

The local bodies responded enthusiastically and in most cases the windfall was expended on what was ostensibly technical instruction; but so liberally was that term interpreted that it was made to cover well-nigh every branch of knowledge, Latin and Greek excepted; and the Science and Art Department by its money grants supported the interpretation. South Kensington naturally attached great importance to the scientific branches, and the net result was that secondary education with a scientific orientation received the impetus instead of that strictly technical instruction for which the "whisky money" was at first intended.

"The amount of residue [that is, the surplus under the Customs and Excise Act] assigned to technical education by English local authorities rose from £472,560 in 1892–3 to £654,463 (out of a total of £775,944) in 1895–6, and in 1900–1 to £863,847 out of £924,360. The sum raised by rates in this country under the Technical Instruction Acts had grown from £12,762 in the first named year to £106,209 in the last, exclusive of £19,439 due to the Public Libraries Acts."[1] The Technical Instruction Acts were repealed by the Education Act of 1902 and that branch of education was merged in the general field over which the local education authorities created by that Act had authority. By the same measure the "whisky money" was assigned to those authorities for the purposes of secondary, including technical, education.

The British Association had not ceased to interest itself in school education and at its meeting in 1887 it appointed a committee to report on the teaching of chemistry in schools. To the Bath meeting in the following year this committee declared that chemistry should be taught in schools "mainly on account of the mental training it affords" and secondly for its practical bearing upon everyday life, that is, as mental discipline and as useful knowledge. Amongst the obstacles to its successful teaching were the absence of qualified teachers, and of good text-books, the pressure of examinations and the insufficient number of hours allotted to it. The committee's report for 1889 stated its opinion that the teaching of chemistry as commonly practised must be "considerably modified if it is to effect the valuable discipline which science teaching can afford". The key to the right method lay in the principle that "the learners should be put in the attitude of discoverers".

[1] Graham Balfour, *Educational Systems of Gt Britain and Ireland* (1903), p. 167, quoting H. of C. paper No. 225, p. vi.

By way of illustration the report printed a scheme whose author was Professor H. E. Armstrong, of the City and Guilds Central Institute, an active member of the committee. Beginning with lessons on common things, the scheme passed to instruction in measurement carried out upon laboratory lines, then to a study of heat. Next followed the problem stage in which pupils were led to find answers to such questions as, What happens when iron rusts, when chalk is burnt in lime, when metal dissolves in acids? A quantitative stage followed and instruction on the physical properties of gases. Professor Armstrong continued this scheme in the report of his committee for 1890 by studies of water, common liquids, chalk and other common solids.

The British Association course for schools propounded by this committee was thus one in elementary physics and chemistry, prefaced by actual measurements in a laboratory, or similar workshop, of lengths, areas, volumes, mass, density, force, temperature, and so on. Each individual pupil was to make these measurements for himself. The scheme was adopted very slowly by the schools, the London school board being the first to introduce it through its peripatetic lecturers aided by the class teachers; in 1897 it was installed in some forty board schools in North and East London, girls as well as boys participating. The classes and corresponding evening courses for the teachers were conducted, first by Mr H. Gordon and later by Mr W. M. Heller.

At the Educational Section of the Health Exhibition, South Kensington (1884), Professor Armstrong had read a paper on the method of teaching elementary science which presented the subject-matter of chemistry as a series of problems for the pupils' solution, the method in fact of the British Association Scheme. At this same Exhibition he had been impressed by a paper advocating the heuristic, or "finding out", method as applied to the teaching of all kinds of subjects, literary as well as scientific. "The heuristic method is the *only* method to be applied in the pure sciences; it is the best method in the teaching of the applied sciences; and it is *a* method" in the study of literature. It is the method of research, the pupil's attitude being that of the discoverer. The author of this paper, Professor Meiklejohn, Professor of Education at St Andrews University, had traced the thought back to Edmund Burke and Pestalozzi; but the idea must have had a still earlier ancestry. It is the essential element of the catechism which Socrates so persistently employed; and, inasmuch as it may be fairly termed the natural mode of learning, it must have had far earlier exponents amongst primitive societies. Professor Armstrong published a very noteworthy article in 1898 under the title "The Heuristic Method of Teaching or the Art of Making Children Think for Themselves",[1] which aroused much controversy and obtained very many converts amongst teachers.

"Heuristic" became a fashion employed enthusiastically in a number of schools, often uncritically, to the almost entire exclusion of the teaching that was stigmatized as "didactic". Obviously, whatever may be said of the child's attitude to his studies, he cannot occupy quite the same position as the researcher in the ordinary sense of that word. Moreover, some knowledge must, overtly or otherwise, be conveyed to the pupil didactically; certain instruments (i.e. crystallized knowledge) must be placed in his hands and, unless an inordinate amount of time be lavished on points of less importance, something must be told. But such considerations do not invalidate the method, nor more especially do they contradict the assertion respecting the pupil's attitude towards knowledge yet to be acquired. Analysis is the first step by which all learn, children or adults, in or out of school; and where there is no analysis, there is no learning. Didactic teaching aids (or hinders) analysis, but is no true substitute for it. Professor Armstrong rendered a much-needed service to schools and to schoolmasters by his insistence on the truth; and his advice to use ordinary objects and experiences in teaching science, so that in effect the classroom was turned into a workshop, brought an element of actuality into schools which was too often a startling novelty.

But the determination to see in "mental discipline" the *raison d'être* of school exercises led to some exaggerated claims for the "finding out" method. It was held, for example, that the continuous use of the balance in school would make the user a stickler for accuracy and truth at large. The girl who "greatly amused and pleased" her teacher by excitedly crying out "Murder!" when weighing some iron "that had been allowed to rust" (i.e. had been "murdered") may have been expressing a sincere conviction which scandalized her scientific conscience. Or—? "Leg-pulling" is not unknown at the expense even of schoolmistresses and professors.

[1] *Special Reports on Educational Subjects*, vol. II, pp. 389 ff., a publication by the Office of Special Inquiries and Reports then recently established under the Education Department.

The Science and Art Department's way of providing scientific education, in spite of its early success and the support lent to it by Huxley, was freely criticized, especially by those who opposed the principle of payment by results. The instruction was given in evening classes and on Saturday mornings, the majority of the students being teachers in elementary schools. The school board gave increases of pay to teachers who gained "Advanced Certificates" in branches of science, and some ambitious teachers, regarding the possession of these certificates as an avenue to promotion, added certificate to certificate until some teachers possessed so many of these documents that one critic drily described them as "memoranda of things to be learned". The instructors of these evening and Saturday classes were almost invariably certificated teachers in elementary schools, duly qualified by the possession of "science certificates" and remunerated by the institution in which they taught from the grant paid in respect of the examination results of their teaching. In some cases the teacher was an absolute free lance who conducted his class, or classes, entirely on his own responsibility, recouping himself by the grant and the pupils' fees, or exacting no fee whatever. The system inevitably concentrated effort upon the examination in a quite unhealthy degree, so that it was said of the pupils "they cram to pass and not to know, they do pass and they don't know". At its best the scheme lacked co-ordination; the student busied himself with his one branch of science with little or no regard for its association with other branches.

In 1872 the Department essayed to improve the position by proposing that Organized Science Schools should be formed by approved local committees, so cutting out the free lance and his uncoordinated teaching; the Schools were to give a three years' course in science, that is in a group of allied sciences, and the grant was to depend partly upon the number of pupils in attendance, partly upon examination successes. But the free lance continued to hold the field for long years after 1872. The Organized Science Schools were very slow in taking root. In 1885 they numbered three only, in 1896, 125; in 1901 there were 212 of them, nearly one fourth of these being attached to board schools.[1]

Huxley's South Kensington courses to teachers soon gave occasion for founding a separate institute, which before the century closed had outgrown the original purpose, the training of teachers. In 1881 the

[1] Graham Balfour, *op. cit.* p. 158.

Normal School of Science was created and the Royal School of Mines was affiliated to it. Both had prescribed courses of study lasting for three or three and a half years, successful students being awarded the title of Associate. The primary purpose of the Normal School was "the instruction of teachers in the various branches of physical science", not their specific training to teach, as the word "normal" implied. In 1890 the title was changed to Royal College of Science, the instruction still being intended for teachers and also for "students of the industrial classes selected by competition in the examination of the Department of Science and Art, but other students are admitted as far as there may be accommodation for them on the payment of fees".[1] The Department's National Art Training School underwent a similar development, becoming in 1896 the Royal College of Art, for the training of teachers of art and of artisans, for whom there was a liberal provision of free places, scholarships, exhibitions and maintenance allowances.[2]

[1] Graham Balfour, *op. cit.*, p. 255, quoting the *Calendar* of the college.
[2] *Ibid.* quoting Command Paper 756.

CHAPTER XV

University Education

The legislation of 1854 and 1856 which followed the Royal Commissions on Oxford and Cambridge effected only a partial advance towards that complete change in academic conditions which university reformers desired. The clerical monopoly of government was broken but not abolished; the relation of the professors to the college teachers and of the University generally to the colleges remained much as before. The Board of Heads and Proctors at Oxford and the Caput at Cambridge were replaced by elected bodies, fellowships and scholarships were set free from some but not all of their ancient restrictions. But modern studies received only a grudging recognition and the Dissenter was not permitted to hold a fellowship or proceed to the master's degree. The prize fellowships, held for life on condition of celibacy but with no obligation to teach, study or reside in the University, continued to absorb money which the reformers would employ for the support of research or for the improvement and cheapening of education. With larger staffs of teachers the colleges could give a more efficient and more comprehensive instruction and concurrently eliminate the private "coach". The man who desired a good place in the tripos almost invariably sought the help of the coach, who made the examination the primary aim of his teaching; his fee at Cambridge ranged from £8 to £10 for each of the three terms and from £15 to £20 during the Long Vacation.[1] The non-resident fellow with his claim upon the college dividend (the amount of which he took part in determining) made it difficult to secure money for new college purposes at the expense of the dividend. The purely personal feature of these fellowships was equally unsatisfactory. "A prize of £200 or £250 a year for perhaps 50 years given merely because a man had been first in one examination was a reward out of all proportion to his industry and ability";[2] twenty or thirty of these "life pensions" were bestowed annually at Oxford.[3]

[1] British Association *Report*, 1862, III, pp. 193 f. Paper on the past and present expenses and social conditions of university education by Rev. W. Emery, Senior Fellow and Tutor, C.C. Coll., Camb.

[2] Abbott and Campbell, *Life and Letters of B. Jowett*, vol. II, p. 122.

[3] Mark Pattison, *Suggestions on Academical Organization* (1868), p. 100.

The changes desired by the Commissioners and sanctioned by Parliament were not made without friction; opponents, albeit in a minority, were still powerful and some were obstructive, while the reformers were not always conciliatory. Feeling was strong, more especially at Oxford, where any novelty was apt to be suspected by the orthodox as a threat to religion. The intolerance of any departure from strict orthodoxy, which in 1853 had driven F. D. Maurice from his chair in King's College, London, was vigorous ten years later. The British Association meeting at Oxford in 1860 became the occasion for a discussion of Darwin's *Origin of Species*, a discussion which was made memorable by the stupid and unmannerly taunt of the Bishop (Wilberforce) and the crushing rejoinder of Huxley. In the same year the appearance of *Essays and Reviews* (to which both Universities contributed) raised a storm of protest which raged mightily until it was intensified by the publication in 1862 of Bishop Colenso's denial that Moses wrote the Pentateuch. For his known sympathy with heterodox opinions and for his share in *Essays and Reviews* Jowett's statutory salary of £40 as Regius Professor of Greek remained for ten years at that sum, until in 1865 Christ Church (which was chargeable with the stipend) changed it at Dr Pusey's instigation to £500.

These adverse circumstances notwithstanding, the Acts of 1854 and 1856, still more the reforming spirit which actuated them, led to noteworthy changes in life at Oxford and Cambridge. The number of residents increased and students were drawn from a wider social area; college teaching was made more efficient. In 1871 the numbers at Oxford were greater than they had been since the sixteenth century. The invidious distinctions drawn between noblemen, gentlemen (or fellow) commoners and commoners (or "pensioners") were abolished. Amongst those who were on the foundation of the colleges, the menial status of "servitor" and "sizar" disappeared, their emoluments becoming exhibitions. The requirement of residence in a college, which had been insisted upon since the fifteenth century as necessary to membership of either University, was abandoned; and the "non-collegiate" or "unattached student" reappeared at Oxford in 1868, at Cambridge in 1869. But the plan was not an unqualified success. As a rule it did not attract the ablest men; the exceptional men who matriculated as *non ascripti* embraced the earliest opportunity of becoming members of a college. Something more than attendance at lecture and admission to an examination was needed to constitute a university education as England understood the term. The better way subsequently adopted was present as an idea to the reformers of the 'sixties', namely, the provision of hostels, whether under the direction of a college or having an independent existence, in which the charges should be considerably lower than those at the cheapest colleges.[1]

Writing in August, 1865, Jowett said: "There is a great change in education at the Universities, especially at Oxford. When I was an undergraduate [1836–9] we were fed upon Bishop Butler and Aristotle's *Ethics* and almost all teaching leaned to the support of authority. Now there are new subjects, modern history and physical science and, more important than these perhaps, is the real study of metaphysics in the *Lit. Hum.* school; every man for the last ten years who goes in for honours has read Bacon, and probably Locke, Mill's *Logic*, Plato, Aristotle and the history of ancient philosophy. See how impossible this makes a return to the old doctrine of authority".[2] Whatever truth lies in the last sentence, the enlargement of the undergraduate's reading is undoubted.

The imposition of religious tests and the relation of the colleges to the University now became the centres around which the struggle for reform was maintained. The disability which lay upon dissenters from the Church of England was strikingly emphasized at Cambridge, where the Senior Wranglers of 1860 and of 1861 were debarred from fellowships by their religious beliefs. Residents at both Universities from 1862 onwards repeatedly petitioned Parliament to remove the test, and Bills to give effect to their prayer were introduced into the Commons' House every year between 1863 and 1870, to be either set aside there or defeated in the House of Lords. The Liberal Government which came into office in December, 1868, was determinedly hostile to privilege, as it showed by the disestablishment of the Church of Ireland, by the abolition of the purchase of Army commissions and the opening of the Civil Service unreservedly to competition. The Elementary

---

[1] Annual cost at Cambridge in 1861–2 estimated at the lowest to be £120, next highest £180, highest £250. Some men "with great economy" lived on £100 a year. "These rates included all university charges and private expenses derived from tradesmen's bills sent in to the tutors." The figures relate only to the academic year of 24–25 weeks. (Mr Emery's paper to the British Association already cited.)

[2] Abbott and Campbell, *op. cit.* vol. I, p. 412.

Education Act of 1870 demonstrated its opinion as to the relation of religion to public education. The series of abortive measures which were designed to give effect to that opinion at the Universities was brought to a close in 1871 when the Prime Minister, Gladstone, made the subject a Government Bill and the Universities' Tests Act abolished these tests in Oxford, Cambridge and Durham. The Act did not apply to the divinity degrees, or chairs, since the divinity professors were virtually engaged in training professionally the clergy of the Church of England. Nor did the Act touch any university or college office which, at the date of its passing (16 July 1871), required the officer to be in Holy Orders; any college not existing at that time was to be deemed outside the scope of the Act. The college chapels and their services remained and religious instruction continued; but attendance was no longer compulsory. Fellowships and, with the foregoing exceptions, degrees and offices in college or university were thrown open without subscription or assent to any formulary of faith or declaration of religious belief. Thus a century of debate, sometimes very hot debate, was brought to an end, and an educational policy which originated with the "Philosophical Radicals" and the French Revolution scored a partial triumph. In the characteristically illogical English manner, this revolution was followed by the institution of halls for men of other religious communions than the Church of England. Some boarded and lodged their students as well as taught them; though no part of the University constitutionally, they were brought more or less within the circle of its teaching. Mansfield College, a non-residential theological hall, was removed from Birmingham to occupy its Oxford home in October, 1889; Manchester College, once University Hall, Gordon Square, London, was domiciled in Oxford in 1893, and later the Benedictines of Ampleforth established Hunter-Blair's Hall there. At Cambridge, Ridley Hall (1879) and Selwyn (1882) were closely associated with the Church of England, St Edmund's House (1896) trained Roman Catholic clergy and Westminster College, Presbyterian ministers. These "public hostels" approximate domestically to the daily life of the colleges, whose neighbours they are.

Reformers on the spot looked for amendment through the solution of a problem which had constantly recurred during the centuries, namely, how to render the relative positions of university and college mutually satisfactory. The success of the examination system and the prevalent confidence in the examination as an ideal made this problem more insistent in the second half of the nineteenth century. In spite of straitened means the Universities had provided new chairs and had rendered possible the pursuit of new studies, made necessary by the conditions of every-day life; but the undergraduate found that the instruction given by his private "coach" and the college lecturer bore directly upon the demands of his "school" or "tripos" and, from that point of view, professorial lectures were superfluous. "The fact that at present the student for honours neglects the professor's lecture room for the private lessons of a tutor only a few years his own senior is an artificial necessity created by the present system of examination."[1] In this way intellectual interests were circumscribed and an unfair advantage accrued to classics, and at Cambridge to mathematics also, as compared with pure science and modern literature. The excessive attention paid to the requirements of the examinations rendered almost impossible that cultivation and extension of knowledge which the reformers regarded as an important duty of the senior university residents. They drew a comparison, unfavourable in this particular to the English universities, between them and the universities of Germany. A German university was a society of learned men engaged quite as much in advancing knowledge as in communicating it; and their teaching was addressed rather to method than to subject-matter. Their aim was to train their students to become knowledge-makers rather than knowledge-absorbers.

Mark Pattison pleaded very forcibly in this sense, but complained that time and labour which should be spent upon independent study were given to the elementary instruction of young men. He described his own University of Oxford as a mere boarding school and an expensive one which made no pretensions to increasing the world's knowledge. His friend, Huxley, in his usual graphic manner, protested that a third-rate, poverty-stricken German university "turned out" more classical lore in one year than "our vast and wealthy foundations" elaborated in ten.[2] There was much debate at that time as to the expediency, or otherwise, of endowing research in the physical sciences; these two reformers were obviously greatly in favour of the principle but, with the existing condition of many fellowships at Oxford and

---

[1] Pattison, *op. cit.* p. 255.
[2] Pattison, *Suggestions*, etc., *passim* and Huxley, *Science and Education*, p. 104.

Cambridge in their minds, they found it better to talk discreetly on the subject. As Pattison would have it, the professor's teaching should be addressed to the advanced student only, "the post-graduate student" in the jargon of to-day, and he should have sufficient leisure to pursue his own studies. But the prevailing attitude towards the professoriate was less than encouraging and the University was too poor to find adequate stipends for the professors. The prize-fellowships continued to absorb college funds which would have been more fruitfully employed in university purposes or in strengthening college teaching. The existing conditions opened to the fellow only a very limited prospect of making academic teaching his life's profession, apart from the bar to his marriage; the hope of securing a college living which had formerly kept the fellow upon the spot was no hope for a lay fellow who did not intend to become a clergyman.

Some colleges, their wealth notwithstanding, gave little or no assistance to the comparatively poor University, whose constitutional paramountcy was obscured by these societies. Reformers inside and outside Oxford and Cambridge now turned their attention to this aspect of the university problem. The Prime Minister in 1871 proposed an inquiry by Royal Commission, or otherwise, into the property possessed by the two Universities and their colleges, and into the distribution of their several funds. Gladstone's proposal was welcomed generally by those concerned; but a memorial sent up from Cambridge deprecated the form of the proposal as likely to delay reforms and preferred to name specifically the matters which required redress. It asked that fellowships which did not entail work should not be allowed a life tenure, that fellows be permitted to marry, that colleges should pool their educational work so as to secure better teaching and leisure for study by the teachers, and that the relations, particularly the financial relations, between the University and its colleges be revised.[1] Cambridge addressed to Parliament more than one memorial to this effect; while seemingly disregarded they accurately anticipated the reforms which were in the end effected.

The *Third Report* of the Devonshire Commission,[2] issued in 1873, dealt with the two Universities. It noted that since 1863 Cambridge had expended £30,000 in erecting a museum and lecture rooms in

[1] See *Henry Sidgwick, a memoir*, by A. S. and E. M. S. (1896), p. 256.
[2] See the preceding chapter.

connexion with natural science and that in both Universities boards of studies had been instituted to organize examinations in science and mathematics. The scientific professorships recently founded comprised, at Oxford, the Waynflete (chemistry), 1854, the Linacre (physiology), 1857, the Hope (zoology), 1861; at Cambridge the Sadlerian chair of pure mathematics, 1863, and two other chairs, zoology and comparative anatomy, 1866, and experimental physics, 1871. Cambridge was said to allow "almost complete freedom to scientific students"; and Oxford, without much difficulty, might so modify its regulations as to secure a like freedom. But no English university regarded original research as one of its functions. "Even the University of London, which has been foremost in advancing experimental science, gives its highest degrees in science without requiring any proof that the candidate possesses the faculty of original research, or is competent to extend the boundaries of the science in which he graduates."[1] Except that Cambridge required elementary mechanics from candidates, nothing was done at either University to make the experimental study of science compulsory.

The Devonshire Commissioners were alive to the necessary connexion between secondary schools and university education. While some critics of the ancient Universities saw in a matriculation examination, like that of London, a guarantee that only competent students would find admission to the University, the Commissioners preferred to leave Oxford and Cambridge as they were in this matter, each college having its own kind of admission test. They would give to the schools a "leaving examination" which would discover those who had satisfactorily completed a course both literary and scientific in its character. The Commissioners based this examination upon a scale of marks which in the scientific subjects would be equitable as compared with the marks which it allotted to literary subjects. The effect of requiring such a certificate would reform the school curriculum and make feasible an advance in the study of science at the Universities, consequences which had followed the institution of the German *Abiturientenexamen* of a century earlier.

The duty of a university with reference to science was, in the Commissioners' opinion, to educate by its medium, to advance knowledge ("research is a primary duty"), to send to first-grade schools

[1] *Third Report*, p. lviii, Dr Frankland's evidence.

highly educated teachers of science, and to give the requisite preliminary scientific instruction required by the professions, e.g. medicine, engineering, chemistry. It was suggested to both Universities that they should instal a complete scientific professoriate; more than one chair is required for a proper study of any one "subject" and every professor requires assistants, as adjoint professors, demonstrators and others. The opinion marks the great development of knowledge which was then taking place, calling for a corresponding development in the organization of teaching. A further suggestion was the institution of research fellowships and the maintenance of research laboratories. Laboratories for undergraduates should be the possession of the university not of a college. Some colleges might have research laboratories for advanced students; more teachers of science were required on the college staffs. University museums and collections should be utilized for more than educational purposes. Finally the example of London should be followed by establishing a doctorate in science.

A Royal Commission on Oxford and Cambridge with the Duke of Cleveland as chairman was appointed in February, 1872, and reported in 1874, when it gave an exhaustive account of university and college properties and of the allocation of their incomes. A general conclusion from the facts, though not formulated in the report, warranted the belief that more might be done for education if the colleges would provide Alma Mater with more money.

A change of Government intervened between the opening of the Commission and the issue of its report, Gladstone making way for Disraeli. In the new Ministry, the Secretary for India, the Marquess of Salisbury, was also the Oxford Chancellor and a very pronounced advocate of reform. In 1876 he introduced a Bill to ensure such a distribution of college funds as would help to improve teaching in the Universities and provide libraries, museums and generally such apparatus as was necessary to the teaching of science; further, the measure was intended to appoint a Commission to discover how best these purposes could be realized.

At this time both Universities had already made substantial provision of the material kind contemplated by this Bill. In the address which he delivered as Lord Rector to the University of Aberdeen in 1874, Huxley was generous in praise of what had been done. "Within the last twenty years Oxford alone has sunk more than a hundred and twenty thousand pounds in building and furnishing physical, chemical and physiological laboratories, and a magnificent museum, arranged with an almost luxurious regard for the needs of the student. Cambridge, less rich, but aided by the munificence of her Chancellor,[1] is taking the same course; and in a few years it will be for no lack of the means and appliances of sound teaching, if the mass of English university men remain in their present state of barbarous ignorance of even the rudiments of scientific culture." But the facilities were insufficiently used.

Although Salisbury's Bill in the form proposed was dropped, the Commission was appointed and in August, 1877, the Universities of Oxford and Cambridge Act became law. The avowed intention of the Act was to cause the colleges to contribute more largely out of their revenues to university purposes, especially with a view to further and better instruction in art, science and other branches of learning, where the same were not taught, or not adequately taught, in the University. The tenure of fellowships and the cost of university education to the individual were also to be considered. With these objects in view the Commissioners were empowered to frame statutes within the period 1877–80 or 1881. Until the end of 1878 the colleges might make their own statutes, subject to the Commission's approval; failing action by a college the Commission was to make the necessary statutes, three college representatives assisting. A right of appeal was granted and the statutes, as is customary, were to be finally approved by the Sovereign in Council.

The Commissioners completed their labours by publishing statutes in 1882 with a supplement in 1888. Briefly, all that the reformers had been contending for was actualized by these statutes. A University Fund was established to which at Oxford the colleges were to contribute on a scheme graduated according to their means, at Cambridge by the same percentage of income from each college; the fund was to pay their stipends to professors, readers and lecturers. The prize life-fellowships were abolished, saving the interests of existing tenants. For all but a few cases the ban on marriage was removed and the general

---

[1] William Cavendish, seventh duke of Devonshire, whose memorial is the great Cavendish Laboratory; Chancellor of the University of Cambridge, 1861–91; chairman of the Devonshire Commission, 1870–5.

effect of the new statutes was to make it possible for the academic teacher to regard his work as his profession for life, if he so desired. The Commissioners noted that the plan of inter-collegiate lectures, that is, the pooling of part of their teaching by two or more colleges, was beginning to work well, although its tendency was "to oust the professors". The non-collegiate organization was making slow progress and ought to be developed. At both Universities a considerable measure of organization was brought into the daily life of these "unattached" undergraduates. Control was exercised at a later time by a delegacy, or syndicate, through a Censor; offices, library, hall, chapel and, at Cambridge, rooms were established for them. They put a boat upon the river and had the customary arrangements for sport. As in the case of the public hostels, all this goes to show how fundamental to the conception of education as understood at Oxford and at Cambridge is the common life of the college.

The statutes made for university and college in the period 1877–82 governed academic organization at Oxford and at Cambridge for the remainder of the century. Subject to the approval of the Sovereign in Council, the Universities and their colleges individually were empowered to make changes in their statutes from time to time as need required, thus rendering impossible the recurrence of the *impasse* which had been created by unmodifiable regulations. The Universities settled down to the work of giving material shape to the ideas and principles which actuated the new conditions.

Closer association was made between the college teachers and the professoriate, and the instruction was co-ordinated and economized by an extension of the scheme of inter-collegiate lectures and by giving to the university teachers, that is, the professors, a real share in under-graduate education. At Oxford the building (1855–60) of the Museum, largely due to the persistent advocacy of H. W. Acland, the Regius Professor of Medicine, had made a home for different branches of natural science and for the pursuit of experimental study. Since 1863 Cambridge had been building a group of institutions in which the university professors and their staffs taught astronomy, physics, botany, chemistry and zoology. To these her Chancellor, William Cavendish, Duke of Devonshire, in 1871 added the Cavendish Laboratory, the University responding to the gift by founding the Cavendish Chair of Experimental Physics. Such facilities as these for the study and advancement of science permitted some reforms to be effected without delay when the new conditions were once established.

Honour courses in new studies were formed and the existing Oxford "schools" and Cambridge triposes underwent changes which limited their scope and introduced greater specialization, changes which signified the development of studies and a further advance of knowledge. Law and history, which had previously constituted a single honours course in both Universities, were made two distinct "schools" or triposes in 1872. The Cambridge syllabus was revised in 1885 so as to emphasize constitutional history and first-hand knowledge of "sources" and original authorities; or, alternatively to the latter, political economy and the principles of law and government. The philosophical element in *Literae Humaniores* was intensified, modern philosophy not being neglected, and at both Universities archaeology attained greater importance in the study of Greek and Roman civilization.[1] In 1881 the Classical Tripos was divided into two parts, to be taken in different years. Part I dealt with classical authors, antiquities, translation. Part II had a compulsory paper in "pure scholarship" thus continuing the Cambridge tradition handed on from Bentley and Porson; additionally there was a choice amongst philosophy, history, law, archaeology, comparative philology, confined of course in all instances to the two civilizations which were the business of the tripos. Theology was made the subject of an honours course leading to the B.A. degree at Oxford in 1870 and at Cambridge in 1874.

Chairs in physiology were founded at the elder University in 1877 and at Cambridge in 1883, in which year a professorship of pathology was added to the equipment of the latter's medical school. In the previous year a chair of animal morphology also had been created. The Cambridge chair of mechanical and applied science, of which James Stuart was the first occupant (1875), eventually became one of engineering.

Candidates for the Indian Civil Service were required from 1878 onwards to spend their probationary period at Oxford or Cambridge before passing to India. In the following year an Indian Languages Tripos (Sanskrit and Hindustani, with Persian and comparative Indo-European grammar) was constituted, while in 1880 Oxford formulated a scheme for an Indian Institution for the probationers, Arnold Toynbee being appointed their tutor. The Semitic Languages Tripos (Arabic, Hebrew,

[1] The British School of Archaeology at Athens was inaugurated in 1886.

Syriac, Chaldee, comparative grammar) was established in 1878; in 1884 Cambridge also instituted an honours course which was destined to become very attractive, the Mediaeval and Modern Languages Tripos. Modern languages (French, German, Italian, Spanish) were taught at Oxford in the Taylorian Institution, a benefaction dating from 1835. From the opening of the building in 1845 until 1868 the work had been under the direction of a Professor of Modern Languages, whose office was abolished in the latter year on the foundation of the Comparative Philology chair. In 1889 a Reader in Slavonic was added to the staff of the Institution. No separate "school" of these languages was formed and the work was largely subsidiary to the fuller study of other subjects, as, for example, of history; the number of students was small. In 1893 the "school" of English (philology, literature and history) was founded.

Following German precedent, the academic teaching of modern languages (English included) during the nineteenth century was chiefly philological, scientific, rather than literary or cultural, that is, concerned with the civilization, the "Kultur" of the people who spoke the particular tongue. The history studied was that of the morphology of language; small attention was paid to the language as spoken, lest there should be any truth in the sneer, "a courier tripos". When the man and woman so taught became teachers in schools their tendency was to tell the tale as it had been told to them. The study of foreign literature as such and the use of the spoken word suffered accordingly in the schoolroom.

The effect of the organization set going by the Statutory Commissioners of 1877–82 is seen not so much in the introduction of studies entirely novel to the Universities, as in the position assigned to them and to their teachers, so that they became substantial, effective factors in the education of large numbers of undergraduates. Modern studies, from being either the hobby or the passing interest of the few, became the primary concern of many.

"Schools", triposes, examinations and degrees do not exhaust the agencies of university education. These are largely individual, with small reference to that common life (their competitive aspect apart) which is the pre-supposition of a collegiate society. Chapel and hall were inseparable from the undergraduate's life in the earlier time. The former had become a matter of voluntary attendance, and the increasing numbers of men seeking admission to the colleges made the authorities less rigid in requiring every man to dine in hall every day. Yet the gathering of congenial spirits for sport, for social intercourse and for those discussions, natural and dear to youth, *de omnibus rebus et quibusdam aliis*, continued to educate in a very real sense those who shared in them. And he was a very exceptional undergraduate who cared for none of these things.

The two Union Societies, in addition to the amenities which, as clubs, they afforded their members, furnished a school of public debate that served as an appropriate apprenticeship to many who in after years were prominent in politics and in other fields of public life. The small and sometimes cliquish societies within the colleges continued to flourish and decay as their predecessors had done. Some had a more prolonged existence. "The Cambridge Conversazione Society", more familiar as "the Apostles", which men of St John's and of Trinity had started in 1820, was still holding its weekly meetings for talk, refreshed by coffee and anchovies on toast, long after its original members had ceased to need any sort of corporal refreshment. Jebb, then a member of thirteen years' standing, joined the annual Richmond dinner of the society in the summer of 1873. Henry Sidgwick declared that the society "had more effect" on his life "than any one thing". Jebb was more explicit: "I have always felt that nothing ever did me more good than belonging to this society, for there was something in its whole spirit and in the peculiar sort of intimacy among its members which helped one, just at the critical time of life, to resist common standards, to aim high and be independent".[1]

Magazines, written and supported by particular colleges or broader based on a university circulation, still experienced the varied fortunes which in such cases invariably end in silence, but which always train some men (and women) to the trade of letters, while giving an opportunity to practise "business" aptitudes, where they exist.

Next to boating, walking was the most general form of exercise at Oxford and Cambridge during the first fifty or sixty years of the nineteenth century; riding at Cambridge in the early 'sixties' was described as the pastime "of a small coterie of the richer sort". But throughout the century boating held first place amongst university sports. There is an Oxford record of a race between college eights in 1815. The first

[1] C. Jebb, *Life and Letters of Sir R. C. Jebb* (1907), p. 116.

boat race between the two Universities took place in 1829; from 1856 the contest was annual, and after that date the race attained an extraordinary popularity throughout the country. The Universities first met on the cricket field in 1827; the match became annual from 1838.

As early as 1868 disgruntled persons like Mark Pattison desired to "strike a heavier blow at the cricket and boating" which, in his opinion, filled the days of 70 per cent. of the Oxford undergraduates; "they are playing all day or preparing for it or refreshing themselves after their fatigues" (*Suggestions*, p. 316). But for the major part of the century cricket and football were exceptional sports for university men when compared with the boats. The change came after the revolution of 1877–82, when increasing numbers and increasing funds made it necessary and possible for the colleges each to possess its own ground. Men who came from the Public Schools continued to play their own form of football at the University; Winchester, Eton, Harrow, Rugby each had its own peculiar game, so making football something of an esoteric mystery to outsiders. But by the 'seventies' the Rugby and Association Games had become organized; the first University matches were held in 1873 (Rugby) and 1874 (Association). Racquets and fives belong to the 'fifties', the first inter-University racquets dates from 1855, tennis (not lawn tennis) from 1859. Lawn tennis belongs to the 'seventies'; the Universities first met across the net in 1881. Oxford and Cambridge "Sports" began in 1864; golf was played in the 'nineties'. Volunteer soldiering and the allied rifle clubs, which were the nation-wide answer to certain foreign threats in 1859, were supported at both Universities from the beginning in that year.

While Vice-Chancellor (1882–6), Jowett made professional actors and their theatre academically respectable at Oxford, where they had suffered more or less of opprobrium for some two and a half centuries. He countenanced the building of a theatre, invited Henry Irving to lecture and formally recognized the undergraduates' amateur dramatic society, which even then had a long history. The corresponding Cambridge society was started in 1855. Jowett also brought John Farmer from Harrow to Balliol to give stimulus and direction to musical societies which in various forms the undergraduates and their seniors had supported long before the nineteenth century. The serious study of music at Oxford and the value of its musical degrees were due to Sir F. A. Gore Ouseley, Professor of Music from 1855 till his death in 1889.

Ruskin's teaching at Oxford cannot in any way be attributed to undergraduate enterprise, but it aroused great enthusiasm amongst the junior members of the University who crowded to his lectures. Felix Slade, in addition to other services to art education, had bequeathed £35,000 to endow chairs of fine art at Oxford, Cambridge and University College, London. Ruskin was the first professor to be appointed; he held the chair from 1870 to 1878, was re-elected in 1883 and resigned in 1885. For many years he had urged that the study of art and the practice of it, at least in the form of drawing, should be an essential part of a liberal education. How far his prelections served to secure that end may be doubted; it is certain that he had a considerable following amongst his Oxford pupils in those "opinions so opposed to Malthus, *The Times* and the city of Manchester" with which he had been charged in 1860.

The last twenty years of the century witnessed a steady development in the higher education of women, some brilliant individual performances and unsuccessful attempts at Oxford and at Cambridge to open the B.A. degree to women. In 1887 Miss Agnata Ramsay of Girton came out first in the first division of the first class of the Classical Tripos. Her success was followed by a memorial to the Senate praying that the degree be granted to women, but that body decided in 1888 to take no action. Miss Philippa Fawcett of Newnham was placed above the Senior Wrangler in 1890 and in the following year she was in the first division of the first class of Part II of the Mathematical Tripos. A second petition for the degree in 1896 led the Senate to appoint a syndicate to consider the question. The report in 1897 proposed that the degree should be given by diploma, a course which would not admit to membership of the University. This was the position accorded to Nonconformists from 1856 to 1871. The Senate rejected the proposal by 1707 votes to 661. The nearer approximation to the men's education which was being effected in this last decade of the century was symbolized by the hockey match between Newnham and Roedean.

At Oxford the Association for the Education of Women, which had been formed in 1878, secured admission to university and college lectures, sanctioned the opening of halls of residence, gave a diploma to women who successfully completed the B.A. course, and was responsible for discipline. In 1893 the Association was represented on the Hebdomadal Council by the Dean of Christ Church. Three new institutions were opened, St Hugh's in 1886, St Hilda's (a hostel giving no teaching) in 1893. The latter was intended originally for students from the Ladies' College, Cheltenham, whose principal, Miss Beale, was its founder. St Hugh's was established by Miss Wordsworth, the principal of Lady Margaret Hall, for students who desired a less expensive collegiate life. Finally, the Home Students, women whose homes were in Oxford and its immediate vicinity, were placed under a principal and governed by a committee of the Association. A memorial in favour of granting the degree to women was rejected by Convocation in 1896.[1]

Oxford and Cambridge "are, as Signor Matteuci called them, *hauts lycées*; and though invaluable in their way as places where the youth of the upper class prolong to a very great age, and under some very admirable influences, their school education, and though in this respect to be envied by the youth of the upper class abroad and if possible instituted for their benefit, yet with their college and tutor system, nay with their examination and degree system, they are still, in fact, *schools*, and do not carry education beyond the stage of general and school education.... The University of London labours under a yet graver defect as an organ of scientific or superior instruction. It is a mere *collegium*, or board, of examiners. It gives no instruction at all but it examines in the different lines of study and gives degrees in them. It has real university examinations (that is, those for Master and Doctor) which Oxford and Cambridge have not; and these examinations are conducted by an independent board, not by college tutors. This is excellent; but nevertheless it falls immensely short of what is needed. The idea of a university is, as I have already said, that of an institution not only offering to young men facilities for graduating in that line of study to which their aptitudes direct them, but offering to them also *facilities for following that line of studies systematically under first-rate instruction*. This second function is of incalculable importance; of far greater importance even than the first. It is impossible to over-value the importance to a young man of being brought

---

[1] In the University of Wales, founded 1893, there was no sex distinction in respect of scholarships, degrees or offices. In 1895 the University of Durham obtained a supplementary charter which threw open its teaching and its degrees to women, divinity degrees excepted.

in contact with a first-rate teacher of his matter of study, and of getting from him a clear notion of what the systematic study of it means. Such instruction is so far from being yet organized in this country, that it even requires a gifted student to feel the want of it; and such a student must go to Paris or Heidelberg or Berlin, because England cannot give him what he wants ".[1]

The reputation of the University of London had grown with the years, the general opinion being that the high standard of its examinations constituted its chief merit. In 1858 these examinations had been opened to candidates irrespective of the place or (the candidates in the Faculty of Medicine excepted) the manner of their education. In the following year a small committee of the Senate, Michael Faraday being a very active member, made an examination scheme for a Faculty of Science, which came into force in 1860. The requirement for the degree of B.Sc. was a good general knowledge of science, that for D.Sc. eminence in one of its branches. An additional charter of 1858 created Convocation, the assembly of graduates, including Bachelors of three years' standing, to whom collectively a certain participation, mainly by assent or veto, was assigned in university affairs. Disraeli's Government in the Reform Act of 1867 gave the University a Parliamentary representative and the Government of Gladstone in 1870 provided it with a home in the specially built Burlington House.[2] The first Parliamentary "burgess" elected by the members of Convocation was Robert Lowe, Chancellor of the Exchequer.

Yet, notwithstanding this development and these tokens of public or at least of official approval, Matthew Arnold was not alone in finding reasons for adverse criticism. The examinations were now being held not only in places distant from London but also overseas, and the wider the "Imperial" connexion became the further removed were the local interests of London. Those institutions, both professional and more general, which were actually conducting the higher teaching of the metropolis stood in no closer relation to its titular University than did a handful of students and their instructor in India. The examinations had no special reference to the instruction which was

[1] Matthew Arnold, *Higher Schools and Universities in Germany* (1868); see pp. 209–11, edition of 1882.

[2] Its headquarters had previously been at Marlborough House and earlier still in Somerset House.

being given at the moment in London, nor indeed could such a reference be expected, seeing the multifarious ways in which the widely dispersed candidates made their preparation. London teachers felt they must either work in fetters or ignore the examinations; and the tendency was towards the second alternative.

The failure of the University, or rather of its Senate, to appreciate its obligations to the metropolis of course had serious financial consequences for the two leading London colleges. It was evident to the Devonshire Commission that University College and King's College were doing their best to meet the demands of the day, especially in science and its application to the professions of the chemist, engineer and architect, without neglecting the older studies or modern languages and literatures. University College had ten, King's College nine, professorships in science which, like the Arts chairs, were "very inadequately paid", notwithstanding the personal distinction of many of the occupants. It was an express condition attached to the "Jodrell" chair of physiology, recently founded at University College, that the professor should give to original research all the time that could be "spared from lecture-room work". The Evening Class Department of King's College provided "a fairly complete course of scientific instruction" for persons unable to attend classes during the day. Of the 550 students in that Department in 1873 about 300 were attending science classes. It was found on inquiry that no artisans attended these classes. Laboratories, fittings and apparatus were inadequate to their purpose on account of the poverty of both colleges. University complained of insufficient endowment, and Dr Alfred Barry, the Principal of King's, told the Commission that the chief impediment to further success was that "we are so extremely poor". The Commission recommended the Government to pay a capital sum to each college and an annual grant in aid. King's College was advised to remove any religious test which might be proposed to a candidate for a scientific chair; it was disclosed in evidence that the only test applied in such cases was a simple affirmation of membership of the Church of England.[1]

While dissatisfaction with the university position was great in these two colleges, it was even greater in the medical schools; the Inns of Court had always held aloof from the University. The medical schools complained of over-elaboration in the syllabuses of examination,

[1] *Fifth Report*, 1874.

especially in the sciences preliminary to the professional medical course. For these their students could afford neither the time nor the money, and in consequence many migrated in their last year, or two, to universities where graduation was easier although opportunity for clinical study was far less. The Convocation of the University itself shared the discontent and as early as 1878 made proposals, which came to nothing, for the addition of a teaching side to the University's operations.

Of all the institutions outside the metropolis affiliated at this date to the University, the chief place was occupied by Owens College, Manchester. Opened in 1851 with a capital sum exceeding £90,000, the bequest (1846) of a Manchester merchant, the college was meant to be the nucleus of a university, the fulfilment of a hope which dated in Manchester from the civil-war period of the seventeenth century. Owens' fortune was to be spent, not on land or buildings, but upon advancing in other ways "such branches of learning and of science as were then and might be hereafter usually taught in English universities", exception being made in the case of theology. In its infant years the college had an uphill struggle, the lack of a suitable building seriously hindering its progress. Yet it was alive to its duty as an educational centre; before the retirement in 1857 of its first principal, A. J. Scott, he and his colleagues had started the Manchester Working Men's College. During the disastrous "Lancashire cotton famine" of 1862 it planned "recreative evenings", including lectures, for the unemployed workmen, a successful scheme which somewhat later gave birth to a series of "science lectures for the people", delivered by Henry Roscoe, Huxley, Tyndall, Huggins, Spottiswoode and other distinguished savants. In the session 1852–3 the college established evening classes for schoolmasters, classics and mathematics being the only subjects taught. In the end these classes absorbed the Working Men's College and both studies and students were of the most general character. In 1867 the position was sufficiently assured to permit the college to state as its purpose "the highest general education leading to degrees in arts and science and the special training required for professional and mercantile life". An appeal for public subscriptions secured £168,300. An Act of Parliament, 1871, gave Owens College a new constitution, which permitted the admission of women to its classes and raised the minimum age of admission from fourteen to fifteen years, in both these matters oversetting the founder's will. When the college reported to the Devonshire Commission it possessed a staff which included twelve professors, of whom six taught branches of science, pure or applied, civil and mechanical engineering being of the number. There were at this time 350 students following, during the day hours, one or other of the systematized courses intended to prepare for a London degree in Arts or Science, a number of students from the medical school receiving their preliminary scientific training, while there were over 900 evening class students. The Commission recommended that the same financial support should be given to Owens College as to the two London colleges.[1]

Principal Greenwood, A. W. Ward, Henry Roscoe and other members of the teaching staff now saw their way to realizing the intention implied a generation earlier in John Owens' bequest. A Press "campaign" was started, the aid of the Lancashire members of Parliament was enlisted and after nearly four years of negotiation Owens College, Manchester, became by charter of 1880 the Victoria University; power was conferred to federate within the University upon equal terms other colleges of suitable standing. At its first meeting (April, 1881) the University Court, the supreme governing body, decided to require from candidates for its science degrees, not Latin or Greek, but a modern language or languages.

The position of the London colleges had now become invidious, that of London University impossible. An Association for Promoting a Teaching University for London was started in 1884 to which University and King's College Councils gave their adhesion in 1886, and thereafter their cordial support. The Association worked steadily towards its objective, Convocation and Senate made schemes and failed to agree with each other. The Senate was obdurate in its refusal to pay especial regard to the higher education of London; if their University was to revert to its early history and take particular institutions, their teachers and students, into consideration, then these must be found all over England and there must be no compulsion to attend courses of instruction or to submit to academic discipline.

At length in the autumn of 1887 University and King's Colleges petitioned the Crown to be incorporated, if possible with the Royal

[1] *Fifth Report*, 1874.

Colleges of Physicians and Surgeons, to form the nucleus of a university for London under the title "the Albert University". But the Royal Colleges ceased to co-operate with the petitioners and asked for a separate charter empowering them to confer academical degrees; the "Albert University" was intended to include the medical schools of the metropolis, the actual teaching bodies. The Senate opposed the "Albert" petition, and in May, 1888, a Royal Commission ("the Selborne Commission") was appointed "to make inquiry whether any and what kind of new university or powers is or are required for the advancement of the higher education of London". This Commission, reporting in April, 1889, approved in general terms the idea of a university which taught as well as examined, but did not specify the precise form which such a university should take; it recommended that a reasonable time be allowed to the Senate and to Convocation to consider whether they would seek for a new charter extending their powers in this direction. In other words the Commission preferred to see one university in the metropolis rather than two; and it believed that the functions of teaching locally and examining on a non-local scale were not incompatible, that the interests of internal students and external examinees could be reconciled. The Senate proposed a *modus vivendi* which satisfied neither Convocation nor the advocates of a new and separate institution.

So the matter dragged along until June, 1891, when the Privy Council decided in favour of the Albert petition. Whereupon the provincial colleges[1] and the provincial medical schools, believing that their vested interests in the University of *London* were threatened, raised a storm of opposition, calling their local members of Parliament to assist. By this time, hopes were entertained in the petitioning colleges that the City Corporation would support the proposed university whose title was changed to the Gresham University, re-calling the merchant prince of the sixteenth century who almost succeeded in founding a University of London in his day and whose benefaction still maintained Gresham College and its seven professors. The petitions in favour of establishing the new university and its draft charter were submitted to Parliament, where the opposition of London graduates and of provincial institutions brought it about that the Crown was asked to withhold consent until further inquiry had been made.

[1] The "University Colleges" described below.

This led, in April, 1892, during the Salisbury Cabinet's period of office, to the appointment of a second Royal Commission, the "Gresham", to consider and, if necessary, "to alter, amend and extend the proposed Charter" so as to form a scheme for establishing "a teaching university for London".

The Commission reported in January, 1894, Gladstone's last Government having in the interval succeeded that of Lord Salisbury, during which time controversy had been heated and prolonged. Amongst other proposals a scheme had been floated for a professorial university into which "all institutions in London of academic rank should be fused and absorbed" into a single teaching body governed by the professors and a number of Crown nominees. The Gresham Commission was in agreement with the first Commission that there should be but one university in London and that its powers should include local teaching and the examination of students from all parts of the British Empire. As the advocates of a teaching body had pointed out, the existing University was powerless directly to encourage research or the advancement of learning, however considerable the *quantum* of knowledge required to pass its examinations. Unlike some universities, it was not concerned with knowledge in the making. The Gresham *Report* asserted that it should not be necessary for advanced students to "cross the Channel in order to find elsewhere what a teaching University of London certainly ought to provide". The Commissioners accordingly recommended that provision of this kind should be made in the newly constituted University; in particular, access should be possible to advanced instruction in languages, in history, in philosophical studies, and for post-graduate research and scientific study, both pure and applied. To these ends, new and independent institutions should be created and new chairs set up. Three of the six Selborne Commissioners had doubted the feasibility of combining local teaching and "Imperial" examining; three of the thirteen Gresham Commissioners thought it inexpedient. The Gresham *Report* recommended that the changes which they had in view as to the constitution, government and studies of the University should be effected not by specific legislation but through a body of commissioners empowered to draw up statutes.

More than four years of controversy followed before the last recommendation took effect in the University of London Act of

August, 1898, which named and assigned their powers to seven commissioners, whose task was completed by the issue of the statutes in February, 1900. Act and statutes combined resulted in the following. The purposes of the University were to encourage regular and liberal courses of education in the United Kingdom and elsewhere, to promote research, to advance science and learning, and to organize and extend higher education within the appointed radius, that is to say, within the circle whose radius extended for thirty miles from the University's headquarters. The supreme governing body, the Senate, was to consist of the Chancellor (chosen for life by Convocation), the Chairman of Convocation, four Crown nominees, sixteen representatives of Convocation, the like number representing the university teachers embodied in "Faculties", and eighteen representatives of institutions, making fifty-six members in all. Of the Senate there were to be three standing committees, the Academic Council having very full advisory powers in reference to the teaching side of the University and the interests of its "Internal" students and affairs generally, the External Council similarly concerned with examinees who were not receiving instruction from the University, and the University Extension Board, whose business was to take over the duties which were being discharged by the "Universities Joint Board of the London Society for the Extension of University Teaching". Eight Faculties were created, namely, theology, arts, laws, music, medicine, science, engineering, and economics and political science (including commerce and industry).

The list is instructive, not only in the light which it throws upon the character of a liberal education and the functions of a university as then understood; the admission of, and the first place uncompromisingly assigned to, theology definitely disregards the educational Radicalism which, throughout the century then closing, had resolutely ignored the study of divinity. The Gresham Commissioners reported (p. xv): "The University of London is by its Charter prohibited from conferring degrees in Theology; and no theological faculty or degree is provided for in the Gresham Charter, although King's College has for many years had a considerable Theological Department connected with it. The divinity degrees now obtainable in England are practically restricted to the clergy of the Established Church....A strong desire was expressed by the representatives of various theological colleges in and near London connected with the Church of England and with

other religious denominations, that the scope of the University might
be enlarged so as to include a Faculty and a Degree in Theological
Science, a term chosen by them to indicate distinctly that the degree had
relation solely to the various branches of learning related to the study
of theology, and implied no test or profession of faith. A similar
proposal received the support of the Convocation of the University of
London. Concurring as we do in the opinion that it is practicable to
conduct theological examinations on the basis proposed, and that the
recognition of the subject by the University must give a valuable
stimulus to the deeper study of this important branch of learning, we
propose that power should be given to the University of London to
teach, examine and confer degrees in Theological Science on the same
footing as in other Faculty subjects". By way of safeguard Statute 22
contained the following: "No religious test shall be adopted or imposed
by any statute, bye-law, regulation or standing order and no applicant
for a university appointment shall be at any disadvantage on the
ground of religious opinions".

The "Schools of the University" comprised University College and
King's College in all the faculties for which they provided instruction,
six theological colleges in their faculty, ten medical schools in their
faculty, Bedford College and the Royal Holloway College in Arts and
Science, the Royal College of Science and the South Eastern Agricultural
College, Wye, in Science, the London School of Economics and
Political Science in its faculty, and in engineering the Central Technical
College of the City and Guilds. The four Inns of Court and the
Incorporated Law Society continued to resist all invitation and almost
urgent persuasion to share the fortunes of the newly reorganized
University.

To return to an earlier stage in the University's history, namely, to
the 'eighties'. By that time the effective demand for the higher education
of women was outgrowing the provision made for it. Other centres
than those at Oxford, Cambridge, London, Cheltenham, became
necessary; and the pioneer colleges were now able to supply the new-
comers with suitable teachers. In 1882 Westfield College, West
Hampstead, was opened "for the higher education of women on
Christian principles"; its first "Mistress", Miss C. L. Maynard, was a
Girtonian, and Westfield, like Girton, was distinctly associated with

the Church of England. Thomas Holloway, the wealthy pill maker, who died in 1883, had long meditated the establishment of a women's university as a memorial to his deceased wife. His project took partial shape in the foundation in 1886 at Egham of the Royal Holloway College for Women, of which the first Principal (1887–97) was Miss M. E. Bishop, who had been educated at Queen's College, London. The addition of the word "Royal" to the founder's name marked the approval of the scheme by Queen Victoria. At the outset it was arranged as a temporary measure that the students should prepare for the London or the Oxford examinations. Ten years later, during the crisis in the fortunes of the University of London, "Holloway" proposed to become a separate and independent university for women, or failing that, that it should form, with other Women's Colleges, a federated university after the pattern of the Victoria University or the University of Wales. Neither proposal was accepted and the college finally became one of the "schools" of the reconstituted London University.

The Ladies' Department (at Kensington) of King's College, London, began with a large number of somewhat dilettante students to whom facilities were given for instruction in divinity, arts, science, drawing, painting, music, sick nursing and "first aid". But from 1895, when some of them read seriously for one or other of the Oxford "schools", studies assumed a more systematic and academic character. In and after 1899 the King's College diploma of "Associate" was conferred upon women who had successfully pursued the required course; in the following year the Department (now organized as "King's College for Women") like its parent society in the Strand, which had always given it the majority of its teachers, became a part of the University of London as constituted by the Act of 1898.

The last two or three decades of the nineteenth century were remarkable in academic history by reason of the rapid and vigorous growth of what came to be known as university colleges. The name itself seems to have been first used in an English connexion at Nottingham in 1877 to describe the building which the town council, stimulated by the Rev. J. B. Paton, Mr Richard Enfield and others, then erected for the purposes of higher instruction.[1] In 1889 Parliament rendered the term

[1] Edith M. Becket, *The History of University College, Nottingham* (1928), p. 37 But University College, Aberystwyth, dates from 1872.

exact by voting an annual sum of £15,000 for distribution in varying sums amongst some dozen colleges on condition that each of them performed an appreciable amount of work of a university standard. Henceforward the title "University College" implied a place on the list of these grantees.[1]

All of these colleges had an earlier history which reflected the different purposes that had animated the advocates of an education beyond the rudimentary stage. Some occupied places which at an earlier date had been filled by a Literary and Philosophical Institution; others represented the survival of a Mechanics' Institute. In some cases a local medical school, associated through its examinations with the University of London, formed the nucleus. Civic pride, the foresight and philanthropy of individual benefactors gave rise to others. Many of them had been fostered by the money grants paid on examination successes by the Science and Art Department. From 1890 they began to assist in the training of teachers; the government grants payable on this account brought a welcome element of stability into their finances and responsibilities. But the most influential forces in creating and shaping the university colleges were University Extension and the agitation for technical education. The success of Extension lectures in Bristol and the desire of the local medical school to equip itself with new buildings resulted in a public meeting, held in 1874, to promote the establishment of a local college, or university, which should house both.[2] The college was opened in 1876, when it was prepared to add teaching in agriculture to its other forms of instruction. Balliol and New College offered to contribute an annual subvention, if the college would admit women to its classes and give adult instruction in the evenings. The promoters of the college at Nottingham were associated with "Extension" in a unique way; Henry Sidgwick, when inaugurating the first course delivered there in the Mechanics' Institute, asserted that it was Notting-

[1] At the close of the century the Parliamentary annual grant was £25,000 distributed amongst the following: Owens College, Manchester; University College, London; Liverpool; Leeds; King's College, London; Birmingham; Newcastle; Bristol; Nottingham; Sheffield; Bedford College, London; the University Extension College, Reading; and Hartley College, Southampton. See Graham Balfour, *The Educational Systems of Great Britain and Ireland* (1903), pp. 251 f. The three Welsh Colleges, Aberystwyth, Cardiff and Bangor, had their own particular government grant.

[2] The University of Bristol was created in 1909.

ham that determined Cambridge to adopt "Extension". "It was the definite, well-thought-out character and practicability of the scheme presented by the Nottingham delegates, and their urgency, which decided the Syndicate to take up the matter.... The idea had existed for some time, but it would have remained an idea, but for the action taken by Nottingham." [1]

All of these colleges at some stage of their history received stimulus and direction from the examination requirements of the University of London, whose degrees were the coveted distinction of their ablest students. Some looked forward to becoming independent universities; most of them outgrew the original limits of their curricula. None gave instruction in divinity, all admitted women as freely as men; but in both respects King's College, London, was exceptional. That college was also exceptional in that it provided college rooms and hall dinner for a few students; chapel was open to all, resident or non-resident. The two London colleges were never purely local but drew some of their members from all parts of the Empire and beyond. Students of university colleges for the most part lived in their own homes; but hostels or halls of residence were added to them at an early time in their history. Most of the colleges became independent universities, or parts of such universities, in the opening years of the twentieth century. They are now centres of culture and disseminators of knowledge amongst the general public as well as amongst their undergraduate members, and they make their due contribution to all forms of research —scientific, historical and literary.

University College, London, King's College, London, and Owens College, Manchester, by seniority and by the standard of their teaching formed a group apart. Hartley College, Southampton, after a troubled history which began in 1859, was admitted by the Board of Education to the category of university colleges in 1902. Bedford College, London, and the University Extension College, Reading, were also recipients of the title and of shares in the annual treasury grant.

Newcastle furnishes an instance of close association between the nucleus of a university college and a local medical school. Reporting to the Devonshire Commission on its scientific labours, the University of Durham stated that it possessed an astronomical observatory,

---

[1] Becket, *op. cit.* p. 31.

maintained chairs of astronomy and mathematics, a lectureship in natural philosophy and was co-operating with the medical school of Newcastle. Attempts to teach applied science in Durham itself had not been satisfactory and, as Newcastle seemed to be better fitted, industrially and topographically, to become the centre of that kind of instruction, the University had undertaken to pay yearly in perpetuity £1000 (a sum subsequently increased) in support of the College of Physical Science in that town. Founded in 1871 and maintained by benefactors' donations and subscriptions, the college was devoted to science, "particularly in its practical application to engineering, mining, manufactures, agriculture". It had professors of pure and applied mathematics, chemistry, experimental physics, geology and biology; there were also lecturers in Greek and Latin, English history and literature, French, German and mechanical drawing. For the session 1873–4, there were seventy-eight students, and the Commission hoped that the college would soon be in a position to claim State aid.[1]

The Paris Exhibition of 1867 greatly perturbed the textile manufacturers of Leeds, and schemes of technical instruction were put into operation, the grants of the Science and Art Department providing a supplement to funds raised locally. The general anxiety about the industrial position, the recognition of the fact that science was being neglected in English education and the native impulse to self-help combined to lend a very practical interest to the discussions of the recently founded Yorkshire Board of Education. In 1869 the Council of this body decided that it was desirable to establish a College of Science and began to collect funds to that end. A capital sum exceeding £25,000 was raised, promise of help was made by the Endowed Schools Commissioners, and the Clothworkers Company (of London) undertook to maintain a chair of technical instruction in the textile industry. The "Yorkshire College of Science", Leeds, opened in October, 1874, with three professors, of experimental physics and mathematics, geology and mining, chemistry. At first competent students came in slowly; but presently requests for help were made by candidates for London examinations and for scholarships at other universities. The academic staff saw that it was expedient to add a literary side to the curriculum and in this opinion they were fortified by Dr Gott, the Vicar of Leeds,

[1] Devonshire Commission, *Fifth Report*, 1874.

and Sir Edward Baines who begged the Council to help University Extension. Chairs of classical literature and history and of modern literature and history were set up and the words "of Science" were dropped from the college's description. New buildings were begun in 1877, the Clothworkers Company voting £10,000 for the erection of the Textile Industries Department.[1]

University College, Liverpool, was established and chartered in October, 1881, its origin being due "not to the munificence of an individual but to the public spirit of many citizens and to the conviction of a community".[2] *Cives posuerunt*, as its lofty tower attests. The aims of its promoters were "to provide such instruction in all branches of a liberal education as would enable residents in the town and neighbourhood to qualify for degrees in arts, science and other subjects at any of the universities granting degrees to non-resident students, and at the same time to give such technical instruction as would be of immediate service in professional and commercial life".

Work began in January, 1881, with a staff of seven endowed professorships and three lectureships; three years later the medical school of the Royal Infirmary was incorporated in the college. In the same year (1884) University College, Liverpool, became the second constituent college of the federal Victoria University, Yorkshire College, Leeds, forming the third in 1887.

The federation had only a brief history. In 1901 Liverpool began to seek an endowment sufficient to justify its existence as a separate, independent university; it convinced the Privy Council of the justice of its claim and the soundness of its finance. In February, 1903, the Council decided that Manchester and Liverpool ought to be made universities and that Leeds should have the opportunity to submit a draft charter with a similar intention. Liverpool secured its university in that year and Leeds followed in 1904.

Mark Firth (1819–80) a wealthy iron-master of Sheffield, was attracted by the University Extension scheme as propounded by Cambridge and determined to make a permanent home for the lectures in Sheffield. The building of Firth College, opened in October, 1879,

[1] See Sir T. E. Thorpe's *The Rt Hon. Sir H. E. Roscoe: a biographical sketch* (1916), to which this account of Leeds "origins" is indebted.

[2] *Case* presented to the Privy Council, 1902.

cost its founder £20,000; to this gift he added a capital sum of £5000 and endowed a chair of chemistry with £150 a year. A technical school, with the assistance of the City and Guilds of London, the Drapers Company of London, the Cutlers Company and the town trustees of Sheffield, was added to Firth College in 1883, of which it was a department until 1889, when it became a separate institution under the corporation of Sheffield. In 1897 the local medical school (founded 1828) and the technical school were amalgamated by charter with Firth College to form University College, Sheffield. Its aims were expressed in terms almost identical with those of Liverpool cited above, except that they include "and generally the promotion and increase of knowledge" while medical education is expressly named with "technical and scientific instruction".[1] The college became the University of Sheffield in 1905.

Birmingham with its strong sense of civic life and pride in the variety and efficiency of its municipal activities, amongst which the provision of elementary and secondary schooling was outstanding, had long enjoyed opportunities for adult advanced instruction. The Birmingham and Midland Institute (founded 1854) excited the enthusiasm of a foreign observer in 1889, who described it as "une sorte d'université populaire".[2] Mason Science College was opened in October, 1880, for purposes exclusively scientific. These were stated to be: (1) regular and systematic instruction for the degrees of B.Sc. and D.Sc. in the University of London, and (2) popular instruction by evening lectures to artisans. The founder, Sir Josiah Mason (1795–1881), would make no provision for teaching theology or "mere literary instruction and education"; but circumstances overruled these intentions. First, the word "Science" was omitted from the college's name; then, when Birmingham took steps to obtain its own university, the property of Mason College formed the nucleus of the required endowment (1898). Joseph Chamberlain, at that time Colonial Secretary in Lord Salisbury's Cabinet, crowned a lifelong series of services to Birmingham by supporting the town's claim to establish a university. The charter was duly obtained in 1900. To the customary faculties of arts, medicine and

---

[1] *Floreamus! A Chronicle of University College, Sheffield* (1897), by members of the academic staff.

[2] Max Leclerc, *L'éducation des classes moyennes et dirigeantes en Angleterre* (1894).

science Birmingham added a fourth, commerce; yet another innovation consisted in admitting brewing to the list of technical studies, a new departure which gave the ill-informed opportunities for cheap witticism. Parliament made the University an annual grant of £2000 in 1901.

A national movement, which secured the support of well-to-do and poor alike, to extend higher education within the bounds of the Principality created the University College of Wales, Aberystwyth, in 1872. A second and more political "cause", Home Rule for Wales, led to the appointment of a Departmental Committee under Lord Aberdare to inquire into Welsh education, intermediate and higher, and to make recommendations[1]. The Committee reported at length in 1881, and, in consequence of its recommendations, university colleges were established at Cardiff and Bangor. "In 1893 the three Colleges were incorporated by royal charter in the University of Wales.... When the petition for this charter was drawn up there were 650 students [of both sexes] attending the three Colleges, and one-eighth of the bachelor's degrees in arts and science granted at the London University during the preceding year were taken by Welsh students."[2] St David's College, Lampeter, founded in 1827 for the education of persons intending to take Holy Orders, is empowered to grant degrees of B.A., B.D. and a licentiateship in divinity; but it is not part of the University of Wales.

A survey of English higher education at the close of the nineteenth century may be fitly closed by a reference to the British Academy. There was a proposal to hold in 1904 an international meeting of academies which concerned themselves with natural science, literature, antiquities and philosophy. This country was represented in the first branch by the Royal Society, but, as the Secretary of that Society pointed out, there was nothing to represent British humanist studies officially. The position was discussed at an informal meeting held in Cambridge at the end of 1899 by Professor R. C. Jebb, Professor H. Sidgwick and Lord Acton, in effect representing classics, philosophy and history. Their deliberations led to the calling of a meeting in London

---

[1] See pp. 448 f. below.
[2] Graham Balfour, *Educational Systems*, etc. p. 257.

in mid-December attended by many distinguished men, when it was resolved to form an academy of history, philosophy, moral and political science. A petition was addressed to the King in January, 1902, and a charter was granted in that year to the "British Academy for the promotion of Historical, Philosophical and Philological Studies", Lord Reay being the first president [1] and Israel Gollancz the first secretary.

[1] Lady C. Jebb, *Life and Letters of Sir R. C. Jebb* (1907), pp. 350 ff.

CHAPTER XVI

Administrative Muddle

During the first half of the nineteenth century the Welsh people had been chary in accepting government grants in aid of education. They preferred to rely upon their own efforts, particularly upon the work of their numerous Sunday schools, which exhibited "a mixture of worship, discussion and elementary education, which the congregation performs for itself, and without other agency than its own".[1] The age-long association of education with religion was maintained as a principle of the first importance and in such an association the State could have no place. As a consequence the number of elementary schools that fulfilled the conditions which qualified for the receipt of public money was comparatively small, and enthusiasm was wanting for such a system as was developing in England. In the 'forties' Wales was fifty or sixty years behind the sister country in respect of public instruction.

The great change which subsequently followed was largely due to the initiative of Hugh Owen (1804–81) who in a *Letter to the Welsh People*, issued in 1843, advocated the establishment of undenominational schools of the "British school" type, to be maintained largely by government grants. In 1846 the Cambrian Educational Society was founded, with Owen as its honorary secretary, in sympathy and active co-operation with the British and Foreign School Society. Parliament then determined to send Commissioners of inquiry into Wales to ascertain the condition of elementary education and in particular the facilities open to children for learning English. After a year's investigation the Commissioners produced a report which presented a deplorable picture not only of the schools but also of the morals and social life of the great bulk of the people. The report was hotly resented, some critics asserting that the Commissioners were sent into Wales with the deliberate purpose of injuring by misrepresentation the nationality, language and nonconforming religious belief of Wales. Critics less vehement

---

[1] *Special Reports on Educational Subjects*, vol. II, p. 4, quoting Lingen in *Report of the Commissioners of Inquiry into the State of Education in Wales* (1847). The schools were for adults as well as for children.

regarded the report as exaggerated, a character which was due in their opinion to incompetence in the inquirers.[1] However, the strictures of the Commissioners, an independent inquiry by the National Society, and the persuasiveness of Hugh Owen aroused attention which did not soon relax. Unlike many enthusiasts for systems of public education, Owen did not confine his vision to its primary grade but urged the establishment of a Welsh college, or colleges, to advance still further the education given in the endowed grammar schools. At a public meeting held in London in 1863 it was resolved to open subscriptions for the purpose and, as the outcome of a national effort in which Welshmen of all classes shared, the University College of Wales was opened at Aberystwyth in 1872.

The Elementary Education Act was a Welsh no less than an English measure, and by it Wales added to her existing voluntary schools, board schools and, in the larger towns, higher grade schools, as in England. In 1880 there were thirty endowed schools of grammar school standing, three of them being for girls. In August of that year Lord Aberdare's Departmental Committee was appointed to inquire into the existing condition of intermediate and higher education in Wales and to recommend measures for improving and supplementing the provision for it. Monmouthshire was subsequently brought within the Committee's purview. The same defects that had formerly hindered higher education in England were noted. Schools were distributed badly with reference to population, their curriculum was unsuitable; a large number of private schools of very varying degrees of efficiency endeavoured to remedy this latter defect by making their courses largely "commercial", that is, by introducing subjects which were chosen and taught with strict reference to the work of the shop and the business office. The schools under public management, grammar schools and their like, were almost exclusively in the hands of the Church and there was a strong prejudice against the Church. The Committee recommended the establishment of two university colleges, the improvement of school premises, the provision of scholarships, a revision of the course of studies and of school fees so that the maximum charge in schools of the first grade

---

[1] A true bill must be returned against the three Commissioners on the score of incompetence at least. The subject is discussed in Dr Frank Smith's *Life of Sir James Kay-Shuttleworth*, pp. 201 ff.

should not exceed £10 a year. The schools should be undenominational and administered by governing bodies popularly elected; they should be financed, as were the board schools, partly by government grants, partly by the local rates.

The University College of South Wales and Monmouthshire at Cardiff and the University College of North Wales at Bangor, each having its charter and an annual Parliamentary subvention of £4000, were fruits of the Committee's report; they were opened respectively in 1883 and 1884.[1] Beyond that, no immediate effect was given to the recommendations.

But a wave of political enthusiasm demanding home rule for Wales was the stimulus to a greater advance and the enactment in 1888 of the Local Government measure creating county councils provided the necessary occasion. The lack of any comprehensive unit of local government, which had hindered the adoption of the principal recommendations of the Departmental Committee, was now removed. The Welsh Intermediate Education Act of 1889 came into operation before the year expired. The Act set up in each county Joint Education Committees with power to initiate school schemes for presentation to the Charity Commissioners, since such schemes were to deal with existing foundations as well as with new schools yet to be created. The schools were to be called "intermediate", as coming between the university colleges on the one side and board and voluntary schools on the other. They were to be financed by the proceeds of a halfpenny rate and by Exchequer grants not exceeding the expenditure from local sources; school fees were to be low. The Technical Instruction Act of 1889 and the Local Taxation (Customs and Excise) Act of 1890 were especially helpful in establishing these new intermediate schools. A Central Welsh Board to co-ordinate the inspection and examination of the new schools was formed, a final monument to faith in external examining bodies.

The intermediate schools were either entirely separate for the sexes or else dual or mixed, according to locality. In the larger towns separate boys' and girls' schools were the rule; in wide rural areas the more economical form of administration was the mixed school and co-education, or the dual school of two departments under one roof

---

[1] The University College of Wales, Aberystwyth, received an annual grant of £2500 in 1884, increased two years later to £4000.

and one head master. Dual or mixed, the teachers were both men and women.

The distribution of population was carefully regarded in planning the site of new schools. The secondary schools of Wales were trebled in number; whereas in 1880 girls' schools to boys' schools had been as one in ten, the ratio in consequence of the Act became two in five. A liberal provision of scholarships from the public elementary to the intermediate schools and from them to the university colleges constituted that "opportunity for all" which had been the democratic demand for a century. In point of fact the majority of students of the University of Wales and of pupils in the intermediate schools began their education in board or voluntary schools. The curriculum of these Welsh secondary schools included languages, ancient and modern, Welsh, mathematics, natural science, and manual instruction. The religious instruction was by statute undenominational.[1] By the federation of the three university colleges in the University of Wales the Principality was thus in possession of a duly articulated national system some ten years in advance of England.

Whereas the legislation of 1888–90 had brought order into the educational affairs of Wales, it had made chaos more confused to the east of Offa's Dyke. While England had long endured a diversity of educational authorities, the Acts of those years had increased their number without diminishing the powers of those already in possession. The county councils and county boroughs were made responsible for the local provision of "technical instruction", an undefined term which, as administered centrally by the Science and Art Department, was a nose of wax. An Act of 1889 empowered the Board of Agriculture to assist this kind of education and it made grants to the university colleges of Leeds, Nottingham, Newcastle, and Reading, as well as to the Cambridge and Counties Agricultural Education Committee. The only titular local authorities for "education" were the school boards; but these had no jurisdiction in secondary or technical education, though most of their schools gave, or attempted to give, both. Centrally two public offices, the Charity Commission and the Science and Art Department dealt with secondary education. The one public office

---

[1] "The Welsh Intermediate Education Act, 1889" in *Special Reports on Educational Subjects*, vol. II (1898).

not formally concerned with it was the *Education* Department; yet that office countenanced by its examinations and aided by Treasury money almost all secondary school studies, Latin not excepted, which public elementary schools could follow under the Department's Code. Again locally, every governing body of an endowed grammar school was an independent corporation with no responsibilities towards any school but its own. The committees which controlled proprietary schools, as also the principals of private schools, were independent not only of other local powers, but of the central authorities likewise. These owed no allegiance to the Charity Commission which to a great extent controlled the endowed grammar schools. No more striking illustration of the national disinclination "to think things out" and of its inevitable consequences can be found than the persistent neglect to define "elementary", "secondary", "technical", as applied to instruction.

The school boards in their zeal for education irrespective of grade or type intensified the confusion, which of course was not merely administrative, but bemused public opinion which in turn reacted upon the work of the schools. Board schools and higher grade schools competed with voluntary schools on the elementary level; and elementary schools, board and voluntary alike, rivalled the poorly endowed secondary schools, whose fees were fixed by the Charity Commission, fees which these schools could not raise in the face of rivals whose fees were either non-existent or trifling. The evening schools, which at an earlier date had been humble adjuncts to the elementary school, were now partly elementary, partly secondary, as their new name, "evening continuation schools", indicated.

The overlapping and waste brought about by this multiplicity of authorities became too obvious to escape attention; the unsatisfactory condition of secondary and technical education and the financial straits in which the poorer schools were plunged called for action. In March, 1894, during Lord Rosebery's Government, a Royal Commission was issued to Mr James Bryce and his colleagues "to consider what are the best methods of establishing a well-organized system of secondary education in England, taking into account existing deficiences, and having regard to such local sources of revenue from endowment or otherwise as are available or may be made available for this purpose, and to make recommendations accordingly". The Bryce Commission included three women in its membership of seventeen, Mrs Henry

Sidgwick and Mrs Sophie Bryant in common with more than half of the members having long and intimate knowledge of English higher education. Although the life of the Commission was not prolonged— it reported in August, 1895—it made inquiry on a liberal scale. Assistant commissioners were sent to make observation in selected, representative areas of England, many persons competent to reply were requested to send in memoranda or answers to questions, and information was sought from most European states, from the United States of America and from British Dominions overseas.[1]

The Commissioners studied the existing provision for secondary instruction from the Public Schools downwards and with a natural reference to the findings of their predecessors of the Schools Inquiry Commission. On the whole they observed signs of progress, and of the increased supply there could be no doubt. In the Public Schools of ancient foundation more serious attention was being paid to modern studies, particularly as part of the preparation of candidates who were looking forward to obtaining Army commissions. The endowed grammar schools were "far better" than in 1867; the number of pupils was greater, the standard of work higher. Many small schools of this kind suffered from an insufficient endowment, from competition by the board schools and from being settled in places whose particular requirements they no longer met. The Commissioners believed that it would be worth while to supplement their meagre endowment or transfer it to other schools of the same kind; their tradition of literary education deserved and, in existing circumstances, needed to be maintained. The proprietary schools were a valuable element, especially when they met a local demand where no endowment existed. The larger schools such as Cheltenham, Clifton, Marlborough, Malvern, Rossall were non-local and their tendency was to pass to the endowed class. Such schools could never be dividend-earning institutions in any real sense and the capital subscribed by their supporters was in effect an endowed fund to meet expenditure and not to earn profits. The educational success of the Girls' Public Day Schools Company, Ltd., with its 7111 pupils in thirty-six schools, had moved other enthusiasts to establish other associations with similar objects. The Boys' Public Day School Company, Ltd., and the Church Schools Company, Ltd., both

[1] *Royal Commission on Secondary Education* (1895), 5 vols: vol. I, Report; vols II, III, IV, Minutes of Evidence; vol. V, Memoranda and Answers to Questions.

inaugurated in 1883, proposed to educate children "above the elementary class", "of all classes above those usually attending public elementary schools". The first-named company aimed at providing "a sound and useful education", including "moral and religious training on a Christian basis" and on the "secular" side instruction in English language and literature, history, geography, mathematics, Latin, French, German, elementary science, drawing, singing, shorthand, book-keeping, drill or gymnastics. It was thought by the Company that the establishment charges could be met, or nearly met, by an annual school fee of £10 per head. The Church Schools Company's object was to combine "a thoroughly efficient secular education" with definite religious teaching "in accordance with the belief and practice of the Church of England". In the schools of both Companies parents might withdraw children from the religious instruction.

In 1894 the Boys' Public Day School Company possessed three schools with accommodation for 680 pupils; two were in London (Kentish Town and Clapham), the third was at South Shields. The Company was short-lived and seems to have been in difficulties from the outset; its funds were insufficient, it suffered from the competition of the higher grade board schools and its projectors had failed to reckon with the improvement in secondary education which had resulted from the labours of the Endowed Schools Commissioners. The Church Schools Company was much more successful. At the date of the *Report*, it had three schools for boys and twenty-four for girls[1]; the boys' schools disappeared, but six of the girls' schools survive in the twentieth century, with three others founded since 1902.

The Devon County School, the pioneer of county boarding schools under proprietary management, founded in 1858, claimed that it had "proved that an outlay of capital not exceeding £100 per boarder will provide well-selected sites, excellent buildings, and all requisite equipment. It has also proved that a revenue of £31 per boarder from parents, or scholarships, will suffice in schools planned for 150 to 200 boarders to provide every reasonable requisite both for board and tuition, and also for interest on the capital".[2] The Trustees believed that the middle classes desired "something more than accurate instruction" and that this something could alone be found in the corporate life of a boarding school. That such a school need not be "an expensive

[1] *Report*, vol. I, p. 50.   [2] *Ibid.* p. 50.

luxury" their own demonstrated; nor was the Devon County School singular amongst county schools. The Woodard Schools and the schools of the Society of Friends, of the Congregational and Wesleyan bodies were evidence to the same effect.

Information respecting private schools as a whole was wanting. In number they were variously estimated at 10,000 to 15,000; the College of Preceptors examined pupils from 3236, but the Commission had obtained information from a little over 2000. The larger schools compared favourably with the public schools. A large proportion of the schools was unsatisfactory, but the proprietors of efficient private schools welcomed public inspection and examination and the official registration of schools and teachers.

London had three higher grade board schools, the rest of England had sixty; fourteen board schools gave special instruction to children who had "passed the standards", that is, had completed the seventh standard course. London had sixty schools with these "tops". The seventy-four schools and classes educated 4606 boys and 2023 girls; the London pupils receiving teaching of the higher grade type numbered 1016. Some voluntary schools also possessed "tops". Of the sixty higher grade schools outside London, forty-nine had chemical laboratories and manual workshops, twenty-eight had art rooms, fifty-four had cookery kitchens, seven had laundries; the London higher grade schools were similarly equipped.

The name "organized science school" did not connote a separate building, but an organization which conformed with the regulations under which the Science and Art Department paid grants. Such a "school" met either in the daytime or in the evening and was but a department attached to a higher grade school, an elementary or an endowed school, a mechanics' institute or a municipal technical school.

The Taunton Commission had divided secondary schools into three grades, those with a "leaving age" of 18–19 being of the first grade, the second and third grades having leaving ages of sixteen and fourteen respectively. The Bryce Commission adopted this nomenclature, but with some misgiving on account of the changed conditions after thirty years. It reported that the supply of second and third grade schools was deficient and that, their popularity notwithstanding, there were very few first grade girls' schools in which the annual cost was as high as £18 or £20 per pupil. An increase both in demand and supply was required in second and third grade girls' schools charging a moderate fee. Higher grade board schools were doing much to provide third grade schooling, but too frequently their classes were unduly large, one of several weaknesses of these schools which came from their connexion with the elementary school system. A greater number of scholarships from grammar schools to the universities and university colleges, and from the elementary schools taking children of 11–12 years of age to secondary schools, was necessary.

Overlapping of function marked secondary education throughout. It occurred between grade and grade, between school and university college, between high schools and the degree examinations of London University. "It is evident that to prepare for the London Matriculation can scarcely be regarded as the proper function of a university college";[1] yet the practice was common. The trespass of the lower institution upon the sphere of the higher is a commonplace of educational history which is inseparable from advance in the standard of instruction; but when the higher institution descends to work proper to a lower, the result is a deterioration of standard and of achievement. The latter sort of overlapping was not confined to any one grade of education, higher or lower. The ill consequence of the overlapping or redundancy of authorities was illustrated by the grants and examinations of the Science and Art Department through which the curriculum of second and third grade schools was unduly biased if not warped.

The Commission appreciated the dangers both of undue centralization and of a series of independent authorities at the centre. Many of the evils noted were the result of the existence of a number of central powers acting independently. The Commission was anxious to safeguard within limits the independence of strictly local authorities; conditions varied too much to make one uniform system throughout the country expedient. Indeed the *Report* in one passage claims to be "founded" on a "decentralising policy" (vol. 1, p. 276). "We conceive in short that some central authority is required, not in order to control but rather to supervise the secondary education of the country, not to override or supersede local action, but to endeavour to bring about among the various agencies which provide that education a harmony and co-operation which are now wanting."[2] "The interference of the State should be confined within narrow limits and virtually restricted

---

[1] *Report*, vol. 1, p. 69.   [2] *Ibid.* p. 257.

to the aiding and advising the local authorities, the prevention of need-less competition or conflict between them, and the protection of private or proprietary schools from any disposition on the part of those authorities, should such a disposition appear, to force competitors out of the field. Such a code of regulations and such a system of examination and inspection as the Education Department has applied to elementary schools would in our view be not only unfitted but positively harmful to secondary education."[1]

The main reference to the Commission was the problem of organization and the solution which it proposed was, first, the establishment of one comprehensive central authority to be entrusted with the formulation of policy and, secondly, the constitution of local authorities invested with considerable executive power. The central authority "ought to consist of a Department of the Executive Government, presided over by a Minister responsible to Parliament, who would obviously be the same Minister as the one to whom the charge of elementary education is entrusted".[2] Attached to the central authority there should be an Educational Council of professional experts not exceeding twelve in number, one-third appointed by the Crown, one member appointed by each of the four Universities, Oxford, Cambridge, London and Victoria, the remainder to be co-opted "from among experienced members of the teaching profession". The chief duties of this Council would be to advise the Minister on purely educational and professional matters, to decide independently of the Minister whether a given school-endowment was local or non-local in application, and to form and maintain "a register of teachers". The phrase was unfortunate. What the public interest required was a register of schoolmasters and schoolmistresses. The less specific word played into the hands of the central authority subsequently created (the Board of Education) whose *personnel* did not welcome the advent of a registered profession such as the medical profession. They did their best to confuse the issue by delay in the first place and, next, by the inclusion of teachers of all kinds, a weakness which hindered the register's success.

Ostensibly the proposed authority was to deal with secondary education only, absorbing the Science and Art Department and the educational functions of the Charity Commissioners, but leaving the Education Department to remain in control of the elementary system.

[1] *Report*, vol. I, p. 266.   [2] *Ibid.* p. 257.

Similarly the school boards and the voluntary school managers were
to continue to administer the elementary schools locally. But this
separation of the two grades of public instruction could not long be
maintained when both were presided over by one and the same Minister.
The Bryce *Report* did not reach the comprehensive scope of the
Education Act of 1902—it would have exceeded its commission had
it done so—but it showed whither instructed opinion was tending and
foreshadowed the future.

The unit of local secondary administration proposed was the county
or county borough, the new system of local government making these
the obvious choice. Passing by the plan of *ad hoc* popular election on
which the school boards were based, the Commission recommended
that in the counties the majority of the local educational authority
should consist of county councillors, the remainder being co-opted
by the central authority and existing members. In county boroughs,
the borough council, the local school board and the central authority
were each to appoint one-third of the educational authority. By such
a system "a fresh set of elections" would be avoided "in a country
where there seem to be already as many elections as can well be attended
to".

The Commission would confer arbitrary power neither upon the
central nor on the local authorities. On the contrary: "We have
proposed the creation of Local Authorities entrusted with large powers
of supervision, but with comparatively little coercive control, in the
belief that it is not so much by superseding as by aiding and focussing
voluntary effort that real progress may be made. Accordingly, while
conceiving that upon this Local Authority the duty of providing an
adequate supply of secondary instruction within its districts must in
the last resort devolve, we have sketched out a plan whereby private
and proprietary schools may be turned to good account, and have
discountenanced any idea of driving them out of the field and thereby
making secondary education purely a matter of State concern".[1]

The provision of secondary schools in a given area should be
determined by the local authority with whom also should rest the details
of curriculum; local conditions are so various that such matters should
be settled upon the spot. But a well-balanced curriculum at the

[1] *Report*, vol. I, p. 324. A bill on these lines was introduced in 1896, only to be
withdrawn.

secondary stage should contain three elements, namely, literary, scientific, technical; "and the last of the three will thrive all the better if the two former receive their fitting meed of recognition".[1] The interpretation of the three terms and their inter-relations are best left to the same local authority. "Having recommended to Your Majesty the constitution of Local and Central Authorities likely, as we venture to believe, to be sensitive to public opinion and willing to obtain light from every source, competent...to try experiments and to profit by their results, we hold it unadvisable to attempt to fetter their discretion by any rigid rules; and we should deplore as certain to be hurtful to educational progress the uniformity of system which such rules would tend to produce."[2]

Technical education was not expressly named in the Commission's reference, but an attempt to define secondary education and to describe the implied course of studies[3] made the consideration of technical instruction inevitable. "The two ['secondary' and 'technical'] are not indeed identical, but they differ as genus and species or as general term and particular name, not as genus and genus or as opposed terms. No definition of technical instruction is possible that does not bring it under the head of secondary education, nor can secondary education be so defined as absolutely to exclude from it the idea of technical instruction."[4] In addition to its humanist, scientific and mathematical studies, a secondary school ought to teach "the practical arts such as the elements of applied mechanics and the subjects connected with agriculture, as well as modern languages and the kinds of knowledge most useful to the merchant or trader".[5] Of course, not every secondary school would attempt to teach all these subjects; and different schools would throw the emphasis upon different branches, humanist, scientific or technical, and combine these branches in different proportions.

All private and proprietary schools ought to be open to sanitary inspection. Such of them as desired the public recognition signified by their inclusion as part of the secondary school supply of their district must satisfy the central authority as to the adequacy of their buildings, teaching staff, curriculum and scale of fees. Equally with the schools publicly provided they must submit to inspection and the examination of their pupils. The head master, or mistress, and a number

[1] *Report*, vol. I, p. 285.   [2] *Ibid.* p. 284.
[3] *Ibid.* pp. 130–6, 284 f.   [4] *Ibid.* p. 136.   [5] *Ibid.* p. 284.

of the assistant teachers should be entered upon the teachers' register; and a statement of salaries should be returned annually. The pupils of these recognized private and proprietary schools should be admissible to all examinations held under rules framed by the central authority, they should be free to compete for all scholarships and exhibitions established or administered by the local authority, and should be permitted to hold their scholarships or exhibitions in a recognized proprietary or private school.

Secondary education in the Commissioners' opinion should not be gratuitous, but fees should be low and there should be a liberal provision of scholarships from the elementary schools. All secondary schools in receipt of public money should provide a number of free places. Scholarships at non-local schools should be merely honorary, power of course being reserved to the governors to make payment in case of need. The endowed schools in rural areas would often require re-organization. Some should be removed from remote sites to railway centres, to some boarding houses might be attached; "secondary tops" should be added to elementary schools situated in small towns or large villages. In certain rural areas the provision of secondary education could only be satisfied by the erection of new schools.

Teachers ought to be specifically prepared for their profession by a training in the theory and practice of education; and this preparation should be sought in universities and in "the leading university colleges". The Commission thus gave its approval to, and extended the scope of, the policy which the Education Department, following the Cross Commission, initiated in 1890. There should be one register for teachers without reference to the grade or character of the schools in which they taught. The central authority should not itself conduct examinations but should "regulate and co-ordinate" those held by the different examining bodies already at work; the certificates of these bodies should be made interchangeable. Throughout the *Report* the principles of elasticity and decentralization are constantly insisted upon; subsequent administrative practice, especially the practice of local authorities, has too often ignored those principles to an extent which has proved injurious to education.

The advance in elementary education achieved since the date of the Newcastle Commission may be inferred from the function assigned to the evening school by the two *Reports* respectively. In 1858–61 the evening school is a makeshift supplement to an elementary education which had been cut short at the age of eleven. In 1894–5 it is a part of secondary education largely used by adults who desired to carry their general education further or to add technical instruction to it.

The *Report* throughout bears witness to a solicitude for the preservation and well-being of all good private schools that could satisfy the simple conditions which the Commissioners regarded as constituting the minimum of efficiency. The comparatively strong professional element on the Commission was alive to the importance attaching to the educational experiments which schools of this kind were making at the close of the nineteenth century. Accordingly a few passages of the *Report* (vol. I, pp. 159–60) are devoted to an experiment which had begun to arouse public interest, namely, co-education, the education of both sexes side by side in the same school, college or university.

The practice of instructing boys and girls together had long been common in rural districts, where administrative economy sufficiently explained the employment of the plan in the small elementary schools which such areas required; and it was followed also in some higher grade schools and in all pupil teacher centres, offshoots both of the elementary school system. A few small endowed schools in the north also admitted girls as well as boys in defiance of their history; but they sacrificed their tradition in this respect for the same reason which caused them to become "organized science schools", their name "grammar schools" notwithstanding. Only so could they support the competition thrust upon them by the school boards. The university colleges almost without exception admitted men and women, and instructed them in common, that plan being adopted to secure a similar economy of money and of labour without reference to any theory of education.

When the Bryce Commission reported, the mixed school had advocates who regarded it as a much more efficient instrument of education than a school for one sex only could ever be; the argument of administrative economy was disregarded. Co-education as thus understood was then commonly believed to be a purely American innovation. But the Commission were told of a private co-educational school conducted in the north of London by the Anderton family for some thirty-five years, counting from before the mid-century.[1] Another

[1] *Report*, vol. v, p. 440.

school of the kind was established at Manchester by the Herford family in 1873 and was flourishing while the Commission sat. Between 1884 and 1892 Miss Alice Woods conducted a similar school at Chiswick. Mr E. Sargant applied the principle in the elementary school for some forty children which he called "School Field", opened (1888) in Hackney. The children paid a weekly fee of twopence; their studies comprised recitation, drawing, composition, arithmetic, and Scripture "absolutely free from doctrinal teaching". They produced a school magazine once a term, and the seniors amongst them had that freedom in disposing of their time and distributing it amongst their studies which is distinctive of the later American "Dalton Plan". "School Field", which was not a commercial venture, differed from the other co-educational schools of the time in that it served children of a humbler social class.[1]

These private schools were small and they tended to become imperfectly co-educational, since the boys usually left the school at a much earlier age than the girls; most parents apparently thought of the schools as preparatory only, where their sons were concerned. Moreover they were not boarding schools. Public opinion on the whole was unfavourable to the experiment of the mixed school and the experimenters themselves were not agreed as to the age and social class of the pupils whom co-education would benefit. But in the history of education it has frequently happened that plans which had been introduced for commonplace, practical reasons, at a later stage have been found, or declared, to possess qualities which erect them into educational principles of the highest rank. Partly owing to the influence of America, whose early public schools for the most obvious reasons taught boys and girls in common, the opinion began to take root in England that co-education in its assimilation to family life was educationally the better way from almost every point of view. George Meredith, whose interest in the process of education had been manifested in so many of his novels, was at this period perhaps at the zenith of his influence in the two countries. In 1894 he published *Lord Ormont and his Aminta* in which Matthew Weyburn is made to plan a new type of school which, for an expressly moral purpose, is to be co-educational. Aminta confesses that she did not know "what to think when the secretary proposed the education and collocation of boys and girls in one group, never separated, declaring it the only way for them to learn to know and to respect one another. They were to learn together, play together, have matches together, as a scheme for stopping the mischief between them".[1] "All the devilry between the sexes begins at their separation. They're foreigners when they meet; and their alliances are not always binding. The chief object in life, if happiness be the aim, and the growing better than we are, is to teach men and women how to be one; for if they're not, then each is a morsel for the other."[2]

Only in the boarding school does co-education come closest to the conditions of home and family life; but a robust faith was needed in parents and in teachers of the late nineteenth century to put the principle to this logical test. In 1898 Mr Cecil Grant opened a boarding school for both sexes at Keswick (later transferred to Harpenden), one of its aims being to combat precisely that menace to sexual purity of thought, word and act which is never entirely absent from societies confined to one sex, particularly when the members are adolescent.[3] The argument advanced is that familiarity with each other from early years outside the family circle renders boys and girls less prone to look upon each other as fascinating mysteries, makes frank and innocent association possible and strengthens in each sex its most distinctive characteristics and virtues.

A mixed day school started at Hampstead in 1898 by Mr and Mrs C. E. Rice proved sufficiently successful to lead its friends to subscribe capital for its maintenance and to associate themselves for the purpose as the King Alfred School Society. The fees varied, according to age, from six to eight guineas per term and the instruction comprised English, mathematics, science, modern languages, singing (under Cecil Sharp), and manual work. The staff contained men and women. Cricket and hockey were played by both girls and boys.[4]

The position of co-education in England in 1903 may be gauged by the list of twenty-nine schools with which Miss Woods closed her *Co-education*. Of these, sixteen at least were grammar schools and other institutions where the economic motive may be not unfairly suspected;

[1] *Lord Ormont and his Aminta*, ed. 1894, vol. II, p. 39.
[2] *Ibid.* vol. III, p. 128.
[3] See the forcible presentation of *The Case of Co-education* (1913), by C. Grant and N. Hodgson.
[4] C. E. Rice in A. Woods' *Co-education*.

that is, the mixed school was a makeshift, not the vindication of a principle. Of the remaining thirteen schools only five were well known.

Before starting the Hampstead school, Mr Rice had been engaged as an assistant master in an experiment of a different nature directed by Mr J. H. Badley. A group of schools, Mr C. Reddie's "Abbotsholme" (1889), Mr Badley's "Bedales" (1893) and Mr A. Devine's "Clayesmore" (1896), have so much in common as to warrant naming them together. "Bedales" became co-educational in 1900. These schools hold in honour the Public School tradition, more especially as it was shaped under Arnold's influence, and they desire to make much of that tradition their own. But in adopting it they discriminate. In curriculum, studies are directed to the demands of the modern world, and the aim is to give a liberal education which recognizes that the boys will pass to commerce, industry and the modern scientific professions on leaving school in much greater numbers than are to be counted of those who go to the universities. Latin and Greek, if taught, become "subjects" in a list including not only mathematics and science, but also music, arts and crafts and, for boys, such heavy outdoor toil as felling timber, road-making, and the construction of cricket pitches. The principle of self-government is carried farther than the Public Schools for the most part carry it; school assemblies or parliaments composed of the pupils are allowed a measure of control and direction of some parts of the school organization. The number of pupils is restricted in order to give individuality its opportunity, while also allowing ample opportunity to the staff to study individuals.

Meredith's Matthew Weyburn seems to have had a vision of these "New Schools" when he established his own with its "cricket and football fields, lake for rowing and swimming, gymnastic fixtures, carpenter's shed, bowling alley and four European languages in the air by turns daily", that is, only one language is to be spoken on one day, another language on the next and so on. It was Weyburn's "grand project to bring the nationalities together and teach Old England to the Continent, the Continent to Old England". This internationalism was partially achieved in the three schools described through the different nationalities represented amongst the pupils; the "New Schools" and the "New Education" soon secured foreign admirers and imitators. In their regard for the individual and for his prospective mode of life and in the broad but liberal culture which they opened to him, Abbotsholme, Bedales and Clayesmore recall the old knightly up-bringing and the "doctrine of courtesy" which directed it. The mingling of the sexes makes the parallel yet closer.[1]

The improved education of teachers in elementary schools experimentally initiated in 1890 by the establishment of "day training colleges" has already been described.[2] Another experiment of this period which proved fruitful in results was the foundation (1887), by Charlotte M. Mason, of the Parents' National Education Union for the study of principles in their application to physical and mental development. By its general conferences of the whole body and by its sectional meetings, held in all parts of the country, the Union has done much to arouse and sustain reflection on the subject in the minds of educated parents who desire to afford their children the best education attainable, yet are critical of the methods usually followed. In the narrower but not less important field of practice, Miss Mason's "House of Education" at Ambleside (1892) trained governesses for young children and started a prolonged course of study for mothers in educational theory and practice.

More particularly concerned with the up-bringing of children between the ages of six and twelve years, Miss Mason was an adverse critic of the curriculum of the Kindergarten and of a certain condescension which it exhibits towards children. The little people should be regarded as persons and treated accordingly; their schooling calls for a generous curriculum, not only of "Things" but also of "Books", "*many living books*". "No education seems to be worth the name which has not made children at home in the world of books."[3] The "Things" to be studied are in the child's everyday surroundings; Miss Mason quotes[4] with approval Richard Dawes' teaching at King's Somborne in the "philosophy (i.e. science) of common things". Nature, handicraft, science, art, all have relation to the child's environment, and ought to be utilized for his instruction. His body calls for a fitting physical development; the great stress which Miss Mason laid upon habit leads her to include in physical training a cultivation of the virtues of chastity,

---

[1] See J. H. Badley, *Bedales, a pioneer school* (1923). Clayesmore is not, and never has been, co-educational.
[2] See Chapter XIII above.
[3] C. M. Mason, *School Education*, ed. 1905, p. 226.
[4] *Home Education*, 5th ed. (1906), p. 268.

fortitude, courage and temperance. Her scheme is permeated by religion. "We do not merely give a religious education...we hold that all education is divine." She finds its fitting symbol in the frescoes of Sta Maria Novella. "We hold in fact that noble conception of education held by the mediaeval church, as pictured upon the walls of the Spanish chapel in Florence. Here we have represented the descent of the Holy Ghost upon the Twelve, and directly under them, fully under the illuminating rays, are the noble figures of the seven liberal arts...and under these again the men who received and expressed, so far as we know, the initial idea in each of those subjects; such men as Pythagoras, Zoroaster, Euclid, whom we might call pagans, but whom the earlier church recognized as divinely taught and illuminated."[1]

The "intolerable strain" upon the voluntary schools which had called the Cross Commission into existence became once more pressing in the 'nineties', when the small and necessitous school boards also shared the pressure. The financial resources of both classes of elementary school were not equal to sustaining the competition caused by the policy of the great school boards and their interpretation of their functions. Yet the supporters of the voluntary system had made strenuous efforts not only to maintain but to improve their position. In 1871 the number of voluntary schools in England and Wales was 8798; in 1890 it was 14,479, after which year it steadily declined. Allowing for the increased population, this latter figure exceeded by 3245 schools the number to be anticipated on that account, an average excess of 129 schools per annum. Between 1870 and 1895 the sums spent upon public elementary education were expended as follows by the sources which provided the money:

					£
By the Government in grants	...	...	...	...	79,895,762
By school boards in local rates	...	...	...	...	73,943,484
By voluntary subscriptions and income of endowments	...				32,922,173
By fees	...	...	...	...	...	32,283,715

making a total exceeding £219,000,000,[2] the several contributors expending in millions 80, 74, 33, and 32. Thus approximately 36 per cent. of the cost was borne by taxes, 34 per cent. by rates and the

---

[1] *Parents and Children, a sequel to "Home Education"* (1897), p. 215.

[2] *Special Reports on Educational Subjects*, vol. I, p. 30.

remaining 30 per cent. roughly in equal parts by voluntary subscriptions and endowment on the one hand, by pupils' fees on the
other.

The "voluntary system" had tended to become a system chiefly
supported by Anglicans, Roman Catholics, and Wesleyans. The undenominational voluntary schools so closely resembled the board
schools that their separate existence was unnecessary and they were
gradually disappearing. Of the 3842 British schools founded in the
nineteenth century, 1703 were closed by 1907, by which year 755 had
been transferred to school boards, 70 had become denominational
schools, 1075 survived as British schools, while the status or the
existence of the remaining 239 schools was in doubt.[1]

Two Acts were passed by Lord Salisbury's Government in 1897
which added somewhat to the resources of the poorer elementary
schools, although they failed to cure the disease from which such
schools inevitably suffered under the conditions of the time. The
Elementary Education Act of 1876 had fixed the maximum annual
grant attainable per pupil at 17s. 6d., except where the local contribution
exceeded that amount, in which case the Treasury was to pay up to
the local range but not beyond it, whatever the sum which a school
"earned" by fulfilling the various conditions on which grants were
paid under the Code of the Education Department. This limit of 17s. 6d.
with the appended condition was abolished by the Voluntary Schools
Act of 1897, which measure also exempted voluntary elementary schools
from the payment of local rates and directed the payment of 5s. per
annum per pupil to associations of voluntary school managers grouped
for the purpose, one more administrative body added to the existing
plethora! Again the Elementary Education Act of 1897 made a supplementary grant *per capita* to necessitous board schools, with a maximum
total grant of 16s. 6d. per pupil.

But the day of tinkering palliatives and the reign of a surplusage of
major authorities were nearing their end. A crisis was brought about
in 1899, when Mr Cockerton, the Local Government Board district
auditor, at the instance of a North London School of Art, surcharged
the London School Board in respect of expenditure on the teaching of
science and art in day schools and evening continuation schools. The

[1] H. B. Binns, *A Century of Education, being the Centenary History of the British
and Foreign School Society*, p. 231 n.

complaint endorsed by the auditor was that the school board was acting *ultra vires* in teaching certain branches of science and art and in teaching adults. Actions at law followed and at the close of the year 1900 the Court of Queen's Bench ruled that the school board could not legally spend public money upon instruction outside the confines of the curriculum laid down in the Education Department's Code, nor in teaching persons who were no longer children. On appeal the ruling was upheld in 1901.

The decision made it clear that the business of school boards from the strictly legal aspect was the elementary instruction of children. It did not define "elementary", but disqualified such local provision as was being made for education beyond the rudimentary stage. By implication the condemnation of the school boards' policy fell likewise upon the Science and Art Department and, less heavily, upon the Education Department, both authorities having abetted that policy. A short Act of 1901 legalized the existing state of illegality and this was repeated in the following year. But it was now obvious that revolutionary measures had become necessary.

In the meantime effect had been given to the principle laid down in the Bryce *Report* that there should be but one comprehensive central authority presiding over the public education of the country. An Act of 1899 had created the Board of Education by amalgamating the Education and the Science and Art Departments and conferring upon the new body the educational functions of the Charity Commission. (The school inspection of Welsh secondary schools was reserved to the Central Welsh Board for Intermediate Education.) The Board of Education is not a Committee of Council, but an independent body of Ministers of the Crown under their own president who is virtually the English Minister of Public Instruction. To that extent the Radical proposal unsuccessfully mooted by Roebuck in the House of Commons sixty-six years earlier took practical shape. The Board of Education Act came into operation in 1900.

The plight of English educational administration during the closing years of the nineteenth century convinced the Government that nothing short of revolution could end the chaos caused by the multiplicity of direction, the poverty of a large number of the schools and the want of clear thinking as to the import of terms in daily use. The Bryce *Report* had given birth to the Board of Education; in essentials it was also the wet nurse of the Education Act of 1902.[1] The Prime Minister (A. J. Balfour) himself took charge of this measure, which for two sessions was the subject of bitter wrangling not only within but also without the walls of Parliament. It was based upon principles which for seventy years and more had been advocated by the Radical party; but the extension of rate aid to voluntary schools, and the very existence of those schools, were repellent to Radical principles as the debates of half a century had shown. Rate aid to denominational schools meant a large public subvention to the elementary schools of the Church of England and this Nonconformists could not tolerate. The bill was forced through its stages and became law on December 18th, 1902, but resistance to its provisions did not cease.

The central authority desired by the Bryce Commission had come into being with control over elementary, secondary and technical instruction and no small measure of influence over those institutions of higher education which became the new universities of the twentieth century. Indeed, Oxford and Cambridge alone excepted, the English universities as a whole came for certain purposes, chiefly financial, within the ambit of the Board's influence. It remained to form the local education authorities proposed by the Commissioners, but this was done on different lines from their planning, since the new authorities, local as well as central, were to supervise not secondary or elementary education, but education.

As drafted, the Bill made the county councils and those of the county boroughs the local education authorities for their respective areas; but local feeling and local politicians made it necessary to give the oversight of elementary education to the councils of non-county boroughs with a population exceeding 10,000 and to urban district councils of which the population was 20,000 and more. The London County Council by its separate Act passed in 1903 was made the sole local education authority for all education within its area. "On July 31st, 1908, there were in England 49 county and 71 county borough education authorities and (for elementary education only)

---

[1] The father of that Act was a former Secretary of the Education Department, Sir Francis R. Sandford, who submitted (April 10th, 1888) a memorandum to the Cross Commission which was the Act in little. Sir Robert Morant, the first Secretary of the Board of Education, by his activity during the passage of the Bill was but giving effect to his Department's policy.

134 borough and 46 urban district authorities, viz. in all, 120 authorities for higher and 300 for elementary education."[1]

The outstanding duty of the councils was, in consultation with the Board of Education, to "promote the general co-ordination of all forms" of education within their areas, thus absorbing the duties formerly discharged by school boards, school attendance committees, technical education committees and all similar bodies. The existence of the central authority implied that the administration of all public education was essentially a unity; the same implication underlay the creation of these local authorities. The community nationally and locally assumed responsibility for all forms ("elementary", "secondary", "technical") of public, secular instruction; national education became possible in a sense never before realized.

Except in striking a rate or negotiating a loan, functions which could only be discharged by itself, a council must exercise its educational powers through a committee, of which the constitution must be approved by the Board of Education. In framing this constitution the following rules must be observed: the majority of the members must also be members of the council, persons experienced in education must be co-opted in addition and some of the members must be women.

For the supplementary grants to elementary schools under the two Acts of 1897 there was substituted one of 4s. per head with increments, where necessary, on a sliding scale to counter-weigh any insufficient local rate. The other and much more considerable grants to these schools remained. The Act of 1902 repealed the Technical Instruction Acts, and the "whisky money" made over to county and borough councils was earmarked for education other than elementary, technical instruction thus being included in secondary or higher education. These councils might raise a rate not exceeding twopence in the pound for higher education. This limit was not imposed upon the London County Council in the Act of 1903; other councils might under the 1902 Act exceed it with the consent of the Local Government Board.

The "board schools" and "voluntary schools" of the nineteenth century became the "provided" and "non-provided schools" of the twentieth, the provision referring to origin and the school buildings, not

---

[1] *Outlines of Education Courses in Manchester University*: Syllabus (by M. E. Sadler) of a course in the history of education in England, 1800–1911, Manchester University Press (1911), p. 86.

to maintenance, since both classes of school were to be equally maintained by the "L.E.A." (local education authority). It was the extension of the rates to the "non-provided" or voluntary schools which was the matter of such hot debate inside and outside the House of Commons while the Bill was being discussed. Nonconformists and the advocates of secular instruction, all in short who represented the Radical tradition, regarded the extension as either a gross injustice to all who stood without the ranks of a particular religious communion, or as a policy which involved State intrusion within the religious domain. On the other hand, denominationalists and Anglicans in particular welcomed the payment as a guarantee that their schools would be firmly established and adequately supported. This appeared to them to be at once good State policy and a thing of simple justice to institutions which had originated the system of popular instruction and had long served the State at considerable sacrifice to themselves.

But the opponents might have profitably pondered the statement, made half a century earlier in Parliament, to the effect that "rate aid" and "voluntary schools" were two incompatibles. Any one who took the long view in 1902 would not have valued the life of the voluntary system at twenty-five years' purchase. For what was its position under the Act? Every non-provided school must have upon its managing committee representatives of the L.E.A., who were in a minority, but who represented the power of the purse. The L.E.A. financed the school's upkeep, including the payment of salaries; all teachers except the head teacher were to be appointed without reference to their membership of the religious body to which ostensibly the school belonged. The managers had to maintain the school buildings, reasonable expenditure on wear and tear apart; but the L.E.A. could require alterations in the buildings. Not many of them could be called "up-to-date" at that time. Where would the voluntary system be when these buildings in structure and planning had become worn out or obsolete? Owing to the great capital cost of replacing the voluntary schools, no statesmen would cheerfully embark upon their immediate suppression. But the 1902 Act inflicted a lingering yet fatal disease upon the system.

The "religious difficulty", which had obstructed the establishment of a State system throughout the century, was not solved, but as in 1870 a compromise was effected. This time, however, the balance came down more heavily on the side of the "undenominationalists" and of the Radical ideal—the school destitute of religious teaching. The L.E.A. while it maintained denominational schools must itself be strictly neutral. In provided schools, as in their predecessors, the board schools, no instruction or worship distinctive of any religious communion could be given or performed. In non-provided schools no pupil could be compelled to attend such worship or instruction; in all schools under the L.E.A., whether elementary or otherwise, a conscience clause protected the pupil without prejudice to his position in the school. This provision in effect was extended to all assistant teachers and pupil teachers of non-provided schools. In short, religious education was treated as a purely individual matter with which the State was not concerned; whereas a hundred years earlier the opinion was almost unanimous that all education was in its nature religious.

But the great achievement of the Act is foreshadowed in its clause outlining the province of the L.E.A. It is "to consider the educational needs of their area and to take such steps as may seem to them desirable after consultation with the Board of Education, to supply or aid the supply of education other than elementary and to promote the general co-ordination of all forms of education". The nineteenth century had been notorious for precisely the lack of that co-ordination; and the problems of the right school in the right place, of the distribution of schools in harmony with the distribution of population, of the ready access of qualified pupils in lower to higher places of education, of overlapping and of wasteful competition, were to find their solution in the authorities created by the Act. The Board of Education was in a position to give a national character to these activities and thus at last allow it to be said that England possessed a State system of education. Central and local authorities between them have created a number of secondary schools for boys and girls, a number which is still being increased, which place advanced instruction within the reach of the major part of the people of England, and a liberal provision of scholarships, exhibitions and maintenance grants has afforded opportunities which would not otherwise have come to many. Intellectual endowment, while it may be made of the highest value to the nation, is not peculiar to any one social rank, to rich, well-to-do or very poor. To foster it and guide it, wherever found, is clearly good State policy; and the schools and other machinery created in the train of the Education Act of 1902 have afforded a means of discovering and training this spiritual power.

CHAPTER XVII

The Schoolmaster's Profession

"To make any progress in the art of education it must be patiently reduced to an experimental science; we are fully sensible of the extent and difficulty of this undertaking, and we have not the arrogance to imagine that we have made any considerable progress in a work which the labours of many generations may, perhaps, be insufficient to complete; but we lay before the public the result of our experiments and in many instances the experiments themselves. In pursuing this part of our plan we have sometimes descended from that elevation of style which the reader might expect in a quarto volume; we have frequently been obliged to record facts concerning children which may seem trifling and to enter into a minuteness of detail which may appear unnecessary. No anecdotes however have been admitted without due deliberation; nothing has been introduced to gratify the idle curiosity of others, or to indulge our own feelings of domestic partiality."[1] Such is the modest introduction of a book which was the outcome of a long series of observations of children and of experiments in teaching them that had occupied the Edgeworth family for many years.

The hope of the Edgeworths was to base the practice of teaching children upon an experimental foundation. A similar purpose actuated the conduct of the Philanthropinum, or Dessau Institute, conducted by J. B. Basedow from 1774 to 1793. Basedow's behaviour and the management of his school were both very blameworthy; but from one point of view the Institute attracted the favourable regard of Kant, who was convinced of the necessity for experimental inquiry in school method. He told his Königsberg students that "the mechanical in the art of education must be transformed into a science and one generation may have to pull down what another had built....Experimental schools must be erected before Normal Schools can be set up....It is supposed that experiment is unnecessary in education and that by reasoning one can judge whether a thing is good or not. But this is a great mistake and experience teaches that the outcome of our experiments is often

---

[1] M. and R. L. Edgeworth, *Practical Education*, 2 vols. (1798), Preface, p. vi.

quite different from what was expected. Thus it is seen experimentally that no generation can present a complete educational scheme. The only experimental school which in a measure has here made a beginning in opening the new road was the Dessau Institute. Notwithstanding the many errors which may be imputed to it, errors which are inseparable from an experimental procedure, this must be put to its credit, that it made more and yet more experiments necessary. It was in a certain fashion the only school in which the teachers were free to work according to their own methods and plans, and where they were in touch with one another and with all the learned men in Germany".[1]

Basedow and the Philanthropinum did very much to discredit experimental pedagogy on the Continent, and the example of the Edgeworths failed to secure a following in this country. But in an age of experimental inquiry and of marked scientific progress it was impossible that the hopes entertained by the Edgeworths could die out. In 1825, James Mill was writing of a "science of education", by which he meant not merely the method of instruction but a body of doctrine which should demonstrate the aims no less than the means of the process. When John Stuart Mill published his *System of Logic* (1843) he added a chapter, by way of suggestion rather than anything more demonstrative, upon "Ethology or the science of the formation of character", which sketches a much more ambitious project than the Edgeworths had imagined. The name "'Ethology' is perhaps etymologically applicable to the entire science of our mental and moral nature; but if, as is usual and convenient, we employ the name, Psychology, for the science of the elementary laws of mind, Ethology will serve for the ulterior science which determines the kind of character produced in conformity to those general laws by any set of circumstances physical and moral. According to this definition, Ethology is the science which corresponds to the art of education in the widest sense of the term, including the formation of national·or collective character as well as individual....While on the one hand Psychology is altogether, or principally, a science of observation and experiment, Ethology as I have conceived it is...altogether deductive....Ethology, the deductive science, is a system of corollaries from Psychology, the experimental science....Ethology is still to be created; but its creation is at length become practicable...". "The subject to be studied is the origin and

[1] Kant, *Schrift über Pädagogik*, ed. Theodor Vogt (1901), paras. 14 and 20.

sources of all those qualities in human beings which are interesting to us, either as facts to be produced, to be avoided or merely to be understood; and the object is to determine from the general laws of mind combined with the general position of our species in the universe, what actual or what possible combinations of circumstances are capable of promoting or of preventing the production of those qualities. A science which possesses middle principles of this kind arranged in the order, not of causes, but of the effects which it is desirable to produce or prevent, is duly prepared to be the foundation of the corresponding art. And when Ethology shall be thus prepared, practical education will be the mere transformation of these principles into a parallel system of precepts and the adaptation of these to the sum total of the individual circumstances which exist in each particular case."[1]

A most important difference exists between the meaning attributed to the conception "education as a science" by the two Mills, and that which satisfied the Edgeworths, Basedow and the early experimentalists generally. These assumed that the purpose of education was one on which men were agreed; experimental inquiry and observation had no concern with it. The end of education, or at least of schooling, was the acquisition of knowledge which could be put to use, with such a discipline of the intellectual powers as would enable the learner the more readily to acquire still more useful knowledge. The aim of experimenting and observing was to discover how best to reach that end; in other words the early experimenters were intent upon establishing an educational method which was "scientific". This, too, is the aim of the present-day educational experimentalist; he is interested in the *how* of educative processes, but is seemingly indifferent as to *why* those processes should be employed at all. J. S. Mill and his father do not so restrict the meaning of the words "education as a science". For them it is at least as important to determine educational aims as educational methods; and the younger Mill saw clearly that, however helpful psychology may be to method, it can throw but little light upon aims, purposes, ends. Indeed, educational theory as such should be much more concerned in discovering the educational end than in improving educative means. The Mills had a more comprehensive view of that theory than was possessed by their predecessors or than their successors take to-day. They looked, not to psychology, but to ethics, political

[1] *System of Logic*, bk. VI, ch. v.

and social theory for an answer to the question, What is the end of education?

However practicable the foundation of a science of ethology appeared to be in the year 1843, it was not founded; nor did Mill return to the subject. There followed the silence of a generation; and the silence was not really broken when Alexander Bain (1818–1903) published *Education as a Science* (1879). These are the very words of James Mill written more than fifty years earlier, and expectation is aroused when the connexion of Bain (who wrote a memoir of James Mill) with the utilitarian doctrine and with the teaching of the Mills is recalled. Yet Bain does not expound a science of education; rather he sets forth the psychological implications of schoolmastering, thus endeavouring to lend a quasi-scientific justification to the schoolmaster's customary practice. His psychology is that of the then predominant associationist school, which, apart from the physiological factors on which Bain and the later members of the school laid stress, assigned little or no place to experiment. *Education as a Science* suffers from the utilitarian obsession which is peculiarly liable to the "information fallacy", and it has much to say respecting the "object lesson", a device which too often became puerile and is now quite discredited. Bain believed that physical training was beyond the school's province (an opinion shared by James Mill) and he regarded "much of the curiosity of children and of others besides children" as "a spurious article". In short, so far as education is concerned, Bain came close to being what Carlyle called a "gerund-grinder".

The doctrine which described mental processes as modes of the "association of ideas", which endeavoured to explain mental development as the consequence of such associations, had long characterized English psychology when Bain finally elaborated it in his *The Senses and the Intellect* (1855) and *The Emotions and the Will* (1859). Its somewhat mechanical conception was not uncongenial to the England of his day; it was the psychological creed of the utilitarians and it had its appropriate place in the sensationist psychology which theorizers on educational method took from Locke and Rousseau. Spencer's *Principles of Psychology* (1855) and Darwin's *Origin of Species* (1859) by their teaching of heredity and evolution modified the pure associationism of the two Mills and of Bain; and the biological "recapitulatory theory"[1] asserted by Spencer was recognized as bearing directly upon

[1] See Chapter XI, p. 296 above.

educational practice. But this new teaching did not immediately affect the psychological basis of educational theory.

Bain distinguished the several intellectual operations under the time-honoured names of "faculties", memory, imagination, judgement, reasoning; the semi-independence which was usually regarded as belonging to these "faculties" supported the principle that the primary, if not the whole, aim of instruction was mental discipline, a principle which was held to justify a curriculum and methods otherwise exposed to very adverse criticism. The paramount importance of training the senses, cultivating the faculties, their precise order of development being specified, and so shaping instruction as to ensure the desired "association of ideas" held their place in orthodox educational psychology long after they had receded in interest for professed psychologists.

The creation in 1846 of the "certificated teacher" made the principal instructors in public elementary schools the most numerous and the most readily organized section of the teaching profession. The recognized status conferred upon them by the holding of qualifications publicly prescribed and publicly tested gave them individually a sense of professional solidarity which had hitherto been wanting amongst teachers generally. So early as 1853 there was a "General Associated Body of Church Schoolmasters in England and Wales" that met annually, the purpose being "the improving the theory and practice of teaching and promoting elementary education in this country".[1] The local associations of Church teachers which existed up and down England found friendly competitors in similar associations of "British" and other voluntary school teachers. A periodical, *Papers for the Schoolmaster*, performed for these teachers a similar service to that discharged by the College of Preceptors' organ, *The Educational Times*, which first appeared in October, 1847.

The courses followed in the training colleges made it necessary to produce technical manuals, and of these by far the most widely read during the second half of the nineteenth century was the work of John Gill of the Cheltenham Training College. Beginning as the *Introductory Textbook to School Management: Government Examination Questions*, of which the second edition is dated 1857, it was at first frankly addressed to the examinee who aspired to the government certificate. But it rapidly passed beyond this humble office and enlarged

[1] *Monthly Paper* of the National Society, September, 1859.

both its range and its quality. It attained its permanent title, *Introductory Textbook to School Education, Method and School Management* in its ninth edition of 1863; the edition of 1872 was the sixteenth and its final form appeared in 1882, having been the *vade mecum* of generations of teachers in elementary schools of all kinds.

On the side of psychology, this popular manual made brief reference to the "order of development of the faculties" and to the principle of association, or "suggestion", as the orthodoxy of the time required; but the reference is slight and allusive only, sufficient to emphasize the dictum that a teacher of children should possess a knowledge of mind (as "intellect", "emotion" and "will") and of the consequent method of instruction, the aim of his labours being the development and culture of the mind and the formation of right habits. No claim is made that education is a science, and the importance of the schoolmaster's office is measured by the trust reposed in him and by the interests involved, and not by his self-importance or by the amount of his stipend. Gill was a pupil of David Stow's.

It was laid down by the *Report* of the Taunton Commission that knowing a subject and knowing how to teach it were two different things and that the first form of knowledge did not necessarily carry the second with it. The professional training of secondary school teachers was accordingly one of the matters about which the Commission deliberated. But the balance of opinion amongst the Commissioners and amongst the teachers themselves was against it; as a substitute the Commission recommended the institution of an examination to test the qualifications of teachers who aspired to head-masterships. A list was to be made of the names of successful candidates which would be in effect a schoolmasters' register. To that extent the charter granted in 1849 to the College of Preceptors found justification.

From its beginning in 1846 it had been a cardinal principle of that College to secure an authoritative register of "persons engaged or desiring to be engaged in the education of youth particularly in the private schools of England and Wales". To that end the College proposed to afford "facilities to the teacher for acquiring a sound knowledge of his profession" and to provide a board of examiners who should certify the competent.[1] Although attention had been diverted from these purposes to the organization of its school examinations,

[1] Royal Charter of Incorporation, March 28th, 1849.

registration and training were never quite forgotten. Joseph Payne (1808–76), a member from the beginning, who had retired from teaching in 1863, devoted himself thenceforth to convincing all whom it concerned that those who taught in secondary no less than those teaching in elementary schools needed, but did not get, a technical course which would prepare them to teach. He read papers to the College, to the Education Department of the Social Science Association and urged the importance of the training of the teacher upon the women's "National Union" for education.

In June, 1864, the College of Preceptors determined to seek reinforcement outside its own ranks in order to obtain the desired register. Its Council reported in the following February the formation of an independent general committee of persons bent upon educational reform, including representatives of various societies. Early in 1866 this committee transformed itself into "The Scholastic Registration Association", making the registering of school teachers its special aim. In the following February it was reported that the Association consisted of 158 members and 14 honorary members, the membership representing the College of Preceptors, the Manchester Board of Schoolmasters, the Association of French Professors, the Associated Body of Church Schoolmasters, the Nottingham Registration Association, the Yorkshire Registration Association and the Wigan Association of Church Schoolmasters.[1] We learn from Joseph Payne that in 1871 the object of the Association (of which he was a member) was "the discouragement of unqualified persons from assuming the office of schoolmaster or teacher", that it had obtained a large share of public approval and that among its members were many head masters and masters of public schools and colleges. He names Haig-Brown (Charterhouse) who was president, Hornby (Eton), Farrar (Harrow), [Prof. B. H.] Kennedy, Rigg (Shrewsbury), Thring (Uppingham), Abbott (City of London School), Collis (Bromsgrove), Mitchinson (King's School, Canterbury), Donaldson (Edinburgh High School) and other prominent men.[2] The Association would seem to have been thoroughly representative, its object was as advantageous to the public as to the

[1] This information has been very kindly furnished by Mr G. Chalmers, Secretary of the College of Preceptors.

[2] Joseph Payne, *Lectures on the Science and Art of Education*, ed. Joseph Frank Payne (1880), p. 39.

teachers; yet its deputations to the Committee of Council were fruitless. Its object did not secure general commendation, enthusiasm cooled and the Association withered, leaving its task to a later generation.

Payne, who had taken part in the deputations, felt that there was a prior problem—how to provide facilities whereby aspirants could be prepared to acquire the technical qualifications which registration would demand. "The real desideratum", he said, "is training colleges for middle class teachers, professorships of education at our leading universities and more, perhaps, than all, a nobler conception of education itself among English teachers."[1] In 1867 he and his friend, C. H. Lake, had induced the College of Preceptors to institute an examination for teachers; the first question papers, which comprised questions in physiology, psychology, logic, morals and a practical paper on lesson-giving, were drawn up by Payne. The College's next step was to address a memorial to the Committee of Council praying that the Government would found professorships of education at the universities. The petition was not complied with; but the Government (of which Gladstone was the head) gave £10,000 to the Bell Trustees[2] to enable them to endow chairs of education at Edinburgh and St Andrews. Whereupon the College itself founded a chair of "the science and art of education", the first of its kind in England, and appointed Joseph Payne its first occupant. This was in 1872; two years later the College appealed for public subscriptions to endow the chair, and to provide a training college, model and practising schools, an educational library, museum and reading room. The scheme, admirable in its design, proved to be too ambitious for its day, and it was only very partially realized. After Payne's death in 1876, his chair had two occupants, each holding office for a very short period with a long interval between the appointments; finally the professorship was put into commission, so to say, by the institution of courses of lectures by various experts who addressed the members of the College during the winter and spring terms.

Payne's addresses, delivered for the most part before the College, were published in the volume, already cited, which was edited in 1880

[1] Joseph Payne, *Lectures on the Science and Art of Education*, ed. Joseph Frank Payne (1880), p. 39.
[2] The trustees of Andrew Bell (of the mutual or monitorial system) who died in 1832 leaving a considerable fortune for the benefit of education.

by his son. The most considerable of these consisted of three lectures given in 1871, their subjects being (i) the theory or science of education, (ii) the practice or art of education, and (iii) educational methods. Payne's use of the word "science" in the term "science of education" does not bear the somewhat arrogant implication which it usually bore in his day. Agreeably to the word's derivation and to its earlier use, "science" for Payne meant any more or less complete body of generalized or organized knowledge, and "theory of education" is interchangeable with "science of education". He conceived that theory to be based upon observation. He did not profess to be a psychologist and does not criticize the current psychology of the time;[1] but in lieu of a study of "the laws of association" and of "the order of development of the faculties", he directs the students to what afterwards came to be named "child study". The development of the child under stress of the social and material environment constitutes his "natural education", and observation of this process shows that therein the child is his own instructor; he is "explorer, experimenter, inventor". It follows that the teaching which is really educative is self-teaching; the teacher's great business is to encourage and suggest the process of "self-learning". Payne in short enunciated the "heuristic method"; he does not employ the phrase but he is as scornful of what he terms *didactic* teaching as is any later writer. He found the method in *Emile*, in the teaching of Pestalozzi and of Froebel, but above all in the practice of Jean-Joseph Jacotot (1770–1840) of whom Payne became a convinced disciple at the outset of his professional life.

The syllabus of the one-year course which Professor Payne delivered in 1873 and 1874 was arranged under three heads. First came the principles, derived from child study, then the practical application of these principles; there was no provision for actual practice, as the students were practising teachers. The third category was truly Miltonic: "A sketch of the history of education from the earliest times and among different nations. With this will be connected a detailed account of the theories of the most eminent writers and teachers in all ages". Seventeen of these, from Plato to Herbert Spencer, are named, with an "etc." to bring up the rear; their theories were to be criticized in the

---

[1] Yet in a College examination paper set in 1871, of which he was probably the author, the question occurs, "Why is a classification of the acts of mind into Memory, Judgement, etc., unsatisfactory?" *Op. cit.* p. 41.

light of the principles established by child study.[1] This pseudo-historical course sins flagrantly against the principle of self-teaching; and, however adroit the lecturer might be, cramming could not be avoided in the circumstances. The names of writers included in the seventeen suggest that all that was meant was the lecturing upon or the reading of R. H. Quick's *Essays on Educational Reformers*, a charming book which, much more than Payne's lectures, succeeded in confusing the history of opinion with the history of education, and set students upon the wrong road. But full responsibility for the misdirection rests neither upon Quick nor upon his friend. The former did not regard his book as a history of education in any sense; training college lecturers, having no text-book, seized upon the *Essays* as a substitute and built upon it a traditional mode of regarding the history of education. Payne again was not an absolutely free agent. He says that the Council of the College "adopted a scheme laid before them by one of their colleagues—a lady—and offered me the first professorship". Who was the lady? If guessing were permissible, one might guess that it was Maria Grey.

On the vexed question of curriculum, ancient *v.* modern, literature *v.* science, Payne took the view of those reformers who thought with Matthew Arnold that classics and science were co-ordinate disciplines; he emphasized the disciplinary value of both.[2] Yet he was in profound disagreement with the way in which the Science and Art Department encouraged the study of science or, rather, with the sort of teaching which the Department's examinations and grants rendered inevitable. In 1871–2, South Kensington was examining some 38,000 students in twenty-three "sciences". Huxley, himself an examiner under the Department, had great confidence in the system. He had laid it down that a man's "science" must be "what he knows of his own knowledge", Payne's own principle of learning through experience. Here is Payne's comment. "After poring over the 91 pages of examination papers [in twenty-three "sciences"] the only question that can be found to answer to the requirement that the learner is to describe 'what he knows of his own knowledge', is one of Professor Huxley's. Here it is: 'How are sniffing and sneezing effected?' This seems to point to practical

---

[1] *Op. cit.* pp. 161–3.

[2] "Curriculum in Modern Education", lecture delivered in 1866, *op. cit.* pp. 233 ff.

experience, but even here there is room for doubt.... We find page after page of the Directory filled up with the titles of books which use the recommendation of 'My Lords' to help to defeat the very conception of scientific teaching.... As things stand these departments [Science and Art, and Education] are perhaps the most powerful promoters of mechanical drill and cram that the world ever knew.... One child only in 63 throughout the primary schools of the country [is] able to pass the 6th Standard; the special mental training, the method of investigation in science, is set aside and treated as worthless."[1]

These years were marked by a clearly discernible growth of the professional sense amongst schoolmasters and schoolmistresses. The consciousness of identity of interests and the pressure of legislation, imminent or actual, led to the formation of societies whose principal object was mutual support in a period of change such as had been unknown in the schools hitherto. The Headmasters' Conference dates from 1869, the Association of Headmistresses from 1874. The independent, purely local societies of those who taught in National, British, Wesleyan or other voluntary elementary schools drew together; a series of meetings held by their members at King's College, London, ended in the institution (1870) of the National Union of Elementary Teachers. Nineteen years later the word "Elementary" was omitted from the name of this Union which, by virtue of its numbers and its political influence, aspired to represent the profession as a whole.

The issue in 1867 of the Schools Inquiry Commission's *Report* and the discussion of the Endowed Schools Bill which followed caused anxiety as to the future of the secondary schools and of the personal standing and interests of their teachers. In these circumstances it occurred to John Mitchinson, Master of the King's School, Canterbury, that a meeting of those concerned was advisable and he convened such a meeting to be held at Freemasons' Tavern in March, 1869. The attendance was not large, but the root idea of the gathering—the defence of professional practice against attacks from those who were ignorant of that practice—greatly commended itself to Edward Thring, who suggested that the meeting should be held annually at the schools of the members in turn. He invited his confrères to begin the rota at Uppingham in the following December. Greatly helped by H. D.

[1] "The true foundations of science teaching" (1872), *op. cit.* pp. 198 f.

Harper, the Master of Sherborne, Thring entered enthusiastically upon the arrangements for this assembly, sending invitations to all the leading schools with the rest. The first Headmasters' Conference was attended by the masters of thirteen schools, ancient as well as modern, although no representative from any of the nine ancient "Public Schools" was present. However, Winchester and Shrewsbury participated in the second Conference (1870), soon followed by Eton and within a short interval of years by all the schools which regularly sent a contingent of boys up to Oxford or Cambridge. In a letter of July, 1875, Thring wrote that the Conference had "utterly broken up the exclusiveness of the old schools and created a feeling of friendliness and union among all schoolmasters".[1]

The Conference of 1873 approved in principle the professional training of teachers and agreed to receive student teachers in its schools. Virtually nothing came of these "resolutions", because the head masters individually did not take the further and logical step of requiring candidates for their assistant masterships to undergo training and submit evidence of technical competence before they were appointed.

The founder and first president (1874–94) of the Association of Headmistresses was Frances Mary Buss, who was succeeded in office by Dorothea Beale, during whose presidency the Association was incorporated (1896). The "Memorandum of Association" was frank and comprehensive. Amongst its objects were these: "To consider all questions affecting the interests of the profession of education, and to initiate and watch over, promote or oppose general or particular measures in Parliament or elsewhere affecting such profession, or the interests of persons engaged in the same, and to promote or procure changes of the law relating to such profession, or to schools, colleges and other educational institutions and matters".

In thanking Thring for entertaining her Association at Uppingham in June, 1887, Miss Buss spoke of him as "one of the leading headmasters of the country". There was no error of overstatement in her words. Next to Arnold of Rugby, Edward Thring (1821–87) was the schoolmaster best known to the general public in the later nineteenth century. Like Arnold, Thring was a personality, with the same strength of religious conviction and an even more autocratic tendency than that which marked the Rugby head master. His conduct was often

[1] G. R. Parkin, *Edward Thring* (1900), p. 178.

arbitrary in his dealings with his staff and with the governing body, but he always acted upon an honest belief of what his position required of him. He ruled Uppingham with a masterful hand for thirty-four years, coming to it in 1853, when it was an ordinary country grammar school of sixty-one boys taught by master and usher, its fortunes at low ebb. He transformed it into a great modern public school of the first rank, endowed with the machinery, landed property and capital which such a school requires.

Working in days when examinations stood high in public esteem and when, as the State incurred an increasing responsibility for education, the number of officials increased proportionately, Thring stood out for individuality and the freedom of the schoolmaster as a responsible craftsman. "A system of examination and inspection in proportion to its power is death to all original teaching, to all progress arising from new methods and even to all improvement which is at all out of the routine track."[1] His opposition to bureaucracy was strenuous because the bureaucratic ideal of uniformity stultified personality, and, with Thring, personality was well-nigh everything.

But individuality expresses itself through instruments, tools; hence the importance of equipment. "Machinery, machinery!" was one of his watchwords. He was a great builder with faith in "the almighty wall", that is, in buildings planned for the school work of to-day, or for modern ideas of housing, arrangements which secured a measure of privacy on occasion to every boy. Carpentry and metalwork were carried on in workshops properly built and fitted, the boys had garden plots to cultivate; in the absence of a natural bathing pool, swimming baths were constructed. The school had its gymnasium and its gymnastic master as early as 1859. Thring, unlike Arnold, was not satisfied to patronize the school games; his eager temperament made him actively join in the school cricket, football and fives. One of his first principles of school management was that success should be measured by the efficiency attained in educating the dull and mediocre, not by performance in examinations or by readiness to conform to official uniformity. "A good teacher with fair play and time ought to rejoice in a stupid boy as an interesting problem and, when good and willing, a delight and reward."[2]

[1] Parkin, *op. cit.* p. 244.
[2] *Ibid.* p. 429.

Thring and his work were appreciated far beyond the confines of the circle which had its centre at the Headmasters' Conference. The year before he died he was elected president of the Education Society, an association not restricted to teachers, which had been founded in 1875, "for the development of the science of education", more especially for the study of psychology as applied to the art of teaching.[1] The Society, which met once a month and for a time maintained periodically a volume of *Transactions*, advocated the training of teachers. Societies with similar aims were multiplied in the closing years of the century; most of them were short-lived and the fruit of their discussions is impossible to discover. But they disseminated ideas respecting education, its aims, processes and history amongst men and women eager to learn and the seed must often have fallen upon good soil. The Society which had Thring for its president was transferred in 1887 to the then newly founded Teachers' Guild, where its activities were maintained for some years longer.

Professional training for secondary school teachers naturally interested Kay-Shuttleworth, the man who had been most influential in framing the system within which elementary school teachers were prepared for their duties. Seeking the co-operation of a few like-minded with himself, he invited a conference at his own house of head masters, training college principals, school inspectors and others. These met in February, 1875, under the chairmanship of Lord Lyttelton, a member of the Taunton Commission and Chief of the Endowed Schools Commissioners under the Act of 1869. A committee was appointed to approach the Charity Commission, the Education Department and the Universities. In the following April a joint meeting of the committee and of members of the Headmasters' Conference approved training in principle, an approval subsequently endorsed by some 200 head and assistant masters. Although nothing tangible came of all this, yet it assisted in creating opinion amongst teachers and the wider public. Shortly before his death in the following year, Kay-Shuttleworth wrote a pamphlet which accurately anticipated the adoption of two rules which were of the highest importance. The weakness of the training college system as applied to elementary school teachers lay in the concurrent study of academic and of purely professional subjects, that is, the mingling of

[1] Alexander Bain was its president in 1879, when he addressed the Society on 'the possibility and the limits of a science of education".

general education with technical instruction, an arrangement which disturbed both branches of study and brought professional problems before the student when he was less well prepared to ponder them. Kay-Shuttleworth's brochure proposed that the technical training should follow the completed degree course (or an equivalent) from which it should be entirely separate, that it should occupy one year and that a university should confer a special diploma upon those who successfully finished the course.[1]

The increase in the number of professional bodies continued. The Teachers' Guild of Great Britain and Ireland (the "Education Guild" of 1921) began a chequered career in 1883 with the aim of unifying and benefiting the whole teaching profession; but the tendency of the times did not favour so catholic a purpose, sectional societies being preferred. The Private Schools Association was founded in 1883 and the Association of Assistant Mistresses in the following year. The National Union of Elementary Teachers became the National Union of Teachers in 1889, and in 1890 the Head Masters' Association was formed by masters of secondary schools who, for the most part, were not members of the Headmasters' Conference; the Head Masters were incorporated in 1894. In 1891 the Assistant Masters' Association (incorporated 1901) began a very vigorous life. The early years of the twentieth century saw the creation of many other more or less sectional societies, including associations of teachers who instructed in particular subjects, or groups of allied subjects. These bodies and the periodicals which they publish testify to the advance in the study of method which was a feature of professional history in the late nineteenth century.

The first practical move to secure training for secondary school teachers was made by women, amongst whom the professional spirit developed sooner and with greater intensity than was the case among schoolmasters. The Girls' Public Day Schools Company intended from the outset to include in each of its schools a group of student teachers who, under the head mistress's direction, would study the theory and practice of their profession. But what was practicable in the schools first established did not prove so in all that followed them. In 1877 Maria Grey and Emily Shirreff induced the National Union for promoting the Education of Women (the parent, as already stated, of the "G.P.D.S. Company") to form a Teachers' Training and Registration

[1] Frank Smith, *Life and Work of Sir James Kay-Shuttleworth* (1923), pp. 312–15.

Society. This body in 1878 opened a training college for women in Bishopsgate, later transferred to Fitzroy Square and finally to Brondesbury. The Maria Grey Training College throughout its history always worked in association with its annexed girls' school. The training department (1879) of the Ladies' College, Cheltenham, has already been mentioned.

In consequence of the receipt of numerous memorials from head masters the Cambridge Senate in 1879 appointed a Teachers' Training Syndicate. This body drew up a scheme of examination in the theory, history and practice of education, which was open to men and women who possessed qualifications of an academical kind. It also arranged courses of lectures delivered in Cambridge; amongst the lecturers James Ward, R. H. Quick and J. G. Fitch were included. Nevertheless training amongst men made little headway. The fact was being lamented as late as 1894–5. Oscar Browning told the Bryce Commission that "the Teachers' Training Syndicate was originally established at the request of the headmasters, and the regulations were drawn up in accordance with their wishes. They have, however, made very little use of the instrument which they themselves created. The matter has been repeatedly brought before the Headmasters' Conference, and negotiations have passed between the Conference and the Syndicate but with no definite result, although the Syndicate have shown themselves in every way desirous to meet the views of the headmasters".[1] Henry Sidgwick wrote to the same effect. "Though fifteen years ago at the request of a committee of headmasters the University of Cambridge established a system of lectures and examinations in the theory, history and practice of education, it has remained almost inoperative up to the present time so far as the schoolmasters for whose benefit it was primarily instituted are concerned; though it has been used to an important extent by women preparing for secondary teaching."[2] The abstention of the men was sometimes accounted for by the expense of undergoing yet another year of unpaid work after the three or four years occupied in reading for a degree. But so long as a graduate could secure a school post without the qualification of training or of a technical certificate, it would only be in very exceptional cases that the training would be undergone or the examination attempted.

[1] Bryce Commission *Report*, vol. v, p. 142.
[2] *Ibid.* p. 247.

And the vicious circle remained closed because most head masters were only half-hearted in supporting training or were sceptical as to its practical worth. In 1894–5 over one hundred women, exclusive of Kindergarten mistresses, were being trained at the Women's Training College, Cambridge, at Bedford College and other university colleges, at the Maria Grey Training College, at the Ladies' College, Cheltenham, at some of the G.P.D.S. Company's Schools, at the Mary Datchelor School, Camberwell, and elsewhere. Unfortunately, the greater number of these women were not in possession of a university degree.[1] Unkind critics asserted that technique was being made to take the place of knowledge, an assertion sometimes not unwarranted by the extravagant claims of enthusiasts for training. Women equally with men were admissible to the "Examination in the Art, Theory and History of Teaching" which the University of London first held in 1883; this examination was open only to graduates of the University.

The manual of psychology which was authoritative amongst educational theorizers and practitioners during the closing nineteenth century was James Sully's *Teacher's Handbook of Psychology* (1886). It is no exaggeration to say that this book directed the main current of thought and writing upon the practice of the schoolmaster's profession in so far as psychology bears upon it. The *Handbook* passed through several editions, revisions and enlargements, of which the most considerable was the last edition of 1909. Yet throughout it remained the lineal successor of the Associationist school and of the "faculty psychology". Sully changed the names, following Hobbes in calling association "suggestion", but kept those laws of contiguity, similarity and contrast very much as the eighteenth-century psychologists had formulated them. "Faculties" reappear as "processes" and, while he himself pointed out that the faculty psychology ignored "the organic unity of the mind", his treatment of these "processes" encouraged adherence to the description which he discredited. His book retained to the end a series of paragraphs distinctly headed "Order of development of faculties" (viz. sensation, perception, memory, imagination, conception, judgement, reasoning). "That this scheme roughly describes the actual order of events is at once apparent." A caution is contained in the next paragraph to the effect that these terms do not connote so many successive periods during each of which a given "faculty" is in

[1] Bryce *Report*, vol. I, pp. 202 f.

predominating and independent activity. But theorizers, anxious to secure a clear-cut scheme which outlined development, ignored the caution, and the compilers of elementary text-books drew up plans of instruction with corresponding aims which could only find justification in a faculty psychology, pure and simple. Mental discipline, to be ensured through a sensationist psychology derived from Locke, associationism and a faculty psychology, ruled discussion on the platform and in the Press and formed a defence for schoolroom practice.

The Bryce Commissioners were not only convinced that service in secondary schools should be preceded by a technical training, they ventured to indicate in general terms the character of the training. In the first place they recognized that it should be individual and consequently expensive; the "ideal college" would restrict its number to forty or fifty students to make careful attention to each possible.[1] Yet the staff of lecturers required for that number would be no less than would be necessary were the number four or five times as great; and the arrangements for practice would include the co-operation of ten, a dozen, or more schools and the collaboration in each of a member, or members, of the school staff with the tutors of the training college. On the theoretical side the related studies upon which educational theory might be based were, in the opinion of the Commission, physiology, psychology, logic and ethics,[2] a comprehensive body of doctrine which rightly repudiates the attempt to base that theory upon psychology alone.

Registration of teachers, the natural consequent of their training, had been described as desirable by a Select Committee of the House of Commons in 1891. A draft scheme was prepared for the Bryce Commission by the Headmasters' Conference and numerous memoranda on the subject were presented to the Commission. Opinion differed as to whether all school teachers should be admitted to the register or only those whose work lay in secondary schools. It was pointed out that by far the greater number of teachers, those engaged in public elementary schools, were in effect registered already; the names, standing and professional history of each were on record in the Education Department. A printed register which included all these particulars would be an ocean in which the secondary school teachers would be engulfed. The solution suggested by the Commissioners was to form

[1] Bryce *Report*, vol. I, p. 202.   [2] *Ibid.* p. 200.

a register of an *élite*; they would admit all who produced evidence of "considerable attainment and practised skill",[1] without respect to the kind of school in which they might be engaged. But the changes in method and curriculum of comparatively recent date had brought into the secondary school specialists who, however well qualified in their own arts, might not satisfy a rigid interpretation of "considerable attainment", a phrase usually construed as meaning the possession of a university degree. Teachers of drawing, music and gymnastic, the Commissioners would register in supplemental lists; even so, the case of the frequently highly skilled Kindergarten mistresses was not met.

In 1898 Lord Salisbury's Government introduced a Teachers' Registration and Organization Bill, but, as in the case of an earlier Secondary School Registration Bill, time was not found to promote it to an Act. The Board of Education Act (1899) assigned to the Board's semi-professional auxiliary, the Consultative or Advisory Committee, the duty of forming and keeping a register of teachers; effect was given to the provision by Orders in Council (March, July, 1902) which set up a Teachers' Registration Council. In the first instance the members of this body represented the Board of Education and the chief associations of teachers, elementary and secondary. The Register, which was to come into force in April, 1906, was to be in two columns, *A* and *B*, registering respectively elementary and secondary school practitioners. Teachers of music, drawing, physical training, manual instruction, cookery and needlework were to have supplementary registers. Column *A* was not to be printed; and registration was not compulsory. The separation of teachers into the two columns was regarded as invidious and it virtually excluded those in column *A* from public recognition; the scheme in this form had to be abandoned as a failure. The subsequent rather chequered history of the register belongs to the twentieth century. But before the preceding century closed a Superannuation Act (1898) established a fund to which elementary school teachers and the State contributed, thus once again in the course of its story assigning a public character to the most numerous section of the teaching profession.

While political measures of this kind were being considered, much attention was bestowed upon the theoretical aspect of education. The connexion between this subject and the British Association was of

---

[1] Bryce *Report*, vol. I, p. 196.

long standing, going back to the days of "social science" conferences and of similar interests. At the Oxford meeting (1860) Edwin Chadwick read a paper "On the physiological as well as psychological limits to mental labour",[1] which made a parade of precision, assigning time limits to the attention to a given topic of which children at ages varying from infancy to fifteen are capable. It asserted also that the attention of Lancashire children was to the attentive power of south country children (county not specified) as 5 is to 4, and that good sanitary surroundings increase the power of attention "by at least one-fifth". The thesis of the paper was that "generally the psychological limit of the capacity of attention and of profitable mental labour is about one-half of the common school-time of children, and that beyond that limit instruction is profitless". These definite conclusions rested upon the opinions of teachers and school inspectors extracted by the writer over a period of ten to twelve years and in reference to from 10,000 to 12,000 pupils. Chadwick's paper is a flagrant instance of those *ex parte* propositions which were often advanced to bolster up the vicious half-time system, of which he was an active and influential supporter.

At the Cambridge meeting of 1862 an astronomer of distinction, the Rev. George Fisher, F.R.S., read a paper "On the numerical mode of estimating educational qualifications as pursued at Greenwich Hospital School",[2] of which he had been head master (1834–60). This was a plea for establishing a numerical standard of attainment in each of the usual school subjects; the idea has been partially realized in some recent American schemes. Mr Fisher in this paper also gave the world an early (and novel) mode of testing intelligence which may be commended to officials who are in search of an expeditious method, applicable to large numbers, of distributing the scholarships offered by county councils. "He had also weighed his boys and divided them into three groups varying from 90 lbs. to upwards of 100 lbs. The result of this was that he found the heavy boys and the light ones, as a rule, to possess much about the same amount of talent, whilst the boys who represented the medium possessed the largest amount." Two years earlier Chadwick had told the Association that "it is reported

[1] British Association *Report*, 1860, Transactions, Statistical Science Section, pp. 185–91.
[2] British Association *Report*, 1862, Transactions, Statistical Science Section, p. 153.

to me" that a division of schoolboys into two groups, the light and the heavy, showed that the attainments "were found to be greatest with the heaviest". "Educational science" at the British Association was no more fortunate in the 'sixties' than in times more recent.

But these were isolated anticipations of an employment of experiment which was in great favour during the 'eighties' and 'nineties', the stimulus to which came from Germany. A number of causes, schoolboy suicides amongst them, led to the belief that overpressure was general in German secondary schools; and psychologists, professed or amateur *ad hoc*, initiated inquiries into mental fatigue in schoolrooms, the fatiguing power of the different studies (an especially futile investigation), attention, the verbal memory and its exercise, and the like topics. Studies in the correlation of subjects, that is, in the relation between attainment in one school subject and attainment in another, were the origin of those inquiries into the nature of intelligence and modes of testing it, of which there have been so many in recent years. Whatever the positive value of these experiments and observations, they certainly stimulated child study and encouraged the hope of establishing a scientific pedagogy. Societies of teachers and others having that object in view flourished.

The "discovery" by American and English educationists of the German philosopher, Herbart (who died in 1841), confirmed the hope. Half a century after his decease, the philosopher-pedagogue underwent a partial revival by translation in America and in England. His chief work, *General Pedagogy derived from the Aim of Education*[1] (1806), was translated by Mr and Mrs Felkin and published in 1892 as *The Science of Education; its general principles deduced from its Aim*. The aims of education as deduced by Herbart are the strengthening of the moral character, the attainment of a many-sided, well-balanced interest, and the preservation of individuality. Had Herbart's modern, English-speaking disciples made a determined study of the master's work and its implications, the tendency to over-emphasize the psychological at the expense of the ethical and philosophical aspects of educational theory would at least have been minimized. But as the late Henry Holman once put it, "These things are made in Germany, translated in America and misunderstood in Great Britain". The American and English seekers for a science of education took the educational aim,

[1] "Allgemeine Pädagogik aus dem Zweck der Erziehung abgeleitet."

or aims, more or less for granted, and concentrated upon method. They looked for light not so much to Herbart himself as to the neo-Herbartians, Stoy (1815–85) of Jena and more especially to Ziller (1817–82) of Leipzig. These made great play with the doctrine of concentration, or the grouping of all studies about one central subject, or "core", with the "culture epochs" or historical steps of culture, a highly artificial application to curriculum and method of the doctrine of recapitulation enunciated by Herbert Spencer and others. The "Five Formal Steps" in particular exemplified Holman's quip; novices tried to squeeze every lesson (at least as figured in their "notes" prepared for the examiner) into the Five, which Herbart never knew and which even Ziller never intended to describe the routine of a single lesson. These vagaries unfortunately diverted attention and energy from the philosophic principles of the master and finally allowed his name to pass into pedagogic oblivion. One fertile principle, that of apperception, remained to help teachers in the business of instruction and to something like a philosophic idea of knowledge, a happy result largely due to the delightful *Herbartian Psychology applied to Education* (1897) of John Adams.

The so-called Day Training Colleges which in their first year (1890) numbered six with an establishment numbering 200 students, all told, had become nineteen in 1902, educating more than 2000 men and women. Their intimate domestic association with their respective universities or university colleges had not only broadened the general education of elementary school teachers, but a more academic character had been given to the theoretical side of their professional training. The change which occurred is strikingly illustrated by a comparison between the manuals, which had hitherto been available to students, and James Welton's *Logical Bases of Education*, which appeared in 1899.

As the 'nineties' advanced, the Day Training Colleges became Departments of Education, those at the head of them attained professorial rank and their operations extended to training for secondary school service. In 1895 Durham (Newcastle College of Science) instituted a Certificate for Secondary Teachers; Oxford followed in 1896 with an examination and diploma in the Theory, History and Practice of Education. But to the very end of the century the training of men for secondary education languished. An inquiry at the close of 1901 showed that Cambridge, Oxford and six university colleges all had schemes for such training. Half of these eight mustered eight students between them, two had just launched their schemes; the remaining two gave no account of themselves.

The twentieth century therefore opened with room and to spare for the organization of the schoolmaster's profession and for a more truly scientific presentation of its task. Yet the dominance of the psychological element continued in spite of the numerous and fundamental changes suffered by psychology itself. The teleological factor was and still is ignored. Educational theory and political principle had brought English education to the same paradoxical situation.

Vagueness of aim finds its appropriate consequence in imperfect achievement. During the past century, more especially during its later part, much zeal, much devoted labour, great expenditure and many laws were lavished upon public instruction. Yet no one pretends that success has been commensurate with the efforts made to attain it; nor is the failure confined to any one grade of instruction.

Aims and methods both seem at fault. The attempt to embrace all knowledge defeats itself by encouraging smattering; and the method usually pursued was of the old academic, bookish kind, which appeals only to the minority. All minds are not of the academic sort; not every one learns best from books. Yet all are compelled to attend school, where the majority are left to do the best they can with experiences which arouse but a tepid interest, when they are not positively repellent. An illustration of what follows is at hand. Within the year ending in September last the recruits to the Regular Army were, in round numbers, 28,000. They were divided in respect of education into five categories; the two lowest comprised men whose education was limited to an imperfect knowledge of the three R's and men who were wholly illiterate. These two classes contained one-fourth of the whole number of recruits, a disturbing fact which has no sufficient counterpoise in the highest category, those who had attained, or had passed beyond, the stage of university matriculation.

Schools, especially those above the purely primary grade, require curricula and methods as varied in scope and nature as are the intellectual types of the children who are compelled to resort to them. Intellectual power of value to the community is not exclusively of the academic type. Not bookish capacity alone but all capacities, which schools can profitably train, should be trained. The old courtly education, as it developed from the tradition of chivalry, repudiated the exclusiveness of the clerkly ideal, and trained boy and girl with an eye to the particular capacity of the individual and to its future employment, by soldier, land-owner, man of affairs or courtier, when training was completed and life in earnest begun. Contradictory as the statement may seem, the aristocratic and not the clerkly principle affords the best model for public education in a democracy.

INDEX

Abbotsholme, 463 f.
Abbott, Edwin Abbott, 257, 475
Aberdare, Lord, 445, 448. *See* Bruce, H. A.
Abingdon Grammar School, 173
"Academies", 48
Accomplishments, 44, 57, 64, 282, 289
Acland, Arthur Herbert Dyke, 408 f.
Acland, Henry Wentworth, 424
"Act", keeping an, 74
Active Powers, The, 101
Acton, Lord, 445
Acts of Parliament:
  Ballot, 325
  Board of Education, 124, 268, 467, 490
  Cambridge University, 171, 194 f., 415 f.
  Charitable Trusts, 195
  Church Rates, 151
  Combination, 14
  Denison's, 352
  Education (1901), 467; (1902), 152, 268, 410, 457, 468 ff.; (1903), 468. Elementary (1870), 130, 205, 325, 334, 340, 350, 353 ff., 364, 369, 417 f.; (1897), 466, 469. Free, 357, 381
  Endowed Schools, 171, 292, 294
  Factory, 16, 33, 319, 352
  Grammar Schools, 44
  Industrial Schools, 352
  Local Government (1888), 151, 368, 449 f.
  Local Taxation and Excise, 409, 449, 469
  London University, 343, 437 f.
  Married Women's Property, 325
  Mundella's (1880), 357
  Municipal Corporations, 150
  Owens College, 433 f.
  Oxford University, 171, 194 f., 415 f.
  Oxford and Cambridge Universities, 422 f.
  Poor Law Amendment, 14, 130
  Public Health, 150
  Public Libraries, 155, 410
  Public Schools, 171, 247, 256
  Reform, First, 14, 31, 87, 131; Second, 323 ff., 333, 347, 431
  Sandon's (1876), 357, 362, 369, 466
  Teachers' Superannuation, 490
  Technical Instruction, 409, 449, 469
  Universities' Tests, 418
  Voluntary Schools, 466, 469
  Welsh Intermediate Education, 449 f.
Adams, John, 493
Address on Education by the Working Men's Association, 158, 161
Admiralty, the, 218
Advice to Young Men, 110
"Affiliated centres", 344
Agriculture, Board of, 450
Airy, George Biddell, 246
Albert, Prince Consort, 162, 178, 190, 291 f., 340, 387 f.
Albert University, proposed, 435
Aldis, William Steadman, 257
Allen, William, 99
Allgemeine Pädagogik, 492
All Sorts and Conditions of Men, 384
Alma Mater, 73, 79
Althorp, Lord, 32, 34
Alton Locke, 165
Analogy of Religion, The, 238, 417
Anderton family, 460
Aniline colours, 403
Anschauung, *see* Intuition.
Anti-clerical opinion, 396
"Apostles", the, 73, 427
Apperception, 493
Apprenticeship, 264, 399
Archaeology, 425
Ardingly, 276
Aristotle, 7, 193, 199, 201, 245, 417
Armstrong, Henry Edward, 411 f.
Armstrong, William, 400

A E